UNIFORMS
OF THE
WORLD

UNIFORMS
OF THE
WORLD

A Compendium of Army,
Navy, and Air Force Uniforms,
1700–1937

REVISED, BROUGHT UP TO DATE, AND ENLARGED BY
HERBERT KNÖTEL, JR., AND HERBERT SIEG

With 1,600 illustrations of uniforms by Richard Knötel and Herbert Knötel, Jr.

Translated from the 1956 edition by Ronald G. Ball, M.A.

CHARLES SCRIBNER'S SONS
NEW YORK

Library of Congress Cataloging in Publication Data

Knötel, Richard, 1857-1914.
      Uniforms of the world.

      Translation of Handbuch der Uniformkunde.
      1. Uniforms, Military—History.   I. Knötel,
Herbert, Date.   joint author.   II. Sieg, Herbert,
joint author.   III. Title.
UC480.K513   355.1′4′09   79-65574
ISBN 0-684-16304-7

   The text of this English version of *Handbuch der Uniformkunde* is
based on a translation by the late Ronald G. Ball, M.A., one-time Research Assistant at the Scottish United Services Museum, Edinburgh.
   The publishers gratefully acknowledge the assistance given by the museum, and the keeper's permission to use the translation.

TRANSLATOR'S PREFACE

In a translation of this sort, which involves the languages of over a score of countries, many of them with their own special idioms and military organization, it is impossible to lay down very strict rules of exact translation. In general, my aim has been to provide an accurate equivalent in all cases.

Certain general rules have, however, been followed. In their organization, the armies of Continental Europe tended to have more in common with each other than with the British army, which developed independently owing to the nation's insular position and to its imperial commitments. Thus the rendering of titles of formations is especially difficult. For example, the concept of guards in the German sense of *Gardekorps* or the French *Garde Impériale*, which were both homogeneous entities embracing all arms of service, had no equivalent in the British Household Cavalry or Foot Guards. Titles as a rule have been translated except for those of the French and German armies, whose formations are known by their indigenous titles (e.g., *Leibregiment* and *Gendarmerie*), and those of some other major armies, except in particular cases where German or French titles were approximately equivalent. In some instances, French titles have been used—for example, for many German states and in northern Italy during the Napoleonic Wars, when these armies were organized after the French model. Precise renderings of formations in some cases defy translation; again, in the case of most armies, these have been left in the original and an equivalent has been given.

The question of reserve forces also poses some problems. Britain was unique among the European Great Powers before 1914 in having a volunteer regular army, with no reserves in the European sense, and in the varying degrees of liability implied by terms like *Landwehr, Landsturm, Landesschützen,* or the *Bans* (levies) of some Balkan forces. They have usually been retained in the original, but some have been translated by the word "militia," though it is an unsatisfactory rendering in the strictly technical sense.

Proper names of persons and places have generally been translated where there are Anglicized equivalents. Ranks of royalty and the nobility have been translated into English where satisfactory words exist.

As for the uniforms themselves, certain foreign expressions have been retained (e.g., *Attila, chenille*) where these are more precise than any English word normally used or where they express in one word what would require a phrase in English. Even so, certain subtleties such as that between *Stutz* and *Busch* (plume) are not satisfactorily translatable, but reference to the illustrations will in most cases make clear, in this case, what form the plume takes. Similarly, the German term *Waffenfarbe*, abbreviated from *Waffengattungfarbe*, the distinctive color of an arm of service, has been used consistently as a conveniently short form.

A further problem concerns the names of formations of certain countries, such as those of Poland, which Professor Knötel translated into German. In cases like these, I have given approximate equivalents to the titles.

One of the most difficult questions in this type of translation is that of ranks and their equivalents. While there are rough parallels throughout the armies, there are variations in the ranks of company officers and general officers. A German *Generalleutnant*, for instance, was the equivalent of a British or U.S. major general and not a lieutenant general. The usual practice has been to translate the rank into its nearest equivalent. But to give the translation a more than insular relevance, subalterns have been called "senior" and "junior" lieutenants, instead of the normal British terms, as usage in some countries differed from British practice (e.g., the Soviet Union had three ranks of lieutenant). The original ranks have been retained in instances where all ranks are listed (e.g., for Austria), and sometimes where the creation of new ranks is mentioned, and in the case of untranslatable ranks. A distinction has been drawn between the concepts of "ranks" and "grades" of officers. "Rank" generally refers to the individual ranks of officers: captain, colonel, etc. "Grade" refers to the type of rank, e.g., company officer, field officer, general officer. Perhaps the most difficult ranks to deal with are those of senior NCOs and warrant officers. In these cases no attempt has been made to give a more precise indication of the ranks than to call them such, since each country had its own special nomenclature. Some countries had a rank, unknown in the British service, which embraced a combination of NCOs' and officers' status and rank distinctions. In some instances the translation of these has been left in the original; in others, the status of the rank has been indicated.

The navies and air forces likewise present some problems with regard to ranks. Flag officers were the naval equivalent of general officers in the army; but the German terms *Stabsoffizier* (field officer) and *Subalternoffizier* (company officer), in both the navies and air forces, have been rendered as "senior officers" and "junior officers," the former denoting captains and all commanders, in the British navy, and the latter, all below. In the air forces, the term "senior officers" is approximately equal, in the British service, to group captains through squadron leaders, and "junior officers" to all below. Air officers, again in the British service, were the equivalent of general officers in the army; but in the German air force and others which had military ranks, the expression "general officer" has been retained to denote this. In the navies, the terms (chief) "petty officer" and "warrant officer" are only approximate equivalents.

One final question is that of the exact translation of orders of dress. As each country has had its own terms for these, and as they have differed from time to time, an approximation has been given. The British term "mess dress" has not been generally used, as the British regimental officers' mess had no counterpart in many other countries; so the expression "evening dress" has been used to denote the uniform worn at formal social functions in the evenings.

My endeavor has been to translate, not to edit, the book. The only countries for which alterations have been made in the text, in the interest of greater preciseness, are Great Britain and France. In addition, a glossary of foreign retentions and technical uniform terms has been included.

Ronald G. Ball
Edinburgh, 1969

FOREWORD

In the foreword to the first edition of this work, which appeared in 1896, Professor Richard Knötel wrote: "Neither in German literature, nor in that of the world as a whole, is there a book that gives the history of the uniforms of all the European armies, although there are some excellent monographs on individual armies and periods." This statement still holds true. The developments of world history in the past few decades have shown the necessity of such a work as this. Just as the study of costume forms an important part of cultural history, so the study of uniforms is an essential part of military history and a valuable branch of the study of armies. Further, a knowledge of the history of uniforms is important for artists and writers, for the theater and cinema, and more generally, for those who wish to portray visually the events of history.

Those considerations have moved the authors, Herbert Knötel, Jr., and the late Herbert Sieg, to bring out a new edition. Professor Richard Knötel's long, profound, and detailed basic work has been thoroughly revised and enlarged in the light of the latest research. In the period up to 1937 the influence of the Great War, the newly created states, the United States of America, and the most important South American and Asiatic states have been described. The navies and air forces have been dealt with in separate sections.

The edition of 1956 is only slightly altered. For technical reasons, the 1937 edition, which in many respects stands at a decisive epoch in the development of uniforms, has been retained. A continuation up to 1956 would necessitate an entirely new edition, and it would be the work of several years to assemble the necessary material.

The text of this English version of *Handbuch der Uniformkunde* is based on a translation by the late Ronald G. Ball, M.A., onetime Research Assistant at the Scottish United Services Museum, Edinburgh.

The publishers gratefully acknowledge the assistance given by the museum, and the keeper's permission to use the translation.

CONTENTS

THE
ARMIES

INTRODUCTION

DRESS, ARMS, AND EQUIPMENT AT THE TIME OF THE THIRTY YEARS' WAR

Even in the Middle Ages there were many instances of the wearing of what is now understood by the term "uniform." The retinues of princes and individual knights appeared in their livery colors just as town officers often wore their town colors. Despite these isolated cases, the uniform in its modern sense originated with the raising of standing armies. Generally speaking, a dress recognizable as a uniform dates from the time of Louis XIV.

During the Thirty Years' War each soldier wore his own clothing. In the cavalry a leather jerkin was favored, mainly on practical grounds. So far as equipment was concerned, there was a certain amount of uniformity. Pikemen (Fig. 1a) wore protective armor consisting of an iron helmet, breast and back plates, gorget, and tassets. They were armed with long pikes and rapiers. Some wore similar armor, but carried a sword and round shield. This latter type of soldier went out of fashion at the beginning of the war. Musketeers (Fig. 1b) usually wore a broad-brimmed hat or sometimes a steel cap. Their arms were the matchlock, to be superseded later by the wheellock and flintlock. The introduction of firearms brought with it the musket rest and the bandolier—a shoulder belt with leather-covered wooden flasks, each containing a charge of powder, with a powder flask and a leather bullet bag suspended from it. Their *arme blanche* was a sword. At the beginning of the war, the cuirassiers wore full plate armor except on the legs, a helmet with visor, and long boots (Fig. 1d). Protection for the arms gradually fell into disuse. Often an iron gauntlet with fingers was worn only on the left hand, while the right hand was protected by a long leather glove. It was covered by the hilt of the sword and, when pistols were used, the iron gauntlet was a hindrance when it came to using the trigger. The visored helmet was later superseded by other types. The erroneously named *Pappenheim* helmet was very popular. It consisted of a bell-shaped skull with protruding peak, ear pieces, long, laméd neck guard, and a single movable nasal piece (Fig. 1c). On the German saddle the cuirassier carried two pistols in holsters, one on each side. The long-bladed sword had an ample guard.

The lancer—a type of solder who disappeared early in the war—was equipped like the cuirassier, but carried in addition a long lance, usually without a pennant (Fig. 1e). Carabiniers and arquebusiers normally wore a lightweight armor without arm pieces, and an iron helmet. The carbine was suspended from a belt over the left shoulder, with its accessories (powder flask, etc.) on a bandolier (Fig. 1f). The other arms were a pistol in a holster on the right side, and a sword. Dragoons—the name was originally applied to mounted infantry—were divided into musketeers and

Fig. 1. Arms, Dress, and Equipment at the Time of the Thirty Years' War.
a: musketeer. b: pikeman. c, d: cuirassiers. e: lancer. f: carabinier. g: trumpeter.
h: dragoon.

pikemen; their arms resembled those of the corresponding types of infantry. They had neither pistols nor spurs. When mounted, the dragoon carried his gun slung over his shoulder (Fig. 1h). Cavalry trumpeters wore no protective armor. Their hanging sleeves, common at the time, survived into the nineteenth century as the distinguishing mark of a trumpeter, and they were called *Flügel*, meaning wings (Fig. 1g). In the course of the Thirty Years' War there were many changes in arms. Gustavus Adolphus, for example, armed his Swedish musketeers with a lighter weapon and was thus able to do away with the cumbersome musket rest. In place of bandoliers with chargers he introduced a form of cartridge pouch.

When a contemporary account mentions a blue or yellow regiment, this can refer to a part of the dress, such as breeches or stockings, but more usually to the color of the standards. References like ''yellow coats'' and ''red coats'' have, of course, that specific meaning.

The volunteers of the Imperial army were the forerunners of the Imperial national border troops of a later epoch, and of the later ubiquitous hussars. Cossacks also took part in the war.

The jacket or jerkin, the principal garment up till then, grew less and less important; it survived during the eighteenth century and into the early nineteenth century as a waistcoat, at first of leather, later of cloth. In its place the coat or surtout, which had hitherto only served as a cloak, assumed greater importance. While colored distinctions were comparatively rare on the jacket, so that regiments had to be identified by breeches and stockings of various colors, the cloth coat had a differently colored lining, which was visible on the turned-back cuffs, skirts, and lapels, and this became the basis of the later conception of uniform—that is, a coat with facings of another color. The colored stitching around the buttonholes, and the colored tape

4

binding sometimes put around them, provided a further means of differentiation and were the origin of regimental lace.

There were no badges of rank in the present sense. Officers were recognizable by the better quality of their dress. In the infantry and dragoons they carried partisans, the precursor of the spontoon. It seems, too, that the sashes worn to distinguish friend from foe were only worn by officers (and perhaps also by the lifeguard companies in the cavalry). The Imperial and Spanish armies from the time of Charles V usually wore bright red sashes; the German Protestants in the Schmalkaldic and Thirty Years' wars had yellow; the Dutch, orange; the Parliamentary troops in the English Civil War had blue or white colors. The French wore blue at first and, from the time of Henry IV, white. In Sweden, yellow field marks were adopted in the reign of Eric XIV "as the cross, which parts our coat of arms, is yellow." Under Gustavus Adolphus, the Swedish field marks were blue. Such distinguishing features were necessary at a time when uniforms were not worn, considering the great proliferation of uniforms later on. At the battle of Warsaw in 1656, the Brandenburgers and Swedes wore wisps of straw in their headdresses, and, at the siege of Vienna in 1683, the Poles, whose dress closely resembled that of the Turks, plaited straw around their waists. The Prussians (or at least the 2nd and 3rd Battalions of the King's Regiment) wore two red hearts in their headdresses at Stralsund in 1715, probably to commemorate the alliance with Saxony. The Württemberg Grenadiers, whose uniforms were almost identical to those of Frederick the Great's army, adopted a white cover to their metal-fronted grenadier caps during the Seven Years' War. In 1762 Frederick introduced white plumes throughout the Prussian cavalry, to distinguish them more easily from the similarly dressed enemy horse. With the great proliferation in uniforms of the armies of the Allies in 1813, a white band was worn on the upper left arm, as a common distinction. In Switzerland uniforms varied greatly from canton to canton. Thus on maneuvers the white Confederation cross on a red band was introduced. In 1864 the Prussians and Austrians again wore white bands, as did the Prussian army of the Main, and its various contingents, in 1866. The South German troops, whose uniforms were rather similar to those of the Prussians, adopted a black, red, and yellow band on the upper left arm.

After the Great War of 1914–1918, various distinctions were frequently worn on the same uniforms to indicate membership of different organizations or groups—for example, the red, white, and blue chevrons of the White Russian Army, worn on the sleeves. Again, various arm bands were adopted during the Spanish Civil War.

The cockade must also be included in general marks of recognition. The international symbol of neutrality, the red cross on a white ground, was promulgated at the Geneva Conference in 1863 and was adopted generally shortly afterward.

SUMMARY OF GENERAL CHARACTERISTICS

Military uniforms of all countries had certain basic similarities at specific periods:

About 1600 to 1670: The main garment was the jacket, with long skirts for the cavalry. Headdress: steel cap or hat. Hair worn long, often with a pointed beard.

About 1670 to 1710: The cut of the long-skirted coat followed civil fashions, and it became the main garment, along with a broad-brimmed hat. Cavalry as a rule still wore the last vestiges of armor. Officers had long perukes; beards were smaller.

About 1710 to 1805: Uniform finally broke away from civilian fashions. Through time the coat became double-breasted and turned back to the chest to form lapels. The skirts, which were similarly turned back, became narrower, and the small collar grew larger. The turned-back cuffs became smaller and the sleeves narrower. The felt hat was turned up at three sides and ornamented with lace. Hair was worn in a queue, and beards were no longer worn.

About 1805 to 1850: A single- or double-breasted coatee, with long or short skirts, was worn. The chaco superseded the hat; the cavalry wore leather helmets with a comb and crest. The queue was abolished.

1850 to 1914: Single- or double-breasted tunic of medium length; spiked helmet or, in many of the Latin countries, a chaco, which was gradually reduced in size.

1914 to 1939: The introduction of a camouflage-colored service dress in almost all countries from the beginning of the twentieth century became universal during the Great War. The steel helmet was introduced. After the end of the war, a British-type service dress was adopted almost universally. It usually had patch pockets on the breast and skirts. The colors ranged from earth brown, through khaki, to gray-green. Steel helmets and fore-and-aft shaped caps were normally worn in service and peaked caps off duty. For walking out and formal occasions, a colored or specially embellished uniform was worn in nearly all countries.

The development of distinctions of rank closely followed the above.

Seventeenth century: Officers were denoted by their sashes and the richer ornamentation of their dress. The exact form of these was largely left to the individual.

Eighteenth century: Distinctions such as gorget, sash, sword knot, and embroidery served as regulation for officers.

Nineteenth century: To the distinctions of an officer as such were added the differentiations of rank, following the French usage, which appeared in the last third of the eighteenth century. The various ways of indicating rank—lace, epaulettes, shoulder straps, etc.—were adopted in all countries.

Twentieth century: The 1914–1918 war brought about a great reduction in the conspicuousness of rank badges. After the war, officers' rank distinctions came back into use in both old and new forms.

ALBANIA

Cockade: red-black-red

During the short existence of the principality of Albania (1912–1914), the army wore a light-blue uniform based on Albanian national dress, with black distinctions and loopings. The badges of rank were on the collar. Fur caps were worn. On service, the men wore national dress (Figs. 2a,b).

Fig. 2. Albania.

a: field officer in full dress. b: auxiliary infantry in national dress. c: field officer. d: NCO.

After the Great War, the army adopted a gray-green service uniform. The jacket had a stand collar with patches in *Waffenfarbe* and slit breast and skirt pockets with scalloped flaps. The peakless Austrian-type field cap had a *Skanderbeghelm* (a round helmet with winged antelope skull) on the top part and piping in *Waffenfarbe* around the flap. The men wore trousers and puttees of basic color, brown leather equipment, and black boots. Officers and NCOs did not wear a sword, either on or off duty, but had a pistol on the left side of the waistbelt, supported by a brace over the right shoulder. NCOs' rank distinctions consisted of one to three narrow vertical gold stripes on the collar patches and, for officers, of one to three silver stars on the collar patches, with a broad stripe of basic color in the center for company officers, and a stripe of basic color around the edge for field officers. On the left side of the field cap rank was denoted by one to three vertical gold stripes, with a fairly broad stripe to the front in addition, for field officers.

The *Waffenfarben* were as follows: general officers and general staff, scarlet; royal guard, dark carmine; infantry, green; artillery, dark blue; and engineers, violet.

In 1929 a service jacket with patch pockets and with shoulder straps piped in *Waffenfarbe* was introduced. The stand collar was entirely of *Waffenfarbe*; NCOs and men wore their detachment number in yellow metal at the ends; NCOs' ranks were denoted by one to three vertical bars to the rear. Officers' ranks were thenceforth distinguished by one to three gold five-pointed stars placed horizontally at the ends of the collar. Field officers wore a narrow gold stripe on the front and lower edges of the collar, as far as the top of the shoulder strap, while general officers had a medium-width gold stripe down the fronts and right around the lower edge of the collar. The double-breasted greatcoat was of basic color without colored distinctions and had a stand-and-fall collar, piped shoulder straps, and a half-belt with two buttons at the back. The gray-green cloak had a turndown collar. The new-pattern cap had a black leather peak and chinstrap and, for officers, piping in *Waffenfarbe* around the bottom and top of the flap and across the top part, with the gold *Skanderbeghelm* on the front. The men had the royal cipher "Z," for Zogu I, and no piping. On the flap, above the peak, officers wore stars as on the collar to denote rank; field officers wore stripes below; general officers had two crossed oak sprigs below which were one or two gold chevrons, points down. The latter also wore red triple stripes on their trousers (Fig. 2c). The steel helmet was similar to the Italian one but had a small comb.

In 1936 there was a further change in the uniform. Officers and men adopted a civilian-style jacket with concealed buttons for the men; officers wore a row of four gilt buttons and pleated patch pockets on the breast and skirts. The collars of the NCOs' and the men's jackets were of basic color with, at the end, a spearhead-shaped patch of *Waffenfarbe*, with a small white metal button in the point and the detachment number below. The collar for officers was of dark blue velvet, piped in *Waffenfarbe* around the outside. General officers and the general staff wore a gold sprig of three oak leaves, in addition, at the ends of the collar. The new steel helmet was hemispherical without embellishments. The peakless pre-1929 field cap was reintroduced with the current rank badges—general officers had a patterned broad gold lace with gold stripes to indicate rank—but without the *Skanderbeghelm*. In its place a black and red cockade with the royal monogram on a red ground was introduced for officers. In undress, and for off-duty wear, a peaked cap like that of the *Reichswehr* was adopted, with a black leather peak and chinstrap. NCOs and men wore a rectangular patch in *Waffenfarbe* on the front, vertical yellow stripes to indicate rank, and above, on the top part, the royal monogram in white (Fig. 2d). The cap band for officers was dark green, with piping around the top and band in *Waffenfarbe*. Rank distinctions were worn on the front, as on the 1929 cap. General officers had gold oakleaf embroidery around the peak and one to three silver stars on the front. Above them was the *Skanderbeghelm* with the royal cipher below in gold embroidery. In full dress a gold double cord was worn instead of the chinstrap; a black-red-black sash worn over the right shoulder; a gold waistbelt with clasp; a sword in a nickel-plated scabbard; and a gold sword knot with thick bullions on a gold double cord. The Royal Guard wore a single cord, looped from the right shoulder to the left hip; in gold for officers, silver for NCOs, and black and red silk for the men. The gray-green shirt was worn with a soft collar and tie; off duty, a white shirt and black tie were worn. The badges of rank were worn on the shoulder straps of the coat, which were piped in *Waffenfarbe*: one to three stripes for NCOs; for officers, one to three five-pointed stars arranged in a triangle at the outer ends, with gold lace all around for field officers; general officers had gold twisted shoulder cords with silver stars on a red backing. In full dress the *Skanderbeghelm* was worn above the rank badges. The greatcoat was now cut Ulster-fashion; otherwise it remained unaltered. Off duty, officers wore a black *Attila* jacket with black fur collar, cuffs, and edging around it, and five rows of black loopings on the breast.

8

ARGENTINA

From 1821: blue-white-blue cockade

Up to the end of Spanish rule, uniforms were based on Spanish ones. The infantry wore white coats with variously colored collars and cuffs. The cavalry had yellow coats with variously colored cuffs, and fur caps; the artillery had dark blue coats with red cuffs and red waistcoats. After independence, British styles predominated, in addition to strong nationalist elements. The infantry wore all-dark-blue coats and trousers, with green as the distinctive color. In Fig. 3a, the coat and overalls are dark blue, the trousers and knapsack white, and the leather equipment black. In Fig. 3b, the jacket is turquoise with red collar, cuffs, waistcoat, and cap, and the trousers are white, with a red edging around the bottom. From the mid-nineteenth century the uniform was strongly influenced by the French (Fig. 3c). The infantry had turquoise-blue tunics and trousers, with green collar, cuffs, epaulettes, and chaco plume; white leather equipment and gaiters; black leather chacos; and yellow metal buttons and insignia. In the same period the artillery had black collars and dark blue cuffs, all piped red, and dark blue trousers with broad red stripes. Camouflage-colored ticken

Fig. 3. Argentina.
a, c, e: infantry. b, d: cavalry (d: horse grenadier).

9

garments, without colored distinctions, were often worn on service. In the 1870s and 1880s the infantry wore red trousers. The cavalry also wore uniforms based on French styles around 1890; they had dark blue dolmans with red collar, pointed cuffs, and epaulettes; red trousers; a red kepi with a red plume; and white leather equipment. The artillery were similarly dressed, but had dark blue trousers with double red stripes and a dark blue kepi with red piping and a red plume. At the turn of the century a black German-type spiked helmet, with a yellow metal plate, was introduced, and the tunic was made double-breasted. The collar, cuffs, and epaulettes were green for infantry, red for artillery, and black for engineers, with natural-colored leather equipment and boots (Fig. 3e). The cavalry, which had white helmet plumes, retained the turquoise dolman with black loopings, red collar and epaulettes, and red trousers. The regiment of horse grenadiers had a distinctive full-dress uniform (Fig. 3d), which remained unchanged from 1821 to the 1930s: blue coatee with blue lapels; red collar, piping, and epaulettes; yellow grenades at the ends of the collar; turquoise trousers with red stripes; and leather chaco with a red band around the top, red plume, and red lines. The service uniform was khaki-colored, with patches in *Waffenfarbe* and the number at the ends of the collar. In 1931 the service uniform was olive green, cut like a blouse for the men, with a stand collar and patches in *Waffenfarbe*. Officers had jackets with arm-of-service badges in silver or gold on the lapels and shoulder straps edged in *Waffenfarbe*. On these were the rank badges, consisting of one to three sunbursts. The *Waffenfarben* were: infantry, dark green; cavalry, dark red; artillery, red; engineers, black; transport corps, golden yellow. The men's gray-green cap had the arm-of-service badge on the front; officers had the national arms with the cockade above, and piping in *Waffenfarbe* around the top and around the band. The greatcoat was double-breasted with roll cuffs and a turndown collar. In full dress and for walking out, a gray-blue uniform with stand collar and piping in *Waffenfarbe* was worn; the men had deep cuffs of basic color, piped in *Waffenfarbe*; officers had pointed cuffs of distinctive color, with their rank badges on them: one to three gold sunbursts. Field officers had an embroidered edging around the cuffs; on the collar was the regimental number or arm-of-service badge, with a gold edging for field officers. The buttons were of yellow metal. General officers had rich oakleaf embroidery on their collars and Swedish cuffs. A U.S.-type peaked cap was worn with this uniform with gray-blue top, piping of *Waffenfarbe* around the top and around the band; and a black leather peak with a single or double row of gold embroidery for colonels and general officers respectively.

General officers' caps had a white top and dark blue band, piped red around the top and bottom. Officers wore shoulder cords, consisting of four plain cords laid side by side: gold for field officers, silver for subalterns, with one to three gold sunbursts; general officers had gold twisted shoulder cords on a red shell with two or three gold sunbursts on them. NCOs and men had gold chevrons, piped in *Waffenfarbe*, on both upper arms of the coat and greatcoat, in both the service uniform and the dress uniform. In full dress the pupils of the Military College wore white flat-topped caps with red piping around the top, and a red band; gray-blue tunics with red collar and pointed cuffs; gray-blue shoulder straps edged with silver and blue double cords; white trousers, gloves, and leather equipment; and black boots.

AUSTRIA-HUNGARY

Cockades: Austria, black and yellow; Hungary, green-white-red

I. GUARDS

Austria had no "guards" in the sense of the German *Gardekorps* or the French *Garde Impériale*; but there were various court and palace guards. The oldest of these was the *Erste Arcieren Leibgarde* (First Lifeguard of Halberdiers). It was raised by Ferdinand II to attend the emperor on his progresses, and to serve as a palace guard. In 1700 (Fig. 4a) its uniform consisted of a gold-laced hat with white plumage, black coat laced with gold, and black waistcoat and undergarments. The coat had red sleeves, all richly ornamented with gold. The arms were a sword and glaive. Later, the hanging sleeves and the hat plumage were done away with, and the undergarments were made white. In 1817 they had a red coatee with black collar and cuffs, and rich gold lace, and gold epaulettes. The black pouch belt was edged gold, and white breeches, high boots, and gold-laced hat with a black feather plume completed the uniform. Up to the end of the monarchy the uniform (Fig. 4d) consisted of a white metal helmet with yellow metal fittings and a white hair plume. The tunic was red, richly ornamented with gold lace, with gold lace and pouch belt. The undergarments were as before. The *Trabanten Leibgarde* (gentlemen at arms) dated from the reign of

Fig. 4. Austria-Hungary—Court Guards.
a, b, c, d: lifeguard (halberdiers). e, f, g: gentlemen at arms. h. Imperial palace guard. i: lifeguard (cavalry). k: lifeguard (infantry). l: Hungarian lifeguard. m: Hungarian Crown Guard.

11

Leopold I; they wore a black and yellow padded costume in old-Swiss style (Fig. 4e) and were armed with a halberd. In 1767 the coat, waistcoat, and breeches were red; the coat had black cuffs and collar. Coat and waistcoat were laced with gold loops. The hat, pouch belt, and waistbelt were all black, embellished with gold lace; gaiters were white. They were armed with a sword and halberd. About 1800 (Fig. 4f) a helmet with comb and chenille was introduced. Black lapels set with gold lace loops, gold epaulettes, and knee boots were added to the uniform. Later, the helmet was again superseded by a hat. Finally, the uniform was changed to one similar to that of the halberdiers; but the coat had black lapels and cuffs, with gold lace (Fig. 4g). The *Leibgarde-Infanterie-Kompanie* was formed from the *Hofburgwache* (Imperial Palace Guard). In 1802 (in which year it was established from the court guard raised by Maria Theresa) the uniform consisted of a plain black hat with small black plume, a gray coat with a row of yellow metal buttons, and black collar, cuffs, shoulder straps, and wings. The pouch belts and undergarments were white, with knee boots. They were armed with a sword and carbine. In 1844 (Fig. 4h) the hat had a gold binding and loop and a black feather plume. The gray coat had a black velvet collar and cuffs with gold lace and gold epaulettes. The trousers were blue with white stripes. The pouch belt was black. In 1890 (Fig. 4k) the uniform consisted of a green double-breated coat with red collar, cuffs, and piping; yellow metal shoulder scales, buttons, uniform consisted of a green double-breasted coat with red collar, cuffs, and piping; yellow metal shoulder scales, buttons, and shoulder cords; gray trousers with red piping; and a black helmet with black hair plume and yellow metal mounts. The black waistbelt had a yellow metal buckle, with sword and bayonet in scabbards. The muskets had black slings. The *Leibgarde-Reiter-Eskedron* (Fig. 4i) was dressed exactly like the infantry, but had white pouch belts and gauntlets, white breeches, and long boots. The *Königliche Ungarische adelige Leibgarde* (Royal Hungarian Nobles' Bodyguard) wore an all-red national costume with rich silver loopings, a panther skin with a silver plate on the breast, and a busby with green bag and white plume. The uniform, in essentials, remained unaltered for a long period (Fig. 4l). The Polish lifeguards (raised 1782, disbanded 1791) wore a richly ornamented version of their national dress, namely a white fur-edged *Konföderatka* (Polish cap) with gold lacing and cords, and red undergarments, of which only the sleeves (which had gold lace and blue cuffs) were visible. In addition, a blue upper garment was worn over this; it had small red lapels and was richly decorated with gold lace. The pouch belt and sash were red and gold; the boots were red; the lances had black and yellow pennants. In 1812 a Bohemian Nobles' Guard was raised. It attended the monarch in 1813–1814 and was then disbanded. This guard wore a white single-breasted uniform with red collar, cuffs, and skirt turnbacks, with gold lace on the collar; gold epaulettes and sash; white breeches and long boots; hat with gold lace and loop and black feather plume; and black pouch belt with yellow mounts.

In 1838 Emperor Ferdinand I formed a Lombard-Venetian lifeguard, which lasted until 1848. The uniform consisted of a red, gold-laced coatee with sky blue collar and cuffs, white trousers with gold lace, and, at first, a hat like that worn by the Bohemian lifeguard but, from 1840, a white metal crested helmet with yellow metal fittings. The last of these guards was the Royal Hungarian Crown Guard (Fig. 4m). They wore a silvered helmet with yellow mounts and an upright feather; madder red *Attila* with silver lace, madder red breeches, and yellow boots; and a black cravat with silver fringe. The arms were a Hungarian saber and a glaive with a scythe-shaped blade with a red fringe below.

II. INFANTRY

Up to the first quarter of the eighteenth century the basic color of the infantry uniform was predominantly pearl gray and later white. The musketeers (Fig. 5a) were partly armed with matchlock muskets with rests to about 1670, when these were superseded by flintlocks. Socket bayonets appeared around 1700, which meant that the musket could thenceforth be fired with bayonet fixed. Grenadiers were first added to the Imperial army in 1664. Their officers carried flintlocks, while those of the rest of the infantry had partisans. At the same time as socket bayonets were introduced, pikemen became superfluous. From about 1670 Montecucculi had been reducing their numbers. Pearl-gray uniforms were ordered to be worn in 1708. In 1718 the only regiments wearing colored uniforms were the eight Dutch national regiments, which had green coats with cherry-colored distinctions. Regiments were distinguished by the colors of the cuffs, linings, waistcoats, breeches, and stockings. The buttons were very often cloth-covered. All NCOs and musicians wore the principal colors reversed. Officers did not wear uniforms until very late—about 1718. Apparently they, too, wore reversed colors to begin with. The sashes were black and yellow, or black and gold for field officers. The officers' partisans were embellished with varying degrees of ornamentation, which formed a distinction of rank. At first, the coat was very long and loose-fitting, with very large cuffs; but about 1710 the whole coat was made closer-fitting, the skirts began to be fastened back, and the turned-back cuffs became smaller. On service, a sprig of greenery was worn in the hat or, in winter, a wisp of straw or other distinction. In a regulation of 1720, the following items were ordered for the men: "A coat made of good, durable cloth

Fig. 5. Austria-Hungary—"German" (Austrian) infantry.
a, b, d, e, g–k: "German" infantry. c, f: officers.

13

Fig. 6. Austria-Hungary—Hungarian infantry.

a, c, d, f, h, i: Hungarian infantry. b, e: officers. g: bugler.

well lined with baize or linen, with waistcoat of the same; a pair of good leather breeches; a pair of strong woolen stockings; a pair of strong shoes made of Russian leather with good soles; a good durable hat; two shirts; two neckcloths or silk cravats; a good knapsack; a pouch with belt attached; a sword and bayonet." Officers had laced hats, coats, and waistcoats. Later, the undergarments became white. In 1735 the coat was again made closer fitting without reaching, however, the Prussian degree of tightness. A shoulder strap was introduced on the left shoulder. From 18 October 1743 to 4 October 1745 the officers' sashes were grass green, embroidered through with gold and silver. In 1755 animal-skin knapsacks, which were in partial use already, were adopted in place of the linen ones. In the early eighteenth century, Hungarian infantry (Figs. 6a,b) wore their national dress, ornamented quite at will. In the Seven Years' War, the "German" infantry (Fig. 5d) wore white coats and waistcoats, some of the latter being single-breasted and some double-breasted. The breeches were white, the gaiters white or black, the latter officially introduced in 1753; but stockings were worn in some cases up to 1767. The coat had lapels and cuffs of various colors, according to regiment. The turned-back skirts were either of basic color or of the distinctive color. The small cloth strap by which the skirts were fastened together varied greatly in shape and color. The hat was bound with white or yellow lace. The grenadiers (Fig. 7c) had fur caps with a colored bag and wore a metal match case on the pouch belt. They also carried a hanger, while the rest of the men only had a bayonet in a scabbard. The neckcloths were red for almost all the "German" infantry and black for the Hungarian infantry. The latter (Fig. 6c) wore a coat without lapels, ornamented with colored lace. The waistcoat was of a different color and had hussar loops; the tight-fitting breeches, of the same color as the waistcoat, were worn in lacing shoes. A hussar sash was worn over the waistcoat. Sabertaches were also worn by a few regiments. The hats were the same as those of the "German" infantry.

14

Line Infantry, 1740–1780

Regimental numbers were introduced for the infantry in 1769.

NO.	NAME OF REGIMENT OR COLONEL	RAISED	DISTINCTIVE COLORS; BUTTONS
1	Infantry Regiment Erbprinz of Lorraine 1726; Duke 1729; Emp. Franz I 1745; Joseph II 1765	1716	red; 1767 pompadour red; yellow metal buttons
2	I. R. Ujváryi 1741; Archduke Karl 1749; Ferdinand 1761	1741	Imperial yellow; yellow buttons
3	I. R. Karl of Lorraine 1736; Archduke Karl 1780	1715	1757 red; 1767 sapphire blue; white buttons
4	I. R. Hoch- und Deutschmeister	1696	sapphire blue; yellow buttons
5	1st Garrison Regiment (1807 became 1st and 2nd Garrison Battalions)	1766	dark blue; white buttons
6	2nd Garrison Regiment (1807, 3rd and 4th Garrison Battalions)	1775	black; white buttons
7	I. R. Neipperg 1717; Harrach 1774	1691	1730 blue yellow; 1743 red; 1748 blue; 1767 dark blue; white buttons
8	I. R. Saxony-Hildburghausen 1732	1647	red; yellow buttons
9	Netherlands I. R. Los-Rios 1725; Clerfayt 1775	1725	apple green; yellow buttons
10	I. R. Brunswick-Wolfenbüttel 1740	1715	1757 red; 1767 green; white buttons
11	I. R. Count Franz Wenz. of Wallis 1739; Count Nich. Joh. of Wallis 1774	1662	1743 blue; 1748 red; 1767 pink-red; white buttons
12	I. R. Botta d'Adorno 1739; Khevenhüller-Metsch 1775	1702	1757 blue; 1767 dark brown; yellow buttons
13	I. R. Moltke 1737; Zettwitz 1780 (disbanded 1809)	1630	1740 red; 1743 blue; 1767 grass green; yellow buttons
14	I. R. Salm-Salm 1733; Ferraris 1770; Tillier 1775	1733	1740 light blue; 1748 black; yellow buttons
15	I. R. Pallavicini 1736; Fabris 1733	1701	1740 blue; 1757 red; 1770 madder red; yellow buttons
16	I. R. Livingstein 1722; Königsegg-Rothenfels 1741; Terzy 1778	1703	1740 blue; 1767 violet; yellow
17	I. R. Kollowrat-Krakovsky 1737; Koch 1773	1675	1740 red; 1767 sulphur yellow; 1770 light brown; white buttons
18	I. R. Sackendorff 1710; Marchal of Biberstein 1742; Brinken 1773	1683	1740 red; 1767 pompadour red; white buttons
19	Hungar, I. R. Palfy 1734; d'Alton 1773	1734	1740 blue; 1767 sapphire blue; white buttons
20	I. R. Diesbach 1719; Colloredo-Waldsee 1744	1682	1740 blue; 1743 red; 1757 blue; 1760 yellow; 1767 lobster red; white buttons
21	I. R. Schulenberg 1734; Arenberg 1754; Gemmingen 1778	1733	1740 blue; 1767 sea green; white buttons; 1778 yellow buttons
22	I. R. Suckow 1734; Roth 1741; Wagenbach 1748; Sprecher of Bernegg 1756; Iacy 1758	1708	1740 red; 1767 imperial yellow; white buttons

(continued)

NO.	NAME OF REGIMENT OR COLONEL	RAISED	DISTINCTIVE COLORS; BUTTONS
23	I. R. Ludw. Gg. of Baden-Baden 1707; Aug. Gg. of, 1761; died 1771; Archduke Ferdinand 1779 (disbanded 1809)	1672	1740 blue; 1767 red; white buttons
24	I. R. Max Adam Count Starhemberg 1703; Em. Mich. Count, 1741; Preiss 1771	1632	1740 blue; 1767 dark blue; white buttons
25	I. R. Wachtendonk 1731; Piccolomini 1741; Thürheim 1757	1672	1740 red; 1742 blue; 1751 red; 1767 sea green; white buttons
26	I. R. Grünne 1737; Puebla 1751; Riese 1776	1717	1740 blue; 1743 red; 1767 green; yellow buttons
27	I. R. Prince Max of Hessen-Cassel 1732; Prince Chrph. of Baden-Durlach 1753	1682	1740 blue; white buttons; 1767 Imperial yellow; yellow buttons
28	I. R. Arenberg 1716; Scherzen 1754; Wied-Runkel 1754; Wartensleben 1779	1698	1740 green; 1743 red; 1748 green; yellow buttons; 1767 grass green; white buttons
29	I. R. Brunswick-Wolfenbüttel 1736; Loudon 1760	1709	1740 red; 1748 blue; 1767 light blue; white buttons
30	Neth. I. R. Prié-Turinetti 1725; Saxony-Gotha 1753; Ligne 1771	1725	1740 blue; 1767 bluish-gray; yellow buttons
31	Hung. I. R. Haller von Hallerstein 1741; Esterhazy 1777; Orosz 1780	1741	1741 blue; 1767 Imperial yellow; white buttons
32	Hung. I. R. Ign. Count Forgáts 1741; Giulay 1773	1741	1741 blue; 1767 sky blue; yellow buttons
33	Hung. I. R. Andrassy 1744; Esterhazy, Prince Nich. of, 1753	1741	1748 yellow; 1762 dark blue; white buttons
34	Hung. I. R. Kökemesdy de Vetés 1734; Bathyany 1756; Ant. Esterhazy 1780	1734	1745 yellow; 1767 madder red; white buttons
35	I. R. Waldeck 1739; Marquire 1763; Hessen-Darmstadt 1767; Wallis 1774	1682	1738 blue; 1743 red; 1767 lobster red; yellow buttons
36	I. R. Ulysses Browne 1737; Jos. Browne 1757; Tillier 1759; Kinsky 1761	1675	1738 light blue; 1767 lilac gray; white buttons
37	Hung. I. R. Szirmay 1741; Count Jos. Esterhazy 1744; Siskovics 1762	1741	red; white buttons
38	Neth. I. R. Ligne 1725; d'Aynse 1766; Kaunitz 1774 (disbanded 1809)	1725	pink-red; yellow buttons
39	Hung. I. R. Palffy 1756; Preysach 1758	1756	red; white buttons
40	I. R. Damnitz 1734; Count Carl Colloredo 1754	1734	1740 blue; 1743 red; 1748 blue; yellow buttons; 1767 carmine; white buttons
41	I. R. Friedr. Prince of Bayreuth 1734; Plunquet 1763; Carl. Eg. of Furstenberg 1770; Belgiojoso 1777; Bender 1778	1701	1740 light blue; 1743 red; 1767 sky blue; 1770 sulphur yellow; white buttons

(*continued*)

NO.	NAME OF REGIMENT OR COLONEL	RAISED	DISTINCTIVE COLORS; BUTTONS
42	I. R. O'Nelly 1734; Gaisruck 1743; Gemmingen 1769; Mathesen 1775	1683	1740 blue; 1743 red; 1757 blue; 1767 orange-yellow; white buttons
43	I. R. Platz 1737; Buttler 1767; Thurn 1775 (disbanded 1809)	1715	1740 blue; 1743 red; 1767 sulphur yellow; yellow buttons
44	Italian I. R. Clerici 1744; Gaisruck 1769; Belgiojoso 1779	1744	1744 madder red; yellow buttons
45	I. R. Heinr. Daun 1711; O'Kelly 1761; Baron Ferd. Bülow 1767; Lattermann 1776 (disbanded 1809)	1682	1740 red; 1767 carmine; yellow buttons
46	Tyrolean Land- und Feld-Regiment Spauer 1745; Ogiloy 1748; Sincere 1751; Marquire 1752; Migazzy 1764 (disbanded 1809)	1745	1745 red; 1767 dark blue; yellow buttons
47	I. R. Count Jos. Harraen 1704; Fr. Chr. Margrave of Bayreuth 1764; Elrichshausen 1769; Kinsky 1779	1682	1740 blue; 1743 red; 1757 blue; 1767 steel green; white buttons
48	Italian I. R. Vasquez de Binas 1734; Luzan 1755; Ried 1765; Caprara 1773 (disbanded 1809)	1721	1740 green; 1767 light brown; yellow buttons
49	I. R. Walsegg 1724; Bärnklau 1743; Kheul 1747; Angern 1758; Pellegrini 1767	1715	1740 red; 1767 bluish-gray; white buttons
50	I. R. Wurmbrand 1727; Harsch 1749; Poniatowsky 1766; Stain 1773 (disbanded 1809)	1642	1740 red; 1767 violet; white buttons
51	Hung. I. R. Count Steph. Gyulay 1735; Count Franz Gyulay 1759	1702	1757 blue; 1767 dark blue; yellow buttons
52	Hung. I. R. Bethlen 1741; Karoly 1763	1741	1743 red; 1748 blue; 1757 light green; 1767 red; yellow buttons
53	Hung. I. R. Simbschen 1756; Beck 1763; Palfy 1768	1756	1756 red; 1767 dark red; white buttons
54	I. R. Königsegg-Rothenfels 1720; Sincere 1751; Callenberg 1769	1661	1740 red; 1767 apple green; white buttons
55	I. R. Arberg 1742; Murray 1768 (disbanded 1809)	1742	1743 red; 1767 light blue; yellow buttons
56	I. R. Phil. Daun 1690; Merci-Argentau 1741; Nugent 1767	1684	1741 blue; 1767 steel green; yellow buttons
57	I. R. Thungen 1735; Andlau 1745; Count Jos. of Colloredo-Waldsee 1769	1689	1740 red; 1767 carmine; yellow buttons
58	Neth. I. R. Vierset 1763	1763	1763 blue; yellow buttons; 1767 black; white buttons
59	I. R. Margrave Leop. Jos. Daun 1740; Franz Daun 1766; Langlois 1771	1682	1741 red; 1767 orange-yellow; yellow buttons

Considerable changes in the uniform were made in 1767. The infantry went into single-breasted coats that were buttoned all the way down the front (Figs. 5e; 6d). The lapels were abolished. The coats had a turndown collar that, together with the cuffs, skirt turnbacks, and the color of the buttons, displayed the distinctive color of the regiment; many regiments retained these colors unchanged up to the Great War. The company distinctive color was shown on the colored muzzle stoppers of their muskets. The men were issued leather *Kasketts*, each of which had an upright front with a brass plate on it. The bag on the grenadier caps was abolished (Fig. 7d). The officers had hats, colored waistcoats, and knee boots. The Hungarian infantry retained their colored close-fitting breeches with long black gaiters. Officers ceased to carry muskets and bayonets in 1760. In 1798 the coat was made with a stand collar. In 1800 a leather helmet was introduced. This had a comb, yellow metal mounts, and a black and yellow *chenille* (Fig. 5g). In 1808 it was changed for a chaco with front and back peaks, pompon, and cockade. In the same year the coat collar was made higher. Queues were abolished in 1804. From that time the Hungarian infantry were distinguished by their light-blue breeches with black and yellow looping and the white lace ornamentation on their cuffs called *Bärentatze*, or bears' paws (Fig. 6e). In the 1830s the ''German'' infantry adopted light-blue pantaloons with white piping. A new-pattern chaco was issued in 1840 (Fig. 6f). At the same time the large brass plate on the grenadier caps was done away with and replaced by a yellow grenade (Fig. 7g). The tunic was introduced in 1894. It was double-breasted, with collar, cuffs, shoulder straps, and piping in the regimental color (Fig. 6g). The Hungarian infantry differed as before in having tight-fitting Hungarian breeches and ''bear's paws'' on their cuffs. Shortly afterward the grenadiers' fur caps were abolished, and their only distinctions from that time were the grenades on the belts and the hanger (Fig. 7h). After the Italian campaign of 1859, a single-breasted tunic

Fig. 7. Austria-Hungary—Grenadiers.
a, b, c, e, g: ''German'' grenadiers. d, h: Hungarian grenadiers.
f: officer, Hungarian grenadiers.

18

with turndown collar was introduced (Fig. 5i). Officers wore their sashes over the shoulder instead of around the waist as previously. A new uniform was introduced in 1868 when the white tunic was superseded by a dark blue one. Generally speaking, this uniform remained in war up to the Great War, although with various changes. It consisted of a single-breasted tunic with differently colored collar, cuffs, shoulder straps, and wings (Fig. 6i). The undress garment was a blue jacket with colored collar patches (Fig. 5k). The greatcoat was gray, double-breasted, with turndown collar and colored collar patches. The trousers were light blue (close-fitting for the Hungarian regiments) with black and yellow loops. The headdress was a chaco with the double eagle plate and cockade. Officers had no shoulder cords, and epaulettes were never generally adopted in the Austrian army. From 1868, officers' sashes were again worn around the waist.

In 1909 a bluish-gray service dress was introduced. The jacket was of the same style as the old blue one but with pleated patch pockets on the breast. The regimental colors of the collar patches remained as before, but for those with ash gray distinctions, dark brown piping was worn around the collar, and no patches were worn. The trousers were also bluish-gray, the Hungarian ones retaining their former shape and ornamentation. Brown leather equipment was introduced. The greatcoat was also made in bluish-gray (Figs. 13a, d, page 36).

In 1914 the distinctive colors were as follows.

DISTINCTIVE COLOR	"GERMAN" REGIMENTS: BUTTONS		HUNGARIAN REGIMENTS: BUTTONS	
	YELLOW	WHITE	YELLOW	WHITE
black	14	58	26	38
white	94	92	—	—
reddish-brown	55	17	68	78
dark brown	93	7	12	83
dark red	1	18	52	53
claret	89	88	—	—
purple	90	95	86	—
madder red	15	74	44	34
cherry red	73	77	43	23
carmine	84	81	96	82
scarlet	45	80	37	39
lobster red	35	20	71	67
pale red	57	36	65	66
pink-red	13	97	5	6
sea green	21	87	70	25
popinjay green	91	10	46	50
apple green	9	54	85	79
grass green	8	28	61	62
seaweed green	102	—	—	—
steel green	56	47	48	60
bluish-gray	30	49	76	69
ash gray	11	24	51	33
orange yellow	59	42	64	63
imperial yellow	27	22	2	31
sulphur yellow	99	41	16	101
light brown	100	98	—	—
light blue	40	75	72	29
sky blue	4	3	32	19

Even before 1915 the service dress was being made from supplies of German field gray cloth, although the former style of uniform was retained. In 1918 the service jacket was made with a very broad turndown collar with narrow vertical cloth stripes in the distinctive color. The rank stars were worn to the front of this. An oilcloth patch with the regimental number painted on it was worn around the outer end of the shoulder straps (Fig. 13f). The steel helmet was the German pattern.

III. NATIONAL BORDER INFANTRY, VOLUNTEERS, *LANDWEHR* AND *HONVED* INFANTRY, BOSNIA-HERZEGOVINA INFANTRY

As a defense against the invasions of the Turks, colonists were settled in the border lands. Their task was to protect the frontiers in return for the promise of toleration and exemption from taxes. The territories were divided into districts, each under a general. By 1699 the Karlstadt, Warasdin, and Banal border generalships were established and, in 1702, the Slavonian. The following were added later: the Banater in 1747; the Szekler in 1764; and the Wallachian in 1766. Up to about 1750 the men from these areas wore their national dress, which varied greatly (Figs. 8a,b). During the Seven Years' War they wore black peakless chacos, looped jackets and waistcoats, and tight-fitting Hungarian breeches. In addition, a hussar sash and a cloak (usually red) were worn (Fig. 8c). Some had coats of the same style as those of the Hungarian infantry.

National Border Infantry, 1762

REGIMENT	COAT	CUFFS	WAISTCOAT	LOOPS	BREECHES
Licaner	red	green	green	yellow	red
Oguliner	blue	yellow	blue	yellow	red
Ottochaner	red	light blue	light blue	yellow	light blue
Creutzer[1]	white	green	green	white	white
Brooder[2]	black-brown	yellow	light blue	yellow	light blue
Szluiner	light blue	red	red	yellow	light blue
St. George	bluish-green	white	?	white	white

[1]Hungarian-style coat with green lace.
[2]Hungarian-style coat, no lace.

At the reclothing of the army in 1767, the border infantry were given gray single-breasted coats like those of the line infantry, with a colored turndown collar and cuffs; white Hungarian breeches and laced shoes; and white leather equipment. Their headdress was a peakless chaco (Fig. 8d).

National Border Infantry, 1812

REGIMENT*	COAT	COLLAR AND CUFFS	BUTTONS
5. (Warasd.) Creutzer	white	lobster red	yellow
6. (Warasd.) St. George	dark brown	lobster red	white
7. (Slav.) Brooder	white	pale red	white
8. (Slav.) Gradiskaner	white	pale red	yellow

(*continued*)

REGIMENT*	COAT	COLLAR AND CUFFS	BUTTONS
9. (Slav.) Peterwardeiner	white	light bluish-gray	yellow
12. (Banat.) Deutschbanatisches	dark brown	sky blue	white
13. (Banat.) Wallachia-Illyria	white	light bluish-gray	white
14. (Siebenburg.) 1st Szekler	white	pink-red	yellow
15. (Siebenburg.) 2nd Szekler	dark brown	pink-red	white
16. (Siebenburg.) 1st Wallachian	white	popinjay green	yellow
17. (Siebenburg.) 2nd Wallachian	white	popinjay green	white

* The Karlstadt (Regiments 1–4) and Banal (Regiments 10 and 11) military border territories were absorbed into the French empire in 1809.

In 1871 the border infantry was absorbed into the line. From 1815 (Fig. 8e) to that year they wore a uniform exactly similar to that of the Hungarian infantry; but the basic color of the short-skirted coatee, and later of the tunic, was dark brown with black leather equipment (Fig. 8f). The distinctions were Imperial yellow, lobster red, pale red, carmine, scarlet, sky blue, or light bluish-gray with white or yellow metal buttons. For a long period the Titler Border Battalion (formerly called the *Tschaikisten*) had a distinctive uniform of light blue with red distinctions and white metal buttons. Among the *Freikorps* (Volunteers) the Pandours are well known, but they did not have a distinctive uniform. In the Seven Years' War there was a Loudon *Freikorps* whose uniform exactly resembled that of the line infantry. The color of the coat, skirt turnbacks, waistcoat, and breeches was green. Cuffs and lapels were red and metal buttons white. The uniform also had white hat lace, black gaiters, and white leather equipment. The *Volontairs von Bock* were similarly dressed, but their collars and cuffs were yellowish-white. During the French Revolution there were a

Fig. 8. Austria-Hungary—Border troops, *Jäger*.
a, b, c, d, e, f: border infantry. g, h, i, k, l: *Jäger*.

21

large number of volunteer corps. Various French *émigré* corps, such as the Royal German Dragoons, wore their former French uniforms while in the Austrian service but adopted black and yellow plumes and cockades. The Archduke Charles Legion in 1749 wore light-gray coats and breeches; white waistcoats; red collar, cuffs, lapels, and skirts; short black gaiters; and helmets with a black crest and plume and white metal badge. The Vienna Volunteers had green uniforms, gray-blue breeches, and Corsican hats. In addition to these, there were other volunteer corps, from which sprang the *Landwehr* formations, which at that time were essentially different from the units of this name in the twentieth century. At the beginning of the nineteenth century, the Austrian *Landwehr* wore white breeches and gray single-breasted coats with white metal buttons. The leather equipment and gaiters were black; the hat, turned up at the left, had the cockade and a yellow metal plate in front. In 1809 the Styrian *Landwehr* wore a green coat cut across in front, with white collar, shoulder straps, cuffs, buttons, breeches, and leather equipment. The headdress was a type of round hat with a cockade on the left. Later on, the uniform of the "German" *Landwehr* was not essentially different from that of the line. The Hungarian units were dressed in blue, with white loopings, short boots, natural-leather belts, and chaco with a cockade and no other device. In 1880 the "German" *Landwehr* had dark blue jackets with red collar patches and shoulder straps, the latter with the regimental number in white, gray service caps, and gray trousers with red piping. In 1892 they were dressed in bluish-gray jackets with green collar patches and dark blue—later bluish-gray—trousers and caps. The *Honved* infantry (Hungarian militia) wore dark blue tunics with dark blue collars and cuffs, and cherry red hussar loopings, edging, shoulder cords, and wings (gold cords for officers). In addition, up to about 1885, they had madder red breeches, which had superseded the former light-blue ones. On them were cherry red loopings. For occasions when the rest of the troops wore an undress jacket, they wore, in place of the tunic, a coat similar to that described above, but without the hussar loopings and edging down the front and around the skirts. The service caps were light blue, but in full dress a red chaco was worn. The 1909 service uniform was similar to that of the Hungarian infantry, but the trouser stripes were dark blue. The Bosnia-Herzegovina infantry wore light-blue tunics and jackets. The distinctions, arranged like those of the rest of the infantry, were madder red (green for *Jäger*) with yellow metal buttons. The headdress was a madder red fez with a dark blue tassel. They also adopted the 1909 pattern of the bluish-gray service uniform but retained their distinctive color. The more general trends followed those of the infantry.

IV. *JÄGER* AND *SCHÜTZEN*

During the Seven Years' War, a *Feldjägerkorps* was formed (Fig. 8g), but it did not last very long. The basic color of the coat, waistcoat, and breeches was gray. The cuffs, turndown collar, and skirt turnbacks were green and the buttons yellow metal; leather equipment and knee boots were black. The headdress was the *Kaskett*, adopted in 1767 by the infantry as a whole. The front part had no metal plate and was edged green. Several *Jäger* corps existed around 1800, but they were volunteers. The first *Jäger* batallions were raised in 1808. The Tyrol *Jäger* Regiment was formed

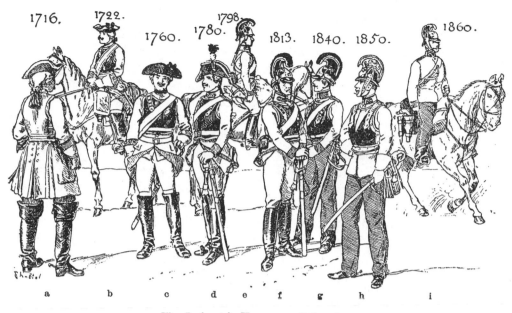

Fig. 9. Austria-Hungary Cuirassiers.
a, b, c, d, e, f, g, i: cuirassiers. h: officer, cuirassiers.

in 1816. The uniform underwent the same changes in style as in the infantry. The color was always a bluish-gray for both coats and trousers. The collar, cuffs, and piping were grass green and the buttons of yellow metal. Black leather equipment was worn. The hat, which was ornamented with a green cock's feather plume, altered in shape on several occasions (Figs. 8i,k,l). The *Landesschützen* were dressed like the "German" *Landwehr*. Officers wore *Jäger* hats. Mounted *Landesschützen* had the same uniform but with cavalry equipment. The *Landesschützen* regiments and *Landwehr* Infantry Regiment No. 4 wore an aluminum *Edelweiss* badge on their collar patches. These mountain troops had a tuft of black and white blackcocks' feathers on the left side of their caps. The jacket had a turndown collar and green shoulder straps edged with silver, and with cipher before the Great War.

The service uniform was of the same style as the infantry, with grass green distinctions.

V. CUIRASSIERS

In 1720 the following was ordered for cuirassiers: "A surtout made of cloth well lined with baize; a pair of good sheepskin or buckskin breeches; a pair of well-made Russian leather boots with strong soles; a good durable hat; two shirts; neckcloths or a good silk cravat; a pouch with belt attached; a good sword with leather belt; a good carbine and two pistols; a good saddle made of seasoned leather well stuffed with horsehair, and with pistol holsters attached; a good martingale and crupper; a velvet girth and headstall; bridle, stirrups, spurs; helmet and cuirass; and a pair of good leather gloves." The iron helmet, however, was soon done away with; but an iron "secret" in the form of a cross was worn, sewn inside the hat, up to 1781. The basic color of the uniform was light gray and, later, white. The cuirass consisted of both breast and back pieces. On the plain front of the cuirass, a gilded inverted wedge-shaped ornament was worn as a distinction of rank; subalterns had them down to the center only, captains to the lower edge; and the same, with a gold inlay at the sides, for field officers. In 1754 these distinctions were simplified. Some regiments had carabinier companies, which were armed with carbines and bayonets.

Up to 1767 all regiments had red distinctions with the exception of the Modena regiment, which had blue. The undergarments were white for some and red for others. The regiments were further distinguished by the color and arrangement of the buttons (Fig. 9c). A black and yellow feather plume was worn after the Seven Years' War. In 1767, as has been seen in the previous sections, new-pattern uniforms were introduced in the army. The white jackets of the cuirassiers were thenceforth single-breasted and fastened across at the top with a cloth tab (Fig. 9d). These, with the cuffs, skirt turnbacks, and edging, showed the distinctive color of the regiment, or *Egalisierungfarbe*, as it was known in Austria. The cuirasses were blackened; the back plate abolished; the shabraques were red with yellow lace and ciphers. In 1798 the hat was superseded by a helmet (Fig. 9e), which was fairly similar to that worn by the Austrian dragoons up to 1914, except that the comb was fitted with a black and yellow *chenille*. Queues were abolished in 1805. The small cloth tab became formalized into a collar patch so that the white collar now had patches in the regimental color (Fig. 9f). The red shabraques, ornamented as before, were covered with a sheepskin. In 1812 the distinctions were as follows.

REGIMENT	JACKET, COLLAR, BREECHES	COLLAR PATCHES, CUFFS, PIPING	BUTTONS
Emperor	white	dark red	white
Archduke Franz Joseph d'Este	white	black	white
Duke Albert of Saxony-Teschen	white	pompadour red	yellow
Crown Prince (Ferdinand)	white	grass green	white
Sommariva	white	light blue	white
Liechtenstein	white	black	yellow
Lorraine	white	dark blue	white
Hohenzollern-Hechingen	white	scarlet	yellow

In 1840 (Fig. 9g) the cuirassiers adopted light-blue trousers in place of white ones. Ten years later the tunic was introduced, and the crest on the helmet was done away with (Fig. 9h). In 1860 the cuirass was abolished (Fig. 9i). The uniform thenceforth was very little different from that of the dragoons. In 1868 cuirassiers were abolished.

VI. DRAGOONS AND *CHEVAU-LÉGERS*

Around 1700 the dragoons were dressed like the cuirassiers, but they wore hats instead of iron helmets and leather jackets, under the coat, instead of cuirasses. The basic colors of the uniform varied considerably until after the Seven Years' War. Horse grenadiers were distinguished by bearskin caps. The Spanish dragoons in the Imperial army in c. 1716 wore the same headdress as the Spanish dragoons, i.e., a type of *Kaskett* with a high front. During the Seven Years' War, the distinctions (Fig. 10c) were as follows.

REGIMENT	COAT	SKIRTS, CUFFS, LAPELS	WAISTCOAT		BUTTONS	BREECHES
			COLOR	ROWS OF BUTTONS		
Bathyany	dark blue	red	dark blue	2	yellow	dark blue
Prince Eugen of Savoy	red	black (blue 1730)	red	2	yellow	red
Liechtenstein	dark blue	red	red	2	yellow	red
Kolowrat	dark blue	red	red	2	white	red
Württemberg	red	black	light yellow	1	yellow	light yellow
Archduke Josef	light green	red	light green	1	yellow	light yellow
Zweibrücken	dark blue	red	dark blue	2	yellow	light yellow
Modena	red	light blue	light blue	2	white	light blue
Saxony-Gotha	red	light blue	light blue	1	yellow	light yellow
Saint Ignon	green	red	red	2	yellow	light yellow
Althann	white	red	white	2	yellow	white
Hessen-Darmstadt*	red	green	light yellow	—	yellow	light yellow
Lowenstein	green	red	red	2	white	red

*No lapels; no buttons on waistcoat; closed by hooks.

The dragoons and *chevau-légers* were dressed alike until after the Seven Years' War. Then the former adopted white uniforms with variously colored distinctions and hats; the latter were dressed in green or white and had *Kasketts* like the infantry (Fig. 10d). Both wore light-colored undergarments and long boots. From that time their uniforms generally followed that of the cuirassiers as regards both headdress and uniform. The collar, however, was wholly colored and not white with colored patches (Fig. 10e). For a short time (1798–1801) all dragoon and *chevau-léger*

Fig. 10. Austria-Hungary—Dragoons and *Chevau-légers*.
a, b, c, e, g, i, k: dragoons.. d, h: *chevau-légers*. f: light dragoon.

25

regiments were turned into light dragoons. As such, they wore green single-breasted jackets with various colored distinctions; helmets with a comb and black and yellow *chenille*; and white breeches with long boots (Fig. 10f).

In 1835 the distinctions were arranged as shown in the table.

REGIMENT	JACKET	COLLAR, CUFFS, SKIRT EDGING	BUTTONS
Dragoons			
1. Archduke Johann	white	black	white
2. King of Bavaria	white	dark blue	white
3. Minutillo	white	dark red	white
4. Windisch-Graetz	white	light red	white
´5. Prince Eugen of Savoy	white	dark green	white
6. Picquelmont	white	light blue	white
Chevau-Légers			
1. Emperor Ferdinand	dark green	light red	yellow
2. Hohenzollern	dark green	light red	white
3. Alberti de Poyn	white	light red	yellow
4. Windisch-Graetz	dark green	dark red	yellow
5. Schneller	white	light blue	yellow
6. Fitzgerald	white	dark red	yellow
7. Nostiz-Rinek	white	crimson	white

In 1840, in place of the white breeches and long boots, long colored trousers were introduced. The dragoons and white-uniformed *chevau-légers* adopted light-blue ones, while the *chevau-légers*, having dark green uniforms, adopted dark green ones (Fig. 10h). In 1850 the tunic was introduced (Fig. 10i). The *chenille* on the helmet was done away with. In 1852 *chevau-légers* were abolished and turned into dragoons and lancers. The dragoon uniform was completely altered in 1868 when the basic color was changed to light blue, with red for the trousers. The uniform generally remained as this up to 1914, although many alterations in detail were made. The helmet, which had yellow metal mounts, retained its shape. In place of the usual dark blue undress jacket the dragoons wore, from the 1890s, a light-blue single-breasted tunic, with collar, round cuffs, and piping in the distinctive color. A light-blue double-breasted coat with fur collar, and colored round cuffs and piping, was slung over the left shoulder (Fig. 10k). The trousers and peakless service cap were red.

From 1868 to 1914 the distinctions were as shown in the table.

DISTINCTIVE COLORS	BUTTONS	
	YELLOW	WHITE
black	6	2
white	15	—
Imperial yellow	12	5
sulphur yellow	10	7
grass green	9	4
dark red	3	1
madder red	14	13
scarlet	8	11

Service dress was first introduced for cavalry during the Great War. To begin with, they wore bluish-gray covers to their headdress and, in 1914, iron-gray trousers were issued to all. An infantry-style service dress jacket was introduced and, more generally during the course of the war, a fur-trimmed coat, the same for all arms of cavalry, was worn: double-breasted, field gray, without colored cuffs or piping.

VII. HUSSARS

Hussars were the national troops of Hungary. There is no record of their having a distinctive dress in the period around 1700. Their principal garment was generally a short coat, noteworthy in that it had no buttonholes but was fastened by loops (Fig. 11a). From this garment developed the dolman. The headdress was either a stockinglike cap with fur edging or the *Heiduckenmütze*—a felt cap, from which the *Flügelmütze* originated. The breeches were close-fitting, and the short boots were frequently of colored leather. In 1734 they were as follows.

REGIMENT	CAP BAG	DOLMAN AND PELISSE	SHABRAQUE
Karoly	red	light blue	light blue
Czungenberg	red	green	green
Steph. Dezsöffy	dark blue	dark blue	red

All had red *Scharawaden* and red loops. Up to 1748, undyed sheepskins were worn. During the Seven Years' War, the hussars wore full uniforms.

Fig. 11. Austria-Hungary—Hussars and Lancers.
a, b, c, d, e, f, g: hussars. h, i, k, l, m: lancers.

27

In 1762 (Fig. 11c) the distinctions were as follows.

REGIMENT	DOLMAN	CUFFS	PELISSE	LOOPS	BUTTONS	BREECHES	CAP BAG
Nadasdy	red	red	dark blue	yellow	yellow	dark blue	red
Baranyay	green	green	green	red	yellow	light blue	red
Szeczeny	dark blue	red	dark blue	red	yellow	dark blue	dark blue
Palffy	light blue	pink	light blue	pink	yellow	light blue	pink
Jos. Dessöffy	light blue	red	light blue	red	white	red	red
Spleny	green	red	green	white/red	white	red	green
Hadik	dark blue	red	dark blue	yellow	yellow	red	red
Bethlen	light blue	pink	light blue	pink	yellow	light blue	pink
Esterhazy	light blue	yellow	light blue	yellow	yellow	red	red
Kalnoky	light blue	light blue	light blue	yellow	yellow	red	red
Emperor Franz	dark blue	yellow	dark blue	yellow	yellow	dark blue	dark blue
Palatinal	light blue	crimson	light blue	white	white	red	crimson
Carlstädter	dark blue	red	dark blue	yellow	yellow	dark blue	red
Kukez	red	red	red	white	white	red	red
Esclavonier	green	green	green	yellow/white	yellow	red	red

The felt cap was introduced generally along with the new uniform of 1767. Only officers, sergeants, and standard bearers retained the fur caps (the last two, up to 1771). The busby bag was of the color of the *Flügelmütze*. The trumpeters were as a rule not dressed as hussars, but as "German" troops. The *Flügelmütze* had the national emblem and cockade in front, a black and yellow plume, and lines. Later, with the addition of a peak, it became a chaco. The color of the headdress varied from regiment to regiment. Toward the end of the eighteenth century, gray buttoned overalls were introduced. From 1770 all regiments had black and yellow loops. In 1812 the regimental colors were as follows.

REGIMENT	CHACO	PELISSE AND DOLMAN	BREECHES	BUTTONS
1. Emperor Franz	black	dark blue	dark blue	yellow
2. Archduke Josef Anton	madder red	light blue	light blue	yellow
3. Archduke Ferdinand Carl d'Este	ash gray	dark blue	dark blue	yellow
4. Hessen-Homburg	light blue	popinjay green	light red	white
5. Radetzky	madder red	dark green	carmine	white
6. Blankenstein	black	cornflower blue	cornflower blue	yellow
7. Liechtenstein	grass green	light blue	light blue	white
8. Elector of Hessen	black	popinjay green	light red	yellow
9. Frimont	black	dark green	carmine	yellow
10. Stipsicz	grass green	light blue	light blue	yellow
11. Szekler	black	dark blue	dark blue	white
12. Palatinal	black	cornflower blue	cornflower blue	white

All regiments wore black and yellow mixed loopings on the pelisse, dolman, and breeches (Fig. 11d).

The sashes were yellow with black knots; the sabertaches red with the ciphers in yellow and yellow-white-black lace edging. The shabraques had the same edging;

they were red and, in most regiments, worn with a fur saddle cover. These shabraques were of the same pattern throughout the cavalry. In 1850 the *Attila* replaced the dolman. Instead of being covered with loops down the front, this, like the pelisse, henceforth had five rows of loops. The chaco was made in a more up-to-date, lower shape. The distinctions were simplified; the *Attila* and breeches were made dark blue or light blue. This, along with the color of the chacos, and the buttons, displayed the regimental distinctions, which in 1854 were as follows.

REGIMENT	CHACO	*ATTILA* AND TROUSERS	BUTTONS
1. Emperor Franz Josef	grass green	dark blue	yellow
2. Grand Duke Nicholas	white	light blue	yellow
3. Prince Carl of Bavaria	white	dark blue	yellow
4. Schlick	scarlet	light blue	white
5. Radetzky	scarlet	dark blue	white
6. King Wilhelm of Württemberg	scarlet	light blue	yellow
7. Prince of Reuss	grass green	light blue	white
8. Elector of Hessen	scarlet	dark blue	yellow
9. Liechtenstein	white	dark blue	white
10. Friedrich Wilhelm III of Prussia	grass green	light blue	yellow
11. Prince Alexander of Württemberg	grass green	dark blue	white
12. Haller	white	light blue	white

When the War of 1866 broke out, the hussars were involved in a change of uniform, which was completed after the war. The *Attila* remained either dark or light blue, while the trousers were made madder red. The headdress was a fur cap with a colored bag called a *kutsma* (Fig. 11f).

Thereafter, the distinctions in 1868 were as follows.

REGIMENT	BAG OF *KUTSMA*	*ATTILA*	TROUSERS	OLIVETTES
1. Emperor Franz Josef	dark blue	dark blue	madder red	yellow
2. Grand Duke Nicholas	white	light blue	madder red	yellow
3. Crenneville	white	dark blue	madder red	yellow
4. Edelsheim	madder red	light blue	madder red	white
5. Radetzky	madder red	light blue	madder red	white
6. King Karl of Württemberg	ash gray	light blue	madder red	yellow
7. Prince Friedrich Carl of Prussia	light blue	light blue	madder red	white
8. Elector of Hessen	madder red	dark blue	madder red	yellow
9. Liechtenstein	white	dark blue	madder red	white
10. Friedrich Wilhelm III of Prussia	light blue	light blue	madder red	yellow
11. Prince Alexander of Württemberg	ash gray	dark blue	madder red	white
12. Haller	white	light blue	madder red	white
13. Iazygier and Kumanier	dark blue	dark blue	madder red	white
14. Hussar Regiment	madder red	dark blue	madder red	yellow

The everyday garment, worn instead of the *Attila*, was a dark blue jacket. Later, however, it was abolished. The fur cap was later superseded by the colored chaco.

In 1914 the regimental distinctions were as follows.

REGIMENT NO.	CHACO	*ATTILA* AND PELISSE	BREECHES	OLIVETTES
1	dark blue	dark blue	madder red	yellow
2	white	light blue	madder red	yellow
3	white	dark blue	madder red	yellow
4	madder red	light blue	madder red	white
5	madder red	dark blue	madder red	white
6	ash gray	light blue	madder red	yellow
7	light blue	light blue	madder red	white
8	madder red	dark blue	madder red	yellow
9	white	dark blue	madder red	white
10	light blue	light blue	madder red	yellow
11	ash gray	dark blue	madder red	white
12	white	light blue	madder red	white
13	dark blue	dark blue	madder red	white
14	madder red	light blue	madder red	yellow
15	ash gray	dark blue	madder red	yellow
16	ash gray	light blue	madder red	white

All regiments had black fur edging to their pelisses; the loops were yellow and black mixed. The chaco had a black plume and black and yellow cords (Fig. 11g). The service caps were red for all cavalry. Officers wore black caps like those of the other arms and grayish-black undress trousers with red piping.

The Hungarian militia (*Honved*) wore hussar uniform; the men had red loops and coats edged with white fur. (For service dress, see the section "Dragoons and *Chevau-légers*" above.) Hussars had dark blue or light-blue collar patches, according to the color of the former *Attila*.

VIII. LANCERS

The first corps of lancers was raised in 1794. It was later split up into divisions of the *chevau-legers* regiments but was reunited in 1791 to form Lancer Regiment No. 1. The 2nd Regiment was formed at the same time from a Galician volunteer corps. The earliest uniform consisted of a light-blue *kurtka* (Fig. 11h) with yellow collar, cuffs, lapels, and skirt turnbacks. The buttons were yellow metal, the waistcoat and breeches light blue. The headdress was a square-topped Polish cap with fur edging around the bottom. The upper part was of yellow cloth. Lance pennants were yellow and black in four squares. In 1785 the basic color of the *kurtka* was changed to white, with dark red distinctions. The undergarments and headdress were as before. In the following year the basic color remained white, but the distinctions became light blue and the undergarments white. In 1792 lancers had green *kurtkas* with red distinctions and yellow metal buttons, green waistcoats, and white breeches. The yellow caps were still worn. Green remained the characteristic basic color of the lancers up to the introduction of the new uniform of 1867. Gradually the Polish cap stiffened into the shape of the familiar lancer cap. The *kurtka* was fastened down the center of the front and had yellow worsted epaulettes. The breeches were changed to green with red stripes. A black and yellow girdle was worn around the waist. This was the uniform as worn in 1809 (Fig. 11i). The lance pennants were black over yellow. The lancer caps, the upper part of which displayed the distinctive color of the regiment, had a black and yellow plume.

In 1812 the distinctions were as follows.

REGIMENT	LANCER CAP	BASIC COLOR	DISTINCTIONS	BUTTONS
1. Merveldt	Imperial yellow	grass green	scarlet	yellow
2. Schwarzenberg	grass green	grass green	scarlet	yellow
3. Archduke Karl	scarlet	dark green	scarlet	yellow

The 4th Regiment, raised in 1813, wore the same uniform as the 3rd Regiment but with a white lancer cap.

The lancer cap itself changed in the meantime. The black and yellow plume was replaced by a drooping black horsehair plume on the left side. No epaulette was worn on the left shoulder, only a yellow shoulder strap (Fig. 11k). In the early 1850s lancers adopted a dark green lancer jacket with red distinctions in place of the *kurtka*. Epaulettes were then worn on both shoulders.

In 1854 the distinctions were as follows.

REGIMENT	LANCER CAP	BUTTONS
1. Civalart	Imperial yellow	yellow
2. Schwarzenberg	dark green	yellow
3. Archduke Karl	scarlet	yellow
4. Emperor Franz Josef	white	yellow
5. Wallmoden-Gimborn	light blue	yellow
6. Emperor Franz Josef	Imperial yellow	white
7. Archduke Karl	dark green	white
8. Archduke Maximilian	scarlet	white
9. Liechtenstein	white	white
10. Clam-Gallas	light blue	white
11. Grand Duke Alexander	carmine	white
12. King of Sicily	carmine	yellow

In 1860 a volunteer lancer regiment was raised. It had a different uniform: a madder red Polish cap (*tatarka*) with an eagle's feather; light-blue lancer jacket and trousers; long boots; and brown greatcoat. In 1865–1866 the other regiments of lancers began to be reclothed in similar uniforms. From 1866 lance pennants were not carried. Issue of the new uniform was completed in 1867 (Fig. 11l).

In 1867 the regiments were distinguished as follows.

REGIMENT	*TATARKA*	LANCER JACKET	CUFFS AND TROUSERS	BUTTONS
1. Grünne	Imperial yellow	light blue	madder red	yellow
2. Schwarzenberg	dark green	light blue	madder red	yellow
3. Minutillo	madder red	light blue	madder red	yellow
4. Emperor Franz Josef	white	light blue	madder red	yellow

(continued)

31

REGIMENT	*TATARKA*	LANCER JACKET	CUFFS AND TROUSERS	BUTTONS
5. Wallmoden-Gimborn	light blue	light blue	madder red	yellow
6. Emperor Franz Josef	Imperial yellow	light blue	madder red	white
7. Archduke Karl	dark green	light blue	madder red	white
8. Emperor of Mexico	madder red	light blue	madder red	white
9. Disbanded	—	—	—	—
10. Clam-Gallas	light blue	light blue	madder red	white
11. Emperor of Russia	dark blue		madder red	white
12. King of Sicily	dark blue		madder red	yellow

The lancer jacket was single-breasted and had a pocket on each side of the chest as well as in the skirts. Later, the lancer cap was reintroduced. The color of the top part varied; there was a black drooping horsehair plume on the left side and a yellow metal plate in front. For everyday use, a dark blue jacket with madder red collar patches was worn. Later, this was abolished and replaced by a light-blue single-breasted lancer jacket. A double-breasted lancer jacket with fur collar, also light blue in color, was slung over the left shoulder (Fig. 11m). This was worn in cold weather. All regiments had madder red trousers.

In 1914 the distinctions were as follows.

LANCER CAP COVER	BUTTONS	
	YELLOW	WHITE
white	4	—
light blue	5	—
dark blue	12	13
dark green	2	6
Imperial yellow	1	6
madder red	3	8
cherry red	—	11

The 9th and 10th Regiments had been disbanded. The *Landwehr* lancers were dressed like the 8th Regiment, with their regimental number on the buttons (Fig. 13b). (For the service dress, see the section "Dragoons and *Chevau-légers*" above.)

IX. ARTILLERY, ENGINEERS, TRANSPORT CORPS, GENERAL OFFICERS, ETC.: DISTINCTIONS OF RANK

The artillery did not have a uniform until relatively late because it was more an independent body than an arm of the service. Illustrations of about 1734 (Fig. 12b) show artillerymen in gray coats with yellow metal buttons and red cuffs; long gray waistcoats; white gaiters; and gold-laced hats. Thereafter the distinctions were always red, but the basic color gradually changed through fawn and "wolf" gray to dark brown. In 1760 coat, waistcoat, and breeches were fawn (Fig. 12c); in 1798, wolf gray. As well as the cuffs, the collar, skirt turnbacks, and officers' waistcoats now displayed the red distinctive color. A hat continued to be worn, but its shape

Fig. 12. Austria-Hungary—Artillery, Pioneers, General Officers.

a, b, c, d, e, f, g: artillery. h, k: pioneers. i: sapper. l, m: general officers in "German"
and Hungarian full dress respectively.

altered several times. In 1840 (Fig. 12f) the uniform was dark brown with light-blue
trousers (the latter having formerly been white). The cut of the coat resembled that of
the infantry. Up to 1850 it was shaped like a coatee; but it was superseded in that year
by a double-breasted tunic and in 1860 by a single-breasted one with turndown collar. Chacos were worn from 1851. From 1868 up to the introduction of service dress,
the foot artillery wore dark brown single-breasted tunics with red distinctions, with
red piping for officers and yellow metal buttons (Fig. 12g). The undress jackets were
dark brown with red collar patches; trousers were light blue; the chacos had a black
horsehair plume. The men's caps were light blue; the stiff officers' caps were
black like those of other officers. The fortress artillery had, in addition, broad red
stripes on the trousers. The dark brown jackets and light-blue trousers were superseded by the bluish-gray service dress, which was similar to that of the infantry in style
and ornamentation. The trouser stripes of the fortress artillery were abolished. The
engineers, pioneers, miners, and pontoon troops of the Austrian army had very
varied uniforms. In 1760 the pioneers wore a black *Kaskett*, gray coat and waistcoat,
with yellow (later white) metal buttons, green collar, cuffs, and skirt turnbacks. The
breeches and leather equipment were white, the gaiters black. In other respects
the uniform generally followed the variations already noted in the infantry uniform.
The hat worn in 1830 was turned up on the left, with the cockade, loop, and black and
yellow plume in front (Fig. 12h). In 1840 it was superseded by a chaco with a black
plume. The trousers were the same color as the coatee. This was superseded by the
tunic in 1850, and from then it followed the same changes in style as the infantry. The
men's tunics, trousers, jackets, and caps were gray, with green distinctions and white
metal buttons. From 1840 the leather equipment was black (Fig. 12k). The service
dress also resembled that of the infantry, except that their former distinctions and

buttons were retained. The pontoon troops were dressed in dark blue with red distinctions and white metal buttons. The sappers had dark blue uniforms with dark red distinctions and yellow metal buttons (Fig. 12i). From 1868 to 1914 the engineers wore light-blue tunics and undress jackets with cherry red distinctions and blue-gray trousers. The service dress was bluish-gray with cherry-colored distinctions. In 1778 the men of the wagon train wore all-white uniforms with yellow collars and a black and yellow band on the upper left arm. In addition, they wore the usual *Kaskett*. Later, the uniform was changed to gray with yellow distinctions and white metal buttons, white trousers, and hats with a black and yellow plume. In 1815 the uniform again became white with yellow distinctions, and a chaco and black leather equipment were introduced. The officers had brown uniforms with yellow distinctions, hats, white trousers, and long boots. In 1840 the distinctions and trousers were made light blue. From then, the uniform remained similar to that of the artillery except that the trousers were madder red, as were the men's caps. As well as the brown tunic with light-blue distinctions, they had dark blue undress jackets. Light-blue distinctions were worn on the bluish-gray service uniform.

General officers did not have a proper uniform until the reign of Empress Maria Theresa, at which time the coat was white, with red distinctions, waistcoats, and breeches, and gold lace ornamentation. This combination of colors was always retained for court dress despite changes in fashion. The undress uniform latterly consisted of a light-gray tunic with red distinctions and gold lace and dark blue trousers with red stripes. In full dress a light-green feather plume was worn in the gold-laced hat (Fig. 12l). Hungarian general officers were ordered to wear a highly ornamented hussar uniform in Maria Theresa's reign. From time to time this uniform was again ordered to be worn, and for generals of cavalry as well, and later, for Hungarian general officers. Since the uniform altered little, that of 1890 will be described (Fig. 12m). The *Attila* and breeches were red with red distinctions and rich gold looping, and the pelisse was white with ornamentation as on the *Attila*. The fur cap had a red bag and a white plume. The undress uniform was a gray *Attila* with red distinctions and gold loops and lace. The pelisse was similar, with black edging. The dark gray trousers had red stripes. The headdress was a hussar chaco, and the universal black officers' cap was also worn. ADCs wore uniforms resembling that for general officers except that the basic color was dark green. The court dress trousers were dark gray with red piping and broad gold stripes. The general staff uniform followed that of general officers in style. The coat was dark green with black velvet collar and cuffs piped red and dark gray trousers with red triple stripes. The court headdress was a hat with a green vulture feather.

General officers wore long red collar patches on their service dress. The rank lace did not extend right to the end of the patch. The collar patches on general staff officers' service dress were of black velvet and red piping with a broad gold stripe at the outer ends.

Rank was denoted by stripes around the collar and cuffs and, in addition, by stars at the ends of the collar. A *Feldmarschall* wore broad waved gold stripes ornamented with embroidered leaves. In the case of other general officers, the stripes were of straight patterned lace, and the stars were silver.

Feldzeugmeister and *General der Kavallerie*: broad lace and 2 stars
Feldmarschallleutnant: 2 stars
Generalmajor: 1 star

For regimental officers, the lace around the collar and cuffs was of gold or silver according to the button color. The rank stars on gold lace were silver, and vice versa.

Oberst: lace and 3 stars
Oberstleutnant: lace and 2 stars
Major: lace and 1 star
Hauptmann: 3 stars
Oberleutnant: 2 stars
Leutnant: 1 star
Fähnrich: narrow gold or silver lace and 1 star
Kadettfeldwebel: narrow gold or silver lace with white or yellow lace above; 3 white stars
Feldwebel: yellow or white silk stripe and 3 white stars
Zugführer: 3 white stars
Korporal: 2 white stars
Gefreiter: 1 white star

The officers' sashes were of yellow and black silk; those of general officers were of gold and black silk. Adjutants wore the sash over the left shoulder. The marksmen's distinction took the form of worsted cords worn across the left breast, red for infantry and green for *Jäger*. Cavalry and artillery officers wore a narrow gold pouch belt with a silver pouch, the flap of which was ornamented with a gilt double eagle. The rank distinctions remained the same on the service uniform, but the stripes took the form of chevrons and were only worn at the ends of the collar and longitudinally on the cuff patches.

REPUBLIC OF AUSTRIA

Cockade: red-white-red

The first corps formed after the end of the Great War was the *Volkswehr*, consisting entirely of infantry, which wore what were left of the wartime uniforms. The universal badge was a round yellow shield, bearing the inscription "Volkswehr," pinned on the left breast. A broad red flash was worn on the collar and left side of the cap (Fig. 13g). The rank distinctions consisted of dark blue chevrons on the upper left arm for NCOs, dark blue horizontal stripes on the lower left arm for officers. When the *Bundesheer* was formed in 1920–1921, the uniform bore a strong similarity to that of the German *Reichswehr*. The universal distinction of the *Bundesheer* was the field gray or silver *Kapelllitze* on a patch of *Waffenfarbe* on the collar of the jacket (Fig. 13k). As well as the German-style steel helmet, a peaked cap like that of the *Reichswehr* was worn, but with a rather smaller top, piped in *Waffenfarbe* around the edges of the band and the top, with a red-white-red cockade and, below, the coat of arms of the republic, or states, stamped in brass (Fig. 13h). The *Waffenfarben* were the same as in the German *Reichswehr*, except that infantry had grass green and

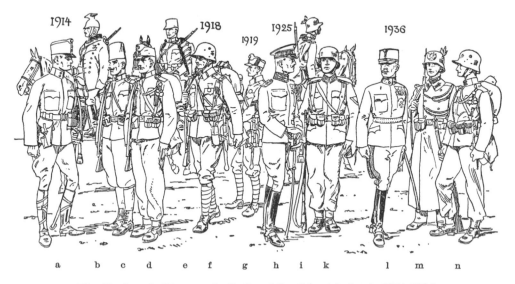

Fig. 13. Austria-Hungary (a–f). Republic of Austria (g–n), 1914–1936.
a: infantry officer. d, f, k, n: infantry. b: lancer. c: Bosnian
infantry. e: hussar. g: corporal of the Volkswehr. h: field officer. i: cavalry. l: general
officer. m: *Gardebataillon*.

Jäger yellowish-green. At first, the officers' rank distinctions took the form of short horizontal silver rank stripes on both lower arms, the uppermost forming a loop, with a patch of *Waffenfarbe* inside it. Subalterns wore one to three narrow stripes; field officers, one medium and one to three narrow; generals, one broad stripe with a narrow one below. Field officers also wore flat silver shoulder cords. The greatcoat had spearhead-shaped patches in *Waffenfarbe* to begin with, with a small button on them for officers and NCOs.

In 1923 the rank distinctions were altered to conform exactly to those of the *Reichswehr*; from the same time, the jacket and greatcoat collars and the cap bands were made of dark green cloth (Fig. 13k). In contradistinction to the *Reichswehr*, the gold general officers' embroidery was placed on a patch of dark green piped red. NCOs had no lace around the collar, and the lace went right around the shoulder straps. The rank stars were in gold. *Offizierstellvertreter* and *Fähnriche* had shoulder straps wholly of *Waffenfarbe*, with a lace stripe down the center as well. In 1923, also, a tunic with six silver buttons, piped in *Waffenfarbe* around the bottom of the collar and around the skirts, was introduced for walking-out dress in the Austrian army. The cuffs were round, without lace. The colored collar patches on the great-coat were discontinued. On service, an old-style peakless cap was worn. The cavalry retained the double-breasted fur-trimmed jacket with fur collar, with no *Waffen-farbe* distinctions but with shoulder straps or cords. It was worn slung over the shoulder (Fig. 13i). The gold officers' sword knot was worn hanging loose.

At the end of 1933, a complete change took place in the uniform of the Austrian *Bundesheer*. Each arm of the service adopted the field gray uniform, as well as the 1914 dress uniform of the arm from which it stemmed (except that the old black and yellow cockade was superseded by the red-white-red one), so that a more detailed description is unnecessary (Fig. 13n). Infantry Regiments 1 to 3 and *Alpenjäger* Regiments 8 and 9 were dressed like the earlier "German" *Landwehr*; Infantry Regiment No. 4, like the former Infantry Regiment No. 4; No. 5 like No. 54; No. 6 like No. 49; No. 7 like the old No. 7; *Alpenjäger* Regiment No. 10 like No. 27; No. 11 like No. 47; No. 12 like No. 59; No. 13 like No. 30; No. 14 like No. 14; No. 15 like No. 99, and the Tyrolean *Landesschützen* Regiment and the mechanized *Jäger*, like the *Jäger*. The distinctive color of the armored troops was black, with a yellow metal button. The peacetime uniform was bluish-gray and the same for mechanized troops. Of the cavalry squadrons, the 6th Squadron perpetuated the mounted *Landes-schützen*. Its distinctive color was grass green. The peacetime tunic was bluish-gray. The other squadrons carried on the traditions of the dragoon regiments: the peacetime tunic was light blue; the distinctive colors were as for Dragoon Regiments 3, 4, 5, 11, and 15 of 1914. With the tunic, the cavalry wore the old red breeches and the red peakless caps. The *Gebirgstruppen* (Mountain Troops) wore a white *Edelweiss* badge on the collar patches and left side of their caps. Mechanized troops had a winged wheel. Above the right breast pocket, armored troops had a gold, silver, or dark gray embroidered knight in armor on a triangular black patch. The rank distinctions were exactly as in the old Austrian army, including the black-and-yellow officers' sashes and the other old appointments (Fig. 13l). *Wachtmeister* and *Stabswachtmeister* had a medium-width lace stripe with a narrow one in silver above;

Offizierstellvertreter had the same lace, but with a brass star; a *Vizeleutnant* had a medium gold lace stripe with a silver star; a *Fähnrich* had the same, with a large button at the end of the patch.

In 1933 a *Gardebataillon* was formed. On the front of the helmet, the National Arms was worn, and looped around the left shoulder, white double cords—gold for officers. The distinctive color was red, with white piping and white metal buttons. The peacetime tunic was dark green (Fig. 13m).

BELGIUM

Cockade: black-yellow-red

I. INFANTRY

Except during the Brabant revolt of 1789, a "Belgian Legion" existed up to 1814. The uniform consisted of a white single-breasted coatee, with green distinctions for the 1st Regiment; yellow for the 2nd; light blue for the 3rd; and red for the 4th. The breeches were light gray. Chacos were worn.

In 1815 the uniforms of Belgian troops differed from those of the rest of the Netherlands in several respects; the main one was that the former wore British-pattern chacos.

The army uniforms of the independent kingdom of Belgium from 1831 were very closely modeled on French ones. Originally the blue infantry uniform had lapels. The fusilier companies had blue shoulder straps; grenadiers had red epaulettes, and *voltigeurs* green. The chaco was of French type; the trousers were gray. The lapels were abolished c. 1840. From then, the uniform consisted of a single-breasted blue coat with blue collar, red piping and cuffs, and yellow metal buttons (Figs. 14a,b). The fusilier companies wore red crescents in place of shoulder straps. The epaulette fringes of the *voltigeurs* were changed to yellow. At the same time, the three *chasseurs à pied* regiments were wearing all-green uniforms. The colored distinctions consisted only of red piping, which went around the collar and cuffs, around the front and hem of the coat, coat skirt, pocket flaps, and trousers. The men's fringed epaulettes were green and red, the buttons yellow metal; the chaco pompon was red, with green tuft above. Equipment was of black leather. The Scheldt Battalion wore a long green coat with yellow metal buttons and yellow piping and green *voltigeur* epaulettes with yellow crescents. The trousers were green; the hat had green cords and a green feather plume. At the end of the 1840s, the uniform was made double-breasted; and (except for grenadiers) epaulettes were abolished, and wings were then worn. The uniform of the line infantry in 1913 (Fig. 14c) consisted of a royal blue coat with two rows of yellow metal buttons. The pointed cuffs were of basic color; the collar was red; and the gray trousers had red piping. The chaco had a yellow metal plate, red plume, and pompon. Equipment was of black leather. Shortly before the Great War the cut of the coat was altered, and the red distinctions were changed to blue-gray. The grenadiers (Fig. 14d) wore the same pattern of coat but had a grenade at the ends of the red collar. They had black trousers with red stripes. Their fur caps had a grenade on the front. They also had red fringed epaulettes. The leather equip-

Fig. 14. Belgium.

a, c: line infantry. b: officer, line infantry. d: grenadier. e: officer,
carabiniers. f: cuirassier. g, i: lancers. h, k: *chasseurs à cheval*. l: guides. m, n: artillery.

ment was white. The carabiniers (Fig. 14e) wore coats like those of the infantry but all green with yellow piping. On the collar were two yellow hunting horns. The trousers were iron-gray, piped yellow. The headdress was a so-called Tyrolean hat. Equipment was of black leather. The *chasseurs* had a similar uniform but without the hunting horns on the collar, and with a chaco instead of the hat.

The Belgian army entered the Great War wearing its peacetime uniform, but later began to be issued—slowly at first—with a khaki-colored service dress of British pattern except that officers also had a stand collar. The steel helmet was of French pattern with the Belgian lion in an oak wreath on the front (Figs. 15a,c). The leather equipment was natural color. The Arm of Service was denoted by a colored scalloped collar patch, brick red for infantry, scarlet for grenadiers. The regimental number was displayed in black on the shoulder straps; grenadiers had a flaming grenade. Rank was indicated by one to three gold stars, with a

Fig. 15. Belgium.

a, c: infantry. b: *chasseurs à cheval*. d: *guides*,
senior lieutenant. e: cavalry officer, full dress.

40

vertical bar at the rear for field officers on the collar patches. NCOs wore short, slanting stripes on the lower arms. *Chasseurs* and carabiniers had green collar patches with the regimental number in yellow and a hunting horn. This uniform continued to be worn, basically unaltered, after the war. From 1935, officers' jackets were open-necked, with a khaki or white shirt. Off duty, British-style forage caps were worn, having the regimental badge, with crown above on the front. In 1930 an evening dress was introduced for officers. The dark blue tunic had a colored collar, slash cuffs of basic color with piping in *Waffenfarbe* for infantry and *chasseurs*, and cuff patches in *Waffenfarbe* for grenadiers and carabiniers (red and green respectively). The trousers were dark blue with red triple stripes, yellow for *chasseurs* and carabiniers. The dark blue forage caps had a black peak, and band and piping around the top in *Waffenfarbe*. The rank badges were on the collar patches, and gold twisted shoulder cords were worn.

II. CAVALRY

Like the infantry, the cavalry closely followed French fashions. Cuirassiers (Fig. 14f)) wore a steel helmet with black horsehair *crinière* and red plume. The blue jacket had a row of white metal buttons. The collar, cuffs, skirt lining, and piping were red for the one regiment, yellow for the other. Trousers were blue with stripes in the distinctive color. They also had red grenadier epaulettes, plain breast and back plates, a white pouch belt, and gauntlets. Both *chasseurs à cheval* regiments (Fig. 14h) were dressed in dark green jackets and trousers, with red distinctions, and tall black chacos with a white hanging plume and white cords. The fringed epaulettes were white. Equipment was of white leather. The shabraques were green and red. The *Guides* regiment wore dark green jackets and breeches with light-carmine collar and cuffs and, at first, light-carmine lapels, skirt edgings, and trouser stripes. The fringed epaulettes, aiguillettes, and leather equipment were white. Fur caps with a red bag and feather plume were worn. Both lancer regiments (Fig. 14g) wore all-blue uniforms: the 1st with carmine distinctions, and 2nd with yellow. Epaulettes and leather equipment were white; the lance pennants were black, red, and yellow.

The two *Guides* regiments (Fig. 14l) in 1914 wore green dolmans with amaranth red pointed cuffs and collar and orange-yellow loopings. The amaranth red breeches had double yellow stripes. Fur caps were worn. Both *chasseurs à cheval* regiments (Fig. 14k) wore, as their main item of dress, a royal blue dolman with white loopings. The breeches were gray-blue with white stripes. The 1st Regiment had yellow chacos, collars, and cuffs; the 2nd scarlet. The chacos were bound with white lace and had a small white plume. They were usually worn with black covers. In 1914 there were four regiments of lancers (Fig. 14i). They wore the same color of dolmans and breeches as the *chasseurs à cheval*. The lancer cap, collar, and cuffs were amaranth red for the 1st Regiment; yellow for the 2nd; white for the 3rd; and ultramarine for the 4th. The loopings were white for the first two regiments and yellow for the 3rd and 4th. Trumpeters had loopings in the distinctive color. The lance pennants were black, yellow, and red, arranged in three triangles.

The *Waffenfarben* on the service dress were white for lancers, yellow for *chasseurs à cheval*, and dark pink with green piping for *Guides*. The evening dress was cut like a lancer jacket.

III. ARTILLERY, ENGINEERS, TRANSPORT CORPS, *GENDARMERIE*, AND GENERAL OFFICERS

The first Belgian artillery uniforms almost exactly resembled French ones in style and color (Fig. 14m). In 1914 chacos were worn only by the heavy batteries. The field artillery had low-crowned fur caps with a red bag. In general, the whole of the uniform was blue; collar, piping, and trouser stripes were red, and buttons were yellow metal. The engineers wore royal blue tunics like the infantry with black collars. The royal blue trousers had red stripes; red fringed epaulettes were also worn, and white leather equipment. The Transport Corps had royal blue coats with ultramarine collar patches and ultramarine stripes on the black trousers. The chaco had both front and back peaks. The *gendarmerie* resembled the *Gendarmes de la Garde* of the French Second Empire in their tall fur caps. The royal blue coat had a row of white metal buttons and red collar and cuff patches. The aiguillettes were white, as was the leather equipment; the trousers, gray-black. General officers' uniforms, likewise, differed little from French ones.

The *Waffenfarben* on the service dress were dark blue with red piping for artillery and general officers; black for pioneers; and light blue for transport troops. To the rear of the rank stars on the collar, and on both sides of the cap badge, general officers wore two vertical bars.

All arms were represented in the *garde civique*. In general, their dress followed that of the regular army. One way in which the uniform of the *garde civique* differed from that of the regular army was in the hat worn by the carabiniers.

42

BRAZIL

Cockade: black up to 1800; blue-red to 1822; from then, green-yellow-blue

From the mid-sixteenth century, Brazil was a Portuguese colony. In 1806 the Portuguese royal house, driven out by Napoleon, settled there, returning to Portugal after Napoleon's downfall. In 1821 Brazil bacame an independent empire, and in 1869 a republic.

I. INFANTRY AND RIFLES

The uniforms of the regiments garrisoned in Brazil during the eighteenth century were of Portuguese style, as were those worn in the period 1806–1822. The Negro regiments wore white coats with red distinctions. In 1823 the infantry adopted a dark blue uniform (Fig. 16a). The distinctions were originally green with yellow piping, with a yellow grenade on the collar for grenadiers; later they were changed to

Fig. 16. Brazil.
a, c, d, f: infantry. b: presidential guard. e: cavalry. g: infantry officer.

red with red piping. Leather equipment was white. The rifle battalions wore dark blue dolmans with black loopings on the chest, a green collar, pointed cuffs, and black leather equipment. In 1834 a low bell-topped chaco with a yellow metal plate was issued to the infantry and rifles. In 1845 the infantry coats were made double-breasted with dark blue cuffs and a narrow scalloped three-button flap of distinctive color. In 1852 single-breasted dark blue tunics, piped red around the collar, collar patches, front, skirt pocket flaps, cuffs, and cuff patches were issued to the infantry. The buttons were yellow metal. Epaulettes were dark blue with a white worsted tuft at the end. Officers' had yellow crescents. White leather crossbelts and a narrow waistbelt were worn. The 1st Fusilier Battalion had gray-blue trousers; the others had dark blue ones without piping. White ones were always worn in summer. The officers' kepi was of French type, piped red, with a band the same color as the cuff patches; from 1850, this was worn by the men as well (Fig. 16c). For rifles, the coat, trousers, and kepi were dark green, piped black, with black leather equipment. The distinctions consisted of variously colored collar and cuff patches as in the following table.

REGIMENT	COLLAR PATCHES	CUFF PATCHES
Fusilier Battalion 1	white	yellow
Fusilier Battalion 2	yellow	light blue
Fusilier Battalion 3	red	yellow
Fusilier Battalion 4	light blue	red
Fusilier Battalion 5	red	light blue
Fusilier Battalion 6	yellow	red
Fusilier Battalion 7	light blue	yellow
Rifle Battalion 8	yellow	white
Rifle Battalion 9	red	red
Rifle Battalion 10	green	green
Rifle Battalion 11	green	red
Rifle Battalion 12	yellow	yellow
Rifle Battalion 13	yellow	green
Rifle Battalion 14	green	yellow

In 1866 the fusiliers adopted dark red collar and cuff patches. The tunic, trousers, and kepi for rifles were changed to dark blue, with dark blue collar and slash cuffs, all piped yellow. The buttons remained yellow as before. On service, khaki-colored ticken clothing was worn, with a white kepi cover, or a broad-brimmed hat, and waistbelt equipment was introduced. In 1871 a tapering chaco with a white and red plume, red cords, and star on the front was introduced for full dress, and dark blue epaulettes with a metal crescent and red fringe. Off duty, a small leather kepi with the number in metal on the front was worn. Rifles had green plumes, cords, epaulette fringes, and a little bugle horn on the chaco.

A completely new uniform (as in Fig. 16d) was introduced in 1889. Tunic and trousers were dark blue, with red collar and cuff patches, piping, loopings, epaulette fringes, and trouser stripes, white leather equipment, black boots, and gaiters. The helmet was of dark blue felt, with black lacquered leather front and back peaks, and a yellow metal plate. Officers had gold loopings on their tunics and a red feather plume on their helmets.

On service, a single-breasted coat with red collar and cuff patches and red shoulder straps was worn and a dark blue kepi with red band and piping. The rifles adopted the same uniform, but their badge was a bugle horn instead of the crossed rifles. In 1894 red trousers with double dark blue stripes were introduced; the collar was altered to red with dark blue patches, and the round red-piped cuffs from then on had a rectangular red three-button patch. The kepi was modeled exactly on the French one and was retained after the Great War. In 1903 single-breasted full dress tunics having seven red loops with buttons on the breast—gold loops for officers— were introduced. A white tropical helmet was worn, with brass spike, chin chain, and arm-of-service badge on the front, and short white gaiters. In 1907 the helmet was abolished, and a red plume added to the kepi for full dress wear plus yellow shoulder scales and single dark blue trouser stripes. From 1908 a light-khaki-colored service uniform was worn: a jacket with a stand collar, without colored distinctions, with pointed shoulder straps; natural-colored leather equipment; a French-style kepi with khaki top part, and broad dark blue band piped red around the top. The arm-of-service badge on the front was in white. The gaiters were brown. In 1917 gray-green webbing waistbelts, cartridge pouches, and straps were introduced (Fig. 16f). Then, too, the kepi was replaced by a khaki-colored U.S.-style forage cap with a darker-colored band, and a khaki peak and chinstrap, with the arm-of-service badge in bronze on the front. The regimental number was worn on the collar. The officers' service jackets had a row of black buttons and patch pockets on the crest and skirts. After the Great War, a single-breasted dark blue tunic, with no loopings—the same for officers—was worn for full dress, and brown leather equipment and black gaiters. In 1931–1933 a completely new uniform was introduced. The field jacket was olive green with pleated patch pockets, and a row of seven black buttons; the stand-and-fall collar, pointed shoulder straps, round cuffs, and trousers were of darker olive green cloth. The leather equipment was brown; officers wore a brace over the right shoulder; the gaiters were gray-green, and the boots black. The French-pattern steel helmet was painted olive green and had a disc in *Waffenfarbe* on the front (Fig. 16g). The service cap was fore-and-aft shaped without colored distinctions. The arm-of-service badge was worn on the collar: crossed rifles with an applied hand grenade and numeral below, in bronze for the men and white silk for the officers. For rifles, the badge was a bugle horn with the number within the coil. Officers had gauntlet cuffs. They also had a walking-out dress: a dark gray four-button jacket with patch pockets, silk girdle with buckle, gauntlet cuffs, pointed shoulder straps piped in *Waffenfarbe* (green for infantry), light-gray trousers with two dark gray stripes down each side, a light-gray or white shirt, and dark gray or black tie. The forage cap was piped around the top in *Waffenfarbe*, with a light-gray celluloid band, dark gray chinstrap, and black leather peak. The national cockade was placed on the band. The gold arm-of-service badge was worn on a small light-gray enamel disc at the ends of the jacket collar. Buttons were yellow metal. In summer, white jackets and trousers, the same color as the gray caps, were worn. Officers had a dark blue evening dress uniform with blue-black velvet collar and round cuffs with gold embroidered edging, scalloped patches in *Waffenfarbe* with the arm-of-service badge in gold; and dark blue forage caps without piping, with a blue-black velvet band, gold chinstrap, embroidered peak for field officers, with the national cockade within a circle of leaves, on the front. The gray walking-out dress for senior NCOs was cut like the officers':

the pointed shoulder straps and round cuffs were dark blue with red piping; the rank distinctions consisted of three to six narrow chevrons on a dark blue backing on the lower arms. The forage caps were dark gray, piped dark blue around the top, with a dark blue band, on the front of which was a semicircular red cloth patch with the arm-of-service badge on it in gold, and with a black leather peak. The trousers were piped red. This uniform was the same for all arms, except for the officers' *Waffenfarbe* and the arm-of-service badges.

II. CAVALRY, ARTILLERY, AND ENGINEERS

From 1822 the cavalry wore the same uniform as the infantry, but with a bell-top chaco and white piping which, up to the late 1930s, was the characteristic distinction of the cavalry. The buttons and shoulder scales were of yellow metal. The collar was green at first, and red later, as were the cuffs. The leather equipment was white. The Presidents' Guard Regiment (Fig. 16b) had single-breasted white jackets with skirts, red collar, pointed cuffs and piping, yellow metal buttons and shoulder scales, white breeches and gauntlets, black leather equipment and boots, and yellow metal crested helmets with a black *crinière*, and green plume on the left, and a winged dragon on the front of the comb. In 1832 the presidential guard was given a black leather helmet with yellow metal comb and plate and a red plume and *crinière*. This uniform was retained by the presidential guard up to the late 1930s. In general, the cavalry uniform developed like that of the infantry. The leather equipment was always white. On the 1852 tunic, all piping was white, the collar patches were red, and the cuff patches red or dark blue, for the four existing regiments of the time. The helmet worn in 1890 was made of red felt; it had a yellow metal comb with a white horsehair *crinière* and small plume at the front, instead of a spike. The piping was white. The trousers were royal blue with broad red stripes. In 1894 red trousers with double medium-blue stripes were introduced. A red plume was added to the left side of the helmet. The arm-of-service badge consisted of two crossed lances. In 1903 royal blue tunics were adopted, with white loopings for the men and gold for officers. A red hair plume was worn on the tropical helmet (Fig. 16e). Royal blue tunics, with white piping on the collar and cuff patches and a white kepi plume, were introduced in 1908. The service uniforms were like those for the infantry, with the appropriate arm-of-service badge. The same was true of the 1933 uniform. In the late 1930s the arm-of-service badge consisted of crossed lances with the numeral below. The *Waffenfarbe* was white.

Up to 1852 the artillery had red distinctions, yellow metal buttons, and black leather equipment; these distinctions remained in use by the horse artillery in the late 1930s. On the tunic, the 1st Battalion had red collar patches and black cuff patches; the 2nd wore these colors reversed. The helmet that went with the 1890 uniform was red with a black and red plume; and red *crinière* for the horse artillery. The trousers were like those for the cavalry. The other changes in uniform followed those in the infantry; the arm-of-service badge on the uniform introduced in 1931–1933 was a flaming grenade, or crossed cannon barrels for the horse artillery; with the numeral below. The *Waffenfarbe* was dark blue.

The engineers in general wore the same uniform as the artillery. The distinctive color up to 1889 was carmine, as well as for the 1890 uniform; the helmet was black, with a black and white feather plume for officers. The trousers were dark blue with broad carmine stripes. The arm-of-service badge was a tower. The *Waffenfarbe* on the 1931–1933-pattern uniform was turquoise.

III. GENERAL OFFICERS AND GENERAL STAFF; RANK DISTINCTIONS

In the late 1930s the uniform of general officers was of the usual style of the period: dark blue, with dark blue collar and cuffs, gold buttons and epaulettes, and rich oakleaf embroidery, the arrangement of which denoted the rank. The full dress headdress up to 1914 was a hat with white plumage and gold lace binding; on service, a dark blue kepi with gold piping and oakleaf embroidery on the band was worn. In 1908 the full dress consisted of a dark blue dolman with black loopings on the breast and lace edging around the outside; the collar and round cuffs were dark blue with rich oakleaf embroidery; the red trousers had gold or dark blue stripes; gold epaulettes with silver rank stars; red kepi with dark blue gold-embroidered band, and piping in gold. On the service uniform, the embroidery on the kepi, and the rank stars on the collar, were white. In 1920 gilt buttons and dark blue shoulder straps with the rank stars in silver were worn on the service uniform; they were also worn on the front of the cap band. On the 1931–1933 uniform a three-leafed oak sprig, in white or gold embroidery, was worn at the ends of the collar of the olive green, gray, and white uniforms. On the evening dress uniform, the collar and cuffs were embroidered with gold oakleaf embroidery, as was the cap peak.

Up to 1933 the uniform of the General Staff was generally the same style as the infantry uniform, but was all dark blue with yellow metal buttons; it was also, for a time, piped white. From 1931 the staff wore the uniform of their former arm, with two crossed oak sprigs in gold embroidery on the lower right arm.

The rank distinctions altered only at long intervals. From 1806 to 1852 they consisted of varying bullions attached to the shoulder scales. Colonels wore thick bullions on both shoulders; lieutenant colonels wore thick ones on the right, thin ones on the left; majors, vice versa. Captains had thin ones on both shoulders; lieutenants, thin ones on the right only and none on the left; ensigns, vice versa. From 1852 to 1889 rank was denoted by lace stripes on the cuffs, running under the patches: ensigns, one narrow one; lieutenants, two; captains, one medium; majors, one medium with one narrow below; lieutenant colonels, two; and colonels, three medium gold stripes. NCOs wore one to four diagonal stripes in the distinctive color, edged black, above the cuffs. From 1889 to 1930 officers wore French-style rank distinctions on the dress uniform: one to six stripes, of the color of the buttons, on the cuffs and on the band of the kepi. On the service uniform, black chevron-shaped cords were worn on the shoulder straps. NCOs' stripes were of the same number, chevron-shaped, above the cuffs, and of black cord on the service uniform. On the 1931–1933 uniform officers wore their rank distinctions on the shoulder straps: for subalterns, one to three five-pointed silver stars with a blue shield applied in the center; field officers all wore three stars on a gold crescent according to rank. General officers had, on their shoulder straps, gold-embroidered stars with the shields in the center and one to three pairs of gold-embroidered crossed sprigs below. NCOs had three to five chevrons on the lower arms, in dark blue silk on the service uniform and in gold on the walking-out dress.

BULGARIA

Cockade: red-green-white

The Bulgarian army stemmed from various volunteer corps. In 1867–1868 the "Holy Legion" wore a uniform with many loops, which bore a strong resemblance to the national dress.

In 1877 the Bulgarian legion was formed, of volunteers of Bulgarian descent in Bucharest and Ploesti. Apart from the turned-down collar, their uniform resembled that worn later (Fig. 17a). The officers of this legion were all Russian. Dress and equipment were exactly like those of the Russian army; indeed, up to the 1950s the uniform was very similar to that of the Russian army.

In 1890 the infantry had dark green coats and trousers (Fig. 17b). The coat was cut in a distinctive way: at the top it was fastened by an oblique line of buttons, and from there down it was closed by hooks. Collar and cuffs were of basic color, and the coat was edged with red piping. The Alexander Regiment had red collars, shoulder straps, and cuff patches with gold embroidery; the Ferdinand Regiment, white; and the Clementine Regiment, light blue. The cap resembled the Russian one and had the Bulgarian cross on the front. The greatcoat, made from a mixture of wool and goat's hair, was earth-gray in color.

The cavalry (Fig. 17d) wore dark blue jackets with red, silver-embroidered collars and cuffs; the edges and seams of the 1st Regiment were piped white; the 2nd, red; the 3rd, yellow; the 4th, blue. A white upright plume was worn on the black lambskin cap.

The artillery wore cavalry-style jackets with collar and cuffs of black velvet, and a red top to the fur cap. Pioneers were dressed like the infantry, but also had black velvet collars and cuffs and white metal buttons. The Prince's lifeguard wore red *Attilas* with white loops and white lambskin caps with a red top.

In summer, white linen uniforms were generally worn, with peaked caps of the same material (Fig. 17c). Officers' rank was denoted by the number of stars on the epaulettes and shoulder straps. The silver, green, and red embroidered sash worn by colonels and senior officers had tassels. Infantry wore two cartridge pouches on a leather waistbelt. Officers, sergeants, and bandsmen carried revolvers. The infantry rank and file carried no sidearms.

About 1900 a lancer-type jacket, with two rows of buttons for officers, was introduced.

In 1914 Infantry Regiments 1, 4, 5, 6, 8, 9, 17, and 22 wore lace, and they had a cipher on the shoulder straps (Fig. 18a).

The cavalry wore lancer jackets: blue for the 1st, 2nd, and 3rd Regiments, green for the 4th. The distinctions of the first three regiments were red, raspberry red for

Fig. 17. Bulgaria.
a: Bulgarian Legion. b, c: infantry. d: cavalry.

the 4th. The piping was white for the 1st and 4th, red for the 2nd and 3rd (Fig. 18b). The old hussar-style uniform was worn by the lifeguard cavalry regiment in the late 1930s (Fig. 18c). Officers had light-blue undress jackets.

From 1908 a gray-green service dress, without colored distinctions, similar to the Russian one, was introduced. German field gray uniforms, with Bulgarian distinctions, were widely worn during the Great War.

After the war a khaki service dress, with collar patches and cap bands in the old *Waffenfarben*, was introduced (Figs. 18d,e). The jacket was single-breasted. Rank distinctions of the old Russian type continued to be worn as before. The green tunic was made single-breasted. White caps were worn by preference. The lifeguard cavalry regiment alone wore the fur cap in the late 1930s, at which time some units were still wearing *Opanken*.

Fig. 18. Bulgaria.
a, e: infantry. b: cavalry. c: lifeguard. d: infantry officer.

CHILE

Cockade: white-red-blue

Around 1820 the infantry wore turquoise blue single-breasted coatees with red collar, pointed cuffs, piping, and epaulettes; white metal buttons; buff-colored trousers (turquoise blue for officers); black gaiters and footwear; and a black felt chaco with leather binding and silver plate on the front with a blue, white, and red pompon above. Officers had silver epaulettes, a silver pompon, and a silver band around the top edge of the chaco (Fig. 19a). The cavalry wore various uniforms: for instance, the hussars of the national guard wore dark blue dolmans with black collar and cuffs and white loopings, and a dark blue pelisse with similar loopings and black fur edging; dark blue breeches with black stripes (silver for officers); white and blue hussar sashes, and leather chacos like the infantry's, but with a tall blue and white plume and black lines (Fig. 19b). Up to the mid-nineteenth century the uniform followed the usual fashions of the period. From then up to the end of the 1880s, it was mainly under French influence. Fig. 19c is an example of the uniform of the 1870s. Ticken clothing was frequently worn on service at that time, with a French-style kepi and

Fig. 19. Chile.
a, c, e, f: infantry. b: hussar. d: officer of the general staff.

51

French distinctions of rank. From 1890 German styles predominated to such an extent that up to the Great War, Chilean army uniforms almost exactly resembled German ones, even in detail (Fig. 19c). In this period the army wore a dark blue tunic with Swedish cuffs that, like the collar, shoulder straps, and piping, were of distinctive color. Infantry and general officers had red, the latter with rich embroidery on the collar and cuffs; artillery, black with red piping; engineers, turquoise with red piping; the military college, black with yellow piping; general staff, gray, with yellow metal buttons, and white, later natural-colored, leather equipment. The tunic worn by the cavalry was light blue. The distinctive color was red and the buttons were white metal. On the blue (later blue-black) trousers the infantry had red stripes, the cavalry and general staff, broad stripes, and artillery and pioneers, triple stripes, the same color as the piping. The headdress was the Prussian spiked helmet with yellow or white metal plate: the flying condor with the Chilean star was mounted on it. Cavalry, artillery, officers on the general staff, and the military college wore seven rows of black loops on the front of the jacket; these were abolished in 1910 (Fig. 19d). Officers wore silver, blue, and red embroidered sashes in full dress; mounted troops wore a pouch belt as well. The shoulder cords were exactly like the German ones, but in gold; subalterns had four cords side by side; field officers had triple plaited cords, the center one of silver, the others of gold, with one to three five-pointed stars on them. In full dress, Prussian-style epaulettes were worn, with bullions for field officers. A metal regimental numeral or arm-of-service badge was worn at the ends of the collar. On service, the men also wore peaked caps, with a small-size national arms badge on the band, with the cockade above. Up to the Great War, the presidential bodyguard wore cuirassier helmets and butcher boots. A gray-green service dress, as depicted in Fig. 19f, was introduced during the war. The coat of arms on the cap was in yellow; the regimental number and rank distinctions of NCOs were green. Subalterns' shoulder straps were edged with a single green cord, those of field officers with three cords. General officers had collar patches of basic color bearing a gold oakleaf, and U.S.-style passants, with a broad gold edging with two or three stars on them. The service uniform underwent a few changes thereafter, as did the dress uniform used up to the late 1930s, for evening wear and walking out. According to the Regulations of 1929, they were as follows.

The service uniform, in a gray-green basic color, consisted of a jacket with stand collar, slit pockets in the breast and skirts with scalloped flaps and small buttons, round cuffs, shoulder straps, or shoulder cords for officers. On the stand collar were four-sided patches, right-angled at the back, in the distinctive color, piped in a different color. On them was placed the regimental number or badge. The forage cap was gray-green with a brown peak and chinstrap, without colored distinctions. On the band was a small-size national coat of arms with button color with, on the upper part, the cockade. The cap had a stiff top for full dress and everyday wear and a soft one for wear on service. The trousers or breeches were gray-green with piping, or triple stripes, in *Waffenfarbe*. The double-breasted greatcoat was gray-green with a turndown collar of the color of the tunic for officers, with roll cuffs, and a belt with a single button at the back. Officers also had three-button pocket flaps in the skirts. Equipment was of brown leather; officers had a brace on the right shoulder. General officers wore no collar patches on the jacket but instead had a large national arms badge in gold or silver according to their former arms and, on the front of the cap, the five-pointed Chilean star, surrounded by two laurel sprigs, all embroidered in gold on a red backing, and red triple trouser stripes. On ceremonial and social occasions officers wore a dress uniform. This consisted of a single-breasted tunic, like that worn by Prussian dragoons. The stand collar was of *Waffenfarbe*, and the Swedish cuffs of basic color were piped in *Waffenfarbe*. The coat was dark blue with gilt buttons for all arms except the cavalry, which had a light-blue one with white metal buttons. The colors of the collar and piping were as follows: general officers and infantry, red; cavalry, red; artillery, black velvet with red piping; the military college, black velvet with yellow piping. The collar patches on the uniform were the same color as the collar, with the appropriate piping. The infantry differed in having red ones with dark blue piping, and the cavalry, light blue with red piping. The dress trousers were black, piped in *Waffenfarbe*. Colonels and general officers wore triple stripes. The headdress was a peaked cap the same as that worn by the German *Reichswehr*; the top part was the same color as the tunic; band and piping were of *Waffenfarbe*. The rest of the ornamentation on the cap was the same as on the service cap. General officers had a black, gold-ornamented chinstrap and leather peak. With this uniform a silver, blue, and red embroidered sash was worn; the cavalry had a similar pouch belt. The saber knot was also silver, blue, and red embroidered. The rank distinctions on all uniforms were the same as on the pre–Great War uniform. The epaulettes worn with the dress uniform had straps and crescents of *Waffenfarbe*, pads of button color, and silver bullions for field officers. The one to three rank stars were placed one above the other on the straps. General officers wore red passants on their service dress. These had a gold embroidered binding, with two or three five-pointed stars in the center. Shoulder cords were not worn on the greatcoat, but rank was denoted by collar patches of the same color as the collar, on which were one to three narrow vertical gold stripes with a five-pointed star to the rear for field officers. General officers had red collar patches, edged with gold embroidery, with two or three gold stars on them. The men's rank distinctions consisted of diagonal stripes of the color of the piping or buttons on both lower arms. The regimental distinctions at the ends of the collar were invariably of the color of the buttons and were as follows: infantry, Arabic numerals; artillery, crossed cannon barrels with the number above; horse artillery, a flaming grenade on its side with the number on the ball; engineers, crossed axe and anchor; signals battalion, flaming fork of lightning; railway regiment, a wheel; transport corps, a vehicle steering wheel with numeral; the military college, the national arms. The regimental distinctions of the cavalry, which remained unchanged for over a century, were, for No. 1, a vertical flaming grenade; No. 2, a hunting horn; No. 3, skull and crossbones; No. 4, the national arms; No. 5, crossed lances with pennants; No. 6, a dragon; No. 7, crossed arrows; No. 8, crossed sabers. General staff officers wore the uniform of their former arms, with a gold laurel wreath around their collar badge and gold double aiguillettes—yellow on the service uniform—on the right shoulder.

CHINA

In the Chinese army, uniforms in the European sense did not appear until after the Boxer Rebellion. Up to that time soldiers wore national dress, with surtouts of various colors, but mainly of dark blue silk ornamented with black bands, with Chinese characters and emblems on the breast and back. Examples are given in Figs. 20a,b,c. Uniforms of Western type, showing an American influence, were first worn by small units of troops (Fig. 20d). During and after the Boxer Rebellion, the regular troops wore dark blue jackets, trousers, and turbanlike caps, with variously colored shoulder straps, and with Chinese characters on the front of the jacket (Fig. 20g). The Boxers wore national dress (Fig. 20f). After the Rebellion, a new military organization was set on foot, with European instructors, and at the same time, a new uniform of European style was introduced. According to the Regulations of c. 1910, the troops had a dark blue winter uniform with dark blue trousers, caps, and double-breasted greatcoats; white gaiters; and brown leather equipment and boots (Fig. 20h). The shoulder straps and cap bands were of *Waffenfarbe*. The men's rank distinctions consisted of one to four red stripes around the cuffs and the same number of narrow black stripes around the cap band. The summer uniform was of the same style but a light khaki color. The *Waffenfarben* were: infantry, red; cavalry, white; artillery, yellow; pioneers, blue; and transport corps, dark brown (Fig. 20h). On service, officers wore dark blue jackets, trousers, and caps (Fig. 20k). The arm of service was denoted by a colored stripe around the lower arm, with the rank distinctions above. These consisted of one to three narrow black stripes and above these, as a means of denoting grade, were one gold disc for subalterns, two for field officers, and three for general officers, placed side by side. The cap did not have a colored band, but had a red pompon on top. Rank was denoted by one to three black stripes around the band, and the grade by one to three vertical stripes at the sides. In front was a round gold disc bearing a dragon device with, in the center, for subalterns, field officers, and general officers respectively, a circular white, blue, or red stone. The guard division was dressed in light gray with shoulder straps and cap bands in *Waffenfarbe*. All had red piping around the top (Fig. 20i). Officers wore Prussian-style shoulder cords with this uniform.

After the Great War a gray-green uniform with collar patches of *Waffenfarbe* was introduced. These were now: infantry, red; cavalry, yellow; artillery, blue; engineers, white; and transport corps, black. The forage caps were gray-green with a device above the peak: troops of the southern states had a white flaming gun on a light-blue ground; and for the northern troops, a five-pointed star with the

Fig. 20. China.

a, c, e, g, h: infantry. b: cavalry. d: infantry officer. f: Boxer. i: guard
cavalry. k: captain, infantry. l: guard infantry. m: infantry of the Northern Army.

republican colors—red, black, white, blue, and yellow (Fig. 20l). The rank distinctions were like the Japanese ones: narrow red cloth passants with one to three yellow stars, with a narrow gold cord down the center for NCOs. Officers wore three lace stripes side by side. For subalterns, the two outer ones were silver, the center, gold; vice versa for field officers; and for general officers, all three stripes were gold. The double-breasted greatcoat was gray-green, fur-lined for winter, with a broad fur collar. The cap was of cloth or leather with turned-up fur-lined peak, neck, and ear flaps. The leather equipment was brown. In summer, light-gray linen uniforms, without color distinctions, were worn. The steel helmets were of various patterns. Troops of the southern states also wore a felt cap similar to that worn by the German Labor Service (Fig. 20m). Rank distinctions were placed at the ends of the collar. In the late 1930s a very low-crowned cap, like a ski cap, was introduced. The cockade was worn on the top part of the front, above the cloth peak.

REPUBLIC OF CZECHOSLOVAKIA

Cockade: white-blue-red

During the Great War, Czech legions were raised from prisoners and deserters and fought on the Allied side in various theaters of the war. The largest was the Russian legion, which was dressed in khaki. The jacket had a row of six bone buttons, breast and skirt pockets (patch type for officers), round cuffs, and, frequently, shoulder straps. Patches, scalloped at the top and back, were worn on the stand-and-fall collar: for infantry, cherry red; artillery, scarlet; cavalry, white piped red. The leather equipment was natural color. The trousers were natural color without piping, and for the cavalry in full dress, red, with white piping. The khaki greatcoat had two rows of six buttons, a turndown collar with patches, and shoulder straps. While the infantry wore khaki Russian-style peaked caps with a diagonal red and white stripe on the front of the band, the cavalry had low-crowned fur caps with a red top and white plume. The rank badges were on a patch of basic color piped red on the upper left arm in the form of chevrons, point up in yellow for NCOs; silver for subalterns; and gold for field officers: one to four narrow or one broad chevron and one to three narrow ones above. Cavalry and officers carried a Russian-pattern saber (Fig. 21a). The Italian legion wore gray-green uniforms; the men's jacket was of Italian style. Officers often wore a jacket with a row of dulled buttons. On the stand-and-fall collar was placed a rectangular white and red patch striped horizontally, with crossed rifles in silver at the front end. The rank distinctions consisted of short horizontal stripes on the lower arm—for NCOs, in violet; for officers, in silver, the same number as in the Russian legion. On the upper left arm was a shield of basic color, piped in violet, with the initials "Č.S." and numeral in violet silk, in silver for officers. The greatcoat was double-breasted and had collar patches as on the jacket. An Alpini hat and Italian-pattern steel helmet were worn. The French legion wore a horizon blue uniform of French pattern. The jacket had a row of dull buttons and patch pockets for officers. The leather equipment and boots were brown. The rank distinctions on the lower arm took the form of short horizontal stripes, of silver for officers, and dark blue silk for NCOs. The collar patches were dark blue with red piping with a red numeral—in silver for NCOs and officers. The steel helmet was the French type, and a dark blue beret was worn. Officers wore a kepi with a red top, and a black velvet band, with silver rank stripes running around it. The greatcoat was double-breasted with collar patches as on the jacket. Rank distinctions were worn on the sleeves. On the shoulder straps of the coat and greatcoat was a dark blue oval patch, edged red, bearing the initials "Č.S." in red or silver. The uniform of these three Czech wartime legions was worn later by the castle guard which formed the presidential bodyguard (Figs. 21a,b,c).

Fig. 21. Republic of Czechoslovakia.
a, b, c: legions in foreign service—Russia, Italy, France.
d, g: infantry. e: officer. f: cavalry.

Early in the 1920s, regulations were promulgated regarding the army uniform and these, in the main, remained unaltered up to the late 1930s. The basic color was khaki. The jacket had a row of seven buttons, patch pockets on the breast and skirts, and round cuffs; officers and NCOs had three small buttons on the hindarm seam. The buttons and all rank badges and insignia were in dull bronze for the men, silver for NCOs, and gold for officers. The arm of service was denoted by variously colored square collar patches, scalloped across the back and top. General officers and general staff officers, however, wore rectangular patches. For generals and general staff, they were scarlet; for the castle guard, infantry, mountain infantry, border *Jäger*, and armored troops, all cherry red; for artillery, scarlet; for cavalry, golden yellow; for transport corps, at first dark green, then orange, and finally yellow like the cavalry; for engineers, dark brown; for signal troops, light brown; and for motorized troops, dark green. General officers' collar patches had gold-embroidered linden leaves on them. The border battalions and mountain troops wore a badge of the button color: a dog's head and a falcon, respectively, on the collar patches. The rank devices were placed on the pointed shoulder straps, which were piped in *Waffenfarbe* for senior NCOs and officers. General officers had straps edged with gold cord with a three-leaf linden sprig in the center. The actual rank was denoted by two, three, or four gold five-pointed stars on the lower arm, French fashion. Up to the early 1930s, field officers wore one to four silver pointed stars one above the other; thereafter, one to four five-pointed gold stars, and a gold cord edging around the shoulder straps. Subalterns at first wore one to four silver transverse bars, and later, one to four three-pointed gold stars. Senior NCOs (*Rottmeister*) at first had one to three silver buttons on a center stripe of *Waffenfarbe* on their shoulder straps; later they wore one to three silver transverse stripes. The grades of other ranks were

57

denoted by one to four silver buttons placed together on stripes in *Waffenfarbe* at the outer ends of the shoulder straps. The regimental distinction was worn on a small metal rectangle of button color on both sides of the collar, in line with the shoulder straps. The khaki trousers had no colored piping; general officers wore red triple stripes; infantry officers off duty wore single broad stripes in *Waffenfarbe* on their trousers. The steel helmet was at first like the German one with a small comb (Fig. 21d), but from 1934 a new, hemispherical type was worn (Fig. 21g). The field cap was fore-and-aft shaped, piped in *Waffenfarbe* around the flap for the men (Fig. 21f). On the left side of the headdress was a small shield with the national arms on it and, to the rear, the rank stars or buttons; for officers likewise. Off duty, officers and NCOs wore a British-style forage cap with a peak; it had piping in *Waffenfarbe* around the top of the band, and the rank stars or buttons at both sides. General officers had gold linden leaf embroidery around the edge of the peak; on the front were the national arms in a metal rhombus, on two crossed swords, of button color. The cap cord was of button color. General officers wore no rank stars on their caps. General staff officers had khaki-colored double silk hanging cords on the right shoulder, and general officers had collar patches without embroidery. Off duty, cavalry regiments and the transport corps wore dark red riding breeches of the old Austrian style. The sword knot had a solid tassel and was of button color. Specialist badges were worn by the men on a patch of the distinctive color on the upper left arm.

DENMARK

Cockade: red-white-red

I. INFANTRY

Red was the color long worn by the Danish army. As Worsaae showed in his book *Dänen und Normannen* (*Danes and Normans*), red was the old Norse favorite color. Around 1700 the grenadier corps wore red coats with sky blue cuffs and sky blue stockings. Their headdress was a grenadier cap with a sky blue bag. The drummer of 1740 (Fig. 22a) wore a red coat with yellow collar, cuffs, waistcoat, and hat lace. Breeches and gaiters were white. The drum had a yellow shell and green hoops. The grenadier (Fig. 22b) wore a red coat with white buttonholes, blue distinctions and waistcoat, white breeches, and black gaiters. The back of the grenadier cap was red, the front blue with a white edging. By about 1750 the red coats of the line infantry had lapels (Fig. 22d). The undergarments were the same color as the distinctions on the coat. The national regiments were dressed in red coats without lapels, red waistcoats, and red breeches. Officers (Fig. 22c), whose rank was denoted by their gorgets, spontoons, and red-and-yellow sashes, worn over the shoulder, wore their swords suspended from a brown leather waistbelt. The men carried their hangers likewise.

In 1762 the distinctions were as shown in the table.

REGIMENT	COLLAR, LAPELS, CUFFS, AND SKIRTS	BUTTONS AND LACE	WAISTCOAT AND BREECHES
Foot Guards	light orange	white	light orange
King's Lifeguard Regiment of Foot	dark blue	white	straw color
Queen's Lifeguard Regiment of Foot	yellow	white	yellow
Crown Prince	green	white	white
Prince Friedrich	yellow	yellow	dark blue
Jutland	white	white	white
Seeland	blue, yellow skirts	white	yellow
Oldborg	white	yellow	green
Bornholm	green	white	green
Schleswig	blue	yellow	white
Holstein	light green	white	straw color
Nordenfield	blue	white	blue
Südenfield	yellow	white	green
Falster	black, straw-colored skirts	white	straw color
Møn	black, white skirts	yellow	white

Fig. 22. Denmark—Infantry.

a: drummer, infantry. b, g: grenadiers. c, e, h: infantry officers. d, f, i, k,
m: infantry. l: grenadier of the guard.

The last two regiments had a white edging around the lapels. The rifles wore
green clothing, very similar to the Prussian uniform. The West Indian troops were
dressed like the line infantry, with yellow distinctions, white lace, and white
undergarments.

Fig. 23. Denmark—Cavalry.

a, d, g: heavy cavalry. b: officer, heavy cavalry. c, l: officers, hussars. f: light
dragoon. e: Bosnian. h, i, k: dragoons.

60

In 1770, the undergarments were white (Fig. 22a). Toward the end of the eighteenth century, a round tapered hat with a plume was introduced. The coat, always red, was made in the style of the Russian *kurtka* of 1786; the short skirts were only turned up in front. Collar, lapels, and cuffs were in the regimental color. The cuff patches were red. The pantaloons were light gray (Fig. 22f). The guard wore long-skirted coats with silver lace. They also had a distinctive hat. The national infantry (i.e., militia) were dressed in plain gray at the time. Types of uniform are shown in the illustrations.

In 1801 the distinctions were as shown in the table.

REGIMENT	COAT	COLLAR, CUFFS, AND LAPELS	PIPING ON COLLAR, CUFFS, LAPELS	SKIRT TURNBACKS	BUTTONS
Guard	red	light blue, no lapels	none	white	white
Danish Lifeguard	red	light yellow	none	white	white
Norwegian Lifeguard	red	light yellow	white	white	white
King's	red	light blue	none	white	white
Queen's	red	light blue	none	white	yellow
Crown Prince	red	light blue	white	white	white
Prince Friedrich	red	green	none	white	white
Fünen	red	white	none	white	white
Seeland	red	green	white	white	white
1st Jutland	red	black	white	white	yellow
2nd Jutland	red	white	none	white	yellow
3rd Jutland	red	black	white	white	white
Oldenborg	red	green	none	white	white
Schleswig	red	light blue	white	white	yellow
Holstein	red	green	white	white	yellow

The grenadiers wore a distinctive form of cap (Fig. 22g). The front part was black, with a yellow metal plate at the base. A white crest ran over the top from one side to the other. The white plume had a colored tip. A colored bag hung down at the back, and a watch case was worn on the shoulder belt. Rifles and light infantry wore the same uniform as the line infantry, but in green, with black lapels, white edging and skirt turnbacks, and yellow metal buttons. Grenadiers of the rifles had a red-over-green plume in their caps (Fig. 24a). As side arms, the light troops carried hangers with a knuckle bow, while grenadiers and sharpshooters had sabers. The rest of the infantry carried only a bayonet in a scabbard. In 1807 the lifeguard rifles (Fig. 24b) wore a black lancer cap with a pentagonal top. The spherical pompon was of green wool. In the same year, the militia (Fig. 24c) wore red coats with white turnbacks and piping, white metal buttons, blue collar and cuffs, and a bright-colored jacket with long skirts under the coat. Headdress and breeches were as worn by the line infantry; the hat plume was green. At that time the guard wore fur caps. Thereafter the uniform remained red with variously colored regimental distinctions. The hat was superseded by a chaco with white cords. In 1813 (Fig. 22i) light-gray undergarments were adopted, and later, sky blue pantaloons. In the 1830s the collar was red, with patches in the regimental color on the front and with two buttons. Crescents were worn on the shoulders (Fig. 22k). The Lauenborg Rifle Corps had green uniforms with red distinctions and yellow metal buttons. In 1842 the line infantry went into red

Fig. 24. Denmark—Miscellaneous.
a: grenadier of rifles. b: lifeguard rifles. c: militia. d: officer, artillery.
e, f, g: artillery. h: officer, engineers. i: private, engineers. k: general officer.

double-breasted jackets with white metal buttons and white-piped, light-blue pointed cuffs and collars. About 1850 a dark blue double-breasted tunic with self-colored collar and red-piped pointed cuffs was introduced. The collar had red patches with two small buttons and embroidered loops, which were later done away with. The leather equipment, which was no longer worn crossed, was changed to black. The trousers remained sky blue; the chaco had white metal fittings. For everyday wear, a dark blue kepi was worn, with red piping and a white and red cockade; this was later replaced by a light-blue kepi without piping. The rifles, which were abolished in 1864, wore the same uniform, but in green. NCOs wore one to three chevrons of the color of the buttons on both lower arms. Officers wore epaulettes, the color of the buttons, with one to three rosettes; field officers had bullions and stars as well. From 1865 twisted shoulder cords were worn, of the color of the buttons for field officers and of button color and *Waffenfarbe* mixed for company officers. The lifeguard regiment retained its red single-breasted tunic, with light-blue collar, shoulder straps, and pointed cuffs, all piped white. It had white guard lace and white leather equipment, worn crossed. Officers had silver embroidery. The light-blue trousers had white stripes, and the fur caps had white metal chinscales and star plate, which bore a gilt coat of arms. This uniform was also worn in court dress up to the 1930s. In daily guard order, dark blue double-breasted tunics were worn; these had red piping on the collar, cuffs, and shoulder straps, with silver lace loops on the collar and cuffs. In 1911 a single-breasted dark blue service jacket, piped red, was introduced, having a stand-and-fall collar and patch pockets on the breast (Fig. 25a). The men wore a red rectangular lace loop with a light of dark blue on the collar. Officers wore their rank stars on the collar and rank was shown on the kepi by one to three narrow or medium-width lace stripes of the color of the buttons. The kepi and trousers remained light blue. During the Great War, a similar uniform, but entirely of stone-gray color, was introduced. In 1923 a khaki-colored service dress was issued but, up to the late 1930s, it was worn only by officers and NCOs. All metal insignia were yellow, as were the rank stars and rosettes worn on the shoulder straps. The arm of service was denoted by a stamped metal badge above the right breast pocket. Leather equipment and the cap peak and chinstrap were light brown. The cap band was greenish-gray. The field cap was fore-and-aft shaped, with lace binding in a darker color. From 1909 the lifeguard regiment wore a greenish-gray service dress, cut like a jacket, without colored distinctions and having yellow metal buttons.

II. CAVALRY

To begin with, the cavalry wore mainly gray uniforms, and, later, red ones. In the early eighteenth century, the heavy cavalry wore gray coats and blackened breast plates and back pieces. The dragoons had dark red coats. In 1740 (Fig. 23a) the heavy cavalry wore red coats with yellow turnbacks. The housings were red with a yellow edging. The lace around the hat was white and the buttons were white metal. The armor was blackened, and the breeches and pouch belts were buff-colored. Heavy cavalry officers had green distinctions in 1750 (Fig. 23b). The straps on the armor were of yellow metal; the waistcoat was white; hat lace, gold; sash, carmine and gold. In 1762 the hussars wore *Flügelmützen*, black dolmans, and red pelisses with white loopings. The hussar officer of 1764 (Fig. 23c) had yellow dolman, sabertache, and boots; dark red cuffs, pelisse, and *Scharawaden*; and white cord loopings. The sash was red and yellow; the shabraque was a panther skin, embroidered in silver. The cap bag was yellow. The cavalryman of 1722 (Fig. 23d) wore sky blue distinctions on the red coat; the skirt turnbacks and undergarments were yellow. Hat lace, buttons, and pouch belt were white; the shabraques, red with a light blue edging. In 1800 the lifeguard of the horse wore yellow jackets with red collar and cuffs, and silver lace. The accoutrements were black leather. They had a black crested helmet with a red and silver turban around the base. The plume was red over white. The red sabertache had silver lace and bore the royal cipher "C7," for Christian VII. Heavy cavalry (Fig. 23g) wore a red coat with yellow skirt lining, yellow leather breeches, and Hungarian boots. Dark blue buttoned overalls were normally worn. The hat had a white plume. Officers wore long-skirted coatees. The red shabraques had a white edging, which was silver for officers.

In 1801 the distinctions were as follows.

REGIMENT	COAT	COLLAR, CUFFS, AND LAPELS	PIPING	SKIRT TURNBACKS	BUTTONS
Lifeguard Cavalry	red	yellow	none	yellow	white
Seeland	red	dark blue	none	yellow	white
Schleswig	red	light blue	none	yellow	white
Holstein	red	light green	yellow	yellow	white

The light dragoons (Fig. 23f) wore a uniform similar to that of the heavy cavalry but had a crested helmet with turban of distinctive color instead of the hat. The lifeguard regiment, however, which had a black collar, etc., had a red turban.

REGIMENT	COAT	COLLAR, CUFFS, AND LAPELS	PIPING	SKIRT TURNBACKS	BUTTONS
Lifeguard Regiment of Light Dragoons	red	black	yellow	yellow	white
Jutland Dragoon	red	green	none	yellow	white
Finnish Dragoon	red	light blue	yellow	yellow	white

The hussars wore light-blue dolmans with carmine collars and cuffs, a carmine pelisse with black piping, white loopings, and a white-and-carmine sash. The breeches were leather. Carmine *Scharawaden*, lacking white, were worn on top. The accoutrements were of brown leather. The black *Flügelmützen* had white lace and a white plume. The shabraques and saber-taches were carmine with a light-blue vandyked edge. The latter bore the initials "C7" in white. The mounted rifles were dressed like the rifles, but had yellow skirt turnbacks. Their green shabraques had a black vandyke. The Bosnian uniform (Fig. 23e) was all light blue with red distinctions. The turban was red with a white band. In 1808 they were converted into lancers, dressed in a light-blue lancer jacket with red distinctions, and a lancer cap with a red upper part. From 1822 until their disbandment in 1842, they had light-blue jackets with white

Fig. 25. Denmark, 1912–1935.
a, c: infantry. b: dragoons. d: officer.

metal buttons and red distinctions. About 1820 the heavy cavalry were converted into cuirassier regiments. The crested helmet they wore had a yellow metal plate; the double-breasted jackets were white with red or light-blue distinctions, white metal buttons, and light-blue trousers. Thereafter, the uniform of the light dragoons remained the same except that the helmet was changed, and the trousers became light blue with leather strappings. Shoulder crescents were worn (Fig. 23h); trumpeters had white fringed epaulettes, and a red crest on their helmet. Later, a helmet with comb was adopted (Fig. 23i). Subsequently, the lapels on the jacket were abolished. With the introduction of the tunic, dragoons adopted light-blue ones, with two rows of white metal buttons. The collar, patches, and piping were dark red; the cloaks, light blue; the helmet had white metal fittings (Fig. 23k). The mounted lifeguard was issued white tunics with red distinctions and white lace. The cuirasses were yellow metal; the helmets yellow metal with white mounts and a black hair plume; and the leather equipment was black. Shabraques were red and white. In court guard order, a red *Superweste* (a sleeveless shell worn over the tunic) with a white star was worn. The mounted lifeguard was abolished in 1868. In 1845 the hussar uniform was made all light blue with white loops; the pelisse was red for the men and carmine for officers. In 1870 an *Attila* jacket, with five rows of loopings on the breast, superseded the dolman (Fig. 23l), and a very low kepi with horizontal peak was introduced. From 1912 a white hair plume was worn with it. From 1889 to 1909 the collar and cuffs were carmine; from then, light blue. In 1889 light-blue hussar breeches and black hussar boots with white edging were adopted. In 1911 the cavalry went into a light-blue tunic without collar lace, piped in *Waffenfarbe*, carmine for dragoons and white for hussars. Later, both adopted stone-gray uniforms without colored piping.

III. ARTILLERY AND ENGINEERS; GENERAL OFFICERS

The engineer officer's uniform, as shown in Fig. 24h for 1750, was all red without colored distinctions; the buttons and lace were yellow. The artillery officer (Fig. 24d) had a red coat with blue collar, cuffs, and skirt lining; yellow buttons and edging; white gaiters; and a carmine-and-yellow sash. The waistcoat and breeches were blue. The men had blue stitched buttonholes. In 1800 the artillery uniform was made exactly the same as that of the infantry except that dark blue breeches and black gaiters were worn. Distinctions and skirt turnbacks were blue, and buttons were yellow metal (Fig. 24e). Officers wore long-skirted carmine-colored coats. As side arms, the men carried a short sword with a yellow metal guard. Later, the hat was replaced by a chaco (Fig. 24f) with a blue pompon for the mounted artillery and a blue plume for officers. After the introduction of the tunic, the artillery uniform was dark blue throughout with carmine collar patches and piping and yellow metal buttons. The black chaco (Fig. 24g) had yellow metal fittings. Equipment was of black leather. In the 1911 service dress, the trousers and kepi were changed to dark blue and the *Waffenfarbe* was carmine, and the same held for the stone-gray service dress. The engineers wore black collar patches with red piping and yellow metal buttons; the blue and gray service dresses were like the artillery's, but the piping was light red and the collar lace was black (Figs. 24h,i).

Up to 1842 general officers wore red coats with light-blue collars and cuffs and gold embroidery. After that date they had dark blue tunics, cut like those of the infantry, with red piping and gold embroidery on the red collar patches and pointed cuffs. Epaulettes were worn at first; later, gold shoulder cords bearing one to three large six-pointed stars. The light-blue trousers had gold stripes. The hat was black with a plume of white feathers (Fig. 24k). The shabraque was light blue, edged gold. The general staff wore the same uniform, but with silver lace and yellow and carmine hat feathers. The service dress was piped in red. The kepi had a gold cord and broad or medium-width stripes, according to rank.

EIRE

The uniform of the Irish army grew out of the dress of the Irish Volunteer Force of 1916–1921. The service dress was of the same pattern for all arms, both regulars and reserve. It was of khaki material with a strong greenish tint. The jacket had two breast and skirt pockets and scalloped buttoned flaps, of patch type for officers, with a row of five buttons (bearing a harp and "I.V."), pointed shoulder straps, and a stand collar. The forage cap had a stiffened top, a peak of material, and a brown leather chinstrap. Cavalry wore a soft beret pulled down to the right. German-type steel helmets were worn. The greatcoat had roll cuffs, shoulder straps, a broad collar, and two rows of buttons, narrowing from the top. Officers' leather equipment, gaiters, and boots were brown, as were the bandolier belts worn over the left shoulder by cavalry. The infantry had gray-green web equipment. The universal army badge was a flaming sun with an eight-pointed star on it with the monogram "FF" (Fianna Feil, meaning the Army of Destiny) in a circle. It was in gold embroidery for general officers and in bronze for others, worn on the cap band and on the left side of the beret. The dull gilt arm-of-service badges were worn at the ends of the jacket and greatcoat collars and were as given in the table in this section. NCOs' rank was shown by one to three red stripes on both upper arms, with a small universal badge in bronze, above, for sergeant majors. Officers' badges were placed on the shoulder straps: for subalterns, one to three bars; commandants and major generals, one bar and one lozenge-shaped star; majors and lieutenant generals, one bar and two stars; colonels and generals, three stars, in gold embroidery for general officers, and in bronze for others, on a colored underlay. The color for general officers and general staff was red; for other staffs, blue; for infantry, purple; and for all the rest, lemon yellow. Caps for general officers and colonels had black leather peaks and edging of gold-embroidered oak leaves, or plain lace, respectively (Fig. 26b).

In 1935, for the first time, a colored full-dress uniform was authorized for officers and musicians. It consisted of a single-breasted tunic—or a double-breasted lancer jacket for mounted troops—with stand collar and three-button cuff slashes of

1933

Fig. 26. Eire.
a: infantry. b: captain, artillery.

Waffenfarbe. The collar was edged around the outside with broad lace and had the arm-of-service badge embroidered at its ends. The twisted shoulder cords had the rank badges on them. All metal insignia were the color of the buttons. The trousers had broad stripes, two for mounted troops. The conical chaco was of the same color as the coat, with top and band around the top of cloth in *Waffenfarbe*. The army badge, of the color of the buttons, was worn above the black lacquered peak. In addition, a black cloak, with lining in *Waffenfarbe* and a black velvet collar, was worn. Other details are given in the table.

For state escorts, etc., the artillery had a blue hussar uniform with saffron yellow loopings, black leather equipment, and fur caps.

For the volunteers, the basic color was gray-green, with dark green for the stand-and-fall collar, the cuffs, and the flap of the fore-and-aft cap, which was worn instead of the peaked cap. The buttons, army badges, arm-of-service badges, and officers' rank badges were silver; the leather equipment (for infantry as well) and the boots were black (Fig. 26a).

SERVICE	TUNIC AND TROUSERS	*WAFFENFARBE* AND BUTTONS	ARM-OF-SERVICE BADGES ON COLLAR
Infantry	dark blue	red, silver	Crossed rifles, battalion number below (at side for reserve units)
Engineers	black	red, silver	Theodolite above crescent
Army Signal Corps	black	green, gold	Mercury on a 12-pointed star
School of Music	dark blue	red, gold	A harp on a lyre
Cavalry	black	red, silver	Cuirass on crossed saber and carbine
Artillery	dark blue	red, gold	Hibernia seated on cannon with scroll below
Supply and Transport	dark blue	red, silver	Roman chariot on shield between laurel sprays, motto below
Army Medical Service			Staff and serpents in laurel wreath above scroll
Military Police Service			Universal badge, with "AP" in center
Army Ordnance Service			Trophy of arms with targe in center, scrolls below
Department of Defense (Administrative Company)			Pierced lozenge, sword hilt in center above scrolls
Military College (Cadets)			Circle, crossed torch, sword and spear in center
Air Corps			Circle, eagle on rock in center above scrolls
General officers	black	red, gold	Red collar patches with gold cord along center, on service jacket and greatcoat

ESTONIA

Cockade: blue-black-white

The nucleus of the Estonian army was formed in 1917 from the Estonian troops of the Russian Imperial army. Thus, the original uniform was substantially the same as the earlier Russian pattern because of the availability of the uniforms. The cap cockade, however, was replaced by an oval-rayed shield inlaid with the national colors. The officers wore Russian-type shoulder straps with small differences. Armbands, in white or in the national colors, were frequently worn. Early in 1919 a Finnish volunteer corps arrived to assist the Estonians in their war of independence against the Bolsheviks, and a Finnish influence was introduced into the uniform. The field jacket remained khaki-colored, with patch pockets on the breast and skirts, and stand-and-fall collar of dark blue velvet, piped white around the outside for officers. The men's collar was of basic color, with the arm-of-service badge at the ends of the collar. Officers' rank badges consisted of one to three large six-pointed stars bearing the national arms, on the

Fig. 27. Estonia.
a: infantry. b: cavalry.
c: general officer.

shoulder straps for company officers. Field officers and generals wore smaller additional six-pointed stars, to denote their grade, at the ends of the collar. The peaked cap was of Russian type; the khaki field service cap was fore-and-aft shaped, with the cockade on the high, turned-up cloth peak, and the neck and ear flaps were buttoned over. Both Russian- and German-pattern steel helmets were worn.

The cavalry early on adopted as a full dress a blue *Attila* jacket with white loopings and black velvet collar; a khaki-colored kepi with blue bag, edged white, falling over to the right; red breeches; and black hussar boots.

About 1925 a British-type peaked cap was introduced for wear in walking out, with gold embroidery on the peak for generals and field officers. The collar was changed to one of basic color with collar patches in *Waffenfarbe*, pointed at the rear, and small buttons, with arm-of-service badges at the ends of the collar. Rank badges were henceforth only worn on the shoulder straps: one to three stars with, in addition, the national arms, with and without an oak wreath, for generals and field officers, respectively (Fig. 27a). The steel helmet was of German type. Equipment was of natural-colored leather; officers wore a Sam Browne.

FINLAND

Cockade: white with light-blue ring

The origin of the Finnish army dates from the raising of the Prussian *Jäger* Battalion No. 27, which was made up of Finns who volunteered to fight on the German side against Russia. In 1918 this extremely efficient and war-tried unit was sent with the German expeditionary force to fight the Reds in Finland. After leaving German service, they continued for some time to wear the 1915-pattern Prussian uniform almost unaltered, with the Finnish national badge. The one to three rank stars were very soon worn, arranged in a triangle, on the collar. The White volunteer troops which were raised all over the country wore various improvised

Fig. 28. Finland.
a, d: infantry. b: Nyland
Dragoons. c: colonel, general staff.

uniforms—including old Russian uniforms, service jackets, and coats of gray Swedish uniform cloth with fur caps, fur greatcoats, and long black soft boots. As a distinctive mark, white armbands with colored devices and inscriptions were often used. The newly raised cavalry regiments wore uniforms whose essential remained unaltered up to the late 1930s. The Kexholm (later Hämeen) Cavalry Regiment wore light-gray coats with brownish-red collar and gauntlet cuffs, piped yellow, and six dark red loopings on the front, and dark red breeches with narrow double yellow stripes. Their brownish-red flat-topped caps were of Russian type with a yellow band and piping around the top. The Nyland (later Uudenmaan) Dragoon Regiment wore a similar uniform, without the loopings, with dark blue distinctions and breeches and gray Swedish-type felt hats, lined dark blue and turned up at three sides, or dark blue fore-and-aft caps with turned-up cloth peak, neck and ear flaps (Fig. 28b). In 1922 a new uniform was introduced. The basic color was light gray, with stand-and-fall collar and cuffs of dark gray (dark blue for the coast artillery). The jacket was the same for all arms and had a row of six dull buttons; officers had pleated patch pockets on the breast and skirts, with scalloped flaps, and two buttons on the waist at the back. The cuffs were of Swedish type for all, except for the artillery, which had pointed ones, and the War Ministry, general staff, and guards (Finland White Guard Regiment, Karelia Guard Regiment, and Guard Rifles Battalion), which had French-type cuffs with a light-gray scalloped slash. The men wore rounded shoulder straps of dark gray, piped in *Waffenfarbe* (except for the infantry); the guards had wholly colored straps: dark blue, dark red, and green piped white, respectively. The arm-of-service badges were worn on them in yellow metal. Officers had twisted gold shoulder cords—gold and silver for general officers—on an underlay of *Waffenfarbe*, with the Finnish lion and arm-of service badge in gold on them. The badges of rank were placed on the stand-and-fall collar. NCOs wore a light-gray, double lace loop with a gray button bearing the national device, edged with one or two light-gray cords according to rank. Sergeants had a broad gold lace stripe across the shoulder straps; company officers wore narrow light-gray silk lace around the outer edge of the collar and one to three small gold roses; field officers had a medium-width and a narrow stripe and one to three large roses; general officers had a broad patterned silk edging and one to three large-size Finnish lions in gold. The leather equipment was natural-colored; officers wore a Sam Browne and, in full dress, a blue-and-silver sash with the tassels on the left side. The sword knot was gold with a gold and black strap. The dark gray trousers and breeches had stripes in *Waffenfarbe*: broad ones for general officers and the general staff, and narrow triple stripes for artillery, cyclists, and technical troops. Other officers wore medium-width stripes. The men had none. The cap was fore-and-aft shaped, with a fur edging in winter (black for technical troops, white for general officers, otherwise, gray). Officers also had a Prussian-type forage cap with a black leather peak. Colonels had one row of gold-embroidered oak sprigs and general officers had two. The chinstrap was of black leather for NCOs and of double gold cord for officers and generals. The band and piping were of dark gray, and the rest of the cap was of basic color. On the band, as on the field cap, was the red Finnish lion badge, and above it, on the top part, was the national cockade. The cavalry tunic had a row of eight buttons and was bound with medium-width light-gray silk trimming around the edges. Tapering from top to bottom down the front were eight narrow straight loopings of the same material. The gauntlet cuffs had two buttons and were edged with lace. The breeches were dark red with two narrow side stripes. In full dress, officers wore a black pouch on a gray, gold-laced pouch belt. In summer, all arms wore a light-gray blouse with turndown collar. Officers wore a light field jacket. The long boots were of soft black leather. The greatcoat, of basic color, was double-breasted and had a broad dark gray turned-down collar. Officers' ranks were denoted by gray silk stripes on the roll cuffs: one to three narrow; one medium-breadth stripe with one to three narrow ones below; one broad stripe with one to three narrow ones above, respectively, according to rank.

In 1927 a new, khaki-colored field uniform was introduced, along with a similarly colored service dress for officers. The gray and khaki uniforms were worn together. The 1927-pattern service jacket was the same for all arms, having leather buttons, patch pockets on the breast and skirts, and a very broad turndown collar with self-colored pointed shoulder straps bearing the arm-of-service badges in yellow or the NCOs' lace chevrons. Officers' and NCOs' distinctions of rank on the collar werc the same as on the 1922-pattern uniform. The 1927 headdress was very similar to that of the German Labor Service: khaki-colored felt with a cloth peak and brown chinstrap (Fig. 28d). Officers' service dress consisted of a British-style jacket with patch pockets on the breast and skirts and a row of four yellow metal buttons. The arm-of-service badges were placed at the ends of the collar; the Finnish heraldic lion and the regimental number appeared in gold on the shoulder straps. The round cuffs had three buttons on the hindarm seam and were piped in *Waffenfarbe*. Rank was denoted by short gold stripes of the same number and arrangement as on the 1922-pattern greatcoat. The khaki-colored forage cap had a light-brown peak. The greatcoat was like the 1922 pattern, but in khaki. The khaki trousers had turnups.

The *Waffenfarbe* were: War Ministry, light blue; general staff, carmine; artillery, red; infantry, light gray; rifles, green; cavalry, yellow; cyclist troops, orange; armored troops, black; transport corps and technical troops, purple. The arm-of-service badges were, for infantry, crossed rifles; for cavalry, crossed sabers; for artillery, a flaming grenade; for rifles, a hunting horn; for cyclist troops, a wheel and crossed skis; for technical troops, a short Roman sword and crossed technical instruments. The steel helmet had always been of thc German pattern.

FRANCE

Cockade: of very varied colors up to 1789. During the Revolution, tricolor, blue-white-red. Under the Restoration, white. From 1830, blue-white-red again.

I. GUARDS

Maison du Roi (Troops of the Royal Household)

Uniforms were traditionally adopted in France in 1670, and Colinen de Frandat is credited with having originated this innovation. The royal guards, however, appear to have had a uniform of sorts even before then. This section deals only with those household troops which performed guard and escort duties; the *Gardes Françaises* and *Gardes Suisses* are discussed later. Blue and red were the uniform colors of the houshold troops. The *Gardes du Corps* (Fig. 29a) was made up of four companies. They wore blue coats with red cuffs and waistcoats and silver buttons and lace. In the eighteenth century variously colored pouch belts were introduced. These, together with the cockade in the hat, denoted the company.

> 1st Company (*compagnie écossaise*): black cockade, silver-and-white checkered pouch belt
> 2nd Company (*première française*): white and green cockade, silver-and-green checkered pouch belt
> 3rd Company (*seconde française*): blue and white cockade, silver-and-blue checkered pouch belt
> 4th Company (*troisième française*): yellow and white cockade, silver-and-yellow checkered pouch belt

Gardes de la Porte (Fig. 29b) wore a blue coat with cuffs of red plush and red lining, waistcoat, stockings, and breeches; gold and silver lace on all seams; and gold-and-silver checkered pouch belt and waistbelt. They had swords and muskets.

Cent-Gardes Suisses wore blue coats with cuffs of red plush with scarlet collar and skirt linings, yellow buttons, and blue or white breeches. The fur caps had a metal plate with the French arms on it. They were armed with dragoon pattern flintlocks and swords. On court guards they wore the Swiss national dress.

Gardes de la Manche (Fig. 29d) wore an all-white uniform except that the shoes had red heels. The embroidery on the cassock was gold and silver. The poles and tassels of the partisans were white.

Gardes de la Prévôté de l'Hôtel (Fig. 29e) wore blue coats laced with gold. The cuffs and lining were red, the waistcoat was red, ornamented with gold, and likewise the breeches and stockings. The hat lace was gold; the cassocks, which were slashed from the waist down, were white, with carnation red, blue, and white stripes. Richly embroidered in gold, the cassocks (called *hoquetons* in French) gave these troops the title of *Hoquetons Ordinaires de sa Majesté*.

Fig. 29. France—Royal Guards.

a, h, i: *Garde du Corps.* b: *Garde de la Porte.* c: *Gendarmes.* d: *Garde de la Manche.* e: *Garde de la Prévôte.* f: *grenadier à cheval.* g: *mousquetaire.*

Of these troops, the *Gardes du Corps* were mounted but also did duty dismounted. The Cavalry of the Guard, later called the *Gendarmes de la Garde du Roi*, wore red coats (Fig. 29c). The cuffs were of black plush; the waistcoats were yellowish, with a rich gold lace edging. The hat, laced with gold, had a black cockade and white plumage. The *chevau-légers* of the Guard wore a similar uniform but with a white hat cockade. The *mousquetaires* consisted of two companies, known as the *mousquetaires gris* and *mousquetaires noirs*, named after the color of their horses (gray and black respectively). The 1st Company wore an all-red uniform richly laced with gold, with white plumage and hat cockade. In the seventeenth century the cassock was the full dress garment of the mounted troops. It was white and loose-fitting like a cloak; early in the eighteenth century, however, it took the form of a blue *soubreveste*, with a white cross having red flames in the angles on the back and front. The *mousquetaires noirs* wore the same uniform, but all lace was silver, and the flames were yellow (Fig. 29g).

Grenadiers à cheval (Fig. 29f) wore light-blue coats with silver lace; red waistcoats, breeches, and cuffs; and red caps edged with black fur (later, bearskin caps with a silver plate). The gaiters were of fawn leather, and the equipment was white.

Under Louis XVI and the ministry of the comte de Saint-Germain, the troops of the *Maison du Roi* were disbanded, and only the *Gardes du Corps* were retained, until the Revolution put an end to their existence as well.

At the Restoration of 1814, the *Maison du Roi* was reestablished as it had existed prior to the Saint-Germain reforms. The *grenadiers*, *Cent-Suisses*, *Gardes du Corps*, *Gardes de la Prévôté* and *de la Porte*, the *gendarmes* and *chevau-légers*, and the two companies of *mousquetaires* were all reraised. The uniforms were the same colors as before but were brought more up to date in style. The hats were largely superseded by helmets. All this splendor, however, came to an end again with Napoleon's return. After the second Restoration, only four companies of the *Gardes du Corps* were raised (Figs. 29h,i). A fifth was added later. The uniform consisted of a blue single-breasted coatee with nine white loops down the front with tassels, white epaulettes, and white aiguillettes. The collar was carmine with one white loop; the skirt turnbacks were carmine; breeches, white; and helmet, steel, with a black turban, black crest, and yellow metal fittings. The plume was white with the base of the company color, which was also displayed on the squares on the pouch belts. These colors were, for the 1st Company, white; for the 2nd, light green; the 3rd, dark blue; the 4th, yellow; and the 5th, carmine.

In 1826 four companies of *Gardes du Corps à pied* were formed. They were dressed in blue coats with nine yellow lace loops, without tassels, down the front; the buttons and epaulettes were yellow, the collar was carmine with a yellow grenade on each side. The cuffs were carmine, as were the skirt turnbacks, which were ornamented with yellow *fleurs de lys*. The fur cap had a white plume, yellow metal plate, and yellow cords. Swords and bayonets were carried. The cartridge boxes had a grenade in each corner of the flap and a plate in the center with a *fleur de lys* on it.

The other regiments of guards—lancers, hussars, etc.—since they were not true household troops, are described under their several arms. The Imperial Guards of the First and Second Empires will be described separately, as they were all troops who fought in the field. Napoleon III's *Cent-Gardes* were the nearest to household troops; but they too are more appropriately listed in the section on cuirassiers.

The premier Regiment of the Guard of the old monarch was the *Gardes Françaises*, whose origins go back to 1558. The uniform colors were the same as for most

Fig. 30. France—Infantry, Royal and Imperial Guards.

a, b: Gardes Françaises. c: pioneer, Gardes Suisses. d, g, h, k: grenadiers of the guard. e: *chasseur* of the guard. f: *voltigeur* of the guard.

of the guard, viz. blue and red; the coat was blue, with red waistcoat and breeches (Fig. 30a). The garments were richly embroidered with white lace. After the Seven Years' War, white breeches were introduced. About 1730 the grenadiers of the regiment adopted fur caps with a plume and were the first in France to do so (Fig. 30b). Later, the grenadiers of all infantry regiments wore them.

The Regiment of *Gardes Suisses* (Fig. 30c) wore red coats with blue lapels, waistcoats, and breeches. The breeches were later changed to white. Coat and waistcoat were ornamented with white lace. While the *Gardes Françaises* espoused the Revolution, the *Gardes Suisses* were all massacred defending their trust.

The Revolution naturally showed little liking for such guards. In 1791, however, a *Garde Constitutionelle* was formed. Its uniform consisted of blue coats with red lapels, cuffs, and skirt turnbacks. The undergarments were white; the hat had white lace and a tricolor cockade. In 1792 a *Garde du Corps Législatif* was formed, having a similar uniform but with a fur cap with no plate, and red plume and cords. More important than these was the *Garde Consulaire*, which was raised in 1799 for duty at the headquarters of the consul and which later formed the basis of the *Garde Impériale*. The uniform of the grenadiers of the *Garde Consulaire* consisted of a royal blue coatee with blue collar without piping, white square-ended lapels, also without piping; red cuffs with white patches, red skirt lining with yellow grenades in the corners, vertical pocket flaps piped red; yellow metal buttons; red epaulettes, and white waistcoats and breeches. The fur caps had a yellow plate and cords, red plume, and tricolor cockade. A copper grenade ornamented the flap of the cartridge box.

The *Garde Impériale* of Napoleon I

For the 1st and 2nd Regiments of *Grenadiers à Pied* (1804–1814) (Fig. 30d), the uniform was as for the grenadiers of the *Garde Consulaire* except that the fur cap had white cords. On the yellow metal cap plate was the Imperial eagle crowned between two grenades; the back part of the cap was red, with a white grenade on it.

The 3rd Regiment of *Grenadiers à Pied* (*Grenadiers Hollandais*) (1810–1813) wore a white coat with carmine collar, skirts, cuffs, and lapels; vertical pocket flaps with carmine edging; white cuff patches; yellow grenades on the skirt turnbacks; yellow metal buttons; red epaulettes; and white undergarments. The fur cap had no plate; it had white cords, red plume, and a red crown with a white cross on it.

Chasseurs à Pied (1804–1814) (Fig. 30e) wore a blue coatee with blue collar, red pointed cuffs piped white, and white lapels tapering to a point. On the four red skirt turnbacks were, alternately, a yellow grenade and a yellow hunting horn; vertical pocket flaps edged red; yellow metal buttons; green epaulettes with red fringes; white undergarments; fur caps without a plate, with white cords, and a red-over-green plume.

Fusiliers-Grenadiers (1806–1814) wore the same coat as for the 1st and 2nd Regiments of grenadiers, as also the undergarments; white epaulettes, the crescents of which were embroidered with two red stripes. The chaco had white chevrons at the sides and a red plume. *Fusiliers-Chasseurs* (1806–1814) wore a coat and undergarments as for *Chasseurs à Pied*, chaco with white cords, and green plume.

Tirailleurs-Grenadiers (1809–1814) wore a blue short-skirted coatee with a red collar edged blue, pointed blue lapels with white piping, red pointed cuffs piped white; red shoulder straps piped white; vertical skirt pocket flaps; red skirt turnbacks piped white, with eagles in white; white undergarments; chaco with white side chevrons, and a green (or red-over-green) plume.

Flanqueurs-Grenadiers (1812–1814) wore a green *habit-veste* with green collar, shoulder straps, and lapels going straight down to the waist. All were piped yellow, as were the vertical pocket flaps. They had red pointed cuffs with yellow piping, red skirt turnbacks piped yellow, with white eagles; yellow metal buttons; and white undergarments. The chaco had white side chevrons, red cords, and a red-over-yellow ball tuft. *Flanqueurs-Chasseurs* (1812–1814) had a *habit-veste* as for the *Flanqueurs-Grenadiers*, except that the cuffs were green and the skirt turnbacks hàd white hunting horns on them; the chaco had white cords and a yellow-over-green pear-shaped pompon.

Conscrits-Grenadiers (1809–1810) wore a blue *habit-veste* with blue collar, lapels, and shoulder straps. All these, and the vertical pocket flaps, were piped red. Cuffs were red with white patches, skirt turnbacks, white with red eagles in the corners; buttons were of yellow metal; undergarments, white; and chaco as for *Fusiliers-Grenadiers*, with red cords. *Conscrits-Chasseurs* (1809–1810) wore the same uniform as *Conscrits-Grenadiers*, but with red collar, green shoulder straps piped red; pointed red cuffs with white piping; blue skirt turnbacks with a green hunting horn on them; chaco with green cords, and a green pear-shaped pompon.

The *Garde Nationale* (1810–1813) wore a short-skirted blue coat with white pointed lapels piped red; white skirt turnbacks piped red, with blue eagles on them; red collar and pointed cuffs piped white; yellow metal buttons; vertical pocket flaps piped red; chaco with white cords, and tuft in the company color; and white undergarments.

Pupilles de la Garde (1811–1814) had the same uniform as the *Flanqueurs-Grenadiers*, with green cuffs and skirt turnbacks, the latter with yellow eagles on them. A chaco with a green cord and yellow pompon was worn.

Vétérans de la Garde (1804–1814) wore the same uniform as the 1st and 2nd Regiments of grenadiers but with red lapels, blue cuff patches, and cross pockets, and a hat with a red pompon.

Marins de la Garde wore a blue dolman with a blue collar, orange-yellow loopings as for hussars; red pointed cuffs; yellow metal shoulder scales; loose blue trousers with orange stripes down the sides and Hungarian knots; and a chaco bound with orange lace, with orange cords, and a red plume.

The chacos of the Garde all bore a yellow metal plate with the Imperial eagle on it, and had chinstraps. The *Flanqueurs-Grenadiers*, *Flanqueurs-Chasseurs*, and *Conscrits* carried no swords, and therefore no sword belts. The bayonet scabbard was attached to the pouch belt.

The Restoration and the July Monarchy

In 1826 the *Garde Royale* consisted of eight infantry regiments, of which the first six were French and the seventh and eighth, Swiss regiments. The distinctions were as follows.

REGIMENT NO.	COAT	COLLAR	CUFFS	CUFF PATCHES	SKIRT TURNBACKS	PIPING
1	blue	blue	crimson	blue	crimson	crimson
2	blue	blue	pink	blue	pink	pink
3	blue	blue	yellow	blue	yellow	yellow
4	blue	blue	blue	crimson	crimson	crimson
5	blue	blue	blue	pink	pink	pink
6	blue	blue	blue	yellow	yellow	yellow
7	red[1]	red	blue	red	white	red
8	red[2]	red	red	blue	white	red

[1]blue lapels [2]blue lapels

All wore single-breasted coatees with white metal buttons. Grenadiers wore fur caps (Fig. 30g); the rest, chacos. Company devices were worn on the skirt turnbacks. The trousers and the leather equipment were white.

The *Garde Impériale* of Napoleon III

By an order of 1st May 1854, a new *Garde Impériale* was formed, comprising three regiments of grenadiers, four of *voltigeurs*, and a regiment of Zouaves. The grenadiers (Fig. 30h) wore a blue coatee with red collar, cuffs, skirt turnbacks, epaulettes with white straps, and white lapels covering the whole of the front of the coat. The buttons were yellow metal. The trousers were blue to begin with, but shortly afterward, madder-red ones, as worn by the line infantry, were adopted. The white leather equipment was worn crossed. The fur caps had a yellow metal plate bearing the eagle, white cords, and a red plume.

The *voltigeurs* (Fig. 30i) wore the same uniform, but with pointed cuffs of basic color, piped yellow, with yellow collar, and yellow crescents to the red epaulettes; the chaco had a yellow metal plate, white lace around the top, and white cords. The plume was yellow over red. The uniform of both was altered in the early 1860s, when the coatee was superseded by a single-breasted tunic; the grenadiers had white loops down the front of theirs (Fig. 30k), the *voltigeurs* had yellow. The leather equipment was now of the same pattern as that worn by the rest of the infantry.

The Zouaves wore blue Zouave jackets and waistcoats with yellow lace. The pointed cuffs were red. Voluminous red trousers were worn, with a light-blue sash around the waist. The fez was red with a yellow tassel and had a white cloth turban around it. The remnants of the regiments of the *garde* were incorporated into the line infantry in 1871.

II. LINE INFANTRY

As mentioned above, the introduction of uniforms dated from 1670, but this only applied to the foreign regiments, and was due to German influence (Jany, *Geschichte der königlichen preussischen Armee*, vol. I, no. 504, p. 340). No definite order is known regarding indigenous regiments until 1690. The earliest uniforms

Fig. 31. France—Line Infantry, 1680–1780.
a: pikeman. b, i: grenadiers. d, e, g, h: fusiliers. c, f: officers.

were fairly dull compared with those of the guards. Neutral colors predominated, such as gray-brown and cream. The turnbacks, however, were colored yellow, red, blue, or green; the breeches and stockings were often of the same color. Pikemen still wore breast plates, but had given up helmets (Fig. 31a). In 1683 cartridge boxes were adopted in place of bandoliers with individual chargers. Up to 1720 the hats were cocked arbitrarily, but after that date, they became uniformly three-cornered. Bayonets were introduced in 1703 to replace the pikes, which had been abolished. About 1715 several regiments (Poitou, Auvergne, Champagne) adopted white coats; gradually, this color became universal for all French infantry regiments, while the *Régiments Étrangers*, as have been seen, wore uniforms of different colors. In 1720 the majority of regiments had black cockades in their hats but some were differently colored or bicolored. Officers first adopted uniforms in 1729. Until 1743 the style of the coat was based on civilian dress. In addition to the colored turnbacks, the pocket flaps of very varied shapes were a further means of distinction. At this period British- and Prussian-type grenadier caps were adopted. About 1757 a large part of the infantry adopted gaiters and, at the same time, a coat with lapels and turned-back skirts. Instead of the hair bag generally worn previously, queues were gradually adopted (Fig. 31d). In 1760 white breeches were introduced for all regiments. Of the foreign regiments, the Swiss and Irish wore red uniforms, and the rest, blue. The *Régiments Royaux* had blue distinctions on their white coats. The distinctions of regiments commanded by royal princes were red.

In 1763 epaulettes were introduced for officers, with the following distinctions: colonel, two epaulettes with rich bullions; lieutenant colonel, a similar one on the left shoulder; major, two epaulettes with a less rich fringe; captain, one such epaulette on the left shoulder; lieutenant and *sous-lieutenant*, one epaulette with lozenge-shaped

French Infantry in 1761
(From a manuscript in the Zeughaus, Berlin)

REGIMENT	COAT	COLLAR	CUFFS	SKIRTS	LAPELS	WAISTCOAT	BREECHES	BUTTONS
Picardie	white[1]	white	white	white	—	red	white	yellow
Champagne	white[2]	white	white	white	—	red	white	yellow
Navarre	white	white	white	white	—	red	white	yellow
Piémont	white	white	black	white	—	white	white	yellow
Normandie	white	black	black	white	—	white[3]	white	white
La Marine	white[5]	black	black[5]	white	—	red	white	yellow
Boisgelin	white	white[8]	white	white	—	white	white	yellow
Bourbonnois	white[2]	—	white	white	—	white	white	yellow
Auvergne	white	—	violet	white	violet	white	white	white
De Rougé	white	—	violet	white	violet	white	white	yellow
Chatellux	white[1]	white	white	white	—	red	white	yellow
Du Roi	white[5]	blue	blue[5]	white	—	blue[5]	white	yellow
Royal	white[2]	blue	blue	white	—	blue	white	white
Poitou	white[2]	blue	blue	white	—	blue	white	yellow
Lionnois	white[3]	red	red	white	—	red	white	yellow
Dauphin	white[1]	—	blue	white	—	blue	white	yellow
Vaubecourt	white	black	black	white	black	red	white	yellow
Touraine	white	blue	blue	white	white	blue	white	white
Aquitaine	white	blue	blue	white	blue	blue	white	yellow
D'Eu	white	blue	blue	white	—	blue	white	yellow
St. Chaumont	white[2]	carmine	carmine	white	carmine	white	white	yellow
Montmorin	white[3]	red	red	white	—	red	white	yellow
Briqueville	white	red	red	white	—	white[4]	white	yellow
La Reine	white	red	red	white	red	blue	white	white
Limousin	white	—	red	white	red	white	white	yellow
Royal Vaisseaux	white[2]	blue	blue	white	—	red	white	yellow
Orléans	white	red	red	white	—	red	white	yellow
La Couronne	white	blue	blue	white	—	blue	white	white
Bretagne	white	—	white	red	black	red	white	yellow
Gardes Lorraines	blue[6]	—	blue	blue	—	blue	blue	white
Artois	white	white	white	white	—	red	white	yellow
Montrevel	white	red	red	white	—	red	white	white
Montmorency	white	white	red	white	—	red	white	white
La Sarre	white	blue	blue	white	—	red	white	yellow
La Ferre	white	red	red	white	—	white	white	white
Alsace	blue	red	red	red	red	white	white	white
Royal Roussillion	white	blue	blue	white	—	blue	white	yellow
Condé	white	red	red	red	—	red	white	yellow
Bourbon	white[2]	red	red	white	—	red	white	white
Grenad. de France	blue	red[9]	blue[6]	red	red[6]	blue[6]	blue	white
Beauvoisis	white[2]	white	white	white	—	red	white	white
Rovergne	white	red	red	white	—	red	white	yellow
Bourgogne	white	white	white	white	—	red	white	yellow
Royal Marne	white	blue	blue	white	—	blue	white	white
Vermandois	white[2]	red	red	white	—	blue	white	yellow
Anhalt	blue	yellow	yellow	yellow	yellow	white	white	white
Royal Artillerie	blue	red	red	red	—	red	red	yellow
Royal Italien	white[5]	light blue	light blue	white	light blue	light blue[5]	white	yellow
Jenner	red[7]	blue	blue	blue	—	blue[9,6]	red	white

(*continued*)

REGIMENT	COAT	COLLAR	CUFFS	SKIRTS	LAPELS	WAISTCOAT	BREECHES	BUTTONS
Boccard	red[7]	blue	blue	blue	red[7]	blue	blue	white
Reding	red[7]	blue	blue	blue	—	blue	blue	white
Castella	red[7]	blue	blue	blue	red[7]	blue	red	white
Languedoc	white	blue	blue	white	blue	white	white	yellow
Aumont	white	white	white	white	—	red	white	yellow
Waldner	red	blue	blue	blue	red	blue	blue	white
Médoc	white	red	red	white	—	red	white	white
Lemps	white	red	red	white	—	red	white	yellow
Bouille	white[2]	—	red	white	—	red	white	yellow
Royal Comtois	white[2]	blue	white	white	—	blue	white	yellow
Lastic	white	carmine	blue	white	carmine	white	white	yellow
Provence	white	red	white	white	—	red	white	yellow
Cambis	white	red	red	white	—	red	white	white and yellow
D'Arbonnier	red[7]	red	red	blue	—	blue[9,6]	blue	white
St. Maurice	white	red	blue[6]	white	—	white[4]	white	yellow
Nice	white[1]	white	red	white	—	red	white	yellow
La Mark	blue[6]	—	white	white	yellow[6]	white	white	white
Penthièvre	white[1]	blue	yellow[6]	white	—	blue	white	white
Guyenne	white	red	blue	white	—	red	white	yellow
Lorraine	white	white	red	white	—	red	white	yellow
Flandres	white	blue	white	white	—	blue	white	white and yellow
Berry	white[2]	red	blue	white	—	red	white	yellow
Béarn	white[2]	red	red	white	—	red	white	yellow
Hainault	white	red	red	white	—	red	white	yellow
Boulonnois	white	blue	red	white	—	blue	white	yellow
Angoumois	white	blue	blue	white	—	blue	white	white
Périgord	white	blue	blue	white	—	red	white	white
Saintonge	white	blue	bluc	white	—	blue	white	yellow
Bigorre	white	blue	blue	white	—	blue	white	yellow
Forez	white	red	red	white	—	red	white	yellow
Cambresis	white	red	red	white	—	red	white	yellow
Tournaisis	white	red	red	white	—	red	white	yellow
Foix	white	red	red	white	—	blue	white	yellow
Bresse	white	—	blue	white	—	blue[3]	blue	yellow
La Marche	white	—	red	white	red	red	white	yellow
Quercy	white	red	red	white	—	red	white	yhellow
La Marche Prince	white	blue	blue	white	blue[6]	blue[6]	white	white
Brie	white[1]	red	red	white	—	red	white	yellow
Soissonnois	white	blue	blue	white	—	blue	white	yellow
Isle de France	white[2]	blue	blue	white	—	blue	white	yellow
Diesbach	red[7]	blue	blue	blue	—	blue[9,6]	blue	white
Courten	red[7]	red	blue	blue	red[7]	blue	blue	white
Bulkeley	red[6]	red	green	red	—	green	white	white
Clare	red	yellow	yellow	yellow	yellow	red[6]	white	white
Dillon	red	—	black	white	—	red[3]	white	yellow
Royal Suédois	blue	light yellow	light yellow	light yellow	light yellow	light yellow	white	yellow
Charres	white	red	red	white	—	red	white	yellow
Conty	white	blue	blue	white	—	blue	white	white
Roth	red[5]	—	blue	blue	—	blue[5]	blue	yellow
Berwick	red[2]	black	black	white	—	red[5]	white	yellow

(*continued*)

REGIMENT	COAT	COLLAR	CUFFS	SKIRTS	LAPELS	WAISTCOAT	BREECHES	BUTTONS
Enghien	white[2]	red	red	white	—	red	white	white
Royal Bavière	light blue	black	black[6]	white	black[6]	light blue[6]	white	white
Salis	red[2]	blue	blue	blue	—	red	red	white
Royal Corse	white	green	green	white	—	red	white	yellow
Royal Écossais	blue[6]	red	red	blue	—	red	white	white
Royal Lorraine	white[2]	white	—	white	black	white	white	yellow
Royal Barrois	white	black	white	white	black	white	white	yellow
Lally	red	green	green	white	—	green	white	yellow
Nassau	blue[6]	red	red[6]	red	red[6]	white	white	white
Royal Cantabres	light blue[10]	red	red, pointed	white	—	white	white	white
O'Gilwy	red	—	blue	blue	—	blue[5]	white	yellow
Lochmann	red	blue	blue	blue	—	blue[9,6]	white	white
Bouillon	white	black	black[6]	white	black[6]	white	white	white
Deuxpont	light blue[6]	carmine	carmine[6]	white	—	white	white	white
Vierzet	white	—	blue	white	blue	white	white	yellow
Horion	blue[5]	—	red[6]	red	red[5]	red[5]	white	yellow
Eptingen	red	red	blue	blue	red	blue	blue	white

[1]vertical pockets [2]double vertical pockets [3]black lapels [4]red lapels [5]yellow loops [6]white loops [7]blue loops [8]red edging [9]white edging [10]white cords

patterned metal and silk lace strap, with fringe intermingled with silk. Gorgets were worn from 1762 in addition to these, as a mark of an officer, not as a rank distinction. Company officers carried a fusil and bayonet (Fig. 31f). In 1762 the uniform, especially the waistcoat, became closer-fitting and shorter, after the Prussian fashion. The sword belt was worn over the waistcoat (Fig. 31e). Grenadiers had worn fur caps for some time; in 1767 these were ordered to be of bearskin with a copper plate, and small feathers or pompons were worn. Dogskin or goatskin knapsacks were introduced in 1767, in place of the ticken ones hitherto carried. In 1775, the Navarre, Flandres, and du Roi regiments adopted helmets, but these were unsuccessful and were later abolished. From 1779 the leather equipment was worn crossed, and only the *gardes* retained the waistbelt. The skirt turnbacks were ornamented with grenades for the grenadiers, and *fleurs de lys* for the fusiliers. The *Régiment Colonel Général*, which wore red distinctions, had as its headdress a black leather helmet with black horsehair *crinière* (Fig. 31h). At the outbreak of the Revolution, all the line infantry regiments, with the exception of the foreign ones, had white coat linings, waistcoats, breeches, and gaiters. The basic color of the coats remained white. From 1791 to 1793 the colored distinctions (collar, cuffs, and lapels) were varied by series: one group of regiments wore black plush distinctions; others, violet, pink, crimson, scarlet, or royal blue. Within each series, each regiment differed in one or more of the following: color of collar, cuffs, cuff patches, buttons, and shape of pocket flaps. The headdress was a hat; grenadiers wore fur grenadier caps (Fig. 31i), now with a metal plate, and plume. The *Garde Nationale* was raised in 1789. Its uniform was a blue coat with white lining, lapels, and cuff patches and red collar and cuffs. The center companies wore hats and also helmets like those worn by the *chasseurs* of the period. The grenadiers had worn fur caps, but as these were too expensive they were replaced for a time by hats with a red plume (Fig. 32b). The fur caps were later revived. In 1793 the line infantry was formed into demibrigades. Each was made up of one line battalion and two battalions of volunteers or *Garde Nationale.* The demibrigades all wore the same uniform: blue coat with scarlet collar and cuffs piped white; white lapels; skirt turnbacks and cuff patches piped scarlet; numbered yellow metal buttons; red epaulettes; white waistcoat; and black hat with red plume. The earlier white uniform continued to be worn for a long time (Fig. 32a). In 1802–1803 the organization was altered again when the infantry was once more divided into regiments.

The First Empire

Up to 1807 the color and cut of the uniform did not change, except that the grenadiers wore larger fur caps than at the time of the Revolution. A copper plate ornamented the front. (Grenadiers of some regiments wore only a copper grenace.) Chacos were introduced in 1804, but it was a long time before all the infantry was issued with them; in the 1806 campaign they still wore hats. The queue, which was supposed to have been abolished in 1805, also continued in use for a time. In 1806 a new white uniform was ordered, and several regiments were issued with it; but, in October 1807, blue was readopted. The distinctions were: Regiments 1–8, Imperial green; 9–16, black plush; 17–24, scarlet; 25–32, *capucine* red; 33–40, violet; 41–48, sky blue; 49–56, pink; 57–64, orange; 65–72, dark blue; 73–80, yellow; 81–88, meadow green; 89–96, madder red; 97–104, crimson; 105–112, iron gray. The arrangement of the colors on lapels, cuffs, collars, and buttons, and the shape of the pocket flaps, indicated the regiment in each series. In 1805 companies of *voltigeurs* were raised in the infantry of the line; these, like the grenadiers, were elite troops. A battalion consisted of a grenadier company, a *voltigeur* company, and four center or fusilier companies. As distinctions, the *voltigeurs* were given yellow or yellow-and-

Fig. 32. France—Line Infantry, 1794–1894.

green fringed epaulettes and a yellow and green or yellow and red plume in their headdress; the grenadiers had a red plume and red epaulettes. On the fusiliers' chacos were pompons with colors varying by company (Fig. 32c). On the cartridge pouch, the grenadiers wore a grenade and, in the corners of the skirts as well, the *voltigeurs* wore a hunting horn. In 1808 the grenadiers' fur caps were replaced by chacos, which had red side chevrons and lace binding. The chacos of the *voltigeurs* had a similar ornamentation, but in yellow. The chaco cords and plumes were abolished in 1810. In 1812 the cut of the coat was altered: The jacket was cut across in front, the lapels ran straight down to the waist, and the skirts were shortened to make a *habit-veste* (Fig. 32d). Because the commanding officers of regiments were allowed to clothe the corps of drums and bands of the *tête de colonne* as they wished, there was a very wide variety of dress. By a decree of 19 January 1812, the uniform of the bandsmen was completely altered. It henceforth consisted of a single-breasted green *habit-veste* with red collar and cuffs; all, including the pockets and skirts, edged with dark green lace, which had green eagles and crowned "N" in green, alternately on a yellow field. There were seven equidistant chevron-shaped darts of the same lace on the sleeves.

At least some of the large number of foreign regiments must be mentioned:

Régiments Suisses: red coatee; collar, cuffs, and lapels yellow for the 1st Regiment; dark blue for the 2nd; black plush for the 3rd; and sky blue for the 4th. They had both chacos and fur caps.

Bataillon Irlandais (1812, 3rd *étranger*): green coatee; yellow collar, cuffs, and piping; chacos.

Portuguese: brown *habit-veste* with red collar, cuffs, and lapels; white piping; headdress of distinctive type.

Vistula Legion (Poles): blue *habit-veste* with yellow collar, cuffs, and lapels; chacos.

The number of foreign units was too great to go into them in more detail.

The Restoration and Louis Philippe

In 1815 Louis XVIII's army was divided into eighty-six departmental legions. The distinctions on the now white uniforms were: 1st–10th Regiments, royal blue; 11th–20th, yellow; 21st–30th, red; 31st–40th, dark pink; 41st–50th, carmine; 51st–60th, orange; 61st–70th, light blue; 71st–80th, dark green; 81st–86th, violet. In each of these series of ten regiments, the first five had yellow metal buttons; the second five, white metal; the 5th and 10th had white lapels; the 2nd, 4th, 7th, and 9th had a white collar. The cuffs and cuff patches also showed the legion distinction (Fig. 32e).

In 1820 the infantry was once more divided into regiments. In this year a blue single-breasted jacket was introduced. From then, the buttons were all of yellow metal. Collars, crescents, cuff patches, skirts, and piping were red and, from 1822, white for the 1st–4th Regiments; 5th–8th, carmine; 9th–12th, yellow; 13th–16th, dark pink; 17th–20th, orange; 21st–24th, light blue; 25th–28th, pale orange; 29th–32nd, light green. Cuffs, skirts, and piping were white for the 33rd–36th Regiments, and so on for each four regiments, as above, up to the 60th. The 29th–60th Regiments had blue collars with patches in the distinctive color.

In 1825 the chaco was changed for a slimmer cylindrical pattern. The distinctions were made red for all regiments in 1828. From 1829 the line infantry wore madder red trousers. This became a long-standing tradition.

Center companies were denoted by red crescents with blue straps, grenadiers and *voltigeurs* by their red and yellow fringed epaulettes respectively. In 1832 the collar was made cut away in front (Fig. 32f). A new pattern of chaco was authorized in 1837, and a further one in 1843, of blue cloth with a band of red lace around the top. In 1845 the coatee was superseded by a single-breasted tunic (*tunique*). This was royal blue, with madder red cuffs and piping and with nine yellow metal buttons, bearing the regimental number, down the front (Fig. 32g). On service, the chacos were worn in covers, which had the regimental number painted on the front. The gray-blue greatcoat was worn as a service dress.

The Second Empire

In 1852 fringed epaulettes were also adopted for the center companies; these were green with a red crescent. A new-pattern chaco was introduced in 1856. The previous year, the collar was changed to yellow piped blue. This piping was done away with in 1860, when the piping and cuff patches were changed to yellow. In the same year, the skirts were made very short and the trousers wide. At the same time, a new-pattern, all-leather chaco was issued (Fig. 32h). In 1867–1868 this uniform was superseded by a double-breasted tunic with round cuffs and a red chaco. On service (Fig. 32i), the red undress kepi, with blue band and the regimental number on it in red, was almost universally worn. The double-breasted tunic had a yellow collar piped blue, and round blue cuffs piped yellow. On the collar, the grenadiers had a red grenade; the *voltigeurs*, a red horn. The buttons were yellow metal. At the beginning of the 1870 campaign, the 1860-pattern chaco was worn, but it disappeared very quickly.

Third Republic: 1871–1915

While the infantry uniform underwent several changes, the overall character remained the same. In 1872 blue patches were added to the yellow collar and, at the same time, the yellow piping on the cuffs was done away with. The kepi was thenceforth made with a scooped instead of a horizontal peak. In 1879 the distinctions between the elite and the other companies were done away with, and all the infantry adopted red grenadier epaulettes. They were no longer worn on service. In 1884 the chaco, which since 1872 had resembled the 1856 pattern, was abolished. Two years later a full-dress kepi was introduced. The equipment adopted in 1892 was arranged similarly to that of the German army, i.e., braces, waistbelt, and three cartridge boxes.

Officers' gorgets were abolished in 1885. In 1883 officers adopted a black dolman. Ten years later a single-breasted tunic was authorized for them. In 1889 the men's tunics also became single-breasted, and the yellow distinctions were replaced by red.

The infantryman had three orders of dress: (1) full dress—blue tunic with red collar and blue patches with the regimental number on them in red, and red epaulettes; (2) drill order—dark blue jacket (*veste*) with narrow blue shoulder straps, and collar with red patches with the regimental number on them in blue; (3) greatcoat (*capote*)—gray-blue with self-colored collar and red collar patches bearing the regimental number in gray-blue (yellow metal buttons throughout). On service, the red trousers were worn either over the gaiters or tucked into them (Fig. 32k).

The reserve army was not issued with tunics, but had the drill order uniform with greatcoats, exactly as for the line, but with white metal buttons and, on the collar patches, white regimental numbers.

1915–1930

A *mignonette* (pale green) service uniform was approved in 1912 but was not adopted; so the army went into the Great War still wearing the colored uniforms, often with the kepi in a light-blue cover (Fig. 41a). As a consequence of the heavy casualties suffered, a camouflage uniform was adopted in 1915; the basic color was horizon blue (a very light gray-blue). The jacket had a row of six yellow metal buttons, horizontal skirt pockets, stand collar with at first yellow, later self-colored, pointed patches with the regimental number in dark blue and two chevrons to the rear; and no shoulder straps or ornamental cuffs. The trousers and puttees were gray-blue, the former piped yellow. The kepi was gray-blue with the regimental number in dark blue on the front, and with no colored trimming. The greatcoat was horizon blue, with cloth rolls on the shoulders and collar patches as on the jacket. The leather equipment was left its natural color. At the same time a steel helmet painted gray-blue was introduced, with a small comb and a flaming grenade above the peak and, also, a fore-and-aft type cap with yellow piping around the flap (Figs. 41e,f). Officers often wore a cloth girdle and had patch pockets on the breast and skirts of the jacket. After the war, the jacket was made with a flat turndown collar, on which were patches, pointed at the rear, with double cords at the back, and shoulder straps. The kepi was made higher and stiffer; dark blue piping was added around the top and band and on the side seams. During, and almost invariably after, the war, officers wore the colored prewar kepi, with a red top, dark blue band, and number and rank lace in gold. The colored kepi was worn by NCOs and regular soldiers from the late 1920s. In the meantime the greatcoat was made double-breasted. See Figure 41, page 114.

From 1935

Shortly after the end of the war, efforts were made to have the horizon blue replaced by the khaki worn by the colonial troops and by Britain. This led in 1930–1934 to the introduction of a new service dress resembling the sky-blue one, but made of khaki cloth. The collars of the jacket and greatcoat were made much broader. In the infantry the regimental number and chevrons on the khaki patches remained dark blue, but were yellow for the machine gun battalions. With the service jacket, a khaki shirt and tie were worn; officers also wore white shirts and a black tie.

Officers likewise adopted the khaki uniform, but continued to wear the colored kepi in place of the now khaki-painted helmet and had a Sam Browne and light khaki-colored riding breeches. The khaki trousers had broad dark khaki stripes down the outsides. On both the horizon-blue and khaki uniforms, officers and NCOs wore the numbers on the collar patches and the insignia on the kepi, embroidered in the color of the buttons. At the same time officers adopted an evening dress that closely resembled the prewar uniform (Fig. 41i). This consisted of a long-skirted blue coat with a row of gilt buttons. The stand collar and scalloped cuff patches were red. The collar patches, which were double-scalloped at the rear and bore the number in gold, were dark blue like the cuffs. Gold passants were worn, and the coat was worn with or without epaulettes. The red trousers had dark blue stripes, and a red kepi with dark blue band, and gold cord, regimental number and rank lace, was worn. The waistcoat was of dark blue silk with two round buckles and a fastener; the saber had a white metal scabbard and was worn on a dark blue sword belt.

III. *INFANTERIE LÉGÈRE* and *CHASSEURS À PIED*

In 1670 Maréchal Broglie formed a company of *chasseurs* in one of the regiments under his command. All infantry regiments were ordered to have a *chasseur* company in 1776. Six *chasseur* battalions were formed in 1784. In 1789 they were formed into fourteen battalions, which were named *demi-brigades légères* in 1794. The organization of these battalions resembled that of the line infantry, except that the grenadiers of the light troops were called *carabiniers*. In 1838 a *chasseur* battalion, the *Tirailleurs de Vincennes*, was raised. Two years later it was renamed *Chasseurs d'Orléans*. Under the Second Empire, a battalion of *Chasseurs à Pied* was formed as part of the *Garde Impériale*, along with twenty line battalions of *chasseurs*. In 1854 the *Infanterie Légère*, which had had an unbroken existence, was disbanded.

Infanterie Légère (Fig. 33b): During the Revolution the basic color of the long-skirted coatee, the waistcoat, and the close-fitting breeches was blue, with red lapels, cuffs, and skirt turnbacks, edged with white piping. In contradistinction to the line infantry, the lapels were tapered to a point at the bottom; the collar was blue, the epaulettes, green with red crescents—all red for the *carabiniers*—and the buttons were white metal. The *carabiniers* wore fur caps with red cords and plume, and a red crown with a white cross on it (Fig. 33c). The rest wore hats. Shortly before the end of the eighteenth century, the light troops adopted a chaco (Fig. 33d). When the *voltigeur* companies were formed in 1804, they adopted jackets with yellow collars piped white, and green epaulettes with yellow crescents. The chaco plume was yellow over green. In 1808 the *carabiniers'* fur caps were superseded by chacos ornamented like those of the line grenadiers (Fig. 33c). There was no *Infanterie Légère* between 1815 and 1820, as each legion consisted of two battalions of line infantry and one battalion of *Chasseurs à Pied*. In 1819 a green uniform was adopted by the light infantry, but in 1820 they went into blue uniforms piped yellow, with yellow collar and skirt turnbacks piped blue. The cuffs were pointed from the start; the buttons were

Fig. 33. France—Light Infantry and *Chasseurs à Pied*.

a, i, k: *chasseurs à pied*. b, d: *chasseurs*, light infantry. c, e, f, g: carabiniers, light
infantry. h: officer, light infantry.

of white metal (Fig. 33f). The legwear underwent the same changes as in the line, and
red trousers were adopted in 1830. Similarly, the different patterns of chaco were as
for the line (Figs. 33g,h).

Chasseurs à Pied (Fig. 33a): In 1784 the *chasseurs* wore green coatees with
variously colored distinctions, buff waistcoats and breeches, and hats. In that year a
distinctive type of shoulder strap was introduced. The colored lapels were replaced
by green ones in 1788. The distinctive colors were red, yellow, pink, carmine. Each
three battalions had one color; the first had it on the collar and cuffs; the second, only on the cuffs; and the third, only on the collar. From 1791 the lapels were piped in
the distinctive color. The hats were superseded by helmets. The 13th and 14th battalions adopted white distinctions. In 1845 their uniform consisted of a blue single-
breasted tunic with blue collar and pointed cuffs. The piping was yellow and the
buttons were of white metal. They wore blue, kepi-type chacos, with yellow piping,
iron-gray trousers, and black leather equipment. The epaulettes were green with
yellow crescents (Fig. 33i). The combination of colors on the uniform remained the
same up to the late 1930s despite the many changes in style in the interval.

The *chasseurs* of Napoleon III's Imperial Guard wore yellow cord loops on the
front of their coats and yellow grenades on the collar.

The *Chasseur Alpins* were raised from the *chasseur* battalions in 1888. At first,
they kept to their old uniform, but they soon adopted Basque berets. The coat was
changed for a single-breasted dark blue jacket with large turndown collar, with a
yellow number on it. In 1891 the kepi was completely abolished.

At the outbreak of the Great War, the *chasseurs* wore a dark blue single-

Fig. 34. France—Cuirassiers.

a, b, d, e, g, i, k: cuirassiers. c: heavy cavalry. f, h: cuirassiers of the guard.

breasted service jacket with a broad turndown collar and round cuffs of basic color, with the battalion number and hunting horn beneath in yellow—or silver for officers—on the collar. The dark blue-gray trousers had yellow piping and were worn with leather half-gaiters. The kepi was blue and red with dark blue piping. The *Chasseurs Alpins* had a medium-blue beret with a yellow hunting horn on the right side; dark blue puttees; and a gray-blue greatcoat with number and hunting horn in the corners of the collar (Fig. 41c). They were to have adopted the horizon-blue uniform, with green numerals and hunting horns on the collar patches, but did not, and the dark blue uniform in its distinctive cut continued to be worn up to the late 1930s. Two yellow chevrons were added at the top of the collar patches, which were of basic color. The steel helmet was painted blue, and the device—a hunting horn—was frequently in green. By the late 1930s, the *chasseurs* were the only troops in the French army who did not have the khaki uniform. The officers' evening dress had collar and cuffs of basic color; all metal insignia were in silver; and the kepi had a black velvet band. See Figure 41, page 114.

IV. HEAVY CAVALRY AND CUIRASSIERS

All cavalry, except the dragoons and hussars, and the *gendarmerie* were called *chasseurs à cheval*.

Following the Regulations of 1690, all regiments were dressed in coats of varying shades of grayish-white red for the *Régiment Colonel-Général* and blue for the royal regiments. These colors were retained up to 1762, when all adopted blue coats. There were frequent changes in distinctions—1740, 1757, 1762, 1767, 1776, and

1786—and only one list, from 1761, can be given here (from the Zeughaus manuscript).

REGIMENT	COAT	CUFFS	SKIRTS	LAPELS	WAISTCOAT	BUTTONS
Colonel-Général	red	black	red	black	light yellow	yellow
Mestre de Camp-Général	gray	black	gray	black	red	yellow
Commissaire Général	light gray	black	light gray	black	light yellow	yellow
Royal[1]	blue	red	blue	red	red	white
Du Roy[2]	blue	red	red	red	red	white
Royal Allemand[3]	blue	red, pointed	red	—	light yellow	white
La Reine	red	blue	blue	blue	red	yellow
Noailles[4]	red	red	red	red	light yellow[1]	white
Fitz James[5]	red	blue	blue	blue	light yellow[1]	white

[1]The same for: Royal étranger; Cuirassiers du roi; Royal Cravattes; Royal Roussillion; Royal Piémont; Royal Pologne; Dauphin; Bourgogne (red collar); Carabiniers de Provence (white piping on lapels, skirts, and cuffs), Artois.

[2]The same for Berry.

[3]white lace

[4]yellow-and-violet checkered lace

[5]white-and-green checkered lace

The following regiments had white coats with red lapels, cuffs, and skirts, and light-yellow waistcoats with the following lace: Royal Lorraine, red and black; Royal Picardie, red and yellow; Royal Champagne, yellow and black; Royal Navarre, crimson and white; Royal Normandie, red and white mixed; Condé, pink; Bourbon, Bourbon lace; Clermont, crimson; Pentievre, yellow and blue mixed (red collar).

The same uniform, but with white skirt turnbacks, was worn by: Orléans, blue lace; Chartres, violet and white; Conty, the same uniform, with red skirts but without lapels; lace, red, white, and blue.

In the French regiments of heavy cavalry, there was only one true cuirassier regiment, the *Cuirassiers du Roi*, raised in 1666. Their uniform (Fig. 34a) was blue with red distinctions and blue undergarments. They wore hats. In 1733 an attempt was made to put all the heavy cavalry into cuirasses, but this did not last long. In 1762 the following uniform was ordered for the cuirassier regiment: blue coat with red cuffs, felt hat with white woolen lace binding, buff leather equipment and breeches, and white metal buttons. In 1767 they had yellow coats edged with red cloth, scarlet cuffs, and a cuirass. At the remodeling of the army in 1791, the regiment was renumbered 8 among the heavy cavalry. In 1802 the 2nd to 7th regiments adopted cuirasses. In 1804 there were twelve regiments of cuirassiers. In 1802 the distinctive helmet with the black horsehair mane was introduced in place of the hat, and so was created the traditional image of the French cuirassier (Fig. 34e). The skull of the helmet was steel with yellow metal comb, chinscales, and turban of black calfskin. The plain breast and back plates, worn by all regiments, had yellow metal straps.

From 1812 a blue *habit-veste* with short skirts was worn; it had a row of white metal buttons, vertical skirt pocket flaps, and blue grenades on the skirt turnbacks. The epaulettes were red. The sleeve linings of the cuirass were red with white piping. The steel helmet had a black turban and *crinière* and a red plume on the left side in full dress. The shabraques and valise were blue with white edging. The former had a white grenade in the rear corners; the latter had the regimental number in white. The saddle was covered with a white sheepskin with a scalloped edge. The officers wore silver epaulettes. Trumpeters mostly wore "fantaisie" and, sometimes, coatees in the reversed colors, with white lace on the front; they did not wear cuirasses. In 1812 the trumpeters adopted the green *habit-veste* with yellow and green lace and a white plume on the helmet.

In 1812 the distinctions were as follows.

REGIMENT	COLLAR AND SKIRT LINING	CUFFS	CUFF PATCHES
1	red	red	red
2	red	red	blue
3	red	blue	red
4	light orange	light orange	light orange
5	light orange	light orange	blue
6	light orange	blue	light orange
7	yellow	yellow	yellow
8	yellow	yellow	blue
9	yellow	blue	yellow
10	pink	pink	pink
11	pink	pink	blue
12	pink	blue	pink
13	lilac-carmine	lilac-carmine	lilac-carmine
14	lilac-carmine	lilac-carmine	blue

These were the same as they had been in 1804, except for the 13th and 14th regiments, raised in 1809.

After Waterloo, Louis XVIII raised six regiments, with the following distinctions on the collar, cuffs, and cuff patches:

1st Régiment de la Reine—scarlet
2nd Régiment du Dauphin—carmine
3rd Régiment d'Angouleme—light orange
4th Régiment de Berri—dark pink
5th Régiment d'Orléans—yellow
6th Régiment de Condé—light orange

In 1815, also, two cuirassier regiments were raised as part of the *Garde Royale* (Fig. 34f). The royal blue jacket had a red collar, red cuffs for the 1st Regiment, red cuff patches for the 2nd; red skirt turnbacks; white buttons and aiguillettes; white breeches; iron breast and back plates, with a yellow metal shield with the coat of arms of France and Navarre on the front. The steel helmet had a black crest and white plume. In full dress, white breeches were worn with high boots; for normal use, long gray trousers were worn. By 1834 there were ten regiments of the line. The uniform remained as before. The distinctions were: 1st Regiment, scarlet; 2nd, carmine; 3rd, light orange; 4th, pink; 5th, yellow; 6th, madder red. The 7th to 10th regiments had cuffs of the same colors as the 1st to 4th regiments, respectively, but with blue collars, piped in the regimental color. From 1830 all wore red trousers. A new-pattern helmet was introduced in 1825. It no longer had a turban, and the *crinière* was replaced by a black *chenille* (Fig. 34g). About 1840 it was changed back to one similar to that worn under the First Empire. In 1842 the distinctive colors were altered as follows.

REGIMENT	COLLAR	COLLAR PIPING	CUFFS	CUFF PIPING	PATCHES	PIPING ON PATCHES
1	orange	blue	blue	orange	orange	blue
2	orange	blue	orange	blue	blue	orange
3	blue	orange	blue	orange	orange	blue
4	blue	orange	orange	blue	blue	orange

The 5th to 8th regiments were the same as the 1st to 4th respectively but, instead of orange distinctions, had yellow ones; the 9th and 10th regiments had red.

In 1860 a tunic was introduced, having a row of white metal buttons, and with madder red collar, cuff patches, and scarlet epaulettes for all regiments (Fig. 34i). The overalls were strapped with leather up to the knee. The cloak was white. Napoleon III formed two cuirassier regiments in the *Garde Impériale* in 1854 and 1855. The 1st Regiment had dark blue tunics, the 2nd, sky blue. Both had scarlet collars and cuffs and turned-back skirts. The epaulettes and aiguillettes were white, and the white breeches were worn with butcher boots. The overalls were madder red, piped in the same color as the coat. Instead of a turban, the helmet had a yellow metal band, with a crowned "N" on the front. The 2nd Cuirassier Regiment of the *Garde Impériale* was disbanded in 1865; the 1st remained up to 1871. The *Escadron des Cent-Gardes à Cheval* on guard and escort duty wore cuirassier uniforms and had white *crinières* on their helmets; the coat was sky blue with amaranth red distinctions, gold-and-red epaulettes, and gold aiguillettes. The breeches were like those for the cuirassiers of the *Garde*. The sword was made to fix onto the carbine.

After the Franco-German War of 1870–1871, the cuirassier helmet was altered: In particular, it had a brass band, and the back peak was lengthened. In general, however, the old shape was still recognizable. The colors remained as in 1860. In 1884 all the piping was changed to dark blue (sky blue in 1888) and blue collar patches bearing the regimental number in red were added.

At the outbreak of war in 1914, helmets and cuirasses were worn, the former with a khaki cover (Fig. 41d). On both the horizon-blue and the khaki uniform, dark blue collar patches with numerals and chevrons in red, and white metal buttons, were worn. The cavalry greatcoat was always single-breasted. The officers' mess dress was as for the infantry except that all insignia were silver. The cavalry wore a flaming grenade on the steel helmet.

V. *GRENADIERS À CHEVAL* AND *CARABINIERS*

Of the heavy cavalry under the old monarch, only one regiment, the *Royal-Allemand*, wore fur caps. In 1785 they were dressed in a long blue Polish-style coat with red turnbacks, white tufted lace loops on the front, and white buttons, epaulettes, and lace. The undergarments were buff-colored. The fur cap had white cords and a red-over-white plume. The *Garde du Corps Législatif*, raised by the National Assembly in 1791 and later becoming the *Garde Consulaire*, wore fur caps with red cords and a red plume. The blue coat had red lapels laced in white. The blue collar had white lace, and the trefoil-shaped epaulettes were edged with white. The buttons were yellow metal; the waistcoat and breeches were also yellow. From this guard originated the regiment of *Grenadiers à Cheval* of the *Garde Impériale* (Fig. 38a). Their fur caps had yellow metal chinscales, red plume, and orange cords. They wore a blue coat with blue collar, white lapels, red cuffs, and red skirt turnbacks with yellow grenades on white patches; gold crescents, aiguillettes, and buttons; and white waistcoat and breeches. The sword hilt was of yellow metal. See Figure 38a, page 104.

During the Restoration, there were two regiments of *Grenadiers à Cheval* in the *Garde Royale* (Fig. 38b). In 1815 the coat, collar, and cuffs were blue, with white grenades on the collar; there were seven white lace loops with tassels down the front; white buttons, aiguillettes, and epaulettes; and three white lace loops on the vertical pocket flaps. The full-dress breeches were white. The 1st Regiment had white piping around the pocket flaps, and the skirt turnbacks and cuff patches were blue. The 2nd Regiment was denoted by carmine piping on the collar, cuffs, and cuff patches. The bearskin cap had a white plume for the 1st Regiment, white and crimson for the 2nd. They were disbanded in 1830.

In 1679 two men in each company of cavalry were armed with carbines. A carabinier company was formed in each regiment in 1690, and in 1693 these were formed into a regiment—the *Régiment Royal de Carabiniers.* The uniform was blue with red distinctions and red (later buff) undergarments. The buttons were arranged in threes on the coat; the sleeves and epaulettes were edged silver; and a silver-laced hat and yellow leather equipment edged silver were also worn. Two regiments were raised in 1788. The uniform was blue with blue collar and red lapels and cuffs. The 1st Regiment had red cuff patches, the 2nd, blue. Fur caps were worn. During the First Empire, the uniform consisted of a blue coat with blue collar, red lapels and skirt turnbacks, red epaulettes, with two longitudinal white strips, and white metal buttons. The undergarments were white, and the leather accoutrements were yellow, edged white. The fur caps were increased in height and had red plumes and yellow metal chinscales (Fig. 38c). This uniform was altered in 1809, when a white coatee with sky blue collar and skirt turnbacks was introduced. The 1st Regiment had red (or possibly sky blue) cuffs piped white, with blue piping on the cuff patches; the 2nd had sky blue cuffs piped white, with blue cuff patches. Red epaulettes were also worn and yellow metal breast and back plates, and a yellow metal helmet with white metal fittings and comb, surmounted by a red *chenille.* The leather equipment remained as before (Fig. 38d). This uniform was retained during the first Restoration, for the *Carabiniers de Monsieur*, but the distinctions were changed to carmine. In 1825 the coat became sky blue without lapels, with red epaulettes. In 1831 they adopted red trousers like the rest of the army. Except for changes in style and the introduction of the tunic in 1860, their uniform remained as before up to 1867, when they were disbanded. In the same year, however, a regiment of carabiniers appeared in the *Garde Impériale* for the first time. They wore a similar uniform, with a white metal sunburst on the breast plate (Fig. 38e). This regiment came to an end in 1871.

VI. DRAGOONS

The dragoons were one of the oldest arms of service in France. In 1676 a coat and "stocking cap" edged with cloth with a heavy nap or fur replaced the leather

Fig. 35. France—Dragoons.

a, b, c, d, e, g, h, k, l, m: dragoons. f, i: dragoons of the guard.

doublet and metal helmet. The basic color was predominantly red, but blue, green, and gray coats were worn by some regiments. White lace loops were added to the coat fronts and cuffs of some of the regiments in 1736. In 1757 epaulettes were introduced on the right shoulder. The headdress was a hat or, more usually, the fur-edged cap.

Regimental Distinctions in 1761
(from the Zeughaus manuscript)

REGIMENT	COAT	WAISTCOAT	CUFFS
1. Colonel-Général[1]	red	blue	blue
2. Mestre de Camp Général[2]	red	red	white
3. Royal[3]	blue	red	red
4. Du Roi	blue	red	white
5. La Reine[4]	red	blue	blue
6. Dauphin	blue	blue	blue
7. Orléans[5]	red	blue	blue
8. Beauffremont	red	red	yellow
9. Choiseul	red	red	dark green
10. D'Autichamps	red	red	light green
11. La Ferronnaye	red	red	red
12. Flammarens	red	red	black
13. Nicolai	red	red	light blue
14. Chapt	red	red	yellow
15. Marboeuf[6]	red	red	red
16. Languedoc[7]	blue	blue	red

[1]white binding to waistcoat   [2]white binding to waistcoat   [3]red skirts   [4]blue skirts   [5]blue skirts
[6]yellow lace loops   [7]red collar

In 1763 a green uniform with collar, lapels, and cuffs of distinctive color was introduced generally, as was a yellow metal helmet with black horsehair plume—white for the colonel's company—like that worn from 1743 by Marshal Saxe's dragoons, and the Schonberg Dragoons raised from them in 1762 (Fig. 35c). The latter were so proud of this headdress that they even refused to take it off in church. Only an order from the king himself could prevent this disobedience. In the Versailles Museum is a helmet which belonged to the Dauphin, the crest of which is of female human hair. The distinctions on the green coats were: 1st, 5th, 6th Regiments, crimson; 2nd, 3rd, 7th, 14th, scarlet; 4th, 10th, pink; 8th, 11th, 16th, buff; 9th, yellowish; 12th, black; 13th, 15th, orange; and 17th, scarlet. The undergarments were a yellowish color. During the revolutionary period, the yellow metal helmet, which had a brown turban and black *crinière*, was fitted with a peak. The coat remained green with variously colored distinctions: 1st–6th Regiments, scarlet; 7th–12th, crimson; 13th–18th, dark pink; 1793, 19th, 20th, 21st, yellow; 1804, 22nd–24th, yellow, 25th–30th, orange. The colors and shape of the pocket flaps were arranged differently for each regiment. During the Empire, the dragoon regiment of the *Garde Impériale* adopted the title *Dragons de l'Impératrice* in 1810 (Fig. 35f). The yellow metal helmet had a turban of panther skin, and a red plume; the coat was green with green collar, white lapels, scarlet skirt turnbacks with yellow grenades, yellow metal buttons, yellow crescents and aiguillettes, and white undergarments. The coat, which was cutaway in front (Fig. 35e), was altered in 1812 to a *habit-veste* with lapels running straight down and much shorter skirts. The buttons were white metal for all regiments, and the helmet was as worn previously. Green epaulettes were worn, piped in the distinctive color. The elite companies were denoted by red grenadier epaulettes and a fur cap with a red plume and red cords.

The undergarments were white. As for regimental distinctions, each series of six regiments wore the same: 1st–6th Regiments, scarlet; 7th–12th, carmine; 13th–18th, pink; 19th–24th, yellow; and 25th–30th, light orange. In each group the differences were as follows.

REGIMENTS	LAPELS AND SKIRTS	COLLAR	CUFFS	CUFF PATCHES	POCKET FLAPS
1, 7, 13, 19, 25	distinctive color	distinctive color	distinctive color	distinctive color	cross
2, 8, 14, 20, 26	distinctive color	green	distinctive color	green	cross
3, 9, 15, 21, 27	distinctive color	distinctive color	green	distinctive color	cross
4, 10, 16, 22, 28	distinctive color	distinctive color	distinctive color	distinctive color	vertical
5, 11, 17, 23, 29	distinctive color	green	distinctive color	green	vertical
6, 12, 18, 24, 30	distinctive color	distinctive color	green	distinctive color	vertical

The shabraques were as for the cuirassiers, but of green, with white edging. Officers were denoted by silver epaulettes and by the absence of pouches. Up to 1812 trumpeters wore differently colored uniforms. Those of the *Dragons de l'Impératrice* wore white with sky blue distinctions, and gold edging to the housings and holster caps. From 1812 trumpeters of line dragoons wore the regulation green *habit-veste* with yellow and green lace. The dragoons of the *Garde Parisienne* had green coatees with red distinctions but, in general, dressed like the line dragoons.

Louis XVIII retained ten dragoon regiments with the following distinctions on the collar, lapels, cuff patches, and skirts:

    1st du Calvados—scarlet
    2nd du Doubs—scarlet
    3rd de la Garonne—yellow
    4th de la Gironde—yellow
    5th de l'Hérault—light orange
    6th de la Loire—light orange
    7th de la Manche—dark pink
    8th du Rhône—dark pink
    9th de la Saône—carmine
    10th de la Seine—carmine

The 2nd, 4th, 6th, 8th, and 10th Regiments had green cuffs and only patches of the regimental color. The odd-numbered regiments had cuffs of the distinctive color.

In 1823 the distinctions were as follows.

REGIMENT	COLLAR	LAPELS AND PIPING	CUFF PATCHES	CUFFS	CRESCENTS
1, 2	dark pink	dark pink	dark pink	green	green
3, 4	green	green	green	dark pink	dark pink
5, 6	yellow	yellow	yellow	green	green
7, 8	yellow	yellow	green	yellow	yellow
9, 10	carmine	carmine	carmine	green	green

The basic color remained green, but the horsehair *crinière* was replaced by a black *chenille*. The overalls were gray, piped in the distinctive color (Fig. 35g).

The regiment of dragoons of the *Garde Royale* wore a green jacket with green collar and cuffs, dark pink lapels, cuff patches and turnbacks, white overalls, and white epaulettes and aiguillettes. Later, the helmet was changed like the cuirassier helmet, from which it was distinguished by being of yellow metal. Madder red trousers were adopted in 1823 (Fig. 35h). The changes up to 1867 were minor. In that year the dragoons adopted dark blue tunics with a row of yellow metal buttons. The collar was white, as were the piping and cuff patches. Epaulettes were scarlet and the trousers, madder red. The helmet was of yellow metal (Fig. 35l).

During the Second Empire, a regiment of dragoons of the *Garde Impériale*—the *Dragons de l'Impératrice* (Fig. 35i)—was formed. The uniform consisted of a light green jacket with red collar, white lapels, epaulettes, aiguillettes, and leather equipment. The pointed cuffs were of basic color, edged with red piping. The skirts, too, were of basic color, with red piping and grenades. The skirt pockets were vertical. The buttons were yellow metal, and the red trousers had green side stripes. The yellow metal helmet had a black *crinière* and a red plume in full dress, but no turban. The cloak was white with four red lace loops on each side of the large turndown collar. Officers had gold epaulettes and trouser stripes. After the war of 1870–1871, the dragoons remained unchanged up to 1884, when a blue dolman with nine black loops, and pointed cuffs, replaced it. The yellow metal helmet was superseded by a white metal one with yellow metal band, mounts, and comb, surmounted by a black horsehair *crinière* of the same type as that worn by the cuirassiers, except that the *houpette* (''shaving brush'') at the point of the comb was not worn. The first rank of all dragoon regiments was armed with the lance, as in the German army (Fig. 35m). The pennants were white and red. In 1907 the dolman was superseded by a tunic. The collar was white, with patches of the basic color, with red numerals. The cuff patches were also white.

The horizon blue and the kahki uniforms had white metal buttons, and dark blue collar patches with white numerals and chevrons; motorized dragoons had a white five-pointed star below the number. The mess dress was like the cuirassiers', but the collar and cuff patches were white.

VII. HUSSARS

These date in France from 1692, when one regiment, the *Hussards Royaux*, was formed, principally of Croatians, Poles, and Turks. It was later disbanded. In 1701 another regiment was formed and in 1720 a further one. Up to 1720 the various hussar formations were dressed almost without exception in light blue. In that year the newly raised Esterhazy Regiment adopted light-yellow dolmans. Fig. 36a shows a hussar of the *Régiment de Bercheny* in 1724 and represents the earliest type of French hussar uniform. The dolman was sky blue with white cords; the red breeches were almost covered by light-blue *Scharawaden*; an animal skin was worn over the shoulders instead of a fur pelisse; the cap had a red bag. The black sabertache bore a white *fleur de lys*. Up to 1740 some of the hussars were armed not with a saber but with a sword that had a long, thin square-section blade.

After the Regulations of 1752 all the hussar regiments—Linden, Bercheny, Turpin de Crissé, Beausobre, Raugrave, Poleraiski, and Ferrari—were dressed in light-blue dolmans, pelisses, and breeches, with white loopings. From that time the regiments wore *mirlitons*, the color and decoration of which denoted the regiment. By 1757 only four regiments still existed. One of these, Nassau-Sarrebrück, was raised in 1756. This regiment was dressed in a quite different manner (Fig. 36b), with black felt caps with a white *fleur de lys* and a black wing edged in orange and white. The dolman and breeches were royal blue, the pelisse, red, and the loops, white. The red sabertache bore a white crowned lion device and was edged in orange and white.

About 1745 several of the volunteer corps had hussar detachments. One of these was the Breton Hussars. They wore light-blue dolmans (with light-brown cuffs), breeches, and *mirlitons*, and light-brown pelisses with dark blue loops. The volunteer hussars of Dauphiné had light-brown dolmans (with light-blue cuffs) and breeches; light-blue pelisses; yellow cords; and black felt caps with a light-blue wing. The hussars of Monet wore all-green uniforms with white loops and a black felt cap. The Cantabres Hussars were dressed all in light blue with red cuffs and white cords. As these instances show, the uniform was very variegated.

After the reorganization of the army in 1763, only three hussar regiments remained; a fourth was added in 1764. The distinctions were now simplified. All four regiments adopted green pelisses and dolmans with white loopings, and red breeches. Sheepskins, with a notched cloth edging, were worn over the saddle. The color of

Fig. 36. France—Hussars.

a, b, c, d, e, g, h, i, k: hussars. f: hussar of the guard.

these edgings, together with the similarly colored cuffs of the dolman and the lining of the wing of the felt caps, displayed the distinguishing color of each regiment, which were: Bercheny Regiment, madder red; Chamborant, black; Royal-Nassau, light orange; and Esterhazy, white. The red sabertaches were ornamented either with a white *fleur de lys* or with the royal cipher intertwined. In 1786 variously colored uniforms were introduced again: the Bercheny Regiment adopted light blue as the basic color of their dolmans; Colonel-Général, royal blue (scarlet pelisse); Chamborant, brown; Conflans (raised from the Conflans Legion Hussars and Nassau Hussars), green; Esterhazy, silver-gray; and the Lauzun Regiment, raised in 1783 from the Lauzun Legion, light blue.

The pattern of uniform did not alter in essentials during the Revolution. In 1791 the regiments lost their names and adopted numbers. There were six regiments.

NO.	FORMER NAME	DOLMAN	PELISSE	LOOPS	BREECHES	*MIRLITON*
1	Bercheny	blue	blue	white	blue	red and black
2	Chamborant	brown	brown	white	light blue	light blue and black
3	Esterhazy	silver-gray	silver-gray	red	silver-gray	white and black
4	Saxe	green	green	yellow	red	green and black
5	Colonel-Général	blue	red	yellow	blue	black
6	Lauzun	blue	white	yellow	blue	blue and black

The officers wore panther skin shabraques and fur caps. The plume on the *mirlitons* was black with a red tip. When the *Saxe-Hussards* Regiment went into exile, the 5th and 6th Regiments were renumbered 4th and 5th. In the years following, there were several renumberings, mostly of short duration. In addition to these regular regiments, there were two Corps of Liberty, the American Hussars, *Hussards à Pied*, *Hussards de Mort* (based on the Prussian *Totenkopfhusaren*), Wildschützen Hussars, *Hussards Libres du Nord* (also called *Hussards Noirs*), *Hussards d'Égalité*, and others. The *Hussards Libres de Paris* were denoted by their yellow dolmans and pelisses, and were nicknamed "canaries." Chacos were worn instead of *mirlitons*. At first the plume, of distinctive color, was worn on the left side of the black chaco; later it was placed in front. Around 1812 the chacos became more cylindrical and were made of colored cloth. In 1804 the regimental distinctions were as follows.

NO.	DOLMAN	COLLAR	CUFFS	PELISSE	LOOPS	BREECHES
1	sky blue	sky blue	red	sky blue	white	sky blue[1]
2	brown	brown	sky blue	brown	white	sky blue
3	gray	gray	red	gray	red	gray
4	royal blue	royal blue	red	red	yellow	royal blue
5	sky blue[2]	sky blue	white	white	yellow	sky blue
6	red[3]	red	red	royal blue	yellow	royal blue
7	dark green	red	red	green	yellow	red
8	dark green	red	red	dark green	white	red
9	red[4]	light blue	light blue	light blue	yellow	light blue
10	sky blue	red	red	sky blue	white	sky blue
11	royal blue	red	red	royal blue	yellow	royal blue

[1]1812—green breeches [2]1812—red dolman [3]1812—dark green dolman [4]1812—blue dolman

The pelisse was edged with black fur, except for the 11th Regiment, which had white fur. The sashes were carmine, with yellow or white barrels according to the color of the loops and buttons. The sabertaches during the Revolution bore a bundle of fasces, topped by the cap of liberty between two wreaths, with the initials "R.F." on a colored background. From 1804, however, they were ornamented with the Imperial eagle. After 1812 they were made of plain black leather, with the regimental number below the eagle (Fig. 36d). In place of the Hungarian breeches, which were only worn in full dress, buttoned overalls, sometimes gray, sometimes of the same color as the breeches, were worn on service and in everyday dress. The elite companies of hussars were distinguished by a fur cap with a red plume. In 1812 green overalls were adopted. In 1813 the regiment then numbered 9 took the number 12, but retained the uniform of the 9th Regiment with white loopings. The 13th Regiment adopted the uniform of the 2nd Regiment with a light-blue collar and red cylindrical chaco.

In addition to the hussar formations of the First Empire, there were four regiments of *Garde d'Honneur*. These existed during 1813–1814 and wore red chacos with white lace and a white metal eagle plate; green pelisses and dolmans with white loopings, the latter having red collar and cuffs; carmine and white sashes; and red Hungarian breeches with white lace, or green buttoned overalls laced red. The black sabertaches had a white eagle badge. The regiments were differentiated by the colored tips of the green plume on the chaco: red for the 1st Regiment; 2nd, blue; 3rd, yellow; and 4th, white. White sheepskin saddle covers with a green cloth edging were worn. A Croatian hussar regiment was raised in 1813. It adopted sky blue dolmans and pelisses, with buff collar and cuffs, white loopings and iron-gray breeches; in general, the uniform closely resembled that of the other regiments.

After the Restoration, six regiments were left:

NO.	TITLE	DOLMAN AND PELISSE	CUFFS	BREECHES
1	Du Jura	sky blue	scarlet	sky blue
2	De la Meurthe	brown	sky blue	sky blue
3	De la Moselle	gray	carmine	carmine
4	Du Nord	light green	scarlet	scarlet
5	Du Bas-Rhin	royal blue	scarlet	scarlet
6	Du Haut-Rhin	dark gray	sky blue	sky blue

The loopings were of the color of the dolman and the breeches, mixed: that is, the 1st Regiment had sky blue and scarlet twisted loopings, and so on. As part of the *Garde Royale* there was one regiment of hussars. They wore royal blue uniforms with amaranth red collar, cuffs, and breeches, and crimson bag and white plume on the fur caps. The loops were white. The fur edging was black (Fig. 36f).

The prevailing fashion in the 1820s and 1830s tended to make the chacos very tall.

In 1834 the distinctive colors were as follows.

NO.	DOLMAN AND PELISSE	BREECHES AND CHACO
1	sky blue	madder red
2	brown	madder red
3	silver-gray	madder red
4	madder red	sky blue; black chaco
5	royal blue	madder red
6	dark green	madder red

In 1845 the distinctions were:

NO.	DOLMAN AND COLLAR; PELISSE	PELISSE EDGING	DOLMAN CUFFS, BREECHES, AND CHACO	LACE
1	light blue	black sheepskin	madder red	white
2	brown	black sheepskin	light blue	white[1]
3	gray	black sheepskin	madder red	mixed
4	madder red	black sheepskin	light blue	white
5	blue	black sheepskin	madder red	mixed
6	green	black sheepskin	madder red	mixed
7	green	gray sheepskin	madder red[2]	mixed
8	white[4]	black sheepskin	light blue	gold
9	black	black sheepskin	light blue	black[3]

[1]In memory of the former Chamboran Hussars.
[2]Green breeches and chaco in memory of Napoleon I's *Guides*.
[3]In memory of the *Hussards de la Mort*.
[4]Sky-blue dolman with red trouser stripes in memory of the Lauzun Hussars.

In 1860 a black fur cap with a red bag and white-and-red plume was introduced.

From 1860 all eight regiments (the 9th was disbanded in 1856) wore red trousers, red collars, and cuffs. The 1st and 8th regiments had sky blue dolmans; 2nd, brown; 3rd and 4th, silver-gray; 5th, dark blue; 6th and 7th, light green. The loopings were white for the first six regiments, yellow for the others. In 1867, in place of the dolmans with many loopings, a sky blue tunic, with only six rows of white loops, was adopted. The sabertaches were black with a copper eagle badge. Officers normally wore a leather kepi with a cover in place of the fur cap.

In 1872 a light-blue *Attila* jacket, with white loopings, was introduced generally. The light-blue collar bore the regimental number in madder red on the white patches. The legwear remained as before. The kepi was light blue with a red band. The full-dress chaco was light blue with white lace and a white Hungarian knot (Fig. 36k). In 1907 a single-breasted light-blue tunic was introduced. It had a light-blue collar with the regimental number in red, light-blue cuff patches, white shoulder cords, and white metal buttons (Fig. 41b). Before the Great War, a few regiments adopted dragoon helmets with a star on the plate as an experimental issue.

At the outbreak of the war, light-blue kepi covers were worn. The 1915 and 1930 service uniforms had dark blue collar patches with light-blue chevrons and numerals, and white metal buttons. The evening dress uniform had all insignia in silver; the collar, collar patches and cuff patches, the triple stripes on the trousers, and the band on the kepi were all light blue.

VIII. *CHASSEURS À CHEVAL*

Chasseurs à Cheval originated from the volunteer corps that were formed shortly after 1740. The first corps of *chasseurs*, called Fischer's, was raised in 1743. The uniform was exactly like that of hussars and consisted of a green dolman and light-red pelisse with yellow loopings and brown fur edging; light-red breeches; yellow and red sashes; and black fur caps with a white feather and cockade (Fig. 37a). A device of three fishes was worn on the sabertache and in the corners of the shabraques, an example of canting heraldry, adopted by the commander, Johann Christian Fischer, who began his career as an ordinary servant. In 1749 green pelisses were adopted, and the device on the sabertache was changed to the royal cipher interwined. Green breeches were taken into wear in 1768. In several of the other volunteer corps, too, there were *Chasseurs à Cheval*. The first six line regiments were formed in the army in 1779. The uniform consisted of a dark green coat, waistcoat and breeches, hussar boots, and a bicorne hat. The cuffs and lapels were scarlet for the 1st Regiment; 2nd, crimson; 3rd, yellow; 4th, buff; 5th, orange; and 6th, white. The breeches were dark green with white lace. During the Revolution a green dolman with white hussar loops was introduced, with similar loops on the collar and cuffs; either the collar or cuffs, or both, according to the regiment, were of the distinctive color. The breeches remained green. The headdress was a crested helmet similar to that worn by the *Chasseurs à Pied* (Fig. 37b). Besides the helmet, a hussar *mirliton* was adopted shortly afterward. The uniform now very much resembled that of hussars (Fig. 37c), but the basic color remained green. Pelisses were not worn. Sabertaches were adopted in 1804 and, in the same year, the looped dolman gave way to a *surtout*: a green coatee with green pointed lapels, piped in the distinctive color (Fig. 37d). The latter color showed on the collor, pointed cuffs, and skirt turnbacks. In 1812 the *surtout* was replaced by a similarly colored *habit-veste*, with green hunting horns on the skirts. The elite companies wore fur caps with a colored bag and red plume, and red epaulettes. Besides the Hungarian breeches, green buttoned overalls were also worn.

Fig. 37. France—*Chasseurs à Cheval.*

a, b, c, d, f, h, k, l: *chasseurs à cheval*. e, h: *chasseurs à cheval*, Imperial guard. i: *guides*.

A regiment of *Chasseurs à Cheval* belonged to the *Garde Impériale* (Fig. 37e). The uniform consisted of a green dolman with green collar, red cuffs, orange loopings, scarlet pelisse edged with black fur; yellow breeches and Hungarian boots; fur caps with a red bag, orange cords, and a red-over-green plume. The sabertaches and shabraques were green, ornamented with yellow and orange respectively. In undress, a green *surtout* with red distinctions and piping was worn. This uniform is well known, since Napoleon himself frequently wore it. Green was his favorite color.

In 1812 all the line regiments wore green jackets with green lapels. The distinctions were as follows.

NO.	COLLAR		CUFFS, TURNBACKS, SHOULDER STRAPS, LAPEL PIPING
	BASIC COLOR	PIPING	
1	scarlet	green	scarlet
2	green	scarlet	scarlet
3	scarlet	green	green
4	yellow	green	yellow
5	green	yellow	yellow
6	yellow	green	green
7	pink	green	pink
8	green	pink	pink
9	pink	green	green
10	carmine	green	carmine
11	green	carmine	carmine
12	carmine	green	green
13	orange	green	orange
14	green	orange	orange
15	orange	green	green
16	sky blue	green	sky blue
17	green	sky blue	sky blue

(*continued*)

| NO. | COLLAR | | CUFFS, TURNBACKS, SHOULDER |
	BASIC COLOR	PIPING	STRAPS, LAPEL PIPING
18	sky blue	green	green
19	light orange	green	light orange
20	green	light orange	light orange
21	light orange	green	green
22	dark orange	green	dark orange
23	green	dark orange	dark orange
24	dark orange	green	green
25	madder red	green	madder red
26	green	madder red	madder red
27	madder red	green	green
28	amaranth red	green	amaranth red
29	green	amaranth red	amaranth red
30	amaranth red	green	green
31	buff	green	buff

The cloak and valise were green. The shabraques were green, edged with stripes of the distinctive color; on service, sheepskin saddle covers were worn. During the Restoration, there were twenty-four line regiments. They wore a tall black chaco and a green jacket with green lapels. The collar, cuffs, and piping were of the distinctive color, with a bugle horn on the turnbacks; the buttons were white metal for all. Green breeches were worn in full dress; for other duties, gray. In 1815 the 19th–21st Regiments adopted violet distinctions, the 22nd–24th, black. In 1818 the distinctions were as follows.

NO.	TITLE	COLLAR	CUFFS
1	De l'Allier	scarlet	scarlet
2	Des Alpes	green	scarlet
3	Des Ardennes	scarlet	green
4	De l'Ariège	yellow	yellow
5	Du Gantal	green	yellow
6	De la Charente	yellow	green
7	De la Corrèze	light orange	light orange
8	De la Côte d'Or	green	light orange
9	De la Dordogne	light orange	green
10	Du Gard	dark pink	dark pink
11	De l'Isère	green	dark pink
12	De la Marne	dark pink	green
13	De la Meuse	carmine	carmine
14	Du Morbihan	green	carmine
15	De l'Oise	carmine	green
16	De l'Orne	sky blue	sky blue
17	Des Pyrénées	green	sky blue
18	De la Sarthe	sky blue	green
19	De la Somme	violet-red	violet-red
20	Du Var	green	violet-red
21	Du Vaucluse	violet-red	green
22	De la Vendée	black	black
23	De la Vienne	green	black
24	Des Vosges	black	green

The last squadron of each regiment was equipped with lances.

The *Chasseurs à Cheval* of the *Garde Royale* in 1815 adopted a black leather helmet with yellow metal comb, black *chenille* and white plume, a green jacket with white collar and skirts piped green, green lapels and cuffs piped white, and white epaulettes and aiguillettes. In 1824 they had red skirts, piping, and trousers, and a red chaco with a white plume.

The uniform of the line *chasseurs* was changed in 1821–1822 (Fig. 37f). It then consisted of a tall black chaco, with lace in the regimental color around the top, and similarly colored lines. The plume was black, with the tip of the regimental color. The green jackets had hussar loopings of green and the distinctive color mixed—officers had silver loops. The collar or cuffs and the skirt turnbacks were of the distinctive color. Those regiments which had green collars had a small scalloped patch of the regimental color on each side. Those regiments which had green cuffs had colored piping around them. The buttons were white metal for all, and the trousers were red.

In 1822 the distinguishing colors were as follows.

NO.	COLLAR	CUFFS
1, 2	scarlet	green
3, 4	green	scarlet
5, 6	yellow	green
7, 8	green	yellow
9, 10	carmine	green
11, 12	green	carmine
13, 14	sky blue	green
15, 16	green	sky blue
17, 18	dark pink	green
19, 20	green	dark pink
21, 22	orange	green
23, 24	green	orange

In 1831 single-breasted jackets and red-fringed epaulettes with green straps were worn. The trousers remained madder red. The chaco was taller, and of cloth, with a black hanging plume (Fig. 37g). A short time later, fur caps without bags were introduced, but these gave way to red chacos in 1848. In 1858 light-green dolmans with eighteen rows of black loopings and three rows of white metal buttons were introduced, as were small fur caps and sabertaches with a copper eagle badge. This was the uniform worn in 1870, except that by then the 1st, 6th, and 9th Regiments were wearing sky blue coats with a row of white metal buttons, and six black loops on the breast; collar and cuffs were sky blue with red piping.

In the *Garde Impériale* of Napoleon III, there was a regiment of *Guides* (Fig. 37i) whose uniform resembled that of the *Chasseurs à Cheval* of Napoleon I's Guard. It comprised a dolman of dark green, with madder red cuffs, and five rows of buttons with yellow loopings. The pelisse was green looped in yellow; the trousers were madder red with golden-yellow stripes; the caps of black fur with a black and white plume; and the sabertache dark green with golden-yellow edging, bearing the Imperial Arms. The new *Chasseurs à Cheval* of Napoleon III's *Garde Impériale* (Fig. 37h) wore a similar uniform, but with white loopings and white trouser stripes. The fur caps were of a rather narrower shape. Both these guard regiments were disbanded in 1871.

In 1873 the *Chasseurs de France (à cheval)* adopted a sky blue *Attila* jacket with nine rows of black loopings and a red collar. At first they had very low red chacos; later they wore light-blue ones, with a yellow *cor de chasse* on the front. In c. 1900 they adopted a dark blue single-breasted tunic with red collar and cuff patches, white trefoil, and white metal buttons. Shortly before the Great War, dragoon helmets, with a *cor de chasse* on the plate, were issued to some of the regiments. On the 1915 and 1930 service dress uniforms, white metal buttons and dark blue collar patches with green chevrons and numerals were worn. The evening dress was like that of the hussars, but with red piping on the outer, double-scalloped ends of the collar patches.

IX. LANCERS

In 1743 Marshal Saxe raised a regiment, the *Uhlans de Saxe*, a part of which was organized after the fashion of the Polish lancers. In the first rank were the lancers, recruited from the nobility, while in the second were the "Pacholks" (valets), whose duty was to care for the horses and the weapons of their masters. The Pacholks were equipped like dragoons, with a sword, a musket, and a pair of pistols. They were dressed in green coats with red collar, lapels, and cuffs; buff waistcoats edged red; Hungarian breeches; and helmets like the lancers. The latter wore all-green uniforms with red girdles and red waistcoats. The yellow metal helmets had a sealskin turban and a horsehair *crinière*, the color of which distinguished the brigades (Fig. 38f). The

Fig. 38. France—*Grenadiers à Cheval*, Carabiniers, Lancers.
a, b: *grenadiers à cheval*. c, d, e: carabiniers. f: lancer. g, i: lancers of the guard. h: *chevau-léger-lancier*. k, l: lancers.

104

saddles were covered by wolf skins. In 1750 the lancers were disbanded, but the rest of the regiment remained in existence.

There were no lancers thereafter until 1807, when the *Chevau-Légers de la Garde Impériale* were formed. Later the title was changed to *Chevau-Légers-Lanciers*. They were first armed with lances in 1809. Their uniform consisted of a royal blue *kurtka* with crimson distinctions edged silver, crimson piping, and white epaulettes, aiguillettes, and buttons. The overalls were crimson with blue stripes. The lancer cap was crimson with white lines and a yellow metal plate (Fig. 38g). The regiment was called also the *Lanciers Polonais*. In 1810 the 2nd *Chevau-Légers-Lanciers* of the guard was formed from the former Dutch Regiment of Horse Guards. The *kurtka*, overalls, and lancer cap were scarlet, with royal blue distinctions and yellow buttons, epaulettes, and aiguillettes. Both regiments had red and white lance pennants. The 3rd Regiment, which only lasted a short time, wore a similar uniform to that of the 1st Regiment, except that insignia were yellow instead of white, and gold instead of silver. The lancer cap was white, with crimson and yellow lines and a crimson plume.

The *Tartares* (Lithuanian Tartars) were dressed distinctively in peaked black fur caps with white turban and red plume and green bag, variously colored sleeveless jackets over richly embroidered crimson Turkish waistcoats, and loose-fitting trousers.

During the First Empire, there were six line regiments of French Lancers and three of Polish. Both had a different uniform. The French regiment of *Chevau-Légers-Lanciers* (Fig. 38h) were formed from dragoon regiments and wore their old dragoon uniforms, but with a *chenille* instead of a *crinière* on the helmet. Collar, lapels, cuffs, and skirt turnbacks were of the distinctive color; the shoulder straps were green, except for the elite companies, who had red fringed epaulettes. The Polish Lancers wore blue chacos with a yellow rayed plate; blue *kurtka* and trousers, with collar and pointed cuffs in the regimental color; white fringed epaulettes for the elite companies, blue shoulder straps piped in the distinctive color for the rest; and white metal buttons. The lance pennants were white and carmine.

In 1812 the distinctive colors were as follows.

NO.	KURTKA, PIPING, AND OVERALLS	BUTTONS	DISTINCTIVE COLOR
1	green	yellow	scarlet
2	green	yellow	light orange
3	green	yellow	pink
4	green	yellow	carmine
5	green	yellow	sky blue
6	green	yellow	red
7	blue[1]	white	yellow
8	blue[2]	white	blue
9	blue[3]	white	buff

[1]blue piping; white skirts
[2]yellow piping; yellow skirts
[3]blue piping; white skirts

105

After the Restoration in 1815, only one regiment was left: the Lancers of the *Garde Royale* (Fig. 38i). The uniform was a green *kurtka* with green collar and cuffs, piped carmine, carmine lapels, and green trousers; white epaulettes and aiguillettes; and a carmine chaco and, from 1816, a carmine lancer cap with yellow metal rayed plate and a white feather plume. In 1830 this regiment was disbanded. The *Lanciers d'Orléans* was formed in the same year. They wore a red lancer cap with yellow cords and lines with a drooping black hair plume. The lancer pennants were red over white over blue.

In 1831 the distinctive colors were as follows.

NO.	COLLAR	CUFFS AND PATCHES	PIPING	LAPELS	SKIRT TURNBACKS
1	blue	blue	red	blue	blue
2	blue	red	red	blue	blue
3	blue	blue	blue	blue	blue
4	blue	blue	red	blue	red
5	blue	red	red	blue	red
6	red	blue	blue	blue	red

The shabraques were red with a blue edging. In 1837 another two regiments were formed, and the uniform was changed. The *kurtka* and lancer cap became blue and the trousers red. The distinctive colors were yellow for the 1st–4th Regiments and madder red for the 5th–8th. In 1839 the hair plume was made red (Fig. 38k). The following table shows the uniform distinctions according to the 1845 regulations. All regiments wore a blue *kurtka* with pointed cuffs and white epaulettes, aiguillettes, and buttons. The passants across the neck of the epaulette straps were blue. The trousers were red with a blue piping, and the lancer cap was blue with a red plume. The lancer pennants were tricolored and, from 1858, white and red.

From 1845 to 1867 the distinctions were as follows.

NO.	LAPELS	COLLAR	CUFFS	SKIRTS, PIPING, LANCER CAP LACE
1	yellow	yellow	blue	yellow
2	yellow	yellow	yellow	yellow
3	yellow	blue	blue	yellow
4	yellow	blue	yellow	yellow
5	red	red	blue	red
6	red	red	red	red
7	red	blue	blue	red
8	red	blue	red	red

In 1856 a regiment of lancers was raised in the *Garde Impériale*. The uniform consisted of a sky blue lancer cap with white lace and yellow metal fittings. The lines and cock's feather plume were red. The trousers were red with sky blue stripes. The white jacket had sky blue collar, cuffs, lapels, piping, and skirt turnbacks, and red epaulettes and aiguillettes. The pennants were white over red. The shabraque and valise were light blue, edged with white, and piped red around the outside. The buttons were white metal.

In 1870 the lancer uniform was in process of being changed, but this was only partially completed. The new uniform, that of the 1867 regulations (Fig. 381), was a dark blue single-breasted tunic with yellow collar, yellow cuff patches, and white buttons and epaulettes. The lancer cap was blue, with yellow lace, and a red plume. The lancers were disbanded in 1871 and not re-formed.

X. *ÉCLAIREURS*

Three regiments of *Éclaireurs* (Scouts) existed in the *Garde Impériale* from 1812 to 1815. The 1st Regiment was divided into (1) *Vieille Garde* and (2) *Jeune Garde*. The first, or "old" Guard, was dressed in a green hussar uniform with red pointed cuffs and white loopings; green trousers; and black chacos with red lace around the top. The "young" Guard was dressed as *Chasseurs à Cheval*, with red piping on the collar, lapels, cuffs, and shoulder straps, and wore the same chaco as the "old" Guard.

The 2nd Regiment wore a single-breasted green jacket with crimson collar and pointed cuffs, green buttoned overalls with crimson stripes, and a tall crimson chaco. Half were armed with carbines and half with lances.

The 3rd Regiment wore the uniform of the Polish Lancers, but with white pompon, blue and white girdles, and blue shabraques without edging. Again, half were armed with carbines and half with lances.

XI. AFRICAN TROOPS

A special section is devoted to these, since from the time of the conquest of Algeria, France kept up various formations in her African possessions, and they were noted for their distinctive uniforms.

Several African corps were involved in Napoleon I's expedition to Egypt. First, there was the Coptic Legion, formed in Egypt in 1799. The uniform (Fig. 39a) consisted of a light-green jacket with self-colored lapels and pointed cuffs. The collar and piping were yellow; the buttons, white metal; and the close-fitting breeches, yellow. Short gray linen gaiters were worn. The hat had a distinctive pompon for each company. The grenadiers had red drooping plumes and red epaulettes. After the evacuation of Egypt, some Mamelukes returned to France, and these provided the nucleus of a squadron which was later incorporated into the *Garde Impériale*. They wore an exotic Oriental costume, which varied very much in color according to the whims of the commanding officers. The unique Dromedary Regiment (Fig. 39b) also dated from the Egyptian expedition. Illustrations show them wearing uniforms of a considerable variety. One, for example, depicts a light-blue dolman and breeches, both looped with white; over this a red pelisse with similar loopings, and with half sleeves; a chaco with yellow fittings and white cords; a white Arabian burnoose; and a black sabertache with the fasces in yellow as a badge. They were armed with hussar sabers and muskets. In the course of the Egyptian campaign, the troops of the regular army were greatly depleted and, as new supplies of uniforms could not be gotten from France, they had recourse to providing their own. The uniforms then showed the most unusual combinations of colors; there were, for instance, dragoons dressed in pink and yellow.

Fig. 39. France—African Troops.

a: Coptic Legion. b: Dromedary Regiment. c, d: Zouaves. e,f: Turcos. g: Spahi. h,
i: *Chasseurs d'Afrique.*

The Zouaves date from 1830, and were first formed from natives and Parisians,
as a battalion called the *Volontairs de la Charte.* In 1842 the battalion was formed
into a regiment and, in 1852, two other regiments were raised. Their uniform was a
dark blue jacket and waistcoat with red lace. On each side the jacket had a false
pocket, or *tombeau,* of red cloth for the 1st Regiment; white for the 2nd; yellow for
the 3rd; and dark blue for the 4th. The baggy trousers were red; the girdle, light blue;
and the fez, red with a white turban (Figs. 39c,d). Before the outbreak of the Great
War, they were already wearing a khaki-colored service dress. Red chevrons and
numerals were worn on the khaki collar patches, and the buttons were yellow metal.
The badge on the steel helmet was a crescent, points uppermost. After the war, all
African native troops wore the old colored uniform for walking out. The regiment of
Zouaves (formed in 1855) in the *Garde Impériale* wore similar dress to the line
Zouaves, but with yellow lace on the jacket and waistcoat, sky blue girdles, and
yellow turbans. In 1870 this became the 4th Regiment of Zouaves.

The *Tirailleurs Algériens,* or *Tirailleurs Indigènes,* or *Turcos,* were raised in
1842 and, from 1852, consisted of three regiments. At first, green jackets,
waistcoats, and cartridge pouches with yellow lace and red trousers were worn. The
girdle and cuffs were light blue (Fig. 39e). In 1845 the French officers and NCOs
wore green tunics, red trousers, and green kepis. From 1858 the *tirailleurs* were
dressed like the Zouaves, but jacket, waistcoat, and trousers were sky blue, with
yellow lace and, later on, had similar distinctions (false pockets): 1st Regiment, red;
2nd, white; 3rd, yellow; 4th, sky blue; and they had a red girdle (Fig. 39f). On the service dress, also khaki, the *Tirailleurs Indigènes (Algériens et Tunisiens)* wore light-
blue chevrons and numerals on their collar patches. The *Tirailleurs Marocains,*

raised during the 1914–1918 war, wore green ones, with the Seal of Solomon (a five-pointed star) in addition. The buttons were yellow metal. After the Great War, the *Tirailleurs Marocains* wore sky blue jackets with green and dark blue lace.

The *Chasseurs d'Afrique* were formed in 1831. To begin with, they wore a long-skirted sky blue coat, red trousers with leather strapping, a small madder red lancer cap with red hanging cords, white gauntlets, and yellow metal crescents (Fig. 39h). The 1st Regiment had yellow collars and pointed cuffs, piped light blue; the 2nd had a light-blue collar with three-pointed yellow patches and light-blue pointed cuffs with yellow piping. The 3rd Regiment (raised in 1832) had a yellow collar with light-blue three-pointed patches and yellow pointed cuffs. The 4th Regiment (1839–1856) had sky blue collars and pointed cuffs. The lance pennants were red, white, and blue. The lances and lancer caps were given up in 1833. From then, red kepis with a light-blue band were worn; in time they became stiffened like chacos, and these were worn up to 1915, frequently with a white cover and sun curtain (Fig. 39i). In 1853 the four regiments adopted all-yellow collars. In 1862 a light-blue dolman with yellow collar, black loopings, and white trefoils and buttons was introduced. On service, and later in all orders of dress, the men wore a short light-blue single-breasted jacket with yellow collar and cuff patches, white trefoil, and red girdle. From about 1900, the officers wore light-blue tunics with yellow collar and cuff patches. The trousers were always red, with light-blue triple stripes for the officers. Dark blue collar patches with yellow chevrons and numerals, and white metal buttons, were worn on the khaki service dress.

The *Spahis* were formed in 1834. In 1845 they mustered three regiments. Their jackets and waistcoats were cut like those of the Zouaves and were red with black lace, with a red sash, blue trousers, and red cloak. The large Arabian cloak, reaching over the head, was called a *haik* and was made of camel hair (Fig. 39g). European officers wore European-style uniforms: red jackets with blue cuffs, yellow metal buttons; light-blue trousers; and light-blue kepis. The regimental number was placed above a crescent, in gold, at the ends of the collar. The khaki uniform had dark blue collar patches with yellow numerals and chevrons and yellow metal buttons. Loose-fitting khaki trousers were worn.

The *Tirailleurs Sénégalais* were dressed like the *Turcos*. About 1890 they adopted navy blue single-breasted jackets. There was yellow lace around the neck and on the pointed cuffs, and it also ornamented the outer edges of the collar and cuffs of the khaki service dress. Yellow foul anchors and chevrons were worn on the khaki collar patches.

In 1831 the Foreign Legion wore the uniform of the line infantry, with a blue collar piped red and blue crescents with red edges. In 1845 they wore infantry uniforms with blue cuffs piped red. In 1858 the 1st Regiment adopted green tunics with yellow collar and red pointed cuffs, the 2nd, dark blue tunics with yellow collar and dark blue pointed cuffs. The chaco was green with yellow lace around the top. The epaulettes were red for grenadiers, yellow for *voltigeurs*, and green with red crescents for the center companies. These last epaulettes were later worn by all. The double-breasted dark blue tunic of 1867 had a red collar.

The collar patches on the khaki uniform were khaki with green chevrons; the men had the regimental number in green; NCOs had gold; the officers had a gold flaming grenade with the regimental number on the bomb. The Cavalry Regiment of the Foreign Legion had dark blue collar patches with green chevrons and a flaming grenade and white metal buttons. The evening dress of the officers was as for the infantry. The collar and cuff patches were dark blue. A flaming grenade was worn on the kepi and on the collar patches, which were piped green on the bottom edge.

The *Infanterie Coloniale* were European troops who served in the colonies. From the 1830s they wore dark blue coats with self-colored collars and cuffs piped red; yellow epaulettes; and a chaco; later, a dark blue kepi with red piping, yellow metal buttons; gray-blue trousers with red piping; and a foul anchor at the ends of the collar and on the kepi band, in red for the men and gold for NCOs and officers. After the Franco-German War, the red collar and coat piping were abolished. The colonial artillery was distinguished from the metropolitan army only by the foul anchor at the ends of the collar instead of the regimental number. On the khaki uniform, the colonial infantry wore khaki collar patches with red numerals, foul anchor, and chevrons. The colonial artillery had red patches with a blue anchor. The badge on the steel helmet was the foul anchor.

XII. *GENDARMERIE*

During the Revolution, the *Gendarmerie Nationale* wore a long-skirted blue coatee with scarlet collar and cuffs (with blue cuff patches) and white metal buttons. The yellow leather accoutrements were edged with white, and the hat was edged with silver lace. The undergarments were buff (Fig. 40a). The equipment of the mounted troops was as for the cavalry, that of the *Gendarmerie à Pied* like the infantry. The same uniform was worn during the First Empire. The *Gendarmerie d'Élite* formed part of the *Garde Impériale* (Fig. 40b). They wore long-skirted dark blue coatees with blue collar; red lapels, cuffs (with blue patches), and skirts; and white buttons, trefoil-shaped epaulettes, and aiguillettes on the left shoulder. Waistcoat, breeches, and gauntlets were buff-colored. The leather equipment was yellow with a white edging. The fur caps had no plates but were furnished with a leather peak, a red plume (white for full dress), and white cords.

In 1811 there was a corps of *Lanciers Gendarmes* in the army in Spain. The uniform consisted of a black chaco with white ornaments and a red plume; blue coatee with blue shoulder straps, red collar and pointed cuffs, and red piping around the pointed lapels; and red skirt turnbacks. The waistcoat was red with hussar loopings. The Hungarian breeches were blue. The valise was blue, and the shabraque was laced with white. The lance pennants were red and white.

During the Restoration, the uniform of the *gendarmerie* remained similar, but the coatee was altered. The silver-laced hats continued to be worn, but the *Gendarmerie de la Corse* wore chacos. The *Gendarmerie d'Élite* wore blue coats with red lapels and skirts and white grenades at the ends of the blue, red-piped collar. The headdress was a white metal helmet with yellow metal comb and leopard-skin turban, with both a black *chenille* and *crinière* and a white plume. In the reign of Louis Philippe, single-breasted coats with a row of nine buttons, no lapels, and red piping were introduced for the *gendarmerie*. The *Élite* adopted fur caps with a red plume.

Fig. 40. France—Gendarmerie, Artillery, Engineers.

a: Gendarmerie Nationale. b: Gendarmerie d'Elite. c: gendarme. d, f: foot artillery. e, g: horse artillery. h, l, k: engineers.

Later the coatee was superseded by a tunic and, from 1843, the trousers were light blue. The *Gendarmerie Coloniale* wore blue *kurtkas* with red skirts and black chacos. The *Escadron des Gendarmes d'Élite* of Napoleon III's *Garde Impériale* wore dark blue coatees with blue collar, cuffs and cuff patches, with white grenades on the collar, red plastron and skirts and yellow leather equipment edged with white. Fur caps with a yellow metal plate and red plume were worn in full dress; in undress, hats with a red plume. In the latter part of the nineteenth century (Fig. 40c) the *Gendarmerie à Cheval* wore a dark blue tunic with self-colored collar bearing white grenades; red skirt turnbacks; white aiguillettes and shoulder cords; a yellow metal helmet with white metal band and black *crinière* and tricolor plume. The *Gendarmerie à Pied* wore the same, but without the depending part of the *crinière*. The hat gave the *gendarmerie* a somewhat old-fashioned appearance. After 1918 a blue jacket was worn for full dress with silver grenades on the collar; white shoulder cords and aiguillettes; blue trousers; and a blue kepi with a black band, bearing the grenade in white.

XIII. ARTILLERY, ENGINEERS, ARMORED TROOPS, AND TRANSPORT CORPS

In 1670 the *Régiment de Fusiliers* was formed to guard the artillery. Up to 1722 they wore grayish-white coats. The uniform from that year was blue, with red collar and cuffs, waistcoat, and breeches. (See the infantry table of 1761.) From 1772 the collar and lapels were blue, edged with red; the shoulder straps, black; the cuffs, skirts, waistcoats, and breeches, red (Fig. 40d). The cuffs had red patches in 1791, and shortly afterward these were changed to blue with red piping. The uniform remained the same during the Revolution and First Empire. Red epaulettes were adopted in 1792 and blue ones in 1812, when a coat with blue collar and lapels and red cuffs was introduced. Chacos were adopted in 1810. From 1792 the *Artillerie à Cheval* wore an all-blue hussar-type uniform with red loopings and, to begin with, a helmet with a crest, like that of the *chasseurs*; but shortly afterward felt caps and chacos were issued, the latter having red cords and plume (Fig. 40e). The *Artillerie à Cheval* of the *Garde Impériale* had a similar uniform but with blue pelisses with red loopings and hussar busbies with a red plume and bag. The *Artillerie à Pied* of the *Garde* wore fur grenadier caps with no plate, but with a peak, and red cords and plume; the rest of the uniform was as for the line. The cut of the uniform subsequently underwent alterations, but the combination of colors remained unchanged, except that the red cuffs were later made pointed (Fig. 40f). The chacos had red plumes and hanging cords. The artillery of the *Garde Impériale* of Napoleon III wore blue dolman and trousers with red loopings and lace, respectively, in them. The buttons were yellow metal. The black fur caps had red bags and cords and white-over-red plumes. The horse artillery wore cavalry equipment with sabertaches (blue with red lace and a yellow eagle); the foot artillery had infantry equipment, knapsack, and carbines. After the Franco-German War, the blue basic color was retained; jackets with seven rows of hussar loopings were adopted by both the horse and foot artillery. The collar and pointed cuffs were red; the buttons yellow metal; and the loopings black. The trousers were blue with red stripes. The blue kepi was piped red (Fig. 40g). About 1900 a single-breasted tunic with red cuff patches and collar was introduced. The Horse Artillery had red trefoils on the cuffs. In 1912 an experimental black leather helmet was issued. It had yellow metal chinscales; a low comb reaching down over the front; and a red feather plume. The artillery mostly wore their drill jackets which, in contrast to the tunics, had blue collars with red patches. On the latter were worn the numerals in blue; in white, for territorial troops. The *Artillerie de Montagne* wore drill jackets and Basque berets. On the horizon-blue and khaki service uniforms, the buttons were yellow metal; the collar patches red with blue chevrons and numerals; the *Artillerie Légère* in addition wore a blue five-pointed star below the numerals. The badge on the steel helmet was a flaming grenade above crossed cannon barrels. The officers' evening dress was as for the infantry, but with dark blue trousers with red triple stripes, instead of red ones, and an all-dark-blue kepi.

Engineers originally consisted only of a corps of officers which, in 1776, was formed into a battalion. In December 1793 a *Corps de Génie* consisting of twelve Sapper battalions and six companies of miners was raised. In 1794 the uniform was a blue coatee, waistcoat, and breeches, with black velvet collar, lapels, and cuffs, red skirt lining, and yellow metal buttons. The uniform remained much the same during the First Empire, but the cuffs were changed from round to slashed ones; red piping was added, and red epaulettes (blue ones with red fringes from 1812). A chaco with red ornaments and pompon superseded the hat previously worn. The *Corps de Génie* of the *Garde Impériale* was dressed similarly, but had steel helmets with yellow metal fittings, a black *chenille*, and a red plume. When engaged in constructing field works under fire, they wore blackened cuirasses and iron helmets. During the Restoration, and up to the Second Empire, the uniform of the line engineers remained much as before. Orange epaulettes, and blue grenades on the skirt turnbacks, were first worn in 1815. Both the coat and chaco altered from time to time, according to the prevailing fashion. The chaco cords were abolished (Fig. 40i). The engineers of Napoleon III's *garde* were distinguished by fur caps without plates, with red cords, and a plume. There were red grenades on the collar. From 1867 the engineers wore dark blue tunics with self-colored collars and cuffs, with black velvet cuff patches; red epaulettes; blue trousers with red stripes; a leather kepi, and black leather equipment. NCOs wore swords instead of sword bayonets. In 1879 a double-breasted dark blue tunic was introduced, with blue collar and cuffs, with black velvet patches on both, and red piping on them; red epaulettes; yellow metal buttons; blue trousers with red triple stripes; and blue kepis with red piping (Fig. 40k). About 1900 a single-breasted tunic was adopted. From c. 1880–1905 officers wore an all-black dolman with black loopings. The men's drill order jackets had dark blue collars with black velvet patches piped red with red numerals.

The collar patches on the 1915 and 1930 service uniforms were black velvet with red numerals and chevrons. The badge on the steel helmet was an armorial helmet and a cuirass. On the officers' evening dress, the black collar patches had gold numerals and red piping at the rear edges. The collar and cuff patches were of basic color. The trousers were dark blue with red triple stripes; the kepi, dark blue.

Chars de Combat (Armored Troops): On the horizon-blue uniform, tank troops wore white metal buttons, sky blue collar patches with green numerals and chevrons, and horizon-blue painted steel helmet with comb and lengthened neck guard, with a leather pad in place of the front peak. Off duty, a small dark blue beret was worn, with the tank troops badge on the front: an armorial helmet with closed visor, above crossed cannon barrels, between the letters "R.F." The same badge was worn on the steel helmet. On the khaki service dress, the dark blue collar patches were edged grayish-blue. The steel helmet had no comb. On the officers' evening dress, the collar, cuff patches, and single broad stripes on the blue-gray trousers were all ash gray; the kepi had a black velvet band.

The *Autos Mitrailleuses de Cavalerie* (motorized machine gun sections of the cavalry) had violet chevrons and numerals on their dark blue collar patches.

Train d'Artillerie, Train des Équipages, etc. (Transport Corps): In 1807 the *Train d'Artillerie* was organized on military lines. The uniform was gray with blue distinctions, gray epaulettes, white metal buttons, yellow undergarments, and chacos with a white metal plate. The *Train des Équipages* of the *Garde Impériale* had gray trousers, the distinctions were piped red, and red crescents were worn. The gray waistcoats had red loopings, and the chaco had a red plume and red cords. The artillery drivers wore the uniform of the *Train*. The gray basic color remained the main characteristic of the uniform, but to note the many variations individually would exceed the scope of this work. The *Train d'Artillerie* had blue distinctions; the *Train des Équipages*, gray distinctions; the *Train du Génie*, black distinctions; the *Train des Parcs d'Artillerie*, blue distinctions. About 1890 the uniform of the *Train des Équipages* had a gray-blue dolman edged with black lace, with black loopings; white metal buttons; cuffs of basic color; and a red collar with the squadron number in red on gray patches; red trousers; red full-dress chaco with red plume; and a dark gray kepi with red band. In 1914 the uniform was a single-breasted dark blue tunic, with white metal buttons, and red collar patches (with numerals in dark blue); red cuff

Fig. 41. France, 1914–1936.

a, e, k: infantry. b: hussar. c: *chasseurs alpins*. d: dragoon. f: officer,
artillery. g: cavalry. h: Tirailleurs Sénégalais. i: officer, infantry. l: fortress
infantry. m: artilleryman in walking-out dress.

patches and trefoils; red trousers; and a red kepi with a blue-gray band. The *Train*
almost invariably wore the drill order jacket with self-colored shoulder straps and
collar, the latter having dark blue patches bearing the numerals in red.

On the 1915 and 1930 service uniforms, the *Train des Équipages* wore white
metal buttons and green collar patches with red chevrons and numerals. The officers'
evening dress was like that of the cuirassiers, but with green collar patches and silver
numerals.

XIV. *GARDES NATIONALES* and *GARDE MOBILE*

The origin of the *Garde Nationale* has been dealt with earlier in the infantry section since its uniform resembled the infantry's. In 1848 the *Garde Mobile* wore blue
coats and trousers with red collar, red epaulettes with green fringes, and a red kepi.
In 1816 the cavalry regiment of the *Garde Nationale* adopted an all-blue uniform
with red collar, cuffs, and piping; white epaulettes and aiguillettes; white pouch belts
with red stripes, sword belts, and trouser stripes; and steel helmets with yellow metal
mounts, black *chenille*, and white feather plume. In 1830 chacos with tricolored
plumes were worn and, in 1843, a lancer cap with red plume. The *Garde Mobile à
Cheval* in 1848 was dressed in blue tunics, with blue collar and cuffs, piped red, white
buttons and epaulettes, and light-blue trousers and kepis, both ornamented with red
stripes. In 1870 the infantry of the *Garde Mobile* wore blue double-breasted jackets
with red distinctions. The trousers and kepis were blue, trimmed with red. After the
Great War, the *Garde Mobile* wore similar uniforms to those of the *gendarmerie*, but
with gold distinctions instead of silver, and with red epaulettes in full dress. Its badge
was a gold grenade.

XV. GENERAL OFFICERS AND STAFF; DISTINCTIONS OF RANK

A regulation uniform was introduced for general officers in 1724. It consisted of a dark blue long-skirted coat with rich gold oakleaf embroidery, single for a *Maréchal de Camp* (*Général de Brigade*) and double for a lieutenant general; on the turndown collar, round cuffs and horizontal pocket flaps with red waistcoat and breeches; long black boots; and a tricorne hat with gold lace and white ostrich feather plumage (Fig. 42a). A *Maréchal de France* in addition carried a baton covered with dark blue velvet, set with golden *fleur de lys*. About 1770 the coat was made with a stand collar, and gold epaulettes with short stiff bullions were adopted, having two five-pointed silver stars for a *Général de Brigade* and three for a *Général de Division*, and for a *Maréchal de France*, two crossed batons, surrounded by a circle of silver stars. Epaulettes were retained, with hardly any

Fig. 42. France—General Officers.

changes, up to the 1930s, as the mark of rank of general officers. From 1791 the waistcoat and breeches were white. From the Revolution to the end of the First Empire, the collar and cuffs of the full-dress coat were red; later, they became blue again; the ornamentation on the pocket flaps was abolished; and the coat was cut like a single-breasted coatee. As distinctions of rank, sashes were worn around the waist, with the gold tassels on the left side: striped white and gold for a *Maréchal*, red and gold for a *Général de Division*, and light blue and gold for a *Général de Brigade* (Fig. 42b). These sashes, too, were retained up to the 1930s, with the full-dress uniform. In 1815 black plumage was added to the hat, which had become very tall. The trousers were changed to dark blue, then back to red in 1831, and later had broad stripes of dark blue. From 1836 on service, and in all orders of dress from 1844, the hat was worn fore-and-aft, not across the head. A *Général de Division*, when commanding a corps, wore white ostrich feather plumage in his hat. In 1844 an all-blue kepi was introduced. Its seams were ornamented with gold and it had one to three rows of gold oakleaf embroidery around the band. The top and sides were red from 1852. A *Général de Division* commanding a corps wore a silver cord, 3 millimeters wide, above the lace around the top. An undress uniform, consisting of a single-breasted long-skirted dark blue coat without embroidery, was authorized in 1847. From 1867 the coat was double-breasted with medium-length skirts with one to three rows of rank embroidery on the collar and cuffs. After the Franco-German War, this coat, together with the hat, sash, and epaulettes, became the full-dress uniform. For normal everyday wear, a black dolman was worn, with five rows of black loopings on the front and black Austrian knots on the sleeves, on which were the stars of rank. Kepis and trousers were red. On the horizon-blue service dress, general officers wore no collar patches but had their rank stars on the lower arms and dark blue triple stripes on the breeches (Fig. 42c). A full-dress uniform was introduced after the Great War, consisting of a long-skirted horizon-blue coat, with gold passants or epaulettes; rank stars on the cuffs; and black collar patches, double-scalloped at the rear, with gold rank embroidery, as on the peacetime uniform. Corps commanders now wore four stars arranged in the form of a diamond; a *Maréchal* had seven stars on each cuff. General officers' ranks were also indicated on the khaki uniform, by the cuff stars. These were also worn on the front of the steel helmet and the service dress kepi. The colored evening dress uniform was similar to the prewar full dress; it also had rank stars on the cuffs, and collar and cuffs were ornamented with broad gold oakleaf embroidery, alike for all ranks.

The uniform of the *État Major* (General Staff) followed that of the general officers; but instead of oakleaf embroidery, they had gold stripes and lace loops on the collar and cuffs respectively which, from 1820 to 1870, had red piping around the edge. From 1870 the General Staff and other staffs wore the uniform of their former arm of service, with a winged thunderbolt or a flaming grenade, respectively, on the collar patches in place of the numerals and variously colored armbands. The same applied to the 1915 and 1930 service uniforms.

From 1775 the *Adjutants Chef* wore dark blue coats without ornamentation, with red epaulettes, waistcoats, and trousers. From 1791 these and the collar of the coat were of a light buff color. During the First Empire, they wore a single-breasted dark blue coatee with light-blue collar and round cuffs, with gold buttons and epaulettes, dark blue breeches, and hat, which was worn fore-and-aft. In 1816 the collar of the coat was again changed to light buff, and buff piping was worn down the front and around the dark blue pointed cuffs. From 1818 the *Adjutants Chef* were dressed like the *État Major*, but with double aiguillettes, of the color of the buttons, on the right shoulder. Feather plumes were worn on the kepi from 1880 to 1914: white for the staff of the president and the Ministry of War; blue-white-and-red for commanders of army corps; red and white for a *Général de Division*; and light-blue for a *Général de Brigade*, with similarly colored silk bands on the upper left arm. The personal aides-de-camp of Napoleon I wore light-blue coats with light-blue pointed cuffs and lapels, all edged with silver lace; red waistcoats with silver loops; light-blue trousers, and hussar boots with silver edging; a hat with black plumage; and silver aiguillettes and epaulettes. The personal aides-de-camp of Napoleon III were dressed similarly, except that they wore single-breasted coatees and red trousers. Napoleon I's marshals dressed their own aides as they wished, mostly in brilliant colors: Berthier's, for example, were dressed in a hussar uniform: white dolman with black collar and cuffs, with narrow gold loopings; black pelisses; red breeches; and red chacos with gold cords.

From about 1860 officers' jackets, although described in regulations as dark blue, were in fact black. This applied also to the colored evening dress uniforms worn in the 1930s.

From 1759 officers wore epaulettes of metal lace of the color of the buttons. For the distinctions in 1763, see under ''Infantry.'' Subalterns had various designs in red silk lace. These were abolished in 1845. From then, the crescents and straps of all of-

116

ficers' epaulettes were of plain metal lace without rank badges. This was denoted as follows by the varying thickness of the bullions and by the ways of wearing the epaulettes. Colonels had two epaulettes with thick twisted bullions; lieutenant colonels the same, but with crescents and straps in contrasting color to that of the buttons; majors, an epaulette on the right shoulder with thick twisted bullions, and a *contre-épaulette* (crescent) on the left; captains, two epaulettes with thin fringes; lieutenants, an epaulette with thin fringe on the left shoulder and a crescent on the right; *sous-lieutenants*, vice versa. Up to 1870 epaulettes were the only distinctions of rank worn on the officers' coatees and tunics (except for the gorget), except in the hussars. Hussar officers wore epaulettes on their greatcoats; but on the dolman and pelisse cuffs, lace rings, pointed on the outside of the arm, were worn as follows in 1843: subalterns, one to three narrow ones; majors, four narrow ones, the lowest of contrasting color; lieutenant colonels and colonels, five (three narrow, the second and fourth being broader), the broader ones being of contrasting color to that of the buttons for lieutenant colonels. From 1845 the rank lace on the undress uniforms of hussar officers, and from the mid 1850s, of officers of *Chasseurs à Cheval* and *Guides* as well, took the form of Austrian knots. On the tunics introduced after the Franco-German War, epaulettes were worn only in full dress; otherwise, lace rings of the same number and type as those of the hussar officers were worn around both lower arms, the three lowest ones running underneath the patches. From 1883 to about 1900, when all officers of the French army wore dolmans, epaulettes fell into disuse. In their place were worn shoulder cords ending in trefoils, of plain cord for company officers and double cord for field officers. The rank lace on the sleeves took the form of Austrian knots. When tunics were reintroduced, for *Chasseurs à Cheval* and hussars as well, rank lace was again worn around the cuffs. Epaulettes were worn as well for full dress. The evening dress uniform worn between the wars had the same rank lace as on the peacetime uniform of 1914. Identical epaulettes were worn on both shoulders, with short bullions for field officers and long, thin ones for subalterns. On the 1915 and 1930 service uniforms, the rank distinctions were in each case on the sleeve and consisted of horizontal stripes 5 centimeters long, of the same color and number as on the tunic in 1914; but field officers had twice as much space between the third and fourth ones. On the kepi, rank was indicated by the width of the lace edging around the top edge. The side seams were ornamented with one cord of button color for subalterns, two for captains, and three for field officers. On the top was an Austrian knot, worked in single or triple metal cord respectively, according to grade.

The rank distinctions of the NCOs and men remained almost unaltered from the middle of the eighteenth century. The rank and file had one to three worsted stripes, mainly of the color of the piping; NCOs, one to three metal lace stripes of the color of the buttons on the lower arms. In the infantry these were usually worn slanting; in the cavalry and *chasseurs*, they were worn as chevrons, point uppermost, above the cuff. On the 1915 and 1930 service uniforms, they took the form of one to three short slanting stripes in dark blue and dark khaki respectively; for NCOs, in metal lace of the color of the buttons. They were worn above the cuffs. On the peacetime uniform, they were of the same number, but chevron-shaped, with the point uppermost. The *adjutants*, who ranked between NCOs and officers, wore the distinctions of a *sous-lieutenant* with narrow red stripes in the center of the lace, which, for the lower rank of *adjutant*, was of contrasting color to that of the buttons.

Officers' sword knots were always gold, with thin fixed bullions and thick ones for field officers and general officers. They were attached to a double gold or black cord. A black leather sword knot was worn latterly on service. Up to 1805, infantry officers wore a gorget of the color of the buttons.

GERMANY

BRANDENBURG-PRUSSIA

I. INFANTRY

One of the earliest sources of information about uniforms dates from 1632, during the reign of the elector George William, when the Prussian lifeguards (consisting of 1,000 on foot and 150 mounted), which had accompanied him to the election of the Polish king, returned to Brandenburg, most of the men were dressed in dark blue. However, we must not be quick to assume that there was great uniformity at this period, for a muster report of 1683 (more than fifty years later), speaking of the livery of the Great Elector's lifeguard, states: "It was first issued fifteen months ago and is now generally wretched and in disorder; some have blue cloth breeches, others, leather breeches; some have light blue coats, and the rest, dark blue." Generally speaking it can be said that the introduction of uniforms on an extensive scale dates from 1670. In 1685 the elector decreed that each regiment was to have flags and clothing of a distinctive color and that each regiment was to select its own special color. Usually, the colonel had a virtually unlimited say in the choice of clothing.

In the infantry the predominant basic color of the coat was dark blue, but at the same time some regiments were dressed in red or gray. The infantry wore felt hats in the fashion of the time, cravats, loose-fitting coats, long waistcoats, stockings coming above the knee, and buckled shoes. The cartridge pouch and powder horn were hung from a shoulder belt. The arms consisted of a musket and straight-bladed sword. The front rank carried swine's feathers—short pikes for sticking into the ground as a defense against cavalry (Fig. 43b). Officers and NCOs generally wore a similar uniform but in varying shades. Occasionally, officers were ordered to wear breast plates; these later tended to fall into disuse. Very many portraits of officers, even of a much later date, show armor, but this was an indication of the social standing of the man rather than a defensive device. The position of the waistline, as indicated by the sword belt and sash, fluctuated. It was fairly high in 1672; at about its natural position in 1675; in 1680–1686 it dropped well down; it was normal again between 1688 and 1695, and later still, it was low down again, below the navel. There it remained almost to the end of the eighteenth century. The officers' sashes and sword knots were always of the Hohenzollern colors: black and white or black and silver, not of the red and silver colors of the electorate of Brandenburg.

Fig. 43. Prussia—Musketeers, prior to 1806.

a: NCO. b, d, e, f, h, i: musketeers. c: drummer. g: officers.

Under Frederick William, the Great Elector (1640–1688), the *Leibgarde zu Fuss* (lifeguard on foot) were dressed in blue coats with white cuffs. The officers probably had red coats. The Electress Dorothea's regiment, according to a detailed inspection return of 1681, wore red coats lined with white, with differently ornamented cuffs for each company: red cloaks lined white, red stockings, leather garters, white cravats tied with a red string, black hats with red-and-white lace, white cartridge pouches with the initials "DCZB" (Dorothea Churfürstin zu Brandenburg) in red, and red-painted swine's feathers with a red-and-white fringe. The NCOs wore jackets of elks leather with blue cuffs ornamented with lace, leather breeches, blue stockings and cloaks, and white or gray hats trimmed with silver. The subalterns were dressed in crimson; captains wore violet; musicians, blue coats with red-and-white lace, and red breeches. In 1686 the regiment was dressed in red uniforms faced green. In 1668 the Anhalt Regiment had blue coats with red linings and cuffs; the NCOs, red coats with silver lace and elks-leather waistcoats; the Kurland and Dohne Regiments, blue coats and cloaks with blue linings. The Kurprinz and Dönhoff Regiment was dressed in blue lined with white; Varenne, blue with yellow.

Under the elector Frederick III (King Frederick I of Prussia, 1701–1713), the uniform generally remained much the same as in the preceding reign. The elks-leather waistcoats were replaced by cloth ones. The officers' gorgets, which had been adopted earlier, were ornamented with the coat of arms of the colonel of the regiment. These arms were also frequently painted on the drums. While the rank and file wore their hair long and loose, officers affected the more fashionable modern hair style, which, especially in the case of the senior officers, formed clusters of perukes. Pikes were completely abolished before the end of the eighteenth century. Grenadiers adopted pointed caps. A brass match case was attached to the belt carrying the grenade bag. The bayonet, which fitted into the muzzle of the musket, was generally

120

worn on a waistbelt along with the sword. In 1691 the elector ordered all battalions to be dressed in blue with white distinctions for those of the guard and red for the rest. From that time other ranks of the line infantry wore blue coats.

In 1705 the uniform of the *Leibgarde zu Fuss* was as follows: for privates, a blue coat lined and turned up with white, leather breeches, white stockings and buttons; NCOs, a red coat with blue lining and turnbacks, gold lace, white stockings; and officers, a red coat and waistcoat, gold lace, red breeches, black stockings, a hat with gold edging and white plumage, and silver gorgets ornamented with the eagle and shield. In that year the regiment was designated "Fusilier Guards." (It was also called the "White Guards.") Fig. 44b shows grenadiers with their distinctive scalloped grenadier caps of blue with white ornamentation with yellow edging. The uniforms of the bandsmen were heavily ornamented with white and red loops. The *Grenadiergarde*, reduced in 1698, had blue uniforms with red turnbacks and crimson grenadier caps. Most regiments appear to have worn blue uniforms turned up with red, but, at the same time, other colors were worn; the Margrave Philip Regiment, for instance, had orange distinctions. The grenadiers of the Anhalt Regiment (Fig. 44a) wore blue coats with self-colored cuffs and red turnbacks; blue waistcoats with red buttonholes; red stockings; white, highly decorated grenadier caps with blue bags; yellow buttons; grenade pouches with white embellishments, and red cravats. In the first decade of the eighteenth century, the whole cut of the uniform gradually began to change in accord with the prevailing fashions (Fig. 43d).

The reign of Frederick William I (1688–1740) came to be one of outstanding importance. The coat, which became closer fitting from that time, and the queue were especially noteworthy. For parades, the hair was powdered. All the men wore red cravats with white edging; officers' cravats were white. The basic color of the coat

Fig. 44. Prussia—Grenadiers, prior to 1806.

a, b, c, d, e, f, g: grenadiers. h: officer.

was blue and remained so; thus it will be unnecessary to mention it again. The coat was frequently made with lapels (though not for all regiments), which could be buttoned across in cold weather. Buttonholes, stitched or edged with lace, served as a further regimental variation; the skirts were generally red and were worn turned back. The undergarments (waistcoat and breeches) were of various shades of red or yellow, or were white. In 1713 the red stockings were replaced by white ones. Later, white gaiters, secured below the knee by garters, were introduced and worn over the stockings. The hat, tacked up at three points, was the distinctive headdress of the musketeers, as also of all officers, including those of the grenadier companies. The officers' hats were edged with gold lace, the men's with a white border. There was a tassel at each side. A tuft was worn on the hat above the left eye (Fig. 43e). The grenadiers were distinguished by their pointed cloth-covered caps, the fronts of which had pierced metal plates (Fig. 44d). The color of the cap varied from regiment to regiment. As a further distinction between the grenadiers and musketeers, the former wore four brass grenades at the corners of their large grenade pouches, a match case on the front of the shoulder belt, and a small cartridge box on the waistbelt (Fig. 44d). The privates' straight-bladed swords were replaced by curved sabers. As marks of rank, officers wore sword knots, gorgets, and sashes and were armed with a sword and spontoon. The NCOs carried the same side arms as the men, and a half pike, which was somewhat longer than a spontoon. The term "half pike" dates from the time when the long pike was in use, when the NCOs carried rather shorter pole arms.

The 1st Battalion of the *Königregiment* (King's Regiment) were dressed in a unique manner (Fig. 44c). The tallest men the king could find were enlisted into this battalion, hence its nickname, *Riesengarde* (Giant Guards). The bag of their caps, their collars, lapels, cuffs, waistcoat, and hat were red, and the buttons yellow. Their accoutrements were of buff leather, as in the rest of the army.

The regiments numbered above 29* did not wear hats, but had oilcloth fusilier caps with yellow fittings instead. These caps differed from those of the grenadiers in that the skull was separate from the pointed front, and was finished with a bell-shaped finial surmounted by a flame; further, it had no tuft on top of the front plate (Fig. 45a).

In the early years of the reign of Frederick the Great, uniforms in general changed little. The pierced shield on the grenadier caps was replaced by one of solid metal. The regimental distinctions were altered frequently. In regiments that the king had inherited from his father, the red cravat continued to be worn, while the newly raised regiments adopted black ones. The new regiments were all fusiliers, as distinct from the older ones, which remained musketeers. Those old regiments which already wore fusilier caps (Nos. 29, 30, 31, 32) became musketeers. After the Second Silesian War (1744–1746) black gaiters were introduced in addition to the white ones; the latter were supposed to be worn in summer and the former in winter. While Frederick William I had no liking for silver buttons and embroidery, Frederick the Great

*Strictly speaking, regiments at this time did not have numbers, but bore their colonels' names. As these frequently changed, it has become customary, for brevity, to identify them by their order of precedence from 1806.

favored this color and, from then on, silver lace and insignia took precedence over gold in the Prussian army.

The marks of rank and weapons of the officers remained as before. The officers of the old regiments were usually distinguished by wearing plain narrow hat lace and white cravats, while those of the newer regiments had broad waved lace and black cravats. Just as no officers wore grenadier caps, so none wore fusilier caps. NCOs and men were allowed to wear moustaches, but not officers.

The distinctions of the Prussian infantry during the Seven Years' War (1756–1763) were as follows.

REGIMENT	CUFFS	LAPELS	BUTTONS	LACE LOOPS	UNDERGARMENTS
1	red	red	white	26 white	white
2	red	red	yellow	6 red	straw
3	red	—	yellow	6 white and black	white
4	red	light straw	yellow	24 white	straw
5	light straw	—	yellow	6 orange	light straw
6	red	—	yellow	22 gold	light straw
7	pinkish-red	pinkish-red	white	—	straw
8	red	red	yellow	32 white with blue stripes	white
9	red	red	yellow	22 white	white
10	yellow	—	white	22 white	yellow
11	red	—	yellow	18 white, vandyked	white
12	red	red	yellow	22 white	straw
13	light straw	light straw	white	10 white	light straw
14	red	red	yellow	16 white with red stripes, vandyked	white
15: 1st Battalion	red	—	white	24 silver	yellow
2nd, 3rd Battalion	red	red	white	18 silver	yellow
16	red	red	yellow	6 white, black, and red	white
17	white	white	yellow	22 white and red	white
18	pinkish-red	pinkish-red	white	18 white	white
19	red	—	yellow	22 white and orange	straw
20	red	red	yellow	white binding	white
21	red	red	yellow	28 white and red	straw
22	red	red	yellow	10 white and orange	white
23	red	—	white	20 white	white
24	red	red	yellow	22 white and red	white
25	red	red	yellow	22 white and blue	white
26	red	—	yellow	22 yellow	white
27	red	red	yellow	white twist edging	white
28	dark blue	—	white	—	straw
29	red	—	white	18 white and red	white
30	red	—	yellow	22 orange	white
31	pinkish-red	—	yellow	—	white
32	dark blue	—	yellow	—	white
33	white	white	yellow	—	white

(*continued*)

123

REGIMENT	CUFFS	LAPELS	BUTTONS	LACE LOOPS	UNDERGARMENTS
34	red	red	white	—	yellow
35	sulphur yellow	—	white	—	sulphur yellow
36	white	—	yellow	—	white
37	red	—	yellow	—	white
38	red	red	yellow	—	white
39	yellow	—	white	—	yellow
40	pinkish-red	—	white	—	pinkish-red
41	light crimson	light crimson	yellow	6 yellow	straw
42	orange	orange	yellow	—	white
43	orange	—	yellow	—	white
44	red	—	yellow	22 red	straw
45	red	—	yellow	22 white	white
46	black	black	yellow	—	straw
47	yellow	yellow	yellow	—	white
48	red	red	yellow	22 white	straw

Fig. 44e shows the equipment worn in marching order on service. The knapsack was slung over the right shoulder, across the pouch belt, with the haversack below. A number of tent pegs were tied to the strap and, in addition, each man carried a pick, axe, or spade. Some of the third rank carried tin water flasks instead of entrenching tools. During Frederick's reign, the coat was increasingly cut away in front, so that in the end the lapels could no longer be buttoned across and became mere ornaments. The queue was supposed to reach down to the two buttons at the waist.

Frederick William II (1786–1797) introduced various innovations. The regiments that previously had not worn lapels were ordered to have them. The undergarments were made white for all. The hat was superseded by a *Kaskett*, a bicorne hat with two fans, which was decorated with white tape and a colored hackle as before, with the king's cipher in metal on the front (Fig. 43h). The grenadiers also adopted this headdress, with a grenade ornament in front. In addition, they were distinguished by a small white plume. The grenades in the corners of the cartridge pouches were done away with. All the infantry regiments were now musketeer regiments. The title "fusilier" took on a new meaning with the reorganization of those troops. Up to now they had been no different from the musketeers, being distinguished only by their headdress. Henceforth, no special fusilier battalions were raised as a kind of light infantry. They adopted green as the basic color of their uniform, with variously colored distinctions. Their headdress was embellished with a metal eagle, and they had black cravats with a white edging. The rest of the uniform was designed as for the infantry (Fig. 45e). The breeches were green for a short time, but later white ones were readopted. Toward the end of the king's reign, black equipment, worn crossed, was introduced.

Several changes took place soon after the accession of Frederick William III (1797–1840). The skirt turnbacks were made permanently fastened up, and the pockets at each side of the coat were abolished. The collar was made higher and developed into a stand collar. The *Kaskett* was superseded by a more up-to-date form of hat. The grenadiers were given caps of a distinctive shape, with a band of cloth of

Fig. 45. Prussia—Fusiliers, up to 1806.

a, b, e, g, h: fusiliers. c: drummer. d: NCO. f: officer.

the regimental color at the back (Fig. 44g). In 1802–1803 the lapels were made to fasten all the way down instead of being cutaway as before (Fig. 43i). From 1806 officers wore their sashes over, instead of under, their coats. Grenadier officers were distinguished by a white feather plume with a black base. Officers had previously given up gaiters for knee boots (Fig. 44h). The men wore linen overalls to protect their breeches (Fig. 43i). The queue had become shorter and shorter, and eventually reached no further than the bottom of the collar. The fusiliers no longer wore their black accoutrements crossed. Their headdress was at first a hat with tuft and eagle badge, and later, a chaco (Figs. 45g,h). In 1806 the coat was cut short, with turned back skirts, and the undergarments were changed back to white.

The distinctions of the Prussian infantry regiments in 1806 were as follows.

REGIMENT	DISTINCTIVE COLOR	BUTTONS	MEN'S LACE	OFFICERS' LACE
1. Kunheim	ponceau red	white	white	silver
2. Rüchel	light brick red	yellow	crimson; white tassels	gold
3. Renouard	ponceau red	yellow	white and black	—
4. Kalckreuth	orange	yellow	white and blue	gold
5. Kleist	pale straw	yellow	orange; white tassels	gold
6. Grenadiergarde	scarlet	yellow	gold	gold
7. Owstein	pink	white	—	—
8. Rüts (or Ruiz, Ruits)	scarlet	yellow	white and blue	gold
9. Schenck	scarlet	yellow	white, rectangular	gold
10. Wedell	lemon yellow	white	white and red	silver
11. Schöning	crimson	white	white, crimson, and blue	silver

(continued)

REGIMENT	DISTINCTIVE COLOR	BUTTONS	MEN'S LACE	OFFICERS' LACE
12. Prince of Brunswick-Oels	light brick red	yellow	white	gold
13. Arnim	white	white	white	silver
14. Besser	light brick red	yellow	white and red, vandyked	gold
15. Guard	ponceau red	white	silver	silver
16. Diericke	light brick red	yellow	white, red, and black	gold
17. Tresckow	white	yellow	white and red	gold
18. King's Regiment	pink	white	white	silver
19. Prince of Orange	orange	white	white	silver
20. Prince Louis Ferdinand	scarlet	yellow	white and blue	gold
21. Duke of Brunswick	scarlet	white	white and red	silver
22. Pirch	ponceau red	yellow	white and red	gold
23. Winning	pinkish-red	white	white and blue	silver
24. Zenge	ponceau red	yellow	white and red (loops and edging)	gold
25. Möllendorf	scarlet	yellow	white and blue	gold
26. Alt-Larisch	light brick red	yellow	orange; white tassels	gold
27. Tschammer	ponceau red	yellow	white waved edging lace	gold
28. Malschitzki	buff	white	—	—
29. Treuenfels	crimson	yellow	white, crimson, and blue	gold
30. Borcke	buff	white	white, red, and blue	silver
31. Kropff	pinkish-red	yellow	—	gold
32. Prince Hohenlohe	buff	yellow	—	—
33. Alvensleben	white	yellow	—	—
34. Prince Ferdinand	ponceau red	white	white	silver
35. Prince Henry	greenish straw	white	—	silver
36. Puttkammer	white	white	—	silver
37. Tschepe	crimson	white	—	silver
38. Pelchrzim	scarlet	yellow	—	—
39. Zastrow	white	yellow	white and red	gold
40. Schimonsky	pinkish-red	white	—	silver
41. Lettow	light crimson	yellow	yellow	gold
42. Plötz	orange	yellow	—	—
43. Strachwitz	dark orange	white	—	silver
44. Hagken	buff	yellow	white and blue	gold
45. Zweiffel	lemon yellow	yellow	white and red	gold
46. Thiele	scarlet	yellow	—	—
47. Grawert	dark lemon yellow	yellow	—	—
48. Elector of Hesse	ponceau red	white	white; crimson tassels	silver
49. Müffling	white	white	white and blue	silver
50. Sanitz	light crimson	white	white	silver
51. Kauffberg	sulphur yellow	white	—	silver
52. Reinhardt	scarlet	white	—	silver
53. Iung-Larisch	light yellow	yellow	—	gold
54. Natzmer	buff	white	white	silver
55. Manstein	crimson	yellow	—	gold
56. Tauentzien	scarlet	white	—	—
57. Grevenitz	light pink	yellow	white and pink	gold
58. Courbiere	light yellow	white	white	silver
59. Wartensleben	white	yellow	—	—
60. Chlebowski	lemon yellow	yellow	—	—

The men's lace was usually set on in pairs below the lapels, on the cuff patches, and between the skirt buttons at the back, and also on the lapels for Regiments 1, 6, 8, 9, 12, 14, 15, 17, 18, 21, 24, 25, and 48; but Nos. 2, 3, 5, 16, 34, 39, 41, 49, 50, and 54 had no lace on the cuffs. In full dress, officers normally had embroidery or waved lace on the cuffs, pocket flaps, below the lapels and on the skirts, and on the lapels for Nos. 1, 6, 8, 12, 15, 16, 17, 18, 20, 22, 31, 35, and 48. Nos. 2, 9, and 27 had an embroidered edging to the lapels and cuffs, with embroidered loops for No. 1. Nos. 13, 15, 46, 47, and 56 wore gold or silver aiguillettes. In 1806 only Regiments 6, 7, 15, 33, 38, 41, 42, 47, 50, 51, and 52 had Swedish cuffs.

The loops had similarly colored tassels; Nos. 1, 6, 8, 9, 14, 15, 22, 24, 41, and 50 had none. Regiments 20, 24, and 27 had lace around the lapels and cuffs; and around the cuffs only for Nos. 9 and 22. The 1st Battalion Guard Regiment No. 15 had lace around the collar and lapels.

The distinctions of the fusilier battalions varied from brigade to brigade and, after many changes, were as follows in 1806:

1st East Prussian Brigade—light green with yellow metal buttons
2nd East Prussian Brigade—light green with white metal buttons
1st Warsaw Brigade—light blue with white metal buttons
2nd Warsaw Brigade—light blue with yellow metal buttons
Upper Silesian Brigade—black with white metal buttons
Lower Silesian Brigade—black with yellow metal buttons
Westphalian Brigade—crimson with white metal buttons
Magdeburg Brigade—crimson with yellow metal buttons

The catastrophe of 1806 and the reorganization of the army brought about a complete change in the uniform. The queue disappeared, the hat was superseded by a chaco, and a new jacket without lapels, and with two rows of buttons down the front, was introduced. The breeches were changed to gray. The knapsack was thenceforth worn on two straps, instead of being slung diagonally over one shoulder as previously. The *Garde zu Fuss* regiment had blue jackets* with red collars and cuffs with white lace loops on them, and white shoulder straps and buttons. The skirt turnbacks were red for all regiments. White breeches were worn in summer, gray in winter, with knee boots. The chaco had a trimming of white lace around the top—silver for NCOs—and the guard star. Tall white horsehair plumes were worn, white for the grenadiers, black for fusiliers. The officers' chacos were edged around the top with silver lace and had small white metal eagles at the sides, to which was fastened the narrow chin chain. They wore feather plumes in place of horsehair ones, of the same color as the men's, but the tips of the white ones were black, and of the black ones, white (Figs. 46a,b). Officers' ranks were denoted by the lace designs on their shoulder straps. The line regiments wore collars and facings of their provincial colors. In each province, the shoulder straps were white for the 1st Regiment, red for the 2nd, yellow for the 3rd, and blue for the 4th. Only East Prussia had four regiments. For East Prussia the collar and cuffs were brick red; West Prussia, crim-

*The principal garment was officially called *Rock*. To avoid confusing it with the *Waffenrock* (tunic), it is here called a "jacket" (after the precedent of von Mila), although properly this refers to the short-skirted cavalry garment.

son; Pomerania, white; Brandenburg, ponceau red; and Silesia, yellow. The buttons were yellow metal for all, the skirt turnbacks red, and the cuff patches of the basic color of the jacket. The grenadiers' chaco had a yellow metal eagle badge in front and a white horsehair plume. The musketeers had an intertwined monogram on the front, the fusiliers, a cockade of ribbon. In addition, the fusiliers were characterized by black equipment and carried a short sword instead of a saber. After the reorganization, the fusiliers were assigned to the infantry regiments as 3rd Battalions and, on the whole, wore the uniform of their respective regiments. The sword belt came generally to be worn over the shoulder, but it was so arranged that for full dress parades it could be worn around the waist (Figs. 46a; 49a,b,c). All officers wore a black, silver-edged cockade on the chaco and, usually, a small chain and eagles as described above, and a band of gold lace around the top. The gray trousers had red stripes down the sides, with a row of yellow metal buttons parallel to them. Musketeer and grenadier officers carried long straight swords; those of the fusiliers had sabers, carried in a leather scabbard (Fig. 49d). Officers as well as men wore oilcloth protective covers over their chacos.

During the Napoleonic Wars the dress of the many newly raised formations varied greatly, particularly in the case of the reserve regiments, whose uniforms were frequently supplied by England. As a headdress, officers made do with an oilcloth-covered cap.

Several alterations took place in 1814. Collars were thenceforth closed in front; the chacos became more ball-shaped with a larger top. The national cockade, previously circular, now became elliptical. Chinscales were introduced gradually, in

Fig. 46. Prussia—Infantry of the Guard, 1810–1893.
a: *Garde-Regiment zu Fuss.* b: officer of same. c: 2nd *Garde-Regiment zu Fuss.* d, e: lst *Garde-Regiment zu Fuss.* f, g, h: *Garde-Regiment zu Fuss.*
i, k, l: guard grenadier regiments.

128

place of the leather chinstrap. In full dress, white cords were worn: black and white for NCOs and black for officers. In addition, the guards wore slender black plumes, with a white tip for officers; bandsmen had red plumes. The 2nd Guard Regiment, raised in 1813, had yellow metal buttons, and cuffs as for the line infantry, to differentiate it from the 1st Regiment (Fig. 46c). In 1814 the regimental distinctions were as follows: collar and cuffs as before in the old provinces; Magdeburg, light blue; Rhineland, madder red; Westphalia, light red. Shoulder straps were white, red, yellow, and blue respectively for the 1st, 2nd, 3rd, and 4th regiments of each province; the cuff patches were all dark blue. In 1817 the collar and cuffs were made red for all regiments, and remained so up to 1914 (except that from 1843 to 1867 only the collar patches, and not the whole collar, were red). Regiments were distinguished from each other by their cuff patches and shoulder straps, and by the regimental numbers worn on the latter. As far as the distinctions were concerned, from 1835 all line regiments adopted red cuff patches; these were edged with white piping on three sides in the case of those army corps with odd numbers:

1st Army Corps—white shoulder straps; white piping on cuff patches
2nd Army Corps—white shoulder straps; no piping on cuff patches
3rd Army Corps—red shoulder straps; white piping on cuff patches
4th Army Corps—red shoulder straps; no piping on cuff patches
5th Army Corps—yellow shoulder straps; white piping on cuff patches
6th Army Corps—yellow shoulder straps; no piping on cuff patches
7th Army Corps—light-blue shoulder straps; white piping on cuff patches
8th Army Corps—light-blue shoulder straps; no piping on cuff patches

In the remainder of this section, the uniforms of the *Gardekorps* will be dealt with first and those of the *Garderegimenter zu Fuss* thereafter. Pointed grenadier caps with a red bag and white base were adopted by the 1st and 2nd battalions of the 1st Guard Regiment in 1824, and by the Fusilier Battalion for the first time in 1848. These caps were only worn on full dress parades, and were only supposed to be worn on occasions when white trousers were also worn (Fig. 46e). They were not a gift from the czar, as is so often maintained. The 2nd Guard Regiment, which had always worn slash cuffs, adopted Swedish cuffs with two loops of white lace in 1834. In 1843 the helmet and tunic were introduced. The distinctions remained as before. The helmet, ornamented with the guard eagle, had a white hair plume for the grenadiers, and black for the fusiliers, in full dress. The trousers were gray with red or white stripes. Equipment remained the same as before (Fig. 46f) until 1848, when the Virchowsche knapsack and *Gürtelrüstung* (equipment in which the knapsack straps were hooked around the waistbelt in front) were introduced. The 3rd and 4th *Garde zu Fuss* regiments, which were raised by William I at his accession, were distinguished by yellow and light-blue shoulder straps respectively. Yellow metal buttons were worn, as in the 2nd Guard Regiment. The Guard Fusilier Regiment adopted the uniform of the Fusilier Battalion of the 1st Guard Regiment, but with yellow shoulder straps.

After the campaign of 1866, the collar, which until then had had only red patches (with loops of guard lace), became completely red, and the helmet was made lighter. Later on, the equipment was altered and the greatcoat was worn strapped around the knapsack. A new pattern of grenadier cap was adopted in 1894 by the 1st Guard Regiment; it was similar to that worn during the reign of Frederick the Great, and the caps then given up were handed over to the Czar Alexander Guard Grenadier Regiment. The 5th *Garde zu Fuss* Regiment, raised in 1897, adopted white shoulder straps and, later, a white pointed lace loop on the collar, dark blue cuff patches with three loops of white lace, and white metal buttons.

Guard Grenadier Regiments: The first two regiments were raised in 1814. They adopted red collars and cuffs with self-colored patches; the Alexander Regiment had white shoulder straps with a red monogram; the Franz Regiment, red with a yellow monogram; chaco as for the guard regiments, but ornamented in front with a flying eagle device. All insignia were of yellow metal (Fig. 46i). In 1834 two loops of white lace were added on each side of the collar. Similar loops were also worn on the collar patches of the 1843-pattern tunic. The Queen Elizabeth and Augusta Regiments, raised by King William I, were distinguished respectively by yellow and light-blue shoulder straps, with red ciphers. In 1874 white lace loops were added to the cuff slashes of each of the four guard grenadier regiments. The rest of the uniform was made as for the *Garde zu Fuss* Regiments; the helmet eagle was later ornamented with a star, like that worn by the *Garde zu Fuss* Regiments. The 5th Guard Grenadier Regiment adopted the same uniform as that of the 5th *Garde zu Fuss* Regiment, but with yellow lace loops and buttons.

In the line regiments, several alterations were made to the chaco fittings. In 1816 the fusiliers of Regiments 1–12 adopted a monogram like the musketeers' and, in 1828, a crown above. All battalions of the regiments numbered from 13 upward, raised since 1813, wore a cockade and brass strip on the front. In 1836 the broad plaited cords were abolished (Fig. 49g). The tunic, which had a self-colored collar with a red patch on each side, was introduced in 1843. The helmet was ornamented with the eagle in yellow metal (Fig. 49h). The Virchowsche knapsack was adopted in 1848. Later the helmet was reduced in height; after the 1866 campaign it was altered by the substitution of a disc mount below the spike in place of the cross or quatrefoil mount. The front peak was rounded off. In 1867 the back peak was done away with, but it was reintroduced after the campaign of 1870–1871. From 1867 the collar of the tunic was wholly red. In the campaigns of 1864, 1866, and 1870–1871 it had become usual to wear the trousers inside the boots while on service (Fig. 49k). In the last years of Emperor William I's reign, the efforts made to lighten the soldiers' load were aggravated in importance by the increasing amount of small-arms ammunition carried, and brought about the introduction of a new equipment. The helmet was lightened again, by the abolition of the peak (later reintroduced) and by the substitution of a leather chinstrap in place of the chinscales (Fig. 49l). Only the guard regiments and the grenadier regiments of the line retained their chinscales. Except for certain arms of service, black leather equipment was generally adopted. In full dress, the line grenadier regiments wore black hair plumes. Gradually, all the grenadier regiments adopted the flying eagle badge on the helmet: Regiments 1–8 and 11 wore cutaway collars with a white lace loop on each side (yellow for the 7th Regiment), and cuff patches with three loops of guard lace. The officers' embroidery was similar to patterns worn by the regiments of Frederick the Great.

In 1914 the regimental distinctions were as follows.

REGIMENT	SHOULDER STRAPS	CUFF PATCHES	CUFF PIPING
1, 3, 4, 5, 33, 41, 43, 44, 45	white	red	white
2, 9, 14, 34, 42, 49, 54, 140, 149	white	red	—
8, 12, 20, 24, 35, 48, 52, 64	red	red	white
26, 27, 36, 66, 72, 93, 153, 165	red	red	—
6, 19, 37, 46, 47, 50, 58, 155	yellow	red	white
10, 11, 22, 23, 38, 51, 62, 63, 157	yellow	red	—
13, 15, 16, 39, 53, 55, 56, 57, 159	light blue	red	white
25, 28, 29, 40, 65, 68, 69, 161	light blue	red	—
31, 75, 76, 84, 85, 86, 163	white	red	yellow
73, 74, 77, 78, 79, 91, 92	white	red	light blue
32, 71, 82, 83, 94, 95, 96, 167	red	red	yellow
99, 132, 136, 143, 172	red	red	light blue
80, 81, 87, 88, 145	light blue	red	yellow
30, 67, 98, 130, 135, 144	yellow	red	yellow
5, 21, 61, 128, 129, 141, 176	yellow	red	light blue
18, 59, 147	light blue	red	light blue
17, 60, 70, 97, 131, 137, 138, 174	light green	red	white
7	yellow	blue	white
154, 156	yellow	white	—
158, 160	light blue	white	—
162	white	white	yellow
164	white	white	light blue
171	red	white	light blue
173	yellow	white	yellow
175	yellow	white	light blue
146, 148, 152	light blue	white	light blue
150	light blue	yellow	light blue
151	light blue	light blue	—
166	light green	white	—

The field gray uniform was introduced in 1910 and was in wear at the outbreak of war in 1914 (Fig. 50b). Jacket, trousers, and cap were of the old pattern, but the basic color was changed to gray. There were sloping pockets in the front skirts, with a flap and button, and dulled buttons bearing a crown. The infantry jacket had a turn-down collar. It, and the cuffs, of unchanged form, were both of the field gray basic color. The front of the jacket, edges of the skirt slashes, collar and cuff edges, and the bottom edge of the latter as well, in the case of the guards, were all piped red. The cuff slash piping was invariably red. The shoulder straps were of basic color piped in the former distinctive colors. All ciphers and regimental numerals were in red. The lace loops on the men's collars and cuffs remained as before. Instead of their former lace and embroidery, the officers wore small double silver lace loops on the collar, on patches the same color as the backing of the shoulder cords (Fig. 50c). Officers' rank insignia and general officers' embroidery remained unchanged. The greatcoat was light gray as before. The helmet was worn with a cover. NCOs' rank was denoted by a narrow lace stripe on the front and bottom edges of the collar. The helmet was worn at the Front in 1915 without the spike. Some were made of field gray felt or tinplate. The jacket had deep roll cuffs without piping. NCOs only wore their lace at the points of the collar (Fig. 50e).

Fig. 47. Prussia—Grenadier Regiments, 1914. NCOs and Men.

a: *Leib-Grenadier* Regiment No. 8, full dress. b: guards, greatcoat. c: fusilier, Guard Grenadier Regiment No. 1, full dress. d, e: grenadiers, marching order. f: guard, undress. g: grenadier regiments, NCO, walking-out dress. h: guard, orderly duty. i: staff sergeant, full dress.

Fig. 48. Prussia—Grenadier Regiments, 1914. Officers.

a: lst *Garde-Regiment zu Fuss*, full dress. b: Guard Grenadier Regiment No. 1, full dress. c: field officer, full dress. d: field officer, service dress. e, f: walking-out dress. g: service dress, greatcoat.

132

Fig. 49. Prussia—Line Infantry, 1810-1894.

a: grenadier. b, e, f, g, h, k: musketeers. c: fusilier. d: fusiliers, officer. i: fusiliers, bandsman. l: line infantry.

At the end of 1915, a new field service uniform was introduced. The stone gray trousers and field gray jacket with turndown collar of dark gray cloth, roll cuffs, and sloping pockets in the front skirts were of the same pattern for all arms (Figs. 50g,k). Those regiments which wore lace now only had a small gray lace loop of the previous pattern on a white patch (yellow for the 5th Guard Grenadiers and 7th Grenadier

Fig. 50. Prussia—Infantry, etc., 1914–1918.

a: line machine gun detachment. b, k: infantry. c: officer, guard infantry. d: officer. e: NCO. f: ski troops. g: infantryman with trench armor. h: infantryman with assault kit and insignia on cuffs. i: NCO.

133

Regiment) on the collar. If the loop was double, it had a red light. Arm-of-service distinctions were denoted only by the shoulder straps; those of the infantry were field gray with white piping. Numerals and letters were in red. The old piping colors were retained only by the guard and guard grenadier regiments, grenadier regiments 7, 8, and 11, and infantry regiments 114 and 115. The buttons on the collar were of dull nickel or tombac. NCOs had light-gray rank stripes on the outer edges of the collar. Officers had matte shoulder cords and small dark gray collar patches with gray lace loops without a colored light; the patches were edged with gold or silver cord, according to the color of the buttons. They wore a dark brown leather waistbelt with a bronze buckle. The leather equipment of other ranks was black. The steel helmet was worn with a cover or was painted gray. The universal-pattern greatcoat was field gray, with a broad turndown collar of dark gray cloth without patches; the shoulder straps and officers' shoulder cords were as on the jacket. NCOs had short vertical matte gray lace loops on the collar. The fatigue cap remained unaltered with colored band and piping around the top. Officers, however, had a field gray leather peak and chinstrap. On service, the colored bands were covered over by a field gray one. Toward the end of the war, a universal field cap was introduced, with band and piping around the top of field gray cloth.

II. *JÄGER*, *SCHÜTZEN*, AND MACHINE GUN DETACHMENTS

Soon after his accesssion in 1740, Frederick the Great raised a corps of *Jäger zu Fuss* and *Jäger zu Pferd*, which underwent many changes in establishment and strength. The uniform for both mounted and dismounted *Jäger* consisted of a canary green coat without lapels and with red collar, cuffs, and skirt turnbacks, with yellow cords on the right shoulder. The waistcoat was the same color as the coat, with yellow buttons; the cravat was black. The breeches were of yellow leather. At first, the heats were edged with gold lace, but this was discontinued later. The *Jäger zu Fuss* wore a brown leather cartridge pouch on the waistbelt (Fig. 51a). They wore gaiters to begin with, but these were later replaced by boots. Under Frederick William II, the coat was made with lapels (like those of the rest of the infantry), which were self-colored. The cuffs were, from that time, of "Brandenburg" type; that is, they were made with a self-colored rectangular patch having three buttons on it. The hat, based on the *Jäger* cap of the period, was ornamented with a green tuft. White undergarments were later adopted. The uniforms followed the same trends as those of the infantry. Officers of the mounted *Jäger* wore gold embroidered loops on their coats.

After the disasters of 1806, two new battalions were formed from the remnants of the former *Feldjäger* Regiment: the Guard *Jäger* Battalion and the East Prussian *Jäger* Battalion. Both had dark green jackets with self-colored skirt turnbacks, red collars, Swedish cuffs, shoulder straps, and piping on the skirts, with yellow metal buttons. In 1811 the guard battalion adopted yellow lace loops on the collar and cuffs. Breeches were gray, and long black boots were worn to begin with. The chaco was similar to that worn by the infantry, but without the lace edging around the top, and it had green cords and a black feather plume. The guard battalion wore a yellow metal star on the front; the East Prussian Battalion, a black and white cockade (Fig.

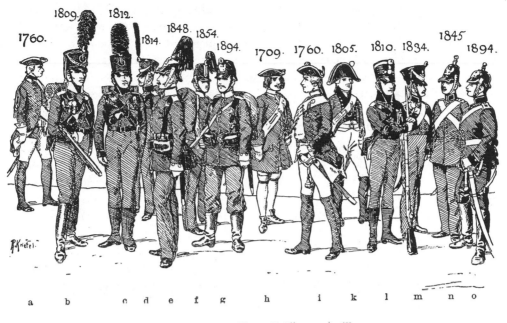

Fig. 51. Prussia—*Jäger, Schützen*, Artillery.

a, b, e, f, g: *Jäger*. c, d: *Schützen*. h, i, k, l, m, n, o: artillery.

51b). The officers' chaco was also like that of the infantry, with black and silver cords. In 1815 another battalion, the Magdeburg Battalion, came into existence; it adopted yellow shoulder straps. In 1821 the East Prussian and Magdeburg battalions were divided into four *Jägerabteilungen* (*Jäger* detachments); all took into wear red shoulder straps with yellow numerals. The chaco followed the same variations of style as in the infantry and, up to its supersession, had a black hair plume, with a white tip for NCOs. Buglers had red plumes. In 1845 the number of detachments was increased when the four former *Schützenabteilungen* (see next section below) were turned into *Jäger*. The tunic introduced in 1843 had a green collar with red patches. The shoulder straps and cuffs were the same as before. The helmet, introduced at the same time as the tunic, had yellow metal fittings. As its device, the guard battalion had the guard eagle with a silver star on its breast, while the Line *Jäger* Battalions had the ordinary eagle. In full dress, all battalions wore black hair plumes (red for the bandsmen) (Fig. 51e).

In 1854 chacos shaped like kepis, with front and back peaks, were introduced, with a silver star plate for the guard battalion; with the crowned royal cipher for battalions Nos. 1, 2, and 6, and a brass loop for battalions Nos. 3, 4, 7, and 8 (Fig. 51f). Black drooping hair plumes were worn in full dress. In 1860 the chaco was made rather lower, and the metal binding around the peak was done away with. The ornamentation remained as before for the guard battalion, while the line battalions adopted a brass eagle; the metal chinscales disappeared for all except officers, a leather chinstrap replacing them. In 1867 the collar became wholly colored. All the subsequent changes—the new equipment of 1848, for example—were as for the infantry (Fig. 51g).

Schützen: In 1808 the Silesian *Schützen* Battalion was raised. Its uniform consisted of a dark green jacket with skirt turnbacks of the same color, black, red-piped collar, and black cuffs with dark green patches without piping. The shoulder straps were likewise black with a red edging. The chaco had no cords and, to begin with, no plume; but in 1810 black horsehair plumes were introduced. It was decorated in front with a cockade and brass loop. Breeches, accoutrements, and buttons were as for the *Jäger* (Fig. 51c). In 1814 the *Garde-Schützenbataillon* was raised in Neufchâtel. The jacket was distinguished by yellow lace loops on the collar, and by the shape of the dark green cuff patches, which were double-scalloped at the back and had red piping around the edge. The chaco was of the same pattern as that worn by the Guard *Jäger* Battalion. In 1815 the Rhine *Schützen* Battalion was formed. It adopted red shoulder straps; at the same time, the Silesian Battalion took white ones into wear; the following year, however, both adopted red ones with yellow numerals. In 1821 both battalions were divided into four detachments. The development of their uniform followed exactly that of the *Jäger*, until 1845, when all the Line *Schützen* were converted into *Jäger* battalions. Thereafter, only the Guard *Schützenbataillon* was left, and it was solely distinguished from the Guard *Jäger* Battalion by the collar and cuffs, which were black with red piping. In 1874 yellow lace loops were added to the collar and to the green cuff patches.

The *Jäger* assumed a completely different appearance with the introduction of the 1910 field service uniform. The basic color was gray-green. The red distinctions disappeared, with the exception of the battalion numbers on the shoulder straps, and green became the distinctive color. The collar patches, which had guard lace on them, also became green. Officers of the guard battalion had green collar patches with red piping and dull silver lace loops. In the Guard *Schützen*, too, the red distinctions gave way to green, but the collar and cuff piping and the cap bands were changed to black.

The 1915-pattern field service uniform jacket was gray-green, with a dark gray-green cloth collar. The shoulder straps were the same color as the jacket, with light-green piping for *Jäger* and black for *Schützen*. Numerals and ciphers remained red. The double gray collar lace worn by the guard regiments had yellow patches, with a light-green light for the Guard *Jäger* and black for the Guard *Schützen*. The rest of the uniform was as for the infantry.

At their formation in 1901, the machine gun detachments wore a gray-green chaco with brown leather fittings and gray-green jackets and trousers (Fig. 50a). The distinctions were red, with all-red turndown collar and cuffs for the men. The 1st Guard Machine Gun Detachment wore lace loops; the 2nd had the distinction of the Guard *Schützen* Battalion. In full dress the line detachments wore black hair plumes and the guard detachments, white.

Service dress differed little from the normal. Collar and cuffs were gray-green with dull buttons. Officers of the guard detachments had collar patches similar to those of the *Jäger* and *Schützen*. The distinctive uniform of the machine gun detachments was abandoned in 1915. Thereafter, they wore the uniforms of the units to which they were attached.

The Volunteer *Jäger* Corps of 1813, which were raised for the duration of the war, both as entire regiments and as independent companies, can only be touched on here. Their uniform was supposed to be similar to those of their respective arms of service, but green in color. There appear, however, to have been many individual variations, due, no doubt, to the circumstances of the time. Equipment was invariably of black leather. Chacos were worn by all units, including the curassiers.

The *Reitende Feldjägerkorps* (whose duties were scouting and gathering intelligence) consisted entirely of officers. From 1809 to 1849 they wore dark green coatees, with two rows of eight yellow metal buttons, a red collar without lace loops, and red Swedish cuffs and skirt edgings. To begin with they had dark green shoulder straps and, later, epaulettes with yellow crescents; hats with a white feather plume; and gray trousers of the pattern worn by cavalry officers. The 1843 tunic had the same distinctions, but it also had gold lace loops on the collar patches and cuffs. An infantry-pattern helmet was worn, and guard eagle plate, with a black hair plume for full dress. The changes in style were as given above: in 1867, for example, the collar became wholly colored. The service dress was of dragoon pattern in gray-green. Piping remained red; the collar patches had no lace loops on them, and the underlay of the shoulder cords was green. In 1915 they adopted the same uniform as the *Jäger*. Dull gold double lace loops were worn on the collar. The underlay of the shoulder cords remained dark green.

III. CUIRASSIERS

Under the Great Elector, from the time of the Thirty Years' War, the main cavalry garment was the well-known leather jacket. Right from the earliest times, the uniforms of the cavalry appear to have been subject to regulations. Armor was no longer worn by the troopers. At this period, the title "Regiment of Horse," not "Cuirassiers," was invariably used.

According to an Inspection Return of 1688, the men of the Anhalt Regiment of Horse wore a jacket with blue cuffs, gray coat, gray cloak with blue lining and collar, leather breeches, black sash with orange-and-white fringe, white cravat with a black band, and a hat with a silver lace edging. A report dated 1700 mentions the *Gensdarmes* Regiment, one of the most distinguished of the cavalry regiments, as wearing blue coats, with silver loops on the sleeves, and silver-laced buttonholes, blue cloth cloaks with gold-laced collars, and hats with silver lace. In the same year the *Garde du Corps* of the elector Frederick III likewise wore blue coats with rich gold lace and crimson shoulder belts ornamented with gold and silver (Fig. 52a). Sashes were crimson and gold. The *Grand-Mousquetaires* wore red, gold-laced coats, while the trumpeters had blue ones.

In the reign of Frederick William I, the cuirassiers' uniform consisted of a leather jacket with fairly long turned-back skirts, leather breeches, high boots, gold-laced hat, and gauntlets. Jacket, waistcoat, and carbine belt were all decorated with lace. From 1735 the yellow leather jackets were gradually given up for ones of a yellowish or straw color made of cloth or kersey. Only the 2nd Regiment retained yellow jackets up to 1806; latterly they became lemon yellow in color; hence the regiment's nickname, *"Die gelbe Reiter"* (the Yellow Cavalry). The yellow jackets, when dirty, were treated with whiting, and thus always tended to become lighter in color. Toward the end of Frederick the Great's reign, jackets, which were white at

Fig. 52. Prussia—Cuirassiers, 1700–1894.

a: *garde du corps*. e: officer.

first, were introduced. Originally, the Yellow Cavalry probably had the same jackets as the other regiments, but treated them with yellow coloring. Possibly at the wish of the prince, their colonel, they retained the basic yellow color. The regulations of 1727 mention red, blue, and dull blue as the only colors for cuffs and, similarly, only gold lace; they expressly forbid silver. White waistcoats, made from the old cloaks, were worn under the jackets. Only the *Gensdarmes* Regiment had blue cloaks and, consequently, blue waistcoats. In 1735 waistcoats of distinctive color, edged with lace, were introduced; the *Gensdarmes* Regiment, however, retained their blue ones. During Frederick the Great's reign, the skirts of the jacket gradually became shorter. After the First Silesian War (1740) a few of the regiments altered their distinctive colors, which thereafter remained unchanged up to the disastrous year of 1806. The hat lace was abolished during the Seven Years' War (1756–1763) but, in 1762, a white plume was introduced, with a black base for officers and a black tip for NCOs (Figs. 52d,e). In the reign of Frederick William I the back plate of the cuirass had already been discarded, and only the breast plate, attached by two cross-straps at the back, was retained. The cravat, red in the previous reign, became black under Frederick the Great. Fig. 52d gives a back view of a cuirassier. The first item to be put on over the jacket was the waistbelt with sword and sabertache attached, and then the sash (of distinctive color). The cuirass was put on next, then the cartridge pouch and belt over the right shoulder, and finally the carbine belt over the left shoulder. The belts were kept in place by narrow shoulder straps of basic color. In the *Garde du Corps* the cuirass was of white metal; those of the other regiments were blackened. Officers wore a more elaborate uniform, their shoulder belts being decorated with metal mounts. On court guard duty in the royal castles, the *Garde du Corps* wore *Supraweste* with the star of the Order of the Black Eagle on the breast and back. Of-

138

ficers of all regiments had white undress and court dress uniforms with colored distinctions and lapels. The court dress always had gold or silver loops, according to the regiment. Only the *Garde du Corps* and *gendarmes* had red court uniforms without lapels.

Under Frederick William II the breast plate was abolished. The officers adopted cartridge pouches and shoulder belts. The jacket skirts became shorter and shorter, but the hat, feather, and collar became higher, especially during Frederick William III's reign (Fig. 52f). In 1806 the distinctions of the regiments were as follows. (The table also applies to the period of the Seven Years' War.)

REGIMENT	BASIC COLOR	DISTINCTIONS	JACKET LACE	OFFICERS' LACE
1. Graf Henckel	white	red	white with 3 red stripes	silver
2. von Beeren	lemon yellow	crimson	crimson; white on waistcoat	silver
3. Leibregiment	white	dark blue	dark blue with white stripes	gold
4. von Wagenfeld	white	black	dark blue-and-white checkered	gold
5. von Bailliodz	white	dull blue	light-blue-and-white checkered	gold
6. von Quitzow	white	light brick red	light brick red-and-white figured	gold
7. von Reitzenstein	white	lemon yellow	white with 3 yellow stripes	silver
8. von Heising*	white	dark blue	white with 2 dark blue stripes	silver
9. von Holzendorf	white	dark crimson	white with 3 crimson stripes	gold
10. Gensdarmes	white	red	red with a broad gold stripe	gold
11. Leib-Karabiniers	white	light blue	white with light-blue worm	silver
12. von Bünting	white	dark orange	orange with white stripe	gold
13. Garde du Corps	white	red	red with silver stripes	silver

*Formerly the famous Seidlitz Regiment.

At the reorganization of the army, four cuirassier regiments were raised. By a Cabinet Order of 1808, their distinctions were as follows.

REGIMENT	DISTINCTIVE COLOR	BUTTONS
Silesian	black	yellow
East Prussian	light blue	white
Brandenburg	red	yellow
Garde du Corps	red	white

The new uniform consisted of a white jacket with white skirts and shoulder straps and two rows each of eight buttons on the front, with collar, Swedish cuffs, and piping around the skirt turnbacks and shoulder straps, all in the regimental color, and gray buttoned overalls. A leather helmet with brass plate was worn, with a high leather comb and black horsehair crest. On the front plate was an eagle, or a star for the *Gardes du Corps.* In undress, a dark blue *Litewka* (a double-breasted surtout) was introduced (Fig. 52h), with white shoulder straps, collar of regimental color, and two rows of buttons down the front. In 1810 the Brandenburg Regiment adopted cornflower blue distinctions on their jackets, but retained red collars on their *Litewkas.* (Up to 1914 the officers of this regiment wore blue distinctions on their dress jackets, but red on their blue undress uniforms.) The *Garde du Corps* had adopted white lace loops on the collar and cuffs. Epaulettes were introduced for officers in 1812. In 1814–1815 all the regiments were issued with cuirasses again, and the old Prussian cavalry sword was replaced by one similar to the French pattern. The side buttons on the overalls were done away with. In 1918 the number of cuirassier regiments was considerably increased. Their distinctions were as follows.

REGIMENT	DISTINCTIVE COLOR	BUTTONS
Garde du Corps	red	white
1st Cuirassier Regiment	black	yellow
2nd Cuirassier Regiment	crimson	white
3rd Cuirassier Regiment	light blue	white
4th Cuirassier Regiment	orange	white
5th Cuirassier Regiment	light red	yellow
6th Cuirassier Regiment	Russian blue	yellow
7th Cuirassier Regiment	yellow	white
8th Cuirassier Regiment	green	yellow

The Guard Cuirassier Regiment was raised in 1821. It adopted cornflower blue distinctions, white buttons, and lace loops. The uniform shown in Fig. 52i was worn up to 1843, when it was superseded by a tunic, which had no buttons down the front, but was fastened with hooks instead, and a metal helmet. The white tunic had a white collar, with collar patches and cuffs of distinctive color. The piping on the sleeves and back seams, edges of the skirt slashes, and around the shoulder straps was also of distinctive color. White lace with stripes of the regimental color running through it ran around the collar and cuffs and down the front of the tunic. Both guard regiments (the *Garde du Corps* and the Guard Cuirassiers) had yellow metal helmets with a white metal guard star on the front, instead of the eagle plate. The 6th Regiment also had a yellow metal helmet. The cuirass was likewise of yellow metal in the guard regiments, and also for the NCOs of the 6th Regiment. In 1856 part of the *Garde du Corps* adopted butcher boots, reaching above the knee; in 1868 these boots were issued to all the regiments, and white pantaloons were introduced in place of the gray trousers. From 1838 (from 1886 in the case of the guard regiments) stiff knee boots were adopted in place of the high soft ones. The 4th Regiment adopted red distinctions in 1870 instead of the orange worn previously. Up to 1914 the cuirass was only worn in full dress. Like all the rest of the cavalry, the cuirassiers were armed with lances. In 1843 the *Gardes du Corps* resumed wearing the *Supraweste*, which they had previously worn to 1797. In certain orders of dress the regiment wore the black cuirasses edged with red, which they had received as a present from the czar of Russia in 1814. In both the guard regiments, a white metal eagle, poised as if to fly, replaced the helmet spike in full dress and court guard order. As a distinction, in June 1895, the 2nd (Pomerian) Cuirassier Regiment adopted gorgets. The 1st Regiment took them into wear in 1896, and the *Garde du Corps* in 1912. In 1901 the 34th Regiment was permitted to wear a distinctive lace on the jacket, of a pattern dating from the reign of Frederick the Great.

The gray service dress introduced in 1910 (Fig. 51b) was cut as the tunic; the col-

Fig. 53. Prussia—Cuirassier Officers, 1914.
a: full dress. b: evening dress. c: court ball dress. d, e: service dress. f: undress, Litewka,
for maneuvers. g: frock coat.

ored piping on the back seams and the lace on the front was abolished, so that lace remained only on the collar and cuffs. The field gray shoulder straps were edged with two rows of piping: the inner one white, the outer one of the regimental color. Collar and cuffs were field gray. Shoulder belts and pouches were abolished throughout the cavalry, and other ranks adopted the infantry equipment, with pouches on the waistbelt, in its place. The shoulder straps of the 1915 jacket were white, with piping in the distinctive color, and yellow ciphers as before. The field gray lace loops on the collar were placed on white patches for both the guard regiments, with a red light for the *Garde du Corps* and a cornflower blue light for the Guard Cuirassiers.

IV. DRAGOONS

In the reign of the Great Elector, dragoons wore leather jackets. The cuffs were generally blue. Later on, white coats were worn. Under Frederick William I, the regimental distinctions were either blue or red, with yellow undergarments and red cravats (Fig. 54c). After the Second Silesian War (1744–1746), light blue was adopted as the color for the coats of all the dragoon regiments. The cravats then became black. The cuffs generally were of Swedish type. Shoulder cords, which were ordered to be of the color of the buttons, were taken into wear on the right shoulder. The hat was similar to that worn by the cuirassiers (Fig. 54d), and the same remarks regarding the lace and plume apply to the dragoons as to the cuirassiers (q.v.). The cartridge pouch was not, as in the case of the cuirassiers, worn on a separate belt, but was attached to the carbine belt. The sword had a brown leather scabbard. The coat was of exactly the same pattern as that worn by the infantry, except that the skirt lining was usually of the distinctive color.

141

Fig. 54. Prussia—Dragoons.

At the death of Frederick the Great in 1786, the distinctions were as follows.

REGIMENT	COLLAR AND CUFFS	LAPELS	SKIRT TURNBACKS	BUTTONS AND SHOULDER CORDS	OFFICERS' EMBROIDERY
1. Count Lottum	black	white	black	yellow	gold
2. von Mahlen	white	pink	white	yellow	gold
3. von Thun	pink	straw	pink	white	silver
4. von Götzen	straw	dark red	straw	white	silver
5. Margrave of Ansbach-Baireuth	dark red	white	dark red	white	silver
6. von Rohr	white	none	white	white	silver
7. von Borcke	scarlet	scarlet	scarlet	yellow	gold
8. von Brausen	scarlet	none*	scarlet	white	silver
9. von Zitzewitz	light blue	none*	blue	white	silver
10. von Rosenbruch	orange	none	orange	white	silver
11. von Bosse	yellow	yellow	yellow	white	silver
12. von Kalckreuth	black	black	yellow	white	silver

*White loops were worn.

Thereafter, the dragoons took into wear jackets, similar in ornamentation to their former coats, except that the skirt turnbacks were of the basic color of the jacket, with piping in the distinctive color. The waistcoat was abolished at the same time. The officers, however, continued to wear coats. In 1797 the equipment was altered, and thenceforth the carbine belt was worn over the left shoulder, and a narrower belt, with the pouch, over the right shoulder. Officers did not wear pouches (Fig. 54f). In 1806 the distinctive colors were as follows.

REGIMENT	COLLAR, CUFFS, AND LAPELS	BUTTONS AND SHOULDER CORDS	OFFICERS' EMBROIDERY
1. King of Bavaria	black	yellow	gold
2. von Prittwitz	white	yellow	gold
3. von Irwing	pink	white	silver
4. von Katte	straw	white	silver
5. Queen's	dark crimson	white	silver
6. von Auer	white	white	silver
7. vac. von Rhein	scarlet	yellow	gold
8. von Esebeck	scarlet	white	silver
9. Count of Herzberg	scarlet	white	silver
10. vac. Manstein	orange	white	silver
11. vac. von Voss	lemon yellow	white	silver
12. vac. von Brüsewitz	black	white	silver
13. vac. von Rouquette	crimson	white	silver
14. von Wobeser	buff	yellow	none

At the reorganization in 1808, the dragoons adopted double breasted light-blue jackets with self-colored skirt turnbacks, piped in the distinctive color, and two rows of eight buttons down the front. Collar, shoulder straps, and cuffs were in the regimental color. The gray overalls had buttons down the sides. The chaco had leather fittings with a circular cockade and eagle plate. To begin with, the chaco had a leather chinstrap: chinscales were supposed to be issued in the event of mobilization. In full dress, thick, bushy white hair plumes were worn. The officers had flowing feather plumes. The chaco cords were yellow or white, according to the color of the buttons. At first the old cavalry sword was carried in a leather scabbard (Fig. 54g), but it was later superseded by a saber.

From 1808 to 1819 the distinctions were as follows.

REGIMENT	COLLAR	BUTTONS
1. Queen's	crimson	white
2. 1st West Prussian	white	white
3. Lithuanian	red	yellow
4. 2nd West Prussian	red	white
5. Brandenburg	black	yellow
6. Neumark	light red	white
7. Rhine (from 1815)	yellow	white
8. Magdeburg (from 1815)	white	yellow

Officers adopted jackets for the first time in 1819. Until then they had worn the *Leibrock*, a form of coatee, but with longer skirts. A light-blue *Litewka*, with collar and shoulder straps of the regimental color, was worn in undress by the other ranks. The buttons on the outer seams of the overalls were abolished in 1814.

In 1819, several of the regiments were turned into cuirassiers, and only four regiments were left, whose distinctions were, from 1819 to 1843, as follows.

REGIMENT	COLLAR	BUTTONS
1. Lithuanian	red	yellow
2. Brandenburg	black	yellow
3. Neumark	light red	white
4. Rhine	white	yellow

In 1826 the chaco cords were made white for all regiments. The plumes, which had become thinner since 1815, were abolished in the same year. The tunic and helmet were introduced in 1842. The collar was of the basic color of the tunic, with patches of the regimental color (Fig. 54i). From 1867 the collar was wholly colored. Originally the Swedish cuffs had been light blue with colored piping, but from October 1866 they were likewise wholly colored. In 1850 the 4th Regiment adopted pompadour red distinctions and yellow metal buttons; these were changed in 1858 to sulphur yellow and white metal. The helmet had the "dragoon eagle" plate (with upswept wings). A black hair plume was worn in full dress. In 1867 a disc replaced the quatrefoil mount below the spike on the helmet, and the peak was made rounded, but this latter change did not apply to the dragoons, who continued to wear their old-pattern helmets. Gray-blue pantaloons and knee boots were taken into wear in 1870. Lances were introduced in 1889 (they were made of steel tubing from 1890), and the 1889-pattern straight-bladed cavalry sword replaced the saber. The sword and carbine were carried vertically on the saddle from 1895. From 1911 the carbine was carried on the left side, the sword on the right, as for all the cavalry. All regiments adopted numerals on the shoulder straps.

The 1st Guard Dragoon Regiment stemmed from the *Normal-Dragoner-Kompanie* raised in 1811, later the Guard Dragoon Squadron, which in 1813 was part of the Guard Light Cavalry Regiment. Its distinctions were red, with yellow guard lace and buttons. The guard star was worn on the chaco, which was unique in having a back peak. This was abolished after the Napoleonic Wars, but in other respects the same distinctions as before were retained. The red collar and cuffs and yellow lace loops were retained on the tunic. The helmet had the guard eagle plate and a white hair plume. During the reorganization of the cavalry under King William I, a 2nd Guard Dragoon Regiment was raised, in 1860. It was differentiated by white buttons, lace loops, and helmet ornament.

In 1897 the 3rd Dragoon Regiment was given the title *Grenadiere zu Pferde* (horse grenadiers), and adopted as a distinction the guard eagle (without the star) on the helmet and a grenade in each corner of the cartridge pouch. In 1913 the 2nd Dragoon Regiment adopted a shield with the electoral scepter and crown above on the eagle helmet plate.

The 1910 service dress was similar to that of the infantry (Fig. 51c), except that the Swedish cuffs were retained and the stand collar was rounded-off in front. All piping was in the distinctive color, as in the table on the next page. Regiments 13 to 16, however, had white collar and cuff piping. The numerals and ciphers were red for all regiments. The 1915-model service dress jacket had cornflower blue shoulder straps piped in the regimental color. Numerals and ciphers were red, except for the 3rd, 7th, and 15th regiments, which had pink, and the 11th and 12th, which had carmine. Similarly colored piping was worn on the trousers. Buttons were white metal,

144

except for the 1st Guard Dragoon Regiment, which had yellow ones. In 1914 the distinctions were as follows.

REGIMENT	DISTINCTIONS	BUTTONS
1st Guard Dragoon[1]	red	yellow
2nd Guard Dragoon[2]	red	white
Dragoon Regiment No. 1	red	yellow
Dragoon Regiment No. 2	black	yellow
Grenadiere zu Pferde No. 3	pink	white
Dragoon Regiment No. 4	light yellow	white
Dragoon Regiment No. 5	red	white
Dragoon Regiment No. 6	black	white
Dragoon Regiment No. 7	pink	yellow
Dragoon Regiment No. 8	yellow	yellow
Dragoon Regiment No. 9	white	yellow
Dragoon Regiment No. 10	white	white
Dragoon Regiment No. 11	carmine	yellow
Dragoon Regiment No. 12	carmine	white
Dragoon Regiment No. 13[3]	red	yellow
Dragoon Regiment No. 14[3]	black	yellow
Dragoon Regiment No. 15[3]	pink	white
Dragoon Regiment No. 16[3]	yellow	white

[1] yellow loops
[2] white loops
[3] white piping around collar and cuffs

V. HUSSARS

The original uniform worn by the Prussian hussars of 1721 is not known. The Beneckendorff *Freikompanie*, raised in 1730, at first wore a white uniform with a *Flügelmütze*. When it was increased to a corps in the following year, light-blue dolmans with red distinctions and pelisses were adopted. Both the Berlin corps and the Prussian corps altered their uniforms in 1732. They began to wear red dolmans with dark blue collars, dark blue pelisses, with white loopings for the men, and gold for the officers; low-crowned bearskin caps with a long hanging *kolpak* (bag), with cords of a different color for each squadron; and leather breeches. *Schalavary* (also called *Scharawaden*), or leggings, of dark blue cloth were worn over the breeches. The Prussian hussars wore rather less ornamental dolmans and pelisses.

The number of hussar regiments was considerably increased during the reign of Frederick the Great. In general, the uniform was of the same style for all. *Flügelmütze* were again worn from 1741, and those regiments which had fur caps appear to have worn a type of *Flügelmütze* in summer. The 1st Regiment had light-green dolmans and *Scharawaden*; dark green pelisses, cap bags, and shabraques, the last having a light-green vandyked edge; twelve white loopings on the front of the dolman; light-green sabertaches; and red and white sashes.

The 2nd, the famous "Zieten" Regiment, wore red dolmans and sabertaches and dark blue pelisses and shabraques, the latter with a red vandyked edging. The officers had eighteen gold loopings, white for the men, on the front of the dolman. The sabertache was red; the sash, dark blue and white. From 1743 the officers wore a tiger-skin "pelisse" in place of the ordinary pelisse on the first day of review and at

Fig. 55. Prussia—Hussars, 1740–1894.

court. The company officers of the regiment wore a bunch of herons' feathers in their fur caps and the field officers a scepter-shaped rod, with an eagle's wing.

The 3rd Regiment dressed in white dolmans with eighteen yellow loops on the front, dark blue pelisses and *Scharawaden*, and fur caps with a white bag, and had dark blue shabraques with a white vandyked edging.

The 4th Regiment had light-blue dolmans, with self-colored collars and cuffs and with fifteen light-blue-and-white loops on the breast; white pelisses with similar loops; light-blue-and-white sashes; and sabertaches with a white face and light-blue edging. From 1752 to 1771, *Flügelmützen* were worn; before then, and after 1771, fur caps, with a light-blue bag, were worn. The shabraque was white, with a light-blue vandyked edge.

The 5th Regiment, the famous *Totenköpfe* (Death's Head), so named from the embroidered skull on the felt cap, originally had an all-black uniform with twelve white loops across the front, but later red collars and cuffs were added. The black shabraques seem to have had a red border from the start. The sabertaches were of black leather without decoration.

The 6th Regiment wore black *Flügelmützen*, an all-brown uniform with yellow loopings, and a yellow-and-white sash.

The 7th Regiment had *Flügelmützen*, yellow dolmans with twelve white loops, and yellow collars and cuffs (light blue from 1771), light-blue pelisses and *Scharawaden*, with light-blue-and-white sashes and sabertaches. The shabraques were light blue with a yellow vandyked edge.

The 8th "Belling," later "Blücher," Regiment, wore an all-black uniform up to 1764, with green collar and cuffs, and green loopings; green sabertache edging; yellow buttons; green-and-yellow sashes; and black leather sabertaches. The *Flügelmützen* bore an embroidered reclining skeleton with an hourglass, with the motto *Vincere aut mori* (Conquer or die). On account of the skeleton, and in contrast to the Death's Head Regiment, this regiment was nicknamed "*Der ganze Tod*" (the

Dead Man). In 1764 the Belling Regiment adopted the uniform of the Gersdorff Regiment (which had been taken prisoner at the battle of Maxen in 1759), which was dark red, with twelve white loopings on the dolman. Black *Flügelmützen* were worn.

The 9th Regiment (Bosnians) was a lancer regiment and will be dealt with later.

The 10th Regiment was raised late in Frederick the Great's reign, in 1773. It wore fur caps with a yellowish bag; yellowish dolmans with dark blue collar and cuffs, and fifteen red loops on the breast; dark blue pelisses and *Scharawaden*; red-and-blue sashes; dark blue sabertaches with yellow vandyked edge and red cipher; and dark blue shabraques with a yellowish vandyked edge. The officers' loops were of silver.

In those regiments which wore *Flügelmützen*, the officers had a silk ribbon cockade on the front, and the "wing" part had an edging of silver or gold lace. Their cord loops were of gold or silver, depending on whether the regiment had yellow or white respectively, except that officers of the Zieten Regiment wore gold lace loops, while the men had white ones. The carbine belt was worn over the left shoulder and the brown pouch belt over the right. The sabertache was worn fairly high up (Fig. 55b). NCOs and men did not wear queues, but instead plaited their hair at the back and on the temples. The uniform as a whole changed little up to 1806, and only the following points are worthy of note. The skirts of the dolman became shorter and the collar higher; the *Scharawaden* were done away with and, later, buttoned overalls were introduced in their place. By 1806 four units had adopted Hungarian cloth breeches: the 6th Regiment and the 11th Hussar Battalion, raised in 1792, both of which had light blue ones; and the 3rd and 10th regiments, which had dark blue. Fur caps were completely abolished in 1796, except for the 2nd Regiment.

Chacos were supposed to be adopted in 1804–1805, but most of the regiments continued to wear the old *Flügelmützen* (at that time called *Schackelhauben*) to 1806. The chaco is shown in Fig. 55d. A woolen cockade was worn in front, with a circle of ribbon below, and a lace loop. The cockade and circle were of the colors of the pelisse and loopings and not the national colors. A cord hung from the right rear of the cap. The white plume was very tall. Hussars had adopted plumes at the same time as the rest of the cavalry in 1762.

The distinctions of some of the regiments had changed, in the meantime and, by 1806, these were as follows.

REGIMENT	DOLMAN	COLLAR AND CUFFS	LOOPS	PELISSE	SASH
1. von Gettkandt	dark green	red	white	dark green	red and white
2. von Rudorff	red	dark blue	white	dark blue	dark blue and white
3. von Pletz	dark blue	yellow	yellow	dark blue	yellow and white
4. Prince Eugen von Württemberg	light blue	red	white	light blue	yellow and white
5. von Prittwitz	black	red	white	black	red and white
6. von Schimmelfennig von der Oeye	dark brown	yellow	yellow	dark brown	yellow and white
7. von Köhler	lemon yellow	light blue	white	light blue	light blue and white
8. von Blücher	dark crimson	black	white	dark crimson	red and white
10. von Usedom	dark blue	straw	white	dark blue	crimson and blue
11. Battalion von Bila	dark green	red	yellow	dark green	red and white

The 5th Regiment wore a skull device on the chaco as well.

During the reorganization of 1808, the following regiments were raised.

REGIMENT	BASIC COLOR	COLLAR AND CUFFS	LACE AND BUTTONS
Leib-Husaren	black	red	white
1st Brandenburg Husaren	dark blue	red	white
2nd Brandenburg Husaren (Schill)	dark blue	red	yellow
Pomeranian Husaren (Blücher)	light blue	black	yellow
Upper Silesian Husaren	brown	yellow	yellow
Lower Silesian Husaren	green	red	white

After 1808 the uniform consisted of dolman, pelisse, gray buttoned overalls, and chaco. A woolen "cockade" and black-and-yellow ribbon cockade and loop were worn on the chaco. The cords were of the color of the loopings. The feather plumes were white, and red for trumpeters. In 1808, too, the *Leibhusaren* Regiment was divided into the 1st and 2nd *Leibhusaren* regiments. Both wore the former chaco ornament—the skull in place of the cockade. The 2nd Brandenburg Regiment was disbanded after participating in the unsuccessful revolt against the French led by its commander, von Schill, in 1809. Its uniform was adopted by the Pomeranian Regiment, but with dark blue collars and cuffs. In 1811 the *Normal-Husaren-Kompanie*, later the *Garde-Normal-Husaren-Eskadron*, was raised; it adopted exactly the same uniform as the former Schill Regiment, but with yellow worsted lace around the collar and cuffs. The chaco was normally worn with a cover while on service. The saber-taches of the *Leibhusaren* were of plain black leather; the other regiments had red cloth ones with a yellow or white edging, ornamented with the crowned royal cipher. The shabraques were of black lambskin edged with red cloth. In 1815 after the *Normal-Eskadron* had become the Guard Hussar Regiment, and a number of new regiments had been raised, the distinctions were as follows.

REGIMENT (LINE REGIMENTS, 1816–1823)	BASIC COLOR OF DOLMAN AND PELISSE	COLLAR AND CUFFS	LOOPS AND BUTTONS
Guard Hussar Regiment	dark blue	red	yellow
1st Hussar Regiment (1st Leibhusaren)	black	red	white
2nd Hussar Regiment (2nd Leibhusaren)	black	black	white
3rd Hussar Regiment (Brandenburg)	dark blue	red	white
4th Hussar Regiment (1st Silesian)	brown	yellow	yellow
5th Hussar Regiment (Pomeranian)	dark blue	dark blue	yellow
6th Hussar Regiment (2nd Silesian)	green	red	yellow
7th Hussar Regiment (West Prussian)	black	red	yellow
8th Hussar Regiment (1st Westphalian)	dark blue	light blue	white
9th Hussar Regiment (Rhine)	cornflower blue	cornflower blue	yellow
10th Hussar Regiment (1st Magdeburg)	green	light blue	yellow
11th Hussar Regiment (2nd Westphalian)	green	red	white
12th Hussar Regiment (2nd Magdeburg)	cornflower blue	cornflower blue	white

The dolman was now made with a closed collar. The buttons down the sides of the overalls were abolished; a more bell-shaped chaco was adopted; and the hair plumes became thinner. The Pomeranian Regiment adopted the same pattern of sabertache as that worn by the *Leibhusaren*. In 1826 the chaco cords became white throughout, and in 1832 the plaited cord across the front was done away with, and the lines became shorter. At the same time, in addition to this, an important change was made: The collar and cuffs of the dolman were altered to the basic color of the garment. As several regiments now had very similar uniforms, the 2nd, 4th, 8th, and 10th regiments adopted chacos of light-blue cloth (Fig. 55h), and the guard regiment took red ones. Hair plumes were no longer worn, the Guard Hussars alone retaining them for foot parades. The pouch belts, formerly black, were made white. In 1836 the cut of the dolman was altered: it was made rather longer, and the officers' loopings were changed from mohair to gold or silver. The year 1843, in which the whole army adopted the tunic and helmet, also brought several changes in the hussar uniform. The guard regiment and the 3rd Regiment were issued with red dolmans with the old loopings, the pelisses remaining blue. The 5th Regiment began to wear blood-red dolmans and pelisses with white loops. The guard and 3rd regiments readopted fur caps, with red bags, with the guard star for the former (Fig. 55i); the other regiments adopted black felt *Flügelmützen* (Fig. 55k). The wing, worn hanging down in full dress, was lined on the inside with colored cloth. Both *Leibhusaren* regiments had skull devices in German silver on their headdress. The upright hair plume was secured in the middle by a brass ring. In 1844 the 10th Regiment took fur caps into wear, to be followed in 1850 by all the other regiments. In 1853 the dolman was superseded by the *Husarka* or *Atilla*, a jacket which had rather longer skirts. In place of the many rows of loops formerly worn, only five loops were retained. The pelisse was completely abolished. In 1849–1850 black leather sabertaches were introduced for the NCOs and men, with the royal cipher in yellow or white metal on them. In 1860 a yellow or white metal scroll was added on the fur cap (Fig. 55l). The 7th Regiment changed its basic color to dark blue in 1854 and to Russian blue (a darkish blue) in 1861. From that year, the royal cipher was also worn on the cap. In 1865 the fur caps became smaller, and a drooping hair plume replaced the upright one. The Guard Hussar Regiment adopted dark blue pelisses at the same time, and the Zieten Regiment did so in 1873. Later, several other regiments took them into wear. In 1867 the leather-strapped gray overalls were replaced by dark blue breeches with white or yellow lace stripes, and hussar boots were introduced. The sashes, up until then of varying colors for each regiment, became black and white for all, with white barrels. The vandyked shabraques, introduced in 1815, were now only worn in full dress. The same equipment, as well as the narrow pouch belt, as for the dragoons, was carried.

The distinctions of the peacetime uniform in 1914 were as follows.

REGIMENT	JACKET	LOOPS	FUR CAP BAG
Leibgarde-Husaren	red	yellow	red
1st Leibhusaren-Regiment No. 1	black	white	red
2nd Leibhusaren-Regiment No. 2	black	white	white
Hussar Regiment No. 3	red	white	red
Hussar Regiment No. 4	brown	yellow	yellow
Hussar Regiment No. 5	dark red	white	dark red
Hussar Regiment No. 6	dark green	yellow	red
Hussar Regiment No. 7	Russian blue	yellow	red
Hussar Regiment No. 8	dark blue	white	cornflower blue

(continued)

149

REGIMENT	JACKET	LOOPS	FUR CAP BAG
Hussar Regiment No. 9	cornflower blue	yellow	cornflower blue
Hussar Regiment No. 10	dark green	yellow	pompadour red
Hussar Regiment No. 11	dark green	white	red
Hussar Regiment No. 12	cornflower blue	white	white
Hussar Regiment No. 13	cornflower blue	white	red
Hussar Regiment No. 14	dark blue	white	red
Hussar Regiment No. 15	dark blue	white	yellow
Hussar Regiment No. 16	cornflower blue	white	yellow

In 1910 a field gray *Attila* jacket without colored distinctions, and with gray loops, was introduced (Fig. 57e). The regimental colors were only displayed on the cap band and shoulder cords—a double cord of the jacket and looping color mixed with the numeral or cipher in the color of the buttons. The *Leibgarde* Hussars adopted a red and yellow double cord forming two loops on the point of the shoulder. The guard lace was gray with red and yellow stripes. The cap band was of the color of the peacetime jacket, the piping, the color of the old loops; in addition, those regiments which had a cap band edging of a different color on the dress cap had a further piping of this latter color above the upper row of piping. Regimental numerals or ciphers were worn on the shoulder straps. The officers' jackets were of the same style as their old undress jackets. Sabertaches and sashes were abolished.

On the 1915 service jacket, the same shoulder cords as on the 1910 uniform were worn, with cord numerals in contrasting color to that of the buttons. The 1st *Leibhusaren* Regiment had a yellow crowned "WR II" cipher. The *Leibgarde-Husaren* adopted red and yellow quadruple cords ending in loops, on the shoulders, and had gray double lace loops with a red light, on yellow patches, on the collar (Fig. 57i). The breeches had yellow or white cord stripes, of the color of the buttons, down the side seams. The officers' shoulder cords were piped in the color of the peacetime jacket.

VI. LANCERS

In 1740–1741 a lancer regiment was raised in Prussia, but it was converted into hussars in 1742. Its uniform included a blue cloth cap edged with fur, a blue jacket and breeches, a long white sleeveless coat, red sash, and a red or blue lance pennant (Fig. 56a). Another lancer corps, the *Bosniaken* (Bosnians), which was originally attached to the *Totenkofp* Hussar Regiment, was raised in 1745. It later became a separate regiment, as the 9th Hussar Regiment. Early illustrations of the costume show a red jacket, edged with white, with long loose red overalls, similarly edged. In addition, a short black overjacket, with wide sleeves reaching only to the elbows, was worn. The headdress was a red cap with a white turban around it. Later, under Frederick the Great, the uniform was all red, with white lace, and a fur cap with no bag. In winter long blue *Katanken* (overcoats) with white ornamentation were worn. Hussar fur caps were adopted in 1796 and, two years later, long red coats with dark blue stand collars and cuffs. The uniform of the Tartar *Pulk* underwent too many changes during its short existence to be detailed here. The colors of the lance pen-

Fig. 56. Prussia—Lancers.

a, e, g, h, i, k, l: lancers. b: Bosnian. c: Towarczy. d: guard lancer. f: guard cossack.

nants varied from squadron to squadron (Fig. 56b). The *Towarczys* Regiment had yellow buttons, the *Towarczys* Battalion, white; both corps had shoulder cords of the respective color of their buttons, which the men of the Bosnian and Tartar corps did not have. In 1805 a chaco with leather peak and fittings was introduced, similar to that worn by the hussars. The *Towarczys* eventually supplanted the Bosnian and Tartar formations. They wore a dark blue uniform with ponceau red distinctions, breeches as for hussars, and red sashes edged with white (Fig. 56c). The men were recruited from the lesser Polish nobility of what were then the provinces of New East Prussia and South Prussia. In 1808 the *Towarczys* were formed into the 1st and 2nd Lancer regiments, to which a third was added in the following year. The principal item of uniform was a double-breasted dark blue jacket with red collar, pointed cuffs, and two rows of yellow metal buttons, with red piping down the right-hand edge of the lapel. The skirts were blue with red edgings. The shoulder straps were white for the 1st Regiment, red for the 2nd, and yellow for the 3rd. The buttoned overalls were gray. The chaco had a tuft, a black-and-white cockade, a black feather plume, yellow cords, and very long lines, which were looped around the neck and across the breast. Around the waist, a blue girdle, edged with red, was worn. The lower parts of the lance pennants were blue, the upper parts of the color of the shoulder straps (Fig. 56e). In 1809 a *Leib-Ulanen-Eskadron* was raised, which wore dark blue jackets with red collars, lapels, pointed cuffs, and red skirt turnbacks-turned up at the sides; red-piped seams; white metal buttons; white worsted epaulettes with loose fringes; and a white girdle with two black stripes. The men wore overalls like the rest of the cavalry (blue with a red stripe for officers), and dark blue lancer caps with a black feather plume. The lance pennants were red over white. In 1810 the title of the unit was changed to *Garde-Ulanen-Eskadron* and the uniform assimilated to that of the line lancer regiments. The jacket had yellow metal buttons,

151

red distinctions (no lapels); yellow guard lace; and epaulettes with white crescent pads and yellow crescents replaced the shoulder straps. The lancer caps now had yellow cords and lines. The lance pennants remained as before (Fig. 56d). All the lancer regiments had black pouch belts and black lambskin shabraques with a red edging. In undress, a dark blue *Litweka* with red collar, and shoulder straps as on the dress jacket, was worn. The chaco was worn in a cover. In 1813 the *Garde-Kosaken-Eskadron* was raised, and together with the *Garde-Dragoner-*, *Garde-Husaren-*, and *Garde-Ulanen-Eskadron* formed the Guard Light Cavalry Regiment. At the same time, a *Garde-Volontär-Kosaken-Eskadron* was raised, which replaced the Volunteer *Jäger* detachments in the *Gardes du Corps*. The uniform was all blue, with a red cap bag; the lances had no pennants (Fig. 56f). In 1815 the number of regiments was increased, and the guard squadron was formed into a regiment.

The distinctions were as follows.

REGIMENTS (LINE REGIMENTS, 1816–1823)	SHOULDER STRAPS	BUTTONS
Guard Lancer Regiment	red crescents	yellow
1st Lancer Regiment (West Prussian)	white	yellow
2nd Lancer Regiment (Silesian)	red	yellow
3rd Lancer Regiment (Brandenburg)	yellow	yellow
4th Lancer Regiment (Pomeranian)	light blue	yellow
5th Lancer Regiment (Westphalian)	white	white
6th Lancer Regiment (2nd West Prussian)	red	white
7th Lancer Regiment (1st Rhine)	yellow	white
8th Lancer Regiment (2nd Rhine)	light blue	white

The lancer caps of the guard regiment had a star plate. The line regiments also adopted lancer caps in place of chacos. In full dress the cap had a tall white hair plume. The sheepskin shabraques were abolished and replaced by dark blue cloth ones with red edging. From 1821 the jackets of the line regiments had red piping on the sleeve and back seams. In 1824 the shoulder straps were replaced by crescents and straps of the same colors as before. The Guard *Landwehr* squadrons had a differing distinctive color for each squadron. The 1st and 2nd Guard Lancer (*Landwehr*) regiments were formed from them in 1826. In 1843 a jacket with different skirts turned up with red at the sides was adopted; it had red lapels that buttoned back in full dress and was also piped red down the left-hand edge. In 1843, too, the four-sided upper part of the lancer cap, which formerly had been dark blue, was made the same color as the crescent straps. The cap had no plate up to 1844, when a white metal or yellow metal eagle was added on the upper part. On this cap, too, a protective cover was worn. A white drooping hair plume was added in full dress (Fig. 56h). Overalls were as for the dragoons. In 1851 both guard regiments adopted red distinctions, with white buttons, lace, and eagle plate for the 1st Regiment, and yellow for the 2nd. Two years later the guard regiments and later, also, the others, adopted the *Ulanka*: a double-breasted tunic of distinctive style. In 1867 a new pattern of lancer cap was introduced, which was made entirely of black lacquered leather, with the eagle on the skull part. From that time, a cover was worn on the upper part in full dress. The oilskin cover was abolished. Since 1815 the lance pennants had been black and white, at first with the black uppermost, and later with the black at the bottom.

A narrower pouch belt and a sword were adopted as in the dragoons and hussars. In 1899 the 13th (King's) Regiment adopted a silver guard eagle and star, with a special cipher on the cartridge pouch and star on the shabraque. In 1913 the 7th Regiment adopted a guard eagle without the star.

In 1914 the distinctions were as follows.

REGIMENT	COLLAR, CUFFS, AND LAPELS	EPAULETTE STRAPS AND CAP COVER	BUTTONS
1st Guard Lancer Regiment[1]	red; white lapels	white	white
2nd Guard Lancer Regiment[2]	red	red	yellow
3rd Guard Lancer Regiment[3]	yellow	yellow	white
Lancer Regiment No. 1	red	white	yellow
Lancer Regiment No. 2	red	red	yellow
Lancer Regiment No. 3	red	yellow	yellow
Lancer Regiment No. 4	red	light blue	yellow
Lancer Regiment No. 5	red	white	white
Lancer Regiment No. 6	red	red	white
Lancer Regiment No. 7	red	yellow	white
Lancer Regiment No. 8	red	light blue	white
Lancer Regiment No. 9	white	white	yellow
Lancer Regiment No. 10	crimson	crimson	yellow
Lancer Regiment No. 11	yellow	yellow	yellow
Lancer Regiment No. 12[4]	light blue	light blue	yellow
Lancer Regiment No. 13	white	white	white
Lancer Regiment No. 14	crimson	crimson	white
Lancer Regiment No. 15	yellow	yellow	white
Lancer Regiment No. 16[5]	light blue	light blue	white

[1]white loops [2]yellow loops [3]white loops [4]white piping [5]white piping

The field gray uniform of 1910 left the lancers still with their distinctive style of uniform (Fig. 57f). The jacket was similar to the full dress one, but with field gray collar and cuffs, piped in the former color of the lapels, except for the 1st Guard Lancer Regiment, which had red. The metal crescents were done away with and were replaced by shoulder straps shaped like them, piped in the color of the old crescents.

On the 1915-pattern service dress, all the lancer regiments had square, chamfered red shoulder straps, with yellow ciphers and numerals, piped in the color of the 1914 cap cover. The three guard lancer regiments had a light of the color of their prewar collar, in their collar loops, and white or yellow patches, according to the color of the buttons on the full dress.

VII. *JÄGER REGIMENTER ZU PFERDE*

The detachments of *Meldereiter* (Dispatch Riders), raised in 1895, were variously dressed. Those attached to the guard had green tunics; to Corps I, blue jackets; and to Corps XV, white *Attilas*. In 1897 they were given the title *Jäger zu Pferde* and a new uniform. This consisted of a gray-green jacket, with light-green collar, Swedish cuffs, and shoulder straps; yellow lace with light-green stripes down the

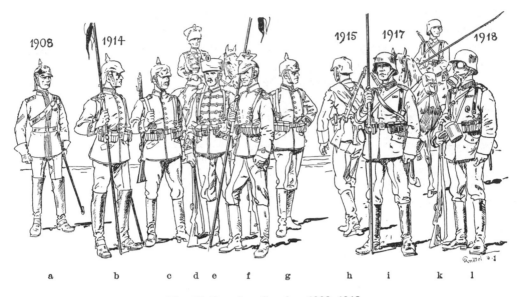

Fig. 57. Prussia—Cavalry, 1908–1918.

a, g: *Jäger zu Pferde*. b: cuirassier. c, h: dragoons. d: officer,
hussars. e: hussar. f: lancer. i: *Leib-Garde* hussar. k, l: cavalry.

front of the jacket; blackened cuirassier-pattern helmets (with a white plume for the guard); and white caps with light-green band and yellow piping. High cuirassier boots reaching above the knee, and pouch belts with brass mounts, whistle, and chain, were worn. All the leather accoutrements were brown. The *Garde-Jäger zu Pferde* had yellow lace loops on their collar and cuffs and the guard star on their helmets and shabraques. In 1905 the detachments were formed into separate regiments. The uniform remained unchanged in essentials (Fig. 57a). The buttons were white metal; the lace, green, with stripes down the center and edges varying in color for each regiment. The shoulder straps were light green, with piping in the regimental color, and red numerals. In 1905 the 1st Regiment adopted a yellow cipher. The caps became gray-green in 1903.

The NCOs and men of the regiments raised in 1913 only had service dress, with the dragoon helmet, blackened equipment, and knee boots as for dragoons. In 1914 the distinctions of the *Jäger zu Pferde* were as follows:

REGIMENT	DISTINCTIVE COLOR*
1, 8	white
2, 9	red
3, 10	yellow
7	pink
4, 11	light blue
5, 12	black
6, 13	dark blue

*White metal insignia for 1st–7th regiments, yellow for 8th–13th.

VIII. ARTILLERY, ENGINEERS, LINES-OF-COMMUNICATIONS TROOPS, AND TRANSPORT CORPS

Generally speaking, artillery uniforms were not subject to regulations during the reign of Frederick William, the Great Elector. According to one source, the artillery of the relief force, which he raised during the Turkish War of 1686, were supposed to have worn brown coats. An Inspection Report of 1709 describes the officers as wearing red coats with gold lace, dull blue cuffs, straw-color waistcoats and breeches, white stockings, and gold-laced hats. The gunners had blue coats, lined straw yellow; straw yellow waistcoats; leather breeches; white stockings; laced hats; and red cravats. Later on, the style of their uniforms exactly resembled those of the infantry and underwent the same changes. In Frederick William I's reign, the officers also were dressed in blue. The artillery coat had no colored distinctions. The cuffs were of the basic color of the coat, and only the skirt turnbacks were red. In 1731 the gunners adopted black oilcloth caps with a brass plate, similar to the fusilier caps. During the reign of Frederick the Great, the uniform consisted of a coat with brass buttons, and a yellow waistcoat, with red cravats for the field artillery (Fig. 51i), and black for the garrison artillery. The officers' waistcoats were ornamented with gold lace and their hats with narrow gold lace. The men's hats were bound with white tape. Frederick the Great was responsible for the formation of the horse artillery, whose uniform was the same as that of the foot artillery, but with breeches and boots as for the cavalry. Under Frederick William II, dark blue lapels were added to the coats. The hat with two fans (the *Kaskett*), which the king introduced, was ornamented with a triple-flamed grenade. In 1798 collar, lapels, and cuffs were changed to black, and a hat like that of the infantry was adopted, the horse artillery taking into wear a

Fig. 58. Prussia—Pioneers, Transport Corps, *Landwehr*, General Officers.

a, b: miners. c, d: pioneers. e, f: transport corps. g, i: *Landwehr* infantry. h: *Landwehr* cavalry. k, l: general officers.

155

cavalry-style hat with a white plume. In 1802 the latter adopted dragoon-pattern jackets. The black distinctions, and the black edging to the skirt turnbacks, were piped with red. The undergarments were white. See Figure 51i, page 135.

During the reorganization of 1808, a dark blue jacket with two rows of yellow metal buttons was introduced. The foot artillery had red skirt turnbacks, black collar and cuffs piped red, and dark blue cuff patches. The shoulder straps were white, red, or yellow, according to brigade. Breeches, gaiters, and chaco were as for the infantry. The chaco had a yellow metal triple-flamed grenade badge. Equipment was black (Fig. 51l). In the horse artillery the skirts of the jackets were of cavalry pattern, of basic color, with a black, red-piped edging. The collar was as for the infantry, but the cuffs were of Swedish type. The leather equipment was white. The chaco was of cavalry pattern, but with the badge of the foot artillery, with a tall white feather plume and yellow cords. The horse and foot artillery of the guard had the same uniforms, but with yellow lace loops and a star in place of the grenade on the chaco. The guard foot artillery had a black hair plume. The shoulder straps were red. The more general changes in style followed those of the other arms of service—in 1814, for example, the shape of the chaco was altered; thinner hair plumes and closed collars were taken on. In 1816 red shoulder straps with yellow numerals were introduced. From 1809 to 1821 an undress *Litewka* of dark blue, with a black collar edged with red, was worn. The chaco cords were red in the guard and henceforth white for the line. In 1843 the tunic was introduced for the artillery also. The collar patches and cuffs were black, piped red; the latter were of Swedish type in the horse artillery and had dark blue patches in the foot artillery. The chaco was replaced by the helmet, which was ornamented with either the guard eagle or the line eagle according to unit (Fig. 51n). White hair plumes were worn in the guard horse artillery, black in the line horse artillery regiments. At first, the helmet had a spike, but this was soon replaced by a ball. All wore white leather accoutrements. The foregoing sections apply to the artillery so far as the more general changes in the uniform are concerned (e.g., the adoption of the *Gürtelrüstung*; the wholly colored collar of 1867, etc.). In 1874 white shoulder straps with red numerals were introduced in the foot artillery. They were issued with rifles. The new equipment was of black leather, except for the guard foot artillery. In 1890 the whole of the field artillery adopted Swedish cuffs. In 1899 their shoulder straps were altered to the corps' colors, which were still worn in 1914; white for the Army Corps I, II, IX, and X; red for III, IV, XI, and XV; yellow for V, VI, XVI, XVII; light blue for VII, VIII, and XVIII; and light green for XXI. The 1910-model service dress was exactly the same as that worn by the infantry, except that the collar and cuffs (the latter of Swedish pattern for the field artillery and guard foot artillery) were piped with black instead of red. The cap band was black, piped with red. On the 1915 field gray jacket, the field artillery regiments wore red shoulder straps with yellow titles. In addition, the 1st Guard Field Artillery Regiment had white piping; the 3rd, lemon yellow; and the 4th, light blue. The shoulder straps of the foot artillery were gold-yellow with red numerals and ciphers, above which all regiments wore two crossed red grenades.

Under Frederick the Great, the miners wore blue coats without lapels, with self-colored cuffs, red-lined skirts, and white metal buttons. Waistcoat and breeches were orange; the cravat was black. A type of low-crowned fusilier cap was worn, with a white front plate and an orange body. In place of the flame-shaped finial, a white tassel was worn (Fig. 58a). The pontooneers wore artillery uniform up to 1806. In Frederick William II's reign, the corps of miners wore blue coats with dark blue lapels, and orange collars and cuffs. The corps of engineers (consisting only of officers and "conductors") under Frederick the Great had blue coats with red collar, cuffs, lapels, skirts, and undergarments. The lace loops were silver, with three on each lapel, with a broad waved lace around the hat. The conductors wore the same uniform, but without the silver lace. Several changes were made in the uniform in Frederick William III's time, prior to 1806. The corps of miners adopted black distinctions, and a pistol was carried on the front of the pouch belt (Fig. 58b). The corps of engineers had dark blue coats with black Manchester velvet distinctions; yellow waistcoats; white breeches; boots; and broad waved silver hat lace. The full-dress uniform had silver lace loops; the undress uniform had none.

In 1808 the pioneers were issued with jackets similar to those of the foot artillery, but with white metal buttons and Swedish cuffs. The shoulder straps were black with red piping; the chaco was ornamented with a cockade and bound with white lace. Accoutrements were of black leather (Fig. 58c). The development of the uniform followed that of the infantry. Ponceau red shoulder straps with yellow numerals were worn from 1830. In 1816 the guard detachments were given white lace loops. The chacos of the guards had upright black hair plumes, and drooping black plumes were worn on the helmet. At their inception in 1866, the railway troops wore the uniform of the guard pioneers with a yellow "E" (*Eisenbahn*) on their shoulder straps; later, when they were augmented, a Roman numeral was added below it. In 1911 the shoulder straps were changed to light gray with a red "E" and numeral. The airship detachment (later battalions) wore an "L" (*Luftschiffer*) on the shoulder straps. In 1895 they adopted *Jäger*-pattern chacos in place of helmets with the guard star in white metal on the front. From 1866 to 1870 the field telegraph detachments wore the uniform of the guard pioneers with a "T" (*Telegraphen*) on their shoulder straps and a Roman numeral below, denoting the detachment. In 1896 the "T" was replaced by a thunderbolt. Chacos were adopted in 1907. The battalions from No. 2 upward wore the same uniform as the line pioneers. In 1911 light-gray shoulder straps were adopted, bearing a red "T" with the battalion numeral in Arabic figures below.

The flying corps, raised in 1912, adopted the uniform of the airship battalions, but with only one loop of lace on the collar. A winged propeller was worn on the gray shoulder straps with the battalion numeral underneath.

The motor battalion wore the uniform of the railway regiments, with a red letter "K" (*Kraftfahr*) on the gray shoulder straps.

The service dress uniform of the pioneers and lines-of-communication troops was based on that of the artillery, with dull silver buttons, and retaining their former distinctions: lace loops, color of shoulder straps (which now became the color of the piping), and headdress. The officers of those detachments whose men did not have lace loops wore none themselves.

On the 1915-pattern field gray jacket, the pioneers wore ponceau red piping on their black shoulder straps. All communications troops wore light-gray shoulder straps, without piping, and with red insignia for all. The lace loops for those units which wore them were gray with a black light on a white patch.

After its reorganization in 1853, the transport corps wore light-blue distinctions and yellow metal buttons (Figs. 58e,f). Spiked helmets were worn at first, but leather kepis were later adopted for the men, the officers retaining their helmets, which were reintroduced for the other ranks in 1903. In full dress, black hair plumes were added. The Guard Transport Battalion was distinguished by white lace loops and, in full dress, by white hair plumes as well. A star ornament was worn on the kepi in place of the eagle by the men; the officers had a guard eagle plate on their helmets. In 1910 a service dress uniform like that of the field artillery was introduced, but with light-blue piping around the collar, cuffs, and shoulder straps. On the 1915 field gray jacket, potassium blue shoulder straps with red numerals were worn. The 2nd Guard Transport Detachment, which had been raised in 1914, had nickel buttons and guard lace loops with a potassium blue light on white patches on the collar.

IX. *LANDWEHR* AND *LANDSTURM* (SEE GLOSSARY)

Infantry: At its raising in 1813, the *Landwehr* adopted a very simple uniform, consisting of a double-breasted dark blue surtout with collar of the provincial color and buttons of varying color:

PROVINCE	COLLAR	BUTTONS
East Prussia	brick red	white
Kurmark	red	yellow
Neumark	red	yellow
West Prussia	black	white
Pomerania	white	yellow
Silesia	yellow	white
Westphalia*	green	white
Rhineland*	madder red	yellow
Elblande*	light blue	yellow

*Raised at the end of 1813.

Within each regiment the color of the shoulder straps varied for each battalion: white, red, yellow, and light blue. During the Armistice in 1813, yellow or red numerals were added on the shoulder straps. The *Landwehr* cap was dark blue, with a broad crown and a peak; the band was of the color of the collar, with a white metal *Landwehr* cross in front (Fig. 58g). Otherwise, there was very little uniformity, especially in legwear. Linen trousers were frequently worn, even in winter, for lack of cloth ones. Greatcoats and knapsacks were often not available at all. To begin with, hardly any of the NCOs had swords. At first, for lack of firearms, the front ranks were armed with spears. Both black and white leather accoutrements were worn, according to what was available. In 1817 the distinctions of the *Landwehr* infantry were assimilated to those of the line infantry, with the difference that the former had a blue piping around the collar. Chacos with the *Landwehr* cross on the front were worn. Too many alterations took place in the dress of individual formations to be dealt with here (see Mila, *Geschichte der Bekleidung und Ausrüstung der Königlich Preussischen Armee in den Jahren 1808 bis 1878*). Helmets and tunics were introduced in 1843 and the *Gürtelrustüng* in 1849. The tunics did not have the red piping

158

down the front. The helmet eagle bore the *Landwehr* cross. Leather kepis replaced the helmets in 1860. On the front they had a black, white-edged oval cockade with the *Landwehr* cross in the center (Fig. 58i). Helmets, of the newer pattern, were reintroduced in 1881, and had the eagle plate, with the cross applied, on the front. The helmet covers of the first line units had an "R" (*Reserve*) above the numeral; those of the second line had the letter "L" (*Landwehr*) above the numeral.

Apart from those on the helmet and helmet covers, the regular, reserve, and *Landwehr* regiments had no further distinctions on their service dress uniforms, except that the grenadier regiments, or those line units of the reserve and *Landwehr* which wore lace loops, had neither lace loops or ciphers.

Landwehr Cavalry: In 1813 the *Landwehr* cavalry adopted a *Litewka* similar to that of the *Landwehr* infantry, with the same provincial distinctions. Overalls were worn as they were by the dragoons; the chacos were mostly worn with covers, which bore the *Landwehr* cross. The pouch belts were black. Lances were carried, without pennants at first but, later, when they were adopted, they were supposed to be of the provincial colors. At that time, however, such details were entirely left to discretion. Black lambskin shabraques, with a cloth edging, were worn (Fig. 58h). In some cases, the uniform differed in many respects from that described above. In 1815 a uniform, similar to that of the lancers, in the cut of the jacket, shape of the cuffs, and girdle, was adopted. The shoulder straps were dark blue with yellow numerals and red piping. Collar and cuffs were of the provincial color. A dragoon-pattern chaco was worn with the *Landwehr* cross on it. The lance pennants were black and white; the shabraques, dark blue with an edging of the distinctive color. In 1822 lancer-pattern chacos with the *Landwehr* cross were adopted. White shoulder belts were introduced in 1830. From 1843 to 1852 tunics and helmets were worn, the latter with yellow metal fittings. The tunic collar was dark blue, with patches and shoulder straps of varying color, according to regiment. The pointed cuffs were of basic color; the girdles, dark blue; all piping was of the color of the collar patches; the buttons were yellow or white metal. The Guard *Landwehr* Lancers became the guard lancers in 1851. In 1852 the *Landwehr* cavalry was reorganized on the same lines as the arms of service of the regular army.

The *Schwere Landwehrreiter* (*Landwehr* Heavy Cavalry) wore dark blue tunics with colored collar patches, shoulder straps, Swedish cuffs, and piping on the seams. The distinctive color was yellow for Regiments Nos. 1 and 5; white for 2 and 4; red for 3 and 6; and light blue for 7 and 8. The buttons were white metal for Nos. 1, 3, 4, and 8, and yellow metal for the remainder. The helmets were similar to those worn by the rest of the cavalry of the period; and swords and white metal shoulder belts were carried. The *Landwehr* dragoons wore tunics like those of the *Landwehr* heavy cavalry, but without the piping on the sleeve and back seams. The cuffs were of basic color. The distinctions were red for Regiments Nos. 1 and 2; white for the 3rd; and yellow for the 4th. The buttons were white metal for No. 1 and yellow metal for the others. An infantry-pattern helmet, with yellow metal fittings, was worn, with the *Landwehr* cross on the eagle plate. The saber was worn on a white waistbelt, and the pouch belt was white. The *Landwehr* hussars had dark blue coats with black-and-white cord loopings. A black *Flügelmütze* was worn, with differently colored linings: white for Regiments Nos. 5, 8, and 11; red for 1 and 3; yellow for 2, 4, and 6; and light blue for 7, 9, 10, and 12. On the front was an upturned flap bearing the regimental number on it in German silver. High on the right side was a cockade, with the *Landwehr* cross below. The *Landwehr* lancers had tunics like those of the *Landwehr* heavy cavalry, but with dark blue pointed cuffs. The sash had an edging of the distinctive color. This latter was white for Regiments Nos. 4 and 5; red for 3 and 8; yellow for 1 and 2; and light blue for 6 and 7. They wore a helmet as for the *Landwehr* dragoons and had a saber and white pouch belt. The lance had a black and white pennant, but in the 4th and 6th Regiments, the NCOs had white pennants with a black eagle on them.

In 1857 the *Landwehr* cavalry adopted the same clothing and equipment as their corresponding mine cavalry regiments, with minor individual differences. In the event of mobilization, the reserve cavalry regiments—which wore the same clothing and equipment as the regular cavalry regiments, on which they had based their uniform (but with the distinction of the *Landwehr* cross on the headdress)—were to be attached to each army corps.

X. *FREIKORPS* AND *NATIONAL-KAVALLERIE-REGIMENTER* (VOLUNTEER CORPS AND NATIONAL CAVALRY REGIMENTS)

The *Freikorps* raised by Frederick the Great during the Seven Years' War for the most part wore the same uniform as the infantry: blue coats, with light-blue distinctions, and yellow or white metal buttons. In some cases, they were distinguished from each other by not having lapels or collars; by the type of cuffs; or by differing lace. Various *Freikorps* often had *Jäger*, who wore green coats, attached to them. Hats were worn by both infantry and *Jäger*; in some of the *Freikorps*, which were partly raised from Austrian deserters, the grenadiers wore fur caps. The *Freikorps* cavalry were dressed in a motley fashion.

The uniform of the *Kleistchen Grünen Frei-Dragoner* (Kleist's Volunteer Green Dragoons), so called because of the color of their uniforms, was especially noteworthy. The distinctions were all green, and the coat was ornamented with white worsted loops. The headdress was a fur cap with a white plate on a green backing. There was also a detachment known as the *Kleistscher Grüner Kroaten*, which wore *Flügelmützen*.

The *Freikorps* of 1807 were a very motley assemblage, largely raised from the remnants of regiments, depots, stragglers, and escaped prisoners, who generally wore their regimental uniforms, which by then were usually in a very bad state. In the later Napoleonic wars, *Freikorps* were again raised, of which the Lützow Regiment is the best known, through its warrior poet, Theodor Körner. Its uniform consisted of a black surtout, with self-colored collar, cuffs, and shoulder straps, piped red, with yellow metal buttons. The chacos were ornamented in a great many ways, which did not, however, matter, since covers were normally worn over them. The trousers were black, and those of the cavalry had buttons down the sides. The hussars wore black dolmans and pelisses, with black loops. The lancer uniform was described above, with lances and with pennants that apparently were red and black. The Tyrol *Jäger* Detachment, which was attached to the *Freikorps*, wore gray jackets and trousers, with green distinctions and lapels; white metal buttons; and an Austrian-type *Jäger* hat with a green plume. All corps had black leather equipment. The Foreign *Jäger-bataillon von Reiche* wore the uniform of the Line *Jäger* Battalions, with light-green shoulder straps and red piping. The infantry of the Hellwig *Freikorps* had dark green jackets with white piping, three rows of white metal buttons down the front, and black collars, pointed cuffs, shoulder straps, and wings. The trousers were gray. The chaco bore a white bugle horn device. Accoutrements were of black leather. The cavalry wore red dolmans and pelisses with blue collars and cuffs on the former. The loopings were white for the men and gold for the officers. The fur caps had blue bags, with a drooping hair plume of the left side. The remainder of the uniform consisted of red-and-yellow sashes, gray breeches, and black sheepskin saddle covers. The front ranks were armed with lances, which had blue-over-red pennants.

The national cavalry regiments can be considered along with the volunteer formations. The individual provinces were responsible for the cost of raising them. The East Prussian National Cavalry Regiment wore long dark blue coats with red collars and pointed cuffs; yellow loopings; and white shoulder straps. The buttoned overalls were dark blue, with two rows of red piping down each side. Sabertaches were black. The chacos had a yellow metal eagle plate and yellow cords. The upper parts of the lance pennants were white; the lower part was white for the 1st Squadron, red for the 2nd, blue for the 3rd, and green for the 4th. The elite detachment wore fur caps with red bags and yellow metal epaulettes. The Pomeranian Regiment had green dragoon pattern jackets with white collars and pointed cuffs and yellow metal buttons. The overalls were gray. The chacos had green cords. The girdle was light green with red edges. The elite detachment had yellow metal shoulder scales. The Silesian National Hussar Regiment wore an all-black hussar uniform, originally with yellow (later with red) collars and cuffs, and red loopings. The hussar-type chacos had cords. The Elbe National Hussar Regiment wore a green line-pattern hussar uniform with light-blue distinctions and yellow loopings. All these regiments had black leather equipment.

XI. GENERAL OFFICERS; RANK DISTINCTIONS; ETC.

In the *alte Armee*, that is, the army prior to 1806, officers had no proper distinctions of rank, except that from 1741, generals wore *Plumage*: an edging of white feathers around the brim of the hat. Toward the end of the eighteenth century a field service dress was introduced for general officers, who previously had always worn their regimental uniforms. It was dark blue, with self-colored lapels and skirt turnbacks, edged with gold. The collar and cuffs were red. In 1806 the coat was cut across at the waist in front. A gold shoulder cord was worn on the right shoulder. The breeches were white, and the boots black. The hat had a feather plume. The red collar and cuffs had gold embroidery on them. This uniform was retained after the reorganization of the army in 1808, except that latterly the hat was worn with a point, and not a fan, to the front. A cord of black and silver thread was worn on the left shoulder. The coat was no longer rounded in front, but was cut across, so that it henceforth had the shape of a coatee. When tunics were adopted in 1843, general officers retained their coatees, and they did not wear tunics until 1856. The tunic worn from that date had twelve buttons down the front, the top eight placed the same as on the usual officer's tunic, and the four lowest from waist to hem. The skirt flaps were edged with gold embroidery. A helmet with the guard eagle superseded the cocked hat in 1843; for full dress it was ornamented with a white hair plume with a black center. Epaulettes or shoulder cords were worn in undress. The trousers had a red piping and two red stripes down the sides. Breeches and long boots were worn from 1888. The full-dress shabraque was of the same color as the tunic, with a gold edging, ornamented with a star and crown in the rear corners; the holster caps bore the same devices. In 1900, a new undress coat, with a sloping collar, was introduced. This had old Prussian embroidery of the pattern worn by the Alt-Larisch Regiment of 1806, on the collar and cuffs. This coat also became the levee and full-dress uniform in 1909. Aiguillettes were worn in these orders of dress. The 1910 service dress jacket for general officers had several peculiarities: red-piped roll cuffs and long red collar patches with gold general officers'-pattern embroidery on them. The usual shoulder cords were worn. Triple red stripes were worn on the field gray trousers. This jacket was permitted to be worn after 1915. The 1915-model service jacket had a collar of darker-colored cloth with dull general's embroidery, in reduced size, on field gray patches; a concealed row of buttons; and red piping around the outer edge of the collar and around the roll cuffs. The trousers stripes were not supposed to be worn while on service at the Front. The 1915-model service dress greatcoat for general officers had red facings on the lapels, and red piping on the cuffs, pockets, and half belt at the back.

The uniform of the general staff resembled that of the general officers in cut and color, being dark blue. The collar and Swedish cuffs and all piping, however, were carmine. The collar and cuffs had two double loops of silver embroidery with bars of a leaf pattern on them. The buttons were white metal. Hats were worn at first, but later helmets as for the guards, with a white metal plate and white plume, were worn. The *Kriegsministerium* (War Ministry) had a similar uniform, but with gold lace. On the 1910-pattern service dress, officers of the general staff lost their embroidered loops, and adopted crimson collar patches, which were done away with on the 1915 jacket. On it, the distinctive embroidered loops, worked in matte silver, were again worn, on patches of darker-colored cloth, on the collar. The triple trousers stripes were carmine as before.

Proper distinctions of rank were not introduced into the army until 1808. Spontoons and gorgets were abolished at that time, but sashes were retained as a mark of rank. The rank distinctions consisted of silver lace with two black stripes through it, arranged in differing ways. Subalterns wore a single stripe down the center of their shoulder straps; *Hauptleute* and *Rittmeister* (captains of infantry and cavalry) had lace along both sides of the straps; field officers had lace all around their straps. In addition, all officers had red piping around the outside of the straps. Cuirassier officers adopted epaulettes in 1812, followed in 1813 by field officers of all arms except hussars; and in 1814 all officers (except the hussars as before) adopted epaulettes with gold or silver crescents. Lieutenants had lace along both outer edges of the strap; captains and field officers had lace on the top edge as well. The latter had all-silver crescents and thin bullions. The shoulder cords that previously had been worn by officers of some arms of service (e.g., the 1st Guard Regiment, *Gardejäger*, and all officers of dragoons) were abolished. In 1830 *Premierleutnants* and lieutenant colonels adopted one star on the epaulette crescents; colonels had two. In 1832 captains also adopted two stars. In addition, all ranks wore a lace edging around the top part of the epaulette strap. Epaulettes were not worn during the short reign of Emperor Frederick III (1883).

In 1914, the badges of rank were as follows:

Leutnant—no stars
Oberleutnant—1 star
Hauptmann (Rittmeister)—2 stars
Major—no stars; thin bullions
Oberstleutnant—1 star; thin bullions
Oberst—2 stars; thin bullions
General officers—thick bullions
Generalmajor—no stars
Generalleutnant—1 star
General (of infantry, cavalry, or artillery)—2 stars
Generaloberst—3 stars
Generaloberst with rank of *General-Feldmarschall*—4 stars
General-Feldmarschall—crossed batons

Shoulder cords, of silver lace with two black stripes, were ordered to be worn during the 1866 campaign. Stars of rank were worn as on the epaulettes. For field officers, they consisted of plaited silver-and-black cords on a colored backing; general officers had similar ones, the outer cords being gold, with no backing. In 1888, the pattern of cords for company officers was altered. These henceforth consisted of four cords laid side by side, not twisted together. Officers' shoulder cords and stars of rank remained unaltered on both the 1910 and 1915 service uniforms and on the 1915 greatcoat. On the greatcoat, however, they were of matte silver and matte gold respectively. On the 1915 uniform, the cords were generally worn on a cloth backing piped in the color of the men's shoulder straps or, if these were field gray, in their piping color. Where the men's shoulder straps had colored piping in addition to the main color, the officers wore the latter in addition as an inner piping on their shoulder cords. Pioneer officers, for example, had a black and red backing.

In the eighteenth century, NCOs were distinguished by their hat plumes (which varied greatly in color from regiment to regiment, but were often of black and white quartered), by their black and white sword knots, and by the gold or silver lace around their hats. In addition, most wore gold or silver lace around their cuffs. There were, however, too many variations for any general rule to be given. Gold or silver lace, around the collar and cuffs, was generally introduced in 1808. Up to 1814, it ran along the lower, not the top, edge of the collar. They also wore a band of gold or silver lace, according to button color, around the top of the chaco. Their rank was also denoted by their plumes: white plumes had a black tip, and black ones a white tip. The distinctions in 1914 were: for a *Gefreiter* (corporal), a button on each side of the collar; for an *Unteroffizier*, lace around the collar and cuffs; for a *Sergeant*, both collar buttons and lace; for a *Vizefeldwebel* (senior sergeant who on mobilization became an officer), the same, but with an officer's sword; for an *etatsmässige Feldwebel* (staff sergeant), a second narrower row of lace above the cuff lace from 1889. The rank of *Offizierstellvertreter* (serving officer cadet) was created in 1887. These adopted the uniform of the *Vizefeldwebel*, with lace of the color of the buttons around the shoulder straps. On the service dress, the distinctions of rank of the *Unteroffizier* and *Gefreiter* remained unaltered. The former's lace on the 1910 service uniform was, however, much narrower. On the 1915 jacket, the collar lace was field gray edged with white; it was frequently only worn chevronwise at the ends of the collar. In 1894 *Schützenschnüre* (marksmen's shoulder cords) were introduced in place of the old *Schiessauszeichnungen* (marksmen's distinctions), which consisted of short black-and-white lace stripes above the cuffs or on the patches. The shoulder cords, in contrast, were of the national, not the Prussian, colors. These cords varied according to degree. In addition, there were a number of other devices: for example in the cavalry, the lance proficiency badges, which took the form of chevrons on the upper arms; and the horseshoe-shaped piece of yellow cloth worn on the lower arms by farriers. The *Einjährig-Freiwilligen* (one-year volunteers) wore a black-and-white cord around their shoulder straps.

THE GERMAN REPUBLIC

When the German army returned home at the end of 1918, it was dressed in every conceivable variation of the service dress uniform worn during the war. In addition, many new temporary rank distinctions, in the form of horizontal dark blue cloth stripes on the left arm, took the place of those formerly worn, for political reasons. NCOs wore one to four narrow stripes above the elbow (Fig. 59a). Company, field, and general officers wore stripes 2.5, 4, and 6 centimeters wide, respectively, with one or two narrow stripes in addition, according to rank, on the lower arms. The numerous *Freikorps* (volunteer corps), raised for defense of the borders and for suppressing internal disorder, were distinguished by metal insignia of their own choice, worn on the collar or on the left upper arm (Figs. 59b,c). Most had an oak sprig, *Edelweiss*, guard star, or appropriate state emblem.

Fig. 59. Germany, 1918–1937.
a: *Vicefeldwebel.* b: *Freikorps.* c, e: privates. d, l: infantry with undress caps. f: NCO in greatcoat. g: cavalry. h: adjutant, service dress. i: officer, evening dress. k: senior private. m: corporal, armored troops.

164

The provisional *Reichswehr* was formed in March 1919. In it, for the first time, the German army had a common uniform for all the federal states. The local distinctions were restricted to the cockade on the cap and the shield on the helmet. The universal-pattern uniform, worn by all ranks and all arms, was of a gray color with a touch of green. The greatcoat and jacket collars, the unusually shaped jacket cuffs, and the cap bands were all of darker green. All buttons were white metal. The universal *Wehrmacht* distinctions consisted of gray double *Kapellenlitzen* (lace loops) on dark green patches on the collar, and the white metal oak wreath on the service cap, which had a black leather peak and chinstrap. On the shoulders of the jacket and greatcoat were worn double cords with two binders, of field gray for the men, matte silver for the regimental officers, and dull gold for general officers. The distinctions of rank, in dull silver lace, were worn on both arms: *Gefreiter*, a short horizontal lace stripe (Fig. 59c); and NCOs, one to four chevrons, point downward, on the upper arms; company officers had one to three horizontal stripes around the lower arms, the top stripe forming a loop; field officers had broad, and general officers very broad, stripes coming to a point; the higher ranks in these grades had in addition one or two narrower stripes above. The sword knot had a silver solid tassel and was worn on a field gray leather strap. The arms of service were distinguished by their *Waffenfarben*, which were generally the same as those still in use in 1937. This was displayed by the piping on the welts of the peaked cap; on the collar patches; and by the edging and inscriptions on the arm patches. Signals troops wore carmine, and airmen wore brown. General officers and the general staff had no arm patches, and wore their old collar embroidery and triple trousers stripes. The universal-pattern greatcoat was double-breasted, with red facings to the lapels for general officers.

The final establishment of the *Reichswehr*, restricted in numbers and armaments, took place in 1921. A new pattern of service jacket, with six buttons and deep roll cuffs of basic color without piping, was introduced. In place of the arm patches and shoulder cords, rounded shoulder straps of basic color, with piping and letters in *Waffenfarbe*, were adopted (Fig. 59e). The signals troops now had light brown. The distinctions of rank were again altered: officers readopted the old matte shoulder cords, without any admixture of the state colors, and with an edging of *Waffenfarbe*. Adjutants wore a single plaited cord aiguillette in matte silver, on the right shoulder (Fig. 59h). Senior NCOs wore dull silver lace around the shoulder straps, with stars, and on the front and lower edges of the collar; corporals wore silver lace chevrons on the upper arm. The state cockade was introduced on the upper part of the peaked cap, and the oval yellow cockade and eagle within the oak wreath, on the band (Fig. 59f). The trousers remained field gray. The soft, field gray service cap had a cloth peak and a dark green band with the state cockade on it. General officers wore gilt buttons on all articles of uniform. In 1927 they adopted red collar patches, and red piping down the front of their jackets; the piping on the peaked cap was gold, and gold double cords with two sliders were worn in place of the chinstrap. All other officers had cap cords and sliders of silver yarn. The six-button service jacket had rounded dark green shoulder straps with piping and devices in *Waffenfarbe*. In service dress, officers wore a leather Sam Browne belt (Fig. 59h), with a side arm buckled to it when off duty. In full dress, double silver aiguillettes—gold for general officers—on the right shoulder, and white gloves, were worn. On their walking-out dress uniform, the men wore collar patches and piping down the front of the jacket and on the trousers, in *Waffenfarbe*, and white metal buttons and lace. The sergeants' collar lace went around the top and front of the collar (Fig. 59f). In 1930, a modified pattern of helmet was introduced.

After Adolf Hitler's rise to power in 1933, the *Hoheitsabzeichen* (eagle and swastika insignia of the National Socialist party) was added to the uniform of the *Reichsheer* in February 1934. Universal military service was reintroduced. By 1937, the following changes had taken place: The basic color of the jacket and greatcoat was changed to gray-green, with collars of dark bluish-green. The jacket had a flat turndown collar; officers had a stand-and-fall collar, and a row of five dull white metal buttons. The patch pockets on the breast and skirts had scalloped flaps, and pleats. It had no cuffs. The pointed shoulder straps were dark green without piping, with letters in *Waffenfarbe*. The eagle-and-swastika badge was in dull gray in the national colors of black, white, and red; on the left was a black shield with the eagle and swastika in white. Black footwear and leather equipment were universally adopted (Figs. 59k,l). The men wore a fore-and-aft shaped forage cap (Fig. 59l). On the flap was a black, white, and red cockade, in the angle of a cord chevron, point uppermost, of *Waffenfarbe*, with the eagle and swastika above. The bayonet and sword knots had a solid gold tassel. Those of the staffs were all gray. Those of NCOs were of green and silver mixed. Corporals wore a matte gray star on the left upper arm, with a single or double lace chevron below, as appropriate. The *Schützenschnur* (marksmen's shoulder cord), in its prewar form, was reintroduced but was now made of woven spun aluminum. The metal lace worn by officers was of the same material. On service, a soft version of the peaked cap, with a leather chinstrap, was worn. The black, white, and red cockade was reintroduced on the cap band, in the oakleaf wreath. The state cockade disappeared, and was replaced by the eagle and swastika.

The *Waffenfarben* of the Wehrmacht were:

General staff officers—carmine
Infantry—white
Jäger—green
Pioneers—black
Cavalry—golden yellow
Signals troops—lemon yellow
Armored and motorized troops—pink
Artillery—red
Smoke troops—deep red
Communications troops—light blue
Recruiting staff—orange

The armored troops had a distinctive service dress (Fig. 59m): an all-black blouse and trousers, with pink piping around the shoulder straps and collar patches, with white metal skulls on the latter. A black beret was worn over the crash helmet in both service dress and full dress. It had the white oakleaf wreath with the cockade on the front, with the eagle and swastika above.

Off duty, stone gray trousers, piped in *Waffenfarbe*, were worn. A gray-green tunic with a row of seven buttons down the front, dark green stand-and-fall collar, and Swedish cuffs were introduced. Silver double lace loops were worn on the collar, and two single loops, on rectangular patches of *Waffenfarbe*, on the cuffs. The collar, front of the coat, cuffs, and scalloped three-button skirt flaps were piped in *Waffenfarbe*; senior NCOs wore lace along the front and upper edges of the collar. General officers and general staff officers wore their respective distinctive embroidered loops in place of the *Kapellenlitzen* on the collar and cuffs. In walking-out dress, officers wore a dagger with an ivory grip, in an aluminum scabbard, suspended by two similarly colored straps buckled under the jacket or hung from the greatcoat pocket.

ANHALT

Cockade: green

Between 1684 and 1689, Anhalt sent troops to the Imperial Army, which was called out against the Turks. The uniform was blue with red turnbacks, red waistcoats and breeches, and white stockings. They wore a hat with a green ribbon. The cavalry was similarly dressed, but in addition had blue cloaks lined red.

During the eighteenth century, the Anhalt-Zerbst Infantry wore white coats with red distinctions and yellow metal buttons. The undergarments were white. The musketeers had hats, and the grenadiers had fur caps.

The first permanently embodied formation in Dessau, the Dessau *Jäger* Corps, was raised in 1795 (Fig. 60a). They wore dark green coats with white buttons, skirt turnbacks, and epaulettes. The cuffs were dark green, the collar was red, and the undergarments and leather equipment were white. The hat had a green plume. During the period of the Rhine Confederation, the Anhalt states together formed a contingent that wore green single-breasted jackets with white metal buttons. The cuffs were green; the collar, shoulder straps, and piping, pink; the leather equipment was black. The gray breeches were worn with black gaiters (Fig. 60b). The grenadiers and *voltigeurs* were distinguished respectively by red and green fringed epaulettes, chaco cords, and pompons. The chaco plates were of white metal. In 1813 Napoleon ordered the raising of a mounted *Jäger* regiment, whose uniform was similar, except that the pointed cuffs were the same color as the collar. It had gray overalls, with stripes of the color of the collar, and white chaco cords and shoulder scales. In 1818, Anhalt-Dessau (Fig. 60d) provided a contingent, a battalion strong, for the Army of the Confederation. The basic color of the jacket and the Swedish cuffs remained dark green; the distinctions were pink, and the buttons white metal. The trousers were at first dark green, and later gray with pink stripes. The chacos had pompons in the company colors (red, white, green, yellow), later in the state colors. In 1818, Anhalt-Köthen (Fig. 60c) also furnished a battalion. These men wore dark green jackets, with self-colored cuff patches and skirt turnbacks, and yellow collars, shoulder straps and cuffs, all piped red. Buttons and chaco plates were white metal. The gray trousers had double red stripes. The leather equipment was black. Anhalt-Bernburg, too, furnished a grenadier company and three *Jäger* companies in 1818. The grenadiers were dressed in dark green jackets with red collar, cuffs, and piping,

Fig. 60. Germany. Anhalt.

a, d: Anhalt-Dessau *Jäger*. b: Anhalt Contingent to the Rhine Confederation. c: Anhalt-Köthen infantry. d: Anhalt-Dessau infantry. e, f: Anhalt Bernburg sharpshooter and *Jäger*. g: Anhalt, infantry.

and white guard lace loops and buttons. The chacos had white metal plates and cords; and the leather equipment was white. The trousers were gray, piped red. The *Jäger* (Fig. 60e) had dark green jackets with self-colored cuff patches, light-green collars, shoulder straps and cuffs, and red piping. The trousers were as for the grenadiers. The leather equipment was black. The chacos had a white metal plate and green (later white) cords and a green plume. In 1846 the *Jäger* adopted dark green Prussian-style tunics (Fig. 60f), with light-green distinctions, red piping, and white metal buttons as worn previously on the jacket. The spiked helmet had a white metal plate and black hair plume. On the cartridge box was a white metal *Schützen* horn. A hanger with a knuckle bow was carried. The other Anhalt states also adopted tunics at the same time, but in their former colors, and spiked helmets with white metal plates. In 1854 Dessau took over the Köthen Contingent, and in 1863 the Bernburg Contingent as well. The Anhalt Regiment dated from this time (Fig. 60g). It had two companies of sharpshooters. Their dark green tunics were entirely Prussian in style, except that the skirt flaps had only two buttons on them. The Swedish cuffs were dark green; the collar, piping, and shoulder straps, pink. The shoulder straps were piped white. The gray trousers had pink piping. The buttons, belt buckle, helmet plate, etc., were of white metal. The straight-bladed sword had a yellow metal guard and chaps. The sharpshooters had hangers with green knots; otherwise their uniform was similar. After the Convention of 28 June 1867, the regiment became the 93rd Infantry Regiment in the Prussian military establishment.

BADEN

*Cockade: black in the eighteenth century; later, red, yellow, and white;
then red and yellow*

Up to the middle of the eighteenth century, the basic color of the uniforms was white; thereafter they were almost exactly the same as those of the Prussian army. In the late eighteenth century dark blue coats with variously colored distinctions, and light-colored undergarments, were worn. Around 1790 the Margrave of the Baden *Leibregiment* wore a uniform that seems to have been based on that of the Prussian Guard Regiment No. 15. The coat had red collar, lapels, Swedish cuffs, and lining, ornamented with white lace and loops; with white metal buttons, and white undergarments. Black stocks were normally worn, except on Sundays and holidays, when red ones were worn. The musketeers wore white-laced hats with a red plume; the grenadiers, caps with a yellow front plate, and blue body with red around the base (Fig. 61a). Also in 1790 the Fusilier Battalion *Erbprinz* had blue single-breasted coats with yellow collar, cuffs, and skirt lining and white undergarments. The fusilier caps had a yellow plate and a blue body (Fig. 61b). The gaiters for all the infantry were white for full-dress wear, otherwise black. As a mark of rank, officers wore gorgets, and silver, red, and yellow embroidered sashes. Company officers wore gaiters up to 1793, and boots from that date. Officers' spontoons were abolished in the same year. In 1803 a new pattern of uniform, with lapels running straight down to the waist, was introduced. The officers' sashes were henceforth worn outside the coat. Queues were abolished in 1806, and NCOs' half pikes. On 21 October 1806, the

Fig. 61. Germany. Baden.

a, b, c, d, e, f, g: infantry. h: *garde du corps*. i, k, l, m: dragoons. n: horse artillery. o: foot artillery.

Leibgrenadier Guard adopted a new uniform, consisting of a dark blue coat with red collar, cuffs, and skirt lining, dark blue cuff patches, and white lace loops on the front, and on the cuff patches. White cords were worn on the right shoulder; white breeches; black gaiters; and fur caps with white metal plates, with white, red, and yellow cords and a white plume (Fig. 61d). Jackets were worn from 1809. In the same year, the line infantry was issued with double-breasted dark blue jackets with self-colored cuff patches; red collar, cuffs, and skirt turnbacks; and no lapels. The buttons were white metal. The breeches were as before (Fig. 61e). A form of crested helmet with yellow metal mounts (white metal for the *Leibregiment*) was introduced in 1806. The *Leibregiment* also had white lace loops on its collars and cuff patches. Officers adopted epaulettes in 1808. Early in 1813, the crested helmets were superseded by chacos; at the same time, distinctive regimental colors were reintroduced. The *Jäger* had dark green uniforms with black distinctions, white piping and buttons, and green epaulettes. Their helmet had a crest and plume. Green trousers and short black gaiters were worn. From the time of the Napoleonic Wars, the uniform was modeled on the Prussian pattern. In 1820 the infantry adopted red collars again, and variously colored shoulder straps, on their dark blue double-breasted coats. In 1833, the regiments had red collars and cuffs and were distinguished by their cuff patches, shoulder straps, and buttons. The *Leibgrenadier* Battalion had silver lace loops.

REGIMENT	CUFF PATCHES AND SHOULDER STRAPS	BUTTONS
No. 1	white	yellow
No. 2	red	white
No. 3	yellow	yellow
No. 4	light blue	yellow

The trousers were gray for the grenadier battalion and dark blue with red piping for the rest of the infantry. The equipment was of black leather. The light battalion had a green uniform, with light-blue collar, cuffs, and skirt edging; yellow metal buttons; light-blue shoulder straps and cuff patches; gray trousers; chacos; and black leather equipment. In 1834, red shoulder straps were again introduced, with white numerals. The chaco had a back peak, and the Baden griffin on the front. In 1843, the coat was made single-breasted. During the year 1849, when the Baden army rose in revolt, chacos and jackets were the normal dress, but at the same time, a completely new uniform was in process of being introduced, although it had not been generally adopted. Some of the mutineers appropriated these and only wore the new uniform. It consisted of a spiked helmet with a yellow metal griffin plate and ball finial, and blue tunics without differently colored distinctions or piping. The collar patches and shoulder straps were red with yellow lace loops for the *Leibgrenadiere*; red for the 1st Regiment; white for the 2nd; yellow for the 3rd; and light blue for the 4th. The gray trousers had no piping. The leather equipment was worn crossed. In 1850 the Prussian spike was introduced in place of the ball finial on the helmet. The infantry was reorganized into separate battalions, and adopted red collar patches and Brandenburg cuffs and white shoulder straps. Shoulder straps of a different color for each battalion were again worn from 1856. The *Leibgrenadiere* wore white metal buttons from 1856 to 1867, yellow metal ones from 1867 to 1885, and white metal ones again from 1885. In 1852 the battalions were forced into regiments once more. The *Jäger* wore dark green tunics with black collar and cuffs, red shoulder straps and piping, and yellow metal buttons. In full dress, the helmet had a black hair plume. Later, hats like those of the Austrian *Jäger*, and black leather equipment, were adopted. The knapsack straps were arranged differently from those in the Prussian army (Fig. 61g). In 1864 the leather equipment was made black for all the infantry. Two years later, the blue field cap with a red band was adopted. Thereafter, the uniforms were identical with those of the Prussian army, except that the helmet plate was the Baden griffin.

In 1914 the regimental distinctions were as follows:

Leibgrenadier-Regiment No. 109: white shoulder straps bearing a red crown; white guard lace; white metal buttons; Swedish cuffs; white metal plate on helmet, with a white hair plume in full dress.

The following regiments all had red cuff patches without piping, and yellow metal buttons.

> No. 110—white shoulder straps with red cipher; white hair plume in full dress
> Nos. 111 and 169—red shoulder straps
> Nos. 112 and 142—yellow shoulder straps
> Nos. 113 and 170—light-blue shoulder straps
> No. 114—green shoulder straps

In 1790 the Margrave of Baden *Garde du Corps* consisted of three companies: a cuirassier company, a *Garde du Corps* company, and a dragoon company.

The *Garde du Corps* had yellow coats with red collars, skirt turnbacks, and sashes, red-and-white lace edging and shoulder cords, leather breeches, and high boots. The hats were laced with silver and had a white plume (Fig. 61h). The white leather pouch belt bore a brass device. The dragoon company wore the same uniform as the Swabian *Kreis-Regiment* of Würtemburg: a blue uniform with black distinctions, yellow metal buttons, and white undergarments. The hat had white lace and a plume. The cuirassier company wore the uniform of the Swabian *Kreis-Regiment* Hohenzollern: the same hat as the dragoons, white coat with red distinctions, and black cuirass lined with red. In 1769 the uniform for all three companies of the *Garde du Corps* was made white with red distinctions, no lapels, and yellow undergarments. The hat had white lace and a plume. In 1799 four silver lace loops were added on the chest. Light-blue coats with dark red collars, lapels, and cuffs, white buttons and shoulder cords, and yellow skirt turnbacks and undergarments were adopted in 1801. The hat plume was white over red. In 1804 white jackets with red collar, and red-and-white lace edging, were introduced, and sabertaches with similar edging, bearing the letters "C.F." crowned; white breeches, and red girdles. A helmet with a white crest was issued in 1806. The jacket had two rows of white metal buttons. Guard lace loops were introduced in 1813, and the red girdle was abolished. A cuirassier helmet of Prussian pattern was adopted in 1810. Toward the end of the eighteenth century, the Margrave of Baden Hussar Regiment was raised. The pelisse and dolman were green, with red collar and cuffs, and yellow loopings.

The green sabertache bore a yellow cipher. The felt caps were black, with a black felt wing. Leather breeches and Hungarian boots were worn. In 1806 chacos with a green plume and red Hungarian breeches were adopted. In the following year, they had dark green breeches with red piping between two narrow red stripes. In 1812 the regiment was almost completely destroyed.

In 1803 the Margrave Charles Frederick, by the cession of new territories on the right bank of the Rhine, acquired a completely equipped Bavarian *chevau-léger* squadron. It was named the Light Dragoon Squadron. Later it was expanded into a regiment. At first, hats with a feather plume, light-blue jackets with red collar, cuffs, and lapels, and white lace loops, white metal buttons, and yellow waistcoats, white breeches, and high boots were worn. In 1805 the Bavarian crested helmet with white metal mounts was introduced, at first only for the men, but for officers as well in 1808. To protect the white breeches, light-blue overalls with red stripes were adopted (Fig. 61i). The lace loops were abolished in 1808, and the lapels in 1810. The jacket was made double-breasted. In 1833 a guard dragoon regiment was established in place of the *Garde du Corps*. There were two regiments of line dragoons. Jacket and trousers were light blue; the helmet had a comb, and black horsehair crest, like the contemporary Prussian cuirassier helmet. The leather equipment was white (Fig. 61k). The guard dragoon regiment had red collar and cuffs with white lace loops and white metal buttons. The 1st Regiment had white cuffs and collars, yellow metal buttons, and no lace loops. The 2nd Regiment had red distinctions, and yellow lace loops and buttons. The uniform was altered in 1834. A new pattern of helmet, with a yellow metal comb and griffin, was adopted, and the black crest was retained (Fig. 61l). All three regiments had light-blue jackets with a row of yellow metal buttons, and light-blue trousers, with white stripes for full dress. Normally, leather-strapped overalls with white piping were worn. The collar, cuffs, shoulder straps, piping, and the edging to the skirt turnbacks were all white. The Grand Duke Regiment had a crown on the shoulder straps; the other two had numerals. The shabraques were light blue, edged with white, and had a crown in the front corners and a crowned cipher in the back corners.

At the reorganization of 1850, light-blue tunics like those of the Prussian dragoons were introduced, along with spiked helmets. The gray trousers had red piping. The 1st Regiment had red collar, cuffs, and piping; the 2nd, yellow; and the 3rd, black distinctions and red piping. All three regiments had white metal buttons and yellow metal helmet ornaments. A jacket was worn in undress. From that time, the uniform more closely resembled the Prussian one. The distinctions remained as before. In 1914 the regiments were numbered 20, 21, and 22. White hair plumes were worn in full dress. When the whole of the German cavalry was equipped with lances, the Baden dragoons adopted yellow and red lance pennants. The 20th Regiment (Baden *Leib-Dragoner* Regiment) had a yellow crown on the shoulder straps. In general, the artillery and pioneers underwent the same changes in uniform as the infantry. At the end of the nineteenth century, the distinctions were black; later, red piping was added (Figs. 61m,n,o). The artillery had yellow metal buttons; the pioneers, white metal ones. The uniforms of the general officers also were of the Prussian pattern.

The 1910 and 1915 models of service dress followed the Prussian ones. The 114th Infantry Regiment had light-green shoulder strap piping, the 22nd Dragoon Regiment, black.

BAVARIA

Cockade: light blue and white

I. INFANTRY

The first sign of any kind of uniformity is to be found in the mid-fifteenth century. Apart from this isolated instance, and from the *Leibgarde*, the beginnings of a distinctive uniform in Bavaria can be taken to date from 1671. The colors varied greatly, often even from company to company within a regiment. White and gray coats prevailed up to 1673, after which date blue became more prominent. At that time, these blue coats were called Savoy coats. In 1683, seven regiments of infantry were raised, as follows.

Berlo (up to 1918, part of 1st and 10th Infantry Regiments)—pearl-gray coats, white cuffs
Puech (disbanded 1688)—green coats, yellow cuffs
Degenfeld (up to 1918, 2nd Infantry Regiment)—pearl-gray coats, dark lilac cuffs
Montfort (disbanded 1688)—dark gray coats, blue cuffs
Perusa (disbanded 1705)—blue coats, violet cuffs
Steinau (disbanded 1705)—blue coats, red cuffs
Preysing (disbanded 1705)—blue coats, yellow cuffs

Blue coats were ordered to be universally worn by a decree of 5 March 1684. They were knee length, and had broad sleeves and very large pockets. The waistcoat was very long, and of the same color as the cuffs. The breeches were red, with gaiters of various colors. During the Turkish wars of the 1680s, the officers frequently wore coats of the same colors as the men's cuffs. The linings were blue, but later were of the same color as the men's. The officers' waistcoats were edged with lace. The sleeves of the NCOs' coats had lace on them. As a mark of rank, officers had a sash of blue taffeta with a silver fringe, worn around the waist at first, later over the right shoulder.

The distinctive colors in 1684 were as follows:

Mercy—white
Steinau—red
Rummel—violet
Preysing—yellow
della Rose—light lilac
Puech—gray coats, blue cuffs
Montfort—gray coats, blue cuffs

The distinctive colors in 1710 were as follows:

Leibregiment—white
Kurprinz—blue
Grenadiers—blue
Lützelburg—red, red waistcoats
Haxthausen—red
Maffei—yellow
Tattenbach—yellow, yellow waistcoats

The first three regiments had white lace loops.

The *Chevalier de Bavière* Regiment had aurora-colored cuffs and waistcoats in 1706 and sulphur yellow ones in 1718.

The hair was worn falling freely (Fig. 62a); later it was tied at the back, and later still, queues were worn. About 1702 the grenadiers adopted sugar-loaf-shaped bearskin caps without plates (Fig. 62b). Shortly after 1700 the *Landfahnen*, an auxiliary force, adopted laced hats; red cravats; blue coats with whitish-gray cuffs; blue waistcoats; white stockings; and yellow pouch belts and waistbelts. The officers were dressed in light gray, without gold or silver lace. They also wore blue stockings, white and blue sashes, silver gorgets, and blue feather plumage in their hats, and carried spontoons. The line troops wore blue breeches at the beginning of the century, but these were changed for yellow ones in 1748. Lapels were often added to the coats. In 1740, a cloth bag was adopted on the backs of the fur caps. In 1748, the stock was made of red leather. On service, officers carried spontoons, and NCOs had short muskets.

Distinctions During the Seven Years' War
(from Gillardone, *Die Zinnfigur*)

REGIMENT	COAT	LAPELS AND CUFFS	BUTTONS	WAISTCOAT	BREECHES
Leibregiment	light blue	white	white	white	light blue
Duke Clemens	light blue	yellow	white	yellow	light blue
Minucci	light blue	buff	yellow	buff	light blue
Morawitzky	light blue	dark red	yellow	dark red	light blue
Kurprinz	light blue	white	yellow	white	light blue
Preysing	light blue	red	white	red	light blue

In 1770 white undergarments were introduced. From that date the hat was made rather smaller in size, and the stocks were black. In 1774 all regiments were ordered to have white linings for their coats, but the colored distinctions remained the same as before. Instead of a sword, the men wore a bayonet on a waistbelt over the waistcoat; the grenadiers had hangers, and the NCOs had straight-bladed cutting swords. The grenadier caps had a plate on the front bearing the electoral arms (Fig. 62d). Beards were only permitted to be worn by NCOs and above. In 1777 the army of the Palatinate was combined with the Bavarian army. The distinctions of the Palatine army, at the time of the union, were as follows.

Leibregiment (in 1914, 1st and 3rd Infantry Regiments): blue coats with red collars and cuffs, red lining, and edged with white lace. The hat lace and undergarments were also white.

Zweibrücken (in 1914, 6th Infantry Regiment): blue coats with red collars, lapels, and lining; white lace edging. Waistcoat, breeches, and buttons were white; officers had silver lace loops.

Birkenfeld (disbanded): blue coats with yellow cuffs, lapels, and linings; white undergarments, hat lace, and buttons.

Effern (transferred): blue coats with red linings, lapels, and cuffs; white undergarments and hat lace; yellow buttons.

Rodenhausen (in 1914, part of 9th Infantry Regiment): dark blue coats with red linings; no lapels; white cuffs, undergarments, loops, and hat lace. Yellow buttons; gold loops for officers.

Leopold von Hohenhausen (in 1914, part of 9th Infantry Regiment): dark blue coats with red lapels, cuffs, and linings; white undergarments and white hat and coat lace; yellow buttons. Silver loops for officers.

Osten (disbanded): dark blue coats without lapels; yellow turnbacks and linings; white undergarments, buttons, and hat lace.

Josef von Hohenhausen (in 1914, part of 3rd Infantry Regiment): blue coats with white lapels, cuffs, and linings; white undergarments and hat lace; yellow buttons. The officers' coats were of a lighter blue color.

Vac. Baden (disbanded): dark blue coats with red lapels, cuffs, and linings; white undergarments; yellow buttons.

The coats of the Palatine regiments were of a lighter blue than those from Bavaria. In 1872 this lighter color was adopted by all the regiments. Officers gave up their spontoons in 1778. Grenadier officers retained the fusils and small cartridge

Fig. 62. Germany. Bavaria—Infantry.

boxes slung over the shoulder, which they had previously carried. Sashes were done away with, but gorgets were introduced. To denote their rank, field officers adopted a gold or silver bullion epaulette on each shoulder, bearing three rose devices for a colonel, two for a lieutenant colonel, and one for a major. Company officers wore a bullion epaulette on the left shoulder, with three transverse strips of lace for a captain, two for a senior lieutenant, and one for a junior lieutenant. Officers had field marks of blue silk and silver at both corners of their hats and at the top, with a broad gold or silver lace binding. NCOs wore an edging of narrow silver lace around the brim, and three blue-and-white silk rosettes; the men wore white hat lace, and blue-and-white worsted tufts. Various regiments had self-colored cuffs, but had collars of the regimental color. The *Leibregiment* and *Kurprinz* regiments had a lace loop around each buttonhole; some regiments had a lace edging around the cuffs; others wore no lace at all. In 1785 white coats were introduced, and the hat lace and officers' epaulettes were abolished (Fig. 62e). A further change took place in 1789. The whole army adopted a universal uniform, varying in color for the several arms of service. A black leather helmet was introduced, with a peak and with a brass plate in front bearing the coat of arms and terminating in a lion's head projecting from the front of the comb. The horsehair *crinière* reached to the nape of the neck (Fig. 62f). It was white for grenadiers and black for fusiliers. The coat was made very close-fitting. The infantry wore white coats; pairs of regiments each had collars, lapels, cuffs, and skirt turnbacks of the same color, and were differentiated by the color of their buttons. Gaiters, shaped like Hungarian boots, were sewn to the close-fitting gray breeches. The leather accoutrements were worn crossed for the first time. At the same time, black leather epaulettes with brass mounts were introduced for the whole army. For officers, the brass part was gilded. The gorget was done away with, and the various ranks were distinguished by the richness of the button loops. In 1799 the basic color of the coat, which by then was cut like a jacket, was changed to light blue, with different distinctions for each regiment. From 1800 to 1806 these were as follows.

REGIMENT	COLLAR, CUFFS, AND LAPELS	BUTTONS
Leibregiment[1]	black (red from 1802)	white
Kurprinz[2]	black (red from 1802)	yellow
Duke Charles	red	yellow
Weichs	sulphur yellow	white
Preysing	pink with red piping	white
Duke William	red	white
Morowitzky	white	yellow
Duke Pius	sulphur yellow	yellow
Ysenburg	scarlet	yellow
Junker	crimson	white

[1]white lace loops   [2]yellow lace loops

A crested helmet was introduced, having a small plate on the front, with crown above, and a small chin chain, fastened at each side by lion's head bosses. Above the peak was a metal band with the name of the regiment on it. In 1803, the grenadiers adopted red hackles and *houpettes* on the helmet; the *Schützen* adopted green ones in the following year. In 1805 the officers took into wear bearskin-crested helmets in place of the hats they had worn until then. Queues were abolished in the same year. In 1806, a white-and-blue cockade was added on the left side of the helmet. The knapsacks were worn on two shoulder straps from November 1807 (Fig. 62g). In 1811 officers gave up gray breeches, and adopted white ones similar to those worn by the men, or light-blue pantaloons.

According to the Army List of 1811, the distinctions were as follows.

REGIMENT	LAPELS AND CUFFS	COLLAR	PIPING	BUTTONS
1. King's	red	red	none	white
2. Crown Prince	red	red	none	yellow
3. Prince Charles	red	red	white	yellow
4. Saxony-Hildburghausen	yellow	yellow	red	white
5. Preysing	pink	pink	none	white
6. Duke William	red	red	white	white
7. Löwenstein-Wertheim	pink	pink	none	yellow
8. Duke Pius	yellow	yellow	red	yellow
9. Isenburg	yellow	red	red	yellow
10. Junker	yellow	red	red	white
11. Kinkel	black	red	red	white
13. No name	black	red	red	yellow

There was no 12th Regiment; it was disbanded after it had mutinied.

The King's and *Kurprinz* regiments respectively had white and yellow lace loops on the lapels and cuffs. The skirt turnbacks were red throughout. The white cloth breeches were worn with black gaiters. The 1st Regiment had a white lace edging to the coat, the 2nd, yellow. The sashes, which had been reintroduced for officers in 1800, were laid aside by an Order of 15 April 1812, when gorgets were again taken into wear. In 1814 all infantry regiments were issued with jackets with red collars, lapels, and cuffs. They were distinguished by the regimental numbers on the yellow metal buttons. The *Grenadier-Garderegiment,* which was raised in the same year, wore the same uniform, with a white lace edging; and had bearskin caps with a feather plume, and cords. The lace which the 1st and 2nd regiments had worn until then was abolished. Shortly afterward, light-blue pantaloons were introduced for the men. As time passed, the crested helmet grew higher. In 1825–1826 a single-breasted jacket without lapels was adopted in place of the lapeled one (Fig. 62h).

The regimental distinctions again took the form of varying colors, which remained unaltered down to 1872.

REGIMENT	CUFFS	BUTTONS
Leibregiment	red	white
No. 1	dark red	yellow
No. 2	black	yellow
No. 3	red	yellow
No. 4	yellow	white
No. 5	pink	white
No. 6	red	white
		(continued)

177

REGIMENT	CUFFS	BUTTONS
No. 7	pink	yellow
No. 8	yellow	yellow
No. 9	crimson	yellow
No. 10	crimson	white
No. 11	black	white
No. 12	orange	white
No. 13	dark green	white
No. 14	dark green	yellow
No. 15	orange	yellow

The *Leibregiment* wore two horizontal lace loops, one above the other, in the cuffs. Piping and skirt turnbacks were red throughout; trousers, light blue, or white in summer. This uniform remained unchanged to 1848, when a single-breasted tunic with red piping and shoulder straps for all regiments was introduced in place of the jacket (Fig. 62i). Those regiments which had black or dark green distinctions wore red piping around the collar and cuffs. The *Kaskett* assumed the form of that already worn by the *Jäger*, and was thenceforth called a helmet. After the disappearance of the brass band and the chin chain, the fittings consisted of a rayed plate bearing the royal cipher. The lion's head bosses at the sides were moved further down, and served as fixings for the chinscales. Up to 1860, the accoutrements, which had been white for the first two battalions in each regiment, and black for the third (*Schützen*) battalion, were worn crossed over on the chest. In that year, however, the *Gürtelrüstung* of black leather for all battalions was introduced. Red padded wings at the point of the shoulder replaced the shoulder straps (Fig. 62k). Later, the rayed plate on the helmet was abolished, leaving only the crowned royal cipher as a device. This remained the regulation uniform to 1872, in which year a tunic of Prussian pattern, of the same basic color as before, was introduced (Fig. 62l). The collar and cuffs, and from that date also the sleeve patches and shoulder straps, were red, the latter having yellow numerals. The Ist Bavarian Army Corps had white piping around the cuff patches; the IInd had none. Buttons were of yellow metal, except for the *Leibregiment*, which had white ones. The latter had Swedish cuffs, and white lace loops on the collar and cuffs. A yellow crown was worn on the shoulder straps. The officers' gorgets were again abolished, and from then they wore a silver-and-blue woven sash. The crested helmet, with leather chinstrap, binding around the peak, and crowned "L" cipher, was superseded in 1886 by a Prussian-type spiked helmet. This had a square peak, cross-shaped mount on top, fluted spike, and the Bavarian coat of arms with supporters on the front, all the mounts being of yellow metal (white for the *Leibregiment*). The trousers were light blue as before, with red piping down the sides. Knapsacks and leather equipment were as in Prussia (Fig. 62m). The IIIrd Bavarian Corps adopted yellow piping on the cuff patches. The helmet had a rounded front peak, and a plain spike latterly.

The first service dress uniform exactly resembled the Prussian pattern, except that the shoulder straps were piped in the color of the former cuff piping, and not in the color of the former shoulder straps. The *Leibregiment* wore Brandenburg cuffs;

these were only supposed to have lace loops on them in peacetime, but in fact the regiment wore them on service in 1914.

The 1915-model uniform also exactly resembled the Prussian pattern, but the trousers and jacket and greatcoat collars were of basic color. The piping on the shoulder straps was white, with red numerals; the *Leibregiment* had a crown. The latter also had gray double lace loops with gold cord around the patches with no light. As a national distinction, the whole of the Bavarian army wore a narrow matte gray lace (matte silver for officers) with an interwoven diamond pattern in light blue, around the outside of the jacket and greatcoat collars.

II. *JÄGER* AND LIGHT INFANTRY

In 1781 the Bavarian *Jäger* Corps wore green coats without lapels, with brick red cuffs, yellow fringed epaulettes, and yellow metal buttons. In the following year, the Mountain *Jäger* Corps had green coats with red edgings, black cuffs and lapels, and white fringed epaulettes and buttons. Both regiments wore bicornes.

In 1805 a mounted and a foot *Jäger* corps were raised. The former had long green coatees with a single row of yellow metal buttons; yellow collar, cuffs, and piping; long green breeches with yellow stripes; yellow epaulettes; tricorne hats with a white-and-blue feather plume; black equipment; saber; sabertache, and green shabraques, pointed at the rear. The uniform of the foot *Jäger* was similar, with an infantry *Kaskett*, artillery saber, and calf leather ammunition pouch. In 1801 the *Jäger* were converted into light battalions. The light infantry uniform consisted of a light-green jacket (changed to dark green in 1809), with black lapels and cuffs, red piping and skirt turnbacks, and long gray breeches. The carabiniers, which were the equivalent of grenadiers in the light infantry, wore green plumes on their helmets. All other features of the uniform were as for the light infantry (Fig. 65a).

After several alterations in the colors, the distinctions in 1811 were as follows.

BATTALION	COLLAR	BUTTONS
1. Gedoni	red	yellow
2. Wrede	red	white
3. Bernclau	black	white
4. Theobald	black	yellow
5. Buttler	yellow	white
6. La Roche	yellow	yellow

In 1815 the light infantry was disbanded, and shortly afterward *Jäger* battalions were raised in its place. They wore the infantry uniform with light-green collars, cuffs, skirt turnbacks, lapels, and pantaloons, and infantry helmets with a green plume. Equipment was of black leather. The cut of the uniform was altered in 1825–1826, as in the infantry. The distinctions remained green; the buttons were changed to yellow metal and the trousers to light blue. A yellow hunting horn was added in the corners of the skirt turnbacks, and chacos with a cockade in front replaced the helmets in 1829 (Fig. 65b). The *Jäger* helmet, as described for the infantry, was adopted in 1845. Green worsted *Schützen* cords were worn from the time of the raising of the battalions. The shoulder straps of the tunic introduced in 1848 were green, as were the padded shoulder wings. The leather accoutrements remained black. In 1872 light-blue Prussian-pattern tunics, with green distinctions and Swedish cuffs, were introduced. Infantry-type helmets were adopted in 1886 and were superseded by *Jäger* chacos ten years later. The 1910-model service dress resembled the Prussian one, except that the basic color was field gray, not gray-green. The 1915 service dress was similar, but with a self-colored collar. The shoulder straps were light green, with the battalion numeral on them in yellow. The machine gun detachment wore the same peacetime and service uniforms as the *Jäger*, but had a Roman numeral I on the shoulder straps.

III. CUIRASSIERS AND HEAVY CAVALRY

In 1682, the following regiments were raised:

Haraucourt—light-gray coats, blue cuffs
Bärtels—uniform unknown
Beauvau—light-gray coats, red cuffs
Schütz—uniform unknown

The headdress was either an iron helmet or a hat. The latter were worn during the War of the Spanish Succession (1701–1713). At that time, the cuirassiers wore light-gray coats; elks-leather waistcoats and gloves; riding cloaks; deerskin breeches, and heavy boots. All ranks wore hats with a gold lace edging. The cuirasses were dull polished. The trumpeters had coats in reversed colors. Hanging sleeves, ornamented with lace, were attached to the shoulders at the back. In 1701 the regimental distinctions were as follows:

Arco—grayish-white coats; blue cuffs, linings, and waistcoats
Weichel—grayish-white coats; carmine cuffs, linings, and waistcoats
La Tour—grayish-white coats; green cuffs, linings, and waistcoats

In 1717 the regiments on their way to Hungary added black cockades to their hats. Later, the cuirassiers adopted white uniforms. The Törring Regiment wore red linings, cuffs, and waistcoats; yellow breeches; and white buttons. The Rechberg Regiment was dressed similarly, but with blue distinctions. The Costa Regiment had green distinctions. A lace loop and button were added on the collar of the coat. The cuffs, skirt edgings, and the lace loop were of the regimental color. Waistcoat and breeches were yellow; long boots and white stockings were worn. The breastplate was worn under the coat. The pouch belt was worn over the coat, and was held in place by a knot of the regimental color, on the left shoulder. The hat was plain, except for two vertical strips of lace at each side. A blue-and-white feather plume was added after the Seven Years' War (Fig. 63b). At the time of the amalgamation of the Palatine army with the Bavarian army in 1777, the Palatine Cavalry Regiment Prince Max wore white coats without lapels, with red linings and red cuffs, and yellow undergarments and buttons. Officers had gold lace around their hats; the men had none. After the

Fig. 63. Germany. Bavaria—Heavy Cavalry, Dragoons.

a, b, c, d, e: cuirassiers. f: heavy cavalry. g, h, i, k, l, m: dragoons.

union of the Palatinate with Bavaria, there were three cuirassier regiments. The Ysenburg Regiment wore white coats, with bright red collar patches, cuffs, and edgings to the skirt turnbacks; epaulettes interwoven with red; white buttons; and light-yellow waistcoats. The Prince Taxis Regiment was dressed similarly to the Ysenburg, but had blue distinctions. The Zweibrücken (later Winkelhausen) Regiment had yellow coats, with red turndown collars, distinctions, and waistcoats, but from 1780 it wore exactly the same uniform as the Ysenburg Regiment, with yellow buttons. In 1785 the cuirassiers delivered their armor into store, and thereafter wore their fairly short coats buttoned up, with the sword on a waistbelt over them. With the introduction of the universal uniform in 1789, the hat was superseded by the *Kaskett*, with a white horsehair *crinière* (Fig. 63c). The coat was as for the infantry, but with a white collar. The waistcoat was white; the breeches were yellow; and knee boots were worn. The epaulettes were like those worn by the infantry. The saber was worn on a white belt over the right shoulder. In 1800 the crested helmet was introduced. The basic color of the coat remained white. In 1804 the cuirassiers, which had latterly numbered only a single regiment, disappeared.

A *Garde du Corps* regiment was raised in 1814. It had light-blue jackets with red distinctions, white breeches, and long boots. The white metal shoulder scales had a red lining and no fringes. The cuirasses were yellow metal, with a red edging, piped white, around the armscye (armhole). The yellow metal helmet had a comb and black crest. Around the skull was a black turban, with a metal oakleaf garland around it for officers. In 1815 the 1st and 2nd Cuirassier Regiments were raised. They adopted a uniform similar to that of the *Garde du Corps*, but with white metal cuirasses and helmets (Fig. 63d). They were differentiated by the color of their buttons. From 1863 to 1867 the 3rd Cuirassier Regiment wore crimson distinctions. The uniforms, despite undergoing a number of changes, retained their general characteristics in

181

style and color until the transformation of the cuirassiers into *schwere Reiter* (heavy cavalry) regiments in 1879. Both regiments thereafter wore light-blue tunics, of the pattern worn by the Prussian dragoons, with red distinctions (Fig. 63f). The 1st Regiment had white metal buttons, the 2nd, yellow. The helmet plate was of the color of the buttons. In full dress, a white hair plume was worn. The breeches were of blue-black cloth, worn in long boots. Accoutrements were of white leather. Like all the German cavalry, the *Reiter* carried lances, with pennants in the national colors. The 1910 service dress was of the Prussian pattern for dragoons, except that the *schwere Reiter* had a stand-and-fall collar, instead of a stand collar. The distinctive colors and the color of the buttons remained as before. In 1915 the *schwere Reiter* adopted yellow as their distinctive color. The shoulder straps were yellow, with steel green piping. Regimental numerals were not worn on them.

IV. DRAGOONS AND *CHEVAU-LÉGERS* (LIGHT HORSE)

In 1683 the dragoons wore either red coats with blue distinctions or blue coats with red distinctions (Fig. 63g). This combination of colors remained in vogue during the years following. The Monasteral Regiment adopted blue coats with green distinctions in 1694. Hats were worn. In 1701 the regiments were distinguished as follows: Fels, blue with red distinctions; Verita, red with green distinctions; Rote, red with yellow distinctions. In 1735 the Hohenzollern Dragoons were dressed in red coats with straw-colored cuffs, linings, and undergarments. There was a row of white buttons down the front of the coat. A white cord on the left shoulder retained the black pouch belt. The hat was laced with silver (Fig. 63h).

The Piosasque Dragoons also wore red coats with straw-colored linings but had blue cuffs, waistcoats, and breeches. The buttons were yellow and the hat lace gold. In 1748 straw-colored waistcoats and breeches were introduced. It appears that the Hohenzollern Dragoons adopted black distinctions in 1768. At the same time, the hat lace was abolished, and a blue-and-white feather plume adopted. Epaulettes of gold or silver for officers were adopted in 1769; the men wore only one epaulette, with stripes in the regimental color, on the left shoulder (Fig. 63i).

In 1780 the distinctions of the four regiments that existed then were as follows.

REGIMENT	CUFFS	SKIRT LININGS	BUTTONS	EPAULETTES
Leibdragoner	black	red	yellow	red and yellow
La Rosée	blue	yellow	yellow	red and blue
Wahl	black	yellow	white	red and black
Leiningen	green	green	white	red and green

The cuffs of the La Rosée and Wahl regiments were of Swedish type; the others had a vertical slit, with two buttons on the cuff and two above.

The order of 11 March 1785, which introduced white uniforms for the army, applied to the dragoons. The men's coats, the skirts of which had been shortened, buttoned all the way down the front (Fig. 63k). The cloak was also white. The *Leibdragoner* and Wahl regiments adopted black collars and cuffs, with white buttons for the latter. The Leiningen and La Rosée regiments had blue distinctions, the latter

Fig. 64. Germany. Bavaria—*Chevau-légers*, Hussars, Lancers.
a, b, c, d, e, f: *chevau-légers*. g: hussar. h, i, k: lancers.

with white buttons. In 1789 only two dragoon regiments were left. The universal pattern of uniform introduced at that time was white for the dragoons as well. The collar was white; the lapels and cuffs were black, with white buttons for the 1st Regiment and yellow for the 2nd. The new *Kaskett* had a white hair *crinière* (Fig. 63l). In 1800 the crested helmet was introduced (Fig. 63m). Both dragoon regiments were turned into *chevau-légers* in 1811.

The *chevau-légers* were a creation of Count Rumford, who reorganized the Bavarian army. They were first raised in 1790 and numbered four regiments to begin with. In reality, however, there were but three, as the 4th Regiment only existed on paper until 1799. The uniform was similar to the universal pattern of the period. The helmet had a green hair *crinière*. Coat and waistcoat were green, as was the collar; the crescents were of black leather with brass mounts, as in the rest of the army. Breeches and shabraques were gray (Fig. 64a). The 1st and 2nd regiments were distinguished by black lapels, cuffs, and skirt turnbacks; those of the 3rd were apple green. The 1st and 3rd regiments had white metal buttons; the 3rd, yellow. Leather equipment was white. A white lambskin with green edging was worn over the shabraque. In 1799 the 4th Regiment was actually formed, but it was disbanded in 1801. A new regiment was raised in its place two years later. The crested helmet was issued in 1800. The coat was cut in the form of a jacket; the skirts were of basic color, with edging in the distinctive color. White shoulder scales were worn, very far to the back at first, so that they were not seen from the front. The helmet had a white plume on the left side. Gloves were worn, with very short tops. The gray breeches were worn with Hungarian boots. The Leiningen Regiment adopted scarlet distinctions, which the *Kurfürst* Regiment already had; the Fugger Regiment, black, and, like the newly raised Bubenhofen Regiment, it was, by an Order of 8 April 1803, to have its black collar, lapels, cuffs,

183

and skirt edgings piped with red. Both the dragoon regiments, which were turned into *chevau-légers* in 1811, adopted scarlet distinctions, but with green collars with red piping; the 1st Regiment had white, the 2nd yellow metal buttons. The jacket was at first of light-green cloth, but was made darker after November 1809. From 1804 officers had worn long gray overalls with stripes in the distinctive color, over their white breeches, to protect them; in the meantime, white breeches had also been introduced for the men (Fig. 64b). The officers' pouch and pouch belt were embroidered from 1802 to 1804, and thereafter the latter were made of silver. The shabraques were red, with silver or gold edging for officers, and white-and-blue checkers for the men. In 1811 the distinctions were as follows.

REGIMENT	LAPELS, CUFFS, SKIRT EDGING	COLLAR	PIPING	BUTTONS
1. No name	red	green	none	white
2. Taxis	red	green	none	yellow
3. Crown Prince	black	black	red	yellow
4. King's	red	red	none	white
5. Leiningen	red	red	none	yellow
6. Bubenhofen	black	black	red	white

After the Napoleonic Wars, the white breeches were replaced by green ones, with red stripes down the sides. In the period 1814–1826, all the regiments wore red distinctions, like the infantry. A few changes were also made. In 1826 regimental colors, by which the regiments were distinguished up to 1914, were adopted anew: crimson for the 1st and 2nd regiments; pink for the 3rd and 6th; and red for the 4th and 5th. The odd-numbered regiments had yellow metal buttons; the even-numbered ones, white metal ones. In the corners of the jackets that were introduced at the same time, the odd-numbered regiments wore a crown, the even-numbered ones, a lion. The shoulder scales were of white metal (Fig. 64c). The jackets were later replaced by tunics. *Jäger* helmets were adopted in place of the crested helmets in 1848; these had white metal bars at the sides, a characteristic of the *chevau-léger* helmet that was retained. A brass binding was added around the front peak. The colored lapels were only worn buttoned back for full dress. On service, a short jacket with cuffs of basic color and collar of the regimental color was worn in place of the tunic (Fig. 64d). Several changes were made in 1872. From that date, the *chevau-légers* wore shoulder straps in the regimental color in place of the white metal shoulder scales. The trousers remained green, but were worn with knee boots in the Prussian fashion. The helmet had a crowned "L" on the front and retained the side bars and peak binding, but in full dress the upright plume was replaced by a drooping one of white horsehair (Fig. 64e). Later the crested helmet was replaced by the spiked helmet, ornamented as for the Bavarian infantry. In full dress it had a white hair plume depending from the spike. The green shabraques, which after 1872 had rounded ends, were edged in the regimental color, with a crown in the corners. They were now only worn for full dress. From 1890 lances, with pennants in the national colors of white and blue, were carried, as in the cavalry as a whole (Fig. 64f). The 7th Regiment (raised 1905) and the 8th (raised 1909) had white distinctions and yellow and white metal buttons respectively. The 1910 service dress for *chevau-légers* had the same cut and distinctive colors as before. The collar was of the stand-and-fall type. On the 1915 uniform, the 1st and 2nd regiments wore orange distinctions in place of carmine. The shoulder straps were wholly colored and bore no numerals. All Bavarian cavalry had steel green piping in memory of the old coat color. The trousers piping was in the distinctive color.

V. HUSSARS AND LANCERS

In 1688 *Generaladjutant* Lidl von Borbula raised a hussar regiment known as the *Baron Lidlische Grännitz-Hungarn zu Pferdt*. The uniform was blue, with red boots. At the beginning of the eighteenth century another regiment, the Hussar Regiment von Locatelli, was formed. It wore blue dolmans with white loopings; white pear-shaped buttons; blue breeches, and silver-and-white worsted sashes. The caps were of fox fur with blue bags; the sabertaches were blue, ornamented with white, and the shabraques were blue, edged with white.

At the end of December 1813 a Bavarian *Land-Husarenkorps* was raised; it was divided into two line hussar regiments in 1815. Like the earlier Bavarian hussars, this corps wore blue dolmans with white loopings. The breeches were blue also. The collar and cuffs were likewise blue; the sash, blue and white. The *Landhusaren* wore white pelisses, which were changed for blue ones in 1814. Both the line hussar regiments also had blue pelisses. The 1st Regiment wore black chacos and the 2nd, red. The chacos and white pelisses had similarly colored cords annd loopings (Fig. 64g). At first the shabraques were blue with white edging stripes, but from the beginning of 1814, red ones with a white edging were worn. The sabertaches were black, with the crowned cipher "MK." The chaco plumes were white over blue. Both regiments were disbanded in 1822.

Lancers: A regiment of lancers was raised in 1813. Its uniform was based on the Austrian pattern. The *kurtka* and overalls were green, the latter having leather strapping around the ankles; the collar, lapels, cuffs, and piping on the back and sleeve seams, as well as the trousers stripes, were light blue at first, but were changed to red in 1814. The lancer cap had a light-yellow top and an upright white horsehair plume for the men, a drooping feather plume for the officers. The shoulder scales and buttons were white metal. The girdle was striped blue and white, and the lances had white-over-blue pennants (Fig. 64h). The lancers were disbanded in 1822 and not reformed until 1863, when two regiments were raised. The uniform was all green, of exactly the same style as that worn by the *chevau-légers*; the distinctions were crimson. The 1st Regiment had yellow metal buttons, the 2nd, white. The lancer cap was covered with red cloth and had the royal cipher in front. A short white horsehair plume was worn; and on service, a cap cover (Fig. 64h). The lancers were disbanded in 1822 and not reformed until 1863, when two regiments were raised. The uniform was all green, of exactly the same style as that worn by the *chevau-légers*; the distinctions were crimson. The 1st Regiment had yellow metal buttons, the 2nd, white. The lancer cap was covered with red cloth and had the royal cipher in front. A short white horsehair plume was worn; and on service, a cap cover (Fig. 64i). In undress, a short jacket, as already described for the *chevau-légers*, was worn. In 1872 the uniform underwent the same changes as for the *chevau-légers*. Shoulder straps were introduced in place of the shoulder scales, but were later in turn superseded by Prussian-type epaulettes. The lancer cap, too, was changed to the Prussian pattern, but the regimental distinctions remained as before. The Bavarian lancers were distinguished from the Prussian ones by their green coats, by the cockade and cap plate, and also by not wearing the girdle; instead, they wore the white sword belt over the lancer jacket (Fig. 64k). On the 1910 service dress they only differed from the Prussians in having a stand-and-fall collar. The 1915 service dress was the same as the Prussian one. The shoulder straps were carmine, with steel green piping and no numerals.

VI. ARTILLERY, PIONEERS, AND TRANSPORT CORPS

The artillery uniform was originally bluish-gray with blue distinctions. From 1791 it was dark blue with black distinctions, and in the same year the Rumford helmet with black horsehair *crinière* was adopted. The light-gray breeches were worn with Hungarian boots. White accoutrements replaced the former yellow ones. Later, red piping was added to the black distinctions. The buttons were yellow metal. The development of the uniform was exactly as in the infantry, except that the various patterns of crested helmet had side bars like those of the *chevau-légers*. The plume on the left side was red (Fig. 65e). The horse artillery, whose jackets were cut like those of the *chevau-légers*, wore drooping hair plumes on their crested helmets. Yellow metal shoulder scales were worn by both the horse and foot artillery. Later, on dismounted parades, the horse artillery wore dark blue trousers with broad red stripes. With the introduction of the tunic, the same changes as described in the foregoing sections were made. In 1872, among other alterations, the shoulder scales were

Fig. 65. Germany. Bavaria—Miscellaneous.
a: light infantry. b: *Jäger*. c, d: halberdiers. e: foot artillery. f, g: horse artillery. h: officer, pontooneers. i: private, engineers. k: pioneer. l: general officer.

186

abolished and red shoulder straps were substituted. A Prussian-pattern helmet was introduced, and the uniform consisted of a dark blue coat and trousers with red piping. Collar, cuffs, and cuff patches were black, piped red; the buttons were yellow metal, and the helmet was as for the Bavarian infantry, with the spike and not a ball. In full dress, the horse artillery wore red plumes. The officers' pouch belts were of red leather, covered with gold lace embroidered through with blue.

The pioneers wore a uniform very similar to that of the artillery, the main difference being that they had white metal buttons. In 1822 a Pontoon Company, Miners Company, and Sapper Company were raised. They adopted a dark blue uniform with black cloth collar and cuffs. The Pontoon Company wore white metal buttons, the others, yellow ones. The crested helmet had a yellow metal plate; the distinctions were, for the Miners, a red-over-black plume and crossed pickaxes on the skirts of the coatee; Sappers, a black-over-red plume and gabions on the skirts; the Pontoon Company, a light-blue plume and anchors on the skirts. Both the Miners and Sappers later adopted white metal buttons. Leather equipment was white. The other changes in uniform were as given above. In 1914 the pioneers' uniform differed from that of the Prussians only in having dark blue trousers and differently shaped helmet plate.

The lines-of-communication troops likewise followed the Prussian pattern, except that the light-gray shoulder straps were introduced at a later date. Transport troops had blue uniforms at first and light-gray ones later, with blue distinctions. The men wore the curved infantry saber on a black belt over the shoulder; officers had cavalry-pattern sabers; and from 1812 a cartridge box with white ornamentation. In 1822 they went into dark blue uniforms with self-colored distinctions and red piping. Yellow metal buttons and shoulder scales were worn. The other developments in their dress were as for the artillery. In 1914 the uniform was almost the same as that of the Prussian Transport Corps, except that the trousers were dark blue like the tunic, and the shabraque was of the Bavarian type. A spiked helmet, similar to that used by the Bavarian infantry, was worn.

All these formations wore the 1910 Prussian-pattern service dress. In the field artillery, the shoulder straps were in the corps color (cf. Bavarian infantry). The 1915 service dress was also of Prussian pattern.

VII. COURT GUARDS AND GENERAL OFFICERS; DISTINCTIONS OF RANK

The *Leibgarde der Hartschiere* (Lifeguard of Halberdiers) was a very old formation whose origins dated back to the Middle Ages. In early times there were carabiniers and grenadiers in addition to the halberdiers. All of these troops were mounted. The uniform was blue, richly ornamented with silver. The halberdiers had red, silver-edged surcoats, the carabiniers and grenadiers, blue ones. Apart from the frequent changes in style, the uniform worn by the halberdiers remained the same from the mid-eighteenth century down to 1852, except that in the early part of the period they had red surtouts and a black cockade and no plume in the hat. They rode black horses. The shabraques were blue, of velvet for officers. Later, the guard was made a permanently dismounted formation, but still retained its riding boots and spurs. Fig. 65c shows the court dress uniform, which was superseded in 1852. The silver-laced hat had a white-over-light-blue plume; the coatee was light blue, with yellow skirt turnbacks, black collar, lapels, and cuffs with silver edging; silver epaulettes without fringes; yellow knee breeches; white stockings; and buckled shoes. The sword was worn on a black, silver-laced belt. A cassock, striped with light blue and black, with silver edging and yellow lining, was worn over the coatee. The normal everyday uniform consisted of a hat, coatee, sword, and sword belt as described above, and white breeches and long riding boots with jack spurs. The black, silver-edged carbine belt and pouch belt were worn crossed. Both a sword and carbine were carried. In court dress, a richly ornamented glaive—a pole-arm with a knife-shaped blade—was carried. Queues were not abolished until 1825.

The 1852-pattern uniform consisted of, for court dress, a light-blue tunic with black collar and cuffs with silver lace loops, and with silver lace loops down the front of the tunic as well. A white *Supraweste*, with the star of the Order of St. Hubert on the front, was worn over the tunic. The padded shoulder wings were silver and light blue. Breeches and gauntlets were white. The long boots were light gray in color. The white metal helmet with yellow metal mounts completed the uniform (Fig. 65d). The glaive, and a sword on a black, silver-laced belt, were carried. For normal dress, the tunic was worn with white breeches, long black boots with jack spurs, and a belt, of the color of the sword belt, over the left shoulder. A white hair plume was worn on the helmet in place of the lion.

With the introduction of the universal uniform in 1790, general officers adopted a uniform that resembled that of the rest of the army in style and color. They were distinguished by having a number of embroidered button loops on the lapels. General officers retained their cocked hats and swords. Blue uniforms were introduced in 1799. The coatee had red collar, lapels, and cuffs, and rich silver embroidery. The hat had a feather plume and lace edging. The general staff wore the same uniform, with violet distinctions, and silver lace loops around their buttonholes. Shoulder cords were worn, and white waistcoats and breeches, and thigh-length boots. Sashes were worn as a mark of rank, and when these were laid aside in 1812, general officers, ADCs, the general staff, and officers of the halberdiers retained them. ADCs wore them over the shoulder. By an Order of 1826, field marshals were to wear light-blue coatees with a row of white metal buttons, and red collars and cuffs with silver embroidery, and with silver embroidery of a distinctive pattern down the front of the coat as well. The hat had silver lace and white plumage. White breeches and riding boots were also worn. General officers wore single-breasted light-blue coatees with red collars and cuffs, with silver embroidery. The silver epaulettes had no bullions. The trousers were light blue with narrow red piping. The unlaced hat had a light-blue-and-white feather plume. The uniforms of general officers and ADCs were similar, but with gold embroidery and yellow metal buttons. Later, the tunic, with the same distinctions as hitherto, replaced the coatee. General officers wore cocked hats with a white-and-blue feather plume up to 1812. In the meantime, the details of the uniform had come more and more to resemble the corresponding Prussian uniform. Broad red stripes were added at each side of the piping on the breeches. The general staff wore crimson distinctions, as in Prussia. On the

1910-pattern service dress, general officers retained their white metal buttons, and Bavarian-pattern generals' embroidery on their collar patches. The 1915 uniform was entirely of the Prussian model, even to the generals' embroidery, but they still had white metal buttons.

The distinctions of rank were latterly as worn throughout the German armies. From 1802 to 1872, however, another system of differentiation of rank obtained. Junior lieutenants had a narrow gold or silver loop on the collar; senior lieutenants had two, and captains of infantry and cavalry, three. Field officers in addition had a gold or silver lace edging around the collar, and majors had one, lieutenant colonels two, and colonels three narrow lace loops. The noncommissioned ranks were denoted in the same way by loops of yellow or white worsted; lance corporals had a narrow loop, corporals the same, but with a narrow yellow or white lace stripe around the edge of the collar; sergeants had two and senior sergeants, three narrow lace loops. Prior to 1872, bandsmen did not wear wings but had lace around their collars and cuffs. In addition, the drum major had shoulder scales. The oboe players had no lace, but wore shoulder scales as well. The director of music wore two lace stripes around the collar and cuffs. Trumpeters in the cavalry and artillery also had hanging sleeves, ornamented with lace.

In 1872 gorgets were abolished and sashes reintroduced for officers.

BRUNSWICK

Cockade: black at first; later, light blue and yellow

In the eighteenth century, because of the close ties between the Brunswick ruling house and the Prussian army, the uniform of the Brunswick troops was exactly like that of Prussia. Fron 1697 the infantry wore blue coats with red, yellow, or white distinctions; these were originally displayed by the waistcoat and stockings, and from 1730 by the lapels.

In 1756 the distinctions were as follows.

REGIMENT	CUFFS, ETC.	BUTTONS
Leib regiment*	red	yellow
Behr	red	white
Imhoff	white	yellow
Zastrow	yellow	white

*no lapels; white lace loops

In 1806 there were two infantry regiments. These were distinguished as follows: Warmstedt, red distinctions and white lace loops; Griesheim, red distinctions, lapels edged with white lace with a blue figure. The 1st Regiment had yellow metal buttons and the 2nd, white. The grenadiers wore Prussian-type fur caps with plate, and patch at the back. The Black Corps had a unique uniform. The corps was raised by

189

Frederick William Duke of Brunswick-Oels in Bohemia in 1809, and achieved fame for its march to the mouth of the Weser. The infantry (Fig. 66a) wore a long-skirted black coat with a light-blue collar and six rows of black loops, with three rows of olivets, across the front. Trousers and leather equipment were also black. The chaco had a drooping black hair plume, and a white metal skull and crossbones on the front. The hussars (Fig. 66i) were similarly dressed but had black dolmans with light-blue collars and cuffs instead of coats. Sashes were light blue and yellow. The lancers (Fig. 66h) had green jackets, girdles, breeches, and shabraques, red distinctions and edgings, yellow metal buttons, and lancer caps with a yellow upper part, yellow lines, and white metal skull badge. The artillery was dressed like the infantry, but in jackets instead of long coats, with black loopings and light-blue skirt turnbacks, cuffs, and shoulder straps. The Black Corps also had a company of sharpshooters (Fig. 66b) who wore green jackets with red distinctions and yellow metal buttons. The hats had a green band and edging. The corps entered British pay and saw service in Spain, Portugal, and Italy. During that time, the officers and NCOs wore British distinctions of rank. Officers and sergeants wore crimson sashes, the latter with a stripe the same color as the collar, along the center. After the return of the Duke to his own territory in 1814, the Brunswick army was reorganized. In 1815 the infantry considered of a Light Infantry Brigade and a Line Brigade. The *Leibbataillon*, which belonged to the former, retained a uniform similar to the former one: black jackets with black loops, light-blue collar and shoulder straps, black trousers, and chacos with a fairly broad crown, black plume, and skull badge. The other light battalions had the same uniform, but with differently colored collars and shoulder straps. On their chacos they had a white metal *Jäger* horn, and a yellow-over-light-blue pear-shaped plume. The distinctions were, for the 1st Battalion, originally light blue, then light orange, and eventually pink; for the 2nd, yellow; and for the 3rd, orange. The line battalions

Fig. 66. Germany. Brunswick.

a, c, e, f, g: infantry. b: sharpshooter. d: *Jäger*. h: lancer. i, k, l: hussars. m: artillery.

190

(Fig. 66c) wore the same uniform, except that on the chaco they had a small white metal plate bearing the rearing horse, and a light-blue-over-yellow plume. The distinctions were red for the 1st Battalion; green for the 2nd; and white for the 3rd. The hussars were dressed exactly as before, except that the cuffs were black. The lancers had black jackets and trousers, light-blue distinctions, and lancer caps. The *Avantgarde* Battalion of *Schützentruppen* had bluish-gray uniforms with green distinctions; green plumes and hat lace, and white metal buttons (Fig. 66d). The artillery had black gaiters with yellow piping and chacos, with the skull and black plume for the horse artillery and with grenade and yellow pear-shaped plume for the foot artillery.

In 1823 a uniform of Prussian-pattern was introduced, the *Leibbataillon* alone retaining the old black and light-blue clothing. In 1830 (Fig. 66f) the infantry wore dark blue jackets with red collar, cuffs, and skirt edging and white guard lace and buttons. The gray trousers had red piping; white ones were worn in summer. The chacos had white cords and white-over-light-blue plumes. The Grenadier Battalion (Fig. 66e) wore Austrian-type fur caps with a red and white backing, and white metal plate and chinscales. The knapsack was worn on very narrow belts, and to distribute the load on the shoulders, there were broad leather pads through which the straps were slotted (Fig. 66f).

In 1843 the infantry adopted a frogged jacket, in memory of the old uniform. It was black in color, like the trousers, and the collar and cuffs were light blue. The buttons were of black glass. A chaco, with horizontal peak and black hair plume, was worn (Fig. 66g). In 1872 this was changed to a kepilike chaco similar to that worn by the Prussian *Jäger*. On 18 March 1866 Prussian pattern uniforms were introduced, but the old ones were permitted to be worn for a time, and they were not finally given up until 11 April 1892. From then, the Brunswick Infantry Regiment No. 92 was differentiated by the star or the skull and crossbones on the helmet eagle, by white shoulder straps with the crowned letter "W," and by light-blue piping around the cuff patches. In the 1830s the hussars (Fig. 66k) wore all-blue uniforms with yellow loopings and red cap bags and trousers piping. In 1850 the basic color was changed to black. Up to 1914 the regimental uniform differed in several respects from that of the Prussian hussars. The skull was worn on the fur cap from 1883; they had black pouch belts; light-blue and white sashes; and red sabertaches bearing a yellow "W" crowned. The regiment was numbered 17. The lance pennants were as in Prussia, and later blue and yellow. In the 1830s, the artillery was dressed like the infantry (Fig. 66m), but with yellow lace and loops and buttons. Crested helmets were worn. Tunics were introduced later, their basic color being changed to black, as in the infantry, in 1850. Yellow piping was worn, in memory of the artillery of the former Black Corps. The Brunswick Artillery adopted its corresponding Prussian-type uniform before the infantry.

GRAND DUCHY OF CLEVE-BERG

Cockade: blue and white

The fortunes of this Grand Duchy during the period of the Rhine Confederation are rather similar to those of the Kingdom of Westphalia. The infantry wore white jackets with light-blue collars, lapels, cuffs, and skirt turnbacks. The buttons were yellow metal, the undergarments white. Chacos were worn; the grenadiers originally wore fur caps with a red plume, and later, chacos. The distinctions of the grenadiers and *voltigeurs* were as in France. The officers had coatees with pointed lapels. From its formation in 1807, the *chevau-légers* regiment wore, in full dress, white *kurtkas*, and in undress gray waistcoats, both with pink distinctions, white epaulettes and white metal buttons, and lancer caps. In 1809, as *chasseurs à cheval*, they were dressed like their French counterpart, in green uniforms with pink distinctions, and chacos. In 1810, as a lancer regiment, they were equipped with lances. After the separation of the regiment into two regiments of *chevau-légers-lanciers*, lancer caps were adopted. The artillery had blue jackets with blue lapels and breeches. Collar, cuffs, skirt lining, and piping were red, with blue cuff patches and yellow metal buttons. The chaco had red cords.

FRANKFURT AM MAIN

Cockade: black; later, red and white

In 1806 Frankfurt am Main, under Prince Primas von Dalberg, had to provide a contingent of troops for the Rhine Confederation. The uniform of the fusiliers (Fig. 67a) consisted of a white Austrian-style coat, with red distinctions and white metal buttons. The leather equipment was white, as were the breeches, with black gaiters. The hat had a black cockade. The *Jäger* (Fig. 67b) wore a coat similar to the French *surtout*, which was green like the breeches. The all-green distinctions had red piping around them. The buttons were white metal; the waistcoat was yellow; the leather equipment and gaiters were black. The green chaco had a black plume and white-and-red cords. In 1808–1809 the uniform was completely assimilated to the French one. The dark blue coat was cut like a *surtout*, and had a self-colored collar. The pointed lapels, cuffs, and skirt linings were red. The piping and buttons were white. The chaco had a small white metal plate on the front and a black cockade. The distinctions of the fusiliers, grenadiers, and *voltigeurs* were as in the French infantry. The blue breeches were worn with black gaiters (Fig. 67c), but blue cloth or white linen overalls were normally worn.

The contingent that Frankfurt raised for the later German Confederation wore dark blue jackets and trousers with red distinctions and piping, white metal buttons, white chaco cords and leather accoutrements, a yellow metal chaco plate, and white pompon with a red tuft (Fig. 67d). The *Schützen* had green collars and cuffs and shoulder straps, with red piping. The chaco cords and pompon were also green. A

Fig. 67. Germany. Frankfurt am Main—Infantry.

yellow metal *Jäger* horn, with a cross in the center of the curl, was worn on the front of the chaco. Equipment was of black leather. Later, tunics and helmets of Prussian type were introduced (Fig. 67c). The basic color of the coat was blue, with red distinctions and white metal buttons, and trousers as in Prussia. The helmet plate was of yellow metal.

HANOVER

Cockade: black up to 1803; after the Napoleonic Wars, black, yellow, and white

I. INFANTRY

Up to 1837 the basic color of the uniform was predominantly red. The distinctive colors of the regiments varied. To begin with, a plain single-breasted coat was worn (Fig. 68a). In 1727 half lapels were introduced (Fig. 68b). In 1730 the cuffs were made the same color as the waistcoat, which had been the means of differentiating the regiments prior to then. The waistcoats and skirt turnbacks were made a light color in 1761. In 1763 the distinctions on the red coats were as follows.

REGIMENT	CUFFS, LAPELS	HAT LACE, BUTTONS, AND LOOPS	SKIRT TURNBACKS AND WAISTCOAT
Guard	dark blue	yellow	light yellow
v. Scheither	green	yellow	light yellow
v. Otten	white	yellow	white
v. Spörcken	dull yellow	yellow	dull yellow
v. Schele	straw yellow	white	straw yellow
v. Reden	black	white	white

(continued)

193

REGIMENT	CUFFS, LAPELS	HAT LACE, BUTTONS, AND LOOPS	SKIRT TURNBACKS AND WAISTCOAT
v. d. Schulenburg	black	yellow	light yellow
v. Bock	dark blue	white	white
v. Craushaar	black	white	light yellow
v. Laffert	yellow	white	white
v. Behr	orange	yellow	light yellow
v. Hardenberg	orange	white	white
v. Linsingen	yellow	white	white
v. Wangenheim	straw yellow	white	straw yellow
v. Plessen	light ocher	yellow	light ocher
v. Rhoeden	white	white	white
v. Block	white	white	white
v. Wurmb	green	white	white
v. Zastrow	green	white	white
Prince of Mecklenburg-Strelitz	green	white	white
1st New Battalion	red	white	white
v. Goldacker	yellow	yellow	dull yellow
de la Chevallerie	yellow	yellow	dull yellow
v. Kielmansegg	grass green	white	white
v. Estorff	grass green	white	white
v. Ahlefeld	blue	white	white
2nd New Battalion	red	white	white

The coats were ordered to have waist-length lapels in 1766 (Fig. 68c). In 1790 a new garment, cut like a coatee, was introduced, and soon after, lapels were abolished altogether for the men. Thenceforth, the coat was fastened by a single row of buttons, with corresponding white lace loops. In 1793 the infantry took into wear greatcoats, long breeches, and half gaiters. The shape of the hat, which was edged with lace, was altered in the same year. From 1800 the coats were made with high stand collars. The grenadiers, who had worn pointed grenadier caps from 1701, adopted bearskin caps in 1785. Leather accoutrements were yellow up to 1785 and thereafter white. From 1705 officers wore yellow sashes over the right shoulder, and from 1773, around the waist. An embroidered epaulette was worn on the right shoulder; field officers (and all officers after 1785) wore two. The hat cockade, which was only worn by officers, was black.

After the occupation of the country by the French in 1803, a great many men of the former regiments escaped to Britain, to join the King's German Legion, which was being formed in British pay. Its uniform was exactly the same as that of the British infantry, and consisted of a red jacket with a row of white metal buttons, blue collar, cuffs, and shoulder straps (in Britain, nearly all "royal" regiments had blue distinctions), with white lace with a blue stripe. The skirt turnbacks were blue; the trousers gray, and the gaiters black. The headdress was the chaco of the pattern worn by the British infantry (Fig. 68d). The battalion companies wore small white worsted fringes on their shoulder straps. The flank companies had dark blue wings ornamented with white lace and a short white fringe. The water bottle was a small barrel painted light blue, and it remained a feature of the Hanoverian army up to its demise in 1866. After the Napoleonic Wars, the uniform altered somewhat. Dark blue cuff patches were added, and two lace loops on each side of the collar. The trousers were changed to light blue. Chacos with yellow metal plates, white cords, and a black, yellow, and white cockade, were worn (Fig. 68e). The Guard Grenadier Battalion had fur caps. In 1837 the uniform was altered to the Prussian model. Dark blue jackets with self-colored cuff patches were introduced (Fig. 68f). Only the Guard Regiment had Swedish cuffs. The collar, cuffs, and skirt turnbacks were red; the shoulder straps were white for the Guard Regiment; red for the 2nd and 3rd infantry regiments, yellow for the 4th and 5th, and light blue for the 6th and 7th. The Guard Regiment had white guard lace loops; the others, yellow. The trousers were gray piped with red. The buttons were the same color as the lace loops. In 1849 (Fig. 68g) tunics of the same colors and spiked helmets were adopted. On the latter, the Guard had the George star; the other regiments, the leaping white horse. In full dress, the Guard wore white hair plumes. In 1858 kepis of the shape of the Austrian chacos were introduced. The braces of the *Gürtelrustüng*, which had been issued in the meantime, were of a distinctive type. In 1866 leather leggings were worn. For everyday use, and on service, the chacos were worn in a cover (Fig. 68h). The flat-topped caps were replaced by caps of Austrian type. Officers left off wearing their epaulettes at the beginning of the campaign of 1866.

II. LIGHT INFANTRY AND *JÄGER*

In 1791 the 14th Light Infantry Regiment had long gray coats with green distinctions, while the *Jäger* had all-green uniforms. Both wore Corsican hats with a red, white, and green plume. The two light battalions of the King's German Legion wore a uniform similar to that of the British Rifle Regiments. The 1st Light Battalion had dark green jackets with a row of white metal buttons; black collar, cuffs, and

Fig. 68. Germany. Hanover—Infantry, *Jäger*, Artillery.
a: infantry corporal. b, c, d, e, f, g, h: infantry. i, k, l: light infantry and *Jäger*.
m, n, o: artillery.

shoulder straps with tufts. The chacos were tapered, and had a short black plume and cords, with a white metal *Jäger* horn. The leather equipment was black. Hangers with plain knuckle bows were carried. The breeches were as for the line infantry. Officers had two rows of white metal buttons, silver wings on the shoulders, black pouch belts, red hussar sashes, and sabers worn on slings. The 2nd Light Battalion differed from the 1st in having three rows of white metal buttons, black worsted fringes on the shoulder straps instead of wings, and black ball tufts instead of plumes (Fig. 68i). The officers were dressed like those of the 1st Battalion, but had black hussar-type loopings and three rows of buttons on their jackets, and no wings. After the Napoleonic Wars, they wore light-blue trousers and chacos like those worn by the line. The basic color of the jackets remained green, with black distinctions, and white metal buttons. The chaco cords were black. The Guard *Jäger* had a single row of buttons on their jackets, a pocket with a button on each breast, and wings on the shoulders. Shoulder belts were worn, and a narrow waistbelt with a cartridge box in front. The hanger had a bayonet scabbard attached to it. Both the other battalions had two rows of buttons, black cuff patches, and black crescents, edged green, on the shoulders (Fig. 68k). Hangers were not carried, only bayonets. In 1837 the Guard *Jäger* adopted red piping around the black distinctions. From that date the trousers were gray, as for the line infantry. Tunics were issued in 1849, the combination of colors remaining black and green, with white metal buttons, and red piping for the Guard *Jäger*. The kepis had a black hair plume, which was always worn (Fig. 68l).

III. CAVALRY

Cuirasses were abolished for heavy cavalry in 1683. In 1698 the uniform of the *Leibreuter* Regiment was red with dark blue distinctions and yellow buttons. The regiment had worn a white and yellow uniform prior to that. The other *Reiter* regiments for the most part had white coats. The distinctive colors varied from regiment to regiment. At the beginning of the eighteenth century, the hats were of white, and later of black, felt (Fig. 69a). Several volunteer corps were raised during the Seven Years' War. The Luckner Hussars wore green, later white, dolmans, with green and red pelisses respectively, with yellow loopings. They had *Flügelmützen* to begin with, and later, fur caps. The Freytag Mounted *Jäger* wore all-green uniforms with white metal buttons, and hats. The Scheither Carabiniers had straw yellow jackets with green distinctions, and hats.

Between 1761 and 1768 the basic color of the uniform was changed to dark blue, except for the mounted *Leibgarde*, which retained its red uniform up to 1799, changing in that year to dark blue. After the Seven Years' War, the light dragoons adopted helmets with a comb and red horsehair plume, like those of the British light dragoons (Fig. 69c). At the dissolution of the army in 1803, the distinctions were as follows.

REGIMENT	DISTINCTIONS	BUTTONS
Leibgarde	red	yellow
1st Cavalry Regiment	red	white
2nd Cavalry Regiment	white	yellow
3rd Cavalry Regiment	yellow	white
		(*continued*)

REGIMENT	DISTINCTIONS	BUTTONS
4th Cavalry Regiment	white	white
5th (Dragoon Regiment)	white	white
6th (Dragoon Regiment)	yellow	white
7th (Dragoon Regiment)	yellow	white
8th (Dragoon Regiment)	red	yellow
9th (Light Dragoon Regiment)	red	yellow
10th (Light Dragoon Regiment)	red	white

In the King's German Legion there were two dragoon regiments that were dressed and equipped as heavy cavalry from 1803 to 1813, and thereafter as light cavalry. From 1803 they wore red jackets with red shoulder straps and wings, with yellow edgings, and yellow lace loops down the front. The 1st Regiment had dark blue distinctions, the 2nd, black. The breeches and leather equipment were white. They wore hats with a red and white feather plume (Fig. 69d). In 1814 the uniform was changed, and both regiments were re-equipped as British light dragoons (Fig. 69e). The new uniform consisted of a dark blue jacket with white breeches; red collar, lapels, cuffs, and skirt turnbacks; and a red and blue girdle. The buttons, epaulettes, and chaco fittings were of yellow metal for the 1st Regiment, white metal for the 2nd. With both the heavy and light cavalry uniforms they wore gray overalls to protect the breeches, which were worn with long boots. Three light dragoon regiments, dressed as hussars, also formed part of the legion (Fig. 69f). The dolman and pelisse were dark blue. White breeches were worn with hussar boots in full dress; gray overalls were worn on service. The 1st Regiment had red collar and cuffs; the 2nd, white; the 3rd, yellow. The loopings were yellow for the 1st and 2nd regiments,

Fig. 69. Germany. Hanover—Cavalry.

a: heavy cavalry. b, k, m: dragoons. c: officer of light dragoons. d: heavy dragoon. e: light dragoon. f, i, l: hussars. g: lancer. h: *Leib-Kurassier*. n: *garde du corps*.

197

and white for the 3rd. The 1st Regiment wore broad-crowned fur caps; the 2nd and 3rd wore narrower ones with leather peaks. All three had red bags and red and white plumes.

In 1813, three new hussar regiments, independent of the legion, were raised. The Lüneburg Regiment wore dark blue dolmans and red pelisses, with red collar and cuffs, and white loopings. The gray trousers had red stripes for the men, and silver for the officers. The gray fur caps had light-blue bags. The Bremen and Verden Hussars had green dolmans with red distinctions, red pelisses, white loopings; the 1st Squadron had chacos with black lace, and the 4th, chacos with red lace. The 2nd and 3rd had gray fur caps with red bags. The trousers were as above. The Duke of Cumberland Volunteer Hussar Regiment was dressed in green dolmans and pelisses, with red collars and cuffs; chacos with yellow lace; and gray trousers with yellow stripes.

In 1816 the cavalry was re-formed. The Guard Cuirassier Regiment (later *Garde du Corps*) wore white jackets with red distinctions and yellow lace; yellow metal cuirasses, and high helmets with a comb and *chenille*. The *Leib* Cuirassier Regiment had white jackets with blue distinctions and yellow lace, black cuirasses, and helmets with a comb and *chenille* (Fig. 69h). The Guard Hussar Regiment wore the uniform of the 1st Hussar Regiment of the King's German Legion; the 2nd and 3rd, the same uniform as the corresponding regiments of the legion, but now with broader-crowned fur caps without peaks. The 4th Hussar Regiment wore dark blue pelisses and dolmans with red distinctions and white loopings, and fur caps as for the other regiments. The 1st Lancer Regiment had green jackets and trousers, with red distinctions, yellow metal buttons, white and yellow girdles, and red lancer caps (Fig. 69g). The 2nd Lancer Regiment was dressed similarly, but with black lancer caps. In 1833 the whole of the cavalry was turned into dragoons. The *Garde du Corps* did away with its cuirasses. Dark blue jackets were introduced, and light-blue trousers. A black helmet with a comb and black *chenille* was worn (Fig. 69k).

REGIMENT	DISTINCTIONS	BUTTONS AND LACE LOOPS
Garde du Corps	red	yellow
King's Dragoons	red	yellow
Queen's Dragoons	white	yellow
Cambridge Dragoons	yellow	white

The new arm was soon increased. In 1838 the *Garde du Corps* wore white jackets with red distinctions and white lace loops, and helmets like those of the Prussian cuirassiers. The Guard Cuirassier Regiment had white jackets with cornflower blue distinctions and yellow lace loops. Both regiments adopted cuirasses again. The Guard Hussar Regiment was dressed in blue pelisses and dolmans, with yellow loopings, and red chacos. The Queen's Hussar Regiment had blue dolmans and pelisses, but with white loopings and crimson chacos. The Cambridge Dragoons wore dark blue jackets with light-blue distinctions and white metal buttons. The Crown Prince Dragoons had dark blue uniforms, white distinctions, and yellow metal buttons. The King's Dragoons wore dark blue, with red distinctions and yellow metal buttons; the *Leib-Dragoner*, dark blue, with yellow distinctions and white metal buttons. All dragoon regiments wore black chacos.

Tunics superseded the jackets in 1849. Those of the *Garde du Corps* were of the same colors as before. They also wore steel helmets with yellow metal mounts. White horsehair plumes were worn in full dress. The cuirasses, as before, were of yellow metal, with a white metal sunburst ornament on the front (Fig. 69n). The Guard Cuirassier Regiment likewise wore its old uniform colors, the same helmets as the *Garde du Corps*, and black cuirasses with a yellow metal star. The Guard Hussars and the Queen's Hussars, too, wore their former uniform colors. From 1847 fur caps, with red and crimson bags respectively, were worn (Fig. 69i). The Cambridge Dragoons had light-blue tunics with crimson distinctions and white buttons and lace loops. Spiked helmets, of black lacquered tin, not leather, with the device of a leaping horse on the front, were worn (Fig. 69m). White horsehair plumes were worn in full dress. The Crown Prince Dragoons had light-blue tunics with white distinctions and spiked helmets. All the cavalry wore gray trousers as in Prussia. In 1840 a section of *Königs-Gensdarmerie* (a type of dispatch rider) was formed. It wore red dolmans, blue pelisses, yellow loopings, and gray trousers. Its chacos were like those of the Hungarian hussars; red to begin with, and from 1859, black.

IV. ARTILLERY AND ENGINEER CORPS

In the eighteenth century the artillery wore light-blue coats of the same style as those of the infantry. In 1743 the distinctions took the form of red half lapels, waistcoats, and skirt turnbacks, black cuff patches, yellow piping and buttons, and embroidered buttonholes. The breeches were yellow. The hat was edged with yellow lace. The powder flask was worn on a red pouch belt edged with yellow (Fig. 68m). Later, the undergarments were changed to white. The uniform remained much the same, but varied in cut, up to the dissolution of the army in 1803. The uniform of the artillery of the King's German Legion was exactly as in Britain: dark blue, with red distinctions and yellow lace. The foot artillery wore infantry chacos, yellow lace on the jacket, and gray trousers; the horse artillery wore crested "Tarleton" helmets, yellow loopings on the jacket, and overalls as for the cavalry. After the Napoleonic Wars, the artillery was dressed in dark blue jackets with red distinctions. The buttons, lace loops on the collar, and epaulettes were yellow. The chaco had yellow cords (Fig. 68n). In 1838 the distinctions were black, and the shoulder straps and piping were red. In 1849 tunics in the former colors were adopted, and spiked helmets with a yellow metal plate bearing a white metal leaping horse. The girdle was surmounted by a ball. The horse artillery had black hair plumes. Austrian-type chacos were adopted in 1859 (Fig. 68o). In 1862 the horse artillery adopted helmets similar to those worn by the horse artillery of the old legion.

Up to 1803 the engineers wore the same uniform as the artillery. From 1808 an Engineer Corps, consisting only of ten officers, formed part of the King's German Legion. They wore dark red coatees with black collar and cuffs, yellow metal buttons, and gray trousers. The hat had a red and white feather plume and gold loop. After the Napoleonic Wars, the uniform was changed to blue with black distinctions, and yellow metal buttons. Chacos were worn. In 1838 they were dressed like the artillery, but with white metal buttons; in 1849 they adopted tunics and helmets with a ball like those of the artillery but with a white metal plate. In 1859 kepis with a black hair plume were adopted. Equipment was of black leather.

199

THE HANSEATIC TOWNS (BREMEN, HAMBURG, LÜBECK)

Cockade: at first black; later, white with a red cross

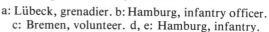

Fig. 70. Germany. Hanseatic Towns

a: Lübeck, grenadier. b: Hamburg, infantry officer. c: Bremen, volunteer. d, e: Hamburg, infantry.

In the eighteenth century the uniform appears to have been generally red. A painted figure of a grenadier in the Museum für Kunst und Kulturgeschichte in Lübeck (Fig. 70a) shows a red coat; white distinctions, undergarments, and buttons; a buff leather pouch belt with yellow metal match case; and a yellow metal cap plate with an orange circle in the center, bearing the Lübeck coat of arms. Fig 70b depicts a Hamburg officer wearing a red coat with a red collar. Collar patches, lapels, and cuffs are light blue, buttons and epaulettes, yellow. The silver gorget bears the Hamburg arms in gilt. The plain hat has a black cockade and gold loop.

Besides the paid troops, there were also Town Guards in the Hanseatic towns. Their uniform, which generally speaking was not subject to any regulations, appears in the case of the officers, at least, to have shown a predilection for red. After Tettenborn and his cossacks had liberated Hamburg, a new Town Guard was formed, the uniform of which, clearly due to the exigencies of the time, appears to have been of a fairly simple kind. For the infantry, it had a long-skirted dark blue coat reaching below the knee, fastened down the front with hooks instead of buttons. The collar and the piping around the dark blue cuffs were light blue; the trousers and peaked cap were dark blue with a light-blue cap band, and there was a white cockade bearing the red Hanseatic cross on the front. The white belts were worn crossed. The artillery wore a similar uniform, but with red instead of light-blue distinctions. The *Jäger* wore long-skirted green coats, with black cord loops across the front, and green caps with a light-blue band and *Jäger* horn, with the cockade and a light-green plume above. The gray trousers had light-green stripes; the cartridge box and sword were worn on a black waistbelt. The dress of the cavalry resembled that of the infantry, except that it had black cord loops across the front of the coat. The cavalry wore a cap like a lancer cap of dark blue, with a light-blue band, yellow cords, white plume, and Hanseatic cockade. The pouch belt was black. When Hamburg was reoccupied by the French, the Town Guard was disbanded.

At the end of 1813, a Hanseatic Town Guard was formed. It adopted dark blue trousers and British-type gray greatcoats and infantry chacos. The infantry had light-blue greatcoat collars and trousers stripes, white helmet cords, and white-over-red plumes. The sharpshooters wore trousers as for the infantry. Their distinctions were green. The artillery had the same distinctions, and red trousers stripes. Their plumes had a white top. They also had red fringed epaulettes. The *Jäger* were dressed like the Hamburg Town Guard, but without the cord loops. The cavalry wore dark blue dolmans and breeches, and flat-topped caps, with light-blue distinctions and black loopings. In addition to sabers, they carried lances with white pennants bearing the red Hanseatic cross. Subsequently, the uniforms of the Hamburg troops changed frequently in detail, but in general the distinctions remained as before: light blue on dark blue for the infantry and cavalry; red for the artillery; and light green on dark green for the *Jäger*. In 1815 the chacos had a very broad crown; from 1853 they were shaped more like a kepi. The Town Guards were disbanded in 1868.

At the same time as the Hamburg Town Guard was raised during the Tettenborn episode, a Hanseatic Legion was formed from volunteers. Its uniform consisted of a long-skirted coat fastened with hooks, trousers, and green flat-topped caps. Collar, sleeve piping, trousers stripes, cap band, and piping around the top were all light blue. The Hanseatic cockade appeared on the cap band. Equipment was of black leather. This uniform was worn by the infantry, artillery, and cavalry, with yellow lace loops on each side of the collar for the infantry and artillery. The cavalry carried lances without pennants. The uniform was altered in 1814. Chacos superseded the caps, and the coats were replaced by jackets. The cavalry was divided into lancers and cossacks. Both wore green uniforms. The lancers had crimson distinctions, white metal buttons, and black lancer caps with a black plume. The lance pennants were red over white. The cossacks had red distinctions and fur caps with a red bag. Their lances had no pennants. The Lübeck Volunteers of 1813 wore long-skirted green coats (hooked down the front) and trousers, with red piping around the green distinctions. They wore high-crowned peaked caps of green basic color with red band and piping, and a yellow metal hunting horn on the band with the Hanseatic cockade above. In 1815 they adopted jackets with red collar and cuffs, gray trousers with red stripes; and similar caps with black plumes. In 1815 the Bremen Volunteer Infantry had black jackets with red distinctions and yellow metal buttons. The chaco had white cords, yellow metal chinscales, and a red-and-white plume (Fig. 70c). The *Jäger* wore dark green jackets with light-blue distinctions, gray trousers with light-green stripes, and Tyrolean hats with a light-green plume like a *chenille*. There was a yellow lace loop on each side of the collar. The cavalry wore long black jackets and trousers, with red distinctions, yellow lace loops on the collar, and yellow metal buttons. They also had black lancer caps and red and white lance pennants. All equipment was of black leather.

During the long peace that followed the Wars of Liberation, the uniforms of all the Hanseatic infantry were green, with red distinctions and yellow metal buttons. The distinctions between Hamburg, Bremen, and Lübeck lay in the different types of pompons, chaco plates, etc. The Hamburg infantry had white leather equipment, the Bremen and Lübeck infantry, black. The chaco cords were white. Gray trousers were worn in winter and white ones in summer (Fig. 70c). The officers had green trousers with red triple stripes. The Hamburg *Schützen* wore green jackets with self-colored shoulder straps and cuff patches, black collar and cuffs, red piping, yellow lace loops on the collar, and yellow metal buttons. The chaco cords and leather equipment were black. The artillery had all-blue uniforms with black distinctions, red piping, red chaco cords, and yellow metal buttons. The cavalry was equipped as dragoons. Its uniform was green with crimson distinctions, white lace loops and epaulettes, and white metal buttons. The trousers were gray, piped with red. The helmet had a comb and black crest. Hamburg had, in addition, a lancer detachment, which wore almost the same uniform, except that it had lancer caps with crimson upper part, white metal mounts, and tall, thin plumes. The crimson girdle was edged with white. The lance pennants were red over white. In the late 1840s and early 1850s the uniform changed with the introduction of the spiked helmet and tunic. The cavalry retained its basic color, but from that time the helmet was of a pattern similar to that worn by the Prussian cuirassiers. The infantry adopted the Virchowsche equipment and, later, kepis in place of helmets (Fig. 70e), the shape of which varied from contingent to contingent. After the Military Convention of 1866, the troops of the Hanseatic Towns formed the 75th and 76th regiments, the uniform distinctions of which are listed under Prussia.

HESSEN-DARMSTADT

Cockade: black up to 1807; thereafter, red and white

The earliest infantry was the *Landausschuss*, a kind of militia, which was organized in 1700 on the lines of the field army. The Obergrafschaft Battalion wore blue coats lined with red baize, with orange cuffs, orange collar four fingers' breadth wide, and orange lapels. There were four pleats in each skirt of the coat, and three dozen tin buttons. The hat had lace four fingers' breadth wide. Breeches and stockings were gray. A musket and sword were carried. The NCOs had blue cuffs and linings. A representation of an officer of the *Landmiliz* (militia) of 1717 shows a dark blue coat with white buttons, white cuffs, and white or silver buttonholes, a white cravat, blue breeches, and red stockings. The hat was edged with silver lace and had red plumage. The sash was silver, red, and blue embroidered. Swords and spontoons were carried. In addition to the sash, officers also wore silver gorgets with the cipher "EL" (Ernst Ludwig) and crown in gold, as a mark of rank. An officer of the Schrautenbach Regiment had a similar uniform, but with red collar and cuffs laced silver (Fig. 71a). At the same period, the Düring Battalion had white uniforms with yellow cuffs; the Dallwig Battalion, white with red; the Lehrbech Battalion, white with blue; the Geismar Battalion, white with green; and the *Kreis-Regiment*, blue with white. This last battalion appears to have worn the same distinctions at the Battle of Rossbach, where it formed part of the Imperial Army and was among the few troops to stand fast. The blue coat had white collar, cuffs, and skirt turnbacks. White lace loops were worn on the chest and on the sleeves above the cuffs. Undergarments, shoulder cords, and buttons were all white. The stock was red. The grenadier caps had pierced yellow metal plates, backed with white; the back part of the cap was red and the tuft white (Fig. 7lb). From 1739 to 1768 the *Leibgrenadierkorps* wore white coats and undergarments, with red collar, lapels,

Fig. 71. Germany. Hessen-Darmstadt.

a: infantry officer. b, c, d, e, f, g: infantry. h: *garde du corps.*
i, k: *chevau-légers.* l: dragoons. m: artillery.

cuffs, and skirt lining, red stocks, yellow buttons, and fur caps with a yellow metal
plate and red bag. The officers wore red undergarments. In other points, the Darm-
stadt infantry was dressed exactly along Prussian lines. Particularly under the *Landgrave* Ludwig IX (1768–1790), who from 1743 to 1757 as *Erbprinz* (heir) was colonel
of the Prussian Infantry Regiment No. 12, even the minor details of dress were made
to correspond to the Prussian fashion, and the Prussian method of drill, and terms of
service, were introduced. The dark blue basic color of the infantry dates from that
period. Toward the end of the eighteenth century, the coat was made more cutaway
in front.

In 1803 the infantry was organized in three brigades, each of three battalions.
All wore white lace, red skirt turnbacks, white undergarments, black gaiters, and a
white-laced hat with red and white tassels at the corners and plume of company color
(Fig. 71c). The little tabs for the button and buttonhole on the turned-back skirts
were of the distinctive color. The 3rd Battalions were called fusiliers, and wore the
distinctive color of the brigade on their green coats. These were: red for the *Leib-
Brigade*; light blue for the *Landgrave*; and yellow for the *Erbprinz*. The knapsack
was worn on a strap over the right shoulder, as in Prussia. During the era of the Confederation of the Rhine, several changes in uniforms were made. In July 1806 the
queue was abolished. Officers were ordered to wear close-fitting breeches in
"Suvarov" boots. Because of frequent misunderstandings on account of their wearing uniforms similar to the Prussians', officers were directed to wear tall black-over-
red feather plumes in their hats, instead of white and black ones, as in Prussia. The
knapsack was provided with two straps and was henceforth worn over both
shoulders. The hat tuft, previously spherical, was now made in the shape of a small
plume, in the company color, as before. Below it was worn the cockade in the ter-

ritorial colors. Previously, only officers had worn a cockade. It had been black. From 1808 the sword belt was worn over the shoulder, not around the waist. In the same year the men adopted blue breeches and shorter gaiters. Long blue or white linen overalls were worn over them on the march. The 3rd (Fusilier) Battalions were disbanded. In 1809 chacos with a leather chinstrap, small white metal plate, and cockade and double pompon were introduced (Fig. 71d). The top part of the pompon was red, the lower part in the company color: 1st Company, white; 2nd, black; 3rd, blue; 4th, red; 5th, yellow and white; 6th, black and white; 7th, blue and white; and 8th, red and white. The brigades were again turned into regiments. The *Leibgarde* Regiment and the *Leibregiment* each consisted of two battalions, each of four companies; but in 1809 the *Erbprinz* Regiment adopted the French organization, i.e., two battalions, each of six companies, with a grenadier company and a *voltigeur* company in each. At the same time, several characteristics of the French uniform were copied. The grenadiers adopted red plumes and chaco cords, and red fringed epaulettes. *Voltigeurs* had green ones, and green epaulettes with yellow crescents. The lapels were only buttoned back for full dress, and the lace edging, except on the lapels, was abolished. This regiment wore Hungarian-type gaiters. The distinctions were yellow; the fusiliers had blue shoulder straps edged with yellow. The *Erbprinz* Regiment fought in this uniform in Spain. The two other regiments, which remained in Germany, retained their lace: seven white loops on each lapel, two below, two on each side pocket, one on each side of the top of the tail vent, and three on the cuff patches. The *Leibgarde* Regiment wore red distinctions, the *Leibregiment*, light blue. Dark blue crescents, edged in the regimental color, without passants, were worn (Fig. 7ld). The officers had single-breasted blue coatees for wear on the march. Officers' epaulettes were silver; subalterns wore one epaulette with bullions, and a crescent. On the march, the men wore blue overalls over their gaiters. In 1812 a provisional Light Infantry Regiment (which became the Guard Fusilier Regiment in 1813) was raised, with scarlet distinctions and white metal buttons. In 1813–1814 the lace seems to have been done away with, except on the lapels. In 1814 the men's crescents were abolished and blue shoulder straps introduced; these the fusiliers of the *Erbprinz* Regiment were already wearing.

The uniform was altered again in 1820. It now included a dark blue jacket with a row of white metal buttons. The collar and cuffs were red, light blue, or yellow, according to regiment. The Guard Fusilier Regiment became the 2nd Guard Regiment and in 1830 adopted pinkish-red distinctions in place of scarlet. White lace loops were worn on the collar and cuffs (silver loops for officers). The trousers were blue or white. The chacos were as before, and no cords were worn (these had not been in use earlier, except in the *Erbprinz* Regiment). Officers wore gorgets to denote their status, but not sashes. In 1824 the officers adopted white trousers in addition to the blue nanking ones. The shoulder straps were changed to the distinctive color in 1827. The officers' "Suvarov" boots were abolished in 1832. In 1834 the chaco was fitted with chinscales (which the guards had worn since 1819) instead of a leather chinstrap (Fig. 71e). From 1836 the field caps had peaks. In 1842 a new type of epaulette was introduced: generals and colonels had boxed bullions; lieutenant colonels and majors, loose ones; captains, one with loose bullions, and one with none on the left shoulder; lieutenants, no bullions at all. The lining was red for all, and the crescent, silver. On the crescents, lieutenants, majors, and major generals had one star; senior lieutenants, lieutenant colonels, and lieutenant generals, two stars; captains and colonels, none; and generals of infantry, three stars. From 1846 the blue trousers were piped in the regimental color. A new uniform was introduced in 1849. It consisted of a dark blue tunic with red piping. The pointed cuffs, also piped red, were of basic color. The shoulder straps were red; the buttons, white metal; and the trousers, gray with red piping. The *Gürtelrüstung*, in white leather, was worn. The helmet was of Prussian pattern with a brass plate. On each side of the collar were two white lace loops with buttons. The collar was red, light blue, or yellow as before. In 1849 the 2nd Regiment changed its pinkish-red distinctions for white. The following year sashes were reintroduced again for officers in place of gorgets. In 1852 they adopted a basket-hilted curved sword in place of the straight-bladed one, with a steel scabbard for mounted oficers and a leather scabbard for dismounted officers. Officers wore shoulder straps on service in 1866. The leather equipment was changed to black in 1867 (Fig. 71f). A new uniform, of Prussian type, was introduced in 1872. The principal differences between it and the Prussian one in 1914 were the cockade, the lion helmet plate, the white metal buttons, and the cuff patches, which were the same color as the shoulder straps (Fig. 71g). Collar and cuffs, as in Prussia, were red. The 115th Regiment had red shoulder straps and cuff patches, and white guard lace. Black hair plumes were worn in full dress. The 116th Regiment had white shoulder straps and cuff pataches, and black hair plumes in full dress; the 117th had Prussian blue distinctions and black hair plumes; the 118th Regiment had yellow distinctions, and the 168th, red. The 115th to 117th regiments wore red ciphers on the shoulder straps; the others had numerals. The 1910 service dress followed the Prussian pattern and had white metal buttons; the 1915 pattern was also similar; the shoulder straps' piping was red for the 115th and 168th regiments; white for the 116th; Prussian blue for the 117th; and yellow for the 118th.

Two *Jäger* battalions existed from 1861 to 1872. They wore a tunic as for the infantry, with green collar, on which the 1st Battalion (*Garde-Jäger* Battalion) had red patches, and the 2nd (*Leib-Jäger* Battalion), white. A white lace loop was worn on the patches. Green padded wings were worn at the points of the shoulders. The chacos had no back peak and had plumes of a different color for each company. In the 1870 campaign, oilcloth covers were always worn.

The *Leibgardekompanie zu Pferd* in the reign of the *Landgrave* Ludwig VI (1661–1678) wore dark blue coats edged with lace, with red linings, crimson fringed sashes; carbine belts covered with red velvet, and dark blue shabraques. A Horse Grenadier Company was formed in 1716. It had blue coats with red cuffs and waistcoats, grenadier caps, and cords on the shoulder. In 1731 the *Garde de Dragons* Regiment was formed from these grenadiers and had a dark blue and red uniform. The regiment adopted white uniforms with red distinctions in 1739. In 1763 a Hussar Corps, dressed in green uniforms, was in existence. The *Garde de Dragons* was disbanded in 1768. The *Garde du Corps* at that time wore a straw-colored uniform with red collar, cuffs, and waistcoat, and white and red lace edging. They also had fur caps with a white metal plate, red patch at the back, a white and light-blue vertically striped plume, and leather breeches (Fig. 71h). Hats replaced the fur caps shortly afterward. At that time, the hussars had light-blue uniforms. A second small hussar detachment had red uniforms. In 1790 the *Landgrave* of Hesse *chevau-léger* regiment was raised. The coat was green, with a red collar, with black patches. Lapels and cuffs were black. These were all edged with white lace. The undergarments were yellowish-colored, the stocks black, and the helmets were of British type. The skirt turnbacks were red and the shabraques green with black van-dyking and a white edging, with ciphers in the rear corners. In general, apart from changes due to fashion, they wore this uniform up to 1872. In 1809 jackets replaced the coats, and the leather equipment was changed from fawn to black. The breeches were green with red piping. The helmet was shaped more like the Bavarian crested helmet (Fig. 71i). The lapels were abolished in 1820, and the jacket was fastened with a row of white metal buttons. Two white lace loops were worn on the black patches of the red collar. The cuffs were of basic color, with a red pointed piping. The green overalls had red side stripes (Fig. 71k). White metal shoulder scales were worn. In 1850 a tunic with similar ornamentation was authorized, but with only single lace loops on the collar, gray trousers with red piping, and helmets with a yellow metal plate. Black hair plumes were worn in full dress. The officers' pouches were normally worn in black leather covers with white metal buttons. The regiment was divided in 1860 and a 2nd Regiment was formed, with white distinctions. From 1872 the uniform was of the same style as that worn by the Prussian dragoons (Fig. 71l). The basic color was dark green. The 1st Regiment—1st Grand Duchy of Hesse Dragoon Regiment (Guard Dragoon Regiment) No.23—had dark green tunics with red collar, shoulder straps, and Swedish cuffs, white guard lace, and white metal buttons, with white letter "L" crowned on the shoulder straps. The helmet had a white metal plate, and a black hair plume in full dress. The leather equipment was black. The sword belt was fastened with a plate bearing a crown instead of a buckle. The 2nd Grand Duchy of Hesse Dragoon Regiment (*Leib-Dragoner* Regiment) No. 24 had a similar uniform, but with white distinctions in place of red, no lace loops, and a red letter "N" and the crown of the czar on the shoulder straps. Both regiments had green shabraques with white crowns in the back corners, and an edging of the regimental color. The breeches were as for the Prussian dragoons. The 1910 and 1915 patterns of service dress uniform were as in Prussia. The shoulder straps were cornflower blue, with a dark green inner piping and outer piping in the distinctive color.

In 1790 the artillery was dressed in dark blue coats with black collars, lapels, and cuffs, red skirt linings, yellow metal buttons, white undergarments, and black gaiters. The officers' hats were edged with broad waved gold lace. Cravats were black. The cuff patches were of basic color. In 1803 the buttons were changed to white metal, and white lace loops were added (Fig. 71m). Later, chacos, red piping around the black distinctions, and dark blue breeches were introduced. The uniform was similar to that of the infantry in style and underwent the same changes. Tunics were introduced in 1850, with blue pointed cuffs, pointed up by the red piping. The black collar had white lace loops, and red piping, white metal buttons, and gray trousers, piped red, were also worn. The helmet was of the Prussian pattern, with a yellow metal lion plate, and spike instead of a ball finial. The officers' pouches were normally worn in black covers with a white metal button, like those of the *chevau-légers*. In 1872 the uniform was ordered to be exactly as in Prussia. A ball finial was added to the helmet. Leather equipment was black. The belt plate had a crown, as for the *chevau-légers*. The blue cuff patches were piped red, and the buttons were henceforth of yellow metal. Everything else was as in Prussia. The Field Artillery Regiment No. 25 had yellow guard lace on white patches. The uniform of the pioneers likewise followed that of the infantry; they had crimson distinctions. The transport corps too was dressed as its Prussian counterpart, but with black leather equipment. In the early period, the general officers wore blue uniforms with red distinctions and silver lace.

HESSEN-HOMBURG

The *Landgrave* of Hessen-Homburg provided a contingent to the army of the German Confederation. It was dressed almost exactly the same as the Hessen-Darmstadt *Erbprinz* Regiment. In 1839 a uniform similar to that of the Prussian Guard *Schützen* Battalion, with white metal buttons, was worn. Helmets and green tunics with carmine distinctions and white metal buttons were introduced in 1849. In 1863 *Jäger*-pattern chacos were adopted.

HESSEN-KASSEL

Cockade: red and white

I. INFANTRY

Up to 1806 the infantry was, generally speaking, dressed in the Prussian fashion. In the eighteenth century the grenadiers wore caps like those of the Prussian grenadiers. The musketeers had laced hats, and the fusiliers had fusilier caps of Prussian type. The basic color of the uniform was blue, with distinctions of various colors. Until about 1750 the breeches were blue. The neckcloths remained white for officers and red for the men up to the end of the Seven Years' War.

In 1759 the regiments were distinguished as follows.

REGIMENT	LAPELS	LACE LOOPS	EDGING TO LAPELS AND CUFFS	BUTTONS
Guard	red	white with red stripes	—	white
Leib grenadiere	red	white	white	white
Leib regiment	—	yellow	—	yellow
Erbprinz	yellow	white	—	white
Prince Ferdinand	red	—	white	white
Prince Charles	red	—	yellow	yellow
Prince Ysenburg	light yellow	white	—	yellow
Mansbach	white	—	—	yellow
Gilsa	red	—	—	yellow
Canitz	yellow	—	—	white
Toll	orange	—	—	yellow
Prince William (Hanau)	carmine	white	—	white

Fig. 72. Germany. Hessen-Kassel.

a, b, c: infantry. d, e, g: dragoons. f, h: hussars. l: horse artillery.

In the course of the following years, the uniform altered frequently. Grenadiers adopted fur caps in 1784. In 1806 the army was disbanded or, as it was said, was "granted leave." Following the expulsion of King Jérôme from Kassel, a new army was raised at the end of 1813. The infantry (Fig. 72a) adopted dark blue double-breasted jackets with red skirt turnbacks. The white breeches were worn with black gaiters that reached to just below the knee.

The *Leibgrenadier Garde* had red collars, shoulder straps, and Swedish cuffs, and white guard lace loops and buttons. The fur caps had a white metal plate and white cords, and a white plume with a red tip. The Guard Grenadier Regiment had a similar uniform but wore chacos with a white grenade on the front, white chinscales and cords, a crimson and white cockade, and plume as for the *Leibgrenadier Garde*. The line infantry had dark blue cuff patches and wore chacos without a plate, but with chinscales, white cords, and a plume. The distinctions were yellow with white metal buttons for the *Kürfurst* (Elector) Regiment; *Kurprinz* (Elector's heir), white with yellow metal buttons; *Landgrave* Charles, red with yellow metal buttons; Solms-Braunfels, crimson with white metal buttons. The equipment was similar to that worn by the Prussian infantry. This uniform was worn up to 1821. In 1813 queues were again ordered to be worn, by all arms, but they were very short, reaching only to the bottom of the collar.

In 1813–1814 the *Landwehr* infantry also saw active service. Its uniform was very similar to that of the Prussian *Landwehr*. The distinctive colors were crimson for the 1st Regiment, black for the 2nd, and red for the 3rd. Buttons were of white metal. The chacos were worn in covers, with the *Landwehr* cross on the front. In 1821 the Swiss *Leibgarde* adopted dark blue jackets and cuff patches, with red collar, lapels, cuffs, and skirt lining. The shoulder straps were white with yellow grenades.

The collar, lapels, and cuff patches were ornamented with white lace loops with tassels. Fur caps with white cords and a white metal plate and chinscales were worn. At the top of the cap was a red patch with a white grenade on it. The *Leibgarde* Regiment wore jackets almost exactly like those of the 1st Prussian Guard Regiment. A yellow crown was worn on the white shoulder straps up to 1832. Trousers, chacos, and leather equipment were as in Prussia, but with the cockade in the national colors. NCOs' cap cords were interwoven with red. The line infantry regiments likewise wore jackets as in Prussia, with white shoulder straps and yellow cuff patches for the 1st Regiment; white shoulder straps and white cuff patches for the 2nd Regiment; and red shoulder straps and light-blue cuff patches for the 3rd Regiment. In addition to the national cockade at the top of the chaco, a further cockade and loop with the electoral cipher was worn below. Chinscales and cords were also worn. In 1832 regimental numbers were introduced on the shoulder straps. The cuff patches and shoulder straps were made one color in the same year (Fig. 72b): yellow for the 1st Regiment; crimson for the 2nd; and red for the 3rd. In 1846 Prussian-type tunics and helmets were adopted. The Swiss *Leibgarde* and the Guard Regiment had white metal helmet plates; the others had yellow metal ones. In full dress, both guard regiments had hair plumes: white for the Swiss *Leibgarde* and black for the Guard Regiment. The tunic differed from the Prussian one in having an all-red collar, and not just red patches (Fig. 72c). Later, the *Gürtelrüstung* was introduced.

II. *JÄGER* AND *SCHÜTZEN*

In 1813 a *Jäger* Battalion was raised. Its uniform resembled that of the infantry in style. The jacket was dark green, with crimson distinctions, white metal buttons, and light-gray trousers. Chacos were worn. In 1814 the volunteer *Jäger* wore dark green jackets with yellow metal buttons, light-blue distinctions, gray trousers, and black leather equipment. The chacos bore the national cockade, yellow metal *Jäger* horn, and green cords and plume. In 1821 the *Jäger* Battalion was redesignated a Guard *Jäger* Battalion. The dark green jackets were of exactly the same style as in Prussia, with red collar, cuffs, and cuff patches, and white lace loops and buttons. The shoulder straps were white with a yellow crown. The chaco had a white metal star plate with green plume and cords. In 1832 the buttons, lace loops, and chaco star were changed to yellow, the shoulder straps to red, and the plume to black. In 1821 a *Schützen* Battalion was raised. Its composition altered frequently. The uniform consisted of green jackets with green cuff patches and skirt turnbacks, light-blue distinctions, yellow lace loops on the collar, yellow metal buttons, and red shoulder straps and piping. The chaco had white cords and plume. The mounts were as in the infantry. Leather equipment was black. Green tunics, and helmets with a yellow metal plate, were adopted in 1846. Black hair plumes were worn in full dress. In the same year, the Guard *Jäger* Battalion adopted green tunics without lace loops, and helmets like the *Schützen*. In 1858 kepis bearing the crowned cipher and a black hair plume were introduced. In 1851 the *Schützen* Battalion was turned into fusiliers (with a blue uniform), but was changed back again to a *Schützen* Battalion in 1856 and as such adopted green tunics with black collar and cuffs, red shoulder straps, and yellow metal buttons. The helmets had a black hair plume. In 1858 these were superseded by kepis like those of the Guard *Jäger*.

III. CAVALRY

During the eighteenth century the cavalry wore uniforms similar to those of the Prussian cavalry, to the extent of being confused with them. In the 1780s, however, the uniform came partly under British influence: the dragoons, for example, were issued British-type helmets (Fig. 72d). In general, though, Prussian fashions remained predominant up to the disappearance of the army in 1806.

The following troops existed in the period 1813–1821:

Garde du Corps: Uniform almost exactly as in Prussia, but with a Bavarian-type crested helmet.

Guard Hussars: Pelisse and dolman dark blue; collar, cuffs, cap bag, and sabertache red, white loopings. The leather breeches were worn with hussar boots.

Leib-Dragoner Regiment (Fig. 72e): Light-blue jackets with two rows of yellow metal buttons; red distinctions; chacos. Breeches as for the hussars.

Hussar Regiment: Uniform as for the Guard Hussars; chacos.

In the years thereafter, the uniform of the *Garde du Corps* developed along the same lines as its Prussian counterpart. Leather helmets with a comb, black horsehair crest, and yellow metal plate bearing a white metal star were adopted in 1821. The distinctions were red with white guard lace loops; the trousers and shabraques were as in Prussia, but the cuirasses were of white metal. White jackets and cuirassier helmets of Prussian type were worn from 1846.

Two hussar regiments existed from 1821 to 1832 (Fig. 72f). The 1st Regiment had dark blue dolmans, pelisses, and shabraques, with red collar and cuffs, and vandyked edges to the shabraques. The loopings were white; the leather equipment was black. The sashes were white and red. The 2nd Regiment had dark brown pelisses and dolmans, and shabraques, the vandyked edges of which were light blue, as were the collars and cuffs. The sabertaches were red, the loopings yellow, the sashes light blue and yellow. Both regiments wore a chaco with a loop, the national cockade, and white cords. The trousers were gray with red stripes. The pelisses and dolmans had shoulder straps of the same color as the collar. These had a narrow chain edging around them and bore the regimental number in the same color as the loopings.

From 1832 to 1845 both regiments were formed into a single regiment, called the *Leib-Dragoner* Regiment (Fig. 72g). They wore light-blue jackets with two rows of yellow metal buttons, red collar, shoulder straps, and Swedish cuffs, with red piping around the skirt turnbacks. The helmet was like that of the Prussian cuirassiers. Accoutrements were of white leather. The trousers were gray with red stripes. From 1845 to 1866 the regiment was again divided into two hussar regiments (Fig. 72h). The 1st wore a light-blue uniform; the 2nd, dark blue. The loopings were white. The cap bag and sabertache were red. The regiments retained these uniform colors when they became the 13th and 14th Hussar Regiments in the Prussian army, except that the sabertaches were changed to plain leather ones.

210

IV. ARTILLERY, PIONEERS, AND TRANSPORT CORPS

The early uniform of the artillery was blue and crimson. These colors were retained after the re-formation of the army in 1813, with the addition of guard lace loops on the collar and yellow metal buttons. Chacos were worn. The foot artillery had white trousers; the horse artillery, dark blue ones with crimson stripes. In 1821 the basic color of the jacket was changed to dark green, with black distinctions, yellow guard lace loops and buttons, and red shoulder straps. The horse artillery had skirts of cavalry fashion: i.e., turnbacks of basic color with an edging in the color of the collar, and red piping; the foot artillery had red turnbacks. The chaco, cartridge boxes, and pouches were ornamented with a yellow grenade. The chaco had yellow chinscales and cords. The horse artillery wore dark green horsehair plumes and white leather accoutrements; the foot artillery had black equipment. In 1832 the collar and cuffs were piped with red (Fig. 72i), and the foot artillery adopted white equipment. The horsehair plumes, which were now issued to the foot artillery as well, were changed to black. In 1846 dark blue Prussian-type tunics and helmets with yellow metal plates were adopted. Black hair plumes were worn in full dress.

The pioneers, which were first made independent of the artillery in 1832, wore the uniform of the foot artillery up to 1846, but with white lace loops, buttons, chaco cords, and plate; black plumes, and black leather equipment. In 1846 tunics as in Prussia were adopted, without lace loops, and the helmets had a white metal plate. Black hair plumes were worn in full dress.

In 1854 the transport corps was formed into a transport corps detachment. They wore dark blue tunics, with crimson distinctions, and yellow metal buttons, and dark blue peaked caps with a crimson band and piping. The side arm was carried on a black belt.

HOHENZOLLERN-HECHINGEN and HOHENZOLLERN-SIGMARINGEN

In 1849 the sovereignty of both the Hohenzollern principalities was transferred to Prussia. The contingent that previously they had jointly sent to the Army of the Confederation wore dark blue jackets and trousers, with red collar, cuffs, and skirt turnbacks. The cuff patches were white for the 1st company; yellow for the 2nd; dark blue for the 3rd; and green for the *Schützen* which were raised in Liechtenstein. The 1st reserve company had light-blue patches, the 2nd, orange. The chacos had a white metal plate and red double pompon. The accoutrements were of white leather, or black for *Schützen*. In the 1840s the collars, cuffs, and shoulder straps were changed to light green with white guard lace loops for all companies. The chacos had a black hair plume, or white for bandsmen. Black leather equipment was introduced. In 1845 dark blue tunics with light-green distinctions and two rows of white metal buttons were introduced. From that date the shoulder straps were dark blue with red piping.

LIPPE-DETMOLD

Cockade: red and yellow

Lippe joined the Rhine Confederation at the same time as Waldeck. Both the Lippe states combined to provide a battalion as their contingent. In 1808 the uniform consisted of a white coat with green collar and cuffs; long gray trousers; low-crowned hats with the brim turned up on one side; and white leather equipment. In 1812 white jackets with white lapels, cuff patches, and shoulder straps were worn. Collar, cuffs, and piping were green, and the trousers, leather equipment, chaco fittings, cords, and buttons were white (Fig. 73d). After the Napoleonic Wars, Detmold had to provide a battalion of infantry for the Army of the Confederation. Its uniform was dark green, with red collar, Swedish cuffs, shoulder straps, and skirt turnbacks. The buttons were yellow metal, and the trousers were gray with red piping (Fig. 73e). In the 1840s tunics and spiked helmets were introduced. The basic color was green, as was the collar. Collar patches, shoulder straps, cuffs, and cuff patches were red. The piping around them was yellow, but that down the front and around the skirt pockets was red. The buttons were yellow metal, and the leather equipment was white. The helmet fittings were of yellow metal. The trousers were as before (Fig. 73f). In 1861 the battalion was turned into fusiliers. The basic color of the coat remained green; the collar (from that date of distinctive color), Swedish cuffs, and shoulder straps were black with red piping. The rest of the piping was red, and the buttons were of white metal. Black leather equipment was adopted. A kepi like that of the Prussian *Jäger* was worn, with a white metal star bearing the rose of Lippe on the front. The state cockade was red, edged yellow (Fig. 73g). The Prince of Lippe

Fig. 73. Germany. Waldeck, Lippe-Detmold, Schaumburg-Lippe.
Waldeck—a, c: infantry. b: *Jäger*. Lippe-Detmold—d, e, f, g: infantry. Schaumburg-Lippe—h, i: carabiniers. k, l: infantry.

Fusilier Battalion wore this uniform in 1866, when it fought on the Prussian side at Kissingen. By the terms of the convention of 26 June 1867, the contingent became part of the Prussian army. Those liable for military service went into the 55th (6th Westphalian) Infantry Regiment and wore the state cockade, in addition to the Prussian one, on their headdress.

MECKLENBURG-SCHWERIN and MECKLENBURG-STRELITZ

Cockade: blue, yellow, and red

Mecklenburg-Schwerin

The earliest uniforms were very varied in color, but up to 1705 predominantly gray uniforms were worn. In 1715 cravats replaced the neckcloths. In general, the uniform followed that of the Prussian army. Fig. 74a depicts a musketeer of 1749. The man has a dark blue coat, with red cravat, lapels, cuffs, skirt linings, and hat plume. Hat lace, buttons, and undergarments are yellow. Fig. 74b shows a similarly colored uniform, except that the hat lace, buttons, and undergarments are white and the gaiters, black. Fig. 74c has red distinctions and white buttons and undergarments.

During the period of the Confederation of the Rhine (1806–1813), the uniforms displayed a remarkable combination of Prussian and French influences. The blue jacket with red distinctions closely resembled the style of the Prussian one, as did the gray breeches and black gaiters. The distinctions of the grenadiers and *voltigeurs*, however, were entirely French. These consisted of red chaco cords, plume, and fringed epaulettes for the grenadiers, and green for the *voltigeurs* (Fig. 74d). The fusiliers carried no swords and were not allowed to grow moustaches. The officers wore the sword on a white belt over the shoulder and had silver epaulettes or crescents, again after the French fashion. They wore gold, red, and blue embroidered sashes around the waist. In 1813 a Foot *Jäger* Regiment and a Mounted *Jäger* Regiment were formed from volunteers. The uniform for both consisted of a dark green jacket with red collar and Swedish cuffs, and gold guard lace loops. The breeches were green. The chacos bore a yellow metal star, and an oval white metal coat of arms.

After the Napoleonic Wars, the infantry went into dark blue jackets with red collar, cuffs, and skirt edging. The buttons were white metal. Gray trousers with red piping were worn in winter, and white ones in summer. The Grenadier Battalion had fur caps with white cords (gold for officers) and a red plume on the left side. The men wore red fringed epaulettes. White lace loops (gold for the officers) were worn on the collar, and cuff patches were dark blue. The line battalions had no lace on their collars or cuff patches. The shoulder straps were white for the 1st Battalion and yellow for the 2nd. The chacos had no cords (Fig. 74e). The Light Battalion was distinguished by green collars and cuffs, red skirt edging, white metal buttons, chacos with green cords, and black leather equipment.

In 1848 tunics with red collar, cuffs, and piping were introduced. The buttons were white metal; the shoulder straps white with red numerals. The spiked helmets

Fig. 74. Germany. Mecklenburg-Schwerin and Mecklenburg-Strelitz.
Mecklenburg-Schwerin—a, b, c, d, e, f, g, h: infantry. i, k: cavalry. Mecklenburg-Strelitz—l: hussar. m, n: infantry.

had a yellow metal plate. White hair plumes were worn in full dress. The trousers were as before (Fig. 74f). In the 1860s dark blue Russian-type caps with a red band and black hair plume superseded the helmets (Fig. 74g). Red cuff patches and black leather equipment were worn from that time. The caps in turn were replaced by helmets bearing the coat of arms of the state and at first had a differently shaped spike. In 1914 Schwerin troops made up the 1st and 3rd battalions of the Grand Duchy of Mecklenburg Regiment No. 89, and Regiment No. 90. The dark blue tunic had red collar, cuffs, and piping. The cuff patches were dark blue with red piping. White lace loops were worn on the collars and cuffs. The white shoulder straps had red numerals. Black hair plumes were worn in full dress. The officers' lace loops were of a special pattern. The crescents of the epaulettes were of silver. The sash and sword knot were in the Mecklenburg colors. Regiment No. 90 wore neither lace nor hair plumes, but instead had red cuff patches, piped yellow, and white buttons and shoulder straps, the latter bearing a red cipher. The helmet plate was of yellow metal; the leather equipment, black. The Light Infantry Battalion (later *Jäger* Battalion No. 14), except for alterations due to fashion and changes in the cuffs, retained its old uniform up to 1890. In that year, it adopted the Prussian *Jäger* uniform with white metal buttons and, in 1899, light-green distinctions piped with red, and white guard lace loops. The 1910 and 1915 service uniforms were of Prussian pattern.

Like the infantry, the dragoons wore whitish-gray coats up to 1705, and blue ones thereafter. From 1719 to 1782 no cavalry existed in Schwerin. In 1809 the *Garde-Reiter* wore yellow jackets with red distinctions. A *chevau-léger* regiment was formed in 1819. Its uniform consisted of a light-blue jacket with red collar, cuffs, skirt turnbacks, and epaulette pads, light-blue cuff patches, yellow lace loops, buttons, and epaulette crescents. The gray trousers were piped red. The helmet was similar to that worn at the time by the Prussian cuirassiers, with yellow metal mounts (Fig. 74i). The horse furniture was of Austrian type and consisted of a red saddle cloth and a black lambskin edged with red. In 1838 the epaulettes were replaced by red shoulder straps. A chaco replaced the helmet, so that from that time the uniform closely resembled that of the Prussian Guard Dragoons. In 1847 tunics, of the same colors as before, were introduced, and German silver helmets with a spike. These were replaced in 1865 by a light-blue cap with a red band (Fig. 74k). A hair plume was worn in full dress. Three years later, spiked helmets made of thin leather were introduced. In 1867 a second dragoon regiment was formed by division. (The regiment from which it originated had been called dragoons since 1837.) The 2nd Regiment was distinguished by Swedish cuffs of basic color with red piping. The 1st Regiment had black lambskin saddle covers, the 2nd white. The uniform underwent many alterations in detail, but developed along Prussian lines. The 2nd Regiment, numbered 18th, altered its distinctive color to black, with white metal buttons and silver guard lace loops. Both regiments had lances with yellow and red pennants, and were numbered 17 and 18 in the dragoon arm of the *Reichsheer*. The 1910 and 1915 service dress followed the Prussian models.

The artillery uniforms always closely resembled those of the Prussian artillery, but the buttons were of white metal. This remained a distinction of the Mecklenburg artillery up to 1918. The collar had red piping around the bottom. General officers had dark blue tunics with carmine distinctions; later, red with silver lace. The distinctive general officers' embroidery was of Russian type.

Mecklenburg-Strelitz

During the period of the Confederation of the Rhine, the Strelitz infantry was dressed almost exactly like the Schwerin infantry, the principal difference being the yellow metal buttons. In the 1830s a dark blue jacket with self-colored cuff patches and red collar, cuffs, shoulder straps, and skirt turnbacks was introduced. The buttons were of yellow metal; and guard lace was worn on the collar and cuff patches (Fig. 74m). The chacos had a yellow metal plate and green cords. Gray trousers with red piping were worn in winter, and white ones in summer. In its general development, the uniform was very similar to the Prussian pattern, except for the green chaco cords. Strelitz provided the 2nd Battalion of the 89th Regiment. It was dressed much as the 1st and 3rd battalions, described above for Schwerin, but the buttons and lace were yellow and the shoulder straps red with a yellow cipher. Officers had double-scalloped cuff patches (Fig. 74n). A hussar regiment existed in Strelitz between 1813 and 1815 (Fig. 74l). The uniform consisted of a black dolman with black collar and cuffs, black pelisse, yellow loopings, light-blue Hungarian breeches, and black and yellow sashes. The black sabertaches bore a yellow "C." The chacos bore the Wendish Cross in yellow metal, and had yellow cords. The gray shabraques had a light-blue vandyked border edged with yellow. Gray buttoned overalls were normally worn to protect the breeches. The volunteer *Jäger* of the regiment had the same uniform, but with green pelisses and dolmans, with black collars and cuffs. The chaco cords were green.

NASSAU

Cockade: black; and blue and orange

From the 1750s the regiment that Nassau-Weilburg contributed to the Upper Rhine District wore blue uniforms with white distinctions and white undergarments, like the majority of troops from the district. The *Leibbataillon* von Todenwarth was formed in 1803. It wore dark green jackets with a single row of yellow metal buttons down the front. The collar, cuffs, skirt turnbacks, and shoulder straps were red, with yellow lace and loops. The undergarments were white, and the equipment of yellow leather. Crested helmets with a black plume were worn (Fig. 75a). In 1808 this battalion was absorbed into the 1st Nassau Infantry Regiment, which was then being raised. A 2nd Regiment was formed at the same time. Both regiments wore single-breasted dark green jackets with self-colored skirt turnbacks and a row of yellow metal buttons. Collar and cuffs were black, with orange lace. The leather equipment was as before. White waistcoats, light-gray breeches with black loopings on the front, and black gaiters were also worn. They had chacos; the officers had hats, but shortly afterward they, too, adopted chacos. As a mark of rank they had French-type gold epaulettes, and gorgets. The sword was carried on a yellow shoulder belt with a small plate bearing the Nassau arms on the front. The grenadiers and *voltigeurs* wore epaulettes and plumes as in the French infantry. The grenadiers are said to have worn the helmets of the old von Todenwarth Battalion (Fig. 75b). The 2nd grenadier company of the 1st Regiment, however, went to Spain in 1809 wearing chacos. In 1810 the crested helmets were entirely abolished, and superseded by fur caps with a red bag, plume, and cords (Fig. 75d). The collar and cuffs were edged with plain yellow

Fig. 75. Germany. Nassau.
a, b, c, d, e, f, g: infantry. h, i: *Jäger*. k: artillery.

216

piping, in place of the orange-colored lace loops and edging, from 1809. The shoulder straps were similarly altered (Fig. 75c). In 1804 the grenadiers and *flanquers (voltigeurs)* adopted red and yellow wings respectively, in place of the fringed epaulettes. Colored pompons, varying for each company, were introduced on the chacos of the center companies.

This uniform was worn unaltered up to 1833, when the distinction between grenadiers and *flanquers* was abolished. The 3rd Battalions were turned into light battalions, and as such were distinguished by a *Jäger* horn instead of the yellow metal rayed plate on the chaco. Dark green jackets and trousers were issued. Officers had gray trousers. The collar and cuffs were black. The chaco cords, shoulder straps, wings, skirt turnbacks, and piping were all red. Leather equipment and buttons were yellow. The cockade on the chaco was blue, with an orange edging (Fig. 75e). The regimental organization came to an end in 1849, when the infantry was divided into seven separate battalions. Dark green tunics with black collars and cuffs, and red shoulder straps and piping, were introduced at the same time. The gray trousers had red piping. Spiked helmets with a distinctively shaped finial and yellow metal mounts were introduced. The buttons, battalion numeral on the shoulder straps, and equipment, were all yellow (Fig. 75f). The infantry was reorganized into regiments in 1855. In 1862–1863, a new uniform, based on the Austrian model, was introduced. It was of the same color as before but was double-breasted. The piping went right around the coat. Kepis like those worn by the Austrian artillery, with a black horsehair plume secured on the right side, were introduced (Fig. 75g). The *Schützen* were denoted by the yellow edging to their shoulder straps and by their swords not having a knuckle bow. The chacos were usually worn in covers. At the beginning of the 1866 Campaign, the yellow equipment was blackened. In 1857 a *Jäger* battalion was raised. It adopted dark green Prussian-style tunics, with black collar and cuffs, white shoulder straps, piping, and buttons. Leather equipment was black, and the trousers were gray with white stripes. The kepis had a black horsehair plume secured on the left side and a white metal star bearing the coat of arms (Fig. 75h). In 1864 all-black jackets and trousers with black loopings, like those of the Brunswick troops, were issued. The collar and cuffs were black as well (Fig. 75i). The headdress remained as before. The officers wore orange sashes; in 1864 the *Jäger* officers adopted hussar-type sashes. From 1862 the distinctions of rank were of Austrian type.

The only cavalry to be formed in Nassau was raised at the time of the Rhine Confederation. It was a regiment of *Jäger zu Pferd*, which wore an all-green uniform with white hussar loopings, black leather accoutrements, and black sabertaches bearing the initials "F.M." and crown in white metal. At first, Bavarian-type crested helmets were worn, and later, fur caps with a red bag. In 1833 the Nassau artillery was dressed exactly like the infantry, except that where the latter had red distinctions, the former had crimson. The trousers were gray with crimson stripes (Fig. 75k). These distinctions also differentiated the artillery during its later changes in uniform, which were based on those of the infantry.

OLDENBURG

Cockade: blue with red cross and white edging; later, blue with red ring

In 1775 a permanent Company of Foot was formed. The uniform was of the Prussian type (Fig. 76a). The coat was dark blue with red distinctions and white metal buttons. The lace loops were white, with a blue-and-red figure with tassels at the ends. They were sewn on below the lapels, above the cuffs, and on the skirts. The undergarments were white and the gaiters black. The hat was laced white and had a red-and-blue tuft. When Oldenburg was constrained to join the Confederation of the Rhine, it had to raise a battalion of infantry, including a grenadier company, a *Schützen* company, and four fusilier companies. They wore dark blue jackets with red distinctions and pip-

Fig. 76. Germany. Oldenburg—Infantry.

ing, white metal buttons, white shoulder straps edged red, gray breeches, and black gaiters. The headdress of the grenadiers was a fur cap with white cords and a red patch at the back. *Schützen* and fusiliers wore felt hats with the brim turned up on the left side (Fig. 76b) surmounted by a plume: white for the fusiliers and green for the *Schützen.*

After the battle of Leipzig, two battalions of the infantry were raised. They had dark blue jackets with red distinctions, white metal buttons, and dark blue trousers without piping (white ones were worn in summer). The shoulder straps and leather equipment were white. The chacos had a yellow metal crowned plate (silver for officers) with white metal chinscales, white cords, and a black plume (Fig. 76c). In 1818 the NCOs' rank distinctions, which previously had been of French type, in the form of chevrons on the cuffs, were replaced by Prussian-type distinctions. Up to 1825 officers wore gorgets, and from that year, red and blue striped gold sashes. The infantry was increased during the 1830s. The 1st Regiment adopted white shoulder straps and buttons; the 2nd, yellow. In 1838 the Virchowsche equipment was introduced. In 1841 red piping was added to the trousers. Blue tunics with blue pointed cuffs and red collar and piping were introduced experimentally in 1843 and superseded the jackets in 1844. The leather equipment remained white. The headdress was a helmet with a distinctively shaped spike (Fig. 76e). The trousers were as before. In 1849 there were four line battalions and one light battalion. This last adopted green collars and shoulder straps, the former with red piping, the latter bearing the numeral 5 in red.

218

The piping elsewhere was green, and the leather equipment black. Kepis with a horsehair plume were worn. In 1855 the infantry was reorganized, and the light companies were abolished. The battalions were formed into a regiment. Prussian-type epaulettes were introduced for the officers in 1858. At the same time, gray trousers, piped red, replaced the blue ones. In 1861 the 3rd Battalion adopted black leather equipment, and the 1st and 2nd followed suit two years later. The bayonets, worn up to then as side arms, were abolished. In 1864 blue Russian-type cloth caps with red piping replaced the helmets (Fig. 76f). In full dress, these had a small white metal plate in front and a black horsehair plume. A military convention was concluded with Prussia in 1867, after which time the infantry bore the regimental number 91 and wore Prussian line infantry uniforms with light-blue piping around the cuff patches and white shoulder straps with a red "P," crowned.

A cavalry regiment was raised in Oldenburg in 1849. The original uniform consisted of greenish-black tunics with light-blue collar, shoulder straps, and pointed cuffs and white metal buttons. All piping, including that around the collar and cuffs, was white. The gray breeches had light-blue piping. Steel helmets similar to those worn by the Prussian cuirassiers, were worn, with yellow metal plates. Leather equipment was white. In 1849 the white piping was replaced by light blue, and in the next year, both the basic and distinctive colors of the uniform were changed. It now consisted of a light-blue tunic with black collar, white shoulder straps, light-blue Swedish cuffs piped black, black piping, and white metal buttons. The breeches were as before, with red piping. The officers had undress coats of light-blue cloth with black hussar-type cords. As in the infantry, the helmets were replaced in 1864 by Russian-type caps. They were light blue with a black band and white piping around the top and had a small silver plate and a white hair plume in full dress. In 1867 helmets, like those worn by the Prussian dragoons, with black plumes for full-dress wear were introduced. The tunic and breeches were as before, except that the Swedish cuffs were now black. The white shoulder straps bore a red letter "A," crowned. The subsequent changes in uniform were as for the Prussian dragoons. The lance pennants were red and blue. The regiment was numbered 19 in the Dragoons of the Imperial Army.

From its formation in 1815, the Oldenburg artillery wore dark blue jackets with self-colored cuff patches and dark blue trousers without piping. Collar and cuffs were black; shoulder straps, skirt turnbacks, and piping were red, and the buttons were yellow metal. The chacos had red cords. The leather equipment was black. Tunics and helmets were introduced later, and in 1858 gray trousers piped with red were adopted. In general, the uniform developed as for the infantry: Russian-type caps that had a small plate and black hair plume in full dress were adopted in 1864. In 1867 both the Oldenburg batteries were formed into the 10th Field Artillery Regiment.

Cockade: black, red, and yellow

The earliest uniforms were white and red (cf. Schwarzburg). In 1750 the basic color was changed to blue, and the uniform thenceforth consisted of a blue coat with red collar, cuffs, and lining, yellow metal buttons, and white undergarments. In 1778 the Greiz-Lobenstein Company adopted red lapels and the Ebersdorf Company, white linings. The former was turned into a grenadier company in 1780 and as such wore bearskin caps with a yellow metal armorial plate. The Lobenstein Contingent adopted *Kasketts*, in place of the hats worn thitherto. In 1807 the Rhine Confederation Contingent (Fig. 77e)—a battalion of three companies—was issued with white coats with yellow metal buttons, light-blue collar, cuffs, and skirt turnbacks, black stocks edged white, and light-blue Hungarian breeches ornamented with a black, yellow, and red braid. The gaiters were black. The chaco had an oval plate bearing an "R." The cords were black, red, and yellow and the plume, red. The leather equipment was white. The uniform remained unchanged after the Second Peace of Paris in 1815. After various minor alterations, the uniform in 1822 consisted of a white coat with a row of eight yellow metal buttons down the front. The distinctions were light blue and the shoulder straps white, piped with light blue. Gray sleeved waistcoats with light-blue distinctions were worn in undress. White trousers were worn in summer and gray ones in winter. The cords were later removed from the chaco (Fig. 77f). The Austrian-type field caps were black with a light-blue edging. The white uniform was abolished in 1845 and replaced by a black tunic (Fig. 77g), with light-blue collar patches, cuff patches, and piping. The black trousers had light-blue welts (white linen trousers were worn in summer). The spiked helmets had a yellow metal plate,

Fig. 77. Germany. Gotha-Altenburg, Reuss, Schwarzburg.

Gotha-Altenburg—a, b, c, d: infantry. Reuss—e, f, g, h: infantry. Schwarzburg—i, k, l, m: infantry.

with a German silver coat of arms on the star. Black hair plumes, red for bandsmen, were worn in full dress. In 1850 officers adopted a saber, hanging from slings worn under the coat. The crossed belts were replaced by the *Gürtelrüstung*, at first white for the musketeers and black for the fusiliers, but black for all from 1861. In 1854 the collar was made wholly of distinctive color (Fig. 77h). From 1867 the Reuss Contingent formed the 2nd Battalion of the 96th Infantry Regiment.

SAXONY

Cockade: white up to 1815; thereafter green and white

I. INFANTRY

In 1683 the clothing of the infantry consisted of a cloth coat with baize lining and tin or brass buttons; hat; cloth stockings of the color of the coat lining, and buckskin breeches. The *Leibregiment* had red coats; the others, gray. The linings were of various colors. The Elector John George III ordered pikes to be left in store, and all the infantry to be equipped with muskets, and swan's feathers, which could be used as musket rests. In 1686, in place of those already existing, another grenadier company was attached to each foot regiment. The grenadiers adopted blue cloth caps. In 1687 the division of the men into musketeers and pikemen came to an end. Red uniforms were introduced in 1695.

In 1701 the distinctions were as follows.

REGIMENT	DISTINCTIONS*
1. Polish Guards	white
2. Saxon Guards	white
3. Queen's	Isabella (cream)
4. Egidy	Isabella (cream)
5. Kurprinz	lemon yellow
6. Thielau	lemon yellow
7. Steinau	green
8. Zeitz	green
9. Biron	not given
10. Tromp	not given
11. Pistoris	pale blue
12. Reuss	pale blue
13. Sacken	moss color
14. Marschall	moss color
15. Fürstenberg	dark blue
16. Löwenhaupt	dark blue
17. Görtz	sea green
18. Rothenburg	sea green
19. Beichlingen	gray
20. Weimar	gray
21. Dönhof	not given
22. Flemming	not given

*After Schuster and Franke.

In 1715 the officers adopted gorgets with the device of a coat of arms in yellow metal, and silver and crimson woven sashes, worn over the right shoulder. The coat had no lapels and was buttoned all the way down the front, so that the waistcoat was not seen (Fig. 78b). In the same year, a Janissary Corps was raised. Its uniform was a lemon yellow coat, red waistcoat, and Hungarian-style breeches ornamented with blue and white lace; yellow half boots, and a Janissary cap (a turban for officers). Equipment was of yellow leather. Green coats and yellow undergarments were worn as an undress uniform. In 1730 the infantry had red coats with variously colored lapels, skirt turnbacks, Swedish cuffs, and waistcoats. The breeches were buff colored, the stockings white. The lace-edged hat had a colored tuft. The cartridge box, worn on a buff-colored shoulder belt, bore no device for the musketeers, but the grenadiers had the coat of arms on their pouches, with grenades in the corners. The latter also wore a match case on the belt and a cartridge box on the waistbelt. Straight-bladed swords were carried. The grenadier cap had a red front with a brass plate, and a colored bag at the back (Fig. 78c). In 1730 the distinctions were as follows.

REGIMENT	COAT	DISTINCTIONS	BUTTONS
Leibgrenadier Garde	lemon yellow	red	white
1st and 2nd Guards	straw	red	white
Crown Prince	red	lemon yellow	white
Weissenfels	red	yellow	white
Marchen	red	white	yellow
Löwendahl	red	pale blue	yellow
Wilcke	red	cinnamon brown	yellow
Saxony-Gotha	red	dark blue	yellow
Böhn	red	straw	white
Caila	red	popinjay green	white
Weimar	red	green	white
Grenadier Company	straw	red	white

Four *Kreisregimenter* (district regiments) were raised in 1733 and lasted to 1756. Their uniform was red, with blue distinctions. In 1734 the infantry adopted white coats; the *Leibgrenadier Garde* alone retained red ones. In 1742 the lapels were abolished, and the coat was made double-breasted, with two rows of six buttons. The cuffs were made plain and round. In 1745 colored collars were added to the coats of the officers and NCOs. The *Kreisregimenter* adopted gray coats. All regiments had white breeches.

In 1754 the distinctions were as follows.

REGIMENT	COAT	DISTINCTIONS	BUTTONS
Leibgrenadier Garde	light red	yellow	white
Foot Guards	white	red	yellow
Queen's	white	cochineal	yellow
Kurprinzessin	white	pale blue	yellow
Frederick Augustus	white	yellow	yellow
Xavier	white	pale blue	yellow
Clemens	white	French blue	yellow

(*continued*)

REGIMENT	COAT	DISTINCTIONS	BUTTONS
Brühl	white	red	yellow
Lubomirsky	white	yellow	white
Rochow	green	red	yellow
Minckwitz	white	French blue	white
Gotha	white	pale blue	white
Friesen	white	green	yellow
1st Kreisregiment	light gray	yellow	white
2nd Kreisregiment	light gray	pale blue	white
3rd Kreisregiment	light gray	red	white
4th Kreisregiment	light gray	green	white

The beginning of the Seven Years' War saw the Saxon army involved in the disaster of Pirns. From those Saxon troops which went into captivity, Frederick the Great raised Prussian regiments, which, however, took every opportunity to flee this enforced service. These deserters for the large part gathered into complete formations of troops, at first in Bohemia and later in Upper Austria and from 1758 were in French pay. The grenadiers adopted bearskin caps in 1761. In 1765, after the war, the army was reorganized and a new uniform was introduced. White coats were adopted by all the infantry with the exception of the *Leibgrenadier Garde*. The skirt turnbacks were white; the collar, lapels, cuffs, and waistcoat were of the distinctive color. The white breeches were close-fitting, with white Austrian knots, and black gaiters in the form of Hungarian boots. The cravat was red. The hat had a white lace binding and a colored tuft (Fig. 78f). In place of swords, the men had bayonets, and the grenadiers, sabers. The officers had a gold or silver edging to their hats and white cockades. Cravats were white, and the gorgets had the electoral cipher in the center

Fig. 78. Germany. Saxony—Infantry.

223

on a colored velvet backing. The silver and red sashes were tied in front on the right side.

In 1765 the distinctions were as follows.

REGIMENT	DISTINCTIONS	BUTTONS
Kurfürst	madder red	yellow
Borcke	madder red	white
Prince Xaver	light blue	yellow
Kurfürstin	light blue	white
Prince Clemens	dark blue	yellow
Prince Anton	dark blue	white
Prince Maximilian	yellow	yellow
Block	yellow	white
Prince Charles	grass green	yellow
Prince Gotha	grass green	white
Count Solms	purple	yellow
Thiele	purple	white

The *Leibgrenadier Garde* retained the red coats with the yellow distinctions and continued to wear these colors until its demise in 1848. In 1771 the breeches and gaiters were changed back to the former style. The uniform altered very little up to 1810, except that the cut changed with the prevailing fashions: the collar became higher, the coat more open in front, the hats rounder, and the queue shorter (Fig. 78g). In 1793 an NCO and eight men from each company of infantry were trained in the role of *Schützen* (rifles) and were distinguished by green feather hackles in their hats. A new uniform was introduced in 1810. It consisted of a jacket with straight turned-back lapels fastened down to the waist, with white skirt turnbacks piped in the regimental color, as were the shoulder straps. The breeches were of white cloth, with short black gaiters. The stock was red. The chacos had a yellow metal plate and chinscales, a white cockade, colored regimental pompon, and white cords (Fig. 78h). The grenadiers had red cords and a red feather plume. The officers had jackets with longer skirts, and Frenon-type epaulettes. They wore gorgets when on duty. The white breeches were worn in knee boots.

According to the 1813 army list, the distinctions were as follows.

REGIMENT	DISTINCTIONS	BUTTONS
King's	red	yellow
Niesemeuschel	red	white
Prince Anton	blue	white
Low	blue	yellow
Prince Maximilian	yellow	yellow
Rechten	yellow	white
Prince Frederick Augustus	green	yellow
Steindel	green	white

In the same year, however, the Prince Frederick Augustus Regiment adopted light-blue distinctions. By the end of 1813, as a result of the rigorous usage of war, the infantry were in the greatest need of new uniforms.

In 1815 the white cockade with green circle was introduced. The infantry adopted white jackets without lapels, but with two rows of yellow metal buttons. The collar and cuffs were green throughout. The guards adopted a narrow lace loop on each side of the collar, and green epaulettes. The cords were removed from the chacos. Green trousers were worn (Fig. 78i). The chacos had a flattened circular pompon with a green edging. The center was green for the *Leibregiment*, blue for the 1st Regiment, black for the 2nd, and red for the 3rd. The company number, from 1 to 12, in yellow metal, was placed on the center. Peaked caps of green cloth were worn on service. In 1832 double-breasted green jackets with yellow metal buttons were taken into wear in place of the white ones. The collar, cuffs, trousers, and field caps were light blue. The piping was red (Fig. 78k). The regimental distinctions consisted of the green pompon, henceforth shaped like a plume, and the shoulder straps, which were red for the *Leibregiment* and light blue for the 1st Regiment, white for the 2nd, green for the 3rd, and black for the Garrison Division. The chaco had a star plate in front, and a back peak. Up to then the ranks of the officers had been denoted by the lace edging on the collar; but from that date they were indicated by means of stars on the epaulettes. Bandsmen had light-blue cloth epaulettes with worsted fringes, and yellow metal crescents. In 1842 the tuft-shaped pompons were replaced by oval ones; and the differently colored shoulder straps were replaced by dark green ones, the same as the coat. In 1849 the infantry was organized into brigades, and the battalions were consecutively numbered throughout the infantry:

1st Brigade—Battalions 1–4
2nd Brigade—Battalions 5–8
3rd Brigade—Battalions 9–12
4th (Leib-) Brigade—Battalions 13–16

At the same time, tunics, with the same distinctions as on the old jackets, were introduced for the infantry. The equipment, which had been white up until then, was replaced by black. The Virchowsche knapsack was also adopted. Tapering chacos were issued in 1846 (Fig. 78l). From 1851 the cartridge box was worn on the shoulder straps; the *Leibregiment* had a crown above as well. Officers wore their sword belts over their coats. Their gorgets were abolished. In 1861 the drums, which had been discontinued in 1849, were reintroduced. In 1862 the color of the tunics was altered; they and the shoulder straps, like the trousers, now became light blue (Fig. 78m). The 1st Brigade had red collars and cuffs; the 2nd, yellow; the 3rd, black; and the 4th, white. The coat was piped red all around, and along the bottom edge of the collar. Peaked forage caps were issued to the infantry in 1866. They were light blue, with band of the brigade color; the piping and the company number above the cockade were red. The battalion number was worn on the shoulder straps. Officers lost their epaulettes, and their stars of rank were placed at the ends of the collar. In 1867 a new pattern of uniform was introduced, very similar to the Prussian model but with many features of Saxony retained. The dark blue tunics were piped red all around; the skirt flaps had only two buttons; the collar and cuffs were red, the latter of their old style, with two buttons on the hind arm seam. A Prussian-pattern helmet was worn, with a star plate bearing the arms of Saxony on the front. The fittings were of yellow metal,

Fig. 79. Germany. Saxony—Cavalry.

a, b, c, d, e: cuirassiers. f: dragoons. g, h: *chevau-légers*. i, k, l, m, n: heavy cavalry. o, p, q: hussars. r: lancer.

like the buttons. The gray trousers had red triple stripes (Fig. 78n). The regiments were denoted by yellow numerals on their shoulder straps, which were of basic color, piped red. The equipment was of black leather. The other changes conformed to the practice in Prussia. The grenadier regiments had lace loops on their collars and Swedish cuffs, and a black hair plume for full dress. The 100th Regiment had white metal buttons. The Saxon infantry formed the following regiments of the *Reichsheer*: 100th, 101st (grenadiers), 102nd, 103rd, 104th, 105th, 106th, 107th, 133rd, 134th, 139th, 177th, 178th, 179th, 181st, and 182nd. The 108th Regiment is discussed in detail in the next section.

On the 1910-pattern service dress, the Saxon infantry retained their distinctive pattern of cuffs, the red piping on the skirts, and the Saxon skirt flaps; but the shoulder straps were of Prussian pattern. The shoulder strap piping was white in the XIIth Army Corps and red in the XIXth. The collar patches on the greatcoat displayed a further peculiarity: only in Saxony were they field gray with colored piping. The Saxon units adopted the 1915-model Prussian greatcoat, jacket, and trousers without any alterations. The Grenadier Regiments Nos. 100 and 101 wore gray double lace loops on white patches, with a red light, on their collars.

II. LIGHT INFANTRY (*JÄGER* AND *SCHÜTZEN*)

In 1809 a corps of light infantry was raised from the *Schützen* attached to the infantry, and in the same year, too, a *Jäger* corps was formed. The uniform for both was dark green with black distinctions and yellow metal buttons of the pattern described for the infantry. The light infantry chacos had a green plume and cords, and yellow metal plate (Fig. 80a); the *Jäger* had white cords, a green plume, and a *Jäger* horn badge. The accoutrements were of black leather. The combination of green, black, and red remained the distinctive feature of light troops. In general, the changes in style and in parts of the uniform followed those of the infantry. The green-edged, disc-shaped pompon introduced in 1822 had a black center with a yellow metal Roman numeral on it. From 1832 the cuff patches and shoulder straps were of a different color for each battalion: red for the 1st; light green for the 2nd; and light blue for the 3rd. The epaulettes, which were introduced for bandsmen in 1832, had black crescent pads and fringes, and yellow metal crescents. The tunic and new-pattern chaco were introduced as described above. After the issue of the new uniform in 1862, the uniform differed little from that of the infantry. The 1867-pattern uniform was very similar to the earlier one. The very low kepi introduced at that time had no back peak, and had a black horsehair plume, which was tacked onto the left side (Fig. 80c). There was red piping along the bottom, but not the top, edge of the collar; the officers' collars were piped all around. The shoulder straps were of basic color, and had a red *Jäger* horn on them, with the numerals below. *Schützen-Füsilier* Regiment No. 108 had yellow metal buttons; *Jäger* Battalions Nos. 12, 13, and 15 (which were disbanded soon afterward) had white metal. The Saxon Machine Gun Detachment wore the uniform of the Prussian detachments with the following differences: Saxon cockade, chaco star, and skirt flaps. The service dress, with corresponding variations, was of the Prussian pattern. The 1910 service dress for *Jäger* and *Schützen* was also based on the Prussian model, with the same differences. The *Schützen* had black piping on collars and cuffs. The collar patches on the greatcoat were gray-green, with a green and black edging for *Jäger* and *Schützen* respectively. The 1915 gray-green service dress resembled that of the

Fig. 80. Germany. Saxony—Miscellaneous.

a, b, c: light infantry (*Jäger*, *Schützen*). d, e, f, i, k: artillery. g, h: horse artillery. l: private, transport corps. m: general officer.

Prussian *Jäger*. The shoulder straps were piped green; the *Jäger* horn and numerals on them were red and buttons remained of white metal. *Schützenregiment* No. 108 retained its yellow metal buttons and had black piping around the shoulder straps.

III. *REITER* AND CUIRASSIERS

In 1695 the basic color of the uniform was red. The cloak was the same color. Hats were worn. The breeches were of yellow leather, worn with long boots.

In 1707 the distinctions were as follows.

REGIMENT	DISTINCTIONS
Leibregiment	white
Queen's	straw
Kurprinz	yellow
Prince Alexander	green
Beust	black
Eichstaedt	coffee brown
Damitz	pale blue

White coats were adopted in 1734; the cuirass was worn underneath. The housings were of the distinctive color. In 1740 straw-colored jackets and waistcoats were taken into wear. NCOs had laced hats. Double-breasted coats with eight buttons in pairs on the lapels were adopted in the following year.

The distinctions in 1754 were as follows.

REGIMENT	COAT	DISTINCTIONS	BUTTONS
Garde du Corps	red	pale blue	yellow
Leibkürassiere	white	bright red	yellow
Crown Prince Cuirassiers	white	pale blue	white
Arnim Cuirassiers	white	crimson	white
Prince Anhalt Cuirassiers	white	yellow	white
Plötz Cuirassiers	white	green	yellow
Vitzthum Cuirassiers	white	dark blue	yellow

During the imprisonment of the Saxon army in the Seven Years' War, after its surrender at Pirns in 1756, the cuirassiers formed themselves into grenadier companies, in French pay. When new uniforms were adopted throughout the army in 1765, the *Gardes du Corps* were issued with yellowish-colored jackets and breeches, with blue collar, cuffs, skirt turnbacks, and waistcoats, all of which were edged with yellow lace with red through it. The cravat was red. The undress uniform, and the officers' levee dress, was red. The Carabinier Regiment wore a similar uniform, but with red distinctions. The *Kürfurst* Cuirassier Regiment had red distinctions on their yellowish jackets, with yellow lace with red through it; the Prince Anhalt Regiment had yellow distinctions, with silver lace for the others (the other regiments had gold). These uniforms were worn up to 1810, except that the men's hat lace was abolished, and a feather plume introduced, with a black base for officers and black tip for NCOs (Figs. 79c,d). Armor consisted only of a blackened breast plate. In 1810 the helmet with comb was introduced: for the *Gardes du Corps* it was of yellow metal with a black band around the base, and a black crest. The jacket was yellow; the collar, cuffs, and skirt turnbacks were blue. The collar, cuffs, skirts, and front of the jacket were edged with lace with blue, red, and yellow stripes. The officers had gold lace, white breeches, and plumes like those formerly worn in the hats. Both the line cuirassier regiments had yellow metal helmets, white jackets and breeches, high boots, gauntlets, black breast plates, and shoulder scales (Fig. 79e). The distinctions were red for the *Leibkürassiere* (formerly King's Cuirassiers), with a red-and-yellow edging; and yellow for the Zastrow (formerly Anhalt) Cuirassiers, with a white-and-black lace edging. In 1815 both regiments were amalgamated; and from them the *Garde-Reiter* Regiment was formed in 1821. The same year, the two other cavalry regiments (hussars and lancers) were equipped as *Reiter* regiments. A similar uniform was authorized for all three regiments: a leather helmet with a yellow metal plate and chinscales, and black comb and crest (Fig. 79i). The jacket was white with two rows of yellow metal buttons; light-blue collar, cuffs, and piping; light-blue trousers, shabraques, and valises; yellow metal shoulder scales; white trousers stripes; and a white edging of hussar pattern on the shabraques. The buttons and the valise ends of the *Garde-Regiment* bore a crown; those of the other two regiments had numbers on them. The *Garde-Regiment* carried the earlier-pattern slightly curved cuirassier saber with a brass hilt; the other two had the light cavalry saber with a steel hilt. The regiments were differentiated by their collar, cuffs, and skirt edgings, which were white for the *Garde Reiter* Regiment, red for the 1st *leichten* (light) *Reiter* Regiment, and crimson for the 2nd. These regimental colors were discontinued in 1840, when all adopted white distinctions, and thereafter the regiments were differentiated only by the cuff patches then introduced, which were white for the Guard Regiment, red for the 1st, and light blue for the 2nd. In 1849 a 3rd Regiment was raised. It adopted yellow (later orange) patches. The crest on the helmet was abolished in the same year. Tunics were introduced in place of the jackets; the shabraques, formerly of hussar type with vandyked edges, now had rounded ends and were edged with stripes of the same color as the cuff patches. White piping was added around the hem of the coat in 1852. The collar, white up to then, was made the same color as the cuffs, which were now of Swedish type with two buttons (Fig. 79l). In 1862 the buttons were removed from the front of the tunic, which was made to fasten with hooks. A lace edging was added down the front. A new pattern of helmet was introduced in 1867, with a small black crest on the comb (Fig. 79m). The distinctions were white for the Guard Regiment, poppy red for the 1st Regiment, purple for the 2nd, and black for the 3rd. The tunic and overalls remained light blue; the leather accoutrements were white; the saddle had a black sheepskin cover. The trumpeters had red crests on their helmets and no wings on their tunics, but had thirteen loops of lace down the front. The officers did not wear sashes. When the two Saxon hussar regiments were formed, only two *Reiter* regiments were left: the *Garde-Reiter* Regiment and the Carabinier Regiment. The former kept its white distinctions; the latter, the black of the 3rd *Reiter* Regiment. A cuirassier helmet of Prussian pattern was worn, of yellow metal with white metal fittings, with a star on the front bearing the arms of Saxony (Fig. 79n). In full dress, a white hair plume was worn. The breeches were worn in high boots. When the cavalry as a whole was equipped with lances, the

229

Saxon Regiment had white and green pennants. At first, they carried wooden lances. From 1907 a silver lion was worn on the helmets of the *Garde-Reiter* Regiment in full dress.

The 1910 service dress was of the pattern worn by the Prussian cuirassiers, but with Saxon skirt flaps. The jacket lace of the Guard Regiment had white, and not light-blue, stripes. The shoulder straps on the 1915 uniform were cornflower blue, with white piping for the Guard Regiment and black for the Carabinier Regiment. The former also wore a yellow cipher on the shoulder straps, and gray double lace loops on white patches, with a cornflower blue light, on the collar. The trouser piping remained red.

IV. DRAGOONS, *CHEVAU-LÉGERS*, LANCERS, AND HUSSARS

In 1695 the Saxon dragoons adopted red coats, yellow leather breeches, and hats. The distinctions in 1707 were as follows.

Baireuth—light blue
Brause—yellow
Schulenburg—straw
Dünewald—green
Goltz—black
Wrangel—coffee brown

Around 1730 grenadiers were also added to the dragoon regiments. They wore caps like the infantry grenadiers. From that date the coats had collars and cuffs (Fig. 79f). The cravats were black. Waistcoats and breeches were buff-colored. The equipment was of fawn leather; the grenadiers wore a match case on the front of their pouch belts.

In 1730 the regimental distinctions were: *Grenadiers à Cheval*, straw color; Arnstadt Regiment, dark blue; Katte, popinjay green; Goldäcker, grass green; and *Chevalier de Saxe*, pale blue. All the regiments had white buttons.

The Mier Dragoon Regiment wore Polish dress. The uniform changed only slightly up to the outbreak of the Seven Years' War. In 1754 the Rutowsky Regiment of Light Dragoons wore red coats with black distinctions, straw-colored waistcoats, and yellow buttons. In 1765 the *chevau-légers* adopted red coats in place of their green ones; with green distinctions for the Albert *chevau-légers*, and blue for the Renard *chevau-légers*. They had yellow metal buttons, and straw-colored waistcoats and breeches. The Kurland *chevau-légers*, which were first uniformly clothed in 1762, wore green coats with red distinctions up to 1767. The Sacken Dragoons had red coats with black distinctions and white metal buttons. The red of the *chevau-légers* uniform was a rather light color. In 1767 red coats were authorized for the Kurland Regiment as well, with cuffs of popinjay green plush and yellow metal buttons. Up to 1810 the uniform of the *chevau-légers* remained in general the same, except that the cut was subject to changing fashions. The lace on the hat was abolished in the meantime and replaced by a white plume (Fig.79g). The shabraques were red. Toward the end of the eighteenth century, black sheepskin saddle covers were introduced. Chacos were authorized in 1810 (Fig. 79h).

As a result of the close relations between Poland and the Electorate of Saxony, lancers were often mentioned in the Saxon army. In 1754 the following Pulks were raised:

Wilczewski—long white coats with red distinctions, and pale blue undergarments
Rudnicki—similar uniform, with pale blue distinctions on the white coats
Bronikowsky—yellow distinctions

All three had yellow metal buttons. These units do not appear to have lasted for very long.

A new lancer regiment was raised in 1813. The uniform was of the then-current style: The jacket and breeches were blue, with black distinctions, red piping, white metal buttons and insignia, and blue lancer caps. The uniform was altered in 1815 to red jackets with light-blue distinctions, trousers, and chacos. In 1821 the regiment was turned into a *Reiter* regiment.

In 1867 two lancer regiments were raised from drafts of other regiments. They adopted a uniform of Prussian pattern. The lancer jacket and overalls were light blue, with crimson collar, cuffs, and lapels, which were buttoned back for full dress, and the overalls had crimson stripes. The 1st Regiment had loops of white guard lace; the 2nd, yellow. The piping was white. Both regiments had yellow metal shoulder scales. The lancer caps had a star in front, and a white cover in the 1st Regiment, and crimson in the 2nd, for full-dress wear. The undress cap was white, with a light-blue band for the 1st Regiment and crimson for the 2nd. In full dress, black sheepskin saddle covers, as for the *Reiter*, were worn. The 3rd Regiment (No. 21), raised in 1905, adopted the uniform of the 1st Regiment (No. 17), but with white metal insignia and light-blue lancer cap covers. The lances had white and green pennants. The regiments were numbered 17, 18, and 21 in the German army.

The 1910 service dress was exactly of the Prussian pattern, except that the shoulder straps were not crescent-shaped but were as in the infantry. The regiments gave up their former distinctive colors and were differentiated by the following colors of piping: white for the 17th Regiment, red for the 18th, and yellow for the 21st. On the 1915 uniform, the lancer regiments wore red shoulder straps with yellow numerals, and colored piping: white for the 17th Regiment, purple for the 18th, and golden yellow for the 21st.

A hussar regiment was raised in 1791. The uniform consisted of light-blue pelisses with black edging and white loopings; white dolmans with light-blue cuffs, collars, lace, and loopings; red sashes; and white undergarments. The black *Flügelmützen* had a white lace edging, and blue lining to the wing. The feather plume was white. The cloaks were blue (Fig. 79o). Later, light-blue dolmans with white loopings and black distinctions were taken into wear. Chacos were introduced in 1810 (Fig. 79p). In 1822 the regiment was converted into *Reiter*.

In 1875 two hussar regiments were raised, the 1st (later No. 18) from the 1st *Reiter* Regiment, and the 2nd (No. 19) from the 2nd, which had been formed from the former hussar regiment of 1791. Both regiments wore light-blue *Attilas* and overalls, with yellow loopings for the 1st Regiment and white for the 2nd. The former had red fur cap bags; the latter, crimson; the bags had a star plate. The sabertaches were light blue, with edging the color of the loops (Fig. 79q). Black sheepskin saddle covers were worn for full dress. The lances had white and green pennants. The 20th Regiment was raised in 1910 and only wore service dress. It adopted a light-blue bag for the fur cap and had a cornflower blue band and white piping on the undress cap. In full dress, a plume and sheepskin saddle covering were worn. Generally speaking, the regiment had no other items of peacetime full dress. The 1910 service dress was of Prussian pattern, but all the regiments wore yellow numerals on their shoulder cords. The Saxon hussar regiments wore the 1915-model Prussian jacket, greatcoat, and trousers, but had shoulder cords as on the previous pattern, with white numerals for the 18th Regiment and golden yellow for the 20th and 21st.

V. ARTILLERY, PIONEERS, AND TRANSPORT CORPS

In 1691 the artillery wore gray coats with red cuffs and collars and red cloth stockings. The hat had a cord around it. In 1717 they had green coats with red collar, lapels, and cuffs, and straw-colored undergarments. The green-and-white uniform was worn up to 1914, except for a short break in 1728–1730, when the field artillery had straw-colored distinctions. The uniform had yellow buttons, with gold embroidery for officers and NCOs, and was very much like that of the infantry in style. The breeches were gray. The horse artillery, which was raised later, adopted a uniform like that of the *chevau-légers*, but of green and red, with yellow metal buttons. Chacos were introduced in 1810 (Fig. 80f). From 1843 to 1867 the horse artillery wore a crested helmet of Bavarian type (Fig. 80h). In 1849 the yellow leather equipment worn up to then by both the horse and foot artillery was replaced by black (Fig. 80i). Green tunics with red collars, yellow metal buttons, and red piping were introduced in 1867. The horse artillery wore piping on the sleeve and back seams. The helmet had the same fittings as for the infantry, but with a ball finial (Fig. 80k). Black hair plumes were worn in full dress. The horse artillery had brass shoulder scales; the foot artillery, green shoulder straps with red piping, regimental number, and grenade with a single burst of flames. The 1910 service dress was of Prussian style, but with Saxon skirts. The shoulder straps of the XIIth Army Corps were piped white, those of the XIXth, red. The Foot Artillery wore white piping on their shoulder straps, and had Saxon cuffs. The 1915 service dress uniform was also of Prussian type. The shoulder straps of the field artillery regiments were red with yellow devices. The 12th and 32nd regiments also wore white piping. Foot Artillery Regiments Nos. 12 and 19 had yellow shoulder straps with red numerals and crossed grenades. The pioneers were distinguished from the artillery principally by their white metal buttons. The lines-of-communication troops wore the blue Prussian-pattern uniform with the usual Saxon characteristics. In 1913 the 7th Telegraph Battalion adopted Saxon skirts. The service dress of the pioneers was of Prussian pattern, but with Saxon skirts, cuffs, and shoulder straps. The 1915 uniform was as in Prussia, with white metal buttons. The Saxon pioneers wore a crossed spade and pickaxe in red above the numerals on their shoulder straps. In 1800 the transport corps wore the same combination of colors as in 1914, i.e., light blue, with black distinctions and red piping. The chaco had no back peak. After the Prussians had introduced helmets for the men of their transport corps in 1910, the Saxons followed suit. The 1910 service dress was of Prussian type, but with Saxon skirts. The 1919 model uniform was also of Prussian pattern. The shoulder straps of the latter were Prussian blue with red numerals.

VI. GENERAL OFFICERS; DISTINCTIONS OF RANK

In 1735 general officers adopted white coats with red linings, and red waistcoats and breeches. The ranks were indicated by the amount of gold or silver embroidery. The coats were changed to blue in 1766, and this color continued in use. The uniform underwent very many changes in detail. Hats were worn up to 1867, and helmets from that date. The full dress was similar to the Prussian one, but with the usual Saxon characteristics. From 1832 ranks were denoted by metal stars worn on the epaulettes. In 1866–1867 these were superseded by stars of rank on the collar, in the Austrian fashion, as described under "Infantry." From that date they were the same as those in the Prussian army. The 1910 and 1915 service uniforms were of Prussian pattern for general officers and the general staff, as were the distinctions of rank.

SAXONY-GOTHA-ALTENBURG:
SAXONY-ALTENBURG from 1826

Cockade: green and white

At the time of the Seven Years' War, the military forces of Gotha wore white coats with red collars and cuffs; red waistcoats and cravats, and white laced hats. About 1780 blue coats with red distinctions and yellow metal buttons and white undergarments were introduced. On 18 April 1807 Saxony-Gotha joined the Confederation of the Rhine and, along with Saxony-Meiningen, had to form two battalions of the Duke of Saxony's Regiment. By agreement between the two ruling houses, the uniform consisted of blue coats with red collar, cuffs, and lapels, white undergarments, short black gaiters, and white-laced tricorne hats with a pompon. The cockade was of black leather with a gold device (Fig. 77a). The grenadiers and light infantry were denoted respectively by red and yellow worsted plumes. From 1809 dark blue pantaloons with red stripes were worn in addition to the white breeches. There were nevertheless a few differences between the dress of the Gotha and Meiningen troops. The former had adopted French-style uniforms with white leather accoutrements; the latter, uniforms of the old Prussian type with black leather equipment. In 1812 complete uniformity, based on the French uniform, was established (Fig. 77b). After the disaster of 1812, the dukes had to raise a new battalion, which was named the Thuringian *Marschbataillon*. It defected to the Confederation at Altenburg on 20 April 1813 and fought, still in its former uniform, against the French on the Katzbach. The uniform consisted of a very wide-skirted dark blue coatee with red collar and light-blue cuffs. The trousers were light gray, as was the greatcoat, which had a narrow cape. The chaco was like that of the Weimar troops. The officers wore oilcloth caps. During the course of the campaign, the battalion took into wear British-style uniforms with light-blue distinctions. To make up for the loss of the battalion that had changed sides, Napoleon then demanded a whole regiment. The uniform was the same as in 1812. After the Second Peace of Paris, the dress was completely altered. Green jackets with a row of yellow metal buttons, black collars, and cuffs with yellow lace loops and red piping were introduced. The musketeers had red shoulder straps; the *Jäger*, black. The trousers were gray in winter, white in summer. The chacos had a yellow metal star and chinscales, white cords, and a green-and-white cockade (Fig. 77c). The musketeers wore white leather equipment; the *Jäger*, black. Officers had gold lace loops, gold epaulettes, and silver chaco cords. They wore gorgets up to 1850. (For Figure 77, see page 220.)

A *Garde du Corps* seventy to seventy-five strong existed up to 1825. They wore a yellow jacket with red collar and cuffs, and white leather breeches; butcher boots with spurs; white cloaks; swords; and carbines. The corps were not mounted.

The uniform was changed in 1845 with the introduction of Prussian-style tunics and of helmets. Collar and cuffs were as before. There were eight yellow metal buttons down the front of the tunic and two at the waist behind. The shoulder straps bore the company number in yellow. The helmet had a yellow metal star. The top of the spike was formed like the *Irmensäule* (the pillar-shaped crest on the coat of arms of Saxony). In full dress, the musketeers had white hair plumes, the *Jäger* black, and bandsmen red. In 1850 the unit was turned into a fusilier battalion. The uniform remained as before, except that the leather equipment was changed to black for all and was no longer worn crossed (Fig. 77d). From 1867 the Altenburg contingent formed the 1st Battalion of the 96th Infantry Regiment.

SAXONY-KOBURG:
SAXONY-KOBURG-GOTHA from 1826

Cockade: green and white

During the period of the Confederation of the Rhine, Koburg provided a contingent for the 4th Rhine Confederation Regiment (that of the Duke of Saxony). The uniform (Fig. 81a) consisted of a dark green jacket with self-colored cuff patches with white lace loops on them, yellow collar and cuffs, and white metal buttons. The skirt turnbacks were red. Light-blue Hungarian breeches with yellow Austrian knots on them and short black gaiters, or long linen trousers, were also worn. Leather accoutrements were white. The chaco had white cords and a yellow metal plate with a *Jäger* horn on it. The grenadiers wore fur caps and red worsted epaulettes with fringes. The officers originally wore hats and later, chacos.

The volunteer *Jäger*, which Koburg put into the field along with Meiningen and Hildburghausen in 1813, had green coats with red cuffs and yellow lace, gray

Fig. 81. Germany. Koburg-Gotha, Meiningen.

Koburg Gotha—a, b, c, d, e: infantry. Saxony-Meiningen—f: *Schütze*. g,
h: fusilier. i: fusilier officer.

trousers piped green, and chacos with green cords. They also wore long butcher
boots with patent leather uppers.

The *Landwehr* had green coats and Swedish-type hats turned up at one side.

In 1826 the ruling house of Saxony-Gotha became extinct. The Koburg and
Gotha Contingent was now formed into a Saxony-Koburg-Gotha Infantry Regiment. The uniform (Fig. 81b) included a dark green jacket with black collar and
cuffs, piped red (the former with yellow lace loops), and red skirt turnbacks. The
shoulder straps were at first black with red piping and later, red piped yellow. The
trousers were green to begin with, then gray, and in summer, white. The chaco cords
were white. In 1846 the contingent was only six companies strong, with a *Jäger*
detachment in addition. They now wore a tunic, of the same colors as before. The
shoulder straps and pointed cuff patches were red, the trousers gray. The crested
helmets had a yellow metal plate and white plume (Fig. 81c). Leather equipment was
white, or black for *Jäger*. A military convention was concluded between Koburg-
Gotha and Prussia in 1861. The uniform up to 1867 (Fig. 81d) consisted of a dark
green tunic with black collar piped red all around, red shoulder straps and cuff
patches, black cuffs and red piping, and yellow metal buttons. The trousers had red
piping. The leather accoutrements were black. The helmet had an unusually shaped
spike, with a small ball on top. In full dress, the 1st Battalion wore white hair plumes,
and the 2nd, black, which depended from this ball (Fig. 81e). In 1866 the Koburg-
Gotha troops fought with the Army of the Main at Langensalza and in various later
battles. In 1867 they were amalgamated with the Meiningen troops and thereafter
bore the regimental number 95. For the uniform, see the section on Prussia.

SAXONY-MEININGEN-HILDBURGHAUSEN

Cockade: green and white

Before 1807 Meiningen troops consisted of *Jäger*. They wore green uniforms with red distinctions, and *Kasketts*. In 1807 they were turned into musketeers and wore the same uniform as described for Saxony-Gotha-Altenburg. The Hildburghausen troops wore the same uniform as those of Weimar. The volunteer *Jäger*, raised in 1814, were dressed like those from Koburg.

A new uniform was introduced in 1821. It consisted of a green coat with blue collar and cuffs and red-piped skirts. The chaco had white cords. In 1826, on the termination of the hereditary ruling house, the Meiningen dynasty acquired Hildburghausen, while the Hildburghausen ruling house took possession of Altenburg, renaming it Saxony-Altenburg. The contingent was now formed into a battalion, with a *Schützen* detachment in addition. From 1827 the uniform consisted of a dark green jacket with black collar, pointed cuffs, shoulder straps, and padded wings, with two rows of yelllow metal buttons down the front, tapering to the waist. The trousers were at first green, later gray; and white linen ones were worn in summer. The chacos had a black horsehair plume and cords (light green for *Schützen*). The whole battalion was turned into *Schützen* in 1827 (Fig. 81f). In 1846 dark green tunics with black collar and cuffs, and red shoulder straps and cuff patches, were introduced. The piping was red and went all around the collar; the buttons, yellow metal; and the trousers, gray with red piping. The battalion number was worn in red on the shoulder straps. Leather equipment was black (later, the *Gürtelrüstung* was worn). The helmet had yellow metal fittings and a white metal star (Fig. 81g). A new pattern of uniform was issued in 1864. It consisted of a dark green tunic with black loops across the front and black buttons (Fig. 81h). The collar, shoulder straps, and pointed cuffs were black; the piping around the collar, cuffs, and shoulder straps was red. In addition, a kepi with a black horsehair plume was supposed to have been introduced, but few, at least among the men, appear to have received it. The officers' uniforms had no red piping but were edged with black lace, and had black cord loops. The officers' silver and green embroidered sashes were similar to those worn in Austria (Fig. 81i). In 1867 a military convention was concluded with Prussia, as a result of which Koburg-Gotha and Meiningen formed the 95th Regiment in the Prussian army.

SAXONY-WEIMAR

Cockade: black, green, and yellow

In the eighteenth century the Weimar troops dressed exactly like the Prussians. The grenadiers adopted fur caps in the late 1780s. In 1788 Duke Charles Augustus raised a *Jäger* battalion, later called the Sharpshooters Battalion. Its uniform (Fig. 82a) in 1790 consisted of a green coatee with self-colored Brandenburg cuffs and collar, yellow collar and skirt turnbacks, and red cravats. The breeches were white, with short black gaiters. The pouch belt was yellowish in color. In 1796 black leather accoutrements were introduced, and the cartridge box was placed on the front of the waistbelt. The breeches, of the same style as before, were green. In 1806 the cartridge box was again moved to the shoulder belt. A form of grenadier cap, rather like the contemporary Prussian one, but with a yellow metal plate on the front and a green plume on the left side, was worn (Fig. 82b). In 1807 a new pattern of hat was introduced (Fig. 82c). It had a small metal plate on the front and yellow binding. The plume was unchanged. The leather equipment was altered to yellow, but to black again in 1809. Long gray overalls were

Fig. 82. Germany. Weimar.
a, b, c, d: sharpshooters.
e: infantry officer.

now worn over the gaiters. Chacos with white cords and a yellow metal horn device were authorized in 1812 (Fig. 82d). The cords were later abolished. Yellow piping was added to the gray trousers; in summer, white trousers were worn. The uniform remained unchanged until the introduction of the tunic. The colors were as before. Collar and cuffs were green with yellow metal fittings. Officers had yellow sashes (Fig. 82e). On 26 June 1867 the Weimar Contingent became the 94th Infantry Regiment. For the distinctions, see the section on Prussia.

There existed up to 1914 a small detachment of hussars, the origins of which went far back into the eighteenth century. Their uniform was almost exactly like that of the Prussian Zieten Hussar Regiment: red dolmans with white loopings, blue pelisses, and blue shabraques with a red vandyked edge. The collars were red and the cuffs, blue. The fur caps had a red bag; later, black *Flügelmützen* were worn, then chacos, and still later fur caps again. The distinctive colors remained unaltered.

At the end of 1813 a volunteer *Jäger* corps was raised. The foot *Jäger* wore dark green coats with yellow collars and cuffs, red shoulder straps, and two rows of yellow metal buttons; gray breeches and gaiters; and chacos with front and back peaks, yellow metal chinscales, and cross, with the black, yellow, and green state cockade above. The mounted *Jäger* wore black coats edged with yellow lace. The breeches were black with yellow stripes. They also had yellow shoulder scales, and chacos as for the foot *Jäger*, with black plumes. Their gauntlets and leather equipment were black.

SCHAUMBURG-LIPPE

Cockade: blue, red, and white; later, red and white

In 1753 the renowned Count William of Schaumburg-Lippe-Bückeburg raised a corps of carabiniers, consisting originally of seventy-five horse and fifty foot, which wore a unique uniform when formed (Fig. 73h, page 212.) The headdress was an iron helmet edged with bearskin, and on the front was a green plate bearing the legend *"Pulchrum mori succurrit in extremis"* (The prospect of a glorious death is a help in time of danger). A black cuirass was worn over the black leather jacket, which was turned up with red. To begin with, black laméd pauldrons were worn on the upper arms. The breeches were of yellow leather. The corps was usually mounted on black Spanish stallions. During the Seven Years' War it fought as mercenaries and retained the same uniform with few alterations, when later it completely changed its role and became a form of military police.

During the period of the Confederation of the Rhine, the Schaumburg and Detmold contingents wore the same uniform. After 1815 Schaumburg provided two companies of infantry. The best of them were formed into a *Jäger* detachment. The distinctive colors were as in Detmold. The *Jäger* were distinguished by green collars and cuffs and black leather equipment. At the end of the 1830s the whole contingent was turned into *Jäger*. Dark green jackets with black collars, cuffs, shoulder straps, and skirt edging, red piping, and yellow metal buttons were introduced. The gray trousers had red piping. Equipment was of black leather. The chacos had a yellow metal plate, white cords, and drooping black feather plume. In the 1840s Prussian-type tunics, in the former colors, were retained. Crested helmets of Bavarian pattern with brass chinscales and star were worn (Fig. 73l). On the star was a German silver plate bearing the Nesselblatt arms. The collar was entirely black. Cuffs and shoulder straps were the same color, and all were piped red. The shoulder straps bore the brass cipher "GA" crowned. Leather equipment was black. In 1866 the contingent formed part of the garrison of Mainz. After the convention of 30 June 1867, those eligible for military service were sent to the 7th Westphalian *Jäger* Battalion.

SCHLESWIG-HOLSTEIN

In 1848–1850, the infantry of Schleswig-Holstein was dressed exactly like the Prussian infantry, except that the collar was all red. The shoulder straps were white, with the battalion number in red. Buttons and leather equipment were white. The Danish-style light-blue trousers had red piping. The spiked helmets bore a yellow metal double eagle on the front, with the Schleswig-Holstein arms on it. The *Jäger* wore similar tunics, but in green, with red distinctions and shoulder straps. The buttons were white metal. The gray trousers had red piping. The leather equipment was black. The kepis had front and back peaks, with a yellow metal double eagle plate, and a long drooping black horsehair plume. The dragoons were dressed in light-blue tunics and trousers, with pink collars, pointed cuffs, and piping. The shoulder straps were white with red numerals. Buttons and leather accoutrements were white. The helmets resembled those of the Prussian cuirassiers and were of white metal with a yellow metal plate. The artillery wore dark blue tunics and light-blue trousers, with crimson distinctions and piping, and yellow metal buttons and helmet plate. The helmet had a ball finial. Leather equipment was white. The pioneers had the same helmet and ball as the artillery. Their tunics were dark blue with self-colored cuffs and black collars and shoulder straps, the former piped red, the latter, white. The rest of the piping was red; the buttons were yellow metal. Black leather equipment was worn. The trousers were as for the infantry.

SCHWARZBURG (SCHWARZBURG-RUDOLSTADT and SCHWARZBURG-SONDERSHAUSEN)

Cockade: white and blue

At the time of the War of the Spanish Succession (1701–1713), Schwarzburg and Reuss together raised an infantry regiment. It wore white coats without collars or lapels, but with red cuffs. In 1733, on the outbreak of the War of the Polish Succession, it was again summoned to the assistance of the Empire. Once more the Schwarzburg and Reuss ruling houses together raised a regiment. It was never formally disbanded, but there was no continued amalgamation of the Schwarzburg and Reuss contingents.

A report of 1791 (printed in von Döring, *Geschichte des 96. Infanterie Regiments*) mentions a *Garde du Corps* in Schwarzburg. They wore blue coats with red collar and cuffs, and straw-colored waistcoats edged with red and blue lace, in addition to bearskin caps. White gaiters were worn for full dress, instead of the normal black ones. Hussars are also mentioned. Their uniform consisted of a green dolman with red cuffs; red pelisse edged with black fur, with white loopings, and yellow leather breeches. The fur caps had a red bag, and a black and white plume. The red shabraques had a green vandyke edged white; the similarly ornamented sabertaches bore the cipher "CF." Pouch belts were yellow.

During the war of the First Coalition against France, Schwarzburg formed a contingent in 1792, which was dressed as follows: blue coats with self-colored red-piped lapels; red linings, collar, and cuffs; yellow metal buttons; and white undergarments. The had white-laced hats with colored plumes varying according to company, and cloth caps as well.

Both of the companies that Schwarzburg had to provide for the *Fürstenbataillon* wore dark green jackets and breeches, with red collar and cuffs, and red stripes on the breeches. (The Battalion of the Princes consisted of: 1st Company, Schwarzburg-Sondershausen; 2nd, Schwarzburg-Rudolstadt; 3rd, Lippe-Detmold; 4th, Lippe-Bückeburg; 5th, Reuss; 6th, Waldeck.) The chacos had white cords and a red plume. The leather equipment was black. Since the rank distinctions of the officers of the several contingents of the battalion varied, French-style officers' epaulettes were adopted throughout. Illustrations show gray breeches and short black gaiters being worn, as well as the green breeches with red stripes (Fig. 77i). After the Napoleonic Wars the uniform was as follows: Russian (dark) green basic color with red collar, cuffs, and skirt edging, and green shoulder straps piped red. Down the front of the jacket was a row of nine yellow metal buttons. The gray trousers had red stripes. White linen ones were worn in summer. The chaco had a yellow metal double eagle plate and chinscales, blue and white cockade, and white cords (Fig. 77k). The undress caps were green with red piping and had no cockade up to 1845. The leather equipment was black. On the cartridge box was a yellow metal oval plate bearing the double eagle. The officers wore gold epaulettes with small white stars denoting rank. Field officers had bullions. In 1845 a green tunic with self-colored cuffs and red collar and piping, and a row of nine yellow metal buttons down the front, was introduced. The headdress was the Bavarian crested helmet with double eagle plate (Fig. 77l). Spiked helmets with similar mounts were adopted later. Equipment continued to be made of black leather. The *Gürtelrüstung* was introduced in the 1850s (Fig. 77m). Officers adopted light sabers carried on slings in place of swords. In 1866, while part of the 2nd Reserve Army Corps of the Army of the Main, the Schwarzburg troops left off wearing helmets, to bring about uniformity throughout the corps, as half only had caps, and the Mecklenburg troops that belonged to it had no other headdress. From 1867 Schwarzburg formed the 3rd Battalion of the 96th Infantry Regiment. (For Figure 77, see page 220.)

WALDECK

Cockade: black, red, and yellow

The Principality of Waldeck was obliged to join the Confederation of the Rhine in April 1807 and to provide a contingent of three companies of infantry for the campaign in Spain. One company was attached to the *Fürstenbataillon* (Schwarzburg-Rudolstadt, Lippe, Reuss). After this had suffered severe losses in the campaign, the remnants joined the 6th Rhine Confederation Regiment, of which the other two Waldeck companies formed part. The uniform (Fig. 73a) consisted of a white jacket with dark blue collar, lapels, and cuffs; yellow metal buttons; chacos with white cords without plumes; and white leather equipment. Yellow cords and a yellow plume were adopted in 1812.

After the Napoleonic Wars, Waldeck had to provide three companies of infantry and a *Jäger* company for the Army of the German Confederation. The infantry adopted dark green jackets with red collars, cuffs, shoulder straps, and skirt turnbacks; yellow metal buttons; gray trousers; black gaiters; and chacos with white cords. The *Jäger* had light-green distinctions and cords. Both infantry and *Jäger* wore black leather equipment (Fig. 73b). The *Jäger* were abolished later. Tunics and Prussian-type helmets were introduced during the 1840s. The collar was green. Collar patches, shoulder straps, Swedish cuffs, and piping were all red. The buttons and helmet plates were yellow metal. Sash and sword knot were silver, embroidered with black and yellow. The tunic cuffs were at first of Brandenburg, later of Swedish, type (Fig. 73c). After the convention of 6 August 1867, the Waldeck contingent was ranked as the 83rd Regiment. Both the Prussian and Waldeck cockades were worn on the headdress. (For Figure 73, see page 212.)

KINGDOM OF WESTPHALIA

Cockade: blue and white

Under Jérôme, Napoleon's brother, the Kingdom of Westphalia (1807–1814) put an impressive army into the field. Even before the end of 1808, fifteen batallions and eight companies of infantry, fourteen squadrons of cavalry, and ten companies of artillery were in existence. The line infantry, originally consisting of eight regiments, was dressed in white. The 1st and 2nd regiments had dark blue collars, lapels, cuffs, and piping. The 3rd and 4th had light-blue distinctions; the 5th and 6th, yellow. The regiments were further distinguished by the odd-numbered ones wearing wholly colored lapels and skirts, while the even-numbered ones had white lapels and skirts piped in the above mentioned colors. As in the French army, the grenadiers were distinguised by red chaco cords, plume, and fringed epaulettes. The *voltigeurs* had green chaco cords, a yellow-over-green plume, and green epaulettes with yellow crescents. The fusiliers (center companies) wore white shoulder straps piped in the distinctive color. The chaco cords were white. The chaco also had a circular pompon with the company number in yellow, and edging in the company color, as in the French army. Similarly, French-type distinctions of rank were worn.

In about 1810 the uniform was simplified in that the colored distinctions were done away with, and the collar, lapels, etc., were changed to dark blue. The buttons were yellow metal (Fig. 83c). In 1812 the Queen's Infantry Regiment was raised. It wore the same uniform as the rest of the infantry—white with dark blue distinctions—but the collar, lapels, and cuff patches had white lace loops on them and the buttons were of white metal. The light infantry at first wore cornflower blue uniforms with orange distinctions, and later wore green single-breasted uniforms with light-blue distinctions and white metal buttons. The carabiniers, which as in France took the place of grenadier companies in the light infantry, were denoted by red grenadier-type distinctions.

In addition to the line infantry, there were a number of guard regiments. The Guard Grenadiers (Fig. 83a) had long-skirted white coatees with red collar, cuffs, lapels, skirt turnbacks, and epaulettes. The collar, cuffs, and lapels were ornamented with gold lace loops. The undergarments were white. The headdress was a fur cap without a plate with red cords, plume, and patch at the back bearing a grenade, and yellow metal chinscales. Officers had a white plume and gold cords on their caps. The Guard *Jäger* (Fig. 83b) had green coatees, breeches, and epaulettes, with green lapels and yellow collar, cuffs, and piping. There were white lace loops on the collar, cuffs, and lapels. The buttons and the loopings on the trousers were white. The gaiters had a white edging. The chaco had a white metal plate, white cords, and a yellow-over-green plume. The *voltigeur-carabiniers* wore all-green uniforms. The

1808 – 1813.

Fig. 83. Germany. Kingdom of Westphalia.

a: guard grenadier. b: guard *Jäger*. c: line infantry. d: officer of light infantry. e: *garde du corps*. f: *chevau-léger* of the guard. g: cuirassier. h: hussar. i: artillery officer.

lace loops on the collar, the piping, and lace were red, as were the crescents of the green epaulettes. Buttons were of yellow metal. The leather equipment was black. The chaco had a yellow metal plate and a red-over-green plume.

The *Garde du Corps* had two uniforms. The full-dress uniform (Fig. 83e) consisted of a dark blue jacket with red distinctions, yellow lace loops and aiguillettes, a steel breast plate with a yellow rayed plate on the front; and a steel helmet with yellow metal mounts, black *chenille*, and white plume. The pouch belt was of black leather with yellow edges, and yellow metal mounts. The white breeches were worn with high boots. On court guard duty a white jacket with blue collar, lapels, and cuffs, all piped red, with gold lace loops and yellow metal shoulder scales, was worn. Short swords were carried. The helmet, leather equipment, and breeches were as previously described. Trumpeters wore red coatees with blue distinctions and gold lace. The helmet had a white *chenille* and red plume. The *chevau-léger-lanciers* of the guard (Fig. 83f) wore green jackets and breeches, with red collar, cuffs, and skirt lining, yellow lace loops, and yellow shoulder cords ending in trefoils. The pouch belt was of fawn leather. The black helmet had a black *chenille* and yellow plate and plume. A line *chevau-léger-lancier* regiment was raised in 1808. It had a similar uniform with orange distinctions, no lace loops, and white metal buttons. In October 1812 a 2nd Regiment was ordered to be formed. The *chevau-léger-lanciers* are said to have adopted lances in 1811. The 1st Cuirassier Regiment was raised in 1808. It adopted white coatees with crimson collar, lapels, cuffs, and skirt lining; white piping and buttons; white breeches; and red grenadier epaulettes. Later it was issued with blue uniforms. The steel helmet had yellow metal mounts, a black *chenille*, and a brown fur turban. Breast plates were not worn at first, but later, white metal ones were issued (Fig. 83g). The 2nd Cuirassier Regiment adopted blue jackets with orange distinctions, a French-style cuirass, and a helmet as for the 1st Regiment, but with a black turban. The 1st Hussar Regiment (Fig. 83h) had an all-green uniform with white loopings, red and white sashes, chacos with white metal mounts and a green plume, black sabertaches bearing a white numeral, and black leather accoutrements. The 2nd Hussar Regiment was dressed all in light blue, with pink collar and cuffs. The rest of the uniform was as for the 1st Regiment. The chaco plume was white. The Jérôme Napoleon Hussar Regiment, raised in 1813, was popularly known as "the Crabs" from its red uniform. The loopings were yellow, pelisse and breeches blue, and chacos red.

The foot artillery (Fig. 83i) had blue coatees with blue lapels and red collar, cuffs, cuff patches, skirts, and piping. Blue breeches, yellow metal buttons and chaco mounts, and yellow grenadier epaulettes were also worn. The transport corps was dressed in gray *surtouts* with gray lapels; red collar, cuffs, and piping; white metal buttons; red waistcoats with white loopings; and gray breeches with white stripes. They also had fawn leather pouch belts, chacos with white plate cords, and a red pear-shaped pompon.

General officers were dressed exactly like those in the French army, in blue uniforms with gold lace. Aides-de-camp wore blue single-breasted coatees with yellow distinctions, gold epaulettes and shoulder cords; yellow and blue sashes around the waist; and white breeches worn with high boots. The hat had a yellow plume. Aides-de-camp to the king were dressed in green coatees with green lapels, and red collars and pointed cuffs. The rich embroidery, the epaulettes, and shoulder cords were all silver. The undergarments were white. The hat had white plumage.

WÜRTTEMBERG

Cockade: black up to the end of the eighteenth century, then red, black, and yellow; red and black from 1817

I. INFANTRY

In the seventeenth century, light-colored uniforms were prevalent. The coats were mainly white, light blue, or yellow. In 1683 the *Leibgarde* had gray coats with yellow cuffs, yellow waistcoats, buff-colored breeches, and gray stockings. Generally speaking, the uniform followed civilian fashions until the 1730s. In 1734 the regimental distinctions on the white coats were as follows (Fig. 84b).

REGIMENT	LAPELS	CUFFS	WAISTCOAT	BUTTONS
Erbprinz	red	red	red	white
Prince Frederick	red	red	red	yellow
Leib regiment	red	red	red	white[1]
Prince Ludwig	—	blue	blue	yellow
Kreis regiment	—	blue	blue	white[2]

[1]red lace loops [2]blue lace loops

In 1745 all regiments with the exception of the *Kreis-Regiment* adopted yellow coats and red waistcoats. Blue coats were introduced in 1752. In 1757 the distinctions were as follows.

REGIMENT	CUFFS AND LAPELS	BUTTONS AND SHOULDER CORDS
Leib regiment[1]	carmine	white
Prince Louis	red	white
Romann	red	yellow
Roeder	pink	white
Prince Frederick William[2]	white	yellow
Truchsess	black	white

[1] silver lace loops and yellow waistcoats
[2] fusilier caps

Bearskin caps were taken into wear in the 1780s. Between then and 1799, the coats were made more cutaway in front. A fundamental change was made in the organization of the infantry in 1798, when the regiments were divided into separate battalions.

BATTALION	COLLAR, CUFFS, LAPELS	SHOULDER STRAPS	BUTTONS AND HAT LACE
Nylius	yellow	yellow	yellow
Obernitz	light blue	light blue	white
Seeger	red	white	white
Beulwitz	pink	pink	white
Perglas	white	white	white

As in Prussia, all battalions had red skirt turnbacks. The uniform was completely changed in 1799. A leather *Kaskett* was adopted, very like the Rumford helmet worn in Bavaria. It had a yellow metal plate, a pompon on the point of the comb, and a black horsehair *crinière* falling to the rear. The distinctive colors at first remained as before, although a new pattern of jacket was adopted (Fig. 84e). It was made very short and had half lapels with two buttons on the front below them. The sword belt was worn over the coat. The breeches and leather equipment were white as before. The gaiters were black. In 1803 the regimental reorganization was restored and various changes were made in the uniform (Fig. 84f). At the end of 1806 a fusilier regiment (von Neubronn) was raised. It adopted a slightly different uniform. The horsehair *crinière* on the helmet was replaced by a black crest. The jacket lapels were not of the red distinctive color, but were blue with red piping. Both of these changes (the crest on the helmet and the blue lapels) were ordered for the infantry as a whole in the following year. This change appears to have been completely implemented by 1811. Chacos were then introduced, gradually at first. They had front and back peaks, a lozenge-shaped plate, and a cockade at the top on the left side. In 1813–1814 they were universally adopted (Fig. 84g).

In 1813 the distinctions were as follows.

REGIMENT	COLLAR, CUFFS, SKIRT TURNBACKS	PIPING	BUTTONS
1	yellow	yellow	white
2	orange	orange	white
3	white	white	white
4	pink	white	white
5	light blue	white	white
6	white	red	yellow
7	red	red	yellow
8	straw yellow	straw yellow	yellow
9	black	black	yellow

In 1814 those regiments which had members of the Royal House as their colonels adopted lace loops.

In 1817 considerable changes were made in the uniforms of the whole army, in the interests of the greatest possible simplicity (Fig. 84h), and they took on a very sober appearance. The chaco was completely without ornament, having only a chinstrap and a cockade at the top in front. The knee-length royal blue coat was fastened down the front with hooks. The cuffs were either red or yellow, and the collar was either of basic color or of the distinctive color. The girdle had a red or yellow edging. The shoulder straps had red, yellow, or blue crescents. The royal blue trousers had no stripes. Equipment was of white leather. A royal blue jacket was worn in undress. Field officers wore the sword belt around the waist; company officers had a white sword belt, with small silver mounts in front, over the right shoulder. A new uniform was introduced in 1821 (Fig. 84i). The chaco had a red pompon, and a small white metal plate with the regimental number on it below the cockade. A royal blue jacket replaced the long-skirted coat. It had two rows of white metal buttons, a red collar, and blue cuffs with red piping. The crescents on the

Fig. 84. Germany. Württemberg—Infantry.

shoulders were white, with blue straps, and the regimental number in white. The coat lining was red. The trousers had red piping. Officers wore silver pompons and epaulettes. In 1836 a soft red tuft was added above the pompon, and the jacket cuffs were changed to red. The jackets were made single-breasted in 1844. In 1846 a new-pattern tapering chaco was introduced. It had a powder blue cloth body, a black leather band around the bottom, and white lace around the top. On the front was the cockade and a white loop. A double blue pompon (green for *Schützen*) was worn above.

Tunics were issued in 1849 (Fig. 84k). They had a row of white metal buttons and were royal blue. Collar, cuffs, shoulder straps, and piping were red. The skirt flaps had three buttons on them. The trousers were royal blue with red stripes as before. The infantry sword was replaced by a pioneer's sword. In 1859 the white crossbelt equipment was abolished and the black leather *Gürtelrüstung* introduced. The uniform changed again in 1864, but the new uniform was at first issued only for full dress, and the men continued to wear the old one up to 1866. They wore dark blue peaked caps with a red band. The full-dress headdress was a kepi-shaped cap of dark blue cloth with a red band and piping, and a small metal plate and the cockade on the front. As a second best and field service headgear, a dark blue cap with red piping and a small cockade was worn (Fig. 84m). The tunic was dark blue, with two rows of white metal buttons; red collar, shoulder straps, and padded wings; and red piping all around. There were two buttons on the skirt flaps. The number of the company was worn on the shoulder straps. The gray trousers had red piping. Leather equipment was black (Fig. 84l). The regimental distinctions consisted of colored collar patches: white for the 1st Regiment; 2nd, black; 3rd, orange; 4th, green; 5th, light blue; 6th, blue; 7th, dark red; 8th, yellow. Officers wore their rank badges on the collar, as in the Austrian army. As a mark of rank, they wore black and red hussar-type sashes with a bow and knot on the left side. These were introduced in 1817. On 1 August 1870 the officers were ordered to adopt shoulder cords of the type worn by Prussian officers. The following year, new uniform regulations, based on Prussian patterns, were promulgated. The infantry adopted the spiked helmet with the Württemberg arms and cockade. The tunic was double-breasted, however, in memory of the old uniform (Fig. 84n). The shoulder straps were red with yellow numerals. The cuffs and cuff patches were red, the latter with a light-blue edging. The buttons were changed to yellow metal. The Grenadier Regiments Nos. 119 and 123 had white lace loops on their collars and Swedish cuffs. From 1892 the tunic had only one row of buttons (Fig. 84o). In full dress, the grenadier regiments wore hair plumes: white for No. 119 and black for No. 123. The Württemberg regiments formed Nos. 119–127 and 180 in the infantry of the *Reichsheer*. Equipment was as in Prussia. The 1910 and 1915 dress uniforms were as in Prussia.

II. *JÄGER* AND LIGHT INFANTRY

In 1799 a Foot *Jäger* Company was raised, and attached to a grenadier battalion. It was formed into an independent *Jäger* corps in the following year. The uniform consisted of a black Corsican hat with the cipher "FII" in yellow and a green hackle; a green jacket of the same cut as that then worn by the infantry, with black collar, cuffs, half lapels, and skirt turnbacks all edged white; yellow metal buttons; green breeches; black sword belt worn around the waist, with a cartridge box in front bearing the royal cipher, and a sword. In 1801 the corps was formed into the von Romann Battalion. The uniform remained as before, except that a chaco, with green band and plume, was introduced (Fig. 86a). A second battalion was raised in 1803; it was distinguished by white metal buttons. From that date the black leather equipment was worn crossed. In 1813 both battalions were amalgamated as the Foot *Jäger* Regiment *König*. From 1811 the uniform had lapels of basic color. Yellow lace loops were added to the collar and cuffs in 1814; the buttons were changed to yellow metal, and a chaco of the pattern worn by the infantry of the line, with white cords and plume, was adopted. The regiment was disbanded in 1815.

In 1805 two battalions of light infantry were raised; these were formed into a light infantry regiment in 1813. The uniform after its formation was as for the infantry, but the basic color was green, with light-blue distinctions, white piping, yellow metal buttons, yellow leather accoutrements, white breeches, and helmet with a black *crinière*. In 1807 a chaco like that of the *Jäger* was adopted, but with a red plume. It was disbanded in 1817.

Much later, another *Jäger* corps was raised. In 1866 it consisted of two battalions; in 1870, three. The uniform was very similar to that authorized for the infantry in 1864, except that the kepi was light green with a blue band and piping, and had a small black hair plume. The tunic was as for the infantry, with green collar patches. Those distinctions which were red in the infantry were green for *Jäger*. Green stripes were worn on the trousers. A green *Schützen* cord was worn across the chest (Fig. 86b). The *Jäger* were disbanded after the Franco-German War. (For Figure 86, see page 252.)

III. *LEIBGARDE ZU PFERD* AND MOUNTED *FELDJÄGERKORPS*

The history of the *Leibgarde zu Pferd* is very involved, and the uniform underwent so many changes that only the most important ones can be mentioned here. Originally the mounted *Leibgarde* was equipped as cuirassiers. During the seventeenth and eighteenth centuries the basic color of the uniform was yellow turned up with red, with silver lace. The breast and back plates were plain. The hat had a silver lace edging. In 1739 the turnbacks were changed to black. In 1776 the *Leibgarde* consisted of three companies with different uniforms:

1st Company: hussar uniform, all dark red, with yellow loopings, light-blue collar, cuffs, sash, and pouch belt. The fur cap bag and the sabertache were dark red; the latter bore the letters "CC" crowned, in yellow.

2nd Company: yellow cuirassier uniform with dark red distinctions and pouch belts. Plain cuirass. Hat with silver lace.

3rd Company: mounted *Jäger*. Green coats with red distinctions and silver lace. The undergarments were white. The hat was bound with waved silver lace and had a white plume. The sabertache was red.

The *Garde* was disbanded in 1794 but was reraised four years later. The uniform then consisted of a yellow jacket with black collar; black *Superweste* with a white star on it, white crossed belts, gauntlets, breeches, and high boots. The helmet had a black *crinière* and white plume. Later, a white metal helmet with a comb and a black crest was worn.

In 1809 the *Leibgarde* was outfitted as follows:

1st Squadron: *Leibjäger*. Fur cap like that of the *Grenadiers à Cheval* of Napoleon I's guard. Green coatee with a single row of yellow metal buttons; yellow fringed epaulettes; black collar, cuffs, and crossed belts; white guantlets and breeches, and high boots.

2nd Squadron: *Garde du Corps*. Yellow jackets; black *Superweste*, helmet, etc., as described above.

3rd and 4th Squadrons: *Grenadiere zu Pferde*. Fur caps as for the 1st Squadron; blue jackets with yellow collar, white epaulettes; gauntlets and breeches; high boots; plain cuirasses.

Each squadron rode horses of a different color. When the regiment marched together, all four squadrons dressed as *Grenadiere zu Pferde* with fur caps and cuirasses, the 1st Squadron in green uniforms, the others in blue. In 1815 these were disbanded, and a *Leibgarde zu Pferd* formed. The uniform adopted was of the very simple type described below for the *Reiter*. The headdress was a very broad fur cap with yellow metal chinscales. The main features of their uniform up to their disbanding were the same as for the rest of the cavalry. The only cavalry regiments after 1817 were *Reiter*. Chacos superseded the fur caps in 1825. All distinctions that were red in the *Reiter* were of a purple color in the *Leibgarde zu Pferd*.

The *Feldjäger* Corps was raised in 1759. They wore green coats, waistcoats, and breeches, with red distinctions, yellow metal buttons, and yellow hat lace. There was a dismounted detachment up to 1765; the mounted corps was disbanded in 1768. In 1782 a new corps, permanently mounted from this date, was raised. The basic color was made darker in 1798, and the buttons were changed to white. The cut of the coat and the *Kaskett* were as for the rest of the army. Equipment was of black leather. Later, crested helmets, black distinctions, and black *Superweste* were introduced (Fig. 86l). In 1815 the corps was dressed as lancers and adopted the title *Leibulanenkorps*. The uniform was green and red with gold lace. In 1817 it was renamed the *Feldjäger* Corps. The uniform thereafter consisted of a long-skirted royal blue coat with black distinctions, and fur caps as for the *Leibgarde*. In 1819 the basic color was changed to dark blue and the distinctions to light blue. The principal features of the development of the uniform followed that of the rest of the cavalry.

IV. *REITER*, CUIRASSIERS, AND *GRENADIERE ZU PFERD*

In 1683 the *Kreis-Regiment zu Pferd von Höhnstedt* was raised in Swabia. It had a blue-gray uniform. A very unusual feature was the leather cuirass, which the regiment is shown wearing according to the illustrations dated 1683 and 1703 in the book by Stadlinger (Fig. 85a). Later, it became a dragoon regiment and in 1775 was amalgamated with the *reitende Grenadiere von Pfull*, whose uniform consisted of red coats turned up with black, with yellow metal buttons and a yellow cord on the shoulder. The undergarments were white. Cuirasses were worn over the waistcoats. The fur caps had a yellow metal plate in front. The Cuirassier Regiment von Pfull

Fig. 85. Germany. Württemberg—Cavalry.

a, g, h, i, k, l: heavy cavalry. b, d, m, n: dragoons. c, e: *chevau-légers*. f: *Jäger zu Pferd*.

was raised in 1758; it was converted into dragoons in 1761. It had yellow coats with red turnbacks and a yellow and red lace edging. The waistcoats were red and the belts white. Thereafter, only dragoons, *chevau-légers*, and mounted *Jäger* regiments were represented in the army; these are dealt with in the following sections.

In 1817 all the cavalry regiments were converted into *Reiter* regiments. The royal blue coat had long skirts and was closed down the front with hooks. The cut was of exactly the same style as for the infantry. The collar and pointed cuffs were self-colored, with red piping. The coat also had red piping down the front, which the infantry did not have. The girdle was likewise edged with red. Yellow metal shoulder scales were worn; the royal blue trousers had red stripes, and the pouch belts were white. The 1st Regiment wore fur caps; the 2nd, 3rd, and 4th had chacos as for the infantry, but of different colors: yellow for the 2nd Regiment; 3rd, dark red; and 4th, red. In 1820 all regiments adopted red chacos and colored pointed cuff patches: 1st Regiment, red; 2nd, yellow; 3rd, royal blue with red piping; and 4th, black.

The uniform was altered in 1821–1823 (Fig. 85h). A red pompon and a small yellow metal shield bearing the regimental number were added to the all-red chacos. The coat was replaced by a royal blue jacket with a self-colored collar, and two rows of yellow metal buttons. Cuffs, skirt edgings, and the piping on the sleeve and back seams were all red. The royal blue trousers had red triple stripes. In 1844 the jackets were made single-breasted, with red pointed collar patches with a button, and red double pompons were added to the chacos. The *Schützen* had green ones. They were equipped with carbines, while the rest of the men carried lances with red-over-black pennants. The edging to the skirts was also altered. In the following year chacos were adopted as in the infantry, but of red cloth, with yellow lace and loop and a black hair plume (Fig. 85i). The 1849-pattern tunic had the same distinctions as the

249

previous jacket. The side stripes on the royal blue trousers were abolished, and only the piping remained. The uniform authorized in 1864 resembled the new infantry uniform of that year (Fig. 85l). The red kepi had a blue band and piping, with a small yellow metal plate bearing the regimental number in white, with a small hair plume above. The dark blue tunic had self-colored collar and cuffs, and red piping, shoulder straps, and padded shoulder wings. The collar patches were light blue for the 1st Regiment, yellow for the 2nd, red for the 3rd, and white for the 4th. The leather accoutrements remained white. The gray trousers had red side stripes. The lance was abolished. Spiked helmets were adopted in 1870. In the following year the regiments were turned into dragoons and lancers.

V. DRAGOONS, *CHEVAU-LÉGERS*, AND *JÄGER ZU PFERD*

The *Reiter* Regiment von Höhnstedt mentioned above was turned into a territorial dragoon regiment, called the Württemberg Regiment, in 1732. Coat and breeches were white; collar, cuffs, lapels, skirt lining, and waistcoat, light blue; and buttons, shoulder cords, and hat lace, yellow (Fig. 85b). In the 1750s a blue uniform with black distinctions and yellowish-white undergarments was introduced. The buttons, etc., were as before. Illustrations of this regiment, however, show considerable variations. Some depict the black distinctions edged with lace, some without; the basic color is variously shown as dark blue or light blue. In the 1790s the uniform was blue with red distinctions and yellow skirt turnbacks, edged with red. Yellow metal shoulder scales were worn. The hat had a black plume. The Cuirassier Regiment von Pfull, mentioned above, was transformed into dragoons in 1761 and disbanded in 1766. They wore a white coat and breeches; red collar, cuffs, and skirt lining; and yellow waistcoat, shoulder cords, waved hat lace, and yellow metal buttons. Toward the end of the eighteenth century the *chevau-légers* were re-formed. The uniform was of the usual style of the period, with half lapels. The basic color was blue. The helmet had a horsehair *crinière*, the white breeches were worn with high boots (Fig. 85c). Soon afterward, the *Jäger zu Pferd* were raised. They had a green uniform. The period 1798–1817 is mainly notable for the frequent changes in formation and uniform. In May 1811 the regiments adopted numbers.

Chevau-Léger-Regiment No.1 (Prince Adam): Blue jackets with self-colored lapels, white piping, yellow collar, skirt turnbacks, girdles, and buttons. The helmet had a comb, with yellow-over-black crest. The leather equipment and breeches were white (Fig. 85e).

Leib-Chevau-Léger-Regiment No. 2: Uniform as above, with brick red distinctions, piping, and girdle. White buttons and lace loops on the collar. The helmet had a black horsehair *crinière*.

Jäger-Regiment zu Pferd No. 3 (Duke Louis): The jacket, collar, lapels, and close-fitting breeches were green; piping and shoulder scales, yellow; buttons, white metal; leather equipment and gauntlets, black. The helmet had a white metal plate and comb with yellow-over-green crest. The boots were of Hungarian type.

Jäger-Regiment zu Pferd No. 4: All-green uniforms as above, with pink collar, white piping, white metal buttons, and green helmet crest.

Dragoon Regiment No. 5 (Crown Prince): Green jackets with white collar and skirt turnbacks; white metal buttons and shoulder scales, red piping, white breeches and leather equipment, and black gauntlets. Chacos as for the infantry, with a white metal plate and white cords (Fig. 85d).

All regiments except the 1st adopted green uniforms in 1814, and chacos. From 1817 the cavalry consisted only of *chevau-légers* and *Jäger zu Pferd*.

In 1871 two dragoon regiments were raised, the 4th *Reiter* Regiment becoming the 1st Dragoon Regiment and the 2nd becoming the 2nd Dragoon Regiment. Both adopted double-breasted light-blue tunics of the same syle as the infantry (single-breasted from 1892). The breeches were as in the Prussian army. The 1st Regiment had white collars, Swedish cuffs, piping, and shoulder straps, the last bearing a red crowned "O." The buttons were yellow metal. White guard lace loops were worn on red collar patches. The spiked helmet had a white metal plate, and a white hair plume in full dress. The 2nd Regiment adopted yellow distinctions, white metal buttons, white metal helmet plate, and a black plume. The shoulder straps bore a red crowned "W." No ornament was worn on the cartridge pouch. Lances, with red-over-black pennants, were adopted in the late 1880s, as in the rest of the cavalry. In 1913 the 1st Regiment (No. 25) adopted silver mounts and small chains on the pouch belt. The 1910-pattern service dress was of Prussian type.

VI. HUSSARS AND LANCERS

Hussars have been mentioned above in the section on *Leibgarde zu Pferd*. A *Leibhusaren* squadron was formed in 1735; it was increased to a regiment in 1758 (von Gorcy; 1763, von Bouwinghausen). It was disbanded in 1798. Dolman and pelisse were green, breeches red, and loopings yellow. Collar and cuffs were black. The fur cap had a red bag; the sash and sabertache were red and yellow. The belts were of fawn leather. After 1798 no further hussar regiments were formed in Württemberg.

The *Leibulanenkorps* of 1815–1817 has been mentioned above under *Feldjäger*. In 1871 the 1st Württemberg Lancer Regiment (No. 19) was formed from the 1st *Reiter* Regiment, and the 2nd (No. 20), from the 3rd *Reiter* Regiment. The uniform resembled that of the Prussian lancers except in the cap plates, cockades, and sword knots. The 1st Regiment had red distinctions; the 2nd, yellow. The buttons and epaulette crescents were of white metal. The 1st Regiment had white guard lace loops. The lance pennants were as for the Württemberg dragoons. The 1910 and 1915 service dress uniforms followed the Prussian patterns.

VII. ARTILLERY, PIONEERS, AND TRANSPORT CORPS

The earliest uniform of the Württemberg artillery appears to have been red. In 1735 the coat was still red, with similarly colored skirt turnbacks, black collar and cuffs; yellow waistcoat, hat lace, and buttons; and white breeches, which were worn with gaiters (Fig. 86c). From the 1750s the uniforms were based on Prussian ones, and light-blue coats were adopted. Collar, lapels, skirt turnbacks, and cuffs were all black. The buttons and hat lace were yellow, and the undergarments, white (Fig. 86d). Up to 1817 the basic color was light blue. The distinctions remained as before, except that the waistcoats were changed to light blue. The Escort Company was distinguished by fur caps with yellow metal plates, and a yellow cord on the shoulder. In 1799 light-blue jackets of the new pattern were introduced, having black half lapels and cuffs, and *Kasketts* with yellow metal fittings and black hair *crinières*. The leather equipment was white as previously. White breeches were worn, with knee boots (Fig. 86e). In 1804 the helmet with the black *crinière* was replaced by a similar one with a black crest. The horse artillery wore a similar uniform, but with light-blue breeches and black girdles. The saber was hung from slings attached to the belt worn over the right shoulder. A white plume was worn on the helmet. The Guard Battery had white lace loops on their black collars and cuffs. At the same time, the horse artillery adopted white metal shoulder scales. In 1811 the half lapels were made light blue like the jacket, and edged with yellow piping; and the breeches of the foot artillery were also made light blue (Fig. 86f). In 1813 chacos with a yellow metal plate and a back peak were introduced. The guard artillery had a white metal plate, and white cords (Fig. 86g). In 1817 the basic color was changed to royal blue. The style was the same as that for the whole army. The coat had a black collar, pointed cuffs, and epaulette crescents; red piping; blue girdle edged red; chaco with vees at the sides and chinscales, and white leather equipment (Fig. 86h). The distinctions remained as before. The uniform underwent the same changes as that of the rest of the army. In 1817 black fur caps with white metal chinscales were introduced for the horse artillery; these were worn until 1838. At that time, red chaco cords were in use for both horse and foot artillery. The new chaco introduced in 1845 was covered with powder blue cloth, with a white band around the top and a black one around the bottom. The fittings consisted of crossed cannon barrels, with the cockade above, a white loop, and a drooping black horsehair plume (Fig. 86i). The 1864 uniform was dark blue, instead of royal blue. The distinctions remained black, with red piping, white metal

Fig. 86. Germany. Württemberg—Miscellaneous.

a, b: *Jäger zu Fuss.* c, d, e, f, h, i: foot artillery. g: guard horse artillery. k: horse artillery. l, m: *Feldjäger.* n: general officer.

buttons, and red padded wings on the shoulders. The full-dress kepi was dark blue with a black band and red piping, and a black horsehair plume. The trousers were the same as in the infantry; those of the horse artillery were as for the *Reiter* regiments. Black leather equipment was introduced. After 1871 the uniforms followed the Prussian models. The distinctions were as in Prussia; the tunic was double-breasted up until 1888 and single-breasted thereafter. The spiked helmets had yellow metal mounts with a ball finial. Leather equipment was black (Fig. 86k). A pioneer company existed from 1815. It wore almost the same uniform as the artillery, but was differentiated by yellow metal buttons and badges. Later, a chaco ornament, consisting of crossed axes in yellow metal, was adopted. The 1854-pattern chaco was bound around the top with yellow lace. From 1871 the uniform was exactly the same as that of the Prussian pioneers, but with the distinctions of Württemberg. From 1871, too, the buttons and insignia were of white metal. The Transport Corps likewise wore the same uniform as its Prussian counterpart, but with black leather equipment. The 1910 and 1915 patterns of service dress for these arms were as in Prussia.

VIII. GENERAL OFFICERS

In the first half of the eighteenth century, general officers had red coats and yellow waistcoats, both edged with gold. The hat had gold lace and white feathers. Later, they had blue coats—light blue from 1782—with black collar, cuffs, and lapels, and silver loops and shoulder cords. Waistcoats were light blue and breeches, white. The hat was laced with silver, and had a white-over-black feather plume. In 1798 dark blue coats with red collars, and lapels buttoned over at the top, all edged with gold, were introduced, with a row of yellow metal buttons down the front. The cocked hat had white plumage and a gold loop; the plume and the breeches were as before, and the boots had stiff tops. Later, dark blue lapels with red edging, rich embroidery, and fringed epaulettes were added to the coats. The epaulettes, and all ornamentation, were gold for generals of the infantry, and silver for generals of the cavalry. The sash was silver, embroidered with red and yellow. In the 1820s a plain hat with a gold loop and black plume was introduced. Red collars and cuffs and floriate embroidery were worn on the coat. The everyday trousers were royal blue with red piping; in full dress, white ones were worn, with high boots. The hussar-type sashes were red and black. Gold stripes were added to the trousers in 1829. The undress uniform had embroidered collar and cuffs, but no gold floral embroidery on the front. The coatee had only a single row of buttons. In 1849 a similarly ornamented tunic was introduced, and in 1851, chacos richly ornamented with gold lace bands (Fig. 86a). The undress uniform had collar and pointed cuffs of basic color piped red; the trousers had red piping instead of gold lace. In 1864 general officers adopted black tunics and caps with red distinctions and gold edgings. The distinctions of rank were of Austrian type. The kepi had a plume of white feathers surrounding red and black ones. Aides-de-camp to the king wore light-blue tunics with silver lace. From 1871 the uniform was of Prussian style as in the rest of the army. The full-dress feather plume was of the same colors as in 1864. The sash was silver embroidered with red and black. The rank distinctions have been described above. Up to 1870 the general staff wore black distinctions, with gold lace loops on the collar and cuffs.

In the eighteenth century, the Wurzburg infantry wore white uniforms, with red distinctions for one regiment, and blue for the other. In 1795 a Wurzburg *Kreiskontingents-Bataillon* (district battalion) was formed. The uniform consisted of a blue coat with white metal buttons, red collar and cuffs, white undergarments, and black hats with black lace. In 1801 white coats were issued, and the battalions were distinguished by red, blue, and green distinctions. The grenadiers wore caps; the fusiliers, *Kasketts*. In the book by Weiland published in 1807, the Wurzburg infantry are given as wearing white Austrian-style coats with red distinctions and yellow

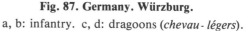

Fig. 87. Germany. Würzburg.

a, b: infantry. c, d: dragoons (*chevau-légers*).

metal buttons (Fig. 87a). Breeches and leather equipment were white; the gaiters, black. Austrian helmets, with a red plume for the grenadiers and green for the *voltigeurs*, were worn. The latter also wore green epaulettes. Somewhat later, chacos were adopted. A French-style uniform, of the same colors as before, was introduced. From that time the lapels were red, and the cuff patches, white. The white distinctions were piped with red; the red, with white. The undergarments remained white. The grenadiers and *voltigeurs* were distinguished by the color of the epaulettes and plumes—red for the former and green and yellow for the latter (Fig. 87b). The artillery uniform was similar, except that the basic color of the coat, waistcoat, and trousers was light gray-brown. Yellow metal shoulder scales were worn. The chaco had a red lace edging. The plume and sash were also red. The red distinctions were not piped. The dragoons (*chevau-legers*) wore green single-breasted jackets with yellow metal buttons and red distinctions. Undergarments and leather accoutrements were white. The helmets had a comb, yellow metal plate, and a red-over-black plume (Fig. 87c). Red fringed epaulettes and chacos with red cords were later introduced; otherwise the uniform remained unchanged. The plume was as before (Fig. 87d). By the terms of the Congress of Vienna, Wurzburg was finally restored to Bavaria.

GREAT BRITAIN

Cockade: black

I. INFANTRY

From the beginning of the standing army, red was the principal basic color of the infantry uniform. The illustrations show the changes in style and equipment. From the mid-seventeenth century to the mid-eighteenth century, breeches and stockings were usually either red or of the facing color. Lace loops and small turned-back lapels were sometimes worn in the 1680s. The grenadier caps had a short hanging bag and small vertical front part; but from about 1700 they became more stiffened and upright. The first general reliable pictorial information is to be found in the "Cloathing Book" of 1742. It shows many variations in the styles of the lapels and cuffs. The infantryman in Fig. 88b had red coat, waistcoat, and breeches; yellow lapels, cuffs, and skirt linings; and white lace loops and hat lace. The leather ac-

Fig. 88. Great Britain—Infantry, 1700–1813.
a, b, e, g, h: line infantry. c, f: grenadiers, foot guards. d: officer of grenadiers.
i: infantry officer.

coutrements and pouches were generally of buff-colored leather, but some regiments had black flaps to their pouches.

Scottish Highland regiments date from 1740, in which year the Black Watch (43rd, later 42nd, Royal Highlanders) was formed. In 1742 the uniform of this regiment consisted of a short red jacket and waistcoat, with buff cuffs, and white buttons and buttonholes (Fig. 90a). The distinctive belted plaid was worn; it was gradually superseded by the "little kilt" (*philibeg* in Gaelic), which later was made in varying sets for the several regiments, the Black Watch, Mackenzie, Gordon, Cameron, and Sutherland tartans being worn up to modern times. The blue bonnets (later diced) worn by these regiments had a red, pompon or tourie. The hose were diced or striped red and white. The foot guards were dressed very like the line infantry. In 1745 the 1st Guards (Fig. 88c) wore red coats and waistcoats, and blue lapels, cuffs, skirt linings, and breeches. The lace loops and hat lace were white. White gaiters were worn in full dress. The grenadiers had red caps with the front part blue, and on the small flap, from about 1714, the white horse of Hanover embroidered on a red field. The devices on the front of the cap were also embroidered.

In 1742 the distinctions were as follows.

REGIMENT	LAPELS AND CUFFS	LACE AND BUTTON LOOPS	SKIRTS	WAISTCOAT	BREECHES
1st Foot Guards	blue	plain white	blue	red	blue[1]
Colstream Guards	blue	plain white	blue	red	blue[1]
3rd Foot Guards	blue	plain white	blue	red	blue[1]
1st Regiment of Foot	blue	white	blue	red	red
2nd Regiment of Foot	green	white with stripes	blue	red	red
3rd Regiment of Foot	buff	white with stripe and worms	buff	red	red
4th Regiment of Foot	blue	white with worm	blue	red	blue
5th Regiment of Foot	light green	white	light green	light green	red
6th Regiment of Foot	yellow	white with worm	yellow	red	red
7th Fusiliers	blue	white with worm	blue	red	blue[2]
8th Regiment	blue	white with stripes	blue	red	blue
9th Regiment	yellow	white with worm	yellow	red	red
10th Regiment	yellow	white	yellow	red	red
11th Regiment	green	yellow and white with worm	green	red	red
12th Regiment	light yellow	white with stripe	light yellow	red	red
13th Regiment	yellow	white with worm	yellow	red	red
14th Regiment	light yellow	none	light yellow	red	red
15th Regiment	yellow	none	yellow	red	red
16th Regiment	yellow	white with worm	yellow	red	red
17th Regiment	gray-white	white with worm	gray	red	red
18th Regiment	blue	yellow	blue	red	blue[3]
19th Regiment	green	white with worm and stripe	green	red	red
20th Regiment	yellow	white	yellow	yellow	red
21st Fusiliers	blue	white with stripe and worm	blue	red	blue[2]
22nd Regiment	pale buff	white with stripe	pale buff	red	red
23rd Fusiliers	blue	yellow and white with stripe	blue	red	blue[2]

(*continued*)

REGIMENT	LAPELS AND CUFFS	LACE AND BUTTON LOOPS	SKIRTS	WAISTCOAT	BREECHES
24th Regiment	dark green	white with stripe	white	red	red
25th Regiment	yellow	white with worm	yellow	red	red
26th Regiment	yellow	none	yellow	red	red[3]
27th Regiment	buff	white with worm	buff	red	red[4]
28th Regiment	yellow	white	yellow	red	red
29th Regiment	light yellow	none; white buttonholes	light yellow	red	red
30th Regiment	yellow	white	yellow	yellow	red
31st Regiment	buff	white with worm	buff	red	red
32nd Regiment	white	white with worm and stripes	white	red	red
33rd Regiment	red	white	white	red	red
34th Regiment	yellow	white with pattern	yellow	red	red
35th Regiment	orange	white	orange	orange	red
36th Regiment	green	white with worm	green	red	red
37th Regiment	yellow	white with worm	yellow	red	red
38th Regiment	yellow	white	yellow	red	red[3]
39th Regiment	green	white with worm	green	green	red
40th Regiment	buff	white with worm	buff	red	red[4]
41st Regiment	green	white	green	red	red
43rd Regiment	light green	none; white buttonholes	violet	red	red
44th Regiment	white	white with stars	white	red	red
45th Regiment	yellow	white	yellow	red	red
46th Regiment	dark green	white with stars	dark green	red	red
47th Regiment	yellow	white with worm	light brown	red	red[1]
48th Regiment	white	white with worm and stars	light brown	red	red
49th Regiment	buff	white with worm and stripe	buff	red	red
50th Regiment	black	white	white	red	red

[1]variously shaped loops [2]grenadier caps [3]no lapels [4]yellow buttons

In 1751 all the grenadiers of the army (except for the 42nd Highlanders) had the white horse on the little flaps of their caps. About 1768 the cloth caps were superseded by fur ones. About the same time, the undergarments were changed to white for almost all regiments (Fig. 88e). The commonest distinctive colors were blue and varying shades of green, yellow, and buff. A light company was added to each regiment in 1771; they wore short jackets, short gaiters, and close-fitting leather caps. From about 1775 the bayonet belt was worn over the shoulder, instead of around the waist, and was ornamented with a metal plate where the shoulder belts crossed. In 1791 field officers adopted two epaulettes, instead of one as formerly. The officers of the flank companies (grenadier and light companies), who already wore two epaulettes, wore on theirs a grenade and bugle horn respectively. In 1799 many of the regiments of volunteers were wearing a crested "Tarleton" helmet. Generally speaking, their uniform varied greatly in color and style. In 1800 the infantry adopted cylindrical chacos in place of hats, although field officers retained their hats up to 1812. Chevrons were introduced for NCOs in 1802. Queues were abolished in 1808. During the Peninsular War, the infantry wore red jackets with white turnbacks; with collar and cuffs of the regimental facing color. The flank companies wore wings on the shoulders, red for the line infantry and blue for the guards, with white lace darts, and a short white fringe. The other companies had white woolen tufts at the ends of the shoulder straps (Figs. 88g,h). In addition to the facing colors, the lace loops on the breast were of distinctive regimental patterns, with variously colored stripes and patterns running through them; and were square, pointed, or bastion-shaped, placed either singly or in pairs. A different chaco was adopted in 1812. It had an upright plate higher than the body, with a metal plate on it, and a peak. On the left side was a plume: white over red, white, or green according to company; with white cords. On service, gray trousers were worn; in full dress, white breeches and stockings, which were abolished in 1823. Each regiment had its number or insignia on the belt plate, worn where the pouch and bayonet belts crossed in front. The light infantry wore a different headdress: a tapering cylindrical chaco with a metal bugle horn badge, and a green plume and green cords. Sergeants carried spontoons up to 1830. The grenadiers' fur caps were not worn on service. The uniform of the rifles was green; for the rifle battalions of the 60th Regiment, green with red facings, white metal buttons, blue breeches, and light infantry chacos. The 95th Regiment (rifles) (Fig. 90f) wore an all-green uniform with black collar and cuffs, edged white, and white metal buttons.

In 1815 the colors of the facings and officers' lace were as follows (F = Fusiliers, H = Highlanders): blue, gold: 1; 4; 7; 8; 18; 21F; 23F; 25; 42H; blue, silver: 2; 86; 97; white, gold: 32; 59; 65; 74H; white, silver: 17; 43; 47; 101; 103; pale yellow, silver: 30; 46; 99; yellow, gold: 12; 57; 80; 83; yellow, silver: 6; 9; 10; 13; 15; 16; 20; 26; 28; 29; 34; 37; 38; 44; 67; 72H; 77; 82; 85; 88; 91; 92H; 93H; 102; deep yellow, silver: 100; orange, silver: 35; buff, gold: 22; 27; 40; 48; 78H; 90; buff, silver: 3: 14; 31; 52; 61; 62; 71H; 81; 96; 98; 104; red, gold: 53; red, silver: 33; 41; 76; purple, silver: 56; black, gold: 58; 64; 70; 89; black, silver: 50; green, gold: 36 (gosling green); 39 (sea green); 51 (grass green); gosling green, silver: 5; 66; green, gold: 19; 49; 55; 69; 87; 94; green, silver: 24; 54 (bottle green); 68; dark green, gold: 11; 73; 79H; dark green, silver: 45; 63.

The rifles wore green coats: 5th Batallion, 60th Regiment, red facings, silver lace; the 95th, black facings, silver lace; and white collar and cuff edgings and loops for the men. The entire 60th Regiment did not adopt green jackets until c. 1813.

From 1829 the infantry wore slash cuffs with red patches. The officers' colored lapels were abolished; and henceforth they wore double-breasted coatees with two loops of lace on the collar, and four on the cuff slashes and skirt pocket flaps. All ranks of the foot guards likewise wore double-breasted coatees, and fur caps (Fig. 89c). The men had white worsted epaulettes—wings for the grenadier companies; the light companies and rifles also wore wings. Officers wore fringed metal epaulettes—wings for flank companies and light infantry regiments—of the color of the buttons (Fig. 89b). In 1830 yellow metal insignia were adopted throughout the regular army. The regimental facing or distinctive colors, displayed on the collars and cuffs, remained almost unaltered up to 1881. Prior to 1929 bandsmen had worn highly laced coats of facing color with red collars and cuffs (although other combinations of colors were worn); from 1829 to 1873 their coats were white, faced in the regimental

Fig. 89. Great Britain—Infantry, 1830–1890.

a: 3rd Foot Guards, light company. b: light infantry officer. c: grenadier guards. d, e, g, h: line infantry. f: officer of fusiliers, undress. i: Highland Light Infantry.

colors. In 1816 the infantry adopted a bell-shaped chaco with a numbered plate on the front, and plume, which was changed to a ball tuft in 1835; this was white, white and red, or green for the grenadier, battalion, and light companies respectively. The fusilier regiments retained their fur caps, for full dress, up to 1842, as did the grenadier companies of the line. In 1836 all regiments adopted plain white lace, arranged as before. Straight-sided chacos, with a back peak, were introduced in 1844: the "Albert" chaco (Fig. 89d). Fusiliers wore a flaming grenade on their plates, and light infantry, a bugle horn. In 1850 bluish-black trousers, with red piping, were introduced.

During the Crimean War, in 1855, a double-breasted tunic (single-breasted from 1856), with medium-length skirts, was introduced. For the infantry it was red, with collar and slash cuffs of facing color, piped with white. The scalloped skirt flaps were also piped white (Fig. 89e). Officers had a single or double row of gold lace around the collar and cuffs for company officers and field officers respectively. Epaulettes were abolished. The crimson silk sash with crimson tassels was worn over the left shoulder, secured by a crimson twisted cord. Sergeants wore crimson worsted sashes over the right shoulder.

In 1878 the collar was changed to red, with patches of the regimental color, pointed at the rear. From 1868 the cuffs had been pointed, with a white trefoil—gold for officers. Scarlet tunics were adopted by the rank and file, in place of the red ones worn hitherto, in 1871. The Albert chaco was abolished in 1855, and from that time it was made smaller and sloped forward, a development that continued with the 1861 and 1869 patterns. A cork helmet, covered with blue cloth (green for light infantry), was issued in 1878. It had yellow metal mounts and a spike (Fig. 89g). The fusilier regiments in the meantime had readopted black fur caps, which had a yellow metal grenade badge, and later, a plume (Fig. 89f).

In 1881 the infantry was reorganized by the linking of many regiments into the two battalions of a single new regiment. The old regimental numbers were abolished. Most regiments took the title of the county forming their recruiting district. The facing color for royal regiments was blue; and for the other English regiments, white; Scottish, yellow; and Irish, green; but later many of the regiments were permitted to wear their old facing colors again. The men's cuffs were round (pointed again from 1902); but officers continued to wear pointed ones, with a single or double lace and braid edging respectively for company officers and field officers, up to 1902. In 1874 most regiments took into wear distinctive badges placed at the ends of the collar. Regimental devices, and the title, were also worn on the crowned star-shaped brass helmet plate. The undress cap of the perior c. 1815–1870 was a dark blue "pork pie" with a colored band, with the regimental number on the front; from 1871 to 1894 a dark blue glengarry was worn; and from then to 1902, an Austrian-pattern cap. From 1905 broad-crowned forage caps were worn for walking out. These were dark blue, with red piping around the top, and a black band—red for royal regiments—and a black leather peak and chinstrap. The regimental badge was worn on the front. The white leather equipment (black for rifles) underwent several changes: Valise Equipment, c. 1879; Slade Wallace Equipment, 1888 (Figs. 89, 90). The foot guards retained their tall bearskin caps, and slash cuffs to the tunics.

Highland Regiments wore their distinctive feather bonnets and kilts, and from 1855 wore doublets with gauntlet cuffs (slash cuffs, 1855–1868), and four large curved skirt flaps with white piping, and white loops and brass buttons. The glengarry cap (diced for some regiments) was worn in undress and off duty. The Scottish Lowland regiments wore line uniforms up to 1881, and from then, doublets, with trews, later of regimental tartan (Figs. 90c,d,e).

Fig. 90. Great Britain—Highlanders and Rifles.
a, b, c, e: Highlanders. d: officer, Highlanders. f, g, h, i: rifles.

From the end of the Napoleonic Wars the rifle regiments wore very dark green uniforms with black buttons, and colored collars and cuffs; officers wore a similarly colored dolman, with pelisse; and from 1855, an *Attila* jacket with black loopings (Figs. 90f–i). They wore chacos as for the line, but in 1873 adopted small black fur busbies; and from 1878 to 1890, dark green spiked helmets; and then busbies again. The undress cap was for the infantry, but in dark green.

The titles, facings, and badges of the foot guards and line infantry regiments, with the old pre-1881 number, in brackets, are given in the following table for 1912. Collar badges were also worn with service dress by some regiments.

Guards: single-breasted scarlet tunic, blue shoulder straps, collar, and slash cuffs; white piping. Black bearskin caps. Dark blue trousers with red piping.

Officers: gold lace on collar, cuffs, shoulder straps (with silver badges); broad red trousers stripes; crimson and gold sashes.

Brass buttons for the men.

REGIMENT	BUTTONS ON TUNIC	CUFFS AND SKIRTS	COLLAR BADGE	CAP PLUME
Grenadier Guards	9 singly	4	flaming grenade	white; left
Colstream Guards	2+2+2+2+2	2+2	Garter star	red; right
Scots Guards	3	3	3	thistle	none
Irish Guards (raised 1900)	4+4+2	4	shamrock	blue; right
Welsh Guards (raised 1915)	5+5	5	leek	white-green-white; left

Line: scarlet tunic, with collar and cuffs of facing color; pointed cuffs; scalloped flaps on skirt; white piping; brass buttons. Blue cloth helmets. Dark blue trousers with red piping.

Officers: gold lace; gilt buttons; and red welts on trousers.

REGIMENT	FACINGS	TUNIC COLLAR BADGE	DISTINCTIONS
Royal Scots (Lothian) (1)	blue	thistle	blue Kilmarnock bonnet, diced, red tourie feather on left; doublet; trews
Queen's (Royal West Surrey) (2)	blue	Paschal lamb	
Buffs (East Kent) (3)	buff	dragon	
King's Own (Royal Lancaster) (4)	blue	lion	
Northumberland Fusiliers (5)	gosling green	grenade	fur cap; red over white plume on left
Royal Warwickshire (6)	blue	antelope	
Royal Fusiliers (City of London) (7)	blue	rose on grenade	fur cap; white plume on right
King's (Liverpool) (8)	blue	leaping horse	
Norfolk (9)	yellow	Britannia	
Lincolnshire (10)	white	sphinx	
Devonshire (11)	Lincoln green	castle on 8-pointed star	
Suffolk (12)	yellow	castle with key above	
Prince Albert's (Somerset Light Inf.) (13)	blue	horn with mural crown	green helmet; sergeants' sashes on left shoulder

(*continued*)

REGIMENT	FACINGS	TUNIC COLLAR BADGE	DISTINCTIONS
Prince of Wales's Own (West Yorkshire) (14)	buff	Prince of Wales plume	
East Yorkshire (15)	white	rose on 8-pointed star	
Bedfordshire (16)	white	hart above scroll	
Leicestershire (17)	white	tiger in wreath	
Royal Irish (18) (disbanded 1922)	blue	Arms of Nassau	
Alexandre, Prince of Wales's Own (Yorkshire) (19)	grass green	Dannebrog cross and cipher "A" with coronet	
Lancashire Fusiliers (20)	white	grenade	fur caps; primrose plume on left
Royal Scots Fusiliers (21)	blue	grenade	fur caps; white plume on right; doublet; trews
Cheshire (22)	buff	oakleaf on 8-pointed star	
Royal Welsh Fusiliers (23)	blue	grenade	fur cap; white plume on right. Black silk flash on collar of tunic and service dress
South Wales Borderers (24)	grass green	sphinx	
King's Own Scottish Borderers (25)	blue	castle	same as for Royal Scots
Cameronians (Scottish Rifles) (26/90)	dark green	none; service dress: horn with star above in thistle wreath sometimes worn	dark green double and chaco with black plume; trews
Royal Inniskilling Fusiliers (27/108)	blue	grenade	fur cap; gray plume on left
Gloucestershire (28/61)	white	sphinx on laurel sprigs	"back" bade on all headdress
Worcestershire (29/36)	white	lion on 8-pointed star	
East Lancashire (30/59)	white	rose	
East Surrey (31/79)	white	Arms of Guilford on 8-pointed star	
Duke of Cornwall's Light Inf. (32/46)	white	Arms of Cornwall; service dress: horn crowned	green helmet
Duke of Wellington's (West Riding) (33/76)	scarlet	elephant	
Border (34/55)	white	Maltese cross on wreath	
Royal Sussex (35/107)	blue	Maltese cross on feather	
Hampshire (37/67)	yellow	rose	
South Staffordshire (38/80)	white	Staffordshire knot	
Dorsetshire (39/54)	grass green	sphinx	
Prince of Wales's Volunteers (South Lancashire) (40/82)	white	plume of Prince of Wales	
Welsh (41/69)	white	plume of Prince of Wales; dragon on service dress	
Black Watch (Royal Highlanders) (42/73)	blue	St. Andrew on cross	diced feather bonnet; red hackle; doublet; Black Watch tartan

(continued)

REGIMENT	FACINGS	TUNIC COLLAR BADGE	DISTINCTIONS
Oxfordshire and Buckinghamshire Light Infantry (43/52)	white	button with cord loop	green helmet
Essex (44/56)	white	shield with county arms	
Sherwood Foresters (Nottingham-shire and Darbyshire) (45/95)	white	stag on Maltese cross	
Loyal North Lancashire (47/81)	white	City of Lincoln arms	
Northamptonshire (48/58)	white	cross on circle in wreath	
Princess Charlotte of Wales's (Royal Berkshire) (49/66)	blue	dragon	
Queen's Own (Royal West Kent) (50/97)	blue	crown with lion above	
King's Own (Yorkshire Light Infantry) (51/105)	blue	horn with rose in center	green helmet
King's (Shropshire Light Infantry) (53/85)	blue	hunting horn with strings	green helmet
Duke of Cambridge's Own (Middlesex) (57/77)	lemon yellow	Prince of Wales's plume	
King's Royal Rifle Corps (60)	scarlet	none	black busby with black and red plume; dark green tunic and trousers; black loopings for officers on tunic
Duke of Edinburgh's Own (Wiltshire) (62/99)	buff	Maltese cross	
Manchester (63/96)	white	sphinx	
Prince of Wales's (North Staffordshire) (64/98)	white	Staffordshire knot	
York and Lancaster (65/84)	white	tiger with rose above	
Durham Light Infantry (68/106)	dark green	hunting horn	green helmet
Highland Light Infantry (71/74)	buff	thistle star and horn	blue diced chaco; doublet; Mackenzie tartan trews
Seaforth Highlanders (Rossshire Buffs, Duke of Albany's) (72/78)	buff	"F" and scroll; elephant	diced feather bonnet, white hackle; doublet; Mackenzie tartan kilt
Gordon Highlanders (75/92)	yellow	tiger	ditto: Gordon tartan
Queen's Own Cameron Highlanders (79)	blue	crowned thistle	ditto; Cameron tartan
Royal Irish Rifles (83/86) (from 1922 Royal Ulster Rifles)	dark green	none	black busby; dark green and black plume; dark green tunic and trousers; black loopings for officers on tunic
Princess Victoria's (Royal Irish Fusiliers) (87/89)	blue	cornet; grenade	fur cap; green plume on left
Connaught Rangers (88/94)	green	elephant	
Princess Louise's (Argyll and Sutherland Highlanders) (91/93)	yellow	boar's head and cat in wreaths	diced feather bonnet; white plume; doublet; kilt of Sutherland tartan

REGIMENT	FACINGS	TUNIC COLLAR BADGE	DISTINCTIONS
Prince of Wales's Leinster (Royal Canadians) (100/109) (disbanded 1922)	blue	Prince of Wales's plume	
Royal Munster Fusiliers (101/104) (disbanded 1922)	blue	tiger on grenade	fur cap; white-over-green plume on left
Royal Dublin Fusiliers (102/103) (disbanded 1922)	blue	tiger and elephant on grenade	fur cap; blue-over-green plume on left
Rifle Brigade	black	none	black busby with black plume; dark green tunic and trousers; black loopings for officers

On service in the colonies from the 1860s, a loose-fitting jacket was worn, latterly with patch pockets, on which the facing color was only worn on the shoulder straps or collar; but when this jacket was adopted for undress wear at home, faced cuffs were worn as well (Fig. 89f). With it was worn a white (later khaki) helmet. Khaki was taken into wear in India in 1846; it was worn in South Africa in the early 1850s; in India during the Mutiny; and on several occasions thereafter. From the early 1880s it began to be generally worn abroad, and experimentally at home. Particularly due to the experience of the South African War, in 1902 this became the sole service dress; and the colored uniform was confined to full dress parades, and walking out (Figs. 95a,d). The service dress altered little up to 1939, and was generally distinguished by the lack of colored insignia. Regimental distinctions were largely confined to the collar badges worn by many units; and the cap badges; and to the abbreviated designations worn on the shoulders or shoulder straps. The buttons and insignia were dull bronze for officers and black for rifle regiments. In 1908 a greenish-colored webbing equipment was taken into wear (Figs. 95c,f,h). After the war, dismounted officers adopted khaki plus fours. Other ranks wore black boots and khaki puttees. The mounted troops also wore a bandolier (Fig. 95d). Officers wore a Sam Browne of brown leather (black for rifles); and after the Great War the service dress jacket was made with pointed cuffs and was worn with a khaki shirt and tie. The Scottish regiments, whose jackets were rounded off in front (with gauntlet cuffs for officers), wore glengarries and kilts up to the early part of the war. The latter were later covered by a khaki apron (Fig. 95e). A khaki Tam o' Shanter bonnet was taken into wear during the war, and this continued to be worn afterward. Steel helmets were introduced in 1916, and remained unchanged between the wars (Fig. 95f). The Imperial troops that served during the Great War were on the whole dressed similarly to the British army. Australian troops, however, mostly wore broad-brimmed slouch hats, turned up at the left side, instead of service dress caps (Fig. 95g, page 275).

After the war, the full-dress scarlet was abolished for the infantry and was only worn by officers at levees and weddings. It was still worn very occasionally on parades, especially by bands. The guards retained scarlet for wear on ceremonial duties (Fig. 95i). For walking out, other ranks were permitted to wear dark blue single-breasted jackets and trousers (dark green for rifles) without colored distinctions, except for the forage cap (Fig. 95l). This uniform was worn at the 1937 coronation. In undress, officers also·wore a very similar uniform.

II. CAVALRY

The cavalry was divided into the following classes: (1) household cavalry, consisting of the 1st and 2nd Lifeguards and the Royal Horse Guards; (2) seven regiments of dragoon guards (formed from regiments of horse in 1746 and 1788), reckoned as heavy cavalry; and (3) twenty-one regiments of cavalry of the line, part dragoons, part hussars, and part lancers. The third category was subdivided by an unusual numbering system. Originally, the cavalry was relatively heavily armed and mounted. With the coming of light cavalry in the mid-eighteenth century, some regiments were converted into light dragoons, without losing their numbers. Similarly, later, some regiments were converted into hussars and lancers. Thus in 1912, the 1st, 2nd, and 6th regiments were dragoons; the 3rd, 4th, 7th, 8th, 10th, 11th, 13th, 14th, 15th, 18th, 19th, and 20th regiments were hussars; and the 5th, 9th, 12th, 16th, 17th, and 21st were lancers.

The original cavalry uniforms were predominantly crimson or scarlet, with variously colored facings; but from the beginning, the Royal Horse Guards wore blue, which gave them the nickname "The Oxford Blues." The lifeguards always had blue facings and rich gold lace. From 1678 to 1788 there were detachments of

Fig. 91. Great Britain—Household Cavalry.
a, d, f: lifeguards. b, e: officers, lifeguards. c: officer, Royal Horse Guards.
g: Royal Horse Guards.

Fig. 92. Great Britain—Heavy Cavalry.

a, d, e, f, g, h, i: dragoons (i: 2nd Dragoons). b, c: officers of dragoons.

horse grenadier guards; these usually wore grenadier caps, later of different colors for the two troops. Trumpeters wore red coats richly ornamented with gold lace, with the royal cipher and crown on the breast and back. Hats were worn generally, their shape conforming to the trends in fashion (Fig. 92a).

In 1742 the distinctions were as follows.

HOUSEHOLD CAVALRY	HOUSINGS AND STRIPES IN LACE
1st Troop of Horse Guards	red
2nd Troop of Horse Guards	white
3rd Troop of Horse Guards	yellow
4th Troop of Horse Guards	blue
1st Troop of Horse Grenadier Guards	blue; yellow and red striped lace
2nd Troop of Horse Grenadier Guards	red; yellow and blue striped lace

REGIMENT	COAT	CUFFS	BREECHES	HOUSINGS
Royal Regiment of Horse Guards	blue	red	blue	red
King's Own Regiment of Horse	red	blue	blue	red
Queen's Own Regiment of Horse	red	buff	buff	red
4th Regiment of Horse	red	white	red	white
5th Regiment of Horse	red	blue	blue	blue
6th Regiment of Horse	red	green	green	red
King's Regiment of Carabiniers	red	light yellow	light yellow	light yellow
8th Regiment of Horse	red	black	buff	buff

All dragoon regiments: red coats without lapels.

266

REGIMENT	BREECHES	CUFFS AND SKIRTS	HOUSINGS
Royal Regiment of Dragoons	red	blue; red skirts	blue
Royal North British Dragoons	blue	blue	red
King's Regiment of Dragoons	light blue	light blue	red
4th Regiment of Dragoons	green	green	green
Royal Irish Regiment of Dragoons	blue	blue	blue
6th Regiment of Dragoons	red	yellow	yellow
Queen's Regiment of Dragoons	white	white	white
8th Regiment of Dragoons	orange	orange	orange
9th Regiment of Dragoons	buff	buff	buff
10th Regiment of Dragoons	yellow	yellow	yellow
11th Regiment of Dragoons	red	white	yellow
12th Regiment of Dragoons	red	white	white
13th Regiment of Dragoons	green	green; buff skirts	buff
14th Regiment of Dragoons	white	light yellow	light yellow

The equipment was of buff leather, except for the Royal North British Dragoons, which had white, In 1742 this regiment was distinguished by grenadier caps (with red body and front plate, and blue flap and turnup). From 1751 the combination of these colors was reversed. The housings of the regiments were highly ornamented, and their colors and devices changed frequently. The light troops added to the dragoon regiments in 1756–1763 wore a distinctive headdress: a small black leather cap with brass comb, and front plate. The Royal North British Dragoons had embroidered caps, for the officers at least.

In 1759 a number of dragoon regiments were turned into light dragoons. They retained their red uniforms (with faced lapels from 1768), and adopted as a headdress

Fig. 93. Great Britain—Light Cavalry.
a, b, c, d, e: light dragoons. f, g, h: hussars. i: officer, lancers. k: lancer.

a form of helmet similar to that previously worn by the light troops (Fig. 93a). In 1784 a blue uniform was issued. The helmet was made with a "caterpillar" crest and was called a "Tarleton" (Figs. 93b,c). In 1812 (Fig. 93d) a jacket with lapels was adopted, in place of the looped dolman worn from 1796. The headdress was changed to a chaco with a white-over-red plume.

The cavalry were dressed as follows in 1812:

Household cavalry and lifeguards: red jacket, hooked down the front, edged with broad gold lace around the outside for all ranks, with blue collar, and cuffs; black leather helmet with yellow metal plate and comb, and black horsehair *crinière*; in 1815, a blue and red *chenille*; white-over-red plume on left (Fig. 91d).

Royal Horse Guards: blue jacket with red collar and cuffs and gold lace. Helmet as for the lifeguards, with blue and red *chenille*.

Dragoon guards: jacket of the same style as the household cavalry. Some illustrations show red patches on the faced collars. The lace around the jacket had a dark blue stripe in it. Black leather helmet with yellow metal plate and comb, and black horsehair *crinière*.

REGIMENT	JACKET	COLLAR AND CUFFS	LACE AND GIRDLE	OFFICERS' LACE
1st King's Dragoon Guards	red	blue	yellow	gold
2nd Queen's Dragoon Guards	red	black	white	silver
3rd Prince of Wales's Dragoon Guards	red	white	yellow	gold
4th Royal Irish Dragoon Guards	red	blue	white	silver
5th Princess Charlotte of Wales's Dragoon Guards	red	green	yellow	gold
6th Carabiniers	red	white	white	silver
7th Princess Royal's Dragoon Guards	red	black	yellow	gold

Dragoons (Fig. 92e): jackets similar to those of the dragoon guards, but with pointed cuffs; and lace on front of collar. Helmet as above, but the 2nd Regiment ("Scots Grays") wore fur caps with a yellow plate and cords; white plume; and black leather peak.

REGIMENT	JACKET	COLLAR AND CUFFS	LACE AND GIRDLE	OFFICERS' LACE
1st Royal	red	blue	yellow	gold
2nd Royal North British (Grays)	red	blue	yellow	gold
3rd King's Own	red	blue	yellow	gold
4th Queen's Own	red	light green	white	silver
6th Inniskilling	red	yellow	white	silver

There was no 5th Regiment at this period. A dark blue stripe ran down the center of the lace, and the girdle had two similar stripes. The remaining regiments, numbered from 7 to 25, were designated light dragoons, of which four were dressed as hussars. (These are dealt with separately below.) The light dragoons (Fig. 93d) wore blue jackets with variously colored collars, pointed cuffs, plastron lapels, and skirt turnbacks. Their girdles were of facing color, with two dark blue stripes. The epaulettes and lace on the chaco were of the color of the buttons. The basic color of the shabraques was blue.

REGIMENT	JACKET	FACINGS	OFFICERS' LACE
8th King's Royal Light Dragoons	blue	red	gold
9th Light Dragoons	blue*	crimson	gold
11th Light Dragoons	blue	buff	silver
12th Prince of Wales's	blue	yellow	silver
13th Light Dragoons	blue	buff	gold
14th Duchess of York's Own Light Dragoons	blue	orange	silver
16th Queen's Light Dragoons	blue	red	silver
17th Light Dragoons	blue	white	silver
19th Light Dragoons	blue	yellow	gold
20th Light Dragoons	blue	orange	gold
21st Light Dragoons	bluc	pink	gold
22nd Light Dragoons	blue	pink	silver
23rd Light Dragoons	blue	crimson	silver
24th Light Dragoons	blue	light gray	gold
25th Light Dragoons	blue	light gray	silver

*yellow girdle with two blue stripes

The hussars (Fig. 93f) wore blue dolmans and pelisses with yellow or white loopings, and variously colored collars and cuffs. The headdress was a fur cap, with a white-over-red plume. The bag was blue for the 18th Regiment, red for the rest. Previously, *Flügelmützen* had also been worn; and chacos were also worn on service.

REGIMENT	COLLAR AND CUFFS	O.R.s GIRDLE	SHABRAQUE	
			COLOR	VANDYK
7th Queen's Own	white	white and blue	blue	white
10th Prince of Wales's Own Royal	red*	red and yellow	red	red
15th King's Hussars	red	red and yellow	blue	red
18th Hussars	white	white and blue	blue	white
*white edging				

All cavalry wore white breeches, and boots; and on service, gray or blue overalls with buttons and colored stripes.

In 1816 the first lancer regiments were formed. The uniform consisted of a dark blue lancer jacket, with collar, pointed cuffs, and lapels of facing color; lancer cap with the top part covered with cloth of facing color; and crimson overalls for full dress, and blue-gray ones for undress (Fig. 93i). The regiments were subsequently increased in number. The lance pennants were white and red. About 1820 dragoon guards and dragoons adopted coatees with a row of buttons down the front; officers wore lace loops across the chest, down to c. 1828. The helmet with *criniere* was superseded by a new pattern, with a *chenille* (Fig. 92f). Yellow metal helmets were adopted in a834. After 1830 all the cavalry wore red uniforms for a while. In the hussars, this only affected the pelisee; the dolman remained blue (Fig. 93g). Light dragoons took into wear red jackets with two rows of buttons close together down the front. Hussars adopted fur busbies again c. 1841, and these remained the characteristic headdress to 1914. In 1840 the light dragoons reverted again to blue; the pattern of chaco was altered several times (Fig. 93e). In 1855 they were issued with *Attila* jackets. Light dragoons as such ceased to exist in 1861, and were turned into hussars and lancers. The dragoon guards and dragoons adopted tunics after the Crimean War. Hussars took *Attilas* into wear, in place of the dolman; pelisses were abolished. The household cavalry retained their red and blue uniforms. In 1821 they redopted cuirasses, of steel (with a yellow metal helmt with black *chenille*; from about 1842 a new pattern, with a horsehair plume falling all around, was worn. From the 1820s to the 1840s a black bearskin cap, with gold cords, and a white plume for the lifeguards, and a red one for the Royal Horse Guards, was also worn (Fig. 91e). Red and blue tunics respectively were adopted in 1856.

The distinctions of the British cavalry in 1912 are given in the following table. The main details applied right back to the Crimean War, after which the uniform altered little. With the full dress uniform, white leather equipment and gauntlets were worn, with laced pouch belts and heavily ornamented pouches for the officers. A single-breasted waist-length jacket with faced collar, and a small round "pillbox" cap with very narrow chinstrap, were worn by the men in undress up to 1914.

The household cavalry wore single-breasted tunics, white metal helmets and cuirasses, white pantaloons with butcher boots, or long dark blue trousers with red stripes (Fig. 91f, g). The men's collar, cuffs, and shoulder straps were of facing color with a gold lace edging. Officers had richly laced tunics. The cap badge worn with service dress was the royal cypher in a crowned corcle, in yellow metal. The cloaks were of the same color as the tunic, with a turndown collar of facing color.

REGIMENT	TUNIC	COLLAR, CUFFS, PIPING	HELMET PLUME	TROUSERS STRIPES
1st Lifeguards	red	dark blue	white	red triple stripes
2nd Lifeguards	red	dark blue	white	red triple stripes
Royal Horse Guards	blue	red	red	broad red stripe

Heavy cavalry (Dragoon Guards) wore single-breasted tunics, red for all regiments except the 6th, which had dark blue; with collar, pointed cuffs, and piping of facing color, Austrian knots in gold or yellow cord on the cuffs, yellow metal helmet with white metal plate, and plume; and dark blue pantaloons and trousers with broad yellow stripes, except where noted. A number of amalgamations of regiments took place in 1922.

REGIMENT	FACINGS	PLUME	COLLAR BADGES AND DISTINCTIONS
1st (King's) Dragoon Guards	blue	red	Austrian eagle: 1914–1937, 8-pointed crowned star with monogram "KDG"
2nd Dragoon Guards (Queen's Bays)	buff	black	"BAYS" in crowned wreath; white trousers stripes

(continued)

270

REGIMENT	FACINGS	PLUME	COLLAR BADGES AND DISTINCTIONS
3rd (Prince of Wales's) Dragoon Guards (1922: 3rd Carabiniers)	yellow	black/red	Prince of Wales's plume; from 1922, same on crossed carbines
4th (Royal Irish) Dragoon Guards (1922: 4/7th Dragoon Guards)	blue	white	star of St. Patrick; from 1922, 8-pointed star
5th (Princess Charlotte of Wales's) Dragoon Guards (1922: 5/6th, later 5th Royal Inniskilling Dragoon Guards)	green	red/white	leaping horse in crowned circle; from 1922, Inniskilling Castle
6th Dragoon Guards (Carabiniers) (to 1922)	white	white	crowned oval on crossed carbines; 2 narrow white trousers stripes
7th (Princess Royal's) Dragoon Guards (to 1922)	black	black/white	demi-lion on coronet with scroll

Dragoons' uniform was as above with red tunics for all. They had a white metal helmet with yellow metal plate, except 2nd Dragoons, which wore a black bearskin cap, with white plume on the left (Figs. 92h, i, page 266).

REGIMENT	FACINGS	PLUME	DISTINCTIONS
1st (Royal) Dragoons	blue	black	eagle on collar; on service dress cap, royal crest and scroll
2nd Dragoons (Royal Scots Grays)	blue	white	grenade on collar; eagle for O.R.s
6th (Inniskilling) Dragoons (from 1922, amalgamated with 5th Dragoon Guards)	primrose yellow	green	castle on collar; primrose yellow trousers stripes

Hussars wore dark blue *Attila* jackets with gold or yellow cord loops; dark blue pantaloons or trousers with two narrow yellow stripes; black fur busbies with plume in front, and bag on right side; gold or yellow lines (Fig. 93h).

REGIMENT	PLUME	BUSBY BAG	REMARKS	COLLAR BADGE
3rd (King's Own) Hussars	white	Garter blue	red collar	white horse
4th (Queen's Own) Hussars	red	yellow		IV in crowned circle with scroll below
7th (Queen's Own) Hussars	white	red		crowned circle with "Q.O." monogram
8th (King's Royal Irish) Hussars	red/white	red		crowned harp
10th (Prince of Wales's Own Royal) Hussars	black/white	red		Prince of Wales's plume
11th (Prince Albert's Own) Hussars	crimson/white	crimson	crimson trousers	crest and motto of Prince Albert

(continued)

REGIMENT	PLUME	BUSBY BAG	REMARKS	COLLAR BADGE
13th Hussars (from 1922, 13/18th)	white	buff	buff collar and trouser stripes	none on tunic
14th (King's) Hussars (from 1922, 14/20th)	white	yellow		Prussian eagle; from 1914, royal crest
15th (King's) Hussars (from 1922, 15/19th	red	red		royal crest with scroll below
18th (Victoria Mary, Princess of Wales's Own) Hussars (from 1922)	red/white	blue		XVIII H in crowned circle on laurel sprays
19th (Queen Alexandra's Own Royal) Hussars (from 1922)	white	white		Dannebrog and "A" intertwined with coronet
20th Hussars (from 1922)	yellow	crimson		crowned figure xHx

Lancers wore a dark blue lancer jacket (red for the 16th Lancers) with collar, lapels, pointed cuffs, and piping of facing color; dark blue pantaloons and trousers with two narrow yellow stripes; lancer cap with the upper part of facing color; and plume (Fig. 93k); girdle of yellow with two crimson stripes. Officers had gold lace on their collars and cuffs.

REGIMENT	FACINGS	PLUME	COLLAR BADGE AND DISTINCTIONS
5th (Royal Irish) Lancers (from 1922)	red	green	harp and crown
9th (Queen's Own) Lancers	red	black/white	crowned "9" over scroll, on crossed lances; cap: upper part blue; black leather top
12th (Prince of Wales's Royal) Lancers	red	red	Prince of Wales's plume and XII on crossed lances
16th (Queen's) Lancers (from 1922, 16/5th)	blue	black	crowned "16" and scroll on crossed lances
17th (Duke of Cambridge's Own) Lancers (from 1922, 17/21st)	white	white	skull and crossbones (on frock coat only); double white trousers stripes
21st (Empress of India's) Lancers (from 1922)	French gray	white	crowned V.R.I. with XXI below on crossed lances

The service dress differed from that of the infantry only in the varying regimental badges and the boots and spurs (Fig. 95d). Leather bandoliers were worn. After 1914 full dress was officially abolished for the line regiments, but continued to be worn on occasions. After 1922 the newly formed amalgamated regiments wore a combination of the distinctions of the old regiments.

III. ARTILLERY, ENGINEERS, ETC.; RANK DISTINCTIONS

The Royal Artillery traditionally wore uniforms of blue, with red facings and gold or yellow lace. The style basically followed that of the infantry (Figs. 94a,b).

The Royal Horse Artillery, raised in 1793, was dressed like light dragoons, i.e., in a looped dolman, white breeches, and boots, and a "Tarleton" crested helmet with a white plume. The jacket was blue with red collar and cuffs, and gold or yellow loopings for officers and O.R.s respectively. Shabraque and valise were both blue. The curved sword was worn on a waistbelt with slings. This was the dress in which the Royal Horse Artillery fought at Waterloo (Fig. 94c). The foot artillery wore jackets and chacos similar to those of the line infantry. The blue coat had red collar, cuffs, and shoulder straps, with gold lace. White breeches and black gaiters were worn for full dress; in undress, blue trousers. Coatees with red facings and red turnbacks were adopted later; these were double-breasted from 1828 (Fig. 94d).

After the Napoleonic Wars, light-blue (in 1847 dark blue) trousers with broad stripes were issued; and white trousers in summer (Figs. 94f,g). After the Crimean War, a dark blue tunic with a red collar, edged with yellow cord, and red piping, was introduced. There were yellow cord Austrian knots above the dark blue pointed cuffs; the shoulder straps were dark blue with red piping. The various headdresses followed those of the infantry; but from 1856 to 1878, a low-crowned black fur busby with red bag and white plume was worn. In 1880–1881, grenade collar badges were introduced; and a blue cloth-covered helmet, with ball finial from 1881, was worn (Fig. 94h). From 1905 dark blue peaked forage caps with a red band were worn for walking out. From 1815 up to the Great War, the Royal Horse Artillery (Figs. 94e,i) continued to wear a dark blue dolman and light-blue (later dark blue) trousers and pantaloons. Collars and cuffs were red, laced with gold, for officers (O.R.s had blue cuffs), narrow gold or yellow loopings respectively on the front, and Austrian

Fig. 94. Great Britain—Artillery, Engineers, General Officers.
a, d, g: artillery, officers. b, f, h: artillerymen. c, e, i: Royal Horse Artillery. k: Royal Engineers. l, m: general officers.

knots on the sleeves. Horizontal grenade badges were worn on the collar from 1880 to 1881. In 1837 black fur busbies, with a red bag, white plume, and gold or yellow lines, were adopted. The khaki service dress was similar to that of the infantry, except for the badge. Busbies were again taken into wear by the officers of the foot artillery for full dress in 1928.

The full-dress uniform of the Royal Engineers was red like that of the infantry, but with collars and cuffs of dark blue velvet, yellow braid, and yellow Austrian knots on the cuffs. The blue spiked helmet was similar to the infantry's (Fig. 94k). The collar badge was a grenade, which was worn on the service dress as well. Military transport was reorganized in 1888, when the Army (later Royal) Service Corps was formed. The ASC adopted a blue helmet with ball, dark blue tunic with white collar and piping, white Austrian knots on the sleeves, and blue trousers with two narrow white stripes. The helmet, cap, and collar badge was an eight-pointed crowned star with "A.S.C." in the center. The specialist troops raised during and after the Great War had the following distinctions.

Royal Tank Corps: The badge was a tank in a crowned wreath, of white metal; an embroidered tank was worn on the right upper arm; the headdress was a black beret with the badge on the left, with in full dress, a brown, red, and green plume.

Royal Corps of Signals: Uniform was similar to that of the Royal Engineers; cap and collar badge: Mercury in a crowned oval.

From the mid-eighteenth century, general officers' uniform consisted of a full-skirted red coat, with blue collar and cuffs, ornamented with rich oakleaf embroidery. The cut of the uniform altered according to the prevailing fashion. In 1800 generals wore their loops equidistant; lieutenant generals, loops in threes; major generals, loops in pairs (Fig. 94l). The tunic adopted after the Crimean War had white piping, and slash cuffs with varying lace, and skirt flaps (Fig. 94m). The undress garment was a dark blue double-breasted frock coat with collar and cuffs of dark blue velvet. The general officers' sash was of crimson silk and gold mixed. The hat had a red and white feather plume, and gold loop. The forage cap was dark blue, with red piping around the top, a red band, and a double row of gold oakleaf embroidery around the peak. The service dress cap had a khaki top and khaki peak. Excepting the cap, they were only distinguished in their blue undress frocks and in service dress by their red gorget patches, pointed at the back, with a small button in the angle, with narrow gold oakleaf embroidery or gimp along the center of the patch.

The uniforms of other staff officers were differentiated from that of general officers by the cut of the coat and the color, arrangement, and shape of the lace loops or embroidery. The black hat had a red and white feather plume. From 1855 to 1897 staff officers wore a red hussar-type jacket with dark blue collar and pointed cuffs, and gold cord loopings on the breast, and gold lace on the collar and sleeves. The trousers were dark blue with broad red stripes. In undress, a dark blue frock coat with black braid loopings was worn. The gorget patches on service dress were of different colors for different staff appointments.

NCOs' rank distinctions, basically unchanged from the early 1800s, consisted of one to four white or metal lace chevrons, point down, worn on both upper arms or, from 1881, on the right arm only in full dress. The higher ranks of NCOs wore a

Fig. 95. Great Britain, 1900–1936.

a: infantry, khaki foreign service uniform. b: sergeant, infantry, walking-out
dress. c: infantry, service dress. d: cavalry, service dress. e: officer, Highlanders, service
dress. f: Canadian infantry, service dress. g: Australian infantry, service
dress. h: Highlander, marching order. i: officer, Welsh Guards, full dress. k: officer, mess
dress. l: infantry, walking-out dress.

crown in addition. On service dress, the chevrons were of khaki braid: lance corporals had one; corporals, two; sergeants, three. The rank distinctions of senior
NCOs and warrant officers were worn below the elbows. From 1918, for example,
regimental sergeant majors wore the royal coat of arms in a wreath above both cuffs.
From 1791 field officers were distinguished by wearing two epaulettes instead of one;
from 1811 these bore a star, crown, and crown and star respectively for majors,
lieutenant colonels, and colonels, in gold or silver, of contrasting color to that of the
epaulettes themselves. These were worn up to 1855. After the introduction of the
tunic, they were worn on the collar, by company officers as well. In 1880 the rank
badges were moved to the shoulder and were in silver on gold twisted cords (black for
rifles); on service dress, in khaki on the cuff slashes, up to around 1917, from which
date rank was indicated by bronzed metal "pips" or stars on the shoulder straps: one
to three stars for company officers; a crown for majors, a crown and a star for lieutenant colonels, and a crown and two stars for colonels. General officers' shoulder
cords were broader; their distinction was a crossed sword and baton. A brigadier
general wore crossed sword and baton (the later brigadier wore a crown over three
stars, arranged as a triangle); major generals wore a star in addition; lieutenant
generals, a crown; and generals, a crown and star. Field marshals wore two crossed
batons in an oak wreath surmounted by a crown. General officers wore their rank
badges on the shoulders in service dress. Their cap badge consisted of a crossed
sword and baton (crossed batons for field marshals) in an oak wreath, crowned.

In the British army, officers wore a special dress when dining in the mess and for
social functions in the evening. An example is illustrated in Fig. 95k. The waist-

length jacket was generally of the basic color of the full-dress uniform, with faced collar and variously shaped cuffs.

INDIA

Before coming under Crown rule in 1858, British India was administered by the Honourable East India Company, a trading concern, which enjoyed substantial royal patronage and protection. The conquest of India proceeded outward from three districts: Bombay, Bengal, and Madras, which in the course of time became autonomous presidencies, maintaining their own establishments of European and native troops. The uniforms of the Indian army were of a very great variety of types and colors and were frequently compounded of a mixture of native costume and European fashion. Only a few instances can be cited here. The dress of the native troops was naturally influenced very strongly by that of the Crown regiments, which from 1754 were garrisoned in India for periods at a time, whereas the uniforms of the European troops of the E.I.C. differed little from those of the British army at home. Changes in pattern followed behind those in Britain, simply because of the slow communications of the time. The coats of the Indian native troops, up to the Mutiny, did not deviate much from the British, as they were usually red, with collar and cuffs of facing color. The differences were mainly in the headdress, and more particularly in the legwear and footwear (Fig. 96a). The cavalry regiments were dressed entirely in British-style uniforms, frequently similar to those of the light cavalry. An example is given in Fig. 96c. In 1812 the facings of the Indian native troops in the pay of the Company were as follows: Infantry (Fig. 96b)—Madras: 2nd, 9th, 12th, 20th Regiments, green; 3rd, 24th, 25th Regiments, white; 4th Regiment, orange; 5th, 14th Regiments, black; 6th, 11th, 19th Regiments, buff; 1st (European), 7th Regiments, light blue; 18th Regiment, dark blue; 8th, 17th, 21st Regiments, yellow; 13th, 16th, 22nd Regiments, light yellow; 3rd, 10th Regiments, red. The 1st, 2nd, 5th, 10th, 11th, 17th, 20–25th Regiments all had yellow metal buttons; the rest, white. Bengal: The 28 regiments all had yellow distinctions and white metal buttons. Bombay: white metal buttons for all; facings— 1st (European) Regiment, yellow; 1st N.I., orange; 2nd, 8th Regiments, dark blue; 3rd, black; 4th, white; 5th, 7th, green; 6th, buff; 9th, light yellow. The coats of all the infantry regiments were red, with white lace loops. The drawers were white, with dark blue vandyked edgings around the legs. The 8th Bengal Cavalry Regiment all had French gray dolmans with orange collars and cuffs, and silver or white loopings and buttons; the headdresses were variously colored turbans. White breeches and knee-length boots were also worn. The Madras cavalry wore red dolmans with white buttons and loopings; officers of the 1st and 2nd Regiments had gold loopings. The collars and cuffs varied: white for the 1st Regiment; 2nd, dark green; 3rd, buff; 4th, deep yellow; 5th, black; 6th, French gray; 7th, yellow; 8th, pale yellow. Later the Madras cavalry wore a black leather helmet with a red *crinière*, later a *chenille* (Fig. 96c). The artillery were all dressed in blue faced red; the horse artillery had heavily braided dolmans and, in 1845, brass helmets with a comb and a long red horsehair *crinière*.

Fig. 96. India.

a, b, e: sepoys. c: officer, Madras Light Cavalry. d: officer, sepoys. f: officer, 16th Bengal Cavalry. g: 45th Rettray's Sikhs. h, k: gurkhas. i: 20th Punjab Infantry.

After the Crown became responsible for the government of India, the Company's native army was taken under British control and was reorganized. Some of the uniforms gave considerable concessions to national dress; and they altered little in essentials from the introduction of the tunic up to the Great War. By the mid-nineteenth century loose khaki linen blouses with long skirts (Fig. 96i) were worn on service, and these were retained up to the 1939–1945 war by the native troops. The full dress was often of the same style: red for the infantry with variously colored piping and collar lace. Single-breasted tunics were also worn (Fig. 96g), with collar, cuffs, and a narrow panel down the front of facing color. The colors and method of folding of the turbans varied from regiment to regiment, and even for each company, according to the ethnic group of the men.

The cavalry regiments wore similarly cut full-dress blouses, mainly dark blue, dark green, or red, with collar, cuffs, and edging down the front of various colors. An example is given in Fig. 96f: the officer had a dark blue *kurtka* with gold lace on the collar and cuffs, and gold embroidery. The coat in Fig. 96g was red, with white facings, yellow metal buttons, and blue-black trousers with red piping, and yellow turban with black stripes.

The ten Ghurka regiments wore a distinctive uniform of dark green, like the British rifle regiments. The collar and cuff piping were red for the first two regiments, and green or black for the rest (Fig. 96h). In general the development of service dress closely followed that of the British army, but was made in drill. The headdress differed. As in the British army, each regiment had special badges. The rank distinctions were much the same as in Britain. Indian officers wore similar uniforms to the European officers in many cases, but with the customary turban.

277

GREECE

Cockade: white and light blue; during the Greek revolution, and from New Year 1822, black, sky blue, and white were chosen as the national colors.

During the Greek War of Liberation, isolated attempts were made to dress various of the volunteer corps in a uniform manner. The *Hierolochiten* wore black coats, and felt caps with a skull and crossbones on them. Such attempts, however, were rare. The army was uniformly dressed for the first time in 1833, when Prince Otto of Bavaria ascended the throne, and uniforms similar to those of the Bavarian army were taken into wear. The infantry (Fig. 97a) adopted single-breasted, short-skirted light-blue jackets, with red collar, cuffs, piping, and skirt turnbacks, and white metal buttons. The trousers were light blue with a red stripe. Chacos were worn. The fusiliers had white shoulder wings and chaco cords; the grenadiers red, and the rifles green. The artillery (Fig. 97c) differed from the infantry in the blue-black basic color of their jackets and trousers. The distinctions and chaco cords were dark red and the buttons, yellow metal. The cavalry (Fig. 97b) were dressed as lancers. Their uniform consisted of a green jacket with carmine collar, lapels, and pointed cuffs; the girdle was white, with two light-blue stripes; the shoulder scales, white metal; and the trousers, green, with carmine stripes. The lancer cap was carmine with a silver rayed plate, and a drooping white hair plume. The green shabraques had a carmine edging, and in the rear corners, the crowned letter "O" in white. White sheepskin covers were worn, with a vandyked carmine cloth edging. The lance pennants were white over light blue. Leather equipment was white. The uniform of the general officers (Fig. 97d) exactly resembled that of Bavarian general officers. In the rear corners of the red, silver-edged shabraques was a crowned "O" in silver. Distinctions of rank were as in Bavaria (Fig. 97d).

In 1851 a conical leather chaco was adopted, with a metal star bearing the crowned "O" on the front; and a double-breasted tunic in the same colors as before. The shoulder straps and round cuffs were of basic color with a colored piping. The infantry wore white leather equipment; all other troops, black. The trousers were light gray with piping; those of the artillery and engineers, dark blue with triple stripes. The soft cloth kepi was of the same color as the tunic, with piping in *Waffen-farben*, and a horizontal black leather peak. The rifles were dressed like the infantry,

Fig. 97. Greece, 1832–1890.
a, c: infantry. b: cavalry. h: cavalry officer. c, g: artillery. d: general officer. f: Evzone.

with light-green distinctions. The cavalry uniform remained unchanged. Field officers and general officers wore fringed epaulettes.

When Prince George of Denmark became king in 1863, the army adopted new uniforms, similar to those of the Danish army (Figs. 97e–h). Black leather equipment was worn by all arms. The cavalry wore a hussar uniform of green, with white loopings, with carmine collar and cuffs on the *Attila*; and carmine piping on the kepi. The rifles (*Evzones*), now the Royal Guard, adopted the old national dress. The small fez was red, with a dark blue tassel on a long cord; waistcoat, red, with a stand collar; jacket, coat (*fustanella*), and gaiters were white; the soft leather shoes, yellow; and the jacket lace, garters, and shoe pompons, all black. The other troops adopted a dark blue single-breasted tunic (double-breasted for artillery officers), with shoulder straps and slash cuffs of basic color, with colored piping. The collar was of *Waffenfarbe*: dark blue for the artillery with red piping and a horizontal flaming grenade in red. The trousers for general officers and infantry were changed to light blue. The kepi was dark blue, piped in *Waffenfarbe*, with a cockade in front and the crown above. In full dress, infantry and engineers wore a white and blue plume (red for artillery); and officers wore a similarly colored feather plume. The *Waffenfarbe* for general officers, infantry, and artillery was red, and for engineers, carmine. The rank distinctions consisted of sloping stripes of the color of the buttons, piped in *Waffenfarbe*, on both lower arms, for NCOs; and one to three rosettes for company officers, small stars for field officers, and large stars for general officers, in the color of the buttons, on the twisted shoulder cords; and in addition, one to three narrow bands, and one broad and one to three narrow bands respectively for company officers and field officers, around the kepi. General officers had broad-patterned gold stripes. The collars and cuffs of general officers' tunics were ornamented with rich embroidery in gold. About 1912 a khaki-colored service dress (Fig. 98a) was introduced, with natural-colored leather equipment. The jacket was single-breasted, with patch pockets on the breast and skirts; the turndown collar and round cuffs were piped in *Waffenfarbe*. The engineers now had light-blue piping. The shoulder straps were wholly colored; but of basic color with piping, for infantry; with the number of the regiment in black (of the color of the buttons for officers) with the rank distinctions: a stripe down the center or the edges for company officers and field

Fig. 98. Greece, 1910–1936.
a, b: infantry. c: captain.

officers respectively, with one to three stars. General officers had gold stripes with large six-pointed silver stars. The men wore white forage caps with piping around the top; the officers wore a kepi with the rank stripes in a dark khaki color. The *Evzones* wore a khaki-colored fez and a long, flared khaki coat, with red shoulder straps and red piping on the collar and cuffs. The service jacket worn in the 1930s had patches, pointed at the rear, of *Waffenfarbe* on the collar, with the badge of the arm of service on them; general offices had a patterned gold stripe. The steel helmet was of British type (Figs. 98b,c).

HUNGARY

Cockade: red-white-green

The first autonomous Hungarian army to wear uniforms different from those of the Royal and Imperial Austrian army was formed in 1848–1849. The distinctive dress, adapted from the national costume, can be only briefly described here. The infantry, artillery, and transport corps wore long-skirted dark brown *Attila* jackets, with red loopings for the men and gold for officers. The olivets and rosettes were yellow for the infantry and artillery, and white for the transport corps. The artillery had white piping on the collar, and white flaming grenades for the men (gold for officers) placed on the collar, in line with the shoulders. The rank distinctions took the form of

1936

Fig. 99. Hungary.
a: officer in greatcoat. b: infantry, major, evening dress. d: Crown Guard.

short horizontal stripes at the ends of the collar, red for the men and of the color of the olivets for officers; and in addition, for field officers, a medium-width gold and silver stripe around the lower edge of the collar and on the cuffs below the Austrian knots. Officers wore a red, white, and green sash, with the tassels at the left, around the waist; on service, it was worn over the right shoulder. Officers had gold sword knots. The trousers were light blue with red knots and red stripes. The chaco was of the same pattern as that worn by the Austrian army (Fig. 6f). It had a leather peak, with the crowned Hungarian arms above, of the color of the olivets; and a red, white, and green cockade above that. Around the top edge was a tricolored cord—tricolored lace for NCOs; and for officers, one to three gold or silver lace bands, with red lights. Off duty, a blue Austrian-pattern field cap was worn (red for the 3rd and 9th Infantry Battalions). General officers had carmine *Attilas* with gold loopings and broad gold collar and cuff lace, and a carmine chaco with broad gold lace around the top and a green heron's feather. Officers of the general staff had dark green *Attilas* with gold loopings. The trousers were dark gray with gold piping down the sides for both.

Of the newly raised cavalry regiments, the Hunyady Hussar Regiment No. 13 had a distinctive uniform in the national dress of the Pandours: a short dark blue jacket with red collar and pointed cuffs and numerous white metal buttons, with a dark blue pelisse with black loopings and fur edging, gray breeches with red stripes, and a felt hat turned up on both sides, with a red feather. The other newly formed hussar regiments adopted cockades and cords on their chacos, in the national colors, with the following distinctions.

REGIMENT	CHACO	DOLMAN	BREECHES	LOOPINGS	OLIVETS
No. 14 Lehel	green	dark blue	dark blue	tricolored; red-	yellow
No. 15 King Mathias	red	blue-gray	blue-gray	white-green, with	white
No. 16 Karoly	light blue-gray	cornflower blue	cornflower blue	red predominating	white
No. 17 Bosckay	light blue	light blue	light blue	white	white
No. 18 Attila	red	light blue	red	tricolored	white

The pelisses were the same color as the dolmans. In the 14th Regiment, officers also wore tricolored loopings (of red, with silver and green threads through them). The 17th Regiment had silver cords, and the others, gold (with red and green through them). The shabraques and sabertaches were red with a green, white, and red edging, and bore the coat of arms. The Lancer Corps Poninski wore light-blue lancer jackets with white collars, pointed cuffs, and lapels, all piped red; light-blue trousers with white stripes; leather lancer caps with blue upper part and a white plume; white and blue lance pennants; and light-blue shabraques edged red. The *Jäger* and pioneers wore blue-gray single-breasted coats with steel-green piping, and six rows of straight loopings on the front, and gold Austrian knots on the cuffs; blue-gray trousers with green piping; with yellow olivets and a hat for the *Jäger*; the pioneers had white olivets, and a chaco with a black plume. The leather equipment was black for the whole army.

In 1919 Hungary became an independent state, with greatly diminished territories, under the leadership of the later regent, Admiral Horthy. The remains of the wartime Austro-Hungarian army were reformed, chiefly from among the White troops. The universal distinction of the new Hungarian armed forces, from that time, was a cord, worn around the outside of the collar patches, which was worn up to the late 1930s. On 1 January 1922, a new service uniform was introduced, of the same pattern for all arms and for all ranks. It remained almost unchanged up to the late 1930s. The basic color was a fairly dark khaki-brown (Fig. 99c). The jacket had a row of five buttons, patch pockets on the breast and skirts, with pleats and scalloped flaps fastened by a small button, and round cuffs, with three small buttons on the hindarm seam for officers and NCOs. The trousers were of basic color, and of the usual cut, without colored piping; but general officers had red triple stripes. In addition to the German-pattern steel helmet, a peakless Austrian-type field cap was worn off duty and in undress. The leather equipment was brown; officers wore a Sam Browne. NCOs and men wore shoulder straps of *Waffenfarbe*, with a small button. Officers wore a gold and red cord on the right shoulder; officers of the mounted arms—cavalry, artillery, transport corps, and ADCs —wore one on the left shoulder as well.

The arms of service were distinguished by the varying colors of the jacket and greatcoat collar patches, the patches on the service cap, and by the men's shoulder straps. The *Waffenfarben* were as follows: general officers, scarlet; general staff, black velvet with scarlet piping; technical general staff, brown velvet with scarlet piping; infantry and bicycle troops, grass green; border troops, green piped with red; hussars, light blue; artillery, scarlet; technical services and communications troops, dark steel green; armored troops, dark blue; transport corps, at first yellow, then from 1922, as motorized troops, brown; medical troops, black; musicians, violet. Officers of the military departments of the regent had white; commisary officers, carmine; and officers in local appointments, orange.

The collar patches, which were pointed at the rear, were edged along the top and bottom with cords, which terminated in a plain loop for other ranks, and a trefoil for officers; while general officers had three eyelets along the converging sides of the point. The cord was of dark khaki silk for the men, silver for NCOs, and gold for officers; as were the buttons, rank badges, and other metal insignia. On the left side of the field cap was a triangular patch, placed pilewise, above which were three narrow horizontal stripes of button color, with rosettes at the ends. In addition, general officers had gold-embroidered oak sprigs along the sides of the triangle. The collar patches on the greatcoat were spearhead-shaped, without cords; officers had a small gold button at the point. General officers' patches were ornamented with gold lace. The greatcoat was double-breasted, with roll cuffs and a turndown collar, the latter made of dark khaki colored velvet for field officers (Fig. 99a).

The cockade was worn on the front top part of the field cap. An upright eagle's feather was often worn on the left side. Boots were black, and the rank and file of the infantry wore dark khaki puttees. In summer, all arms wore white linen clothing. Mounted troops, however, wore breeches of khaki cloth.

The rank distinctions were worn on the collar, and in addition to the various cords, took the form of one to three six-pointed stars: white for the men; silver for NCOs, field officers, and general officers; and gold for company officers. NCOs' collar patches had, forward of the point, a medium-width scalloped silver stripe. Junior lieutenants wore a silver star on a narrow vertical gold stripe. Ensigns, who wore officers' cords on their patches, had a silver star, with a short horizontal gold stripe, pointed at the rear, behind it. Field officers and general officers had a broad gold stripe on their collar patches, of such a width as to allow the *Waffenfarbe* to appear like piping along the top and bottom and at the point. In addition, general officers wore two crossed oak sprigs embroidered in gold, on the red pointed part of their collar patches. The officers' gold sword knots had loose bullions and, on the acorn, a red, white, and green overlay with the coat of arms on it. In all orders of dress off duty, all officers wore a black cap like that worn by Austrian officers prior to 1914, with the Hungarian cockade at the top front, and a gold and red cord loop below. Off duty, officers wore black trousers with red piping, and for formal occasions, an *Attila*; otherwise, the undress *Attila* was worn. The colors of the *Attilas* were: general officers, light blue; infantry, dark green; hussars, dark blue; artillery and transport troops, brown; all other arms, black. General officers and artillery had red collars and pointed cuffs; general staff officers wore the *Attilas* of their former arm, with black velvet collars and cuffs, piped red. Company officers and field officers wore the old-style Austrian rank distinctions on their collars, i.e., field officers had lace right around their collars. The loopings on the full-dress *Attila* were the same as on the earlier Prussian *Attila*; the undress version had five short straight loops on the front and a plain trefoil on the sleeves. The loopings were invariably gold (Fig. 99b).

The Royal Hungarian Crown Guard, and the other guards—Trabant; lifeguard cavalry; lifeguard infantry (Castle Guard); and the parliament guard—were part of the army. Their Court Guard uniform resembled the old Hungarian dress; in red and green for the Crown Guard; cherry red and silver for the parliament guard; and red and white for the other guards (Fig. 99d). Off duty, the men also wore officers'-type caps with silver cord loops, and colored *Attilas* with cherry red loopings—dark blue for the lifeguard cavalry and parliament guard—and dark green for the rest; with black trousers with cherry red piping.

ITALY

KINGDOM OF SARDINIA

Cockade: cornflower blue

I. HOUSEHOLD TROOPS

The longest-established guard was the *Gardes du Corps*, which stemmed from the *Compagnia Archieri Guardia* of the sixteenth century. In 1707 they are referred to as the *Gentiluomini Archieri Savojardi*. As the *Guardie del Corpo*, in 1685, the company wore a silver-laced hat with red and blue feathers, black cravat, and plain breast plate, with red lining, edged with white, around the armpits. The leather jacket was lined with red and had red, silver-laced cuffs and yellow metal buttons. The shoulder belt was of fawn leather. The waistcoat was red, laced with silver; breeches and gauntlets were likewise red. In 1745 a gold-laced hat, white cravat, and red coat with gold lace and light-blue cuffs and skirt turnbacks were worn. Waistcoat and breeches were light blue, and stockings were red. The carbine belt was light blue with a gold edging. The shabraque was also light blue, edged gold. In 1774 the uniform was cut in the close-fitting fashion of the time: the coat was dark blue with gold lace loops, and red collar, cuffs, and skirt lining. The hat had gold lace; the under-garments were dull yellow. The waistcoat was laced with gold. The pouch belt was red with gold lace. Gauntlets and jack spurs were worn; and the arms consisted of a sword, and a halberd with blue tassel and shaft thickly studded with yellow metal nails. The uniform was of the same colors in 1815; but the cut was different. Gold epaulettes were now worn; and the hat had a sky blue plume. In 1832 the uniform consisted of a hat with cock's feather plume, dark blue coatee and trousers, with two silver lace loops on the collar and cuffs, and red skirt turnbacks and trousers stripes, and white metal buttons; sky blue sash; and silver pouch belt. A tunic of the same color replaced the coatee in 1844.

Archibusieri Guardie: In 1713, this guard wore a gold-laced hat with white plumage, and a white neckcloth; the coat was red with white lining, yellow metal buttons, and gold lace edging; cuffs, waistcoat, stockings, and sash were all sky blue, the last having gold tassels. The pouch belt was sky blue and gold. In the spearhead of the partisan was the intertwined cipher "VA" (Vittorio Amadeo II). The tassel was yellow. In 1775 the uniform consisted of a gold-laced hat without feather plumage, a dark blue coat with gold lace loops, red collar, and cuffs with gold lace loops. The waistcoat was red, the breeches blue, and stockings, white. The pouch belt was red with a gold edging. In 1816 they wore a gold-laced hat, and dark blue coatee with lace on the front, and red collar, cuffs, and skirt turnbacks. The dark blue trousers were worn with low boots. A small pouch was worn on the front of the waistbelt. The pouch belt was as before; and sword and musket were carried. In 1832, as the *Guardie del Reale Palazzo*, they wore: hat across the head, with broad gold lace loop; a double-breasted coatee with red collar, cuffs, and skirt lining, with a yellow lace loop on the collar and cuffs. The buttons were yellow metal. The epaulettes had no fringes. The dark blue trousers had red stripes; the gold-laced pouch belt had silver mounts; and sword and musket and bayonet were carried. Tunics were introduced in 1844.

Allabardieri Guardie: In 1719–1744 they wore exactly the same uniform as the *Archibusieri Guardie*, but without plumage around the hat, and no sash; and silver lace edging. The halberd had a red tassel.

Guardia Swizzera: In 1816 they were dressed like the *Archibusieri Guardie*, but without lace on the hat. The breeches were white and the epaulettes silver.

The Corps of *Carabinieri Reali* (Royal Carabiniers) wore hats with black lace and a silver loop; and dark blue single-breasted coatees with red skirt turnbacks, and sky blue collar patches and pointed cuffs, with a white lace loop on each. The fringed epaulettes were sky blue with white crescents. The buttons were white, as were the leather crossbelts. The black gaiters reached to just below the knee. The mounted carabiniers were distinguished by a sky blue plume and white epaulettes, and carbine belt and pouch belt worn one below the other. There was a yellow grenade badge on the pouch. Knee boots were worn. In 1832 a red-over-sky-blue drooping feather plume was worn. Two white lace loops were worn on the collar, and two on the (now dark blue) cuffs. The sky blue collar patches were done away with. White epaulettes and aiguillettes were worn. The blue trousers had two red stripes. This uniform was worn by both the mounted and dismounted carabiniers.

II. INFANTRY

By and large, up to about 1770, the uniform was the same general style as that in France. Until the mid-seventeenth century, the basic color was usually white; then blue came into use, and this remained the predominant color for full-dress uniforms in the Italian army. Details were as follows.

An illustration, believed to be of 1659, shows the *Granatieri Guardie* (Grenadier Guards) wearing a blue coat turned up with red, with yellow buttons, and red undergarments. At the beginning of the eighteenth century, the line infantry wore an ample-fitting white coat with cuffs, waistcoat, and breeches in the regimental color, red cravat, white stockings, and gold- or silver-laced hat (Fig. 100a). The Regiment *della Marina* had red coats with white lining and green cuffs, green undergarments, and yellow buttons. The pouch belt was of fawn leather and had a large buckle on the front. Illustrations of 1744 show the same combination of colors, but the style had changed in accord with the fashion of the period. Around 1758 the whole infantry was dressed in dark blue (Fig. 100b). The different distinctions were as follows.

286

REGIMENT	HAT LACE	COLLAR, CUFFS, LAPELS, SKIRTS	WAISTCOAT AND BREECHES	BUTTONS
Granatieri Guardie	white	red[1]	red[1]	white
Savoia	white	white	dark blue	yellow
Piemonte	white	red	red	white
Aosta	yellow	red	red	yellow
Della Marina	white	yellowish-white	dark blue	yellow
La Regina	white	red[2]	dark blue	yellow
Sardegna	white	light yellow	light yellow	yellow

[1]white lace loops on cuffs, lapels, waistcoat
[2]white twist buttonholes on lapels and cuffs

Hangers were only carried by the *Granatieri Guardie*; the rest had bayonets in scabbards. The pouches had a red binding. The gaiters were white for all. In 1775 the *Granatieri Guardie* adopted bearskin caps. The undergarments were changed to white, or yellowish-white, for all in 1787 (Fig. 100c). Thereafter the cut of the uniform changed several times, without altering in essentials. In 1803 a single-breasted coatee, cut rounded at the front, was introduced. With it went blue breeches and black gaiters, and a helmet with yellow metal plate and sky blue crest, based on the then current Austrian helmet; the whole uniform, in fact, was very similar to the Austrian one. In 1814 all the infantry was dressed in this manner (Fig. 100d). The shoulder straps were dark blue, the white leather belts were worn crossed, with a brass match case for the grenadiers. The grenadiers also wore fur caps.

In 1814 the distinctions of the regiments were as follows.

REGIMENT	COLLAR AND CUFFS	SKIRT TURNBACKS	BUTTONS
Granatieri Guardie	red	red	white[1]
Savoia	black	red	yellow
Piemonte	red	red	yellow
Aosta	dark red	yellow	white
Cuneo	crimson	white	white
La Regina	white	dark red	white
Sardegna	red	red	white[2]

[1]9 white lace loops on breast; 3 above each cuff
[2]lace loops without tassels, arranged as for Granatieri Guardie

In 1821 the crested helmet was superseded by a chaco (Fig. 100e). This had yellow metal chinscales and heart-shaped plate in front, with an eagle with the arms of the House of Savoy on its breast. The short plume was blue over red. The breeches were white; the greatcoat was gray-brown. The chacos were changed about 1833. The grenadiers adopted them as well. The grenadiers had red padded wings on their shoulders, and the *voltigeurs*, green one. About this time the infantry had gray trousers with a red stripe; in 1839 dark blue ones, also with a red stripe, were introduced (Fig. 100f). A complete change took place in 1843–1844. The coatee was

Fig. 100. Italy. Sardinia—Infantry.

a, b, c, d, e, f, g: line infantry. i: infantry officer. h: *Bersaglieri*.

superseded by a double-breasted tunic, with white metal buttons for all regiments. The fusilier companies now adopted wings, which were dark blue like the tunic. The elite companies retained their green and red ones. The new-pattern chaco had a plate in front with the regimental number on it (Fig. 100g). The elite companies had a grenade or hunting horn on theirs, for the grenadier and *voltigeur* companies respectively. The crossbelts wee abolished and superseded by a waistbelt with a short sword, and a bayonet in a scabbard; the leather equipment was black, except for the grenadiers and light infantry of the guard.

In 1844 the uniforms were as follows.

REGIMENT	COLLAR AND CUFFS	PIPING
Granatieri Guardie[1]	red	red
Brigata Savoia (1st and 2nd Infantry Regiments)	black, piped red	red
Brigata Piemonte (3rd and 4th Infantry Regiments)	red	red
Brigata Aosta (5th and 6th Infantry Regiments)	red	dark red
Brigata Cuneo (7th and 8th Infantry Regiments)	crimson	crimson
Brigata La Regina (9th and 10th Infantry Regiments)	white	white
Cacciatori Guardie (Light Infantry of the Guard; previously Sardegna Regiment)[2]	red	red
Brigata Casale (11th and 12th Infantry Regiments)	light yellow	light yellow

(continued)

288

REGIMENT	COLLAR AND CUFFS	PIPING
Brigata Pinerola (13th and 14th Infantry Regiments)	black; piping on front and bottom of collar and on top of cuff	red
Brigata Savona (15th and 16th Infantry Regiments)	white	red
Brigata Acqui (17th and 18th Infantry Regiments)	dark yellow	dark yellow

[1] fur caps with yellow grenade and red cords; white lace loops on collar and cuffs; red wings
[2] chaco with red-over-white drooping plume; white lace loops on collar and cuffs; green wings

The *Bersaglieri*, which was formed in 1836, adopted a uniform of the same style as the infantry: of dark blue, with carmine collar and cuffs and yellow metal buttons; and the famous hat with cocks feather plume (Fig. 100h). In the early 1850s, the infantry adopted a single-breasted tunic: the wings were abolished, and a new pattern of chaco was issued.

These were the uniforms worn in 1860, when Sardinia assumed the hegemony of Italy.

III. CAVALRY

Toward the end of the seventeenth century, three dragoon regiments were raised. They were called the Yellow, Blue, and Green Dragoons, after the colors of their coats. All had red cuffs and undergarments, and white buttons (Fig. 101a). The heavy cavalry was dressed in blue, with red turnbacks and undergarments. In 1744 the Piemonte Dragoons (Fig. 101b) were wearing red coats, breeches, and cravats, white hat lace, white collars, lapels, cuffs, skirt turnbacks, and waistcoats; and white metal buttons. The crossed shoulder belts and the waistbelt were yellow. The uniform was changed later to a dark blue coat with red distinctions, yellow metal buttons, and yellow undergarments. Sky blue sashes were worn over the waistcoats. All dragoons wore hats except the dragoon grenadiers, which had fur caps with a yellow metal plate. This regiment was dressed in this manner in 1774. The heavy cavalry retained their blue coats. In 1744 the undergarments were made dull yellow. Metal shoulder scales were taken into wear in 1789. In the same year, the Piemonte Cavalry Regiment adopted red collars, cuffs, and linings and yellow metal buttons on the coats; sky blue sashes, and white shoulder belts. The hats had yellow lace. The Savoia Cavalry (Fig. 101c) had yellow hat lace, black collars, and cuffs (no lapels), red lining, and white metal buttons. The shabraques were of white sheepskin; the holster covers bore the Sardinian arms in color on a blue field, with a white edging, the latter having a blue vandyke through it. In 1816 the cavalry was issued with helmets with a yellow metal plate and comb, and sky blue *chenille*; some had single-breasted, others double-breasted, jackets; with red distinctions for the Piemonte Regiment, and black, piped red, for the Savoia Regiment. They also wore blue breeches, knee boots, and yellow epaulettes (Fig. 101d). In 1822 a helmet entirely of yellow metal, with a black horsehair *crinière*, was introduced (Fig. 101f). The light

Fig. 101. Italy. Sardinia—Cavalry, Artillery, Engineers.

a, b: dragoons. c, d, f, g: heavy cavalry. e, h: light cavalry. i, k: artillery. l, m: engineers.

cavalry had the same uniform, with red chacos (Fig. 101e). Tunics were worn from 1843 (Fig. 101g). These had a colored collar and cuffs, two rows of white metal buttons, and white epaulettes. The gray-blue trousers had colored double stripes. The saber had a white metal hilt. Sky blue pennons were fitted to the lances. The helmet was white metal with a black band, bearing the white cross of Savoy on the front. Comb and chinscales were yellow metal.

The regimental distinctions of the heavy cavalry in 1844 were as follows.

REGIMENT	COLLAR AND CUFFS	TROUSERS STRIPES
Nizza	carmine	carmine
Savoia	black[1]	red
Piemonte Reale	red[2]	red
Genova	light yellow	light yellow
Novara	white	white
Aosta	red	red

[1] red piping around collar and cuffs
[2] piping down the front

The *Cavallegieri* (Light Cavalry) Regiment wore an all-dark-blue uniform with light-blue distinctions, trouser stripes, and chacos. In 1843 tunics, blue-gray trousers, and chacos with a black drooping horsehair plume were introduced (Fig. 101h). The officers wore a blue pelisse over the shoulder. The Piacenza Regiment, which was raised during the reign of Victor Emanuel, wore a green uniform with red loopings. The Guides Regiment also wore a hussar uniform, of light blue with black loopings, and fur caps with a bag.

IV. ARTILLERY AND ENGINEERS

Toward the end of the seventeenth century, the artillery wore all-blue clothing, yellow-laced hats, red cravats, and red stockings. They had the same color of uniform in 1733, but with white stockings. In 1758, coat, breeches, and waistcoat were likewise blue, but with black lapels and cuffs, but blue skirt turnbacks. Black gaiters were worn, with white knee pieces. The buttons were yellow; the shoulder belts were yellow; and the hats had a cockade. On the waistbelt were worn the sword and a pouch with red edging and a yellow metal badge (Fig. 101i). The officers had broad waved hat lace. Lapels, cuffs, and waistcoat were ornamented with lace loops, which were alternately gold and silver. The silver shoulder straps had a mixed silver and gold fringe. In 1816 the uniform was similar to that of the infantry, but all dark blue, with black distinctions and yellow metal buttons. The chaco had a yellow metal eagle plate above crossed cannon barrels, yellow metal chinscales, and a yellow flame-shaped plume. In 1832, the coat was made with two rows of yellow metal buttons, yellow piping, and epaulettes with a short fringe; and a drooping black horsehair plume on the chaco (Fig. 101k). Double-breasted tunics were introduced in 1845. A white cross was adopted on the chaco in place of the eagle; the leather equipment was yellow. The horse artillery was dressed similarly. An illustration of an engineer officer in 1752 shows a silver-laced hat, white cravat, dark blue coat, waistcoat, and breeches, with collar, lapels, and cuffs of a dull yellow color. The buttons were alternately silver and gold. In 1775 the engineers had carmine distinctions, yellow lining, and white undergarments. The buttonholes were laced alternately with gold and silver. The hat lace and epaulettes were silver and gold mixed. In 1816 the uniform was single-breasted with silver lace. The men wore chacos from 1816, with a drooping black plume from 1838. The padded wings on the shoulders were carmine, and were ornamented with two crossed axes. Equipment was of black leather. The rest of the uniform was as for the infantry, and remained unaltered up to the introduction of the tunic. Shortly before 1848, the chaco was replaced by a hat with a drooping plume (Fig. 101m). The officers wore tricornes with black feathers.

PAPAL STATES—THE VATICAN

Cockade: white and yellow

In 1870, after the occupation of Rome, the army was disbanded, and only those troops specifically connected with the Palace were retained as a Vatican Guard.

The oldest established troops were the Swiss Guards, which dated back to the Middle Ages. Their undress uniforms were frequently altered; but the full dress was little affected by changing fashions. It consisted of a slashed doublet and breeches, of blue, red, and yellow, based on old Swiss costume. The hat was decorated with red feathers (Fig. 102b). In court dress, cuirasses, and helmets with a red plume, were worn (Fig. 102a). The drummers, fifers, and NCOs were dressed differently. The Noble Guard wore red coatees richly ornamented with gold lace, helmets with a horsehair *crinière*, and white breeches and long boots (Fig. 102k). The Palatine Guard of Honor had a French-style uniform: blue tunic with black collar and cuffs,

Fig. 102. Italy. Papal States—The Vatican.

a, b: Swiss Guard. c: line infantry. d: cavalry. e: officer of
grenadiers. f: carabinier. g: line infantry. h: Zouave. i: Palatine Guard of
Honor. k: Noble Guard.

and madder red piping and epaulettes. The buttons were yellow metal; the trousers, madder red; and the chaco, blue, with madder red lace (Fig. 102i). Officers had gold epaulettes and lace. The Gendarmes were dressed in blue; and in full dress, had tall fur caps, white breeches, and long boots. The epaulettes and buttons were white, and the cap plume was red.

The former army was originally dressed like the Austrian army, with the characteristic white basic color. In 1816 the infantry adopted chacos. Single-breasted coatees were introduced in 1830; and the chacos were made lower, with a very large bell top. From 1848 to 1870 the uniforms were based on French styles. In 1820 (Fig. 102c) the infantry had a white jacket and trousers, with dark blue distinctions for the 1st Regiment, and orange for the 2nd. The chaco plume and cords, and the epaulettes, were red for the grenadiers, and green and yellow for the *voltigeurs*. The cavalry (Fig. 102d) had green jackets with red distinctions, and helmet with yellow metal plate. Fig. 102e shows a grenadier officer in an all-white uniform with red piping and collar patches, yellow metal buttons, and a yellow and white sash. The plume on the fur cap was red. The carabinier (Fig. 102f) had a green coatee, piped carmine, with white lace loops, epaulettes, aiguillettes, and buttons. The undergarments were white. The fur cap had white cords and a red plume. In the 1860s the infantry was dressed exactly like the French, in blue with red trousers (Fig. 102g). The *carabinieri* were dressed like the French *chasseurs à pied*. The *carabinieri indigeni*, recruited from Italians, had red piping; the *carabinieri esteri*, made up of foreigners, had yellow. The Zouaves had gray jackets, waistcoats, trousers, and peaked caps, with red lace. The girdle was red also (Fig. 102h). The dragoons had green coatees, with red distinctions, and Italian helmets with a comb. In 1908 the Swiss Guard took medieval-style morions into wear, in place of the spiked helmets.

NAPLES

Cockade: under King Murat (1808–1815), white and carmine. Under the Bourbons, all red. (From June 1820, when the Constitution was adopted, to the restoration of the absolute monarchy in March 1821, the Carbonari *colors of black, red, and sky blue were worn. In Sicily, during the same period, the yellow Sicilian cockade was worn.)*

In the eighteenth century the uniforms closely resembled the Austrian and Spanish types. The Swiss troops, however, wore red coats.

Joseph Napoleon (1806–1808) straightaway introduced French-style uniforms. During his short reign, and that of his splendor-loving successor Joachim Murat (1808–1815), the uniforms were ornamented with a profusion of lace. The dress of the line infantry (Fig. 103c) closely resembled that of the French infantry, except that the basic color was white. In 1812 the distinctions of the regiments were as follows: 1st Regiment, sky blue; 2nd, light red; 3rd, black; 4th, amaranth red; 5th, green; 6th, orange; 7th, yellow; 8th, pink; in 1815: 9th Regiment, light blue; 10th, blue; 11th, amaranth red; 12th, green. The 7th Regiment was made up of Negroes. The uniform of the light infantry was very much in the French style, but the blue was of a rather lighter color, and the collar and cuffs were variously colored. The grenadiers of the guard had blue uniforms with carmine distinctions and gold lace loops. In addition to the lace, the officers of the guard had a gold edging to their collars, lapels, and cuffs. The *velites* (light infantry) wore white uniforms, with carmine distinctions, and gold lace loops for the 1st Regiment, and pink distinctions for the 2nd.

Fusiliers, *voltigeurs*, and grenadiers were distinguished in the same way as in France. In 1813 the line cavalry was dressed as follows: 1st *chevau légers* Regiment, light blue with red piping on collar, shoulder straps, lapels, and pointed cuffs, and amaranth red skirts and trouser stripes; 2nd *chevau-légers* Regiments, green with red distinctions and breeches; 3rd Regiment, green with yellow distinctions.

The cavalry of the guard cannot be dealt with in detail, as the units frequently altered; and, moreover, different uniforms were often worn within the same regiment.

The artillery of the guard was dressed almost exactly like the French artillery, but had amaranth red distinctions. The mounted and foot artillery of the line, as well as the transport corps, resembled very much the corresponding French units of the period. Apart from the cockade, the main difference lay in the distinctive chaco plate. The decoration around the top of the officers' chacos of the transport corps, which was in the form of waved lace, is also worth mentioning.

After the Bourbon Restoration (the period of the Kingdom of the Two Sicilies), an English influence prevailed on the uniform of the guard. The basic color was red, with blue distinctions, white lace loops and wings, and white metal buttons (Fig. 103f). The line infantry had single-breasted blue uniforms with variously colored distinctions (Fig. 103e). The undergarments were white. The officers' sashes were red and silver.

The legionaries wore single-breasted green jackets with black distinctions, and white metal buttons. The chacos were ornamented with a white metal plate and a green plume. The gray trousers had a red piping and black stripes down the sides.

Fig. 103. Italy. Naples.

Naples under Joachim Murat—a: *chasseurs à cheval*. b: grenadier of the guard. c: line infantry. Kingdom of the Two Sicilies—e: infantry officer. f, i: grenadiers of the guard. g, k: *chasseurs*. h: grenadier. d, l: dragoons.

The men wore green fringed epaulettes; the officers had silver ones. Equipment was of white leather. The National Guard of Naples wore green jackets with a row of yellow metal buttons, red distinctions, fringed epaulettes and cords, and red trousers stripes; and white leather equipment. The Provincial Militia likewise wore green coatees, with a row of white metal buttons, with yellow collars and cuffs, and green and white shoulder wings. The trousers were white. The chaco had yellow metal mounts, with white cords and plume. The dragoons (Fig. 103d) wore green jackets with green collars and shoulder straps, yellow collar patches, piping, and wings. The buttons and helmet plate were yellow metal; the helmet crest, black; and the trousers, white. Equipment was of white leather. The lancers of the National Guard were dressed very like the Polish lancers of Napoleon I's *Garde Impériale*, but had green uniforms, with green collar, and amaranth red lapels and piping; and yellow aiguillettes and buttons. The helmet was like that worn by the French dragoons, but with a black *chenille* instead of the horsehair *crinière* and white plume. The artillery wore blue uniforms with red collar and cuffs and had yellow grenades on the collar. The buttons were yellow metal, and the trousers, white. In more general aspects, the uniforms more closely resembled French ones.

In the 1840s the *chasseurs* (Fig. 103g) wore tapering conical chacos; green jackets with black loopings and three rows of white buttons, with yellow collars and cuffs; white trousers; and white leather equipment. In the late 1850s the army was dressed as follows.

Foot *Garde du Corps*: blue coatees with red collars, cuffs, and skirt turnbacks; white cuff patches, and white lace loops down the front; yellow metal buttons; red epaulettes with white fringes; white leather equipment; straw-colored trousers; and long black gaiters. Fur caps with a yellow metal shield, red cords, and white plume. White grenades were worn at the ends of the collar.

Grenadiers of the guard (Fig. 103i): coatees as for the Foot *Garde du Corps*, but without the grenades on the collar; blue cuff patches and skirt turnbacks; red fringed epaulettes and long red trousers. The white leather equipment was worn crossed.

Chasseurs (Fig. 103k): green jackets with green pointed cuffs and collar patches. Yellow collar and piping; epaulettes with yellow crescent pads and straps, and green crescents and fringes. The marksmen's cords were also green. The leather waistbelt equipment was white, as were the trousers; the kepi was green with yellow lace, pompon, and hunting horn.

Swiss infantry: red coatees, with red cuff patches; with light-blue collar and cuffs for the 1st Regiment; 2nd, yellow; 3rd, dark blue; and 4th, black; a single row of yellow metal buttons down the front; a loop of yellow lace on each side of the collar; sky blue trousers; white epaulettes; white leather equipment, worn crossed; black kepi with yellow metal plate, red lace, and double pompon.

Mounted *Garde du Corps*: blue coatees, with white lace down the front; white collars, red lapels, piping, and skirt turnbacks; red fringed epaulettes; and white metal buttons. White pouch belts, ornamented with squares of a different color for each squadron; white breeches and gauntlets; high boots; white metal helmets with a panther-skin turban, yellow metal comb, black *chenille*, and white plume.

Carabiniers: blue jackets with a row of white metal buttons, white collar, blue cuffs and cuff patches, all piped red. Red fringed epaulettes with blue straps. White aiguillettes, breeches, and leather equipment. White metal helmets with a black turban, yellow metal mounts and comb, and black horsehair *crinière*, with a small *houpette* on the front of the comb, and a red plume on the left side.

Dragoons (Fig. 103l): exactly similar jackets, with red collars and cuff patches; helmets similar, but with a black *chenille* instead of the horsehair *crinière* and *houpette*.

Hussars of the guard: light-blue dolmans with light-blue collars, red cuffs, and white loopings. Red trousers. Red kepis with a black horsehair plume and white lace.

Lancers: blue jackets with blue collar patches, red collars, pointed cuffs, lapels, and trousers. The buttons, fringed epaulettes, and leather equipment were all white. Lancer caps with a yellow metal plate, red upper part, and black hair plume.

Swiss artillery: blue jackets, cuff patches, and trousers. Red collar, cuffs, piping, skirt turnbacks, and fringed epaulettes; a single row of yellow metal buttons in front; black kepi with red lace and double pompon, and yellow metal fittings; white leather equipment.

The transport corps wore almost exactly the same uniform as that of the French *Artillerie à Cheval* of the period, except that the pointed cuffs were of the blue basic color, and not red.

With the surrender of the fortress of Gaeta, the last stronghold of Francis II, in 1861, the army ceased to exist.

MODENA

Cockade: sky blue-white

In 1814 the infantry uniform was almost identical to that of the Austrian army. In 1850 double-breasted dark blue tunics were worn, and bluish-gray trousers, piped white. The men wore Austrian-type chacos with a cockade and blue rosette, and white leather equipment (Fig. 104b). Officers had black coats and gold-laced chacos. The *Jäger* were dressed in blue-gray tunics with grass green cuffs, blue-gray trousers, and Corsican hats with a black feather plume. The buttons were white metal. Equipment was of black leather. The dragoons had medium-blue tunics and trousers with yellow distinctions and piping. The black helmets had a brass comb and plate; in full dress, a blue and white *chenille* was worn. Buttons were white metal; and the leather equipment was white (Fig. 104c). The artillery was dressed in dark blue with black distinctions piped red; and hats as for the *Jäger*. The leather equipment was white. The

Fig. 104. Italy. Modena.
a, b: infantry.
c: dragoons.

pioneers wore dark blue coats with cherry red distinctions, and blue-gray trousers with cherry red piping. The chacos had black feather plumes, and the equipment was of black leather. The officers wore gold-laced hats. General officers had dark blue coats with red distinctions and hats with green feather plumes; with rank insignia as in the Austrian army. In 1860 the duchy was united with Italy. Up to 1863 the troops of the small states formed a separate brigade, the *Brigate Estense*, in the service of the Duke of Modena. The uniform remained as before. On service, linen coats were worn.

PARMA

Cockade: red-white; 1840, blue-gold; from 1851, red-blue-gold

In 1814 the infantry wore light-blue single-breasted jackets with red distinctions. In 1830 low, bell-shaped chacos were adopted. Double-breasted coatees, dark blue trousers, and cylindrical chacos were introduced in 1840 (Fig. 105a). The grenadiers wore Austrian-type fur caps and had yellow metal buttons. The artillery and engineers had carmine distinctions.

In 1852 the infantry was dressed in blue Prussian-style tunics with yellow metal buttons, the shoulder straps, cuff slashes, and skirt pocket flaps being light blue for the 1st Regiment; white for the 2nd; and yellow for the 3rd. The spiked helmets had yellow metal mounts; and the crossbelts were white. The trousers were light blue (Fig. 105c). In 1859 the grenadiers of the guard had all-red distinctions, with yellow lace loops on the collar and cuff patches, and red hair plumes (white for field officers and NCOs). The musketeers of the guard wore a similar uniform, but with black hair plumes, white lace loops, and white leather equipment.

In 1859 the cuff patches were abolished. The officers adopted Austrian rank distinctions, but kept their epaulettes. The *Jäger* had green tunics with black distinctions piped red; black hair plumes; and black leather equipment. The red piping was done away with in 1859; and the light-blue trousers were superseded by green ones.

In 1850 the *guides* (cavalry) wore dark blue double-breasted tunics with red distinctions; spiked helmets with a white hair plume, and a white pouch belt and girdle. The lances had small red, yellow, and blue pennants (Fig. 105b). In 1859 the spiked helmets were replaced by kepis similar to those worn by the Sardinian cavalry; and yellow fringed epaulettes and aiguillettes were adopted. In 1853 the artillery had black collars with yellow lace loops and red piping. The lace was discontinued six years later. In that year, the horse artillery were wearing double-breasted tunics with red-piped seams, and fawn leather pouch belts and waistbelts. The engineers were dressed like the artillery, but had white metal buttons and black leather equipment.

General officers wore dark blue tunics, with red collars and cuffs ornamented with gold embroidery, a row of yellow metal buttons, gold aiguillettes, and gold sashes. The spiked helmets had a yellow metal plate and white feather plume. The trousers were light blue. The greatcoats were white and resembled those of the Austrian artillery. Up to 1859 the officers' rank distinctions consisted of one to three stripes along the tops of the cuffs, with lilies on the epaulettes instead of rank stars. Field officers wore fringed epaulettes and had waved stripes. On 18 March 1860, Parma was united with Italy.

Fig. 105. Italy. Parma.
a, c: infantry. b: *guides* (cavalry).

Fig. 106. Italy. Tuscany.
a, b, c: infantry.

TUSCANY

Cockade: white-red

During the Restoration, the infantry wore white jackets with lapels running down to the waist, white trousers, and chacos (Fig. 106a). In full dress, the grenadiers wore fur caps with cords and epaulettes, as in France. The distinctions varied by regiment. The cavalry had green double-breasted jackets, with light-blue distinctions and yellow metal buttons; yellow shoulder scales with red fringes; gray trousers with light-blue stripes; and white leather equipment. The chacos had yellow mounts and a red-over-white-over-green plume.

In 1848 the infantry was dressed in single-breasted white jackets, very broad-topped chacos, and light-blue trousers (Fig. 106b). In the following year a double-breasted tunic with Saxon cuffs was introduced, as well as Austrian-type rank distinctions (Fig. 106c). General officers, cavalry, and infantry all had red collars, cuffs, and piping, with white metal buttons for the infantry. Equipment was of white leather. The trousers were light blue with red piping; general officers and cavalry had red triple stripes. The *Velites* Guard Battalion had red trousers. General officers wore gold-laced hats with a green feather plume. The cavalry helmets were of black leather, with a brass comb and plate; the infantry and artillery wore chacos, with a red plume for the *Velites*. The Field and Fortress Artillery had yellow and red piping respectively, on their collars and cuffs, light-gray trousers with the corresponding piping; and fawn leather equipment.

All arms of service adopted yellow metal buttons in 1859. The tunic was now also piped around the skirts; and there were two buttons above the cuffs. The *Jäger* Battalion wore an Austrian-type *Jäger* uniform, except for the cockade.

On 22 March 1860 Tuscany was absorbed into the Kingdom of Italy.

THE CISALPINE REPUBLIC (1797–1804) and THE KINGDOM OF ITALY UNDER VICEROY EUGÈNE De BEAUHARNAIS (1805–1814)

Cockade: green-white-red

In 1796 a Lombard and Cisalpine Legion was formed. The uniform consisted of a dark green coat like that worn at the time by the Polish army, but with a stand collar, a row of white metal buttons instead of lapels, and white piping, down the front. The shoulder straps, front of the coat, and pointed cuffs were red. The green breeches had red stripes and were worn with short black gaiters. The headdress was a black hat, turned up on the left, with a yellow metal plate in front of the legend "*Viva la liberta.*" The cockade and a yellow loop were placed on the upturned brim, with the white-over-red-over-green plume above. The white leather shoulder belts were worn crossed.

The Cisalpine Hussars wore an all-green uniform with white loopings. Their headdress was a type of conical chaco (like a *Flügelmutze*) with white lace, and a plume on the front, of the same colors as that on the infantry hat.

The Cispadane *chasseurs à cheval* were dressed in similar uniforms. Their headdress was a black felt cap with a yellow wing and a small black peak.

Later, the line infantry wore French-style green coats, waistcoats, and breeches, with red collars, cuffs, and skirt turnbacks with white piping, white lapels with red piping, and white metal buttons; long black gaiters; and white leather equipment worn crossed. The hats were as for the French infantry and were ornamented with a cockade. In 1801 there were two hussar regiments: the 1st had red dolmans with light-green collar and cuffs; light-green pelisses; and red trousers. The loopings, chaco cords, lozenge-shaped plates, and leather equipment were all white. A red-over-green plume was worn on the front of the chaco. The 2nd Regiment was dressed all in green, with red collar and cuffs, and red pelisses; and chacos as for the 1st Regiment, but with a cockade and loop instead of the lozenge-shaped plate. The foot artillery was dressed like the infantry, but the collar, cuffs, cuff slashes, and lapels were black piped red.

Under Napoleon's viceroy, Eugène de Beauharnais, the distinctions of the army were as follows.

The grenadiers of the guard wore the same uniform as the grenadiers of Napoleon's *Garde Ancienne*, but with green substituted for blue. The buttons and fur cap plate were white metal. The uniform of the carabiniers of the guard exactly resembled that of the *chasseurs à pied* of Napoleon's *Garde Ancienne*, except that it was green where the latter was blue; and had white metal buttons instead of yellow ones. The *Velites* Grenadiers wore similar uniforms, but in white; with green distinctions, and yellow metal buttons. The *Velites* Carabiniers had pointed lapels and cuffs, and fur caps and epaulettes as for the carabiniers, but the rest of the uniform was like that of the *Velites* Grenadiers.

The *chasseurs* of the guard wore green uniforms with green lapels, red collars and cuff patches; white piping; yellow metal buttons; chacos edged with white lace with white cords and eagle plate; and green epaulettes with red crescents and fringes. The line infantry had uniforms of the same pattern as the French infantry. From 1806 the basic color was white. Chacos were introduced in 1807; in 1810 the cords around them were abolished.

The distinctions were as follows.

REGIMENT	COLLAR	LAPELS	CUFFS	CUFF PATCHES	SKIRT TURNBACKS
No. 1	green	red	red	green	red
No. 2	white	red	white	red	white
No. 3	red	red	red	red	red
No. 4	red	white	white	green	white
No. 5	red	green	green	red	white
No. 6	white	green	white	green	white
No. 7	green	white	red	none	white

All the red or green distinctions were piped white; and all the white ones were piped green or red. The buttons were yellow metal, except for the 4th, 5th, and 7th Regiments, which had white metal ones. This last regiment had pointed cuffs and no cuff patches. The shoulder straps were the same color as the lapels. The *voltigeurs* wore the same uniform as the French line infantry, but the basic color was green. On service, a single-breasted coat with slash cuffs was usually worn.

The light infantry wore green coats with green lapels cut pointed, green trousers, and yellow metal buttons. The carabiniers, which took the place of the grenadiers, were distinguished, as in France, by fur caps and epaulettes.

REGIMENT	COLLAR, CUFFS, AND PIPING	WAISTCOAT	SKIRT TURNBACKS
No. 1	red	green	white
No. 2	yellow	yellow	yellow
No. 3	white	white	white
No. 4	light blue	light blue	light blue

The Guards of Honor took first place among the cavalry. Green coats were worn, similar to those of the French dragoons. The collar, lapels, and cuffs were set with white lace loops. The buttons were white metal and the shoulder scales, yellow metal; waistcoat, breeches, and leather equipment were white and worn with high boots. The yellow metal helmet had white metal mounts, a yellow metal comb in the shape of an eagle, black *chenille*, and white plume on the left. The collar, cuffs, lapels, skirt turnbacks, and piping around the vertical pocket flaps varied in color for each company: 1st Company, Mailand, pink; 2nd, Bologna, yellow; 3rd, Brescia, buff; 4th, Romagna, scarlet; 5th, Venice, orange.

The Dragoons of the Guard wore exactly the same uniform as their French counterparts, except that the buttons and aiguillettes were white.

Both regiments of line dragoons were dressed exactly like the French dragoons. The coats and shoulder straps were green; undergarments, leather equipment, and buttons, white. The 1st Regiment (*Dragoni Regina*) had pink collars, cuffs, and lapels, skirt lining, and piping. The helmet was like that of the French dragoons, with a green plume on the left. The 2nd Regiment (*Dragoni Napoleone*) had carmine distinctions (red, with a green collar, in 1812) and helmets similar to those of the French dragoons, but with turbans of black fur instead of panther skin. On the left side was a black plume with carmine tip.

The *chasseurs à cheval* wore green jackets and Hungarian breeches. The jackets were closed down the front with a row of white metal buttons and were ornamented with white lace loops. The breeches had white Austrian knots and piping down the sides. The Hungarian boots had white binding around the tops. The 1st, 2nd, and 4th Regiments had chacos with a cockade and loop at the top of the front, and white lace chevrons, point uppermost, at the sides. The chinscales were white metal. Above the cockade was a green plume with the tip in the regimental color. The 3rd Regiment wore fur caps, with the cockade high up on the front and a red plume above. The collars, cuffs, and skirt turnbacks were yellow for the 1st Regiment; red for the 2nd and 3rd; and violet-carmine for the 4th.

The foot artillery wore the old uniform colors, and had peakless chacos with red cords. The horse artillery wore green jackets with green collars and pointed cuffs; with red piping, lace loops on the breast, skirt turnbacks, and fringed epaulettes; and green breeches. It had lancer caps, with black fur around the bottom, and a red plume. The Foot Artillery of the Guard was dressed like the line infantry, but had red fringed epaulettes and fur caps with a red plume and cords. The Horse Artillery of the Guard wore a dark blue hussar uniform, with red loopings and yellow metal buttons, like the corresponding French troops; and wore the same headdress as the latter. The engineers were dressed like the artillery, but had chacos with peaks, red epaulettes, and black pointed cuffs. The Transport Corps of the Guard had gray uniforms with green distinctions and loops of lace on the breast; the Transport Corps of the Horse Artillery wore lancer caps. The line artillery transport corps wore the same uniform as the artillery, but with green collar and lapels piped red, red pointed cuffs, and chacos with peaks and no red lace. The Transport Corps of the Horse Artillery was dressed like the horse artillery, but with chacos; the Transport Train had green single-breasted coats with red collars, shoulder straps, and pointed cuffs. The Engineer Transport Corps was clothed like that of the horse artillery, but had green cuffs and collars, red epaulettes, and white metal insignia. All units of the service corps wore leather breeches.

The general officers were dressed like those in France, but had green coatees instead of blue; and silver instead of gold buttons and embroidery. The full-dress uniform had amaranth red collar and cuffs and embroidered loops down the front.

As a result of the events of 1814, the army was disbanded.

THE KINGDOM OF ITALY

Cockade: green-white-red

To begin with, the army of the unified kingdom retained the old Sardinian uniform. A new uniform was introduced in 1871. The universal badge of the Italian regular armed forces from that time was the five-pointed star, worn at the ends of the collar. It was invariably white or silver, except for general officers, who had gold stars. All officers on duty, and with the service dress as well up to 1915, wore a light-blue silk sash with tassels of the same material, across the right shoulder, and tied fairly high up on the left hip.

I. INFANTRY

1871–1903

As the uniform introduced for all arms of the service was of the same basic style, it will be described in detail for the infantry, and only the differences will be given for the other arms. The dark blue tunic was faily short-skirted, single-breasted for the men, double-breasted for officers, with white metal buttons, a turndown collar, and pointed cuffs (Figs. 107c,d). It was piped in *Waffenfarbe*—red for infantry—on the front of the coat, around the collar and cuffs, skirts, vertical two-button skirt pocket flaps, and the rounded shoulder straps, and around the wings of the infantry. The collar and cuffs were dark blue for the infantry. The scalloped collar patches were black, as were the wings and shoulder straps, which bore the regimental number in white. The collar and cuffs of the officers' double-breasted tunics were black, piped red. In addition, they wore variously ornamented epaulettes of the color of the buttons with thin or thick fringes, according to rank; and on service and off duty, single or double shoulder cords, according to rank, of the button color. The Grenadier Brigade, consisting of the 1st and 2nd Grenadier Regiments, had red collar patches; and the officers had red collars and cuffs, with a silver loop of Prussian-type guard

Fig. 107. Kingdom of Italy, 1890.
a: *Bersaglieri.* b: *Alpini.* c: infantry. d: infantry officer. e: line cavalry
officer. f: lancer. g: light cavalry. h: artillery officer. i: carabinier. k: officer,
cuirassiers. l: general officer.

lace on the collar. The trousers were blue-gray with red piping for the men and red
stripes for the officers. The conical chaco was covered with dark blue cloth and had a
black lacquered peak, with a five-pointed crowned star bearing the regimental
number, on the front; and a red pompon with the company number in white, and red
cords; officers had silver ornamentation. The dark gray-blue greatcoat was single-
breasted for the men and double-breasted for the officers, and had a turndown collar
bearing the regular star. The men's coats had shoulder straps and wings as on the
tunic. On service, the skirts were worn fastened back. Equipment was of white
leather, with a black cartridge box. Off duty, a dark blue kepi was worn. It was piped
in *Waffenfarbe*, with the arm-of-service badge on the front: infantry, crossed rifles
with a crown above; and grenadiers, a vertical flaming grenade. Officers had rank
stripes around the band.

The infantry regiments, numbered from 1 to 94, were linked in pairs to form
brigades, which bore the names of districts. This organization was retained up to the
1930s.

The *Bersaglieri* Regiments, numbered from 1 to 12, had carmine piping and collar patches, which were swallow-tailed at the rear. The officers' cuffs were carmine
as well. The buttons were of yellow metal. The trousers were dark blue. A round
black leather hat with a broad flat brim was worn, with a yellow hunting horn and a
flaming grenade on a large silk cockade in front, and on the right side, a long drooping plume of green cock's feathers (Fig. 107a). Instead of the usual undress cap, the
men wore a soft red fez with a blue tassel. Leather equipment and gloves were black.
Short dark blue capes were worn instead of greatcoats.

The *Alpini* Battalions had red piping and green swallow-tailed collar patches

302

and the officers had green cuffs. The rest was as for the infantry. Instead of the chaco, a black leather hat with crowned eagle badge on the front was worn, and a large cockade. A brown eagle's feather was worn upright on the left side (Fig. 107b). The leather equipment and dark blue cape were as for the *Bersaglieri*.

On service, all arms wore white cloth covers over their headdress, with the regimental or battalion number on the front. Ticken trousers were often worn.

1903–1915

The tunic was made with rather longer skirts, and the colored piping was done away with. The collar was changed to a stand-and-fall type. Patches, varying in color for each brigade, were worn at the ends of the collar. They were pointed at the rear and had a small button (Fig. 108a). The color and design of the patches, which were worn up to the 1939–1945 war, were as follows.

COLOR OF COLLAR PATCHES	PATCHES WITH NARROW CENTER STRIPE	PATCHES WITH NARROW EDGING
white Brigade Regina (Regiments 9, 10)	red: Bologna (39, 40) green: Puglia (71, 72) black: Savona (15, 16) carmine: Napoli (75, 76) blue: Lombardia (73, 74)	red: Ravenna (37, 38) carmine: Modena (41,42) blue: Forli (43,44) green: Reggio (45,46) black: Valtelina (65, 66)
yellow Casale (Regiments 11, 12)	black: Acqui (17, 18)	black: Ancona (69, 70) red: Messina (93, 94)
red Piemonte (Regiments 3, 4)	black: Aosta (5, 6) green: Calabria (59, 60) white: Toscana (77, 78)	black: Pinerolo (13, 14) green: Sicilia (61, 62) white: Cagliari (63, 64) yellow: Roma (79, 80)
carmine Cuneo (Regiments 7, 8)	black: Brescia (19, 20) blue: Venetia (83, 84) white: Basilicata (91, 92)	white: Salerno (89, 90)
blue Como (Regiments 23, 24)	red: Bergamo (25, 26) white: Marche (55, 56) yellow: Torino (81, 82) black: Friuli (87, 88)	red: Ferrara (47, 48) white: Parma (49, 50) black: Palermo (67, 68) yellow: Verona (85, 86)
orange Livorno (Regiments 33, 34)	black: Pistola (35, 36)	
black		red: Re (1, 2) yellow: Siena (31, 32)
green Alpi (Regiments 51, 52)	red: Pavia (27, 28) white: Umbria (53, 54) black: Abruzzi (57, 58)	red: Cremona (21, 22) black: Pisa (29, 30)

The grenadiers adopted all-red collars and cuffs. White or silver guard lace, according to rank, was worn on the collar. The leather equipment was black for all. On service, officers of all arms wore a dark blue jacket with self-colored pointed cuffs and shoulder straps, and collar as on the tunic. The rank distinctions were worn on the shoulder straps. In the *Bersaglieri* and *Alpini*, the colored piping on the coat and collar were abolished. The *Alpini* adopted green piping on the cuffs, shoulder straps and wings, and trousers.

1915–1934

With the entry of Italy into the Great War, a gray-green service dress, which had been on trial since 1908, was introduced. The service jacket had pointed cuffs, shoulder straps, and a stand collar (Fig. 108c). The *Bersaglieri* had a stand-and-fall collar with colored collar patches. Officers had patch pockets on the breast and skirts. The leather equipment was gray-black, later field gray. The colored trouser piping and stripes were not worn to begin with, but were later reintroduced in another form. The brigades that were raised during the war took into wear patches with variously colored horizontal or vertical stripes. Of these new units, only the following remained up to the late 1930s: Sassari (151, 152), red with white horizontal stripe; Liguria (157), orange with blue horizontal stripe; Arezzo (285), yellow with blue vertical stripe; Avellino (231, 232), red with yellow vertical stripe.

With the service dress went a kepi, with the arm-of-service badge on the front, a gray (later black) leather peak, and a very broad chinstrap. The officers' rank badges were of silver, but of gray-green silk during the war. The *Bersaglieri* retained their carmine swallow-tailed collar patches; and had gold rank badges; and wore leather hats with gray covers (Fig. 108e). The *Alpini* had green swallow-tailed collar patches, gray puttees, and gray felt hats with the brim turned up at the back and sides, the badge on the front (a hunting horn on crossed rifles, with an eagle with outstretched wings above) and an eagle's feather on the left (Fig. 108f). French-pattern steel helmets were worn, without badges (Fig. 108d). After the war, the officers' collars were changed to black, with colored patches. The infantry also had a red piping around the outside edge. The kepi was made much taller, with piping in *Waffenfarbe* around the upper band and on the side seams. The trousers had black double stripes with piping in the distinctive color for the officers, and piping only for NCOs.

In 1934 an entirely new style of uniform was introduced. In place of the kepi, a gray-green forage cap without colored adornment was issued to all arms. It had a black leather peak and chinstrap, with the arm-of-service badge on the band: for infantry, crowned crossed rifles with the regimental number in the center, with rank stripes around the band for officers. The service jacket, the same for all arms, was of British style, with patch pockets on the breast and skirts. It was fastened with four buttons. Officers had black, red-piped collars, and the colored collar patches, as in the foregoing table, were retained. These, however, were now rectangular, without the button at the outer end. On the gray-green pointed shoulder straps, piped in *Waffenfarbe*, were the arm-of-service badges in yellow metal. Field officers wore a gold cord edging to their shoulder straps. The officers' rank distinctions took the form of short lace stripes on the cuffs. At the same time, all officers up to the rank of colonel, inclusive, adopted gold buttons, arm-of-service badges, and rank lace. The cuffs were round, and for officers of the fighting arms were piped in *Waffenfarbe*—red in this case. At the same time, but with their respective *Waffenfarben*, the *Bersaglieri* and *Alpini* adopted the same uniform. Their badges were respectively a hunting horn with a flaming grenade on crossed rifles, and a crowned hunting horn on crossed rifles. After the 1st to 3rd Grenadier Regiments were formed into a division, they retained their white or silver lace loops on the red collar. Their arm-of-service badge was a flaming grenade.

Also in 1934 a white uniform, of the same style as the service dress but without the colored collar or the stripes on the trousers, was introduced for officers of all arms; and a black evening dress as well. This last consisted of a black forage cap with the arm-of-service badge and rank stripes on it, but no colored ornamentation and a medium-length double-breasted tunic with stand-and-fall collar, with piping and collar patches and cuffs that, in general, were of the same color as those on the 1903–1915 tunic. For the infantry the black velvet collar was piped with red but had no brigade patches. With this uniform were worn either pointed black shoulder straps with the arm-of-service badges in gold, and rank stars, and gold edging for field officers, or epaulettes, which were now invariably of gold. Infantry and grenadiers wore two red stripes on their trousers. The epaulettes were also worn with the gray-green uniform in full dress; and by the *Bersaglieri* and *Alpini*, together with the pre-1915 leather and felt hats respectively.

In 1935 a new-pattern close-fitting brimless steel helmet was adopted, with the arm-of-service badge in yellow metal on the front; and a fore-and-aft field service cap with turned-up cloth peak and ear and neck flaps, all piped in the distinctive color, with the arm-of-service badge on the upturned peak and the badges of rank on the left side (Figs. 108h,i).

The armored corps, which became an independent arm after the Great War, wore the infantry uniform from its formation, with red swallow-tailed collar patches instead of brigade patches.

Fig. 108. Italy, 1908–1936.
a, c, d, g, h: infantry. b: cavalry. e: *Bersaglieri*. f: *Alpini* officer. i: infantry officer. k: general officer. l: *Askari* NCO.

II. CAVALRY

After the unification of Italy, the light cavalry was greatly increased. The cavalry tunic was similar to the infantry one. The buttons were white metal for all regiments. Equipment was of white leather. Officers had silver-laced pouch belts with richly ornamented pouches. On the gray-blue trousers, officers wore two medium-width stripes of the color of the piping; the men had two black stripes. The collar patches of the cavalry had three long, slightly curved, rounded points at the rear. The distinctions of the cavalry regiments between 1871 and 1903 are given in the following table.

REGIMENTS	COLLAR	CUFFS	PIPING
1. Nizza	carmine	carmine	carmine; white on collar
2. Piemonte	red	red	red
3. Savoya	black	black	red
4. Genoa	yellow	yellow	yellow
5. Novara	white	black	white
6. Aosta	red	black	red
7. Milano	carmine	black	carmine
8. Montebello	green	green	red
9. Firenze	orange	black	orange
10. Vittorio Emanuele II	yellow	black	yellow
11. Foggia	red; black patch	red	red
12. Saluzzo	black; yellow patch	black	yellow
13. Monferrato	black; carmine patch	black	carmine
14. Alessandria	black; orange patch	black	orange
15. Lodi	red; black patch	black	red; white on collar
16. Lucca	white; black patch	black	white
17. Caserta	black; red patch	black	red
18. Piacenza	black; green patch	black	green
19. Guide	light blue; white patch	light blue	white
20. Roma	black; white patch	black	white
21. Padua	carmine; black patch	black	carmine
22. Catania	red; black patch	black	red
23. Umberto I	white; light blue patch	white	light blue
24. Vicenza	white; red patch	white	red

Nos. 1–4: White metal helmet with yellow metal comb and chinscales; black turban; white cross. White grenade on kepi and shoulder straps. *Cavalleria di Linea.*

Nos. 5–10: Dark fur caps with brown feather and cords of color of piping. White crossed lances crowned badge. *Lancieri.*

Nos. 11–24: Fur caps as for *Lancieri.* Badge: crowned hunting horn. *Cavalleggeri.*

Regiments 1–4 (*Cavalleria di Linea*, Fig. 107e) and 5–10 (*Lancieri*, Fig. 107f) carried lances with royal blue swallow-tailed pennants; 11–24 (*Cavalleggeri*, Fig. 107g) only had sabers and carbines.

In 1903 the cavalry uniform underwent the same changes as for the infantry. The regiments, except for the 3rd, lost their collar piping. The officers' trousers stripes were of the same color as the collar patches. The 22nd Catania Regiment adopted orange as its distinctive color. The colored cuff piping of the 19th Guide, 23rd Umberto I, and 24th Vicenza Regiments was abolished. The cords (which were of the color of the piping) on the fur caps of the lancers and light cavalry regiments were done away with. The gray-green cavalry service dress was the same as that of the infantry in style and ornament. The stand collar remained as on the tunic. The 2nd Piemonte Regiment adopted black piping. Before the introduction of steel helmets, a gray-green tropical-pattern helmet, with the arm-of-service badge on the front, was worn (Fig. 108b). Shortly before the outbreak of the Great War, the cavalry was increased by five regiments. Their distinctions were as follows on the field gray service jacket:

Lancieri di Mantura—black collar with white piping
Lancieri di Vercelli—light-blue collar with red piping
Cavalleggeri di Acquila—carmine collar with white patches
Cavalleggeri di Treviso—light-blue collar with red patches
Cavalleggeri di Udine—white collar with green patches

The development of the uniform followed that of the infantry. After the Great War, only the 1st–6th, 9th, 10th, 12th, 13th, 14th, and 19th Regiments remained, with their old numbers, names, and distinctions. In 1934 yellow metal insignia were adopted throughout the cavalry as well as the infantry. The 3rd Savoya Regiment lost its red collar piping. The crested helmets and fur caps were retained for full-dress occasions. The black evening dress was of the same pattern as for the infantry. The collar and cuffs were of the colors worn in the period 1903–1915. The trousers had triple stripes of the distinctive color. In addition to the regular regiments, there was also a guard of cuirassiers (Fig. 107k), which did bodyguard duty for the king. Their tunic was dark blue with red distinctions and white metal buttons; the officers had silver embroidery on the collar and cuffs; the men had white lace. Dark blue trousers with red stripes were worn for everyday parades; and for full dress, white breeches with high boots; a white metal cuirass; and silver epaulettes. The white metal helmet had a yellow metal comb, plate, and chinscales, with a black horsehair *crinière* and a white metal plume on the left.

III. ARTILLERY, ENGINEERS, AND CARABINIERI

The development of the artillery uniform closely followed that of the infantry in style and ornament, except that the buttons were yellow metal, and the piping, orange-yellow. The trousers were dark blue. The cloth chaco worn in the period 1871–1903 had an upright black plume above the pompon (Fig. 107h). The horse artillery had a long black horsehair plume on the right side of the chaco. The arm-of-service badge consisted of crossed cannon with a flaming grenade above, on the kepi. Up to 1903 the leather equipment was fawn yellow in color; and black from that date. The horse artillery had a shoulder belt and pouch. The engineers wore the same uniform as the artillery, but with carmine piping instead of yellow.

On the stand collar of the gray-green service dress, the artillery and engineers had black collar patches piped in *Waffenfarbe*, ending in a point; and from the 1920s, an all-black collar piped as before.

The *Carabinieri Reali* counted as part of the armed forces, and accordingly also wore the regular star. The hat was worn across the head by the men, and fore-and-aft by the officers. The plume, which was of drooping feathers for the officers, was red over light blue. The coatee was dark blue with black cuffs and collar, which were ornamented with silver embroidery for officers and with white lace for the men. The buttons, epaulettes, and aiguillettes, which were worn looped across the breast, were white. The cuff piping and the stripes on the dark blue trousers were red (Fig. 107i).

IV. GENERAL OFFICERS AND GENERAL STAFF

The characteristic distinctions of general officers consisted of the silver embroidery known as *Greca*, which was arranged in a rectangular vandyked pattern, with a stylized floral design in the upper and lower vandykes; and of the regular star in gold.

1871–1903

The dark blue double-breasted coat had patterned silver buttons and black velvet collar and cuffs, piped red. The edges of the collar and cuffs were ornamented around the inside with *Greca*; this was repeated twice or thrice on the cuffs of senior general officers, according to rank. In full dress, trefoil-shaped silver braided shoulder cords were worn with a double aiguillette running from the left shoulder across to the right breast; and in undress only, fairly broad black, silver-embroidered passants were worn. The light gray-blue trousers had double silver stripes. The full-dress headdress was a black leather helmet with a gold crowned five-pointed star on a large rayed silver plate, with a gold eagle instead of a spike, and a white plume, and a feather *crinière* falling to the rear. The kepi had *Greca* around the band, with one to three narrow silver cords above (Fig. 107l).

1903–1915

The helmet and the piping around the outside of the coat were abolished. The kepi was made taller and stiffer, and in full dress a tall white ostrich feather plume was worn. The general officers' service jacket was like the infantry one, with a black velvet collar piped red and no further ornamentation. The pointed cuffs were dark blue, piped red. Rank distinctions were denoted by silver braid shoulder straps, on which were one to three rank stars in gold. On service, trousers with red double stripes were worn.

1915–1934

The gray-green uniform was of the same style as that worn by all arms. During the course of the war, the field gray collars, which only had the star on them, were changed to ones of turquoise-blue velvet. The trousers were made with double black stripes with a silver piping between. The kepi had *Greca* around it, with the rank stripes above, and silver piping on the sides. During the war, dark gray-green silk piping was worn instead. Marshals adopted as their rank badge four stars, worn on the shoulder straps, and four cords above the *Greca* on the kepi. From 1934 general officers had black, red-piped collars on their jackets; the buttons and rank stripes remained silver. The forage caps had rank embroidery around the band. On the front of the kepi worn up to 1934, and on the forage cap then adopted, a flying eagle badge, in silver, was worn. From the same date, a black silk-felt cocked hat was worn. It had black ostrich feather plumage and was bound around the edges with silver *Greca*. Silver rank stars were worn on the left side. On all full-dress headdress, including the steel helmet, general officers and colonels commandant wore a tall white ostrich feather plume as a mark of command. It was worn on the left side of the cocked hat. The silver shoulder cords on the jacket only had the flying eagle on them; the distinctions of rank, of the same form, color, and number as on the cap, were introduced on the cuffs (Fig. 108k). On the black evening uniform, the collar and cuffs were of black velvet with red piping, with *Greca* on the collar as well. The shoulder scales, introduced in 1903, were of silver, with large stiff bullions, and gold rank stars on the strap. Very broad silver lace stripes, with red silk piping down the center, were worn on the black trousers.

The uniform of the general staff resembled that of the infantry, but the buttons and rank distinctions were invariably gold, and the collar and cuffs were turquoise blue—but on the service jacket, only the collar was blue. Gold guard lace was worn on the collar from 1934. The service dress trousers had black stripes with gold piping down the center; those on the black uniform were gold with a turquoise-blue center one. The general staff and other staffs wore the blue silk sash over the left shoulder.

V. COLONIAL TROOPS

The main distinction of the colonial native troops was the tall red fez, with the star near the top, and a dark blue tassel; the red girdle; and the chevron shaped NCOs' rank distinctions, worn on the upper arms (Fig.108l). The European officers and NCOs of the native troops wore the same uniform as the home army, made in light-gray-green material, with only the star on the collar, and the arm-of-service distinctions on the shoulder straps.

VI. FASCIST MILITIA

The part of the Fascist forces that was liable for active service wore the gray-green infantry uniform, with black swallow-tailed patches on the self-colored collar, and instead of the star, a fasces in yellow metal; the same device was also worn on the steel helmet. The rank distinctions were worn on the lower arms. A black shirt and black tie were worn. The trousers stripes of the officers and the trousers piping of the NCOs were black. Off duty, a low-crowned stiff black fez was worn, with a drooping black plume, yellow fasces in front, and rank insignia on the left side.

VII. RANK DISTINCTIONS

The distinctions of rank of officers and NCOs remained basically unchanged, and were the same for all arms at the same period.

1871–1903

Officers' rank distinctions took the form of metal lace stripes, which were worn above the pointed cuffs of the coat and greatcoat. Company officers had one to three narrow stripes; field officers, a medium-width stripe with one to three narrow stripes above. The topmost stripe of the cuff lace formed a large Austrian knot, which was the mark of a commissioned officer. The same arrangement of stripes was also worn around the edge of the kepi. A further indication of rank was the varying ornamentation of the shoulder scales, which were of button color, with thin or thick fringes according to grade. The end scale, forming the crescent, had one to three grooves around the circumference for company officers, and one to three engraved vandykes for field officers. In the distinctions of the other ranks, the Austrian knot was invariably of the color of the piping. Those of the rank and file were denoted by one medium-width and one to three narrow worsted stripes above the cuffs, of the color of the piping; and those of the NCOs by the same number of stripes, of button color. Trumpeters wore a red hunting horn on the sleeves of the tunic. The one-year volunteers had a narrow cord, of button color, on the collar.

1903–1915

The rank distinctions on the officers' cuffs were abolished. Rank was denoted on the tunic by the epaulettes, which were always worn with it from 1903. On the blue service jacket and greatcoat it was shown by three stars on the pointed dark blue shoulder straps, which had a cord binding and one to three stars of button color, for field officers. The other ranks' distinctions remained as before, except that the Austrian knot was abolished.

1915–1934

During the Great War, officers' rank stars and field officers' cord binding were worn on the pointed cuffs of the service jacket. After the war, they were again worn on the gray-green shoulder straps, which were piped in *Waffenfarbe*. Other ranks wore black chevrons on the sleeves.

In 1934, the officers' rank distinctions were again changed, this time to 8-centimeter-long stripes on the cuffs, of the same number and arrangement as on the kepi, and, from that date, on the forage cap as well. The topmost stripe formed a curl. NCOs' rank insignia remained as before. The rank of *Marescialli*, intermediate between officers and NCOs, which was created during the war, wore as a distinction of rank one to three cords lengthways on the shoulder straps. Around the kepi, and the center of the forage cap band, they wore a medium-width stripe, of button color up to 1934 and of gold thereafter, embroidered with black.

The officers' sword knot, worn on a gold cord, had fixed bullions, and was gold regardless of the buttons' color. With service dress, black leather ones were worn.

JAPAN

Up to the middle of the nineteenth century, Japan was a closed country to all foreigners. Its soldiers, particularly the Samurai, were dressed in armor, which had developed along national lines without a break for centuries. Uniforms in the European sense were not known before c. 1860. After that time, the army was organized anew, and dressed on European and American lines. The medieval weapons were superseded by rifle, saber, and leather equipment. While many features of the national dress were retained at first, dark blue soon became the basic color (Fig. 109a). At first, loosely cut jackets and plain American-style kepis without ornamentation were worn (Fig. 109b). The officers' uniforms, and also the earliest clothing of other ranks, showed a marked French influence. The uniforms introduced after the reorganization of the army in 1880 altered little up to the Great War. The main item of the men's dress was a dark blue single-breasted tunic with five buttons. The collar and piping were of *Waffenfarbe*. The dark blue trousers had piping; equipment was of black leather; the peaked caps were dark blue, with a narrow top, and wide band in *Waffenfarbe* with a five-pointed brass star in front, above the peak and the chinstrap (Fig. 109c). The guard infantry wore white lace loops on the breast for a short time; later they had two crossed cherry sprigs below the brass cap star. In full dress, a dark blue chaco—red for the guards— with black peak and white and red drooping plume—later a tuft—was worn (Fig. 109c). The *Waffenfarben* were: guard infantry, red; infantry, yellow; artillery, white (the guard artillery had a red stripe around the cap); engineers, dark red; transport corps, light blue. After the Russo-Japanese War, the whole of the infantry adopted red as its *Waffenfarbe*, and the artillery, yellow. The rank distinctions consisted, for rank and file, of one to three cords in *Waffenfarbe* around the round cuffs, with a broad *Waffenfarbe* stripe below for NCOs. Senior sergeants also had a narrow stripe of button color below their other rank stripes. The basic color of the officers' uniform was blue-black. They normally wore an *Attila* jacket with five rows of black silk loopings on the breast, and no colored distinctions. Rank was denoted by one to six black silk cords above the cuffs, forming an elongated trefoil. The dark blue trousers had broad stripes of *Waffenfarbe*. Their caps were similar to those worn by the men, with narrow black stripes around the band: two for company officers, three for field officers, and four for general officers. In the Russo-Japanese War they often wore privates' jackets, with stars denoting rank on the shoulder straps. The *Waffenfarbe* for general officers was red, with triple stripes on the trousers and triple Austrian knots with a broad lace edging around the cuffs, all in black silk, on the service *Attila* jacket.

Fig. 109. Japan, 1863–1935.
a, b, c, e, g: infantry. d, f: cavalry. h, i: infantry officers.

The officers' full-dress uniform, with small variations dictated by fashion, was worn up to the late 1930s. It consisted of a double-breasted tunic with medium-length skirts. The stand collar, pointed cuffs, and piping were of *Waffenfarbe*, which from the beginning was red for infantry officers. The collar was edged with plain or figured gold lace according to rank; those of general officers were covered by gold lace. The cords on the cuff denoting rank were gold. The sash was red and white—red and gold for general officers—with red tassels on the left side. Single, double, and triple twisted gold cords, with one to three five-pointed silver stars, were worn on the shoulders, according to rank. The rank intermediate between lieutenant and sergeant wore officers'-pattern service dress and full-dress uniforms, with no lace on the sleeves or rank stars on the shoulders. General officers and general staff officers wore the uniform of their arm of service, with gold aiguillettes on the right shoulder. The trousers were the same as those worn with the service uniform; the blue-black kepi tapered inward to the top at first, and later had straight sides and top, with no colored distinctions other than the gold cords on all the seams. Around the band, starting from the bottom, were one to nine gold cords, for all ranks up to field marshal; and on the top was a star-shaped pattern. A tall white and red plume was worn, with a gold stylized chrysanthemum above the black leather peak (Fig. 109i).

The cavalry wore a dark blue *Attila*, with white loopings for the line and red for the guard, and red trousers with green stripes down the sides. The rest was as for the infantry (Fig. 109d). The loopings on the officers' *Attilas* were black; the same on the full dress; the collar and cuffs were of *Waffenfarbe*—green for cavalry. The three rows of buttons, the collar lace, and the rank stripes were silver for the line and gold for the guard. White (later khaki) uniforms without colored distinctions were worn in summer (Fig. 109f).

The service dress worn after the Great War consisted of a khaki jacket with five

312

dull buttons, stand collar with patches in *Waffenfarbe*, swallow-tailed at the rear, bearing the regimental number in brass, or the arm-of-service badge; trousers without colored piping, puttees, brown leather equipment and footwear—later, black was often worn—and khaki British-style service dress caps, unstiffened at the front up to 1935. The band and piping around the top were of *Waffenfarbe*. A five-pointed brass star was worn on the front, above the black peak and chinstrap. From 1916 the *Waffenfarben* were as follows: infantry, red; cavalry, green; artillery, yellow; engineers (and airmen), dark brown; and transport corps, blue. Across the end of each shoulder was worn a narrow red cloth stripe, like a passant. On these were one to three brass stars denoting rank; NCOs also had a narrow gold cord down the center (Fig. 109g). The officers had slit pockets with scalloped flaps in the breast and skirts; gold buttons; and black knee boots. In addition to the one to three stars, their red shoulder stripes had varying arrangements of lace: company officers, a gold stripe down the center and gold piping on the outer edges; field officers, two gold stripes down the center and piping along the edges; general officers, broad gold stripes with an interwoven red piping on the longest sides. The steel helmet was of a distinctive pattern, with a star on the front (Fig. 109h).

In winter dress, especially in Manchuria in the mid-1930s, medium-length fur-lined greatcoats were worn, with a full collar, and fur-lined caps with broad turned-up peak, neck flaps, and ear flaps.

JUGOSLAVIA

SERBIA

Cockade: red-blue-white

Around 1850 the army wore double-breasted dark blue tunics with red distinctions and yellow metal buttons, and forage caps. About 1880 the infantry adopted single-breasted dark blue tunics with green distinctions, gray-blue trousers (Fig. 110a), and a dark blue kepi piped green, with a green plume for full dress. On service, gray-blue peakless field caps were worn. These, like the greatcoat, resembled the Austrian patterns.

At the end of the nineteenth century the single-breasted tunic was abolished, and a coat and jacket were introduced. The coat was made in the same color as before. The dark blue jacket originally had no colored distinctions other than the regimental number in white on the shoulder straps. The leather equipment was changed to brown. Officers and senior NCOs wore dark blue Russian-type forage caps with a green band. The officers' silver sashes had two red and blue stripes in the center, and a rectangular metal clasp in front. The officers' coats were double-breasted. Their jacket was the same as the men's and was always worn on duty and on service. In 1901 the blue jacket and the coat (both the men's fly-fronted one and the officers' double-breasted one) were made with madder red distinctions. Fur caps replaced the kepis for winter wear and in full dress. The trousers were changed to black; but the gray-blue ones continued to be worn with the jacket. The forage caps had a madder red band. The officers' lambskin caps had gold cords and a white plume in full dress. With full dress, officers wore epaulettes. The distinctions of rank were as follows: general officers, plaited thick gold shoulder cords without stars. Field officers, triple stripes of the distinctive color on the trousers, shoulder straps completely covered with gold or silver lace. Colonels, three stars; lieutenant colonels, two; majors, one. Captains and subalterns, shoulder straps of *Waffenfarbe*, with gold or silver lace around the outside. Captains, four small stars; 2nd captains, three small ones; lieutenants, two; 2nd lieutenants, one.

The 2nd and 3rd Ban or Levies wore brown peasant costume and field caps of the appropriate arm of service—gray-blue for the infantry. The rank distinctions were placed on the collar patches (which were of *Waffenfarbe*) in the form of yellow or white lace for the men and gold or silver for the officers.

The regimental bands of music wore light-blue *Attilas* with yellow loopings; busbies with a red bag and white plume; and black trousers and long boots. The guard had bluish-gray *Attilas* with black loopings and red booted overalls.

314

Fig. 110. Serbia, 1890.
a: infantry. b: cavalry. c: artillery officer
(undress). d: officer of engineers.

Fig. 111. Serbia.
a, c: infantry. b: field officer,
line cavalry.

The service dress was cut in the style of the earlier jacket, but the basic color was changed to khaki (Figs. 111a,c). The distinctions remained madder red. The men had collar patches; the officers had fully colored collars, and colored piping around the top of the roll cuffs. Henceforth, officers also wore service caps, but with a peak, colored piping, and cockade; with one narrow stripe around the top for field officers and two for general officers (Figs. 112a,d).

To begin with, the cavalry wore blue *Attilas* with red distinctions and yellow loopings, and fur caps, but about 1880 they had single-breasted light-blue tunics and kepis (with a red plume), dark blue distinctions, white metal buttons; and madder red trousers (Fig. 110b). The jackets and service caps were also light blue without colored distinctions, with the regimental number in white on the shoulder straps.

At the end of the nineteenth century black lambskin caps were introduced for full dress. As well as the jacket, officers had a double-breasted light-blue tunic, and a light-blue forage cap with a dark blue band (Fig. 111b). In 1901 the jacket, too, was made with a dark blue collar and shoulder straps, the latter having the regimental number in yellow. The cavalry of the guard wore a dark green *Attila* jacket with yellow loopings, a light-blue pelisse edged with black fur without loops; madder red trousers with a yellow stripe; hussar boots edged with yellow lace; and black lambskin caps with a yellow top, and a madder red bag for officers (Fig. 112b). The green jackets of the officers were piped yellow, around the breast pocket as well; and had yellow Austrian knots on the cuffs. There were yellow olivets instead of buttons down the front. The green forage caps had a yellow band (Fig. 112c). The dark blue distinctive color of the cavalry was retained on the khaki uniform. The officers' service caps had a brown chinstrap.

The artillery uniform resembled that of the infantry, but the distinctions were black, as were the service caps. Officers had black velvet collars, and red piping on

315

their trousers (Fig. 110c). The khaki uniform had black distinctions. The engineers had cherry red distinctions and white metal buttons. The service caps were cherry red (Fig. 110d).

General officers wore blue jackets and blue double-breasted tunics with red distinctions and gold embroidery; they also had single-breasted red tunics with blue distinctions and gold embroidery for wear at court. The cap was red with a blue band. They also had white lambskin caps, and black trousers with red triple stripes. The general staff had pomegranate-red distinctions and trousers.

The 2nd and 3rd Levies of the cavalry were dressed like those of the infantry, but had red trousers and red service caps.

After the Great War, the Kingdom of Serbia became part of the Kingdom of Jugoslavia, the territory of which was much larger, owing to the incorporation of Montenegro, Bosnia and Herzegovina, Dalmatia, Croatia, and Slavonia. The uniforms of the army remained unchanged in general and retained their national characteristics up to the late 1930s.

Fig. 112. Jugoslavia.
a: infantry. b: guard cavalry, full dress.
c: field officer of the guard cavalry
(undress). d: infantry officer (full dress).

Fig. 113. Montenegro.
a: infantry. b: officer, full dress.

MONTENEGRO

As the principality originally only had a militia force, there was at first no special uniform. The soldiers drilled and fought in their own clothing, which was the distinctive national dress. It consisted of a braided jacket with loose hanging sleeves, broad knee breeches, white stockings, and ankle boots. The headdress was a low-crowned round cap with a badge on the front, which served to denote both the rank and the arm of service.

With the creation of the Kingdom of Montenegro in 1910, a universal uniform was introduced. The officers' was almost identical to the Russian service dress. Epaulettes were worn in full dress. The old cap devices were retained on the new field caps (Fig. 113b). The men were issued with a field gray jacket, which had colored piped shoulder straps for officers and NCOs: general officers, dark red; infantry, scarlet; machine gun troops, light blue; artillery, yellow; and engineers, green. Legwear, footwear, and headdress remained of the same style as before but were made in field gray (Fig. 113a). The Royal Escort wore a gray-blue uniform with black loopings, based on the national dress.

LATVIA

In 1918–1919, two Latvian divisions from Courland and Livonia were engaged in fighting the Russians. After Latvia achieved independence, the army was reorganized. The earliest uniforms were field gray, with no shoulder straps on the jacket, and with peaked caps. The rank distinctions—four- and five-pointed stars for officers and vertical stripes for NCOs—were worn on the collar patches, which were cherry red with a white diagonal stripe. The first pattern of cap was like the Russian forage cap, but was higher and had straight sides. Later, the army was clothed in a fairly dark khaki color, tending to green. From 1923 a distinctively shaped kepi was worn. The top part was of *Waffenfarbe*, with a khaki-colored band coming to a high point at the front. Above the peak was a rayed cockade. Instead of a chin-strap, the officers wore a double cord, the upper one looped above the cockade. The coat was piped

1925   1932

Fig. 114. Latvia.
a, b: infantry. c: lieutenant.

in *Waffenfarbe* on the collar and shoulder straps (Fig. 114a). The khaki-painted German steel helmets worn up to then were superseded by French ones, painted khaki, with an "L" and three stars on the front (Fig. 114b). The *Waffenfarben* were: war ministry, bluish-white; infantry, dark cherry; cavalry, orange; artillery, blue; technical troops, black; lines-of-communication troops, green. Leather equipment was brown; and officers wore a Sam Browne. In 1929 the jacket was altered. The cuffs were changed to slash ones of basic color, with piping in *Waffenfarbe*; the pocket flaps on the breast were similarly piped. Armored troops wore black uniforms. The kepi was of a different shape, with band, and piping on the edges, sides, and top in the distinctive color (Fig. 114c). The men wore single-breasted great-coats; officers, double-breasted ones, with colored collar patches and piping around the bottom edge of the collar. The buttons and rank stars were yellow for the arms, and white for the administrative services. The sword knot was silver, on a silver and carmine strap. The rank badges took the form of stripes on the collar patches. The stripes were always gold for officers, white for the men, and yellow for junior NCOs. On the stripes of the collar patches generals wore three four-pointed stars; colonels, two; and lieutenant colonels, one; company officers had one to three small five-

318

pointed gold stars. NCOs had vertical gold stripes and junior NCOs, yellow stripes. Senior sergeants wore a broad gold lace, and the rank of ensign (coming between lieutenant and sergeant) had a gold lace and a five-pointed gold star. Around their cuffs and cuff slashes, NCOs had narrow gold lace; and the same on the greatcoat. The peaks of the officers' kepis were bound with gold lace. On service, a fore-and-aft-shaped field cap with turned-up neck and ear flaps, and a cockade on the front, was worn.

From 1931 the *Waffenfarben* were as follows.

ARM OF SERVICE	PIPING ON COATS, CAPS, AND TROUSERS	COLLAR PATCHES AND CAP BAND
General Officers; General Staff; Ministry of War	bluish-white	bluish-white
Divisional Staffs and Infantry Regiments	dark cherry red	dark cherry red
Artillery Regiments	blue	blue
Cavalry Regiments and Divisional Cavalry	orange	orange
Technical Division (Pioneers and Signal Troops)	orange	dark cherry red
Armored Troops (black uniform)	dark cherry red	dark cherry red

LITHUANIA

From the creation of Lithuania as an independent state, the army was dressed in khaki. The uniforms were mainly based on Russian ones, although there were some British influences. The jacket was single-breasted, with a stand-and-fall collar; a short time later, patch pockets were added to the breast and skirts. Leather buttons were worn to begin with, but metal ones were taken into wear later. The characteristic distinction of the Lithuanian army was the national coat of arms, shaped like a triangle, worn at the ends of the collar, with a triangular cord edging for officers. At first, the caps were like the Russian style of forage cap, with the coat of arms in the center of an oak wreath.

In the 1920s a new khaki service uniform, of the same pattern for all arms, was introduced. The national arms, which had cord binding for the officers, was worn on a patch of *Waffenfarbe* at the ends of the collar. On the cuffs were rectangular patches in *Waffenfarbe*, with two buttons. The service caps were straight-sided and shaped like a low-crowned kepi, with a horizontal peak, and band and side piping in *Waffenfarbe*, with the national arms on the front (Fig. 115a). On service, fore-and-aft caps with the national arms on the front were worn. The equipment was of brown leather; the buttons, yellow metal. Officers wore a Sam Browne over the right shoulder. They also had narrow gold embroidery around the band of the kepi; a single row for subalterns, two for field officers, and three for general officers. The officers' rank distinctions were worn on the shoulder straps. Generals had two large gold stars, and brigadier generals, one; field officers had one to three gold stars on round gold discs; and company officers, one to three small gold stars. The ranks of NCOs and men were denoted by small chevrons, point down, worn on the upper arm.

The *Waffenfarben* were: red for general officers and engineers; orange for infantry; white for cavalry; and black for artillery and for the general staff. The double-breasted greatcoat was khaki-colored, with a broad turndown collar. General officers wore triple red stripes on their trousers (Fig. 115b).

1926   1934

a   b

Fig. 115. Lithuania.
a: artillery officer, service dress. b: general officer, full dress.

320

LUXEMBURG

Cockade: orange-blue-white-red;
from 1898, orange with a blue circle

In 1841 the infantry wore long-skirted double-breasted green tunics like those worn by the Dutch army, with carmine distinctions and pointed cuffs; white metal buttons; white epaulettes; tall green chacos with a white metal hunting horn badge and chinscales; and light-blue trousers with broad carmine stripes (Fig. 116a).

The *chasseurs à cheval* wore a similar uniform, except that they had jackets instead of tunics, and white pouch belts. The artillery, too, was dressed like the infantry. On their chacos they wore a device of crossed cannon barrels.

In 1847 the infantry was turned into *chasseurs* and adopted single-breasted tunics with light-blue distinctions. The white epaulettes were retained. Green trousers with light-blue stripes were adopted. In 1858 the chaco was made smaller, and light-blue shoulder straps and wings were taken into wear in place of the epaulettes. In 1876 the tunics became double-breasted again with red distinctions, and gray trousers were worn. The shoulders were ornamented with a white plaited cord of distinctive shape. The chaco was thenceforth green, with red piping.

From 1888 the uniform of the volunteer companies was blue with red distinctions, as was the kepi (Fig. 116b). Later, a single-breasted blue tunic was worn. The cuffs, which had been pointed on all previous uniforms, were then changed to round ones. Soft kepis, similar to those worn in France in 1914, were adopted. The rank distinctions were the same as those in the French army (Fig. 116c).

1845 1888 1935

Fig. 116. Luxemburg.
a, b, c: infantry.

MEXICO

Cockade: green-white-red

In the early 1820s, when Mexico declared its independence from Spanish rule, the infantry wore single-breasted turquoise coats with red collars, round cuffs, and wings; and black leather chacos with a yellow metal plate, with the top painted in the national colors of green, white, and red, like the cockade. The trousers, short gaiters, and leather equipment were all white. The militia had white coats with red distinctions (Fig. 117a). In the years following, turquoise blue remained the basic color. Lapels were added to the coat; the distinctive color varied for each regiment. The grenadiers of the guard wore red coats with light-blue collar, cuffs, and skirt turnbacks, white lapels with eight yellow-laced buttonholes, yellow shoulder straps, white piping; light-blue trousers with white piping; and large fur caps with a brass grenade. From the first, the cavalry regiments were dressed in various colors: yellow, blue, red, and green *kurtkas* with distinctions and piping of very varied colors. From 1823 to c. 1845 the hussars of the guard had red dolmans with light-blue collar and cuffs; white buttons and loopings; light-blue trousers with broad white stripes; black boots; light-blue pelisses with a black fur edging and white loopings; and red chacos with a yellow metal plate on the front, chinscales, and edging around the top, a light-blue plume, and white lines. Equipment was of white leather. The Tulacingo Cuirassiers were dressed in light-blue coats with carmine collar and cuffs; carmine trousers with light-blue stripes; yellow metal helmet with white plate and black crest; and white leather equipment (Fig. 117b).

In 1848 a universal uniform was adopted throughout the army. It consisted of a single-breasted blue coat, with red collar, round cuffs, and piping; yellow metal buttons; and blue shoulder straps, with the regimental number or initial of the arm of service in yellow metal on the collar. The working dress was cut like a jacket and was blue or gray, worn with blue trousers in winter, and white in summer. In 1856 the army was made up of two battalions of rifles, six of infantry, one of engineers, three regiments of cavalry, a battalion of field artillery, a detachment of fortress artillery, a detachment of horse artillery, and a company of transport corps. For full dress, a dark blue double-breasted tunic with red collar and round cuffs was worn; dark blue trousers with red stripes; and black leather chaco with red band around the edge, and red pompon, and yellow metal plate bearing the number or arm-of-service badge. The cavalry and horse artillery had gray jackets with light-green collar, cuffs, and skirt turnbacks; gray trousers with light-green stripes, strapped with leather around the bottom; and chacos like the infantry's. The service uniform at that time consisted of a linen jacket with dark blue piping and plain buttons, and a leather kepi, worn with or without a cover. Later, the piping was discontinued, and red patches were added at the ends of the collar (Fig. 117c). With few alterations, the uniform introduced in 1856 remained as the full dress for the infantry up to the end of the nineteenth century. Black leather equipment was introduced and underwent various modifications (Fig. 117d). Following the Uniform Regulations of 1900, dark blue double-breasted coats with red piping around the collar, round cuffs, and front of the coat were issued to the men. The trousers were dark blue with red piping. The dark blue kepi had a loop and small button, and red piping around the top; the greatcoat was dark blue with red piping. In the artillery, all piping was carmine; the trousers had triple stripes. The engineers had carmine piping, and black velvet collars and cuffs and edging to the kepi. The Presidential Guard was dressed in dark blue *Attila* jackets with light-blue loopings and light-blue trouser stripes and kepi band. Infantry officers wore a dark blue tunic with red piping on the self-colored collar, round cuffs, and scalloped skirt pocket flaps, which had three buttons. The trousers and kepi were as for the men, the latter bearing the rank distinctions. Cavalry officers wore a dark blue dolman with black loopings, red piping on the shoulder straps and cuffs, and trousers and kepi like the men's. Artillery officers, too, wore a similar *Attila*, but with carmine piping. The officers of the engineers and Presidential Guard were dressed like the men. At this time, the rank distinctions were: colonel, shoulder straps of basic color with gold edging and a large gold five-pointed star in the center and three medium-width gold stripes around the kepi and cuffs; lieutenant colonel, shoulder straps with two gold bars in the center, two medium stripes with a narrow one down the center, on the kepi and cuffs; major, one bar on the shoulder straps, two narrow stripes, with a medium-width one in the center, on the kepi and cuffs; captain, 1st class, three narrow stripes on the shoulder straps and around the cuffs and kepi; captain, 2nd class, the same, but with the center stripe of silver or gold, according to the arm of the service; lieutenant, two stripes; 2nd lieutenant, one stripe.

Fig. 117. Mexico, 1826–1935.

a, c, d, e: infantry. c: cavalry. f: cavalry officer. g: Belgian relief corps, *voltigeur*. h: Austrian Volunteer Brigade, *Jäger*.

Sergeants, 1st class, wore three diagonal stripes on the lower arms; sergeants, 2nd class, two; and corporals, one stripe. General officers, who wore dark blue coats with red (later dark blue) distinctions, in all orders of dress, had broad gold embroidery around the outer edges of the collar and cuffs; and their rank was indicated by silver stars on the epaulettes and the white plumage in the hat. About 1910 a Prussian-style spiked helmet was introduced and was worn in addition to the kepi. General staff officers at that time wore an *Attila* jacket with black loopings, and three short gold lace loops, pointed at the top, above the cuffs, and a single gold aiguillette on the right shoulder. At the same time, the army adopted for full dress a uniform very like that of the Prussian infantry, with Brandenburg cuffs, spiked helmets with black plumes, and white leather equipment (Fig. 117e).

Special mention must be made of the uniforms worn during the Emperor Maximilian's expedition of 1864–1867. That of the regular army has been dealt with above; the frequently embodied militia troops generally wore the same uniform, but with white metal buttons. Emperor Maximilian himself wore a single-breasted dark blue coat with red piping on the front, dark blue trousers with red piping; and white metal buttons. The collar and cuffs were edged with silver lace embroidered with red. The passants were of the same lace. His headdress was a large gray felt sombrero with broad silver lace around the edge. At his overthrow, an Austrian and a Belgian relief corps were sent out. The Belgian one consisted of a grenadier battalion and a *voltigeur* battalion, dressed in a distinctive fashion (Fig. 117g). The coat was dark blue; the trousers, light blue; gaiters, white; and leather equipment, black. The lace loops on the front of the coat and the hat cords were red for the grenadiers, green for *voltigeurs*, and white for bandsmen. The officers wore dark blue hussar *Attilas* with black silk or gold loopings according to rank; the French-style rank distinctions were worn on the lower arms. A dark blue kepi with gold edging and rank stripes was worn as well as the hat. A green cock's feather plume was worn in the latter. The Austrian volunteer brigade consisted of three *Jäger* battalions, a hussar regiment, and a lancer regiment. All wore red field caps (shaped like the Austrian cavalry cap) and brown double-breasted greatcoats. The rest of the uniform consisted of a plain dark blue jacket with red trousers, and a light-gray hat with variously colored feathers—*Jäger*, light gray; artillery, red; pioneers, white—and black leather equipment. The hussars wore dark green dolmans with white loopings; the lancers, dark green lancer jackets of Austrian type with red collar patches and piping, dark green trousers with broad red stripes, and a type of lancer cap. The rank distinctions were like those in the Austrian army (Fig. 117h).

After the Great War, the uniforms of the Mexican army were greatly influenced by United States patterns. From 1925 up to the late 1930s, a gray-brown service dress was worn. The jacket had a row of seven large buttons, patch pockets on the breast and skirts, and a stand-and-fall collar. The collar shoulder straps, Brandenburg cuffs, and trousers were piped in *Waffenfarbe*. The leather equipment was brown. Officers wore a Sam Browne, with the brace over the left shoulder. The cap was of basic color without colored distinctions, with a brown leather peak and chinstrap. The arm-of-service badge in bronze was worn at the ends of the collar of the jacket, and on the front of the cap band. The greatcoat was double-breasted with a broad turndown collar without colored piping. The rank badges, in bronze, were worn on the shoulder straps of the jacket and greatcoat. NCOs and men wore one to three narrow bands in *Waffenfarbe* above the outer ends of the shoulder straps; company officers had one to three diagonal bars; field officers, one to three stars, one above the other; a brigadier general wore the Mexican eagle in a laurel wreath; a major general had, in addition, a silver star above and below (Fig. 117f). In full dress and off duty, a black uniform was worn. It consisted of a single-breasted tunic with collar patches of *Waffenfarbe*; and trousers stripes and cap bands also of *Waffenfarbe*. The French-type cuffs were of basic color. On the collar patches and front of the cap was worn the arm-of-service badge, in button color; with the national cockade above, on the top part of the cap. On this uniform, the rank distinctions of the NCOs and men consisted of one to three diagonal stripes of button color on the lower arms. Officers wore epaulettes of button color—with no fringes for company officers—and rank badges, as on the service jacket, on the crescent, with, in addition, stripes of button color around the cuffs and cap band: company officers, one to three narrow ones; field officers, one to three medium ones, with a narrow additional one below for majors and lieutenant colonels. General officers wore the device of a sprig of laurel.

ARM OF SERVICE	DISTINCTIVE COLOR	ARM-OF-SERVICE BADGE	BUTTONS ON BLACK UNIFORM
General Staff	light blue with red piping	crossed sword and key on sunburst	gold
Infantry	red	crossed rifles and horn	gold
Cavalry	light blue	crossed swords	silver
Artillery	carmine	flaming grenade on crossed cannon	gold
Engineers	red	crossed hammer, spade, and torch	gold

NETHERLANDS

Cockade: orange

I. INFANTRY

Uniforms in the accepted sense were introduced in 1680. The infantry had iron-gray coats and the guards, blue. Several regiments wore red coats. In 1730 blue was also adopted by some of the line regiments, and gray (by then almost a white color) was latterly worn less and less. By 1750 only a few regiments still wore it; and finally, in 1753, all the infantry regiments were dressed in blue. The only exceptions thereafter were the Scots, who wore red. The distinctive colors were gray, red, madder red, white, and yellow. The Swiss Regiments wore blue coats like the line. In the mid-eighteenth century the uniform was very similar to that of the British army. Very large cuffs were still being worn in 1752. The guards wore laced hats and had richly laced lapels, cuffs, and pouch belts. The grenadier caps had a red plate ornamented with silver (Fig. 118a). The officers did not wear turned-back skirts. As a mark of rank, they had gilded gorgets, orange sashes worn over the right shoulder, and spontoons; NCOs wore their sashes around the waist and carried carbines. The waistcoats and breeches were colored; later, they were all white or yellowish-white. The distinc-

Fig. 118. Netherlands—Infantry.

a, e: grenadiers of the guard. c: line grenadier. b, d, f, g, h, i, k: line infantry.
h: Swiss infantry.

tions of the coats varied greatly in color. The Swiss Guards wore fur grenadier caps; later, this headdress was adopted by grenadiers throughout the army. In 1760 the fur caps had a plate on the front; by 1790 they had none (Fig. 118c). Officers were denoted by cords on the shoulders. During the War of the French Revolution, the infantry regiments wore helmets. A specimen of one, in the Zeughaus, had a black skull, brass mounts, and a red horsehair plume. A small chain hung down at the back, to protect the neck. On the left side was a cockade of ribbon of indeterminate color. Latterly, it was almost gray-green, but it had originally been orange. When the Netherlands became the Batavian Republic in 1795, blue French-style uniforms were adopted. The coat skirts were lengthened, and the collar was made higher and the hat bigger (Fig. 118d). The infantry adopted the French organization into demibrigades of three battalions each. Epaulettes were introduced for the officers. The cockade, orange up to 1795, was changed to black. At the end of 1796, the distinctions were as follows.

FORMATION	COLLAR, LAPELS, AND CUFFS	SKIRTS	PIPING
1st Demibrigade	red	red	white
2nd Demibrigade	carmine	white	white
3rd Demibrigade	white	white	white
4th Demibrigade	white (red collar piped white)	red	red
5th Demibrigade	light blue	light blue	white
6th Demibrigade	light blue	white	white
7th Demibrigade	yellow	yellow	white
Regiment Waldeck	yellow	yellow	white
Regiment Saxony-Gotha	red	red	red

The rifles had green coats with variously colored distinctions, and black leather equipment.

In 1803 the infantry distinctions were changed: Henceforth, all battalions wore different colors. When Napoleon declared the Batavian Republic a kingdom, the color and pattern of the uniforms were changed. In this period (1806–1810) the infantry (Fig. 118f) wore white coats, breeches, and waistcoats. The color of the collar, lapels, cuffs, and skirt turnbacks varied from regiment to regiment.

1st Regiment (Guards)—carmine
2nd Regiment—light blue
3rd Regiment—red
4th Regiment—pink
5th Regiment—dark green
6th Regiment—grass green
7th Regiment—yellow
8th Regiment—light violet
9th Regiment—black

The greatcoats were light blue. The black chacos had a brass loop on the left, with a pompon in the regimental color above, and the regimental number in metal on the front. The fusilier companies had white cords; the grenadiers and *voltigeurs* had red and green cords respectively, as in the French army. The fusiliers wore a bayonet and scabbard; and the grenadiers, *voltigeurs*, and NCOs had a hanger. The guard

(Fig. 118e) had seven yellow lace loops with tassels at the ends, on each lapel. The top loop was set diagonally, and there were two similar loops on the collar. Red fringed epaulettes were also worn. The fur caps had a red patch, with a white grenade on it, at the top of the back. The feather plume was red and the cords, white. White leather equipment was worn by all regiments. As a mark of rank, officers wore gorgets, but no sashes. The sword knot was gold. The boots had yellow turned-over tops. The epaulettes resembled those worn by French officers; and similarly, the NCOs' chevrons. The uniform of the light infantry was of the same style. Coat, lapels, waistcoat, breeches, pompon, cords, and shoulder straps were dark green. The collar, pointed cuffs, skirts, and piping were light blue for the 2nd Regiment and yellow for the 3rd; the buttons were yellow metal for all. The leather equipment and gaiters were black. (The *chasseur* battalion of the guard ranked as the 1st Regiment; it was dressed like the grenadiers, with the distinctions of the *chasseurs*.)

When Napoleon incorporated the Kingdom of Holland into the Empire in 1810, the Dutch regiments were assimilated into the French army and adopted French uniforms. Only the guard regiment retained its white uniforms; but the yellow lace on them was abolished. It was numbered as the 3rd Regiment of *grenadiers à pied* of the *Garde Impériale*. In 1814/1815, the country again became independent as the Kingdom of the United Netherlands. The infantry (Fig. 118g) adopted blue single-breasted British-style coats with blue cuff slashes and shoulder straps. The collar, cuffs, and piping were differently colored; the buttons, yellow metal; the trousers, light gray. The chaco had front and back peaks, a small yellow metal shield plate, an orange cockade, and a white plume. The flank companies wore blue wings with white piping. The distinctive colors were:

    1st and 9th Battalions—orange
    2nd and 10th Battalions—yellow
    3rd and 11th Battalions—white
    4th and 12th Battalions—red
    5th and 13th Battalions—carmine
    6th and 14th Battalions—light green
    7th and 15th Battalions—light blue
    8th and 16th Battalions—pink

In 1815 a new pattern of chaco was issued (Fig. 118h). It had a brass plate shaped like a diadem; an orange cockade; and no plume. The rifles wore uniforms of a similar style but in green, with green cuff patches and shoulder straps. The collar, piping, cuffs, and buttons were yellow. The skirt turnbacks were red. The chaco was as worn by the line, with a green plume, and the battalion number in yellow, over a yellow hunting horn. Their equipment was of black leather. Officers readopted orange sashes and wore long-skirted coats.

The national militia had blue coats with blue shoulder straps and Swedish cuffs, and orange collars and piping. The skirt linings and buttons were white. The chacos were of British type and had a white plate and plume and an orange cockade. This uniform was worn throughout the 1820s.

In 1819 the whole of the infantry adopted short, single-breasted coats with white collars and piping, and yellow metal buttons with the number of the formation on them.

The four Swiss Regiments (29th–32nd Regiments, all disbanded in 1829) were (with the exception of the Nassau-Orange Regiment) the only infantry units that were organized as regiments—the rest only formed independently numbered battalions or detachments. They were dressed in ornamented uniforms, with variously colored collars, cuffs, and skirt turnbacks. There were nine lace loops down the front (Fig. 118h).

REGIMENT	DISTINCTIONS	BUTTONS, LACE, AND FLANK COMPANY WINGS	SKIRT TURNBACKS
29th	red	white	red
30th	orange	white	orange
31st	light blue	white	light blue
32nd	yellow	yellow	red

In 1831 the infantry adopted fairly low-crowned bell-shaped chacos. Later, tall, tapering chacos were worn; these gradually decreased in height. A new pattern of uniform was introduced in 1854. The line infantry adopted low-crowned chacos, like kepis, with a red drooping plume. The Prussian-style single-breasted tunic then introduced was dark blue, with a white collar, shoulder straps, cuff patches, and piping. The light-blue trousers had red stripes. The buttons were yellow metal, and the leather equipment, black.

The regiment "Grenadiers and *Jäger*" wore a similar uniform, except that the grenadiers had white chaco cords, red distinctions, red shoulder wings, and yellow lace loops on the collar and Swedish cuffs, and white shoulder straps with a yellow grenade on them. The *Jäger* wore all-green uniforms with green distinctions, and yellow lace loops and piping. In 1890 the line infantry (Fig. 118k) was dressed in double-breasted dark blue coats with self-colored collar and cuffs. Yellow piping went around the collar, pointed cuffs, and skirt pockets; the shoulder straps and tasseled loops were yellow. Light-blue trousers with yellow piping were worn. The chaco was shaped like a kepi, and had an orange cockade, and yellow metal chinscales and plate. The small plume was white. The grenadiers had red collars, cuffs, and piping. The leather equipment remained black as before. The *Jäger* wore all-green uniforms of the same style as the rest of the infantry; with yellow piping. In 1897 the yellow distinctions of the infantry were superseded by red; and the collar became all red. In place of the chaco, a blue cloth kepi was introduced.

About 1900 a single-breasted blue tunic (green for *Jäger*) with breast pockets was introduced for all dismounted troops, for wear on service and in undress. No colored distinctions or piping were worn on it. The collar bore the regimental number in red. The old uniform was retained for full dress (Fig. 120a).

After the introduction of the gray service dress, a colored evening dress and walking-out uniform, of the same style for all arms (except cavalry), was introduced for officers and NCOs. It consisted of a single-breasted blue-black tunic with yellow metal buttons; and red piping around the dark blue stand collar, pointed cuffs, and three-button skirt pocket flaps. The shoulder straps were blue-black; officers had gold plaited shoulder cords. Dark blue trousers, piped with red, were worn with the tunic. The kepi was dark blue, with a black lacquered leather peak and chinstrap, and an orange cockade with a yellow cord binding. The piping around the top and the two stripes around the band were in *Waffenfarbe*—red in this case—but of metal lace for officers. Either the old dark blue greatcoat or the gray service coat was worn with this uniform. The grenadiers (who had light-blue trousers) and *Jäger* (green coat and trousers and yellow piping) wore a grenade and a hunting horn respectively, in yellow embroidery on the collar, and retained the old chaco for full-dress wear. The officers of both regiments continued to wear the old-pattern tunic in full dress, up to the late 1930s. The lace was gold. The Brandenburg cuffs had three lace loops on them.

The former national militia was replaced by a form of reserve forces, the *Schutterij*, which was dressed in dark blue tunics and trousers, with red collars and cuffs, and white shoulder straps and buttons. As a mark of rank, all officers of dismounted units wore orange-yellow sashes.

II. CAVALRY

From 1680 the cavalry, as well as the infantry, was dressed in gray; and the guards, in blue. The heavy cavalry retained this color (which latterly became white); but the dragoons wore blue coats from 1752. The color of the lining was changed often: Almost every new colonel gave his regiment a different distinctive color; and the officers frequently wore a special embroidery as well. In 1752 the horse guards (Fig. 119a) were dressed in blue British-style coats with red turnbacks and rich silver ornamentation. The detachments of horse grenadiers wore fur caps (Fig. 119c). In imitation of the Prussians, white plumes were added to the hats in the 1760s. The breeches and pouch belts were buff-colored. The 2nd Heavy Cavalry Regiment, called carabiniers, had yellowish-white coats. In all, there were six heavy regiments in 1752. Their distinctions were green, light blue, red, pink, black, and red respectively. The 3rd and 6th regiments were differentiated by the colors of their buttons. There were two dragoon regiments, dressed in blue and pink respectively. The waistcoats and breeches were white. The horse guards and guard dragoons wore dark blue uniforms with red distinctions and silver lace. During the early years of the Batavian Republic, there were only two heavy cavalry regiments, one dragoon, and one hussar regiment. The heavy cavalry wore white coats, with black distinctions and epaulettes for the 1st Regiment, and blue for the 2nd. The hussars had blue dolmans with red distinctions and yellow loopings. The dragoons had dark blue coats with pink distinctions.

In 1802 the light cavalry wore black helmets with a black crest, red and white turban, and white plume; short white coats, with black distinctions for the 1st Regiment and light blue for the 2nd; with white lace loops on the collar, lapels, and cuffs for both regiments. In 1804 these helmets were replaced by French dragoon-pattern helmets with a comb. In 1805 dark blue coats with a light-red collar and distinctions were introduced. On service, all the cavalry wore blue buttoned overalls. At the reorganization of the army in 1806, a guard cavalry regiment (horse grenadiers) was raised. It adopted the uniform of the foot guards: white with carmine distinctions and yellow lace loops. Yellow shoulder cords were worn in place of epaulettes. The fur caps had white cords and a red plume. Long boots were worn. The cuirassiers (Fig. 119d) wore a yellow metal helmet with a black horsehair *crinière* and a red

Fig. 119. Netherlands Cavalry.

a: horse guards. b: heavy cavalry. c: guard dragoons (grenadier). d,
k: cuirassiers. e: hussars. g, i: light dragoons. f, h: heavy dragoons. l: lancer.
m: light cavalry. n: dragoon.

plume. The jacket was white, with light-blue collar, cuffs, lapels, and skirts; red
epaulettes; and yellow leather equipment. The hussars were dressed entirely in dark
blue or light blue with red collars and cuffs, and yellow loopings (Fig. 119e). The
guard hussars wore red dolmans with white loopings and white pelisses. During the
last part of King Louis Napoleon's "reign," the cavalry uniforms were constantly
being changed, so that there was hardly time for them to be adopted by all. In 1814
two regiments of heavy dragoons were raised (Fig. 119f). They were dressed in long-
skirted blue coats, with pink collars and lapels for the 1st Regiment and yellow for
the 2nd. The uniform was altered in 1815, in which year the cavalry consisted of eight
regiments, of which the heavy dragoons were called cuirassiers.

REGIMENT	COAT	COLLAR AND CUFFS	SKIRT LINING	TROUSERS	BUTTONS	REMARKS
1st Carabiniers	blue	red, blue collar	red	white	white	steel helmet with black *chenille*
2nd Carabiniers	blue	red, blue collar	red	white	white	helmet as above; red lapels and epaulettes
3rd Carabiniers	blue	yellow	red	white	white	helmet as above
4th Light Dragoons	blue	red	red	white	white	black chaco
5th Light Dragoons	green	yellow	yellow	gray	white	green chaco
6th Hussars	light blue	red	none	light blue	white	black chaco
8th Hussars	light blue	light blue	none	light blue	yellow	black chaco

All the cavalry regiments wore gray overalls on service, except for the hussars,
which had dark blue ones. The trumpeters were dressed in red, except for those of the
5th Light Dragoons, who wore yellow (Fig. 119g). The 7th Regiment, which is not
listed in the table, was serving in the East Indies. The carabiniers were turned into

cuirassiers in 1816 (Fig. 119k). They kept their blue jackets and colored distinctions, and wore plain cuirasses. The steel helmet had a black *chenille* and, as before, a yellow metal comb and chinscales, with a lion's head on the front. Shoulder wings, of the color of the collar, were introduced. In 1810 all four corps of cuirassiers were dressed in blue single-breasted coats with red distinctions and yellow metal buttons. A new-pattern helmet was issued to them in 1821. In the 1820s the light dragoons (Fig. 119i) had blue jackets with blue lapels, blue trousers and shabraques, orange-colored collars and piping, white metal buttons, and white lace on the trousers and shabraques. The black chaco bore the regimental number in white and had a white band around the top, and white cords, black plume, and orange cockade. The hussars had light-blue dolmans and pelisses with yellow loopings. The sabertaches were black, with the regimental number in metal.

The lancers, raised in 1822 (Fig. 119l), had dark green *kurtkas* with dark green collars and lapels, trousers, shabraques, and valises; orange lace and piping; white metal buttons and shoulder scales; and green lancer caps with a white plume. The lance pennants were orange over white. The trumpeters wore white jackets with green distinctions. In the broader aspects of fashion, the uniform generally resembled French ones. In 1841, a second lancer regiment was formed; it adopted blue jackets.

The four cavalry regiments were renamed dragoons in 1849. All adopted lapels. The 1st and 4th were dressed as light cavalry; and the 2nd and 3rd as heavy cavalry. The 1st and 3rd Regiments had red distinctions; the 2nd, white; and the 4th, light blue. The chacos of the 1st and 4th Regiments were of the distinctive color (Fig. 119n). The 2nd and 3rd Regiments wore cuirassier helmets with a lion's head device on the front. All had white epaulettes. In 1867 a comprehensive change took place. All four cavalry regiments adopted a hussar uniform (Fig. 119o). From that time, they wore blue-black *Attila* jackets and trousers. The 1st, 2nd, and 4th Regiments had light-blue (later dark blue) loopings, and the 3rd Regiment, red. The fur caps had white metal chinscales, with a pompon, of the color of the loopings, on the front. The buttons were white, as were the lines and tassels worn over the shoulder. The black sabertache bore the regimental number in white. In the four half-regiments to which the cavalry was reduced in 1922, the officers and NCOs retained the old uniform unaltered for evening wear and walking out, up to the late 1930s. A double-breasted light-blue greatcoat, or a light-blue jacket edged with black fur, was worn with it.

III. ARTILLERY AND ENGINEERS

In the eighteenth century the uniforms of the artillery and engineers were like those of the infantry, but the waistcoats and trousers were blue like the coat. The artillery had red cuffs, and the pioneers, black. In 1752 the undergarments were red. The horse artillery, formed in 1793, wore cavalry uniform: a dark blue coat with blue lapels, red collar and cuffs, yellow breeches, long boots, and dragoon hats. At the reorganization of the army of the Kingdom of Holland in 1806, the foot artillery was issued with uniforms like those of the Dutch infantry in style. Coat, waistcoat, breeches, and lapels and shoulder straps were dark blue; with red collar, cuffs, piping, and chaco cords. The pompon on the left side of the chaco varied in color according to the battalion: red; white; blue; or yellow. The device on the chaco consisted of a yellow crown above crossed cannon barrels. Buttons were yellow metal; leather equipment was white, with black gaiters. The horse artillery wore an all-blue hussar uniform with red loopings, yellow metal buttons, and black leather equipment. The bands around the chaco, cords, and plume were all red. In 1815 the Dutch artillery adopted dark blue single-breasted jackets with dark blue cuff patches, black collar and cuffs, red piping, and yellow metal buttons; gray trousers with red stripes; and red chaco cords and black plumes. The transport corps wore a similar style of uniform, but in gray, with black collar and cuffs, red piping, and white metal buttons. In its more general aspects, the development of the artillery uniform resembled that of the infantry. In 1900 the uniforms of the field and garrison artillery consisted of a double-breasted blue coat, with black collar piped red, self-colored cuffs also piped red; and dark blue trousers with red stripes. The tasseled loops and shoulder cords were red. The chaco had a yellow metal plate, red pompon, and a black plume.

The colored walking-out dress worn in the 1930s was the same as that of the infantry, with collar badges consisting of crossed cannon barrels. From the 1820s, the horse artillery wore a British-style all-dark-blue hussar dolman, with narrow yellow loopings. The tall fur caps had a red bag and pompon and yellow lines. The loopings on the officers' dolmans were gold, with rich sleeve lacing; blue-black loopings were worn on the undress uniform. This continued to be worn up to the 1930s for evening wear and walking out (Fig. 120b).

The engineers followed the changing patterns of the infantry uniforms, but had collars of basic color, and red piping. The men always wore two yellow lace loops on the collar; officers had an armorial helmet in gold embroidery. On the walking-out dress worn during the 1920s, NCOs wore only one loop on the collar and had a red embroidered helmet device on the shoulder straps.

IV. GENERAL OFFICERS AND GENERAL STAFF; RANK DISTINCTIONS

The successive uniforms worn by general officers were dark blue, with red distinctions and rich gold embroidery. In 1815 they had single-breasted dark blue coatees, with red collars and round cuffs with broad gold lace on the outer edges, gold epaulettes, and white (later dark blue) trousers (gray in undress) with broad gold stripes. The hat had white feather plumage and plume, and an orange cockade and gold loop on the right side. In the mid-1840s, the gold lace was done away with, and the collar and cuffs were ornamented with rich gold embroidery. During the next decade, general officers wore a single-breasted tunic with the same ornamentation. On the undress uniform, there was no embroidery on the red collar; the cuffs were dark blue, gold epaulettes were worn, and

Fig. 120. Netherlands.
a, c: infantry. b: officer of horse artillery. d: colonial infantry.

333

the chaco had broad gold lace around the top. From 1869 to the end of the century, general officers wore a hussar uniform consisting of a blue-black *Attila* jacket, with red collar with broad gold lace on it, gold loopings, and gold pointed lace with red piping, on the cuffs. On the undress uniform, the loops on the breast were dark blue. An orange hussar sash, and dark blue trousers with broad gold stripes (later with red piping), were worn. The fur caps had an oval orange cockade, gold chinstrap, and lines. A white plume, and red bag edged with gold, were worn for full dress. The red sabertaches bore stars denoting rank and had a gold edging.

From about 1900 up to the late 1930s a blue-black double-breasted coat with red collar and round cuffs with rich oakleaf embroidery was worn, with gold epaulettes and an orange sash with the tassels on the left side. The dark blue trousers had two narrow red stripes; and the black hat had an orange cockade, gold loop, and white feather plume. The undress coat had dark blue roll cuffs piped red. The red collar was edged with narrow gold embroidery; and a gold plaited shoulder cord was worn. The dark blue kepi had a red band with gold embroidery, gold cord piping on the sides and top, black peak and chinstrap, and an orange cockade in a laurel wreath on the band. The full-dress coat was not worn after 1912, after which year a single-breasted undress one was the only coat worn. The rank stars were placed on the collar. Epaulettes and the hat were retained for full dress.

The uniform of the general staff on the whole followed that of general officers, but with carmine distinctions and narrow gold lace instead of oakleaf embroidery. From 1868 up to the late 1930s the general staff also wore a hussar uniform: a blue-black *Attila* jacket with carmine collar and dark blue loopings. The trousers and fur caps were similar to those of general officers, but with carmine piping; the sabertaches were black.

Up to about 1830, except during the Napoleonic era, officers' rank insignia were as follows: general officers and field officers had two epaulettes with thick bullions of button color, with two to four six-pointed silver stars on the crescent, according to rank, for the former; colonels had plain crescents; lieutenant colonels and majors had one or two longitudinal stripes in contrasting color to that of the buttons. Captains had one epaulette with thick bullions—subalterns likewise, but with thin bullions—on the right shoulder. From about 1830, company officers, like field officers, wore epaulettes on both shoulders, but with thin bullions. Epaulettes were abolished in the mid-1860s. From that time, the distinctions of rank were as follows: company officers, one to three six-pointed stars at the ends of the collar, in contrasting color to that of the buttons; field officers, similar stars, on a broad lace stripe of button color, on the collar. Warrant officers had a round button, in contrasting metal to the buttons, at the ends of the collar. A further distinction of rank consisted of a single cord running from the left shoulder to the right hip, the tassels of which were fixed on the left breast. Lieutenants had two or three tassels with thin bullions; captains, two tassels with thick bullions; majors, three; colonels, four, with thick bullions. Lieutenant colonels also had four tassels, the upper two of contrasting color to that of the buttons. General officers had one or two silver stars, according to rank, on the upper tassels. The sword knot was silver with an orange core. From 1900 general officers wore epaulettes similar to those in use in 1815 and, on the collar, four silver stars for lieutenant generals, and two silver and two gold for major generals. The NCOs and men's ranks were indicated by one or two chevron-shaped metal lace or worsted stripes of the color of the buttons, above the cuffs.

V. THE GRAY SERVICE DRESS UNIFORM AND ITS ARM-OF-SERVICE AND RANK INSIGNIA

From about 1912 the Dutch army had a protective-colored service dress that was worn on service, and for everyday wear by the men liable for military service. It remained unaltered in essentials up to the late 1930s. The cut and color were the same for all arms of the service. The jacket had a row of seven buttons, breast and skirt pockets—of patch type for officers and NCOs with scalloped flaps and small buttons—and gray shoulder straps. The stand collar was piped all around, and the round cuffs were piped along the top in *Waffenfarbe*. Breeches, piped down the sides, were worn, with puttees for dismounted troops and riding boots for the rest. The footwear was black; leather equipment, brown. Officers wore Sam Brownes (Fig. 120c). The steel helmet was of a design peculiar to the Dutch army, and had the national arms on the front. The stiff kepi, which narrowed toward the top, had a cloth peak and brown chinstrap and, at distances of 2 and 4 centimeters from the bottom, piping in *Waffenfarbe*. The regimental badge in bronze was worn between these on the front. On the upper part was an oval orange cockade with a white or yellow cord binding (silver or gold for officers) forming a small loop below it. Senior NCOs wore a metal cord in place of the lower piping, and officers wore two cords of metal lace instead. The kepi was piped gray around the top, except for field officers, who wore a metal lace cord. A fore-and-aft-shaped field service cap was worn on service, with metal cord around the flap for officers. The men wore piping in *Waffenfarbe* on the cap up to 1934. The regimental device in orange was worn on the left side. The double-breasted greatcoat had a turndown collar, roll cuffs, and a half belt with two buttons at the back. All buttons on the service uniforms were bronze and bore the crowned lion. The *Waffenfarben* and distinctions, as they were in 1934, are given in the table below. The rank distinctions resembled those on the dress uniform. Field officers wore vertical bars of button color to the rear of the stars on their collars, instead of their former lace. The same rank badges were worn on the collar of the greatcoat. In addition, general officers had two or three silver stars, according to rank, on the greatcoat sleeves. The men had small straight lace stripes, of the same number and color as on the cuffs, at the end of the collar.

ARM OF SERVICE	EDGING OF COCKADE ON KEPI	KEPI BADGE (BRONZE)	PIPING ON KEPI AND TROUSERS	PIPING ON COLLAR AND CUFFS	REMARKS
Grenadiers	yellow	flaming grenade	red	red	yellow grenade on collar
Jäger	yellow	hunting horn	green	green	yellow hunting horn on collar
Infantry	yellow	Arabic number	blue	blue	
Cyclists	yellow	lion	blue	blue	yellow wheel on collar

(continued)

ARM OF SERVICE	EDGING OF COCKADE ON KEPI	KEPI BADGE (BRONZE)	PIPING ON KEPI AND TROUSERS	PIPING ON COLLAR AND CUFFS	REMARKS
Hussars	—	—	—	—	staff of 1st Hussar Regiment as for 1st Half Regiment; staff of 2nd Hussar Regiment as for 3rd Half Regiment
1st, 2nd, 4th Half Regiments	white	Arabic number	blue	—	
3rd Half Regiment	white	Arabic number	red	—	
Artillery	yellow	Arabic number	red	red	yellow crossed cannon barrels on collar
Anti-aircraft Artillery	yellow	lion	red	red	propeller on crossed cannon barrels on collar
Horse Artillery	yellow	lion	yellow	—	crossed cannon barrels on collar
Engineers	yellow	lion	blue	blue	yellow armorial helmet on collar
Bridging Units	yellow	lion	red	red	yellow foul anchor on collar
Air Force	yellow	lion	red	red	no piping on officers' jacket
General Staff	gold	lion	carmine on trousers	carmine on collar	six-pointed gold star with lion on left breast
General Officers	orange cockade in gold laurel wreath		gold on kepi, also on side seams; two narrow red stripes on trousers	—	collar edged with serrated lace

VI. THE COLONIAL ARMY IN THE DUTCH INDIES

Up to the end of the 1860s, the uniform worn by the colonial troops very closely resembled those worn by the army at home. Thereafter, they were dressed in all dark blue *Attila* jackets, with piping in *Waffenfarbe* in the shape of a plastron on the front, and piping around the collar and pointed cuffs as well (Fig. 120d). The tropical helmet was dark blue, with star plate and coat of arms, and a spike for full-dress wear. The dark blue trousers had piping in *Waffenfarbe*. Six horizontal loopings in *Waffenfarbe* adorned the front of the dress coat. Officers wore black silk loops on all their uniforms. This uniform continued to be worn, with minor alterations, for walking out, up to the late 1930s. The jacket then worn by all arms of service was an *Attila*, with black loops on the front, and black Austrian knots on the sleeves for officers. The helmet was abolished, and replaced by a low-crowned dark blue cloth chaco with a cord of button color around the bottom and piping in *Waffenfarbe* around the top. The distinctions of rank were the same as in the Dutch home army. The uniform worn by general officers was of the same pattern as that worn in the Netherlands in the period 1868–1900. The *Waffenfarben* and button colors of the main arms of service remained unaltered up to the 1930s, as follows: infantry, orange and gold; cavalry, red and silver; artillery, red and gold; engineers, red and gold, with an armorial helmet on the collar.

On service, from the beginning of the present century, a gray-green uniform with a row of black bronze buttons was worn. On the gray-green shoulder straps were placed the arm-of-service badges in black bronze: crossed rifles, sabers, or cannon, or an armorial helmet. The rank badges were worn on the black double-scalloped patches of the stand-and-fall collar. The rank stars and buttons were of the same number as for the home army but were invariably of silver. Company officers had a gold cord edging to their collar patches; field officers and general officers had broad gold stripes on theirs. Steel helmets, of the same pattern as at home, were worn; and gray-green fore-and-aft field service caps; or gray-green British-style forage caps, with a darker-colored band, and a round cockade on the front above the leather peak.

NORWAY

Cockade: blue-white-red

I. INFANTRY

Up to 1814, Norway was under Danish rule. During the period of the "personal union" with the Swedish crown (1814–1905), the uniforms bore a general resemblance to Swedish ones in cut and color. Thus, in 1830, the infantry (Fig. 121a) wore short-skirted dark blue coatees with red collars, cuff patches, skirt turnbacks, and piping. The yellow sashes had two blue stripes. The buttons were yellow metal. The chacos had yellow fittings. The trousers were blue, but white ones were worn in summer. About 1860 (Fig. 121b) the uniform consisted of a dark blue tunic with dark blue distinctions, red piping, yellow metal buttons; gray trousers with red piping; and a blue kepi with a red band and pompon. A blue, white, and red cockade was worn. The rifles (Fig. 121c) wore an all-green short-skirted jacket without distinctions; white metal buttons; and gray trousers. They wore a hat like that worn by the Italian *Bersaglieri*, with a cockade and black plume. Around 1890 the sharpshooters of the guard (Fig. 121d) were dressed in a similar hat and in a short dark blue tunic with self-colored collar and cuffs, white buttons, and lace loops, with red piping all around the jacket; green fringed epaulettes with white crescents; and gray trousers with double white stripes. Later, dark blue epaulettes, without fringes, were worn, and dark blue trousers. Officers' lace was silver. In 1890 the infantry was dressed in a light-blue tunic with self-colored turndown collar and cuffs. All distinctions were piped red, and the jacket itself had piping down the front and around the skirts. There was similar piping on the light-blue trousers. The buttons were white metal. The black leather helmet had a white metal plate (Fig. 121e). About 1900 the infantry uniform was changed. A dark blue jacket with a stand collar, piped red around the outside, and with pointed cuffs for the men, was introduced. A dark blue kepi with red piping on the side seams was adopted in place of the helmet (Fig. 122a). This dark blue uniform was retained up to the 1930s and was allowed to be worn by all arms, as well as the service uniform. In addition, the guards, when off duty, wore a fore-and-aft field service cap with broad silver binding around the flap and a small tassel on the front.

II. CAVALRY

The basic color of the uniform up to the 1930s was green. In 1830 (Fig. 121f) the jacket had green collar, cuffs, and lapels with red piping, and white metal buttons. A red stripe was worn on the green trousers. The chaco had a black plume, and white

338

Fig. 121. Norway, 1830–1890.

a: infantry officer. b, e: infantry. c: rifles. d: bandsman of the guard. f: cavalry
officer. g, h: cavalrymen. i: artillery officer. k: artilleryman. l: engineer officer.

plate and cords. In 1860 (Fig. 121g) they had a red kepi with red pompon and white
ornaments. The green coat had green cuffs and lapels, a red collar, and red piping
around the shoulder straps, lapels, cuffs, skirts, sleeve, and back seams; white guard
lace; and white metal buttons. The trousers were green with a red stripe, and black
leather strappings. The green shabraques had a red vandyked edge and a white crown
in the rear corners. In 1890 the uniform was similar in cut and color, but the kepi
then worn was green, with carmine piping, a white metal plate, and black plume.
Dark green breeches were worn, with knee boots. The officers had triple carmine
stripes on the breeches, a black pouch and belt, and epaulettes. All the red distinctions were changed to carmine (Fig. 121h). The shabraques had a plain carmine edging, and the crowns in the rear corners were also carmine.

III. ARTILLERY, ENGINEERS, AND TRANSPORT CORPS

In 1830 the artillery uniform (Fig. 121i) was all blue, with blue distinctions and
carmine piping. The buttons were of yellow metal. The chaco had a yellow grenade
and chinscales and a black plume. In 1860 blue tunics were worn, with self-colored
cuffs; carmine cuff patches, collars, and piping, and yellow buttons and leather
equipment. The trousers were gray with red piping; the chacos, blue, with a carmine
band, pompon, and lines. The cockade was placed on the front, with a yellow
grenade below (Fig. 121k). Later, a dark blue kepi with carmine piping, and dark
blue trousers with carmine piping, were worn. Officers had triple trousers stripes,
and gold pouch belts. The transport corps had the same uniform, but with dark blue
collar and cuffs with carmine piping. In 1890 the engineers wore uniforms similar to
those of the infantry, but with black piping. About 1900 the basic color was changed
to dark blue, with light-blue stand collar, cuff patches, and piping (Fig. 121l).

IV. GENERAL OFFICERS AND GENERAL STAFF; DISTINCTIONS OF RANK

The uniforms of the general officers were always very similar to the Swedish ones but had red piping and triple stripes on the trousers. A blue and red feather plume was worn in the hat. The general staff wore the same uniforms as general officers, but without the oakleaf embroidery on the collar and cuffs, and with double gold aiguillettes on the right shoulder.

The ranks of the officers, within each grade, were denoted by one to three five-pointed stars. Up to about 1860, and again in the 1930s with the full dress only, the rank stars were worn on epaulettes. These had thin bullions for field officers and thick ones for general officers. From the 1860s to the 1930s, on the everyday uniform the rank stars, of button color, were worn side by side at the ends of the collar. Field officers, in addition, had a narrow stripe of button color around the outer edge of the collar. The collars of general officers had broad gold lace, with the rank stars in silver. The side piping on the kepi was of button color. Around the band were worn one to three narrow rank stripes of button color, and for field officers, one medium-width stripe, and one to three narrow stripes below. All general officers had a broad gold stripe around the kepi band, and a gold cap cord. All officers wore a carmine silk sash, with the tassels on the left. The sword knot was of gold woven with dark blue silk, with a rigid pendant. NCOs' rank distinctions consisted of one to three cords in *Waffenfarbe* around the cuffs and kepi band.

V. THE FIELD GRAY UNIFORM

A protective-colored service uniform had been on trial since 1903, and it was introduced in 1912. In the 1930s it was the only uniform worn by the conscripts and was the everyday uniform of the permanent corps of officers and NCOs. It was of gray-green basic color, of the same style for all arms and for all ranks. The jacket had patch pockets on the breast and skirts, with pleats and scalloped flaps, and stand-and-fall collar and roll cuffs, both piped red. The breeches and trousers had red piping. The leather equipment was brown; officers wore Sam Brownes. The boots were black (Figs. 122b,c). The gray double-breasted greatcoat had a turndown collar; the shoulder straps, roll cuffs, and collar were all piped red. The kepi was of basic color and had a black lacquered leather peak and chinstrap; with red piping for the men, and cords of button color for officers, on the side seams. The cockade was placed at the top in front, with a loop below, secured by a button bearing the coat of arms. Officers' buttons were of red enamel, with a gold lion *appliqué*. The arms of service were denoted only by the differing colors of, and devices on, the buttons. General officers, artillery, and the transport corps had yellow metal buttons; the rest, white. The rank badges on the service dress were the same as on the colored uniforms. The collar lace worn by field officers only extended back as far as the shoulder.

1903 1936

**Fig. 122.
Norway—Infantry.**

a   b   c

POLAND

Cockade: from the eighteenth century, white

At the time of the relief of Vienna in 1683, the Polish army under John Sobieski consisted of infantry (called "foreign," but in fact composed only of Poles), and three kinds of cavalry: heavy hussars, *Panzerny* (light cavalry), and dragoons (formerly mounted infantry). In addition, there were artillery, organized after the Western European model, and the usual auxiliary troops of the period. Except for the household troops and court guards, there is no evidence of much uniformity at that time.

Infantry were supposed to wear the livery colors of the district from which they came. A specified number of households had to provide the clothing, weapons, subsistence, and a cart for five persons for six months. The infantry did not wear armor, but had hats, fur caps, or light iron helmets. After the abolition of pikes, their arms consisted of a heavy wheellock and the so-called *berdysz*—a small axe with a long haft, which was introduced by Sobieski as a weapon for the infantry and dragoons. It could also be used as a digging tool and as a weapon, and was carried on a belt across the back.

The cavalry was organized into units of 20 to 100 horsemen, led by captains designated in writing by the king. These captains carried long lances with various pennants; the rest of the weapons and equipment were the property of the individuals. The hussars, and the cavalry that wore armor, were recruited only from the nobility. Each horseman had his own attendants, provisions, cart, and horses. The dragoons were organized on the same basis as the infantry. The principal weapons of the hussars were lances, about 5 to 6 meters in length, with variously colored pennants and a long sword, carried on the saddle below the knee. Each lance bore a name, and if it was found unbroken on the battlefield, the owner had to relinquish his position among the troops. The jacket was of chamois leather or cloth. Armor was worn over it. The helmet had a movable nasal. Two (or sometimes one) "wings" of wood staves, with eagles' feathers stuck into them, were worn on the back (Fig. 123a). The helmet with metal wings was still worn in the early eighteenth century, but was later superseded by a fur hussar cap. The only armor that was retained as time passed was the breast plate, secured by two straps crossing over on the back. A tiger or leopard skin, or a plain wolfskin, attached by a metal buckle on the breast, was worn over the left shoulder. The gorget, or right side of the breast plate, was often ornamented with a gilt cross, with a representation of the Virgin Mary in gilt on the left. The saddlery and horse furniture were richly ornamented, and an embroidered horsecloth was worn. The *Panzerny* were responsible for all reconnaissance and policing duties. They were armed with a saber and holster pistols;

Fig. 123. Kingdom of Poland.

a: hussar. b: aide-de-camp. c, g, k: lancers. d: officer of the Warsaw Crown
Guard. e: dragoon of the lifeguard. f, h: line infantry. i: grenadier of the
guard. l: billman. m: Sandomierz Volunteers. n: light cavalry. o: Masovian Volunteers.

almost every rider carried obsolete arms as well: a bow and a quiver of arrows, and a
shield called a *kalkan* made of woven reeds or fig branches, hung at the side of the
saddle. The *kalkan* and quiver were more traditional items of equipment. A short
lance, without a pennant, was often carried. The small, round metal helmet had a
mail tippet reaching to the shoulders. Like the hussars, the *Panzerny* wore a thigh-
length coat of mail with short sleeves over the jacket, and a pair of ornamented iron
gauntlets called *karawasche*. As in the case of the hussars, this dress was not a regulation uniform, and so there were very many variations of it. The dragoons, which
were organized like the infantry, had no armor, and their headdress was a fur cap,
hat, or light iron helmet; a jacket of leather or cloth; a saber or sword, a carbine on a
shoulder belt, a *berdysz* on the back, and often holster pistols as well. The horses
were of moderate size.

During the course of the eighteenth century the uniforms and equipment of the
Polish army showed two different influences: that of Saxony on the one hand, and
that of the national Polish costume on the other—the latter particularly in the case of
the cavalry. The infantry retained the old red Saxon color of uniform long after
white ones had been introduced in Saxony itself.

One type of soldier that had almost completely disappeared in Western Europe
remained in existence in Poland, namely lancers. These had a distinctive organization. In the first rank were the *Towarzysz*, who were recruited from the nobility and
whose only arms were lances. In the second rank were the *Pacholks*, the servants of
the *Towarzysz*, whose primary duty was to wait on the *Towarzysz* and their horses.
The uniform of the first rank is given in the table below. The *Pacholks* wore, as a

rule, the same uniform, except that the headdress was of a different type, the boots were black, not yellow, and aiguillettes and epaulettes were not worn.

The distinctions of the cavalry in 1775 were as follows.

REGIMENT	HEADDRESS	KURTKA	COLLAR AND LAPELS	WAISTCOAT	TROUSERS	BUTTONS
Narodowi 1st Brigade	purple	light blue	purple	white	purple	white
Narodowi 2nd Brigade	dark blue	dark blue	red	white	dark blue	white
Narodowi 3rd Brigade	light blue	light blue	crimson	white	light blue	white
Narodowi 4th Brigade	red	dark blue	red	white	red	white
Przdny Straz 1st Regiment	red	dark blue	red	white	dark blue	white
Przdny Straz 2nd Regiment	green	green	black	red	red	yellow
King's Hussar Brigade	red	dark blue	red	white	dark blue	yellow
National Cavalry	orange	dark blue cassocks	orange	white	white	white
1st Lancer Regiment	yellow	white	yellow	yellow	yellow	white
2nd Lancer Regiment	dark blue	white	dark blue	dark blue	dark blue	yellow
3rd Lancer Regiment	red	white	red	red	red	yellow
4th Lancer Regiment	green	white	green	green	green	yellow
5th Lancer Regiment	orange	white	orange	orange	orange	white

The regiments of the *Przdny Straz* (vanguard) wore *kurtkas* with short sleeves, revealing the sleeves of the waistcoat, which had pointed cuffs. The 1st Regiment had dark blue *kurtkas* with red cuffs; the 2nd, dark green with black cuffs. The last seven regiments in the table did not have waistcoats, but wore long Polish coats. The lancers had short-sleeved *kurtkas* (Fig. 123c).

The Lifeguard Regiment of Dragoons was dressed in the Saxon manner, like all the dragoon regiments. They wore tricorne hats with a white feather, red coats with blue distinctions, no lapels, white lace loops on the breast; white waistcoats; and buff-colored breeches. The line dragoons wore green coats with yellow aiguillettes and yellow metal buttons. The Royal Commander in Chief Regiment had black collars, lapels, and cuffs, and buff colored skirts, waistcoats, and trousers. The Deputy Commander in Chief Regiment had pompadour red cuffs, but white skirts and waistcoats. The Koszlowski Dragoon Regiment had red collars, lapels, cuffs, and skirts, and white waistcoats. The yellow-laced hat had a red plume. The Lifeguard Dragoons (not to be confused with the Lifeguard Regiment of Dragoons) wore red coats with blue distinctions and yellow buttons.

The infantry was also dressed in Saxon-style uniforms. In 1775 the regiments were distinguished as follows.

REGIMENT	COAT	COLLAR, LAPELS, AND CUFFS	SKIRTS	BUTTONS
Crown Guard Grenadier Regiment	red	dark blue	dark blue	yellow
Witten Grenadier Regiment	red	dark blue	white	yellow
Royal Commander in Chief Infantry Regiment	red	green	green	yellow
Royal Deputy Commander in Chief Infantry Regiment	red	light blue	light blue	white
Queen Hedwig Infantry Regiment	red	black	white	white

(continued)

343

REGIMENT	COAT	COLLAR, LAPELS, AND CUFFS	SKIRTS	BUTTONS
Crown Prince Infantry Regiment	red	white	white	white
Lanowi Infantry Regiment	red	light green	white	white
Czapski Infantry Regiment	red	dark green	white	yellow
Raczinski Infantry Regimen	red	light blue	white	white
Potoozki Infantry Regiment	red	dark blue	white	white
Ordination of Ostrog Infantry Regiment	red	black	white	yellow
Ordination of Reissen Infantry Regiment	red	yellow	white	white
Kalixt Poninski Infantry Regiment	red	light green	white	yellow
Lithuanian Lifeguard Grenadier Regiment	red	dark blue	white	yellow
Commander in Chief 1st Infantry Regiment	light blue	white	white	yellow
Commander in Chief 2nd Infantry Regiment	light blue	yellow	yellow	white
Deputy Commander in Chief 1st Infantry Regiment	light blue	black	white	yellow
Deputy Commander in Chief 2nd Infantry Regiment	light blue	red	red	white
Grabowski Infantry Regiment	light blue	yellow	yellow	white
Massalski Infantry Battalion	light blue	red	white	white

The Crown Guard Grenadier Regiment wore brown fur caps with a brass plate; the Witten Grenadier Regiment wore a cap similar to the Prussian fusilier cap, but with a pompon at the top of the front plate as well; the Lithuanian Lifeguard Grenadier Regiment had Russian-style grenadier caps. The Hungarian regiments were dressed in varying ways. The Warsaw Hungarian Company wore light-blue coats with orange-colored distinctions, white undergarments, Hungarian boots, and fusilier caps. The Royal Commander in Chief Hungarian Company had fur caps with a red bag, green coats with four rows of buttons, red collars, pointed cuffs, and skirts; white waistcoats with red loops; and red sabertaches with a green edging and the Polish eagle badge. The Deputy Commander in Chief Hungarian Company was dressed in a similar manner, except that the colors were reversed: cap with a green bag; red coat with green distinctions; white waistcoat with green loopings; and green sabertaches with a red edging. The buttons were white; the former company had yellow ones. The officers of both these corps wore *Flügelmützen*.

All the infantry of the line wore white-laced tricorne hats. The pompons were of white and the distinctive color. The Lanowi Regiment had white vandyked lace. Officers had small epaulettes of the color of the buttons, and Saxon-style sashes and sword knots.

In 1775 the artillery was dressed in green coats with black collars, lapels, and cuffs, white skirt turnbacks, and white undergarments.

The men of all arms wore red cravats; but officers and the front ranks of the cavalry wore black ones. In 1790 the Crown Guard in Warsaw was dressed in the following uniform: hats with a white cockade (the officers' hats were ornamented with broad silver waved lace); red coats with dark blue collar, lapels, cuffs, and skirt lining, and white metal buttons. The officers' epaulettes and braid were silver. The gilded gorget bore the eagle in silver. The undergarments were dull-yellowish. The Lifeguard Dragoon Regiment (Fig. 123e) wore hats with silver waved lace, white cockade, and a white-over-red plume. The jacket and breeches were dull yellow; and the collar, skirt turnbacks, and shabraques, all of which were ornamented with silver, were red. Silver shoulder cords shaped like epaulettes on a red backing, and a carmine pouch belt ornamented with silver, were worn. General officers' uniforms resembled Saxon ones, except that they were purple where the latter were red, and silver where the latter were gold. The undergarments were white. These remained the colors of general officers' uniforms up to 1831.

At the time of the Polish rising (1794) that preceded the Third Partition of Poland (1794–1795), almost the whole army wore a uniform that was clearly derived from the Russian one introduced by Queen Catherine II in 1786. The *kurtka* was almost exactly like the Russian model. The infantry (Fig. 123f) wore a dark blue *kurtka* and trousers. The collar, cuffs, lapels, and the skirts, which were turned back at the front, were of a different color for each regiment. The Stanislaus Potocki Regiment, for example, had light-blue distinctions with yellow metal buttons. The Ozarowski Regiment had orange distinctions and silver lace; the Wodzicki Regiment, orange and gold; Grand Commander in Chief, green and gold; Deputy Commander in Chief, light buff and silver; Fusilier Regiment, black and gold; Lancwy, popinjay green and silver; Czapski, green and silver; Racryski, pink and silver; Dziasynski, pink and gold; Jlinski, light buff and gold; Queen Hedwig, bright yellow and white; Ordination of Ostro, black and gold; and Malczewski, popinjay green and gold. The distinctive headdress took the form of a black cylindrical cap with a peak, and a white metal plate with the Polish eagle on it, on the front. Behind this was a black leather plate coming to a point at the top and edged with lace. A featherlike plume of black or white horsehair, fixed at the back, curled up and forward over the top. Some regiments had black leather equipment; others, white.

From this time, the officers and men of all arms wore white cravats. The officers' sashes were now tied on the left side, not on the right as before. The *konföderatka* (Polish cap) was worn by all officers.

The cavalry wore uniforms of the same syle as the infantry, and also the *konföderatka*. The King's Lancer Regiment (Fig. 123g) was dressed all in blue, with yellow undergarments. The blue shabraques had a yellow edging. The sword belt was black and the pouch belt, white. The mounted National Guard was dressed in a similar fashion, but with bright red substituted for carmine, and with yellow metal buttons. During the popular rising of 1794 and the later revolutions, a great many of the hurriedly raised troops wore the national dress, particularly those armed with bills (*Kosziniere*).

The artillery wore green *kurtkas* with black distinctions and trousers and yellow metal buttons. The headdress was a round broad-brimmed hat with a white feather; officers wore a black *konföderatka*. The pontooneers wore a green *kurtka* and trousers, with white distinctions, yellow metal buttons, and brown leather equipment.

When, after the end of the campaign of 1807, the Army of the Grand Duchy of Warsaw was reorganized, French-style uniforms were generally adopted, although a great number of national peculiarities were retained. The infantry was issued with dark blue coats cut as jackets, with short lapels. The distinctions were of very varied colors: e.g., dark blue collars with red piping; amaranth red collars, lapels, and cuffs (8th Regiment); and also light blue, and dark red, collars and cuffs. The *voltigeurs* frequently wore yellow collars. Fusilier and *voltigeur* companies wore square-topped chacos (Fig. 123h), which were apparently only regulation for the fusiliers. The grenadiers had fur caps with peaks. Grenadiers and *voltigeurs* wore epaulettes similar to those of their French counterparts. The leather equipment was white, as were the undergarments. The National Guard wore a round-topped chaco with a light-blue pompon, red plume, and red cords. The chinscales and the plate were yellow metal. The blue jacket had a light-blue collar, with small white patches at the front. The short lapels and the skirt turnbacks were white, piped with light blue; light-blue cuffs; and white cuff patches piped red. The epaulettes were red; the buttons, yellow metal; and the undergarments and shoulder belts, white. The cuirassiers (14th Regiment) were dressed exactly like the French ones, but were distinguished from the French by having yellow metal shoulder scales with red fringes, and by red shabraques ornamented with yellow lace. The lancers wore dark blue *kurtkas* and trousers with variously colored distinctions and lance pennants. The French-type elite companies, which the lancer regiments had as well, wore fur caps with red cords and plume; the rest of the lancers wore fur caps.

Lancers 1810–1814

REGIMENT	BUTTONS	COLLAR	COLLAR PIPING	LAPELS	LAPEL PIPING	TROUSERS STRIPES
2nd	yellow	red	white	dark blue	yellow	yellow
3rd	yellow	carmine	white	dark blue	white	yellow
6th	yellow	white	carmine	dark blue	carmine	carmine
7th	yellow	yellow	red	dark blue	red	yellow
8th	yellow	red	red	dark blue	red	red
9th	yellow	red	dark blue	dark blue	white	red
11th	yellow	carmine	white	carmine	white	carmine
12th	yellow	carmine	white	dark blue	white	carmine
15th	yellow	carmine	white	carmine	white	carmine
16th, 17th, 18th	yellow	carmine	white	dark blue	carmine	carmine
19th, 20th	yellow	yellow	yellow	dark blue	yellow	yellow
21st	yellow	orange	orange	dark blue	orange	orange

The *chasseurs à cheval* had chacos, green single-breasted jackets with yellow metal buttons, and green trousers with stripes of the distinctive color. These were: 1st Regiment, red; 4th, carmine; and 5th, light orange. The hussars wore light-blue chacos with black drooping plumes, dark blue dolmans and pelisses (with black fur trimming), and carmine collars and cuffs. The 1st Regiment (No. 10) had yellow loopings, the 2nd (No. 13), white. The elite companies of the hussars also wore fur caps. The artillery were dressed entirely in green; with black collar, lapels, and cuffs, all piped red. The buttons were yellow metal. The foot artillery wore chacos and the horse artillery, fur caps.

After the Second Peace of Paris, the kingdom of Poland achieved a certain measure of autonomy, although under the Russian crown. The uniforms accordingly came under Russian influence, and were based on Russian styles. The basic color was blue for the infantry, with yellow distinctions and white metal buttons. The regiments were distinguished by their shoulder straps. Each regiment of the two divisions had distinctions arranged as follows: yellow (1st and 3rd); white (2nd and 4th); light blue (5th and 7th); dark blue, edged with yellow (6th and 8th). On the shoulder straps, the 1st Regiment had a cipher, and the divisional number 1 for the 1st, 2nd, 5th, and 6th Regiments; and 2 for the 3rd, 4th, 7th, and 8th Regiments. In addition, the buttons bore the regimental number. The rifle regiments had similar uniforms, but with black leather equipment, and dark blue collars, lapels, and cuffs, all piped yellow. The guard (Fig. 123i) was distinguished by white guard lace. The chaco was of the Russian type, with the Polish eagle in white on the front. The uniform of the lancers (Fig. 123k) was likewise exactly of Russian style. The *kurtka* and trousers were dark blue. The distinctions and chaco varied from regiment to regiment. The colors of the lance pennants were, at the top: 1st Regiment, carmine; 2nd, dark blue; 3rd, yellow; 4th, blue; and below, white for all four regiments, with a narrow longitudinal stripe of the upper color through the white. The shabraques were of black sheepskin with an edging of the distinctive color: 2nd Lancer Regiment, dark blue; 2nd Light Horse, dark green; Light Horse of the Guard, yellow; with two white stripes around the edge. The officers had the Imperial cipher in the rear corners. The Light Horse Regiment (Fig. 123n) wore green jackets and trousers. The green collar had colored patches at the front. The patches, pointed cuffs, piping, and trouser stripes were all carmine for the 1st Regiment; 2nd, white; 3rd, yellow; and 4th, sky blue. These distinctive colors were also worn by the four lancer regiments. The chaco had a white eagle plate, chinscales, and pompon; buttons, epaulettes, and leather equipment were also white. The shabraques were similar to those worn by the lancers. The Light Horse of the Guard had yellow distinctions, and white lace loops on the collar patches. The shabraques were of dark green cloth. The artillery uniform, which resembled the Prussian one, was made in the old colors.

During the insurrection of 1831, a large number of volunteer corps were raised, of which many wore bizarre uniforms. For instance, the Sandomierz Volunteers formed by Grotthus (Fig. 123m) wore fur caps with a white metal eagle plate and yellow metal chinscales, green knee-length coats with black collar and cuffs and red piping, yellow metal buttons, green epaulettes; green trousers with red stripes; natural-colored waistbelt with a small pouch at the front, and with cartridge loops around it. Two pistols and a dagger were worn at the front of the belt. Cartridge loops were worn Circassian fashion on the breast. The knapsack straps were black. The saber was worn on slings. The Podlasie Volunteers formed under Colonel Kuszell (Fig. 123o) wore green *konföderatkas*, with a white metal oval plate in front bearing a cross, with a skull and crossbones below. The feather plume was green over red. The long gray coat had green collar, cuffs, and epaulettes. The gray trousers had green piping. Gloves were black. Waistbelt, pistols, dagger, and cartridge loops on the breast were worn, as described above. The Cracow Billmen wore red *konföderatkas* and long blue coats with carmine collars, cuffs, and piping. There were carmine sloping pocket flaps on the breast. The buttons were white metal; the trousers, blue; and the leather equipment, black. The Kalisch Volunteer Lancers wore long black single-breasted coats with light-blue collars, pointed cuffs, and piping; carmine waistbelt; white buttons; and white leather equipment. The trousers were black with light-blue stripes. The lancer cap had a light-blue top part. The lancer pennants were carmine over light blue. The National Guard was dressed in long single-breasted coats with red collars and cuffs; dark blue trousers, and *konföderatkas*; and black leather equipment. During the rebellion of 1863, many attempts were made to dress individual corps alike; but generally there was no uniformity to speak of.

REPUBLIC OF POLAND

With the outbreak of the Great War, there arose the possibility of an independent Poland, and a number of legions were formed, under Austrian command, mainly in the Austrian part of Poland. These fought on the side of the Central Powers. Marshal Pilsudski was closely connected with their formation and organization. The uniform, made at first from Austrian and later from German cloth, bore a strong resemblance to the Polish national styles from the beginning. Characteristic of these troops was the lancer-caplike headdress: either a cap with a square top, or with a raised top like a lancer cap (Figs. 124 a,b). The collar patches and piping were red for all, with white metal buttons; rank was indicated by white or silver stars on the collar patches. From an early date, the white Polish eagle, in cloth or metal, was worn on the upper part of the cap. The distinctive lace on the collar patches, which was to continue to be a distinguishing feature of Polish troops and which dated from the Napoleonic Wars, was introduced. It consisted of a vandyke along the outer edge of the collar, in worsted or metal lace, which was often red, but more usually white.

In the course of the war a Polish legion was formed in France under General Haller. It was dressed in the normal French horizon blue uniform. Here, too, a square-topped cap, with no peak for other ranks, was worn (Fig. 124c). The piping was dark blue (light green for rifles). The rank badges were of French style; and the officers wore French kepis.

After the end of the war and the Treaty of Versailles, the newly organized Polish army was dressed in the uniforms formerly worn, so that items of Austrian, German, and Russian styles were worn in colorful confusion. By this time, the universal distinctions of the armed forces were the white Polish eagle above a semicircular shield, on the cap, and the lace on the edges of the collar, in white or silver according to rank.

The cavalry had no collar patches, but had small silk-embroidered lance pennants at the ends of the collar, of collars wholly of the distinctive color. Very frequently at that time, officers of cavalry regiments wore field gray lancer jackets with carmine, blue, red, or white piping, wholly colored collars, and cap band, or a collar of basic color piped in the distinctive color with small silk-embroidered lance pennants at the ends (Fig. 124d). The dark blue trousers had triple stripes of the distinctive color. Rank was denoted by the trefoil-ended silver shoulder cords, piped in *Waffenfarbe*, with gold stars on them.

In November 1919 the first regulations for the army uniform were promulgated. The dress remained basically the same up to 1939, except that the distinctions of specific units differed from those given in the table below. Thus general officers and

Fig. 124. Republic of Poland.

a, b: cavalry and infantry of the Polish legion in the Austrian army. c: infantry of Haller's Legion. d: officer, lancers. e, h: infantry. f: infantry officer. g: cavalryman.

the general staff wore pomegranate-red collar patches, double-scalloped at the end, and piped in carmine; the infantry had pomegranate red with yellow piping; light horse, carmine with white piping; mounted rifles, carmine with dark green piping; tartar cavalry, carmine with light-blue piping; motorized troops, black with yellow piping; transport corps, chocolate brown with sky blue piping. The lancer regiments had all-carmine collars.

During the 1920s a slightly different uniform, with altered *Waffenfarben*, was introduced. It continued to be worn throughout the 1930s. The basic color of the jacket, which was similar in cut and style for all arms, was gray-green. The men's jacket had a stand-and-fall collar, a row of five buttons, and sloping slit pockets, with flap and button, in the front skirts. The officers' jacket had a row of six buttons, and patch pockets on the breast and skirts, the former having pleats. All ranks had round cuffs, closed by a small button at the hindarm seam. The trousers were of basic color without piping, and the men's puttees were also of basic color. Officers and mounted troops had black footwear; the equipment was of natural-colored brown leather. The greatcoat had a broad turndown collar and deep roll cuffs, with a loop for fastening them more tightly, a row of six buttons, point shoulder straps, and a half belt with two buttons at the back. The officers' greatcoats were double-breasted. French steel helmets were worn up to 1936 (Fig. 124e), when a new pattern was introduced (Fig. 124h). The fore-and-aft field service cap was of basic color without piping, and had the Polish eagle on the front of the flap in white embroidery for rank and file, and silver for all others (Fig. 124g). Also characteristic of the Polish army was the forage cap (Fig. 124f). It had a square top, which was inclined sharply down to the rear, and a very long peak, of black leather, which was bound with white metal for officers. The top and sides were of basic color, and the band was of *Waffenfarbe*, as given in the next table. The only exception to this was the British-style forage cap worn by the light horse regiments. For evening wear, officers had a dull silver waistbelt with a silver buckle, and colored trousers, with triple stripes for officers, and with a broad colored stripe for NCOs. The universal distinction of the Polish army was the silver or white lace vandyke on the front and lower edges of the collar. The arm of service was denoted by the embellishments on the collar. The infantry had large colored collar patches, double-scalloped at the rear, frequently piped in a different color; mounted troops had small silk-embroidered lace pennants. The number of the regiment or unit was embroidered in silver on the coat and greatcoat shoulder straps for all except the rank and file, who had theirs painted in yellow.

The mounted troops wore small pennants at the ends of the greatcoat collar, as on the jacket. Other troops had a band of the color of the collar patches across the corners of the collar; if the collar patches were piped in another color, this band had that piping along the upper edge of the band. There was no vandyked lace on the collar of the greatcoat.

The Mountain Troops (21st and 22nd Divisions) wore a swastika of fir twigs, in white metal, on their collar patches. Their headdress was a round felt hat with an eagle's feather on the left side, and bore the same device as on the collar. Regiments that perpetuated the traditions of the old legions bore appropriate badges: the Polish eagle, numerals, or similar devices, on their shoulder straps or collar patches. Officers of the general staff wore the uniforms of their former arms, with a silver eagle with outspread wings across the corners of the collar, and double silver aiguillettes on the right shoulder. General officers wore similar badges on the collar.

The colored distinctions, which had hardly changed since the introduction of the uniform, are given in the following table as they were in 1935.

| ARM OF SERVICE | COLLAR PATCHES | | CAP BAND | WALKING-OUT DRESS TROUSERS | |
	COLOR	PIPING		COLOR	STRIPES
General officers	dark blue velvet	carmine	gray-green	gray-green	dark blue
Infantry	dark blue	dark yellow	dark blue	dark blue	dark yellow
Rifle Battalions	dark blue	green	dark blue	dark blue	dark yellow
Field Artillery	dark green velvet	black	dark green velvet	dark green	red
Heavy Artillery	dark green velvet	red	dark green velvet	dark green	red
Antiaircraft Artillery	dark green velvet	dark yellow	dark green velvet	dark green	red
Engineers	black velvet	carmine	black velvet	green	carmine
Signals Troops	black velvet	light blue	black velvet	green	light blue

| MOUNTED TROOPS | SWALLOW-TAILED LANCE PENNANT (COLLAR) | | CAP BAND | WALKING-OUT TROUSERS | |
	TOP AND BOTTOM	CENTER		COLOR	STRIPES
1st Light Horse	silver	carmine	carmine	dark blue	carmine; white center piping
2nd Light Horse	silver	carmine	white	dark blue	white
3rd Light Horse	silver	yellow	yellow	dark blue	yellow
1st Lancers	carmine, white	—	carmine	dark blue	carmine
2nd Lancers	white, dark blue	—	white	dark blue	white
3rd Lancers	yellow, white	—	yellow	dark blue	yellow

(continued)

351

MOUNTED TROOPS	SWALLOW-TAILED LANCE PENNANT (COLLAR)		CAP BAND	WALKING-OUT TROUSERS	
	TOP AND BOTTOM	CENTER		COLOR	STRIPES
4th Lancers	light blue, white	—	light blue	dark blue	light blue
5th Lancers	red-brown, white	—	red-brown	dark blue	red-brown
6th Lancers	light blue	white	light blue	dark blue	light blue
7th Lancers	carmine, white, carmine	—	carmine	dark blue	carmine; white center piping
8th Lancers	dark yellow	—	dark yellow	dark blue	dark yellow
9th Lancers	carmine, white	white, carmine	carmine	dark blue	carmine; white center piping
10th Lancers	carmine, white	white, dark blue	carmine	dark blue	carmine
11th Lancers	carmine	white	white	dark blue	white
12th Lancers	carmine	dark blue	white	dark blue	carmine
13th Lancers	pink	light blue	pink	dark blue	pink
14th Lancers	yellow	white	yellow	dark blue	yellow
15th Lancers	white, red	—	red	dark blue	red
16th Lancers	dark blue, white	red	white	dark blue	white
17th Lancers	white, yellow	red	yellow	dark blue	yellow
18th Lancers	white, light blue	red	light blue	dark blue	light blue
19th Lancers	dark blue, white, dark blue	—	dark blue	dark blue	white
20th Lancers	carmine	white, dark blue	carmine	dark blue	carmine
21st Lancers	light blue	yellowish-white	light blue	dark blue	light blue
22nd Lancers	white, carmine, white	—	white	dark blue	white
23rd Lancers	orange, white	white, orange	orange	dark blue	orange
24th Lancers	white	yellow	white	dark blue	white
25th Lancers	white, red	light blue	red	dark blue	red
26th Lancers	pink, white	light blue	pink	dark blue	pink
27th Lancers	yellow, white	white	yellow	dark blue	yellow
1st Mounted Rifles	green, carmine	—	carmine	dark blue	carmine
2nd Mounted Rifles	green, carmine	light blue	carmine	dark blue	carmine
3rd Mounted Rifles	green, carmine	yellow	carmine	dark blue	carmine
4th Mounted Rifles	green, carmine	white	carmine	dark blue	carmine
5th Mounted Rifles	green, white	carmine	white	dark blue	white
6th Mounted Rifles	green, white	—	white	dark blue	white
7th Mounted Rifles	green, white	yellow	white	dark blue	white
8th Mounted Rifles	green, white	light blue	white	dark blue	white
9th Mounted Rifles	green, yellow	carmine	yellow	dark blue	yellow
10th Mounted Rifles	green, yellow	white	yellow	dark blue	yellow
Horse Artillery	black, red velvet	—	black velvet	dark blue	red
Mounted Pioneers	red, black	—	red	dark blue	red
Transport Corps	light blue	carmine	light blue	dark blue	light blue with carmine center piping
Armored Troops	pointed pennant, black, orange velvet	—	orange velvet	dark blue	orange

Badges denoting rank and grade were worn on the pointed shoulder straps of the jacket and greatcoat, the cap band, and on the collar patches. General officers wore a broad-patterned vandyked silver lace around the cap band, across the outer ends of the shoulder straps, on the front and lower edges of the collar patches, and on the jacket and greatcoat cuffs, with the silver Polish eagle with spread wings across the front corners of the collar patches. Field officers had double silver braid around the top edge of the cap band and across the outer ends of the shoulder straps. Company officers had only one row of silver braid around the upper edge of the cap band. Officers had a double silver vandyked cord on the front and lower edges of their collars; a white metal edging to their cap peaks; and silver braid running diagonally from corner to corner of the square tops. Within all grades, the individual ranks were denoted by one to three five-pointed silver stars, worn on the front of the cap band and on the shoulder straps (Fig. 124f). NCOs had narrow silver lace, edged with red, on their shoulder straps, and one to two small silver lace chevrons, piped red, point down, on the cap band. The rank and file were distinguished by one to three silver lace stripes, piped red, across the outer ends of the shoulder straps; and the same, in reduced size, on the cap band. The vandyk at the ends of the other ranks' collars was of single narrow silver lace.

PORTUGAL

Cockade: at first blue with a red ring; from 1821, blue with a white ring; and from 1910, green with a red ring

I. INFANTRY AND RIFLES

Information on the dress of the Portuguese army in the eighteenth century is sparse. The uniforms tended, however, to be rather out of date in style. Thus in 1740 the infantry wore long coats with very large cuffs and a row of buttons right down the front, and a very large broad-brimmed tricorne hat. The grenadiers had tall fur caps with no plate. From an early date the coat was dark blue for the whole army, with predominantly white or yellow undergarments. Officers were denoted by crimson silk sashes, a distinction of rank they retained in full dress up to the 1930s. By about 1800 the infantry uniform fairly closely resembled the prevailing continental fashions (Fig. 125a). The distinctions were as follows.

REGIMENT	COLLAR	LAPELS	BUTTONS AND EPAULETTES	SKIRTS	WAISTCOATS	PLUME
Lippe	red	blue[1]	white	white	white	white
Albuquerque	blue; white cuffs	white	yellow	white	white	red
Minas	red[2]	red[1]	white	white	white	white
1st Armada	red[2]	red	yellow	red	red	red
2nd Armada	red[2]	red	white	red	red	white
Cascaes	blue	blue	yellow	blue	white	carmine
de Setubal	yellow	blue[1]	white	yellow	white	red
Peniche	white[2]	blue[1]; white lace	yellow	white	white	red
1st Elvas	red	red	yellow	blue	blue	white
2nd Elvas	red[2]	red[1]; white loops	white	red	white	white
Colonial, Rio de Janeiro	red	none; white loops	white	white	white	chacos
Serpa	red	yellow	white	red	yellow	red
1st Olivenca	orange	orange; white lace	white	red	white	light blue
2nd Olivenca	orange; white cuffs	orange; white lace	white	red	white	red
Campo Major	blue[2]	blue[1]; white loops	white	red	red	black
Castello de Vide	blue; white cuffs	blue	yellow	red	white	—
Colonial Moira, Rio de Janeiro	yellow	none	white	yellow	yellow	white *Kaskett*
Lagos	white	white	white	white	blue	red
Faro	red	blue	yellow	blue	white	—

(continued)

354

REGIMENT	COLLAR	LAPELS	BUTTONS AND EPAULETTES	SKIRTS	WAISTCOATS	PLUME
1st Porto	red	red	white	yellow	yellow	—
2nd Porto	blue	yellow	white	red	red	—
Vianna	yellow; white cuffs	yellow	yellow	red	white	—
Valença	yellow	yellow	white	red	blue	—
Almeida	red	red	white	red	yellow	—
Gena Major	yellow	yellow	white	yellow	yellow	—
Chares	white	red	yellow	white	red	—
Bragança Colonial	red	white	yellow	red	white	—
Bragança	light yellow	light yellow	white	white	white	—

¹lapels edged with lace of button color; with two or three loops below
²cuffs edged with lace, and with lace loops, of the button color

In the period 1809–1814 the infantry distinctions were as follows.

REGIMENT	COLLAR	CUFFS	EDGING
1	blue	white	white
2	blue	white	red
3	blue	white	yellow
4	blue	red	white
5	blue	red	red
6	blue	red	yellow
7	blue	yellow	white
8	blue	yellow	red
9	blue	yellow	yellow
10	blue	light blue	white
11	blue	light blue	red
12	blue	light blue	yellow
13	white	white	white
14	white	white	red
15	white	white	yellow
16	red	red	white
17	red	red	red
18	red	red	yellow
19	yellow	yellow	white
20	yellow	yellow	red
21	yellow	yellow	yellow
22	light blue	light blue	white
23	light blue	light blue	red
24	light blue	light blue	yellow

All wore blue coats, with the exception of the two armada regiments, which had green coats and breeches. The breeches were blue for the other regiments, with the following exceptions: Colonial Moira, 2nd Porto, and Almeida, yellow; 1st Porto, red; Valença, white. The small bicorne hat was worn across the head, sloping forward. The binding, and the tassels depending from the corners, were of button color.

Fig. 125. Portugal, 1802–1890.

a, c: infantry officers. b: cavalryman of the Alcantara Regiment. d: cavalryman of the
Alorgna Legion. e, i: infantry. f, m: lancers. g: light
cavalry. h: rifles. k: artillery. l: engineer officer.

In 1809 the infantry adopted short single-breasted blue jackets with nine yellow
metal buttons, blue or white breeches, and black half gaiters, and British-type chacos
with cockade and white plume at the front, with the regimental number on it. The
leather equipment, which was worn crossed, was white. Piping ran around the top
and front of the collar, down the front and around the bottom of the jacket, and
along the skirt edges, and also around the shoulder straps (which were blue for all)
and the round cuffs. A hunting horn was worn on the chaco and green fringes on the
shoulders. The rifles wore a brown uniform and had a small horn badge above the
chaco plate, and a green plume. The first three battalions had brown collars, the 4th
through 6th had theirs of the distinctive color. These were: 1st and 4th Battalions,
blue; 2nd and 5th, red; and 3rd and 6th, yellow. Leather equipment was black.

The National Regiments (auxiliary troops) were not uniformly dressed. They,
like the other units, wore many items of British provenance.

In 1814 a double-breasted jacket with epaulettes was introduced. The latter were
white for fusiliers, red for grenadiers, and green for light infantry. As time passed,
the British influence became more marked. The chacos had larger tops and a more
pronounced curve at the sides. The cuffs were changed to blue, with colored French-
type slashes. Gray trousers were worn.

In 1835 the rifles were dressed in brown jackets with red collars, black lapels,
black cuffs with red patches, black epaulettes with yellow crescents, and brown
trousers, and black leather equipment.

In 1848 single-breasted jackets were again taken into wear by the infantry. The chaco became more conical in shape (Fig. 125a). The distinctions remained as before, i.e., with differently colored collar and cuff patches in the infantry; purple with white piping for the grenadiers. Officers adopted gold lace loops on their cuffs; field officers had crowns on their epaulettes. In the 1860s the chacos, following French fashions, became lower and lower. Single-breasted tunics were introduced, which at first were dark blue for the infantry, and later brown, as for the rifles; the infantry had red distinctions and white leather equipment; the rifles, black distinctions and black leather equipment. The blue-black trousers had piping; white ticken ones were worn on service. The chaco plume was black for infantry, dark green for rifles (Fig. 125h). About 1885 a Prussian-style spiked helmet with yellow metal plate, with a short black hair plume for full dress, was introduced throughout the army. In 1895 the basic color of the infantry coat was changed again to dark blue; with dark blue pointed cuffs and shoulder straps with red piping. The buttons were, and remained, of yellow metal (Fig. 125i). The officers' undress tunic had broad black lace around the collar and cuffs, with six rows of similar lace across the front. After 1900 the spiked helmet was abolished and superseded by a small low-crowned kepi, with a white cover for wear on service and in the colonies. The double-breasted greatcoat was dark blue—brown for rifles—with collar patches of the distinctive color bearing the regimental number.

The service dress that was introduced during the Great War was of British style, but in gray-blue cloth; with it were worn early-British-pattern steel helmets and forage caps (Fig. 126a). The bronze arm-of-service badge on the cap band and ends of the collar consisted of two crossed rifles. The men wore the regimental number in black on the upper arm. The waistbelt, pouches, and straps were of gray-green webbing. Brown leather equipment was worn from 1920. The men's jacket was made with a stand-and-fall collar (Fig. 126b); and a fore-and-aft service cap of basic color with the cockade on the front was introduced. Instead of the normal service jacket, officers frequently wore a four-button jacket with patch pockets. At the same time, a uniform for full dress and evening dress, of the same style throughout the army, was introduced for officers. It consisted of a dark blue tunic with a row of eight buttons, gold passants, and shoulder scales with fringes; black collar and cuffs; with red scalloped collar and cuff patches. The arm-of-service badge in gold was worn on the collar, and also on the dark blue forage caps. These had red piping around the top, a red band with the national cockade on the front, and a gold chinstrap (Fig. 126c). The peak was black, with a gold lace edging for field officers. The trousers were light blue with double red stripes. NCOs had a somewhat simplified version of the same uniform, with broad stripes on their trousers. In 1935 a new-pattern steel helmet was introduced, bearing the arm-of-service badge; the service jacket had collar patches and cuff piping in *Waffenfarbe* (Fig. 126d).

II. CAVALRY

In 1800 the uniform of the cavalry consisted of a blue jacket, yellow leather breeches, long boots, and a white metal cuirass. The leather equipment was black in some regiments, red in others. The Caés and Moira regiments wore sabertaches.

The several distinctions are given in the following table.

REGIMENT	COLLAR, CUFFS, AND SKIRTS	SASH	HEADDRESS	LACE LOOPS ABOVE CUFFS
Caés	carmine; white loops	crimson with white edges	bicorne; white lace; red plume	—
Alcantara	pink; white loops on collar	pink with white edges and vandyk	crested helmet with white metal mounts	3 white chevron-shaped loops
Mecklenburg	light blue	red with two narrow stripes	black helmet with red crest extending down at rear	3 white V loops
Elvas	red	red, blue edges, and center stripe	bicorne; yellow lace; white plume	4 yellow chevron-shaped loops
Evora	white	yellow-blue-yellow	black peakless helmet with yellow comb and red crest	—
Moira	yellow	as for Mecklenburg	bicorne	—
Olivença	blue	white-crimson-black	chaco with white lines and crimson feather	—
Almeida	light blue	black, white edges piped light blue	white metal helmet with red crest	—
Castello Branco	orange	as for Mecklenburg	black helmet with white comb and crimson crest	3 white chevron-shaped loops
Miranda	brick red	brick red with white edges	black *Kaskett* with red feather rising from rear	—
Chaves	carmine	carmine	bicorne with red feather	—
Bragança	blue	as for Mecklenburg	black helmet with red feather rising from rear	—

The Legion of Light Troops was dressed differently. Its uniform consisted of a short blue coatee with black collar and black pointed cuffs, with loops of yellow lace on the collar and on the breast. The collar and cuffs were edged with yellow and had yellow chevron-shaped loops. They also had cylindrical chacos with yellow cords, white breeches, and hussar boots.

In 1809 the uniforms, which were supplied from Britain, were simplified. The twelve regiments wore blue uniforms with the following distinctions: 1–3, white; 4–6, red; 7–9, yellow; and 10–12, blue. They wore helmets with combs and a crest; and yellow metal shoulder scales. After the Napoleonic Wars, the uniforms and equipment were modeled exactly on British styles. Up to 1837 the lancers wore dark blue *kurtkas* with two rows of buttons close together running straight down the front; red collar with yellow lace loops; red pointed cuffs edged with yellow lace; yellow metal shoulder scales; gray trousers with red triple stripes; white leather equipment; and a yellow girdle with two dark blue stripes. The headdress was a chaco of British type, with red binding and a black drooping plume. The stripes on the officers' girdles were carmine. The light cavalry had the same uniform, but with light-blue distinctions and chacos with yellow lace around the edge, yellow metal chin chain, and a red tuft (red plume for officers).

NO.	COLLAR AND CUFFS	SKIRTS AND LINING	DESIGNATION
1	red	red	lancers
2	carmine	carmine	lancers
3	white	white	light cavalry
4	light blue	light blue	light cavalry
5	orange	orange	light cavalry
6	yellow	yellow	light cavalry
7	red	white	lancers
8	carmine	white	lancers

In 1837 the number and distinctions of the cavalry regiments were altered; but the coats remained dark blue, with yellow metal buttons and insignia.

In 1848 the 7th and 8th Regiments also were turned into light cavalry. At the same time, the uniforms were changed. The lancers retained their *kurtkas* but without the edging to the cuffs; and the trousers were made with two broad stripes, of the same color as the collar. The light cavalry wore a single-breasted jacket with no lace on the collar and cuffs. The cavalry headdresses were made smaller; the light cavalry had black plumes. The metal shoulder scales were replaced by worsted epaulettes. All officers discontinued wearing the girdle, and adopted a carmine silk sash in its place. The distinctions then were as follows.

REGIMENT	COLLAR	CUFFS	PIPING ON SKIRT TURNBACKS
1st Lancers	carmine	blue	carmine
2nd Lancers	carmine	carmine	carmine
3rd Light Cavalry	white	white	yellow
4th Light Cavalry	white	red	yellow
5th Light Cavalry	red	light blue	yellow
6th Light Cavalry	red	red	yellow
7th Light Cavalry	light blue	light blue	yellow
8th Light Cavalry	light blue	red	yellow

1st–2nd Lancers: yellow girdle with 2 longitudinal carmine stripes
3rd–8th Light Cavalry: yellow girdle with 2 longitudinal dark blue stripes

About 1855 the cavalry jacket was made with a front like a lancer jacket with lapels. The lancers adopted carmine distinctions with yellow piping; the light cavalry, red, with white piping (Figs. 125f,g). The girdle was abolished. The small lance pennants were yellow. The light cavalry chaco was made with a dark blue cloth covering, with white lace around the top. In 1890 the cavalry wore a tunic with a row of nine yellow metal buttons; with red collar and pointed cuffs, and red piping around the skirts; yellow metal shoulder scales; white leather equipment; blue-black trousers with red stripes; and spiked helmets with a yellow metal plate. The 1st and 2nd Lancer Regiments had white helmet plumes; the 3rd–12th Light Cavalry Regiments, black ones. At the ends of their collars the lancers wore a rectangle of yellow worsted lace; the light cavalry had black lace, bearing the regimental number. The small lance pennants were light blue and white (Fig. 125m). Field and company officers had gold, and black silk, collar lace respectively, bearing the arm-of-service badge: two crossed lances, or crossed sabers, respectively, in a laurel wreath. Their six-button jacket was edged with broad black silk lace all around and had six horizontal loops on the front, and a trefoil above the cuffs. After 1900 the spiked helmet was abolished and superseded by a dark blue kepi with red band. The dark blue double-breasted greatcoat worn in the 1930s had red collar patches.

On the gray-blue service dress, the arm-of-service badges took the form of two crossed lances, or sabers, with the number below. The officers' evening dress uniform had red collar, cuff patches, cap band, and piping; and at the ends of the collar a gold or black silk rectangular lace loop with a similarly colored cord binding, which formed a loop at the rear.

III. ARTILLERY AND ENGINEERS

In the eighteenth century the uniforms were usually blue with black distinctions. About 1800 the coats and waistcoats were blue, with red skirt turnbacks.

REGIMENT	COLLAR, CUFFS, AND LAPELS	BUTTONS AND EPAULETTES	BREECHES
Lissabon[1]	black with white edges	white	blue
Estremoz	black; blue cuffs	white	blue with white stripes
Algarve	blue[2]	white	blue
Porto	black[3]	white	black

[1] red hat plume
[2] white lace loops on front
[3] 2 white lace loops below lapels

In 1808 an all-blue uniform with yellow metal buttons was introduced. After the Napoleonic Wars, the uniform, double-breasted from that time, had a red collar (with yellow lace and yellow grenades), and cuff piping, skirts, skirt edging, and broad trousers stripes all in red. The same patterns of chaco were worn as in the infantry. The plume was red, and the leather equipment, white.

In 1848 a long-skirted coat was introduced for the foot artillery. The earlier distinctions were retained. When the tunic was introduced, that for the artillery was dark blue, with a single row of yellow metal buttons—two rows for officers. The collar, shoulder straps, and the piping on the pointed cuffs were red, with yellow grenades on the collar; the blue-black trousers had a single broad red stripe; officers had double stripes. The equipment was of white leather. The plume on the helmet was red (Fig. 125k). The arm-of-service badge on the service dress of the field artillery consisted of two crossed cannon barrels; that of the foot artillery, a bursting grenade. The post–Great War dress uniform was like that of the infantry, but had an all-red collar.

Engineers: In 1835 the officers wore infantry uniform with white cuffs and skirt turnbacks, black velvet collar and cuffs with a narrow gold lace edging, and dark blue trousers with white piping. The men's chacos had a white worsted plume, with the arm-of-service badge—a tower—instead of the regimental number, and yellow metal buttons. After the introduction of the tunic, the piping was changed to red, and medium-width yellow lace (gold for officers) was added on the front and bottom edges of the collar. The helmet plume was black issuing from red at the top. The trousers were as for the artillery (Fig. 125l). The arm-of-service badge remained a tower, on the service uniform. The evening dress uniform of the 1930s had a black velvet collar with red piping, and gold lace on the front and lower edges; with the arm-of-service badge in gold at the ends of the collar. The cuff patches were of black velvet, piped red, as was the cap band.

IV. GENERAL OFFICERS AND GENERAL STAFF; DISTINCTIONS OF RANK

In 1855 the uniform worn by general officers consisted of a long dark blue coat, with dark blue collar and cuffs with rich gold embroidery, and white skirt turnbacks; hat with gold lace loop and black plumage; dark blue trousers with gold lace; and gold epaulettes. Rank was indicated by silver stars on the epaulettes, and by varying embroidery on the collar and cuffs. On service, a dark blue coat without embroidery was worn, and a hat with no feathers. With the introduction of the tunic, the collar and cuffs were changed to red. From 1890 general officers wore dark blue double-breasted tunics with red collar and cuffs edged with waved gold lace, dark blue trousers with double broad red stripes; gold epaulettes with stiff

Fig. 126. Portugal, 1917–1935.
a, b, d: infantry.
c: officer in dress uniform.

bullions with two or three silver stars on the crescent, and a silver crown on the strap. The helmet had a silver device in front, and a gilt plate, and light-blue-over-white feather plume. The sash was carmine and gold. With the everyday uniform was worn a dark blue straight-sided kepi with two broad gold lace bands around the top. The dark blue dolman had black lace loopings and edging, and a red collar with the rank stars at the ends, and embroidered laurel leaves on the pointed dark blue cuffs. After the abolition of the helmet, a black hat was worn, with white feather plumage, and from 1911, a green and red silk rectangle on the right side, with a gold loop. The service dress cap badge was a large silver five-pointed star; three similar stars were worn on the collar and cuffs. There was only one rank of general officer. The colored evening dress uniform worn after the Great War was similar to the prewar uniform.

General Staff: In 1855 they had a dark blue coat with green velvet collar and cuffs, with gold lace around the edges. The hat had a white and red feather plume. In 1890 a dark blue double-breasted tunic with red collar and pointed cuffs was worn, with blue-black trousers with broad red stripes. The helmet plume was red over white. A gold double lace loop, with three silver oak leaves on it, was worn as an arm-of-service distinction on the collar of the tunic; this was also worn on the service dress uniform, and on the colored evening dress uniform after 1918. The latter

361

uniform had a royal blue velvet collar, cuff patches, and cap band. The trousers were light blue, with two dark blue stripes.

From 1847 the several ranks of officers were denoted by gold stripes along the top of the cuffs: junior lieutenant, one narrow stripe; senior lieutenant, two narrow; captain, one medium; lieutenant colonel, two; and colonel, three medium-width stripes. From the same time, the ranks of the NCOs and men were indicated by one to four chevrons, point down, of the color of the piping, worn on the upper arm. The rifles had dark green chevrons.

With the introduction of service dress, the number and arrangement of the officers' rank stripes were altered, to horizontal stripes, 5 centimeters long, one to three narrow ones for company officers, with a medium-width one above for field officers. On the colored evening dress uniform, the stripes ran around the cuff, below the patches. NCOs' stripes were black on the service dress uniform, and on the summer uniform were worn across the shoulder straps. Warrant officers wore officers'-pattern service dress and full-dress uniforms, without any rank lace, but instead had the coat of arms within a circle, all in gold, on the lower arms.

From the eighteenth century up to the 1930s, all officers wore a carmine sash with the tassels tied on the left side, around the waist, and a gold sword knot.

RUMANIA

Cockade: blue-gold-red

The principalities of Moldavia and Wallachia, independent from 1830, were united into one principality in 1861, and became a kingdom in 1866.

I. INFANTRY, RIFLES, *DOROBANZE* AND BORDER TROOPS, AND GUARDS

Moldavia: In 1830 the infantry was dressed in long dark blue coats with a row of yellow metal buttons (Fig. 127a). The collar was edged red all around, as were the round cuffs and front of the coat, with red lace ornamentation, and gold for officers. Dark blue trousers with red piping, and black leather equipment, were worn. The chacos had a red bag on the right side. The greatcoat was dark gray. In 1835 the lace was abolished, and the dark blue round cuffs were changed to Brandenburg-type ones, with red piping. The officers adopted gold guard lace on the collar and cuff patches, and gold sashes with tassels on the left. In 1847 single-breasted dark blue coatees with red collars and cuff patches were introduced. The trousers were gray-blue with red piping; the helmet had a Russian-style spike, and yellow metal plate in the shape of an ox-head, and a black horsehair plume. The leather equipment was worn crossed (Fig. 127b). In 1854, a dark blue tunic was adopted, with red collar, Brandenburg cuffs, shoulder straps bearing the battalion number in black, and piping; with white waistbelt equipment; and dark blue trousers with red piping. The officers' guard lace was abolished.

Fig. 127. Rumania—
Infantry, 1830, 1850.
a: Moldavia. b: Wallachia.

Wallachia, 1830–1861: Dark blue single-breasted tunics and trousers were worn, with yellow piping around the collar, Brandenburg cuffs, and skirt pockets down the front of the coat (Fig. 127b). The shoulder straps were red for the 1st Regiment; 2nd, yellow; and 3rd, light blue. Officers had guard lace on the cuff patches; gold epaulettes; and sashes with the tassels on the left side. The chacos were ball-topped at first, but from 1847, tapered to the top, with a yellow metal plate. The border guards wore brown coats with green piping and white metal buttons; low-crowned fur caps with a green bag; black leather equipment; and *Opanken*.

United Principalities: In 1861 the infantry adopted a dark blue single-breasted tunic with yellow metal buttons and red piping. The collar and pointed cuffs were of basic color with red piping; and red wings were worn on the shoulders. The dark blue cloth chaco had red edging and side piping, with the numeral in red on the front, and cockade, red loop, and double pompon; officers had gold instead of red ornamentation, and gold epaulettes and gorgets; and gold, blue, and red embroidered sashes. The dark blue trousers had red piping. The leather equipment was black.

In 1868 dark blue shoulder straps with red piping and numerals were added to the coat; the trousers were changed to dark gray; and the chaco was superseded by a dark blue kepi with red piping, and a horizontal peak. The gray double-breasted greatcoat had red spearhead-shaped collar patches, and red piping on the collar and roll cuffs.

In 1878 the coat was made with rectangular red collar patches, red shoulder straps and pointed cuffs; and a red band was added to the kepi. In 1891 a dark blue turndown collar with red spearhead-shaped patches, and piping, was added to the jacket, and the shoulder straps and pointed cuffs were changed to basic color with red piping. The full-dress headdress was a soft fur cap inclining to the right at the top, with the royal cipher and crown on the front, and the cockade and an eagle's feather on the left. In 1916 the service dress uniform, which had been on trial since 1912, was adopted. The basic color was bluish-gray to begin with, and from 1917, a lightish blue. The men's jackets had slit pockets, rounded shoulder straps, pointed cuffs, and a stand-and-fall collar. The officers' jacket was single-breasted, with patch pockets on the breast and skirts. All had yellow metal buttons. The arm of service was denoted by the spearhead-shaped collar patches, the collar piping, and the numeral on the shoulder strap, in either *Waffenfarbe* or the regimental color—red for the infantry. Equipment was of brown leather; the trousers were gray, piped in *Waffenfarbe*, and were worn with gray puttees. The field gray greatcoat was made in the former style. The men wore a soft cap, high at the front and back, and low in the middle, with red piping and a numeral on the front above the cloth peak (Fig. 129a). In addition, from 1916, French-pattern steel helmets were worn, with the crowned royal cipher on the front. The officers had a stiff gray kepi with gray top and side piping, with the cockade on the front and the cipher below. In 1921 the basic color of the service dress was changed to khaki; but it was of the same style, and had the same insignia, as before. In 1931 a British-type peaked service dress cap with a red band and khaki peak was introduced, with one and two rows of oakleaf embroidery for field officers and general officers respectively, around the peak. The regimental number, within a crowned oakleaf wreath for officers, was placed on the front. In addition to the service jacket, officers had another khaki jacket, with which a khaki-colored or white shirt was worn.

From 1861 to the 1930s the uniform of the rifles consisted of a brown double-breasted coat, piped green all around, with yellow metal buttons, pointed green cuffs, with a green hunting horn (gold for officers) on the brown, green-piped stand-and-fall collar. The dark gray trousers had green piping and were worn with white gaiters, which were later abolished. The equipment was of black leather. The round black leather hat was tacked up at the sides, with the cockade and a green cock's feather plume on the right, and the cipher in front. The service uniform of the rifles was like that of the infantry. The distinctive color was green. The men wore a green hunting horn in place of the patch on the collar (Fig. 128b).

From 1866 the border guards were dressed like the infantry, their distinctive color being light green. In 1912 they wore spiked helmets with a yellow metal plate.

In 1870 the *Dorobanze* (auxiliary infantry) wore the infantry uniform, with light-blue distinctions for officers. To begin with, the men wore white jackers with light-blue collar, cuffs, and stripes down the front; white trousers; *Opankan*; and fur caps. From 1879 they wore infantry uniform with light-blue distinctions (Fig. 128c). The Moslem *Dorobanze* had a red fez with a blue tassel, and the crowned cipher in gold on the front.

In 1931 the Guard Division adopted distinctive dress and field service uniforms. The dress tunic was dark blue, with collar, cuff patches of the Brandenburg cuffs, and piping, as well as the officers' shoulder straps and epaulette crescents, in *Waffenfarbe*. The collar and cuffs were edged with yellow cord (gold for officers). The men had yellow guard lace on their collars and cuff patches; officers had a floral pattern gold embroidery (Fig. 129b).

REGIMENT	DISTINCTIVE COLOR	TROUSERS	FULL-DRESS HEADDRESS	AIGUILLETTE ON RIGHT SHOULDER
Michael Viteacu Guard Infantry Regiment	light yellow	light gray with piping— triple stripes for officers—in distinctive color	fur caps	yellow and blue
Palace Guard	white		white cuirassier helmet with yellow mounts,	white and blue
Royal Escort	black		and white plume	yellow and black

On the khaki-colored service dress, the men wore a yellow metal button at the rear ends of the collar patches, and a vertical patch in *Waffenfarbe* with two buttons, on the cuffs. Officers had embroidery, as on the tunic, on their collar patches, and on the basic collar patches of the Brandenburg cuffs. A yellow metal crown badge, within an oakleaf wreath for officers, was worn on the peaked cap.

II. CAVALRY

Moldavia: In 1830 the cavalry was dressed like the infantry, with pointed, red-piped cuffs, and had red-and-blue checkered lance pennants. In 1847 they were dressed as lancers, in dark blue jackets with red collar, pointed cuffs, lapels, and piping; white metal buttons; and white guard lace on the collar. The trousers were dark blue with red triple stripes. A black leather lancer cap was worn, with red top part, silver coat of arms on the front, and a white hair plume. The white metal shoulder scales had white fringes. Equipment was of white leather.

Wallachia: At first, infantry uniform was worn. In 1852 the cavalry adopted a lancer uniform of dark blue with white distinctions, and yellow metal buttons, and light-blue trousers with white piping. The lancer cap top was red. The lance pennants were yellow, red, and blue.

In 1860 the cavalry wore lancer jackets with a red, yellow, and blue girdle, dark blue trousers with broad stripes, and lancer caps with a white hair plume. The 1st Regiment had red distinctions, white metal buttons and epaulettes; and the 2nd, white distinctions, yellow metal buttons, and red epaulettes. In 1861 the distinctions were made red for both regiments.

In 1868 all the cavalry went into a hussar uniform. The three *Rosiori* (regular) regiments, expanded to ten in 1912, had red dolmans and white breeches, with black loopings; black fur caps with the royal cipher, cockade and white feather plume in front, yellow lines, and bag of the regimental color, on the left side. The equipment was of white leather, and later of natural color (Fig. 128d). Officers had a black kepi with band of the distinctive color. From 1884 the cavalry carried lances, the pennants of which were of the regimental color at the top, and red below; and had gray double-breasted greatcoats, with spearhead-shaped patches of the regimental color on the red collar.

The service dress was as worn by the infantry, with collar patches and piping of the regimental color. The distinctive colors of the *Rosiori* regiments were: 1, yellow; 2, white; 3, green; 4, light blue; 5, light green; 6, dark blue; 7, light brown; 8, lilac; 9, pink; and 10, light gray. From 1868 the *Calarasi* (auxiliary cavalry) wore dark blue dolmans with red loopings and red fur cap bags. They did not carry lances. The piping on the service uniform was red, and the collar patches were red, with black piping; the rest of the uniform was as for the infantry (Fig. 128e).

III. ARTILLERY, TRANSPORT CORPS, ENGINEERS, AND ARMORED TROOPS

In 1848 the artillery of the principality of Moldavia wore the infantry uniform, but with dark blue collar and cuffs, carmine cuff patches, shoulder straps, and piping; and helmet with a ball finial and the device of crossed cannon barrels below the coat of arms on the front. In 1854 they wore tunics, and black hair helmet plumes. The Wallachian artillery was dressed like that of Moldavia from 1852.

In 1860 the artillery of the United Principalities wore a dark blue double-breasted tunic. The collar and pointed cuffs were black, piped with red. A red grenade (gold for officers) was worn on the collar; red epaulettes; black leather equipment, chaco with a red hair plume, and badge consisting of two crossed cannon barrels. Brown coats and gray trousers were introduced in 1868, and dark blue kepis with black band and red piping, in place of the chacos. Officers had triple red trousers stripes (Fig. 128f). Black piping and black collar patches were worn on the service dress; in 1931 the heavy artillery adopted yellow piping, and the horse artillery, carmine distinctions with black piping. The mountain artillery had green piping; and the anti-aircraft artillery, sky blue.

From 1868 to 1915 the transport corps was dressed like the artillery, but with white metal buttons and rank distinctions, and single-breasted jackets. The service dress uniform had red piping, black collar patches, and yellow metal buttons.

The engineers from 1861 wore a dark blue single-breasted jacket with black collar and pointed cuffs, with red piping and grenades on the collar, and black leather equipment. The kepi was red with a black band and side seams. A dark blue band was worn from 1885; and dark blue trousers with red piping, or with triple stripes for officers (Fig. 128g). Black piping and black collar patches, piped red, were worn on the 1912 service uniform. In 1923 the collar patches and piping were light brown, but from 1931 were as in 1912.

On the 1931 service dress uniform, armored troops wore ash-gray piping and collar patches, the latter with red piping.

Fig. 128. Rumania, 1890.

a: infantry. b: rifles. c: Dorobanze. d. regular cavalry. e: auxiliary
cavalry. f: artillery. g: soldier of engineers. h: mounted *gendarmerie*. i: general officer.

IV. GENERAL OFFICERS AND GENERAL STAFF; RANK DISTINCTIONS

Moldavia, 1859: The general wore a black hat with white plume, dark blue single-breasted coatee with red collar and Brandenburg cuffs with gold oakleaf embroidery, red piping, gold epaulettes and sash, and gray trousers with red triple stripes.

Wallachia: A hat with blue, gold, and red plume; dark blue single-breasted tunic, skirts lined white, yellow piping, black collar and Brandenburg cuffs with rich gold embroidery; dark blue trousers with yellow triple stripes, and gold epaulettes and sash were worn. In 1860 general officers of the United Principalities wore a black hat with gold lace and black ostrich feather plumage (white for generals of divisions). The coat was dark blue, single-breasted, with dark blue collar and Brandenburg cuffs with rich oakleaf embroidery, gold epaulettes and sash, and red trousers with double gold or dark blue stripes. The general staff wore black collars and cuffs, edged with gold. The feather plume on the hat was red and yellow; otherwise they wore the same uniform as general officers.

In 1868 the collar and the now-pointed cuffs were changed to red and were ornamented with oakleaf embroidery. The trousers were dark blue; and on service dark gray, with red triple stripes. Off duty, a dark blue kepi with a red band was worn. The dark gray double-breasted greatcoat was piped red. The general staff wore the same uniform as the infantry, with a thunderbolt device on the collar, and a red kepi with dark blue band, and red, yellow, and blue feather plume.

In 1871 the general officers' hat was abolished, and a white feather plume was added to the kepi, and on the band above the peak, a silver sunburst. In the mid-1880s the dark blue regulation cloth became black (as in France), for generals as

367

well as for the officers of the rest of the army (Fig. 128i). For the general staff the red piping was abolished, and black velvet collar, cuffs, and kepi band, with a white kepi cover, and carmine triple trousers stripes, were taken into wear.

On the 1912 service dress, general officers wore red collar patches, piping, and triple trousers stripes, and a silver sunburst on the kepi. On the khaki service uniform, the red distinctive color was retained, and the silver sunburst, in smaller size, was worn on the band of the peaked cap, which had double oakleaf embroidery around the peak.

The uniforms of the general staff followed the lines of the rest of the army. Black velvet collar patches and piping were worn at first; later, these were of the *Waffenfarbe* of the former arm of service, bearing a gilt-winged thunderbolt in both cases. Aiguillettes were worn with the full-dress uniform.

The rank distinctions up to the Union of the Principalities were of Russian type. Officers wore epaulettes, with bullions for field officers. Colonels and captains had plain crescents; with two stars for majors and senior lieutenants and one for junior lieutenants. NCOs had one to three narrow red stripes across the inner end of the shoulder straps. From 1860 to 1916 officers wore epaulettes of button color in full dress, with long thin bullions for company officers, and short thick ones for field officers and general officers, bearing one to three silver stars on the strap. In addition, general officers had a silver sunburst on the crescent. On the service dress officers wore shoulder cords, consisting of from one to three metal lace cords, ending in a trefoil on the point of the shoulder. They also wore rank stripes on the lower arms; from 1889 these were worn in all orders of dress. Company officers wore one to three stripes above the cuffs, in the shape of a spearhead: field officers had an additional medium-width stripe below; general officers had a very broad additional oakleaf pattern stripe on the pointed cuffs. Field officers of cavalry also had a medium-width stripe along the front and lower edges of the collar. Company officers wore one to three narrow rank stripes above the band of the kepi; field officers had an additional medium-width stripe around the top of the kepi band; white for general officers, the whole band was covered with broad patterned lace. The side seams were set with one to three cords.

On the service dress, the distinctions of rank were worn only on the rounded shoulder straps, and from 1921 to 1931 also on the kepi, as previously. Company officers had one to three gold cords across the shoulder straps. Field officers had a medium-width stripe along the center as well. General officers' shoulder cords were completely covered with patterned lace; in addition, a field marshal had four diagonal cords. From 1860 to 1916 NCOs

Fig. 129. Rumania—Infantry, 1915, 1931.
b: Guard Regiment Michael the Brave.

and men wore one or two worsted or metal lace stripes of button color above the edge of the cuffs; the senior rank of NCOs in addition had a narrow chevron above, of contrasting color to that of the buttons. On the service dress, the rank distinctions took the form of one to three broad stripes in silver of *Waffenfarbe* across the shoulder straps.

After 1931, officers took into wear a colored full-dress and evening-dress uniform, which in general resembled the prewar dress uniform. Dismounted troops had Brandenburg cuffs with a patch of *Waffenfarbe*, edged with gold cord. The rank stripes ran around the cuffs and under the patches. *Calarasi* officers wore their prewar uniform; *Rosiori* officers had a dark blue dolman with black loopings and double-scalloped collar patches in the regimental color, and black trousers.

RUSSIA

Cockade: black-orange-white

I. INFANTRY

The first uniformly dressed troops were the *Strelitz*, which first appear in the middle of the sixteenth century. Their clothing and arms were supplied by the state. The main item of uniform was a kaftan ornamented with colored lace; the headdress was a fur-edged velvet cap, or an iron helmet. The arms were a matchlock, curved sword, and a long-handled *gisarme* (Fig. 130b). Officers had gold or silver lace on their kaftans and a crown-shaped device on the cap (Fig. 130a). As a mark of rank, they wore a stock, and officers and standard bearers wore long gloves.

A return of 1674 lists the distinctive colors of the various *Pulks* as follows.

PULK	CAP	KAFTAN	LACE	BOOTS
1. Jegor Lutochin	iron gray	red	red	yellow
2. Ivan Poltev	red	light gray	red	yellow
3. Vassili Buchvostoff	red	light green	red	yellow
4. Fedor Golovlinski	dark gray	cherry red	black	yellow
5. Fedor Alexandroff	dark gray	aloe color	cherry red	yellow
6. Nikifor Koloboff	dark gray	yellow	cherry red	red
7. Stefan Janoff	red	sky blue	black	yellow
8. Timofei Poltev	cherry red	orange	black	green
9. Peter Lupochin	cherry red	cherry red	black	yellow
10. Fedor Lupochin	red	dark yellow	red	yellow
11. David Woronzoff	cinnamon	red	black	yellow
12. Ivan Naramanski	red	cherry red	black	yellow
13. Lagosskin	green	dark red	black	yellow
14. Afanass Levschin	red	light green	black	yellow

The superiority of the *Strelitz* over other more heavily armed and equipped troops, together with their feeling of being indispensable, caused a spirit to grow up which was reminiscent of the Praetorian Guard and the Janissaries. The *Strelitz* revolt of 1698–1699 was bloodily suppressed by Czar Peter, who hurriedly returned from abroad. They were not reraised. Immediately after their destruction, Peter the Great began to rebuild the army. In the space of three months, twenty-nine regiments, two of them dragoons, were raised. The infantry uniform comprised coats, long-skirted waistcoats, knee breeches, stockings, and shoes. Only the cap was distinctive, in that it had flaps able to be turned down (Figs. 130c,d). The colors were left to the colonels of the regiments, with the result that the army had a variegated appearance. The Preobraschenski Regiment wore dark green coats; the Semenov Regiment, light-blue ones (Fig. 130g); both had dark green, and occasionally also dark red, breeches and waistcoats, red coat lining and cuffs, and red stitched buttonholes. Laced hats were worn. The grenadiers of these regiments (Fig. 130h) had a grenade pouch on a shoulder belt and a cartridge pouch on a waistbelt. Their headdress was a black leather cap, with neck guard, and front flap, bearing a double eagle device on the front. The cap was ornamented with a white feather, colored red around the edges. The officers (Fig. 130f) of these regiments wore the same uniform as the men, with the following distinctions: gold lace on all the seams of the coat; laced hat, with white and red plumage around the brim. Their status was shown by a red, green, and white sash worn over the right shoulder, gorget, and spontoon. The grenadiers of the other regiments had cloth caps of the familiar "sugar loaf" shape (Fig. 130e). In 1720 the uniform was changed. The colored cloth caps of the infantry were replaced by hats. The line infantry regiments adopted dark green coats. The collar, cuffs, binding of the buttonholes, waistcoats, and breeches were red; the cravats, black; and the stockings, white. The shoes were cut square. Boots were worn on active service. The guard regiments had dark green coats, waistcoats, and breeches. The cuffs, lining, and binding around the buttonholes were red. The two regiments were distinguished by the color of the collar: red for the Preobraschenski Regiment, and blue for the Semenov Regiment. The color of the collar remained as the main distinction up to 1914. After 1730, various innovations, of Prussian origin, were introduced—powder, hair curls, queues; cuff frills; and white gaiters. All wore white cravats. The grenadiers wore their pointed caps as before, but a metal plate with the regimental badge (the coat of arms of the town after which the regiment was named) was added to the front. The officers wore the same uniform as the men, but had

Fig. 130. Russia—Infantry, 1670–1700.
a: Strelitz, officer. b: Strelitz. c, d: line infantry. e: line grenadier. f, g, h: officer, musketeer, and grenadier of the guard.

green instead of red breeches. Their hats had a gold lace edging. They wore gorgets, and sashes of yellow and black silk, and had spontoons and swords. In 1743 the coat and waistcoat were made closer-fitting, and the skirts were worn permanently fastened back. From 1756 officers' sashes were worn around the waist instead of over the shoulder. On service, they were armed with a musket, and a red leather cartridge box, having the regimental badge, worn on the front of the waistbelt (Fig. 131c). The grenadiers adopted a distinctive cap with front plate and neck guard, and a brass plate and side bars (Fig. 131e). In addition, the grenadiers of the guards wore a large ostrich feather plume. Under Peter III the coat remained green and the lining red.

In 1760 lapels were introduced, which, together with the collar and cuffs, varied in color according to the regiment (Fig. 131f). According to F. von Stein, *Geschichte des russischen Heeres*, these colors varied considerably, as their choice was left to the colonels:

> In addition to black and white, there were red, green, blue, and gray in all shades, and to distinguish these colors, which were hardly different to the eye, names were given, like fire, iron, sand, brick, cherry, apricot, celadon, puce, mohair color. The waistcoat and breeches were yellow, white, orange or straw color. Similarly, the buttons were either yellow or white metal, as the colonel wished. The buttons were arranged six on each lapel, with two closer together, below. The buttonholes were laced with white or blue, and sometimes had small tassels or bows attached. On the right shoulder was worn an aiguillette, of the same color as the loops. The hats became somewhat elongated; the guards were provided with sword knots. The leather equipment, which hitherto had been of natural color, was now pipeclayed white, and the cartridge boxes, which had earlier been worn on the right side, were now worn to the rear. Officers adopted gold or silver aiguillettes, and loops on the coat, the latter often ornamentally embroidered. They carried spontoons, very similar to those of Prussian officers, in place of muskets. The guards took into wear light-green coats, without lapels, set with a number of loops. The cuffs remained red, and the collars, of different colors. The waistcoats and breeches were red, and the cravats, white. Officers wore all-green coats, richly decorated with gold lace.

On 24 April 1763, Catherine II issued new clothing regulations. The infantry coats were changed to a rather lighter green color, with round cuffs. All regiments were to have red collars, cuffs, and lapels. Aiguillettes were abolished, and a shoulder strap with fringe was introduced on the left shoulder. As a regimental distinction, their form and color were left to the colonel of the regiment to decide. The waistcoat was made with a small turndown collar, and cuffs, of green cloth. In full dress, the cravat was red; otherwise, black ones were worn. The breeches were red; the summer ones were of white linen. The gaiters were black. The hat was bound with scalloped white lace. The grenadier caps resembled the contemporary Prussian ones. At the same time, rank distinctions, in the form of small stars on the shoulder straps, of gold or silver combined with the regimental color, were introduced for officers.

The new uniform of 1786 is noteworthy in that almost the whole army adopted a common pattern, and the same headdress. This uniform was quite different from the prevailing fashions of the period (Figs. 131g,h). The infantry wore a short-skirted green coat, with the red-edged skirts turned back at the front only. The collar, lapels, and cuffs were all red. On the left shoulder was an epaulette, as previously worn. The

Fig. 131. Russia—Infantry, 1732–1796.
a: grenadier, guard. b: grenadier officer, guard. c, d, e: officer, musketeer, and grenadier
of the line. f: grenadier of the line. g, h: musketeers. i: grenadier.

trousers were red, with scalloped yellow stripes, with leather bootings around the
bottom. The headdress was formed of a felt skull, with a small peak, which was
edged with leather. On the front was a brass circlet. A broad yellow worsted crest ran
transversely across the helmet. A red cloth turban, edged with yellow cord, was
placed around the base of the skull. From the back depended two black cloth bands,
with yellow tassels at the ends. These cloth tails were intended to protect the neck,
and in cold weather could be tied over the ears. On the left side were a white bow and
a small black plume. A white edging was added to the black cravat. The unpowdered
hair was cut straight across at the back. Bayonets in scabbards were worn instead of
hangers. NCOs adopted lace on their collars and cuffs. The grenadiers wore the same
headdress, with a larger circular plate; they also wore a hanger on slings. Officers retained the uniform they had previously. The aforementioned changes did not apply
to the guards. In 1788 officers also adopted the new uniform, but did not have the
pendant tails at the back of their helmets.

When Czar Paul came to the throne in 1796, the old uniform, together with hair
powder, queues, gaiters, etc., was reintroduced. The coats sloped away in front (Fig.
131i). Regimental distinctions, of various colors, were reintroduced. The epaulette
on the left shoulder was replaced by a shoulder strap. The fusiliers adopted a headdress very like that of the Prussian fusiliers in the reign of Frederick the Great. In
1802 Alexander I introduced a headdress that closely resembled that worn up to 1796
but was wider and taller, for the guard regiments (Figs. 132a,b). The cloth band at
the back and the pendant tails were red for the Preobraschenski Regiment, light blue
for the Semenov Regiment, and white for the Ismailov Regiment. The officers wore
hats with feathers; and a gold aiguillette on the right shoulder (Fig. 132c).

In 1803 chacos, with a cockade and tuft on the front, were introduced. At first

Fig. 132. Russia—Infantry, 1802–1840.

a, b, c: grenadiers and officer of the guard. d, f, h: grenadiers of the line. e, g,
k: musketeers of the line and officer. i: NCO of the guard.

this headdress was only worn by the musketeers, but in 1805 it was adopted by the
grenadiers and fusiliers as well (Fig. 132d). For a time, officers retained their hats; to
these, very high feathers were added. Queues were abolished in 1806. In 1807
epaulettes were introduced for officers, at first in place of the strap on the left
shoulder. Spontoons were abolished. All grenadier and musketeer regiments took into wear red collars, cuffs, and skirt turnbacks. The shoulder straps varied, so that in
each division the 1st regiment had red; 2nd, white; 3rd, yellow; 4th, dark green with
red piping; and 5th, light blue. From 15 December 1807, the divisional number was
worn on the shoulder straps and on the epaulettes of the officers. The leather equipment was now worn crossed. White cloth trousers, with leather strapping around the
bottom, were worn in winter (Fig. 132e); in summer, they were of linen, cut with a
vamp, like gaiters (Fig. 132f). In 1809 officers adopted an epaulette on the right
shoulder also. Aiguillettes were accordingly abolished. The greatcoat was worn
rolled below the knapsack straps (Fig. 132g). In the same year, white cords were added to the chaco. In 1812 the shape of the chaco (*kiver*) was completely altered.
The broad crown was swept upward at the front and back (Fig. 132h). From 1796 the
Pavlov Regiment wore plain grenadier caps. The cap plate was altered in 1802. The
back of the cap was red, with a white band around the bottom. Chinscales were added after the Napoleonic Wars. The Pavlov Regiment retained their grenadier caps for
full-dress wear up to 1914. When the caps themselves were renewed, the plates were
used again; they often bore the marks of bullets on them.

The *kiver* of the guard had a double eagle plate; grenadier regiments and the
grenadier companies of the line had a three-flamed grenade. All metal insignia were
of red copper in the guards; brass in the line. The cartridge boxes bore the same

devices as on the *kiver*, except that the guards had the star of St. Andrew on theirs. The guards also had deep yellow lace loops, and variously colored collars. In 1813 these were: Preobraschenski and Lithuania Regiments, red; Semenov and Guard Grenadiers, light blue with red piping; and Ismailov and Pavlov, green with red piping. In 1812 the Guard Grenadiers and Pavlov Regiment belonged to the Grenadier Corps and up to 1813 wore the grenadier uniform; in addition, the former regiment, and the Kexholm Grenadier Regiment, both had white guard lace.

From 1812 fully closed collars were worn, but this change came so late that during the 1812 campaign, many regiments still had collars of the old open shape, and the tall chacos. In the following year, the Lithuania, Guard Grenadier, Pavlov, and Kexholm Regiments all adopted red lapels. The winter trousers were made of white cloth, booted with soft leather below the knee. In summer, white linen trousers, cut with a vamp the length of gaiters, were worn (Fig. 132h). In addition to their epaulettes (which had bullions for field officers), officers also wore gorgets: silver for ensigns; silver with a gilt edge for junior lieutenants; silver with a gilt double eagle for senior lieutenants; silver with a gilt edge and double eagle for staff captains; gilded with a silver double eagle for captains. The marine regiments, which were transferred to the army in this year, wore rifles' uniforms with white piping.

In 1816 new-pattern chacos were introduced, with a pompon of the battalion and company colors. The knapsack, formerly of black leather, was now made of untanned calfskin. The line infantry adopted single-breasted jackets. White trousers were worn in summer, and dark green ones in winter. In 1846 the spiked helmet (Figs. 133a,b,c) was introduced, with a black plume for the guards. Tunics were not adopted until after the Crimean War (Fig. 133d). In 1855 the line infantry adopted chacos having a front peak only; the guards retained their helmets until 1862, when a kepilike cloth cap, similar to the French one, was introduced (Figs. 133f,g). A black plume was worn with it in full dress. The cap was dark green, edged with the distinctive color.

In 1882 a form of national dress was introduced as a uniform (Figs. 133h,i). Except for the shoulder straps, the dark green coat had no buttons, and was fastened down the front with hooks. The dark green trousers were worn in long boots. In full dress only, low-crowned black lambskin caps were worn; and for everyday wear, dark green forage caps. In the line infantry, the colored distinctions were confined to the collar patches and piping, shoulder straps, and cap band and piping. The two brigades in each division were differentiated by the color of their shoulder straps: red for the 1st Brigade and blue for the 2nd. The four regiments in each division were distinguished by the color of their collar patches and cap bands: 1st Regiment, red; 2nd, blue; 3rd, white; and 4th, dark green. All had red piping. A few regiments were denoted by guard lace. The grenadier regiments wore the same uniform, but had yellow shoulder straps with colored piping: 1st Grenadier Division, red; 2nd, blue; 3rd, white; 4th, yellow. The waist girdles were black for all regiments.

After this complete change in the uniform, the guards had a quite different appearance. The fur caps were superseded by chacos; later, in addition, colored lapels were worn on the full-dress uniform. A black or white waistbelt was introduced in place of the girdle (Fig. 139c). In 1914 the guard regiments were distinguished as follows.

REGIMENT	COLLAR	CUFFS*	CUFF PATCHES
Lifeguard Regiment Preobraschenski	red	red, white piping	red, white piping
Lifeguard Regiment Semenov	light blue, red piping	red, white piping	red, white piping
Lifeguard Regiment Ismailov	dark green, red piping	red, white piping	red, white piping
Lifeguard Rifles Regiment	dark green, red piping	dark green, red piping	red, white piping
Lifeguard Regiment Moscow	red	red	red
Lifeguard Grenadier Regiment	light blue, red piping	red	red
Lifeguard Regiment Paul	dark green, red piping	red	red
Lifeguard Regiment Finland	dark green, red piping	dark green, red piping	red
Lifeguard Regiment Lithuania	yellow, dark green piping	yellow	yellow
Kexholm Grenadier Regiment	light blue, yellow piping	yellow	yellow
St. Petersburg Grenadier Regiment	dark green, yellow piping	yellow	yellow
Lifeguard Regiment Wollonia	dark green, yellow piping	dark green, yellow piping	yellow

*Lapels were exactly as cuffs, except for the Lifeguard Rifles Regiment, which had light-green lapels with white piping.

The last four regiments had yellow trousers stripes and white metal buttons; the rest, red stripes and yellow metal buttons. All regiments had yellow lace loops on the collar, and cuff patches. The cap bands and the lower band around the chaco were of the same color as the collar, except that the 3rd Regiment of each division had white. The Pavlov Regiment (Lifeguard Regiment Paul) continued to wear their tall grenadier caps in full dress (Fig. 133e). The guard regiments adopted regimental badges, worn on the breast, like the stars of orders; these were also worn on the greatcoat and service dress.

The universal greatcoat was earth gray in color. A new equipment was also introduced in 1883 (Figs. 133h,i). The men wore no sidearms. In 1910 the grenadier divisions and line infantry stopped wearing fur caps and adopted double-breasted jackets.

At the same time as the new uniform was introduced, all troops were issued with service dress as well. As a general rule, the guard was distinguished by wearing their knapsacks on the back, while the line wore theirs on the hip. The service dress was gray-green, the leather cap peak being of the same color. Only the higher ranks of NCOs and officers had chinstraps. The guards were distinguished by colored piping around the cuffs (1st Division, white; 2nd, red; 3rd, yellow) and by the lace edging on the shoulder straps, which was of the same color as the old cap band. Officers had breast pockets, the flaps of which, for officers of the guards, were piped the same color as the piping on the shoulder straps (Fig. 139g). The shoulder straps were exactly like those on the peacetime uniform on one side, and on the reverse side, field green with a numeral or cipher, in yellow for all regiments. The infantry had no colored distinctions.

Fig. 133. Russia—Infantry, 1846–1882.
a: drum major of the guard. b, d, f: guard infantry (d: NCO). e, g: officers of the guard. c, h, i: line infantry.

A new-pattern full dress was introduced for the line infantry on 9 March 1913. It was intended to be in general use by 1915; but by the outbreak of war, it had only been issued to a few regiments. It was similar to the service uniform, with hooked collar and lapels. Officers had two loops of gold lace on their collars. In each division, the colors of the collars were: 1st Regiment, red; 2nd, blue; 3rd, white; and 4th, light green. A gray lambskin cap (*papacha*), with the double eagle badge, was worn with it (Fig. 139f).

II. RIFLES

In 1769 detachments of light troops were added to the infantry regiments. Their uniforms consisted of a short green jacket with green collar and pointed cuffs, and close-fitting green breeches. They had black loopings like hussars'. On the left shoulder was worn the aiguillette denoting the regiment to which they belonged. The greatcoats were green. Short boots were worn. The headdress was a green cap, with black upturned flaps front and back, edged with green indented lace. On the left side was a white worsted tuft. A cartridge box was worn on the front of the black waistbelt, with a bayonet and scabbard on the left. The new-pattern uniform of 1786 resembled that of the infantry in style. It was all green in color, except that the breeches had black stripes. The buttons were yellow metal. The helmet had a black crest; the hoop-shaped plate was painted green. The pendent cloth tails were also green.

The rifles detachments of the three guards regiments were dressed in a distinctive manner. In the Preobraschenski Regiment the uniform consisted of a black felt cap with green cords. The green coat had dark green lapels and cuffs edged with red.

There was a green epaulette on the left shoulder. The dark green breeches, and the black gaiters too, had red stripes down the sides. The rifles detachment of the Semenov Regiment wore green caps with a black fur edging, like the Polish konföderatka, with a white cockade and small black plume on the left side. The dark green uniform had no colored edgings. The headdress of the Ismailov Regiment detachment resembled the helmet of the period. The front plate, binding of the peak, band around the back, and the crest were green. There was a white cockade and black plume. The short-skirted coat was edged red all around, and so were the so-called "half" lapels; the pointed cuffs were of basic color, edged with red. The green trousers and black gaiters had red stripes. In 1796, as in the rest of the army, the old style of uniform was reintroduced. The breeches were changed to white. Light-green ones were readopted in 1801. The collar and cuffs varied from regiment to regiment. The cartridge pouches, which were now worn on a waistbelt, almost went all the way around the body. In 1802 a new-pattern hat was introduced in place of the tricorne issued under Czar Paul. It was shaped roughly like a top hat. In the center in front was a black cockade with an orange edging and a yellow metal button. The loop and pompon were of the same color as the collar and shoulder straps. Above was a tuft, of the battalion and company colors. Chacos were adopted in 1807. In the previous year, the cartridge boxes had been reduced in size.

During the Napoleonic Wars, the headdress was a fur cap. The uniform exactly resembled that of the infantry, which is dealt with in the foregoing section. The rifles were characterized by their black leather equipment and the dark green, red-piped collar and cuffs. The shoulder straps were of the distinctive color. It is interesting that the national uniform, which the infantry wore from 1882, was based on the dress worn by the huntsmen of the Imperial family in the 1850s. The army rifle regiments wore an all-green uniform with red shoulder straps, and carmine collar and cuff piping. The forage caps were likewise all dark green with red piping. The lambskin caps were as in the line infantry. The Finnish rifle battalions had a different pattern of fur cap; otherwise they were dressed like the rest of the rifles. Their shoulder straps were light blue. There were four guard rifle battalions. These had guard lace on their collars and Swedish cuffs, and lambskin caps bearing a yellow metal star.

In 1892, the distinctions were as follows.

BATTALION	LACE	BUTTONS	SHOULDER STRAPS
1st Lifeguard Rifles Battalion	yellow	yellow	raspberry red
2nd Lifeguard Rifles Battalion	white	white	raspberry red
3rd Finnish Lifeguard Rifles Battalion	yellow	yellow	light blue
4th Lifeguard Rifles Battalion	white	yellow	raspberry red

The guard rifles wore green girdles; the others, black. About 1900 the first three battalions adopted Brandenburg cuffs and all-yellow lace. In 1910 rifles adopted the guards' kiver, and lapels were added to their jackets. The distinctions were changed to raspberry red for all four battalions. The 1st Battalion had raspberry red collars, and cap and kiver bands; these were dark green for the 2nd and 3rd Battalions. The 1st and 3rd had white metal buttons. The 4th Battalion wore a distinctive uniform reminiscent of the national dress. In 1911 the battalions were enlarged and formed into regiments.

On the service dress, the officers' shoulder strap lace and pocket piping was raspberry red; the cuff piping was white, green, raspberry red, and field green, respectively. The peacetime uniform of the army rifle regiments altered little. In 1910 double-breasted jackets were introduced. The low-crowned fur caps were superseded by taller black lambskin *papachas*. The rifles were distinguished by the raspberry-red-colored devices on their shoulder straps in service dress (Fig. 139i).

III. CUIRASSIERS

Cuirassiers in the Russian army date from 1731. Their dress at that time was a leather jacket, with turndown collar and turned-back skirts; leather waistcoat and breeches. The jacket collar, cuffs, and skirts and the waistcoat were edged with red cloth. The cuirass was lacquered black and had the crown and cipher on the front. This uniform was only worn in full dress; otherwise, long-skirted red waistcoats were worn. The hat was bound with gold lace, and had an iron "secret." The horse guards, the first regiment of the guard cavalry, which later was to become so numerous, also wore cuirassier uniform, but their everyday breeches were red, and the jacket and waistcoat were edged with gold lace instead of red cloth. The cuirasses were of plain steel; the leather accoutrements were faced with red cloth, and edged with yellow lace for other ranks, and with gold lace for officers. In 1763 the cuirassiers adopted green waistcoats and buff-colored jackets with green collars and cuffs. The lace was of green and white worsted. The hat was edged with gold lace, and sabertaches shaped like those of hussars were carried: They were green, with white lace, and the cipher in yellow. The Chevalier Guard (Fig. 134c) had a particularly ornate uniform: red coats and breeches, with dark blue velvet trimmings

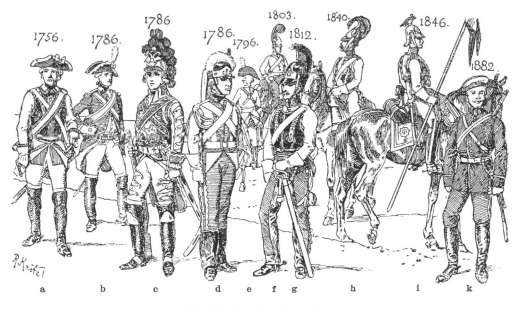

Fig. 134. Russia—Cuirassiers.
a, d, f, g, h: cuirassiers. b: horse guards. c: chevalier guard. e: officer.
i, k: guard cuirassiers.

and *Superweste*. All were heavily laced with gold and silver. Black ostrich feathers were worn with the silvered helmets. With the introduction of the universal uniform of 1786 (Fig. 134d), the cuirassiers adopted light-yellow jackets. The colors of the edgings and breeches variedfrom regiment to regiment. The helmet had a white crest and a broad brass band. The cloth band at the back was of the distinctive color. The pendent tails were made of yellow cloth. The officers retained the old uniform for a short time.

> Lifeguard Cuirassiers—green distinctions (collar, cuffs, piping) and breeches
> Order Regiment—black distinctions and yellow breeches
> Novostroitsk—light-blue distinctions and light-blue breeches
> Kasan—dark blue distinctions and dark blue breeches

All regiments wore their shoulder belts crossed. The Crown Prince Regiment, which had retained the old uniform, similar to that of the cuirassiers of Frederick the Great, had red distinctions and a hat with a white plume. Cuirasses were no longer worn. The horse guards (Fig. 134b) had gold-laced hats with a white plume, a blue old-style coat with red collar and cuffs, and a red waistcoat. The epaulettes had gold fringes; the red shoulder belts had yellow edgings and were worn crossed. The breeches were of yellow leather. In 1796 the old-style uniform was reintroduced for the cuirassiers as for everyone else, and the cuirass was readopted (Fig. 134e). In 1801 white jackets were introduced. For everyday wear, and on the march, gray buttoned overalls were worn. In 1803 a new headdress was adopted: a leather helmet with brass plate, leather comb, and a full *chenille* (Fig. 134f). Soon after, this was replaced by a bristlelike horsehair plume. This was the uniform worn by the cuirassiers during the Napoleonic Wars (Fig. 134g).

In 1813–1814 the distinctions were as follows.

REGIMENT	COLLAR, CUFFS, AND SHABRAQUES	BUTTONS AND SHABRAQUE EDGING	REMARKS
Chevalier Guard	red[1]	white[2]	yellow loops
Horse Guards	red[1]	yellow[3]	yellow loops
Lifeguard Cuirassiers	light blue[1]	white[4]	white loops
Czarina's Lifeguard Cuirassiers	dark pink[1]	white	white metal cuirasses
Jekaterinoslaff	orange	white	
Pskoff	dark red	yellow	white metal cuirasses; yellow for officers
Gluchow	blue	yellow	
Astrakan	yellow	white	
Order Regiment	black	yellow	
Little Russia	dark green	yellow	
Novgorod	light red	white	
Starodub	light blue	yellow	

[1]stars on the shabraque [2]yellow-blue-yellow shabraque edging [3]yellow-red-yellow shabraque edging
[4]silver-white-silver shabraque edging

The officers' lace loops were of the color of the buttons. Both the first two regiments wore the star of the Order of St. Andrew in yellow metal (silver for officers) on their helmets; the 3rd had a white metal double eagle plate (a silver star for officers); the other regiments had a yellow metal double eagle, with the exception of the Order Regiment, in which all ranks wore the yellow metal star of the Order of St. George. In 1814 the buttons on the gray-brown overalls were abolished, and triple stripes, of the color of the jacket collar, were added.

This uniform remained in wear, largely unaltered, up to 1846. In 1840 the guard and line cuirassiers were wearing white jackets with collar, cuffs, shoulder straps, and skirt edging in the regimental color. The shabraques and holster covers of the guard regiments were pointed and bore the guard star; those of the line were rounded, with the Imperial cipher. The guards' helmets had a star plate; those of the line regiments, a double eagle (Fig. 134h). In 1846 a Prussian-type cuirassier helmet was introduced. White jackets were adopted after the Crimean War. The first rank was armed with lances (Fig. 134i).

In 1882 the whole of the cavalry was turned into dragoons, with the exception of the guard cavalry. The coat, and its collar, cuffs, and shoulder straps, were dark green; and the trousers, gray, with colored stripes. The Chevalier Guard of the Czarina had red piping around the collar, cuffs, and shoulder straps, red trousers stripes, and white metal buttons. The lifeguard of horse also had red piping, and yellow metal buttons. The Czar's Lifeguard Regiment had yellow piping and white metal buttons; and that of the Czarina, light-blue piping and yellow metal buttons. The band and the piping around the top, of the peakless white forage caps, were of the distinctive color (Fig. 134k). The helmet was yellow metal with white metal fittings and a spike. In full dress, the Czarina Chevalier Regiment had a double eagle of the color of the buttons, in place of the spike. From 1910 this ornament was worn by all four regiments. In full dress was worn a white jacket, with collar and shoulder straps of the color of the piping on the everyday jackets, yellow lace with a red or light-blue center stripe, and yellow lace loops on the collar and cuffs. Accoutrements were of white leather. In gala dress, red *Superweste* with the star of the Order of St. Andrew, or a double eagle of the color of the buttons were worn respectively by the Chevalier Guard and the lifeguard, together with white breeches and long boots. Black shoulder straps, piped like the everyday dress, were worn on the service dress. In 1910 line cuirassier regiments were re-formed. For their uniform, see below under "Dragoons."

IV. DRAGOONS, HORSE GRENADIERS, CARABINIERS, LIGHT HORSE, AND MOUNTED RIFLES

During the reign of Peter the Great, the color of the dragoon uniform, as in the infantry, was left to the colonel's fancy. The style resembled that of the infantry. Hats were worn; and when mounted, heavy riding boots (Fig. 135a). In 1720 all regiments adopted blue coats with white linings and lace. Leather waistcoats and breeches were worn, and black cravats. By 1730 the linings and edgings were red. The horse grenadiers were dressed like the dragoons, at first with blue turnbacks, later with red. They also wore pointed cloth caps like those of the infantry grenadiers, but these were cornflower blue, not green as for the infantry. Subsequently, these caps

Fig. 135. Russia—Dragoons.

a, c, d, e, f, g, h, l: dragoons. b: officer, horse grenadiers. i: officer.
k: mounted guard grenadier.

were changed, and later they had an upright front plate and a neck guard (Fig. 135b). When the infantry adopted lapels on their coats, this fashion was not followed by the dragoons, but they did adopt infantry-type aiguillettes. The waistcoats and the housings were changed to cornflower blue, the same color as the coat. The hats were bound with white lace. In 1763 the carabinier regiments wore the same uniform, except that they had lapels and narrow gold lace around the hat, and carried carbines, whereas the dragoons had muskets and bayonets. In 1775 the dragoons adopted green coats with red collars and cuffs, yellowish waistcoats and breeches, boots, and short white cloaks. The sword was superseded by a saber, and in place of the German saddles, Hungarian ones, and shabraques were adopted. When the universal uniform of 1786 was introduced, that of the dragoons resembled the infantry's; except that they had yellow aiguillettes and gauntlets, and cavalry arms and equipment (Fig. 135d). The carabiniers were dressed similarly, but in dark blue coats instead of green ones, with red distinctions and breeches. The buttons were of yellow metal; the stripes on the breeches, white. No aiguillettes were worn. The light horse, likewise, wore blue coats with red distinctions and breeches, white metal buttons and trousers stripes, and white aiguillettes. The crest on the helmet was yellow for the dragoons, white for the carabiniers and light horse; the pendent cloth tails were black. In the late 1780s mounted rifles were raised; they had an all-green uniform with white aiguillettes and buttons, black felt caps with a white plume, and black pouch belts and sashes. In 1796 the old uniform, along with the hat, was reintroduced. In 1801 the dragoons had light-green coats with fairly short skirts; the collar, cuffs, and strap on the left shoulder varied in color for each regiment. Their arms were a musket and bayonet, and a sword. Like the cuirassiers, the dragoons adopted gray buttoned overalls. Cuirassier helmets were introduced in 1803 (Fig. 135e).

382

REGIMENT	COLLAR	CUFFS	BUTTONS	COLLAR PIPING
Lifeguard	red, yellow loops	red, yellow loops	yellow	
Riga*	red	red	yellow	
Yamburg	green	red	white	red
Kasan*	carmine	carmine	yellow	
Nyeschin	green	light blue	yellow	light blue
Pskoff	orange	orange	yellow	
Moscow*	pink	pink	white	
Kargopol*	orange	orange	white	
Ingermanland*	black	black	white	
Courland*	light blue	light blue	yellow	
Orenburg	black	black	yellow	
Siberia	white	white	white	
Irkutsk	white	white	yellow	
Kharkov*	dark yellow	dark yellow	yellow	
Chernigov	blue	blue	white	
Kiev*	carmine	carmine	white	
New Russia*	light blue	light blue	white	
Starodub	red	red	white	
Tver*	blue	blue	yellow	
Shitomir	red	red	white	white
Arsamass	green	light blue	white	light blue
St. Petersburg*	pink	pink	yellow	
Livonia	red	red	yellow	white
Syeversk	dark yellow	dark yellow	white	
Kinburn*	yellow	yellow	white	
Smolensk*	yellow	yellow	yellow	
Pereyeslav	green	carmine	white	carmine
Tiraspol	green	red	yellow	red
Dorpat	green	yellow	white	yellow
Vladimir	green	white	yellow	white
Taganrok	green	pink	yellow	pink
Serpuchov	green	yellow	yellow	yellow
Nishagorod*	green	white	white	white
Narva*	green	pink	white	pink
Borissoglebsk*	green	carmine	yellow	carmine
Finland*	white	white	yellow	red
Mitau*	white	white	white	red

*These regiments remained in existence after 1813 and retained the above uniforms for some time, while the other regiments were converted into other arms of service. The Lifeguard Dragoon Regiment had red lapels in addition to the distinctions listed. The green shabraques were edged with a strip of the color of the cuffs, for all regiments; the Guard Regiment had a broad stripe, edged yellow on both sides.

After the Napoleonic Wars, chacos with red pompons, white plumes, and plate of the metal of the buttons were introduced (Fig. 135f). The jacket was fastened by a row of nine buttons down the front. The trousers were changed to dark green with broad colored stripes. The shoulder straps were replaced by worsted epaulettes with short fringes of white or yellow, according to the color of the buttons. The mounted rifles wore a *kiver* with green cords; green jackets with green collars, green trousers with double broad stripes of the distinctive color, and white metal buttons. In 1813–1814, the colors of the collar piping, shoulder straps, and skirt edgings were as follows: Nyeshin, blue-green; Tshernigoff, blue; Asamass, light blue; Seversk, orange; Livonia, dark red; Pereyeslaff, pink; Tiraspol, yellow; and Dorpat, light red. The Lifeguard Mounted Rifles, raised in 1814, had, in addition to red distinctions, white lace loops, and white cords and a white metal double eagle in place of the cockade, on the *kiver*. In 1817 the collars were changed to green with colored patches; and white epaulettes were adopted. By 1840 the dragoon uniform had altered somewhat. The collar was piped, and had patches, the latter bearing a button. The epaulettes were of metal lace; the cuffs, formerly of Swedish type, were now of Brandenburg shape. A green girdle, with edging stripes of the regimental color, was worn around the waist (Fig. 135g).

In 1840 the distinctions were as follows.

REGIMENT	DISTINCTIVE COLOR	COLLAR	COLLAR PATCHES	HORSES
Moscow	carmine	green	carmine	chestnut
Kargopol	white	green	white	white
Kinburn	yellow	green	yellow	brown
New Russia	sky blue	green	sky blue	black
Kasan	dark red	dark red	green	brown
Riga	white	white	green	white
Finland	yellow	yellow	green	black
Tver	sky blue	sky blue	green	black

The Novgorod Regiment had a uniform of a different style. It had a red collar; the cartridge pouch belt was carried over the shoulder; and peaked fur caps were worn instead of chacos, which in all the regiments were henceforth worn with a spherical pompon instead of the plume.

During the Crimean War, the uniform as described above was worn, but with a helmet like that worn by the infantry (Fig. 135h). The front ranks carried lances. After the war, tunics, and later infantry-type kepis, were taken into wear (Fig. 135i).

In 1870 the distinctions were as follows.

REGIMENT	COLLAR	COLLAR PATCHES	CUFFS	BUTTONS
1	green	red	red	yellow
2	green	pink	pink	white
3	green	light blue	light blue	yellow
4	green	light blue	light blue	white
5	green	white	white	yellow
6	green	white	white	white
7	green	yellow	yellow	yellow
8	green	yellow	yellow	white
9	red	green	red	yellow
10	red	green	red	white
11	light blue	green	light blue	yellow
12	light blue	green	light blue	white
13	orange	green	orange	yellow
14	yellow	green	yellow	white
15	green	carmine	carmine	yellow
16	crimson	green	carmine	yellow
17	green	carmine	carmine	white
18	crimson	green	carmine	white

Regiments 1 and 2: white lace
Regiments 16 and 17: double yellow lace loops

In 1882 the dragoon arm was greatly increased, as all the line cavalry regiments were turned into dragoons, with the exception of the cossacks. The everyday head-dress was a peakless green forage cap; in full dress, a lambskin cap with a colored crown was worn. The fur edging was cut out in a vee, front and back. The double eagle badge, in white or yellow metal, was placed on the front. The collar was either of the green basic color (in which case it had differently colored patches) or colored, with green patches. The cuffs were outlined by pointed piping in the distinctive color. The girdle and shoulder straps were of the color of the piping. Trousers were gray. The sword had a different means of suspension from usual: The sling rings were on the front, and not the back, edge of the scabbard—an old Slavonic method of carriage (Fig. 135l). The Lifeguard Dragoon Regiment (Fig. 135k) formed part of the guards. Their headdress was the same as that worn by the line. The lining was red; the plate was in the form of a yellow metal star; and from 1897, a white metal star with a scroll above. The green tunic had a red collar, pointed cuffs, and shoulder straps, and red piping down the front. Yellow guard lace was worn on the collar and cuffs; and red lapels; a red girdle; white metal shoulder scales with red fringes; and white metal buttons. In 1910 they were issued with a black *kiver*, with double eagle badge; and white leather equipment. The trousers were gray with red piping. The Lifeguard Grenadier Regiment of Horse wore the same uniform, but with yellow metal shoulder scales and buttons. The full-dress headdress was rather like the helmet of 1786. The pendent tail was red, with a yellow edging. In 1897 the line dragoons changed to a double-breasted tunic, like the one adopted by the infantry in 1910 (Fig. 139a).

At the reorganization of 1910, the appearance of the dragoons changed completely. Their new headdress was a helmet resembling that of the Lifeguard Grenadiers of Horse, but without the pendent tail. The jacket was single-breasted. The distinctions again approximated to those given in the table for 1870. Regiments Nos. 2, 4, 6, 8, 9, 10, 12, and 14 perpetuated the traditions of the former cuirassiers, and were denoted by a white helmet crest, collar and cuffs of distinctive color, and lace on the collar and cuffs and down the front. The 13th Regiment wore black jackets with white distinctions, black and orange lace, black collar patches with yellow metal grenades, a white helmet crest, and a yellow metal star instead of the usual double eagle (Fig. 139e). The 16th to 18th Regiments adopted fur caps.

The cavalry service dress resembld that of the infantry, except that the coat had pointed cuffs of basic color and the trousers remained blue with colored piping. The gray-green shoulder straps of the line bore the numeral and the Russian initial for the arm of service in light blue: "D," dragoons; "Y," lancers; "T," hussars. The Horse Grenadier Guard and the Guard Dragoon Regiment had respectively red and dark green cuff piping; and both had dark green piping on their shoulder straps.

V. HUSSARS

There were hussars in existence during Peter the Great's time, but detailed descriptions of them are lacking. In 1740–1741, five regiments of hussars were raised. In the reign of the Czarina Elizabeth (1741–1762), the uniform consisted of a dolman, pelisse, close-fitting breeches, sash, sabertache, and felt or fur cap. The pouch belt and carbine belt were of plain black leather, worn croseed. The hair was worn in two strands over the temples (Figs. 136a,b).

At this period, the distinctions were as follows.

REGIMENT	HEADDRESS	DOLMAN AND BREECHES	LOOPS ON DOLMAN AND BREECHES	PELISSE	LOOPS ON PELISSE
Slobodisch	white *Flügelmütze*	dark blue	white	white	dark blue
Serbian	fur cap with light-blue bag	sky blue	black	sky blue	black
Hungarian	fur cap with red bag	red	black	red	black
Grusinisch	fur cap with red bag	red	blue	blue	red
Yellow	yellow *Flügelmütze*	yellow	black	yellow	black

The sabertaches bore the crowned cipher "E.P." The front was the same color as the pelisse, the edging was that of the pelisse loopings. The sash was of the color of the dolman, and the dolman loopings, mixed. All five regiments had yellow buttons.

In 1765 the colors were changed as follows.

REGIMENT	DOLMAN	PELISSE	BREECHES	CUFFS	LOOPINGS	REMARKS*
Serbian	blue	blue	blue	black	white	
Hungarian	red	red	red	black	yellow	
Grusinisch	yellow	yellow	red	black	red	yellow loops on breeches
Moldavian	dark blue	white	dark blue	yellow	yellow	blue sabertaches
Black	black	white	black	white	yellow	
Yellow	yellow	white	yellow	yellow	black	yellow sabertaches
Bachmut	green	white	green	white	yellow	
Ostrogerski	dark blue	black	dark blue	black	yellow	
Isum	red	black	red	black	black	yellow loops on pelisse; blue sabertaches
Sumsk	light blue	black	light blue	black	yellow	light-blue sabertaches
Kharkov	blue	black	blue	black	black	yellow loops on pelisse; blue sabertaches
Achtyrka	green	black	green	black	black	green loops on pelisse; blue sabertaches

*Except where noted, the sabertaches were black.

In the reign of Czarina Catherine II, the lifeguard hussars (Fig. 136c) wore a fur cap with red bag, red and silver lines, and a white plume. The plume was retained by a silver socket in the shape of a double eagle. The dolman and pelisse were green with silver loops, with white fur edging; and a white pouch belt. The cuffs were red; the sash, red and silver; the breeches, red with silver looping, and the boots, yellow. The red sabertaches were edged with silver and bore the intertwined crowned cipher "E.J." In 1776 all the line hussar regiments wore black pelisses with yellow loopings and white fur edging, and the distinctions were as follows.

REGIMENT	DOLMAN	BREECHES	CUFFS	LOOPINGS
Ostrogorski	raspberry red	raspberry red	white	yellow
Kharkov	yellow	yellow	white	white
Achtyrka	green	green	yellow	yellow
Sumsk	blue	blue	black	yellow
Isum	red	red	black	yellow

(continued)

REGIMENT	DOLMAN	BREECHES	CUFFS	LOOPINGS
White Russia	black	black	?	yellow
Ukraine	orange-yellow	orange-yellow	blue	black
Hungarian	black	black	white	yellow
Slavonic	green	green	black	yellow
Bulgarian	brown	brown	white	yellow
Moldavian	brown	brown	white	yellow
Macedonian	yellow	yellow	red	black
Dalmatian	orange-yellow	orange-yellow	green	black
Illyrian	raspberry red	raspberry red	dark blue	yellow
Serbian	blue	blue	white	yellow

From 1783 to the death of Catherine in 1796, there were no line hussars.

In about 1802 gray overalls were introduced. The headdress for all regiments was a black felt cap with a wing; with a cockade and white plume. The cut of the uniform had altered in accord with the fashion of the period: the high collar came into wear at the turn of the century.

In 1802 the distinctions for each regiment were as follows.

REGIMENT	DOLMAN	COLLAR AND CUFFS	PELISSE	LOOPINGS
Alexandria	carmine	carmine	carmine	white
Pavlograd	green	light blue	light blue	yellow
Mariupol	white	yellow	light blue	yellow
Olviopol	green	green	green	white
Elizabethgrad	yellow	red	yellow	yellow
Sumsk	yellow	light blue	light blue	white
Isum	red	dark blue	dark blue	white
Achtirsk	brown	yellow	brown	yellow

Fig. 136. Russia—Hussars and Lancers.

a, b, d, e, f, h: hussars. c: lifeguard hussar. g, i: hussars of the guard.
k, l: lancers. m: lancer of the guard.

Queues were abolished in 1806, together with the long strands of hair. The head-dress now introduced was the chaco (Fig. 136d). The pouch belts were of Russian leather; the carbine belts of white leather.

According to a handwritten report of the Prussian King Frederick William III, which corresponds exactly with the regulations, the distinctions of the hussars in 1813 were as follows.

REGIMENT	PELISSE	DOLMAN	COLLAR AND CUFFS	LOOPINGS	BUTTONS	PELISSE EDGING
Isum	blue	red	blue	white	white	white
Grodno	blue	blue	light blue	white	white	white
Lubenski	blue	blue	yellow	white	white	white
Mariupol	blue	blue	yellow	yellow	yellow	white
Bieloserk	brown	blue	red	white	white	black
Achtirsk	red	brown	yellow	yellow	yellow	white
Alexandria	black	black	red	white	white	white
Pavlograd	sky blue	green	sky blue	red	yellow	white
Elizabethgrad	gray	gray	gray	red	yellow	black
Sumsk	gray	gray	red	white	white	white
Olviopol	green	green	red	white	white	white

In the period following, the hussar uniform did not differ much from that of the West European armies (Fig. 136e). The chaco went through the same changes as in the infantry. In the 1820s the collar and cuffs were changed to the basic color of the dolman. The chaco was covered with colored cloth. The hair plumes were abolished. In 1840 (Fig. 136f) the distinctions were as follows.

REGIMENT	DOLMAN	PELISSE	LOOPS; SHABRAQUE AND SABERTACHE EDGING	CHACO AND SABERTACHE	SHABRAQUE	HORSES
1. Sumsk	gray	gray	white	red	gray	brown
2. Klästiz	dark blue	dark blue	white	light blue	dark blue	white
3. Elizabethgrad	gray	gray	orange-yellow	gray	gray	chestnut
4. Luben	dark blue	dark blue	white	yellow	dark blue	black
5. Prince Wittgenstein	dark blue	dark blue	orange-yellow	yellow	dark blue	brown
6. Prince of Orange	light blue	red	white	light blue	light blue	white
7. Pavlograd	green	light blue	orange-yellow	light blue	green	brown
8. Archduke Ferdinand	red	dark blue	white	red	dark blue	white
9. Achtirsk	brown	brown	orange-yellow	yellow	brown	chestnut
10. Alexandria	dark blue	dark blue	white	red	dark blue	black
11. Kiev	green	green	orange-yellow	red	green	chestnut
12. Ingermanland	light blue	light blue	orange-yellow	light blue	light blue	black
13. Crown Prince Michael Pavlovitch	light blue	light blue	white	light blue	light blue	brown
14. King of Wurttemberg	green	green	white	light blue	green	white

The shabraques no longer had a vandyked border, but were edged instead with a plain stripe of the color of the loopings; the sabertaches likewise. On the latter, and at the rear corners of the shabraques, was the Imperial cipher. The color of the sash was a combination of the color of the chaco and that of the loopings. The pelisses had a gray edging. The pouch belts were white. The gray trousers were piped in the color of the chaco. After the Crimean War, an *Attila* jacket, and a kepi with drooping black plume, were introduced.

In 1870 the distinctions were as follows.

REGIMENT	ATTILA	KEPI	LOOPINGS
1	light blue	red	yellow
2*	green	light blue	yellow
3	light blue	white	yellow
4	blue	yellow	yellow
5	black	red	white
6	blue	light blue	white
7	light blue	white	white
8	blue	yellow	white
9	green	red	yellow
10	light blue	light blue	yellow
11	blue	white	yellow
12	brown	yellow	yellow
13	light blue	yellow	white
14	green	yellow	white

*broad white lace with a blue stripe on the collar and cuffs

The Guard Hussar Regiment, which was mounted on white horses, had red kepis, dolmans and sabertaches, and dark blue pelisses and shabraques. The loopings were orange-yellow. The Grodno Hussar Regiment, which also belonged to the guard, had the same uniform, but with white loopings and a light-blue kepi. They rode brown horses. Later, both the guard regiments adopted fur caps. While the Grodno Regiment took into wear green *Attilas* and pelisses with white loopings, and carmine breeches, the Lifeguard Hussar Regiment retained its former uniform, but adopted white pelisses with yellow loopings. Between 1882 and 1910 these two regiments were the only hussars in the Russian army (Figs. 136g,i).

With the reorganization of 1910, hussar regiments were reraised (Fig. 139d). The old uniforms were reintroduced (cf. table for 1870). The kepis gave way to fur caps with an upright white plume. The bag was of the same color as the former kepi; except that the 2nd Regiment adopted a light-green one; and the 11th (in 1911), a red one. The 15th Regiment had light-red *Attilas*, with white loopings and light-blue bags; the 16th had green *Attilas*, with yellow loopings and carmine bags; the 17th likewise, but with white bags; and the 18th, green *Attilas* with white loopings and light-blue bags. All regiments had red breeches except the 5th, which wore black. For the 1910-pattern service dress, see under "Dragoons": the only difference being that instead of shoulder straps, the lifeguard hussars had a yellow aiguillette, and the Grodno Lifeguard Hussar Regiment, a white one.

VI. LANCERS

Lancers date from 1803 in Russia. The uniform at that time consisted of a dark blue *kurtka* with buttoning-over lapels, blue trousers, and lancer caps, the upper part of which was of varying colors according to regiment. Gray buttoned overalls were usually worn (Fig. 136k).

In 1812 the distinctions were as follows.

REGIMENT	COLLAR	LAPELS AND OTHER DISTINCTIONS	BUTTONS AND EPAULETTES	SIDES OF LANCER CAP
Lifeguard	red with yellow loops	red	yellow	blue
Polish	carmine	carmine	white	carmine
Lithuanian	blue	carmine	white	white
Tartar	blue	carmine	white	carmine
Wollonian	carmine	carmine	yellow	carmine
Chuguyev	red	red	white	red

The number of lancer regiments was increased within a short time; but generally speaking, the same distinctive colors were still in use in 1813. The lapels were either red or carmine. Some of the new regiments that wore blue collars had no piping on them. The upper part of the cap was now ornamented with yellow and red lines in addition to the white ones. Further distinctive colors were introduced in 1817: light yellow, light blue, green, and orange.

In 1825 the 1st Division had red distinctions. The 2nd had the same, but with dark blue patches on the collar. The several regiments were distinguished by the color of the upper part of their lancer caps: red for the 1st Regiment; 2nd, white; 3rd, yellow; and 4th, light blue. In the other three divisions, the regiments had distinctions and lancer caps of the same color, which were orange, white, yellow, and light blue in the 3rd and Bug Divisions, while the individual regiments of the Lithuanian Division had carmine, white, and light-blue distinctions. Around 1840 the lancers wore blue *kurtkas* (Fig.136l). The colored collar had dark blue patches with a button, or if the regiment had a dark blue collar, patches of the regimental color. The lapels, pointed cuffs, edging of the girdles, and of the shabraques, were of the regimental color. All regiments wore white metal shoulder scales and buttons. In 1840 the colors were as follows.

REGIMENT	COLLAR	PATCHES	CUFFS, LAPELS, ETC.	LANCER CAP	HORSES
1. St. Petersburg	yellow	blue	yellow	yellow	chestnut
2. Kurland	light blue	blue	light blue	light blue	black
3. Smolensk	orange	blue	orange	orange	light brown
4. Karkov	white	blue	white	white	white
5. Duke of Nassau	blue	yellow	yellow	yellow	chestnut
6. Wollonia	blue	light blue	light blue	light blue	black
7. Olviopol	blue	none	light blue	light blue	white
8. Wosnessenski	blue	none	yellow	yellow	light brown
9. Bug	blue	none	orange	orange	chestnut
10. Odessa	blue	none	white	white	black
11. Orenburg	blue	orange	orange	orange	light brown
12. Siberia	blue	white	white	white	white
13. Crown Prince Michael	yellow	none	yellow	yellow	chestnut
14. Iamburg	light blue	none	light blue	light blue	black

(continued)

REGIMENT	COLLAR	PATCHES	CUFFS, LAPELS, ETC.	LANCER CAP	HORSES
15. Belgorod	red	none	red	red	light brown
16. Chuguyev	red	none	red	white	white
17. Borisoglebsk	red	none	red	yellow	chestnut
18. Serpukoff	red	none	red	yellow	black
19. Ikraine	blue	none	red	red	light brown
20. Novoarchangel	blue	none	red	white	white
21. Novomirgorod	blue	none	red	yellow	chestnut
22. Elizabethgrad	blue	none	red	light blue	black

The lancers of the guard had red distinctions, and as a further variation, yellow metal buttons and shoulder scales. The lancer caps were red. The regiment was mounted on chestnuts. The Guard Lancer Regiment of the Crown Prince wore red distinctions and white lace loops, and yellow lancer caps. Its horses were brown.

During the Crimean War, the uniform remained as before. The lancer caps were altered in shape, and the lancer jacket was superseded by a *kurtka*.

In 1870 the distinctions were as follows.

REGIMENT	COLLAR	COLLAR PATCHES	LAPELS, CUFFS, LANCER CAP SIDES	BUTTONS
1	blue	red	red	yellow
2*	blue	light blue	light blue	yellow
3	blue	white	white	yellow
4	blue	yellow	yellow	yellow
5	blue	red	red	white
6	blue	light blue	light blue	white
7	blue	white	white	white
8	blue	yellow	yellow	white
9	red	blue	red	yellow
10	light blue	blue	light blue	yellow
11	white	blue	white	yellow
12	yellow	blue	yellow	yellow
13	yellow	—	yellow	white
14	light blue	—	light blue	white

*white lace loops

From 1882 to 1910 there were only the two guard regiments of lancers (Fig. 136m). The Lifeguard Lancer Regiment wore a blue lancer jacket with red collar, shoulder straps, piping, pointed cuffs, and girdle. The cap band and piping were red, as were the sides of the lancer cap. The buttons and guard lace were yellow. The gray trousers were piped red. The Lifeguard Lancer Regiment of the Czar (2nd Guard Lancer Regiment) wore the same uniform, but with white lace loops, and yellow sides to the lancer cap. The undress cap had a yellow band. The 1910-pattern service dress is described under "Dragoons." The Lifeguard Lancer Regiment of the Czarina had dark blue piping on the shoulder straps and cuffs; that of the Czar was yellow.

Lancer regiments of the line were reraised in 1910. Their uniform fairly closely resembled that given in the table for 1870. The 15th Regiment had carmine distinctions, blue collars with carmine patches, and white metal buttons; the 16th had red distinctions and white metal buttons; and the 17th had carmine distinctions and yellow metal buttons.

VII. COSSACKS

The cossacks' uniform was a development from their national costumes. In the eighteenth century they wore long coats of whatever color they wished, long waistcoats, white trousers in short boots, colored girdles, and tall cylindrical caps of gray lambskin with a colored cloth bag. Their arms consisted of lances, sabers, and muskets without bayonets, or carbines and pistols (Figs. 137a,b). Now and again during the century, coats of the same color were worn. Nevertheless, during the Napoleonic Wars, a common uniform is known to have been worn by only a few regiments. As a rule, blue and dark green were the most popular colors for the coats.

Although during the Napoleonic Wars there was a great variety of uniform, there exists a brief mention of regulations. The most usual dress consisted of a short jacket (demikaftan) over which the cossack coat (*chekmen*) was worn. It was the same color as the demikaftan, and took the place of the greatcoat, which was only a regulation garment in the guard cossacks. The *kolpak* (fur cap) was of black lambskin with a colored bag, and white lines, as in the infantry. The service cap, which is depicted in many contemporary pictures, was not a regulation item, and appears to have been the old 1809-pattern cap for noncombatants. In 1812 the uniform colors were as follows (Figs. 137c,d).

REGIMENT	CAP BAG	EDGINGS	WAIST SASH	TROUSERS STRIPES
Ataman	light blue	light blue	light blue	light blue
Other Don Regiments	red	red	light blue	red
Ural	carmine	carmine	light blue	carmine double stripes
Orenburg and Tyetyaren	carmine	carmine	white	carmine double stripes
Kalmücken	yellow top to lancer cap	yellow	yellow	yellow
Bug	white	white	white	white

The Bug regiments are said to have worn green double-breasted jackets. All the others wore dark blue garments. Equipment was of black leather; all metal insignia was white.

The lifeguard cossacks, which were uniformly dressed, had red demikaftans, with yellow lace loops on the collar and cuffs, yellow epaulettes; white girdles; white leather equipment; red cap bags and yellow lines; and blue trousers without stripes. The Black Sea *Sotnie* (formation) had a similar uniform, but with black collar and cuffs with white piping; later they wore half sleeves like those of the demikaftan. The illustrations give details of the styles.

Around 1840 the Don Guard Cossacks wore all-blue uniforms with yellow lace loops and epaulettes; red cap bags; and red shabraques with white lace. The girdles were white. The Black Sea Guard Cossacks wore the same uniform, but with red cuffs, and blue shabraques with white lace. The Guard Cossack Regiment of the

Fig. 137. Russia — Cossacks.

a, b, c, d, e, i, k: cossacks. f: officer, guard cossacks. g: guard cossack. h: officer.

Crown Prince (Fig. 137f) wore an all-light-blue jacket with white epaulettes and a white cap; dark blue trousers; and a white girdle. The Ural Guard Cossacks wore all-dark-blue uniforms with white lace loops and epaulettes, and a light-blue sash. Both the last two regiments had light-blue cap bags. In 1840 the distinctions were as follows (Fig. 137e).

REGIMENT	JACKET AND TROUSERS	COLLAR	PIPING	SHOULDER STRAPS	GIRDLE	CAP BAG
Don	blue	blue	red	blue	black	red
Black Sea	blue	blue	red	blue	white	red
Astrakan	blue	blue	yellow	yellow	yellow	yellow
Little Russia	green	green	red	red	black	red
Azoff	blue	blue	white	blue	white	red
Danube	blue	blue	dark red	blue	dark red	dark red
Ural	blue	blue	light blue	light blue	light blue	light blue
Stavropol	blue	red	blue	red	red	red
Mesherya	blue	blue	blue	blue	black	light blue
Orenburg	green	green	light blue	light blue	light blue	red
Siberia	blue	blue	blue	red	red	red
Tobolsk	blue	red	blue	red	black	blue
Tomsk	blue	red	blue	red	black	blue
Yeniseisk	blue	red	blue	red	black	blue
Irkutsk	blue	red	blue	red	black	blue
Sabaikal	blue	red	blue	red	black	blue
Yakutsk	blue	red	blue	red	black	blue
Tartar	blue	red	blue	red	black	blue

The Caucasian regiments had a different uniform. The main garment was the *cherkesska*, a form of collarless open-necked kaftan. Below it was worn the undergarment—the *beshmet*. This had a stand collar. There were cartridge loops across the front of the *cherkesska*. The round cloth cap had a fur edging. The shoulder straps on the *cherkesska* were of the same color as the *beshmet*. In 1840 these colors were as follows.

REGIMENT	CHERKESSKA	BESHMET, SHOULDER STRAPS, AND CAP
Caucasus	blue	red
Kuban	blue	white
Coper	blue	yellow
Volga	blue	light blue
Stavropol	blue	gray-green
Gor	brown	red
Greben	brown	yellow
Mosdak	brown	white
Kislar	brown	light blue

With the passing of time, the headdress underwent many changes. Up to 1914 it consisted of a fur cap, rather pointed at the top, with a colored crown (Fig. 137h). Flat-topped forage caps were worn in everyday dress. The coat had no buttons and was hooked down the front. The trousers were of the basic color of the coat. In 1890 the distinctions were as follows.

REGIMENT	COAT, TROUSERS, COLLAR, AND CUFFS	PIPING, TROUSER STRIPES, WAIST GIRDLE, AND CAP CROWN	SHOULDER STRAPS
Don	blue	red	blue
Orenburg	green	light blue	light blue
Ural	blue	carmine	carmine
Astrakan	blue	yellow	yellow
Transbaikal	green	yellow	yellow
Ussuri	green	yellow	yellow
Siberia	green	red	red
Semiretshensk	green	carmine	carmine
Amur	green	yellow	green

The last Amur Regiment had a cap like that described for the Caucasian cossacks and wore the *cherkesska* and *beshmet*. The conical fur cap was fairly tall. In 1890 the Caucasian cossacks were dressed as follows.

REGIMENT	CHERKESSKA	SHOULDER STRAPS	BASIC COLOR OF BESHMET	PIPING OF BESHMET	CROWN OF FUR CAP
Kuban	gray-brown	red	red	red	red
Kuban Foot Cossacks	gray-brown	carmine	gray	carmine	carmine
Terek Cossacks	gray-brown	light blue	light blue	light blue	light blue

The Lifeguard Cossack Regiment of the Czar formed part of the guard; it wore blue coats and trousers with red piping; red shoulder straps and girdle; yellow guard lace; and red crowns to the caps. The forage caps were red with blue band and piping. The Lifeguard Ataman Cossack Regiment of the Crown Prince had the same uniform, but with light-blue shoulder straps. The forage caps were light blue with dark blue band and piping. The Combined Lifeguard Cossack Regiment wore dark blue demikaftans with yellow guard lace, in everyday dress. The piping, shoulder straps, and caps were of the color of the respective army, from which the *Sotnie* originated. In full dress, they wore variously colored demikaftans. The cossacks of the Imperial Escort wore a red *cherkesska*, white *beshmet*, and yellow stripes on their trousers. In 1911 the lace was changed to white. Blue kaftans and *beshmets* were worn in undress; on these the lace remained yellow. The crowns of the tall fur caps were red. The Lifeguard Kuban and Terek Cossack Squadrons wore the same uniforms as detailed above under the Kuban and Terek Regiments; these units disappeared with the raising of the Combined Regiment.

In addition to the regular Russian army, many Bashkir, Kalmuck, Kirghiz, Tartars, and other cavalry fought during the Napoleonic Wars. There is no record of their having had a uniform; they wore their various national costumes.

For the 1910-pattern service dress, see under "Dragoons" (Fig. 139h). The devices on the shoulder straps were dark blue; the broad colored stripes were retained on the trousers. The rifles were carried slung over the right shoulder. The guard cossack regiments had red and light-blue piping respectively, on their shoulder straps.

VIII. ARTILLERY, ENGINEERS, TRANSPORT CORPS, GENDARMERIE, AND GENERAL OFFICERS

Under Peter the Great, the artillery was dressed in red coats, waistcoats, and breeches. The cuffs and linings were cornflower blue; the cravats, black. The gunners wore the same sort of cap as the grenadiers of the guard. Later, the distinctions were changed to black. During the reign of Elizabeth (1741–1762), the gunners' caps were changed for new ones, which were ornamented with a brass garlandlike comb (Fig. 138c). Peter III (1762) gave the artillery green uniforms with green collars, red linings, and yellow metal buttons. The other ranks' lapels and cuffs were of cloth; and of velvet for officers. The engineers wore the same uniform, but with white metal buttons. Under Czarina Catherine II, the artillery regiments of the infantry wore the uniforms of their respective formations, but with black collars, lapels, and cuffs. After the introduction of the universal uniform of 1786, they wore red *kurtkas* and trousers; black lapels, cuffs, and edging; and yellow trousers stripes and buttons. The helmet had a yellow metal plate and a white crest (Fig. 138d). The engineers had a similar uniform, but with white buttons and trousers stripes. The newly formed horse artillery were dressed in a like manner, but with hats rather like top hats, with the left side of the brim turned up, and ornamented with a white cockade and feather plume. On the upper part of the flap was a small brass griffon; at the back depended two cloth tails. The old uniform was reintroduced in 1796, as in the rest of the army.

Fig. 138. Russia—Artillery.

a: artillery fusilier. b: gunner. c: drummer. d, e, f, k: artillery. g: horse artillery of the guard. h: officer, horse artillery of the guard. i: artillery officer. l: general officer.

From the accession of Alexander I in 1801, the uniform resembled that of the infantry. The basic color was green, with black distinctions, red piping, and yellow metal buttons. Chacos were adopted in about 1807 (Fig. 138e); and helmets in 1846 (Fig. 138h). Later, kepis were worn, and later still, lambskin caps (Figs. 138i,k). Only the horse artillery adopted the cuirassier helmet concurrently with the dragoons, but it was given up in 1815. Up to 1909 the artillery uniform consisted of dark green jackets hooked down the front, with green collar and cuffs (officers had black collar and cuffs with gold lace loops), red piping and shoulder straps, dark green trousers, black girdle, and black lambskin caps with a yellow metal plate. From 1910 they wore caps and double-breasted tunics like the infantry. The horse artillery had dragoon helmets and pointed cuffs. The guard field artillery had yellow guard lace and red cuff patches with piping of varying color—white, black, or yellow—for each brigade. The service dress had the same piping on the cuffs, and red piping around the bottom of the collar. In the horse artillery, the cuffs and collar were green, the trousers blue. The cut of the uniform, and the headdress, were the same as those of the dragoons. The artillery service dress was the same as that of the infantry, but with the devices on the shoulder straps (crossed cannon barrels with the number below) in red, and in light blue for the horse artillery. The engineers also wore the same uniform as the artillery, but with white metal buttons and headdress badge. The engineer units of the guard invariably wore yellow lace loops as well. The service dress was as for the infantry, with red-brown shoulder strap devices; the guard had white piping on the cuffs. For a time, too, there was a unit of mounted pioneers. This wore a similar uniform.

The transport corps battalions of the peacetime establishment had gray jackets and trousers, with light-blue collars, cuffs, and shoulder straps. These formations disappeared around 1900. The battalions of the war establishment were dressed all in green, with light-blue shoulder straps and collar piping. In 1910 they adopted the infantry uniform, with light-blue collar patches and white metal buttons; the shoulder strap devices on the service dress were white.

The gendarmerie wore light-blue uniforms with red shoulder straps and piping, and gray trousers.

The uniforms worn by general officers resembled those of infantry officers in style. The colors were dark green with red distinctions and gold lace; and for the general staff, dark green, black, and silver. Rich embroidery ornamented the collars and cuffs; general officers had oakleaf embroidery. The piping was red. The full-dress headdress for general officers was originally the cocked hat, then the helmet, and later the fur cap (Fig. 138l). These latter were black, but white for general officers and aides-de-camp to the czar. The service dress was as for the infantry, with shoulder straps denoting rank. The majority of general officers wore blue trousers with red triple stripes.

IX. RANK DISTINCTIONS

The distinctions of rank remained largely unchanged in essentials from the beginning of the nineteenth century up to 1917.

Epaulettes were introduced for general and other officers about 1810, which in their appearance was based on those worn in the Prussian army, and later in the Ger-

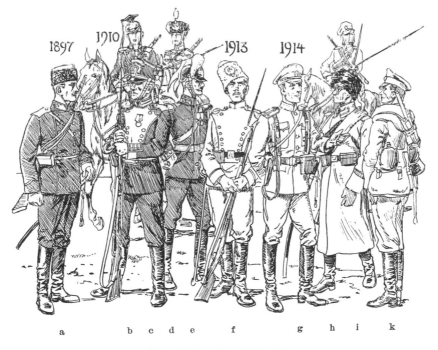

Fig. 139. Russia, 1897–1914.
a: dragoon. b: lancer. c: infantry of the guard. d: hussar. e: dragoon (cuirassier) officer (see text). f: infantry. g: infantry officer. h: cossack. i: rifles. k: infantry.

man army. For general officers and officers of the guards, the crescent pads and straps were of metal lace of the button color; the crescent was of metal; general officers had thick, stiff bullions; field officers, thinner, flexible ones; company officers, none. For line officers, the crescents and straps were of the cloth of the men's shoulder straps. The badges were worn on the crescent of the epaulette and took the form of small five-pointed stars of button color; on metal epaulettes they were of contrasting color. The highest rank in each grade—general, colonel, and captain—wore no stars. Marshals wore gold crossed batons. Hussar officers' grades were denoted by lace of varying widths on the collar and cuffs; the ranks were shown by small loops on the shoulder cords bearing raised stars. In the last third of the nineteenth century, shoulder straps were introduced on the everyday dress; and they were retained unaltered on the 1910 service dress. They were broad, long, and squared off at the top. On these were two longitudinal stripes for subalterns, and three for field officers, of narrow metal lace of the button color, showing the basic color of the shoulder strap between the stripes. The red shoulder straps of general officers had broader, vandyked gold lace, completely covering the straps, except for a narrow red edging. On the shoulder straps were worn the same devices of rank as on the epaulettes.

The rank distinctions of NCOs were denoted by lace of button color on the collar and cuffs, Prussian fashion, and also by transverse stripes near the top of the shoulder straps. Sergeant majors had a broad metal lace stripe of button color; sergeants had two and three narrow worsted stripes of button color; corporals had single narrow worsted stripes.

The sword knot, which at first had loose, and later fixed, bullions, was of silver with a black and orange core. The officers' sashes, and the girdles worn up to the end of the nineteenth century, were silver, with black and orange silk threads running through them.

U.S.S.R.

Cockade: five-pointed red star with hammer and sickle

The uniforms of the Soviet army were dark khaki (earth brown) in color. The winter dress consisted of a long double-breasted greatcoat with broad turndown collar and roll cuffs; and a single-breasted five-button service jacket with patch pockets on the breast, stand-and-fall collar, and round cuffs, and felt helmet coming to a blunt point, with cloth peak, and turned-up neck guard (Fig. 140a). Breeches and long black boots were worn. The equipment was of brown leather. In summer, a dark khaki blouse, with patch pockets on the breast, and a stand-and-fall collar, was worn in place of the jacket. In addition, a soft khaki peaked forage cap, with close-fitting crown and brown chinstrap, was worn (Fig. 140b). The steel helmet was of French type (Fig. 140c). The cavalry wore dark blue riding breeches. The cossacks latterly readopted a dress similar to that worn considerably earlier (Fig. 140d). The several arms were differentiated by various *Waffenfarben* displayed on the rectangular jacket and blouse collar patches, and on the pointed patches on the greatcoat. The *Waffenfarben* were: infantry and higher staffs, cherry red; cavalry, blue; technical troops, black, with variously colored pipings: red for artillery; steel blue for tank troops; blue for engineers; and black for gas troops. A large five-pointed star in *Waffenfarbe* was worn on the felt cap, on which was worn the universal badge of the armed forces, a small five-pointed red star with applied hammer and sickle in yellow. This also appeared on the *Waffenfarbe*-colored band of the service cap introduced in 1935. The distinguishing insignia of certain troops were worn on the collar patches, as were the rank badges, which took the form of small red enamel devices edged black. The ranks of NCOs and men were denoted by one to four triangles; subalterns by one to four squares; field officers by one to three vertical bars; and general officers by one to four diamonds. From 1935 special ornamentation was worn by all grades of officers on their walking-out uniform, consisting mainly of gold cord edging to the collar patches, and chevrons, point down, and stars, on the lower arms—in gold for general officers, and in red for other officers.

Fig. 140. U.S.S.R.
a, c: infantry.
b: infantry officer. d: cavalry

SPAIN

Cockade: red; later, red-yellow-red

I. INFANTRY

In Spain a kind of uniform was established at an early date. In about 1668 the infantry wore a close-fitting jacket called a *justacor* (or *justaucorps*), with large cuffs. The front of the coat was turned back on the chest, like lapels. Musicians had a checkered lace in the Austrian royal house colors (red and white) on the edge of the coat and around the pocket flaps. They also wore false sleeves hanging from the shoulders. The neckcloth was of white linen. The rest of the uniform consisted of knee breeches and stockings, usually red in color, and shoes. The headdress was a hat. The hair was parted down the center, and worn long. The long straight sword was carried in a shoulder belt. Pikemen were clad in breast and back plates.

The army was organized by and large in *tercios* and not in regiments. In 1694 ten *tercios* were raised in the standing army, formed from various towns and districts. These *tercios* and their distinguishing colors were as follows: Burgos, turquoise; Valladolid, emerald green; Cuenca, bottle green; León, yellow; Murcia, sky blue; Sevilla, scarlet; Gibraltar, flame red; Jaen, mouse-gray; Toledo, violet; and Segovia, silver-gray.

Around 1710 the uniform consisted of a white coat with variously colored cuffs and shoulder cords; waistcoat of the distinctive color; and white breeches; white or red stockings; black buckled shoes; white cravat; and black hat with white lace and a red cockade. The belts were of fawn leather. On the cartridge pouch flap was worn the royal coat of arms with the Burgundian cross in yellow metal (Fig. 141a). The grenadiers carried their hand grenades in a leather pouch; the pouch belt had a brass match case on it. A linen haversack was carried instead of a knapsack. The hair was tied in a leather bag at the back. Grenadiers wore a bearskin cap having a black cloth-covered plate in front, edged with sheepskin. The royal arms in metal ornamented the front plate. The red cloth bag had yellow-piped seams and a yellow tuft. Arms consisted of a musket, bayonet, and straight sword (Fig. 141b). Sergeants carried halberds instead of muskets. Colonels could, if they wished, clothe the musicians in the livery of their servants. In about 1730 the uniform was altered in some respects (Figs. 141c,d). The basic color remained white, except for the guards and Swiss, which had blue coats. The coat was worn open at the top, with the waistcoat buttoned right up. The hat lace was yellow or white, according to the color of the buttons. The neckcloth was superseded by a black tie. White gaiters with black garters were adopted. Officers wore gorgets as a mark of rank. Colonels carried a gold-topped cane, and a spontoon. Later, the skirts of the coat were turned back; and the

Fig. 141. Spain—Infantry, 1704–1793.
a, d, g, h: fusiliers. b, c, f, i: grenadiers. e: light infantry.

shape of the grenadier caps was altered. Light infantry (Fig. 141e) wore a more national style of dress: a red waistcoat with slit cuffs, blue breeches, and white stockings. In bad weather, a blue greatcoat (*gambeto*) was worn; normally it was carried slung over the left shoulder. The rest of this very distinctive dress is shown in the illustration. From 1767 the line infantry coats were made with a turndown collar and curved lapels, and turned-back skirts; and the cartridge box was worn on the front of the waistbelt (Fig. 141f). The colonels' spontoons and the sergeants' halberds were abolished. The latter adopted muskets. As distinctions, they wore worsted *dragonas* (shoulder cords) or *charreteras* (epaulettes). The hair was worn in two rolls on the temples. The lapels were shortly afterward done away with, and the yellow leather equipment was worn crossed. The hats were superseded by black felt helmets with a brass comb, and a red plume on the left (Fig. 141g). The grenadiers continued to wear their caps, which had richly ornamented bags. In 1779–1780 the helmets were given up and hats again taken into wear (Fig. 141h). The yellow leather equipment was replaced by white. In 1793 the hat lace was abolished. Lapels were again introduced, and black gaiters and black garters adopted (Fig. 141i). The light infantry wore green coats with red cuffs and lapels, white undergarments, brown leather gaiters, and blue greatcoats (Fig. 142a). In 1800 the uniform was blue and red; and the greatcoat, green and red. In 1802 green jackets with yellow loops and red distinctions were worn, and a crested helmet with green plume (Fig. 142c). For the line infantry the coat, which continued to be white, was altered, and made with straight vertical lapels. For a short time the hat was superseded by a form of grenadier cap, which had a lace-edged front plate with a red pompon above, with the royal coat of arms in the center (Fig. 142b). In 1806 the uniform consisted of an unlaced hat with a white or yellow loop and button and a red cockade. The white coat had variously colored distinctions. The shortened skirts had white turnbacks, with an edging in the regimental color. Heart-shaped cloth patches, also in the regimental color, were worn in the four corners of the skirts. The shoulder straps were white, with colored piping; the cuff slashes had four buttons on them. The undergarments were white; and the gaiters, reaching to below the knee, were black (Fig. 142d).

In the following table, all the colored distinctions were piped white, while white distinctions were piped in the regimental color. The regiments that had sky blue coats had all-yellow skirt turnbacks.

REGIMENT	COAT	COLLAR	CUFFS AND PATCHES	LAPELS	BUTTONS
Rey	white	violet	violet	violet	yellow
Reyna	white	violet	violet	violet	white
Principe	white	white	violet	violet	yellow
Soria	white	white	violet	violet	white
La Princesa	white	violet	violet	white	white
Saboya	white	black	black	black	yellow
La Cronoa	white	black	black	black	white
Africa	white	white	black	black	yellow
Zamora	white	white	black	black	white
Sevilla	white	black	black	white	white
Granada	white	light blue	light blue	light blue	yellow
Valencia	white	light blue	light blue	light blue	white
Toledo	white	white	light blue	light blue	yellow
Murcia	white	white	light blue	light blue	white
Cantabria	white	light blue	light blue	white	white
Cordova	white	red	red	red	yellow
Guadalaxara	white	red	red	red	white
Mallorca	white	white	red	red	yellow
León	white	white	red	red	white
Aragon	white	red	red	white	white
Saragoza	white	green	green	green	yellow
España	white	green	green	green	white
Burgos	white	white	green	green	yellow
Asturia	white	white	green	green	white
Fixo de Cueta	white	green	green	white	white
Navarra	white	dark blue	dark blue	dark blue	yellow
America	white	dark blue	dark blue	dark blue	white
Malaga	white	white	dark blue	dark blue	yellow
Jaen	white	white	dark blue	dark blue	white
Las Ordines Militares	white	dark blue	dark blue	white	white
Estremadura	white	carmine	carmine	carmine	yellow
Voluntarios de Castilla	white	carmine	carmine	carmine	white
Voluntarios de Estado	white	white	carmine	carmine	yellow
Voluntarios de Corona	white	white	carmine	carmine	white
Voluntarios de Borbon	white	carmine	carmine	white	white
Irlanda	sky blue	yellow	yellow	yellow	yellow
Hibernia	sky blue	sky blue	yellow	yellow	white
Ultonia	sky blue	yellow	yellow	sky blue	yellow
Neapolis	sky blue	yellow	yellow	yellow	white

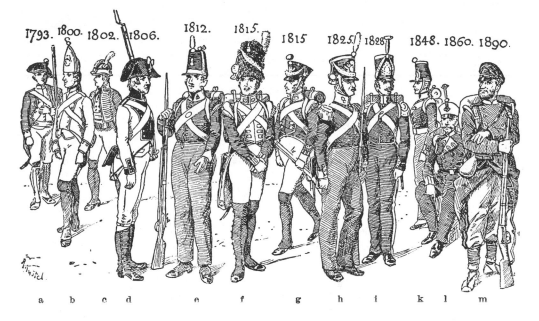

Fig. 142. Spain—Infantry, 1793–1890.

b, d, k, l, m: fusiliers. e, f, h: grenadiers. g: rifles. a, c, i: light infantry.

The light infantry (*infanteria lisa*) was dressed in general like the line, except that the coats were dark blue. The waistcoats were double-breasted. The greatcoats were brown.

REGIMENT	COAT	COLLAR	CUFFS AND PATCHES	LAPELS	BUTTONS
Primero de Voluntarios de Aragon	dark blue	red	red	red	white
Primero de Voluntarios de Cataluña	dark blue	yellow	yellow	yellow	yellow
Secundo de Voluntarios de Cataluña	dark blue	dark blue	yellow	yellow	yellow
Taragona	dark blue	yellow	yellow	dark blue	yellow
Voluntarios de Gerona	dark blue	yellow	yellow	yellow	white
Secundo de Barcelona	dark blue	dark blue	yellow	yellow	white
Secundo de Aragon	dark blue	dark blue	red	red	yellow
Primero de Barcelona	dark blue	yellow	yellow	dark blue	white
Cazadores de Barbastro	dark blue	red	red	dark blue	white
Voluntarios de Valencia	dark blue	carmine	carmine	carmine	white
Voluntarios de Campo Major	dark blue	dark blue	carmine	carmine	white
Voluntarios de Navarra	dark blue	carmine	carmine	carmine	white

The Provincial Militia wore white uniforms with red distinctions and skirt turn-backs, the latter having white heart-shaped patches on them. During the war against Napoleon and the kingdom he established, a bewildering array of uniforms appeared, as was so often the case with hastily raised troops. Gray, yellow, blue, and green uniforms, broad trousers, short knee breeches, round hats, chacos, and helmets of very varied types were worn. In 1812, with the help of British money, an

403

attempt was made to bring about some uniformity. The infantry adopted a blue short-skirted coatee with a row of yellow metal buttons, and red collar, cuffs, piping, and skirt edging. The initial of the regiment was worn on the sides of the collar. The headdress was a tapering British-style chaco (Fig. 142e). On the front it had a grenade for grenadiers, a hunting horn for rifles, and a lion for fusiliers, all in yellow metal. The fusiliers wore blue shoulder straps piped with red, and a black chaco band; the grenadiers wore blue wings with red fringes, and red chaco lace; the rifles had the same, but with green instead of red. The trousers were blue-gray. The light infantry had the same uniform, with a blue collar, and white skirt linings with a blue edging. The knapsack was made of oilcloth. The greatcoat was of gray cloth. In 1815 the regulation infantry uniform was as follows.

The line infantry wore a turquoise blue coatee with red lining and variously colored lapels, skirt edging, collar, and shoulder straps, white or yellow piping, and white or yellow lace loops and buttons on the lapels; white undergarments, black gaiters, and blue or white trousers. All the light infantry had turquoise linings and blue lapels. The grenadiers wore bearskin caps with white or red cords, and a red plume (Fig. 142f); the rest of the infantry wore chacos with a brass plate, and white cords and a red pompon (green cords and a green pompon for rifles) (Fig.142g). A number of changes were made in 1821. The lapels were abolished, and the coatee was made single-breasted, with a row of yellow metal buttons. The collar was changed to carmine, and the cuffs, piping, and lining to scarlet. The shoulder straps were of the distinctive color, and the regimental number was placed on the collar and buttons. Gray trousers were worn in winter. The grenadier caps were superseded by chacos with red lace, cords, and plume. Later the grenadiers were distinguished by red fringed epaulettes (Fig. 142h) and the rifles by green ones. The latter had green ornaments on the chaco. The light infantry had short green coatees, with carmine collars and scarlet cuffs and piping, and green trousers. By 1842 other changes had taken place. The chaco had become more cylindrical, and the collar was changed to the basic color of the coatee. The trousers were made blue. Patches were worn on the front of the collar, and these, together with the cuff patches and piping, were of the regimental color. These colors were: 1st and 2nd Regiments, carmine; 3rd and 4th, blue; 5th and 6th, yellow; and 7th and 8th, orange. The distinctions of the grenadiers and rifles were as before. The light infantry wore a uniform of the same style, but their coatees and trousers were dark green, with yellow epaulettes and white metal buttons.

In the 1840s the line infantry had green coatees, with green distinctions and lapels, white metal buttons, yellow piping, and blue-gray trousers. This green uniform did not, however, last very long; and by 1847 they had reverted to short single-breasted blue coatees. The cuffs, collar, skirts, and piping were henceforward white; the collar patches, blue; and the buttons, yellow metal. White trousers were worn in summer, and in winter, gray-blue ones (Fig. 142k). About 1850 the infantry adopted short dark blue tunics, with red collar, cuffs, and piping, and yellow metal buttons bearing the regimental or battalion number; gray-blue cloth trousers, black cloth gaiters, and gray-blue greatcoats with red collars. The low-crowned chaco was black, with lace around the top: red for grenadiers; green for rifles; and yellow for fusiliers. The pompon was the same color as the lace and bore the regimental number. Except for the 27th Regiment and the rifle battalions, which wore black leather equipment, the infantry wore white. Generally speaking, the changes of uniform followed those of the French army: the chacos became very tall; tunics replaced the coatees; and the crossbelts were abolished. A distinctive headdress called the *ros* was introduced in the 1850s, and was for a long time a characteristic of the Spanish army. It normally had a black or white cover. The trousers were madder red, as in the French army. In the field, a gray-blue French-style greatcoat was worn (Fig. 142m). The tunic had red shoulder wings. The rifles were distinguished by green wings, green piping on the shoulder straps, and green collars. In the 1890s officers adopted a dark blue dolman with black loopings. On service, a single-breasted tunic was worn. Officers wore their gorgets in all orders of dress. The dress cords on the *ros* were abolished in the 1880s; it had red piping around the top for the men, and gold lace for officers. In about 1900 the officers' dolmans were changed for tunics. Buglers had a special distinction of dress, which consisted of an Austrian knot of red cord, repeated three times at the sides, on the lower arms. A simple loop only was worn from 1910. On the collar of the tunic was placed the regimental number in metal.

The summer service uniform up to about 1920 consisted of a loosely cut jacket and trousers of blue and white ticken. It was also worn by officers (Fig. 146a).

The dress uniforms were retained for full dress and walking out even after the introduction of the service uniform throughout the army, and up to the abdication of Alfonso XIII in 1931, with few changes. In brief, they were as follows (for all arms) around 1930: dark blue tunic with a row of seven yellow metal buttons, red stand collar (and red round cuffs for officers), dark blue shoulder straps, the regimental number—or a distinctive badge for some regiments—on the collar; red trousers with dark blue double stripes; gray *ros* with red piping around the top, and red plume in front with the cockade and national arms below, with black peak and chinstrap; natural-colored leather equipment. The men's greatcoat was dark blue, double-breasted, with a red stand collar bearing the regimental number, and red wings. In full dress, officers wore gilt shoulder scales without fringes or rank badges, and a red and gold sash. For everyday wear, they had British-style forage caps of dark blue, with a red band and piping around the top; gold chinstrap; and the arm-of-service badge on the front: for infantry, crossed rifles with applied hunting horn with crown above, in gilt. A dark blue double-breasted greatcoat with dark blue turndown collar, or a dark blue fur coat with black loopings and black fur collar, cuffs, and edging, was worn. This fur coat was worn by officers of all arms and was the same color as their tunics.

For rifles, the distinctive color was green; on the collar was a yellow hunting horn with the number in the coil; above the cuffs were three small vertical green lace loops (gold for officers) pointed at the top, called *sardineten*. The trousers were dark blue with double green stripes.

The greenish-khaki service uniform was of the same pattern for all arms. The men's service jacket had a stand-and-fall collar; officers had a four-button jacket with patch pockets. Buttons and leather equipment were brown; and a khaki shirt, khaki trousers, and a double-breasted khaki greatcoat with turndown collar, were worn. The forage caps had a brown peak and chinstrap. Basque caps were worn by mountain troops (Fig. 146d). The bronze arm-of-service badges were worn at the ends of the collar and on the cap band: a hunting horn on crossed rifles for infantry; a hunting horn for rifles. After Spain became a republic, the uniform generally remained unchanged, except that the "royal" devices, such as the crown, were abolished. During the Civil War, a fore-and-aft cap with variously colored pipings and tassels was worn; and the Nationalist troops frequently wore their shirt collars outside their jackets (Fig. 146f). A new-pattern steel helmet was introduced (Fig. 146g).

II. CAVALRY

At the end of the seventeenth century, the Spanish cavalry (consisting of cuirassiers and dragoons) were dressed in yellow, with red distinctions. The cuirassiers wore breast plates and helmets; the dragoons, white felt hats. Musicians wore uniforms of reversed colors. In the late seventeenth and early eighteenth centuries, variously colored distinctions were introduced for the regiments. Shortly after 1700 the dragoons adopted green coats and green caps (Fig. 143b). The colors of the distinctions and undergarments varied for each regiment. A knot of yellow cord hung from the right shoulder. The housings were of the distinctive color, edged with green lace. Sheepskin covers were also worn: white for the grenadiers, and black for the other dragoons. The line (heavy) cavalry (Fig. 143a), formed from the cuirassier regiments, had white coats with variously colored distinctions. In 1719 the color and style of the uniform were altered. Henceforth, yellow coats with broad colored lapels, and white-laced hats, were worn. In 1748 a cockade was worn on the horse's halter, below the left ear. For a time around the middle of the eighteenth century, dragoons wore fur caps with a colored bag (Fig. 143c). Hats were later reintroduced. The basic color remained yellow—white for the heavy cavalry.

Fig. 143. Spain—Cavalry, 1702–1806.
a, e, h: line (heavy) cavalry. b, c, d, f: dragoons. g: hussar. i: light cavalry.

406

In 1805 a new uniform was introduced. For the line cavalry, this consisted of a hat with white or yellow lace, and a red cockade. The basic color of the coat was blue, with red skirt turnbacks, black stock, and chamois-colored undergarments. On the collar was a white lion (yellow for the 4th Regiment). On the cuffs were three white *fleurs de lys* (yellow for the 4th Regiment) (Fig. 143h).

REGIMENT	COLLAR	CUFFS	LAPELS	BUTTONS	REMARKS
1. Rey	red	red	red	yellow	white piping, yellow loops on lapels
2. Reyna	light blue	light blue	light blue	white	red piping, white loops on lapels
3. Principe	red	red	red	white	white piping, white loops on lapels
4. Infante	white	white	white	yellow	yellow piping, yellow loops on lapels
5. Borbon	red	red	red	white	white piping
6. Farnesio	red	red	red	white	yellow piping
7. Alcantara	red	red	light green	white	light-green piping on red distinctions; red on light green
8. España	yellow	carmine	carmine	white	yellow piping
9. Algarbe	yellow	yellow	light blue	yellow	red piping
10. Calatrava	red	light blue	light blue	white	red piping
11. Sanjago	carmine	carmine	carmine	white	scarlet piping
12. Montesa	carmine	carmine	white	white	white piping

The dragoons had white-laced hats with a red cockade. Coat, lining, and undergarments were yellow. At the ends of the collar was a device consisting of a crossed saber and palm branch, probably cut out of white cloth. The cuffs had flaps with four buttons, with white lace loops on them for all regiments (Fig. 143f). The 4th, 6th, and 8th Regiments had yellow collars; for the others, the collar, together with the lapels, cuffs, cuff patches, and pocket piping, was of the regimental color.

The distinctions were all piped white and were as follows for the eight dragoon regiments in 1806: 1st, Rey—carmine; 2nd, Reyna—light red; 3rd, Almansa—light blue; 4th, Pavis—red; and 8th, Lusitania—black.

The mounted rifles (Fig. 143i) wore a black chaco with white fittings and a red plume; and green dolman, breeches, and shabraques, with white loopings and buttons. The Olivencia Regiment had red collar, cuffs, and trouser stripes, and light-blue and red girdles. The regiment Cazadores Voluntarios de España had light-blue collars, cuffs, and trousers stripes, and light-blue and white girdles. At the ends of the collars they wore the same badges as for the dragoons.

Hussars (Fig. 143g) had the same chaco as for mounted rifles. The rest of the uniform was like that described above, but a pelisse was also worn. The María Luisa Hussar Regiment wore red dolmans with light-blue collar and cuffs, light-blue pelisses with red collars and cuff patches, and black fur edging. The loopings and buttons were white. The breeches and shabraques were light blue, laced with white.

During the war against Napoleon, very brightly colored nonregulation uniforms were worn. Order was not brought to this chaos until 1815. The 1st Regiment of heavy cavalry, the King's Cuirassiers, wore a complete French cuirassier uniform, but in red, without epaulettes; and with blue shabraques edged with white lace (Fig.

Fig. 144. Spain—Cavalry, 1815–1890.
a: cuirassier. b: dragoon. c: hussar. d, f, g, k: light cavalry. e, h: line cavalry.
i, l: lancers. m: officer, hussars.

144a). The dragoons retained their yellow basic color, and the rifles, green (Figs. 144b,d). The dragoons disappeared from the Spanish army shortly afterward. The heavy cavalry then adopted the yellow basic color; and for a time they wore red, and later light-blue, trousers. The helmet was originally of cuirassier type, but later crested helmets with combs were worn (Fig. 144e,h). In about 1835 the cavalry was armed with lances. The light cavalry, which wore green uniforms up to 1828, had short light-blue jackets with red distinctions and white shoulder wings by 1830. The trousers were dark blue (Fig. 144f). In 1835 green jackets were reintroduced, with red trousers. In 1844 there was only one cuirassier regiment in the cavalry, the rest being *lanceros* (lancers) and *cazadores* (mounted rifles). The cuirassiers wore yellow metal helmets with a black plume; red jackets with light-blue distinctions; yellow epaulettes; light-blue trousers; and steel cuirasses with yellow metal fittings. At the same period the lancers (Fig. 144i) wore helmets with a comb, yellow fittings, a black *chenille*, and a red plume. The Almansa Regiment had a green jacket with red distinctions and lapels (carmine for the Calatrava Regiment), yellow shoulder wings, and blue-gray trousers. The mounted rifles wore white metal dragoon helmets with a yellow metal plate; and later, chacos; they had green jackets like the lancers, but these were single-breasted without lapels.

The uniform of the hussars altered little. In 1815 the chaco was superseded by a fur cap; this in turn was replaced by a chaco, the shape of which altered frequently. For a while the 1st Hussar Regiment was dressed all in light blue; the 2nd adopted white dolmans, but otherwise had the same uniform as the 1st Regiment, except that the sheepskin shabraques were black instead of white. The dolman had short skirts. In the 1850s, the lancers adopted steel helmets like those worn by British heavy cavalry, with a white hair plume; at that time, their uniform consisted of a blue tunic with red collar, shoulder wings, and sleeve piping; white metal buttons; and madder red trousers. The lance pennants were always of the Spanish colors: red over yellow. The cuirassiers had a similar uniform, but with yellow collar and epaulettes, and a cuirass. In about 1890 the tunic was superseded by a light-blue dolman with black loopings and white metal buttons. The collar and cuffs were red. The red trousers had light-blue stripes. The helmets were steel, with yellow metal mounts (Fig. 144l). Around 1900 they had light-blue single-breasted tunics and light-blue trousers with double white stripes. For a time the mounted rifles wore the same uniform but had light-blue kepis, bound with red lace around the top, instead of helmets (Fig. 144k). The cuirassiers later formed the Palace Guard. Their uniform consisted of a short blue tunic with carmine distinctions and silver lace, and white breeches worn in tall boots, cuirassier helmets, and breast and back plates. The Princess's Hussar Regiment had an all-light-blue uniform with a white pelisse. The loopings were yellow and the kepi, white (Fig. 144m). The Pavia Hussar Regiment was dressed likewise, but had red dolmans and a light-blue pelisse and blue kepi. Both regiments adopted fur caps in about 1910 (Fig. 146c). The pelisses of the Pavia Regiment had large Austrian knots on the sleeves. The newly raised dragoons adopted the lancer uniform, with red collars and red pointed cuffs. The helmet of the lancers was latterly the same shape as the Prussian cuirassier helmet (Fig. 146b).

The dress uniforms in 1930 were as follows.

Lancer Regiments 1–8: Nickel-plated cuirassier helmet with yellow metal plate bearing the regimental device, with white plume in gala dress; and for everyday wear, light-blue and red British-style forage caps; the same for the men. The tunic was light blue and red, with pointed cuffs. The buttons and leather equipment were white. The regimental badge (usually a coat of arms) in metal was worn on the collar of the tunic, with crown above, and on the cap, without the crown. The trousers were light blue with double red stripes. The cloak was light blue with red piping around the collar and down the front. The undress tunic was all light blue. Officers wore braided silver shoulder cords; those of the men consisted of four red cords side by side. The trumpeters had a red feather plume. Their tunic had hussar-type loopings of distinctive color at the first, third, fifth, and seventh buttonholes.

Dragoon Regiments 9–11: The uniform of the dragoon regiments was exactly the same as that of the lancers except that the distinctive color was yellow, and the buttons were yellow metal. The trumpeters had a black feather plume.

Mounted Rifles Regiments 12–18, 21–30: The 12th, 24th, and 27th Regiments had tall brown fur caps; the 17th and 22nd Regiments, black ones; the rest had light-blue chacos with a black leather peak and broad white lace around the top edge. The fur caps had chinscales of the button color, a bag of distinctive color, and a feather plume of varying colors. Off duty, the regiments having fur caps wore British-type forage caps with a band of the distinctive color; the other regiments wore the chaco in an oilskin cover. The tunic worn in court dress was the same as for the other cavalry regiments. The distinctive color was generally white, but some regiments wore red with a white collar with red or blue piping. The regiments with fur caps wore hussar sashes of the button color and distinctive color mixed. The regimental badge was worn on the collar and on the front of the fur caps. The trousers were light blue with double stripes of the distinctive color. The Mounted Rifle Regiment No. 12 Lusitania had as a badge a skull and crossbones. The fur caps were brown, with yellow metal chinscales, yellow cap bags, and white and black heron's feathers. The tunic was light blue and black with yellow piping on the coat and collar, yellow and black hussar sashes, yellow metal buttons, and black pouch belts. The trousers were light blue with yellow piping. The forage caps were light blue with a black band, and yellow piping around the top. The badge on the cap and collar was a silver skull, with a gilt crown above on the cap. The mounted rifles' cloaks were light blue with no colored piping. The undress tunic was the same as for the other cavalry regiments.

Hussars: Regiment No. 19 Princesa. Black fur caps with cockade, gilt regimental device, and chin chain. White cap bag with gold cords and tassels, and a white feather plume. In undress, a chaco in a black oilskin cover was worn, and a light-blue dolman with three rows of yellow metal buttons, and narrow yellow loopings. The cuffs were pointed with double Austrian knots. The dolman was edged with yellow lace on all the seams, and on the top and bottom of the collar. The hussar sash was yellow with red barrels. The trousers were light blue, with yellow piping down the sides with two narrow yellow stripes as well. Double yellow cords were worn on the shoulders. The pelisse was white with the same loopings as on the dolman. The collar, front, cuffs, and hem were edged with black fur. The pouch belt was black. All officers' lace was gold. Single-breasted light-blue jackets without loopings were worn in undress. They had yellow cords on the collar and seams. The cloak was light blue. Trumpeters wore a blue feather plume and blue cap bag, white dolman with blue collar and cuffs, and a blue pelisse.

Regiment No. 20 Pavia. Fur caps as for No. 19, but with red bags. Red dolman with light-blue collar and cuffs and yellow loopings. The sash was yellow with blue barrels. The pelisse was light blue with yellow loopings and black fur edging. The remainder of the uniform was like that of the 19th Regiment. The trumpeters had blue fur cap bags; white plumes; light-blue dolmans with red collar and cuffs; and red pelisses with yellow loopings. The arm-of-service badge on the service dress consisted of crossed lances with superimposed crossed sabers (with a crown above up to 1931).

III. PALACE GUARDS, ARTILLERY, AND ENGINEERS

The halberdiers formed the Palace Guard (Fig. 145g). They retained their eighteenth-century uniform up to 1931. It consisted of a blue coat with red lapels, cuffs, and skirt lining; silver lace; and red, silver-laced waistcoat. The breeches were white, with black gaiters. The silver-laced hat had a red cockade. They were armed with a sword and halberd, the latter having a red fringe. The cuirassiers that formed the Royal Escort have been dealt with in the "Cavalry" section above. In court dress, the blue coatee had broad carmine lapels, without lace and silver epaulettes from about 1895 (Fig. 145h). The helmet had a white hair plume. On duty, when mounted, the guards wore the helmet without a plume; and a blue single-breasted tunic with carmine distinctions and wings, blue trousers with broad carmine stripes, and "butcher" boots, and gauntlets, were worn.

The gendarmerie wore a blue coatee with red collar, lapels, cuffs, and skirt turnbacks. The breeches were white; and worn with long boots. The hat resembled that of the halberdiers. The buttons were white metal (Fig. 145i). Trumpeters wore red coatees with blue distinctions.

The artillery always wore dark blue uniforms with red distinctions and yellow metal buttons, and their badge was a yellow grenade. In general they followed the changes of the infantry uniforms. The full dress worn in 1930 was almost the same as that worn during the preceding fifty years. The *ros* was white with red lace and a red feather plume. The tunic was dark blue and red, with yellow metal buttons; and the collar badge was a vertical flaming grenade. Double red cords were worn on the shoulders. The trousers were dark blue with single broad red stripes. The equipment was of white leather. The men's greatcoat was like the infantry's, but the collar badge was the grenade. The arm-of-service badge on the service uniform consisted of crossed cannon barrels (Figs. 145a–c).

The engineers had the same uniform as the artillery, but the buttons and insignia were of white metal. The arm-of-service badge worn on the service dress was a tower (Figs. 145d–f).

IV. GENERAL OFFICERS AND GENERAL STAFF; DISTINCTIONS OF RANK

The uniform of the general officers followed the usual style: a dark blue double-breasted coat with red collar and cuffs which were ornamented with one to three rows of patterned gold lace, according to rank. Up to the introduction of the tunic, the collar was worn closed, with the lapels buttoned back at the top to show the red facings, which were edged with broad gold lace. In court dress, up to about 1880, a

Fig. 145. Spain—Miscellaneous.

a: artillery officer. b, c: artillery. d, e, f: engineers. g: halberdier. h: officer of the Royal Escort. i: officer, *gendarmerie*. k: general officer.

black hat with black plumage was worn (white plumage for a general). About 1870 a long single-breasted dark blue coat without embroidery or colored distinctions was introduced as a service uniform, and a white *ros* with one to three broad gold lace bands around the bottom. In all orders of dress a red silk sash with gold knot and red tassels was worn, even in the late 1930s, as the distinction of general officers. From the 1880s their dress uniform consisted of the following: for court dress, a single-breasted dark blue tunic with rich gold oakleaf embroidery on the red stand collar, round red cuffs with one to three broad gold stripes according to rank, gold epaulettes (later gold shoulder cords), gold and red sash with gold tassels, dark blue trousers with broad gold lace stripes, black leather helmet with a gilt plate and white feather plume (Fig. 145k), and, from about 1910, a similarly ornamented white metal cuirassier helmet. The everyday uniform was, to begin with, a dark blue single-breasted coat without colored embroidery and distinctions, with gold shoulder cords; and a white *ros*; red sash; and red trousers with two medium-width dark blue stripes. From about 1910 a dark blue tunic with self-colored, red-piped collar and round cuffs was worn. The rank distinctions, consisting of a crossed saber and baton, with one to three gold stars, were placed at the ends of the collar. The British-style forage caps had a red band, and red piping around the top. The band had gold embroidery around it, and one to three rank stars, with a crown above, on the front. The general officers' service dress differed from that of the other officers, in being fastened right up, with seven gilt buttons, with a stand collar, and patch pockets on the breast. Their badge (with the crown above up to 1931) and the rank stars were worn on scalloped patches of basic color on the collar, on the cuffs, and on the front of the

Fig. 146. Spain, 1912–1936.
a, d, g: infantry. b: lancer. c: officer, Pavia Hussars, full dress. e: general
officer. f. foreign legion

cap. The general officers' red sash was also worn with service dress. During the Civil War, they frequently wore the more usual pattern of jacket (Fig. 146e).

From the mid-nineteenth century, the uniform of the general staff followed, in style and ornamentation, the infantry uniform; but their distinctive color was light blue, as were their silk sashes. The trousers worn with the dress uniform were always dark blue with two broad light-blue stripes. The full-dress headdress up to 1910 was the white *ros* with gold lace around the top, and a light-blue feather plume; and from that date, a white metal cuirassier helmet with yellow metal arm-of-service badge on the front, and also a yellow metal plate, and a light-blue feather plume. The arm-of-service badge consisted of a five-pointed star between two sprigs of laurel.

The distinctions of rank remained unaltered from about the middle of the nineteenth century. They were worn on both sleeves of the dress and service uniforms, and consisted of: for subalterns, one to three six-pointed stars of button color; field officers, one to three eight-pointed stars, on the cuffs of the coat, greatcoat, and fur-lined jacket. The cuffs of the dress tunic worn up to about 1910 had one to three narrow metal lace stripes of button color around the edge. Latterly, the Nationalist troops, especially, wore their rank stars on the front of the band on the peaked cap, with the arm-of-service badge above, and on the front of the fore-and-aft cap. The rank distinctions of the NCOs and men consisted of one to three diagonal stripes of the button color or of the color of the piping respectively, above the cuff. The sword knot was gold.

SWEDEN

Cockade: blue, with yellow ring

I. INFANTRY

Uniforms were generally introduced by Charles X in 1655. Some regiments wore coats, and others wore jackets. The breeches were the same color as the coats in some regiments, and of different colors in others. As the combinations of colors were derived from the coat of arms of the province from which the men came, this was very frequently red, but red-brown, brown, yellow, blue, and green were also worn (Figs. 147a,b).

According to a regulation of 1675, the infantry wore the following.

REGIMENT	COAT	CUFFS
Uppland	red	yellow
Skaraborg	yellow	black
Åbo	gray	yellow
Södermanland	yellow	blue
Kronoberg	yellow	red
Jönköping	gray	red
Björneborg	red	blue
Dal	blue	red
Östgöta	red	black
Tavastehus	red	yellow
Hälsinge	red	green
Elfsborg	gray	Isabel (buff)
Viborg	blue	red
Nyslott	green	white
Västgöta	gray	yellow
Västmanland	green	red
Västerbotten	blue	white
Kalmar	gray	green
Nyland	gray	red
Närke-Värmland	red	white
Österbotten	gray	blue
Jämtland	gray	green
Colonial Regiment	red	black
Mountain Regiment	gray	green

Blue uniforms were universally introduced around 1690. Under Charles XII the regimental distinctions took the form of variously colored breeches and stockings, and buttonholes in colored stitching. Yellow lapels were worn by the lifeguard of foot. The grenadier caps, which varied from regiment to regiment, had a distinctive shape (Fig. 148a). On service, the officers usually wore gray uniforms. These were also worn by some of the Tremännings regiments. The waistcoats were still made of leather. The coat was flared. Up to the end of the Seven Years' War, the uniform altered little, so that the army had a rather old-fashioned appearance. In 1748 twenty-three regiments had yellow distinctions; five regiments, white; and four regiments, red. The uniform was further simplified in 1756.

Fig. 147. Sweden—Infantry, 1655-1683.

It is a curious fact that before almost every war, the Swedish army made changes in its uniform, which could usually scarcely be implemented on account of the outbreak of hostilities and the great distances concerned.

In 1765 the uniform again became varied in style, color, and ornamentation. The coat was now made double-breasted for most of the regiments. A few of them adopted lapels. The closer-fitting Prussian fashion and the Prussian grenadier caps were copied.

In 1779 Gustavus III introduced the "Swedish style" of uniform. With it the appearance of the army completely changed. The infantry went into short coats with a low stand collar, ornamented in very varying ways. *Schurzwaden* were taken into wear. The hat had a feather, of a varying combination of colors for each regiment, on the left side (Fig. 148c). In general, blue and yellow remained the most common uniform colors. The cravats were red for some, black for others. Under Gustavus IV (1792–1809) the coat was somewhat simplified, so that it approximated that worn by the Danish infantry c. 1800 (Fig. 148d). The basic color was, however, blue, usually with yellow distinctions, but also with various other colors, e.g., yellow lapels with red collar and cuffs; or yellow lapels and cuffs with white collar, and so on. Two other distinctive colors were also worn: white and pink.

In 1802 the *Konungens Svea Lif Garde* (Royal Swedish Lifeguard) wore white-laced hats with a white plume, blue coats with yellow distinctions and white lace loops, and yellow breeches (Fig. 148e). In 1807 they adopted white undergarments, white epaulettes, and a crested helmet with a white plume. The crest ran obliquely from back to front. In 1798 the 2nd Lifeguard had yellowish-white collars, cuffs, and skirt turnbacks, and yellow ocher lapels, all piped red. The helmets had yellow metal mounts and a white crest. The undergarments were light-colored. In 1806 they had white-laced hats with a white plume; red lapels and skirt turnbacks, yellow collars and cuffs, and white lace loops and epaulettes. The lifeguard grenadier regiments had red lapels and cuffs, white collars, skirt turnbacks, and undergarments; and fur caps with a yellow metal plate and red bag.

Fig. 148. Sweden—Infantry, Artillery, 1700-1890.

a, b, c, d, g, h, i, k, l: line infantry (a: grenadier). e, f: lifeguard. m: artillery.

The uniforms of a number of regiments were greatly simplified in 1807. The coat and breeches were changed to gray, with dark blue collar, cuffs, and skirt turnbacks, blue and yellow sashes, and black leather equipment. The hat was turned up on the left, with yellow fittings and plume (Fig. 148g). The regiments were distinguished by their cockades. The Kronoberg Regiment had an orange one with a dark blue cross; Elfborg, orange with a red cross; Västgöta Dahl, red with a yellow cross; Kalmar, orange, the vertical arm of the cross, dark blue and the horizontal arm, red. A whole succession of new clothing regulations failed to bring about any order. In the 1807 campaign the Swedish troops in Stralsund presented a very mixed appearance. The riflemen of the Bohuslän Regiment, for example, were dressed in a light-blue coatee with yellow lapels and a red collar, with green ornamentation on the hat. Because of this combination of colors, they were nicknamed "parrots" by friend and foe alike.

In 1810 a blue uniform was reintroduced and almost all of the regiments of the line had red distinctions, Brandenburg cuffs, and yellow skirt turnbacks. The knapsack was worn on the back. During the 1813-1814 campaign in Germany, Russian-type chacos were worn. Several styles of uniform were worn in this campaign. The Uppland Regiment was still dressed in the tricolored uniform of 1800; the Kronoberg Regiment had the gray uniform of 1807; but most of the troops had the 1810 uniform, although with very varied regimental idiosyncrasies. From the reign of Gustavus III up to their going into the Prussian army, both the "German" regiments retained their individual distinctions.

In 1816 the Swedish Lifeguard wore yellow distinctions, and fur caps with a white plume and red cords. The 2nd Lifeguard had red distinctions, and hats with an oblique crest. From 1816 the coats were made to button down the front. In the previous year all the line infantry (Fig. 148h) had blue double-breasted jackets with yellow skirt turnbacks; cuff patches and shoulder straps of basic color; and collar and cuffs of red, dark blue, yellow, or orange; the trousers were gray with stripes and Austrian knots of the distinctive color. The chaco had white cords and a yellow metal plate. The pompon varied in color from regiment to regiment. In 1838 (Fig. 148i) the line infantry all had blue single-breasted jackets with yellow skirt lining; red collar, cuff patches, and piping; and yellow metal buttons; yellow girdles with two blue stripes; and blue trousers with red piping. The distinctive colors appeared on the shoulder straps and chaco pompon.

In 1845 a single-breasted dark blue tunic was introduced. The Swedish Lifeguard had yellow collars and cuff patches, dark blue cuffs and shoulder straps, yellow piping, and white guard lace; the 2nd Lifeguard had red collars, cuff patches, shoulder straps, and piping; and both regiments wore a crowned "O" (for Oscar I) on their shoulder straps. All the other regiments had blue collars with patches at the front; these were ornamented with lace loops for the grenadiers. The line infantry (Fig. 148k) had yellow collar patches; dark blue cuffs and cuff patches piped yellow; and dark blue trousers with yellow piping. The shoulder straps were variously colored, with the regimental number in red. The headdress was a spiked helmet, with a black plume for both the lifeguard regiments. White leather shoulder belts were worn. In 1845 the regiments were dressed as follows.

NO.	REGIMENT	COLLAR	PATCHES	SHOULDER STRAPS	PIPING	CUFFS	PATCHES	REMARKS
1	Konungens Svea Lif Garde	yellow	yellow	blue	yellow	blue	yellow	white guard lace
2	Konungens Andra Lif Garde	red	red	red	—	blue	red	white guard lace
3	Lif Regementets Grenadier Corps	blue	white	white	—	blue	white	yellow guard lace; no number on shoulder straps
4	1st Lif Grenadier	blue	red	light blue	red	blue	red	white guard lace; no number on shoulder straps
5	Andra Lif Grenadier	blue	red	light blue	red	blue	red	white guard lace; no number on shoulder straps
6	Västgöta	blue	yellow	yellow	blue	blue	red	red numerals
7	Smålands Grenadier Battalion	blue	blue	light blue	red	blue	red	yellow guard lace
8	Upplands	blue	yellow	white	blue	blue	red	red numerals
9	Skaraborgs	blue	yellow	yellow	blue	blue	red	red numerals
10	Södermanlands	blue	yellow	light blue	red	blue	red	red numerals
11	Kronobergs	blue	yellow	light blue	red	blue	red	red numerals
12	Jönköpings	blue	yellow	light blue	red	blue	red	red numerals
13	Dahl	blue	yellow	white	blue	blue	red	red numerals
14	Helsinge	blue	yellow	light blue	red	blue	red	red numerals
15	Elfborgs	blue	yellow	yellow	blue	blue	red	red numerals
16	Västgöta Dahls	blue	yellow	yellow	blue	blue	red	red numerals
17	Bohus Läns	blue	yellow	yellow	blue	blue	red	red numerals
18	Westmanlands	blue	yellow	white	blue	blue	red	red numerals
19	Norbottens Fält Jägare Corps	green	red	green	red	green	green	red numerals

(continued)

NO.	REGIMENT	COLLAR	PATCHES	SHOULDER STRAPS	PIPING	CUFFS	PATCHES	REMARKS
XIX	Westbottens Fält Jägare Corps	green	red	green	red	green	green	red numerals
20	Calmare	blue	yellow	light blue	red	blue	blue	red numerals
21	Nerikes	blue	yellow	white	blue	blue	blue	red numerals
22	Wermlands	blue	yellow	white	blue	blue	blue	red numerals
23	Jemtlands Fält Jägare	green	light blue	green	red	green	green	red numerals
24	Norra Skanska Jägare	blue	yellow	light blue	yellow	blue	blue	red numerals
25	Södra Skånska Jägare	blue	yellow	light blue	yellow	blue	blue	red numerals
26	Wermlands Fält Jägare	green	black	red	—	green	green	white numerals

The *Jägare* troops have been included in the above table for the sake of completeness. They wore trousers of the basic color of the tunic with piping of the color of the collar patches; with yellow metal buttons; and black leather equipment. In general, the development of the uniform of the *Jägare* troops followed that of the rest of the infantry. They were divided into *Jägare* of the army (formed into groups of regiments) and *Jägare Corps* (or regiments).

In 1856 the kepis ordered in 1854 were issued. In 1860 the line infantry tunic was made double-breasted (Fig. 148l), and yellow lace loops were added. The Wermlands Fält Jägare Corps adopted a *Bersaglieri*-like hat, which was abolished in 1901. Only the guard and the grenadiers had colored distinctions, while the line wore the universal uniform. In 1886 the tunic reverted to being single-breasted.

The first service dress was introduced in 1910. It was of the same pattern for all arms. The headdress was a form of tricorne hat (called a "Charles XII hat"—Fig. 149b). All regimental distinctions, with the exception of the buttons, disappeared. The uniform was modified in 1916, when shoulder straps and cords were adopted, and distinctions of rank on the sleeves were abolished. The blue chevrons on the lower arms were retained by all ranks.

In 1923 a new service dress, of earth brown color and of the same style for all arms and ranks, was introduced. It consisted of a single-breasted six-button tunic with a stand collar, patch pockets on the breast and skirt for officers—slit pockets for other ranks—with straight-cut flaps and pointed shoulder straps of basic color;

Fig. 149. Sweden—Infantry, 1914–1937.
a: infantry, full dress. c: officer.

trousers of basic color—breeches for officers—and a double-breasted greatcoat with flat turndown collar and shoulder straps. The buttons were of dull bronze, with various devices for each corps and regiment. The only arm-of-service distinctions were the colored regimental numbers or arm-of-service badges in yellow on the shoulder straps. These were also worn by officers. Equipment was of brown leather; officers wore Sam Brownes (Figs. 149c,d).

The rank distinctions, in silver, were the same for all arms. On the collar, company officers wore one to three medium-sized five-pointed stars; field officers, in addition, had a medium-width stripe along the front and upper edges of the collar; general officers wore a broad figured stripe, bearing one to three large gilt five-pointed stars. Officers on probation wore a star on a small crescent; NCOs had two or three small chevrons, point forward; the senior grades of private wore one to three vertical stripes. The kepi had a heraldic button on the front, with a blue enamel cockade on the upper band for officers; and a black lacquered leather peak and chinstrap. NCOs had no distinctions of rank on the cap; warrant officers and all other officers wore double silver cords on the vertical seams of the cap. Subalterns wore one to three narrow silver stripes around the upper band; field officers wore a broad one with one to three narrow ones below; general officers had one broad patterned silver lace stripe that covered the whole band. On the greatcoat, the collar badges were worn on the shoulder straps. General officers' lace covered the whole of their shoulder straps; field officers' lace ran around the edges. The rank stars were placed in a row above the regimental number. The old blue uniform was retained for wear in full dress and off duty. The full-dress headdress was abolished and a blue kepi was introduced, on which the rank badges were the same as on the service cap. Shoulder cords, and not epaulettes, were worn: for company officers, these consisted of four flat cords laid side by side, and for field officers, of two plaited cords; all were of button color, with rank stars and regimental devices of contrasting color. Warrant officers had shoulder cords without rank stars; NCOs and men had shoulder straps of distinctive color, or of basic color piped in the distinctive color. Rank was denoted by narrow metal or worsted stripes of the button color on the upper edges of the collar and cuffs. In full dress, with both the service dress and the peacetime uniform, officers had yellow silk sashes with a blue center stripe and gold tassels; NCOs and men had a leather belt and bayonet frog covered with a yellow-blue-yellow silk weave.

II. CAVALRY

In the eighteenth century the cavalry wore leather jackets made of elk skin. From Charles XII's reign, a single-breasted blue coat, like that worn by the infantry, was worn on top (Figs. 150a,b). The gentlemen at arms were distinguished by yellow cuffs and skirt turnbacks and by gold lace. White, yellow, red, blue, and buff distinctions were worn in 1748. All regiments had blue coats with the exception of the Bohuslän Dragoons, which had green. In 1756 the lifeguard regiment adopted a light-blue uniform with white distinctions. The main means of identification lay in the shabraques. The Mörner Hussar Regiment (Fig. 150c) had an all-blue uniform with yellow loopings; the *Flügelmütze* had a yellow lining and white plume. It divided and formed a second regiment, which wore a black dolman and *Scharawaden*, yellow pelisse, and white loopings. The fur caps had yellow bags, and a skull and crossbones on the front. The plume was white. In 1779 uniforms of the same style as worn by the infantry were issued to the cavalry (Fig. 150d). The Konungens Life Garde till Häst (Royal Lifeguard of Horse) had white uniforms with blue distinctions and white lace loops; blue *Scharawaden*; yellow sashes; and black caps with a white badge, and yellow plume. The dragoons (Fig. 150e) were dressed in blue with variously colored distinctions and with hats. The mounted rifles had green uniforms with yellow distinctions, and hats. Around 1800 the dragoons and carabiniers wore hats with a white plume; the lifeguard cuirassiers (Fig. 150f) had a buff-colored uniform without colored distinctions, and helmets with yellow metal mounts. All the cavalry had blue sabertaches with the three yellow crowns of Sweden on them. The headdresses, as illustrations show, varied greatly in color. The hussar uniform was always primarily dark blue; the collar, cuffs, and loopings displayed the regimental distinctions. The lifeguard of horse was very elaborately dressed. Its establishment and uniform were altered frequently.

In 1813 the uniforms were as follows: Lifeguard of Horse—short white jackets with light-blue distinctions, and crested hats; and from the autumn of 1813, chacos. Lifeguard Regiment of Dragoons—blue, with white distinctions, helmets; autumn 1813, chacos. Schonisch Carabinier Regiment—blue with yellow distinctions, bicornes; autumn 1813, chacos. These three regiments also wore short jackets in colors opposite to their dress ones. Smalands Dragoons—blue with yellow distinctions; chacos. Hussars—as the early Mörner Regiment, with black edging to the pelisse (white for the Schonisch Regiment).

The uniform underwent many changes. Thus the lifeguard of horse was dressed in hussar uniforms in 1820; in dragoon uniforms in 1845; in lancer uniforms in 1852; and in cuirassier uniforms from 1879. The colors, however, generally remained the same. The style of the jacket, and the headdress, approximated those of the infantry.

In 1914 the distinctions of the cavalry were as follows.

REGIMENT	TUNIC OR DOLMAN	COLLAR	LACE	HEADDRESS
Lifeguard of Horse	light blue	light blue, white lace loops	white	cuirassier helmet
Lifeguard Dragoons	light blue	white	white	dragoon helmet
Schonisch Dragoons	light blue	yellow	white	dragoon helmet
Norrlands Dragoons	light blue	orange	white	dragoon helmet
Lifeguard Hussars	dark blue	white	white	kepi
Schonisch Hussars	dark blue	light blue	yellow	kepi
Smålands Hussars	dark blue	yellow	yellow	kepi
Crown Prince Hussars	dark blue	dark blue	yellow	kepi

The service dress uniform resembled that of the infantry. In 1927 there were only four cavalry regiments: Lifeguard of Horse; Lifeguard Hussars; Schonisch Hussars; and Norrland Dragoons. The arm-of-service distinctions on the 1923-pattern service dress consisted of the regimental number in white. Off duty, the pre-1914 blue uniform was worn, with the exception of the full-dress headdress and epaulettes.

Fig. 150. Sweden—Cavalry.

a, b, d, e, h, l, k: dragoons. c, l, m, o: hussars. f: lifeguard cuirassier. g: mounted lifeguard. n: light cavalry.

III. ARTILLERY, ENGINEERS, TRANSPORT CORPS; GENERAL OFFICERS

During Charles XII's reign, the artillery uniform was all blue without colored distinctions. In 1779 they adopted a coat similar to that of the infantry. The shoulder straps were yellow; the remainder, including the breeches, were dark blue. The buttons were yellow metal. The hat had a white band and yellow plume. In 1794 the Finnish Artillery Regiment wore an all-blue uniform with red collar, and yellow-piped dark blue cuffs and shoulder straps. The buttons were yellow metal. The hat had a yellow plate, loop, and plume. In 1808 the Wendisch Artillery Regiment had an all-blue uniform with yellow metal buttons, and white collars with yellow lace loops. The leather equipment was yellow. The chaco had a yellow metal plate, black binding around the upper edge, and a white plume. In 1816 the uniform of this regiment was changed, and black hussar loopings and yellow metal buttons were added to the jacket. The lace loops on the collar were abolished. Blue sashes, and yellow stripes on the blue trousers, were also worn. The chaco had a yellow metal plate and black plume. The Göta Artillery Regiment wore an all-blue uniform with yellow collar, yellow piping around the shoulder straps, yellow trousers stripes, and bright yellow lace on the collar. The helmet had yellow metal mounts and a black crest. After the introduction of the tunic in 1845, the Svea (Swedish) Artillery Regiment wore a blue uniform with self-colored collar and cuffs, yellow guard lace, yellow trousers stripes, and yellow metal buttons. The shoulder straps were white. Leather equipment was yellow. The crested helmet had yellow metal fittings. In 1914 the artillery wore dark blue dolmans with black hussar loopings and yellow metal buttons, cuffs of basic color, and blue kepis with a black plume and yellow fittings. A colored triangle was let into each side of the kepi; these, and the jacket collar, were of the regimental color (Fig. 148m). These were: Regiment No. 1 (Svea), light blue; No. 2 (Göta), yellow; No. 3 (Vendes), white; No. 4 (Norrland), orange; No. 5 (Uppland), carmine; No. 6 (Småland), red; No. 7 (Gotland), green. The Fortress Artillery had yellow collar patches. The engineers wore single-breasted sky blue tunics with black collars and yellow lace loops, black cuff patches, and a light-blue kepi. The transport corps was dressed in dark blue uniforms with light-blue collars, pointed dark blue cuffs with lace loops, white metal buttons, and a leather helmet.

General officers had an all-dark-blue uniform with gold embroidery and gold epaulettes, and broad yellow trousers stripes. The cocked hat had a yellow and blue feather plume. The general staff was dressed similarly, but without gold embroidery, and had narrow yellow trousers stripes.

The arm-of-service devices worn on the service uniform were: artillery, regimental number in red; engineers, black letter "F"; transport corps, light-blue initial "T." The blue dress uniform was as worn in 1914, with the kepi. On the 1923-pattern uniform, general officers wore crossed marshals' batons, as did the general staff. This device was not worn on the shoulder straps of the greatcoat by general officers. The blue dress uniform remained unaltered up to the 1930s, but the cocked hat and epaulettes were abolished. A gold sash with a blue silk stripe down the center, and gold tassels, was worn with both the full dress and the service dress.

SWITZERLAND

Cockade: red and white

I. INFANTRY

Because of the peculiar political circumstances of Switzerland, the uniforms worn during the eighteenth century were very varied. Of considerable importance for the study of military dress in this period are two series of engravings: *Neujahrsgeschenk der Züricher Konstabler-Gesellschaft* (New Year's Gift of the Zurich Company of Constables), and the *Militarischen Gesellschaft zu Zürich* (Military Company of Zurich). These first appeared around 1689, and cover about a century. These are unfortunately uncolored but have been utilized for Figs. 151a–d. The short accompanying text to the New Year plate of 1763, showing the *Finalexercitii* of 1760, mentions "Red" and "Blue" Grenadiers. The dress of the Helvetian Legion is described in the *Revolutionsalmanach* of 1800 (published by J. Ch. Dieterich, Göttingen), as follows: "The uniform consists of a dark green jacket, with black collar and cuffs, a row of yellow metal buttons, long green breeches, short boots, round hats turned up on the left à la Henri IV, with a scarlet cockade, and a scarlet band on the upper left arm. Grenadiers are distinguished by lemon yellow epaulettes—gold for officers" (Fig. 151e).

After the Congress of Vienna, in 1814–1815, the question of a common uniform for the militia army as a whole began to be considered for the first time. Only the colors for the uniforms of the various arms, however, were laid down: blue and red for the line infantry, and green and black for rifles. Accordingly, up to about 1860, there were very many variations in dress and equipment among the cantons. Coatees, in various styles, sometimes single-, sometimes double-breasted, were worn as well as tunics. In 1862 the infantry adopted long skirted double-breasted tunics with a stand collar, and piping down the front, around the cuffs and the three-button skirt flaps—dark blue and red with white metal buttons for fusiliers; dark green and black with yellow metal buttons for rifles—with gray-blue trousers with piping; white gaiters; and black leather equipment and footwear. The men had epaulettes of *Waffenfarbe*; the officers' were of the color of their buttons. The fusiliers wore a low-crowned leather chaco with a red pompon (Fig. 151l); the rifles, a black leather hat turned up at the sides, with a green cock's feather plume on the left. The greatcoat was gray-blue, double-breasted, with double-scalloped collar patches in *Waffenfarbe*. In 1869, gray-black trousers with piping, and a black cloth-covered chaco with front and back peaks, were adopted. The chaco had the arm-of-service badge with the regimental number below, on the front; above was the canton cockade and pom-

423

Fig. 151. Switzerland, 1693–1869.

a: Zurich artillery. b, c, d: Zurich infantry. e: infantry of the Helvetian Republic. g: Vaud infantry. h: Basel infantry. i, l, n: infantry. f, k, o: cavalry. m, p: artillery (m: officer).

pon in the company color: 1st, green; 3rd, orange; and 5th, red; 2nd, 4th, and 6th, respectively the same, but with a white band around the center. The collar was for a short time turned down. Officers wore a tall, soft kepi of the same cloth as the coat, with band, and piping on the top and sides, in *Waffenfarbe*, a black leather peak, and a broad chinstrap. From 1897 the coat skirts were very short, with piping around the hem as well. The skirt flaps were vertical with two buttons. On the shoulder straps were colored patches bearing the detachment number. Cyclist troops were issued with a dark blue single-breasted tunic with five yellow metal buttons, with carmine piping, stand-and-fall collar with carmine patches, and fore-and-aft caps. From the 1870s a dark blue jacket was worn—by the rifles as well—on service. It had slit pockets in the skirts. Officers had collar patches in *Waffenfarbe*. The machine gun sections wore the uniform of their original arm of service, with three-button vertical cuff patches of *Waffenfarbe*, double-scalloped to the rear. The officers likewise wore them on their jackets. Natural-colored leather equipment was adopted in 1910. From the 1870s the fortress infantry wore the normal infantry uniform, but with yellow metal buttons and rank distinctions.

II. CAVALRY, ARTILLERY, AND TRANSPORT CORPS

After the Congress of Vienna, it was laid down that the cavalry was to wear green uniforms with red distinctions. The differences in uniform between the individual cantons were even greater than in the case of the infantry. As well as coats with lapels, single-breasted jackets were worn, and tall and bell-shaped chacos, tall upright black plumes and white drooping ones, and so on. In the 1850s the cavalry was dressed fairly generally in green jackets and trousers, with green shabraques and valises; the distinctions were red. The helmet (Fig. 151k) had a yellow metal plate, and a black crest for dragoons, and a yellow one for *guides*. White metal shoulder scales were worn; and black leather gloves instead of gauntlets. A low-crowned French-type leather chaco with horizontal peak was introduced in the early 1860s, and was changed in 1869 for one of the same pattern as that then adopted by the infantry (Fig. 152a). This had a black forward-drooping plume for dragoons—white for *guides*—with black cap lines for the former, and carmine for the latter. A further change took place in 1880 (Fig. 151b). The chaco worn from then up to 1918 had black leather front and back peaks. The body was covered with dark green cloth, and the top edge and side seams were covered by nickel bands. On the front was a white eight-pointed star with the Swiss cross applied, in nickel, and the squadron number in black; with a black hair plume for the dragoons, and white for the *guides* and machine gun squadron. The chin chain was of white metal. The coat, dark green with two rows of white metal buttons, followed in style the development of the infantry uniform. In 1869 the shoulder straps and stand-and-fall collar were dark green, piped carmine, the latter having carmine patches. Officers had passants. In 1880 the jacket had a carmine stand collar, and white metal shoulder scales. The gray-black trousers were piped red. From the 1880s dark green jackets with carmine collar patches were worn on service. The collar patches were also worn on the gray-blue greatcoat. The officers' greatcoat had, in addition, piping on the collar, cuffs, pocket flaps; and a cloth belt at the back. Natural-colored leather equipment, with the cartridge pouches on a bandolier, was adopted in 1910.

The artillery uniform almost exactly resembled the French one in cut and style: it was blue, with red distinctions and yellow metal buttons, red fringed epaulettes, and blue-gray trousers piped red. In the early 1870s a dark blue tunic with two rows of yellow metal buttons, and red piping, was introduced. On the dark blue collar were worn self-colored, red piping collar patches, pointed at the rear. The chaco plate was yellow metal; and the arm-of-service badge consisted of two crossed cannon barrels. The trousers were gray-black with red piping. From 1897 the collar was all red, with a dark blue grenade—gold for officers—worn slanting at the ends. The pompon on the chaco was red. The dark blue undress jacket had red collar patches without the grenades. The greatcoat was similar.

Up to the late 1860s the engineers wore long dark blue double-breasted tunics with yellow metal buttons, and carmine collar and piping. Their headdress was a round black leather hat with the confederation arms on the front, and a black hair plume on the left. The trousers were blue-gray. Thereafter, a dark blue tunic with two rows of yellow metal buttons, dark blue collar, and red piping was worn. The chaco badge consisted of two crossed axes. Black collar patches, double-scalloped at the rear, were added to the tunic service jacket and greatcoat in 1897. The trousers were dark gray, with red piping.

From the same period the transport corps wore dark blue double-breasted tunics, piped red all around, with a short yellow horizontal lace loop, piped red, on the cuffs, and on the unpiped dark blue collar. Officers had gold loops.

III. COMMANDERS OF GENERAL OFFICER RANK AND GENERAL STAFF; RANK DISTINCTIONS

In Switzerland, up to the 1930s the grade of general officer only existed in times of national emergency, when the militia was mobilized. Then, colonels were specially invested with the ranks of general officers. Consequently, there was no special uniform for that grade. The general staff uniform, with the rank distinctions of a colonel, and a white feather plume in the hat, was worn. In 1869 commanders of higher formations adopted a special uniform, consisting of a dark blue double-breasted tunic with black velvet collar, red piping, and yellow metal buttons, with the rank badges of a colonel; a general had an additional gold band around the upper part of the kepi. Generals and colonels of corps had a white feather plume in the kepi; colonels of divisions and brigades had green ones. In 1897 the collars were changed to red; and single broad red stripes were added to the black trousers. The tunic was also piped around the hem; and the feather plumes were abolished and superseded by gold pompons. A further distinction of generals and colonels of corps was their silver and red sash, with bows and tassels on the left side. The field service jacket worn by commanders of higher formations was blue-black with red collar patches. In the 1930s colonels of brigades wore infantry uniforms with broad red stripes on the trousers.

The uniform of the general staff was green with carmine collar and piping and yellow metal buttons up to 1869; and from then to 1897, dark blue, with a black velvet collar and red piping. From 1897 they wore dark blue coats with yellow metal buttons and carmine collars and piping, with carmine trousers stripes. The field service jacket was dark blue, with carmine collar patches.

Commanders of higher formations, the general staff, and unattached officers wore the cross of the confederation on the lower band of the kepi, with the confederation cockade above.

Rank Distinctions: Up to 1869, the rank distinctions of officers and NCOs were exactly the same as in the French army. From that year, cavalry officers wore one to three silver rank stars on their epaulettes. Those of company officers had a plain crescent; those of field officers had ornamental ones. The crescent pad was carmine for company officers, and black for field officers. Officers of all other arms wore passants on the shoulders of their tunics and jackets: transverse black velvet stripes piped red, edged with metal lace of the button color for subalterns, with broader lace for field officers, and with one to three stars in the center. Around the bottom edge of the chaco, and around the upper band of the kepi, lace of button color was worn to denote rank: company officers, one to three narrow stripes; field officers, one to three medium-width ones. In 1897 the passants were replaced by shoulder straps of gold or silver lace running along the shoulder, piped in the distinctive color, with an ornamental edge for field officers. One to three stars of contrasting color were worn one above the other, with the detachment number as well. These straps were also worn by cavalry officers on the field service jacket. The rank badges remained unchanged. The rank distinctions of corporals and senior corporals consisted of worsted sloping stripes of the button color, piped in *Waffenfarbe*, above the cuff; and for sergeants, of one or two chevrons, point up, in metal lace of the button color,

426

piped in *Waffenfarbe*. Sergeant majors and quartermaster sergeants had in addition a diagonal stripe of button color on the upper arm. These distinctions remained unaltered up to the introduction of the field gray uniform.

IV. THE FIELD GRAY UNIFORM AND ITS ARM-OF-SERVICE AND RANK BADGES

First experimentally issued in 1914, the field gray uniform was introduced in 1917 and, with only a few small changes, was still being worn in the late 1930s. The basic color was greenish gray, the same pattern for all arms and all ranks. The jacket had a row of six field gray buttons, patch pockets on the breast and skirts, and marengo ("dark mouse gray") piping around the pointed cuffs and rounded shoulder straps. The arm of service was denoted by colored patches, double-scalloped at the back, on the stand collar, and by straight-sides patches, 4 centimeters wide, running from the bottom to the apex of the pointed

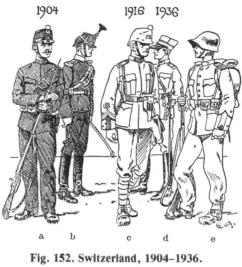

Fig. 152. Switzerland, 1904–1936.
a, c, d, e: infantry (c: sergeant;
d: lieutenant). b: dragoon.

cuffs, and by patches across the outer ends of the shoulder straps. The *Waffenfarben* were: commanders of higher formations and general staff, black; infantry, dark green (the rifle battalions wore all-dark-green cuffs with field gray patches); cavalry, lemon yellow; artillery, brick red; engineers, marengo; transport corps, brown; motorized troops, wine red. The engineers differed from all other arms in having the whole collar in *Waffenfarbe*. The machine gun detachments wore cuff patches with double-scalloped rear edges. Mountain troops had a black triangle as the lower end of their cuff patches. Officers had gold-embroidered triangles. The rank badges were of gilt metal for all except the cavalry, which had silver. Company officers had one to three five-pointed stars on their collar patches. Field officers had, in addition, a metal embroidered binding, 1 centimeter wide, on the front and top edges of their patches. Colonels of divisions wore dull gold laurel leaf embroidery on the collar patches, which were edged with gold cord along the front and top; colonels of corps and generals had, in addition, one and two silver stars respectively. For walking out, officers were permitted to wear a tunic without patch pockets, and with gilt or silver buttons. Company officers and other ranks wore their formation number on their shoulder straps. The trousers were of basic color, piped marengo. The greatcoat had two rows of five buttons, with two side pockets without flaps, and a half belt. The German model of steel helmet was worn up to 1935, when a new pattern was introduced (Fig. 152e). The peakless service caps had turned-up neck and ear flaps, and piping of marengo cloth. Senior NCOs and officers wore a kepi with a black leather peak and a very broad black leather chinstrap. The band, top, and side piping was marengo. Rank stripes were worn on the upper band, as on the dress kepi. The kepis of colonels of higher formations and general staff officers had the lower band of black cloth, which was ornamented with plain laurel leaf embroidery for colonels of divisions, with an additional gold embroidered stripe around the upper band of the kepi for colonels of corps. A general had two rows of narrow laurel leaf embroidery. Colonels of higher formations also had two black stripes on their trousers; and general staff officers had one. The ranks of corporal and sergeant were denoted by chevrons on the lower arms, of field gray and white lace, and of field gray and yellow in the case of the cavalry. Corporals wore a short chevron, senior corporals a longer one, with, in addition, a field gray coat of arms and two laurel sprays above the cuff, for sergeants. Senior sergeants had two chevrons and the coat of arms; and sergeant majors had a further chevron on the upper arm. All NCOs wore gold or silver lace, piped black, around the top edge of their collar.

The sword knot was silver, and was worn on a silver-and-red embroidered strap. Generals and colonels of corps wore a silver sash embroidered with red, with tassels on the left, as a distinction of rank. Adjutants wore a double silver cord on the right shoulder.

On maneuvers, before 1914, all troops wore a red band with the white cross of the confederation on it, on the left upper arm.

TURKEY

In the late seventeenth century, the Janissaries (*Jeni-Zeri* = new warriors) formed the core of the Turkish infantry. As described by Dr. Brock in *Die Brandenburger bei Szlankamen und im Türkenkriege 1691–1697* (Rathenow, 1891):

Long ago, they were recruited mainly from Christian children or prisoners of war; and a number of them still continue to be incorporated. The majority were Turkish professional soldiers, mainly from the European parts of their empire. They were a closely knit corps, organized into *ortas,* and lived in *odas* (garrisons), to which they were confined, under the absolute command of the Janissary *Agasi.* Each year, at Ramadan, they were given a new *dolman* or long coat with short sleeves, fastened around the waist by a *kusak*, a brightly colored girdle with gold or silver fringes at the ends. Over this they wore a *spahi* or overcoat of blue cloth. The headdress was a tall cap of white felt (*zarcola*), the top part of which was shaped like a long bag and hung down at the back (a fashion said to be in memory of the holy dervish Hadschi Bektasch, who consecrated the corps). On ceremonial occasions it was ornamented with a long feather plume, worn in a socket [Fig. 153a]. Their arms were a musket, saber, and a dagger stuck through the waistbelt, with the powder horn hanging on a strap from the waistbelt. The match was carried twisted around the left hand. The *Solaks* or Guards of the Sultan, 400 strong, were similarly dressed, in silk *spahis* and gold-trimmed caps. They were ordered to tuck the skirts of their *dolmans* into their waistbelts, to give them greater freedom of movement. Below this they wore close-fitting breeches of ticken or buckskin. The *Ichoglans* or officers were dressed similarly; they were former slaves. The *Sipahis* or regular cavalry were different from the *Zaims* and *Timariots*, which had feudal-type obligations. They were armed with sabers, *dscherid* (lances), and firearms. The first corps carried a yellow standard; the second, a red one; the others had red and white; white and yellow; green; and white, standards. The *Dellis* or "hot-headed ones" wore panther skins, and eagles' tail feathers in their caps, and had eagles' wings on their shields; and pointed yellow boots with spurs a foot long. They were volunteers, and often formed the bodyguards of the Begler Beys (governors). The *Sokbans*, a kind of dragoons, guarded the baggage. The *Acanzi* or *Azapas* were volunteers, and carried bows and arrows. The *Petits Tartares* wore long trousers like sailors, a plain cloak, long pointed woolen cap, and were armed with sabers, bows and arrows, and a *durd* (throwing spear). As the vanguard was not regarded as a position of honor in the Turkish army, it was formed of irregulars, Kurds, Tartars, and the like, whose main occupation was plundering and laying waste. The *Guastadours* or pioneers were for the most part Armenians or Turks. The artillery was held in great esteem in Turkey, not as elsewhere in Europe, where they had a long struggle to gain respect, the men being looked on as laborers. Up to the end, the *Topshu* or gunners formed one of the Sultan's most reliable bodies of troops. They were commanded by the *Topshu Baschi*, or grand master of artillery. At the head of the army was the *Vizier Azem* or Grand Vizier. His deputy was the *Kaimakan.* They, like the Pashas of Baghdad, Cairo, and Buda were entitled to carry three tugs or horsehair tails; the other Pashas, two; the Beys, one.

Fig. 153. Turkey, 1680–1890.

a, b: janissaries. d, e, g, h: infantry. c, f, i: cavalry. k: artillery officer. l: pasha.

There are no records of uniform clothing being worn during the eighteenth century. The army was first organized on Western European lines by Sultan Mahmud, in the 1820s. An order was given that 150 men be reduced from each of the Janissary battalions to form new units. This infuriated these privileged elite troops, and in 1826 they rebelled. The Sultan unfurled the banner of the Prophet, and suppressed the uprising in a sanguinary war. A ruthless slaughter ensued, and 20,000 Janissaries are said to have been executed or otherwise put to death. In Constantinople, it took two days to throw the corpses into the Bosphorus.

Scarcely had the rising been put down than the training of the new army began, and the Sultan discarded the turban and loose-fitting garments of his predecessors and took to wearing Western European dress: jacket, close-fitting trousers, and boots, with a fez. In illustrations of this period the Turkish infantry (Fig. 153d) is depicted as dressed all in blue. A close-fitting cap was worn. Artillerymen wore light-blue jackets and dark blue trousers. Cavalry wore tall red-and-yellow striped caps, and green jackets with red and white loopings, red girdles, and blue trousers. In 1832 the *Berliner Stadt- und Landbote* gave the following description of the dress of the Turkish army:

> In general the uniform is of the same style for all arms. Generals' and other officers' uniforms are mainly red, with gold embroidery varying according to rank. The distinctions of rank are as follows: lieutenant general, two crescents set with diamonds, with three stars, also set with diamonds, in the middle; brigadier generals wear similar crescents, but with only two stars. Lieutenant colonels have a plain gold crescent with gold stars. Captains have silver stars; senior and junior lieutenants wear plain silver crescents. These distinctions are worn on the breast on each side. The surgeons wear a light-blue coat, with a low collar, and carmine cuffs. Field apothecaries have plain ash-

colored coats. The cadets of the general staff wear the uniform of the infantry officers, without crescents and with differing embroidery. The pupils of the cavalry school wear scarlet officers' uniforms. The dress of the infantry is of exactly the same style for all, but the color of the coat varies from regiment to regiment: dark blue, light blue, red, and chestnut brown coats all being worn. The headdress is a *tarbuche* or Greek cap, and the *tequi*, a close-fitting cap, which is worn underneath it, with a part projecting down all around. The shoes are of red Morocco leather. The girdle is white. The artillery and engineer corps are dressed in red, with a leather waistbelt, the rest of the uniform being as in the infantry. The guard infantry regiment wears a chestnut brown uniform with more silk embroidery than the line. The bands of music in all corps wear blue coats, with scarlet collars, and lace of the same color, with yellow silk embroidery. The guards have gold embroidery. The fifers, drummers, and trumpeters are, up to now, dressed like the other troops. The cavalry wear a dolman with a brightly colored lace, five rows of white buttons, red cuffs, mameluke trousers of the same color as the dolman, and a red girdle. The headdress, as in the infantry, are the *tarbuche* and *tequi*. The boots are of black leather, the spurs of blackened iron, as in the French army. The four cavalry brigades wear green, chestnut brown, dark blue, and light-blue uniforms; and the guards, scarlet. All arms have an undress uniform of white linen, ornamented with blue lace. The infantry is equipped with muskets and bayonets and sabers, and have cartridge boxes of lacquered leather, and white belts. The artillery also carry muskets, but have a French-type sword bayonet instead of a saber. The arms of the cavalry are a carbine, pouch, and French-pattern saber, with white accoutrements.

Later, all the infantry changed to a dark blue uniform with a red stand collar. The principal garment was a waist-length jacket, fastened with one row of buttons. The cartridge box and bayonet were worn on white crossed belts—black belts for rifles. This was the uniform worn by the infantry in the Crimean War. The cavalry at that time was dressed in dark blue tunics, with hussar loopings and three rows of buttons. Woolen trousers, and gaiters, or boots reaching to just below the knee, were also worn. The officers had blue coats with fur-trimmed collars and cuffs. The greatcoat, the use of which was not confined just to the infantry, was gray-brown and had a hood (Fig. 153f). A white-striped woolen blanket was carried across the hindquarters of the horse. The cavalry was equipped partly with carbines, partly with lances.

With the exception of the fez, the uniform was of Western European type; but later a more national style of dress was adopted. During the Russo-Turkish War of 1877–1878, the whole regular army wore zouave jackets and waistcoats, baggy trousers reaching below the knee, and stockings (Fig. 153g). The basic color was dark blue throughout. Infantry, artillery, and cavalry had red lace on their jackets and waistcoats; the rifles, green. The stiff red fez with a dark blue tassel was worn unaltered by the infantry until during the Great War.

The uniform of the regular army, which was influenced by successive military missions, again came to resemble more closely those of Western Europe. In 1890 the infantry was dressed in dark blue single-breasted tunics with collar patches, shoulder straps, and vertical rectangular cuff patches with a single button, of *Waffenfarbe*, with piping on the front of the coat, on the skirt pocket flaps, and around the sleeves in line with the top edges of the cuff patches; dark blue trousers with piping in *Waffenfarbe*; and black leather equipment. The *Waffenfarben* were: infantry, red; rifles, dark green; engineers, light blue. In the late 1880s the cuffs were frequently pointed, of basic color, with piping in *Waffenfarbe*. The officers' tunics were usually double-breasted with collar and pointed cuffs of *Waffenfarbe*, with gold lace on the shoulder straps, also of *Waffenfarbe*. Later, Prussian-type epaulettes were worn. Off duty, a long dark blue double-breasted frock coat with collar of *Waffenfarbe* and deep, piped roll cuffs was worn. The cavalry regiments wore light-blue *Attilas* with black loopings to begin with; but from about 1890, they had dark blue single-breasted tunics with collar and pointed cuffs of distinctive color, varying by regiment, but usually red or green; yellow metal shoulder scales; light-gray trousers with colored piping, and black leather equipment. The carbine belt was worn over the left shoulder. The headdress was a *kolpak*: a fairly tall, round peakless black fur cap with the crown of *Waffenfarbe*, ornamented with lace. The officers' uniform was like the men's. The two elite regiments—the Guard Lancers and the Ertugrul Lifeguard Regiment—wore the fur cap with a dark blue lancer uniform with red distinctions. The Guard Lancers also had red lapels, with white buttons and guard lace on the collar and cuffs; dark blue trousers with broad red stripes, and lances with red pennants. The artillery had dark blue, black-looped *Attilas* with red collar and pointed cuffs, yellow metal buttons; gray trousers with broad red stripes, fur cap, and black leather equipment (Fig. 153k). In full dress, general officers wore the fez, with a long-skirted single-breasted coat with red collar and cuffs (both completely covered with rich gold embroidery), with broad gold embroidery on the front; and dark blue trousers with broad gold stripes (Fig. 153l). From the mid-1890s, heavy gold epaulettes with stiff fringes were also worn. In everyday dress, they wore a long-skirted double-breasted dark blue frock coat with red collar, with gold embroidery at the ends, and deep, red-piped roll cuffs; dark blue trousers with red triple stripes, and high boots; red shoulder straps ornamented with broad gold lace stripes, and from the beginning of the present century, plaited gold shoulder cords. Generals of cavalry wore gray trousers with triple red stripes; and the black cavalry-pattern fur cap. The rank distinctions of general officers were placed on the cuffs of the frock coat. All generals wore, along the top of the cuff, four medium-width gold loops, and above these, slanting medium-width gold stripes: four for a marshal, three for a general commanding a division, and two for a general commanding a brigade.

Officers of the general staff wore the undress uniform of a general officer: the dark blue double-breasted frock coat, with red piping, gold-embroidered crossed rifles and flags at the ends of the collar; a double gold aiguillette on the right shoulder; and triple stripes on the trousers. The rank distinctions of the NCOs and men consisted of one to three fairly large chevrons in *Waffenfarbe*, point up, on the upper arm; sergeants wore in addition a fourth gold one below. Officers' ranks were denoted by metal lace stripes, according to rank, around the top of the cuffs: colonels wore four medium-width ones of button color; lieutenant colonels likewise, the first and third from the top being of contrasting color; majors, three medium-width stripes; captains, two; senior lieutenants, one; lieutenants, one in contrasting color.

In the years immediately before 1914, the German Military Mission exerted a noticeable influence on the uniforms. The cut of the tunic came more and more to resemble the German one. Officers wore single-breasted tunics like the men.

A khaki service dress was introduced in 1909. It consisted of a single-breasted jacket with a stand-and-fall collar, breeches and puttees, and brown leather equip-

Fig. 154. Turkey, 1916–1930.

a, d: infantry. b, c: infantry officers. e: cavalry. f: field officer, full dress.

ment and footwear. The headdress, somewhat resembling a tropical helmet, was made of khaki-colored cloth (Fig. 154a). With this uniform, however, officers and cavalry wore a gray fur cap. The arm of service was denoted by the varying colors of the collar, and crown of the fur cap: infantry, khaki; rifles, olive green; cavalry, light gray; artillery, dark blue; engineers, light blue; transport corps, red; general officers, scarlet; general staff, carmine. The men's rank distinctions were unchanged, but were worn in reduced size, on the upper arm. Officers had gold shoulder cords of German type, with silver stars on them (Fig. 154b). After the war, several alterations were made to the uniform. A peakless kepi with crescent and star on the front was introduced; and triangular patches of *Waffenfarbe* on the collar; with gold rank stars on them for officers, and gold rank stripes around the kepi (Fig. 154c). About 1930 a khaki-colored cap with cloth peak was taken into wear, and the collar patches were altered (Figs. 154 d,e). In full dress and off duty, officers wore a jacket with patch pockets on the breast and skirts, stand-and-fall collar, and gold plaited shoulder cords. With it was worn a British-style peaked cap. Rank was denoted by varying lace on the collar patches and the cap band. On the collar patches, company officers, field officers, and general officers wore one to three horizontal medium-width gold stripes respectively, and above them, according to rank, one to three gold stars together (Fig. 154f).

UNITED STATES OF AMERICA

I. INFANTRY

The first uniformed troops in North America were the militia raised by the governors and towns. At the beginning of the Revolution, these corps fought in their varied uniforms, which frequently resembled British ones. The newly raised volunteers were dressed and equipped in so many ways in this period that only a few instances can be given. "America" at the time consisted only of thirteen colonies, and had no indigenous clothing manufactories. Thus, the earliest levies frequently had to serve in their civilian clothes. The trappers and hunters were better off, their everyday dress being suitable for campaigning (Fig. 155a). Some examples of the uniforms worn are given below.

1772–1775. The Battalion of Independent Foot Companies of Militia, New York City: Grenadier company, blue with red distinctions; fusiliers, blue with red distinctions, and fur caps with the legend "Fusiliers—*salus populi suprema lex*." The German fusiliers were dressed similarly, but had silver lace in addition, and the inscription "German Fusiliers" on their cap plates. The Union, Light Infantry Company, and Oswego Rangers also wore blue uniforms with red distinctions, and white undergarments. The Bold Foresters had green coats, and round hats turned up at the sides, with a plate in front with "Freedom" on it. The Sportsmans Company and the Corsicans and Rangers were dressed in green coats with buff and carmine distinctions respectively. The New York Independent Companies of Rangers wore blue uniforms with white distinctions, and a helmet with a skull and crossbones and "Liberty" below, painted in white on the front. The Massachusetts and Connecticut militias mainly wore red coats. The majority of the corps, however, adopted the dress worn by the trappers and huntsmen. The Maryland Rifles were mostly dressed in green hunting shirts. Morgan's Riflemen, the 1st Virginia Regiment of Infantry, and the 5th Regiment of South Carolina Riflemen wore white hunting shirts, which they supplied at their own expense, so that some sort of uniformity ensued. General Washington himself recommended this dress to all those who could not obtain a military uniform, as with it they would give the enemy the impression that every man was a marksman. In 1774 the 1st Company of Governor's Foot Guards of Connecticut wore red coats with black lapels, with yellow lace, white skirt turnbacks, straw-yellow breeches and waistcoats, and fur caps with a red plume. The 2nd Company had red coats with buff distinctions and white metal buttons, and white waistcoats and breeches. In 1775 the Light Company of the 1st Philadelphia Battalion wore light-blue coats with buff distinctions.

In 1775 the troops were ordered to adopt brown uniforms with variously colored distinctions for each regiment. In that year the uniforms worn by the New York infantry were as follows:

> 1st Regiment—blue coats with carmine distinctions
> 2nd Regiment—light brown with blue distinctions
> 3rd Regiment—gray with green distinctions
> 4th Regiment—dark brown with scarlet distinctions

In Connecticut the prewar red coats continued to be worn.
In Pennsylvania the uniforms were:

> 1st Regiment—brown with buff distinctions
> 2nd Regiment—blue with red; round black hats
> 3rd Regiment—brown with white; tricorne with white lace
> 4th Regiment—blue with white
> 5th Regiment—blue with white
> 6th Regiment—blue with red

In New Jersey blue uniforms were usually worn, but red coats with buff distinctions were also in evidence. The Declaration of Independence was signed in 1776. In 1777 the colors of uniforms had become so varied that in August of that year, green sprigs were ordered to be worn in the headdress as a universal badge. Baron von Steuben reported that the officers wore coats of all colors and styles. In 1777 the following colors are noted: blue and white; red with black distinctions; brown uniforms with sea green distinctions, lined white, with silver lace; gray coats with buff lapels and cuffs. The Pennsylvania regiments were distinguished by their plain yellowish-brown coats. They were nicknamed the "Quaker Brigade."

Fig. 155. United States of America, 1775–1861.
a: rifleman. c, d, f, g, h, i, k: infantry. b, e: cavalry. l: artillery.
m: infantry officer, full dress.

On 2 October 1779, the following distinctions are mentioned:

Blue with white distinctions: New Hampshire, Massachusetts, Rhode Island, Connecticut
Blue and buff, white skirt turnbacks and undergarments: New York, New Jersey
Blue and red: Pennsylvania, Delaware, Maryland, Virginia
Blue with blue distinctions: North Carolina, South Carolina, Georgia

From that time, a universal black and white cockade was worn: the white part was included as a compliment to France (Fig. 155c). Officers and NCOs carried staff weapons. The rank distinctions are given in Part III. Bandsmen were normally dressed in uniforms of the reversed colors. Washington's Commander in Chief's Guard wore blue coats with white distinctions, white undergarments, black half gaiters, and hats with a blue and white feather.

In 1782 an order was promulgated that the infantry and cavalry were for the future to wear blue uniforms with red distinctions, with white linings, and white metal buttons. These distinctions do not appear to have been universally adopted until 1796. Bandmen wore red coats with blue distinctions and undergarments. In 1799 the black and white cockade was replaced by a black one with a white eagle on it. Cocked hats were abolished in 1802 and superseded by a crested helmet. The winter trousers were changed to blue, and white ones were thenceforth worn in summer (Fig. 155d). In 1808 the long coat was superseded by a single-breasted coatee with silver lace loops down the front. The headdress was a cylindrical hat with a cockade and a plume on the left side. Sergeants wore a yellow epaulette on the right shoulder; corporals, one on the left. The red distinctions were abolished in 1812. The blue jacket was fastened by ten white metal buttons, with black twist loops. The blue collar was edged with white, and had two narrow white lace loops and buttons. The blue cuffs had three white metal buttons with black loops on them. The chaco had a yellow metal eagle plate, and a white plume and white cords and chinscales (Fig. 155f).

The rifles wore all-gray uniforms. The loops on the front were sloped, with the buttons forming the apex of a vee. Similarly shaped loops corresponded to the three buttons, placed one above the other, on the cuffs. The collar was as for the infantry, but gray, with black loops and lace. The buttons were of yellow metal. The leather equipment was white, as for the infantry. The chaco was similar to that worn by the line infantry, but had a yellow metal hunting horn badge, green plume and cords, and yellow metal chinscales. The 4th Rifle Regiment wore this uniform in the Battle of Chippewa, at Niagara. To commemorate this victory, the cadets at West Point Military Academy still wear this uniform. Officers of infantry and rifles wore long-skirted coatees and tall bicornes.

In 1821 blue was decreed to be the national color. There was a noticeable striving for simplification. Red coats were only to be worn by bandsmen. From this time, the NCOs' rank distinctions were worn on the sleeves.

In 1835 the chaco was made more straight-sided and the cords were abolished. White epaulettes replaced the blue shoulder straps. The skirt turnbacks were made white. The loops on the front of the coat were abolished, and gray-blue trousers introduced. The chaco emblem was changed to a white metal eagle with a hunting horn below. The cuff patches were unusual. There was no actual cuff; the rectangular patches were piped white on three sides, with only two buttons and loops (Fig. 155g). A distinctive service uniform was worn as well at this time. It consisted of a gray-blue shell jacket and trousers. The sleeves were made without patches, but had two buttons on the hindarm seam. In general it resembled the uniform described above; with it was worn a soft blue forage cap (Fig. 155h).

In 1851 a completely new uniform was introduced. It consisted of a dark blue tunic without piping, with a light-blue collar bearing the regimental number in yellow at the ends, light-blue pointed cuffs, and light-blue epaulettes. In full dress, bandsmen wore a plastron-shaped lapel. A tall dark blue kepi with a light-blue band and light-blue pompon was introduced in place of the chaco. The trousers were as before, but blue stripes were added. The leather equipment was changed to black. Officers had neither colored distinctions nor lapels. In undress and off duty, officers wore passants on their shoulders. On these and on the straps of the epaulettes were placed the rank distinctions: colonel, a silver eagle; lieutenant colonel, a silver leaf; major, a gold leaf; captain, two gold bars; 1st lieutenant, one gold bar; 2nd lieutenant, none. The regimental numeral in yellow was worn on the oval, raised cloth crescent of the epaulettes, and on the kepi band was worn the number and a bugle horn badge. The men retained their undress jackets (Fig. 155i). The epaulettes and bandsmen's lapels were abolished in 1855. The colored band on the kepi was superseded by colored piping. The bandsmen's red coats were done away with in 1857.

In 1861 the collar and cuffs were dark blue with light-blue piping. Yellow metal shoulder scales were worn. The full-dress trousers were changed to dark blue. The stiff kepi was abolished. A black lacquered hat, turned up on the left side, with the regimental device and a black feather, was introduced (Fig. 155m). The service dress consisted of a low crowned dark blue kepi, a short-skirted dark blue jacket with self-colored turndown collar, without colored distinctions, and the old gray-blue trousers without piping. This comprised the dress of the federal troops during the Civil War (Fig. 155k).

On the outbreak of war, the small army had to be greatly expanded. With the calling out of the very colorful and frequently very showily dressed militias, and the raising of volunteer formations, the northern armies assumed a very varied appearance. The 1st Division of New York Militia wore Scottish highland dress. The 2nd Regiment, like various other corps, still wore a tall kepi similar to the 1851 pattern, and double-breasted coats with epaulettes. The Ohio Regiment wore short open jackets. The French Zouave uniform was especially popular, and was worn by the following units: 55th Regiment New York State Militia (French Zouaves), New York State Volunteers (New York Zouaves), the New York Firemen, the Vanguard, the National Zouaves, the Young Zouaves, and others. Each corps varied in the cut and color of its uniform; the trousers were red or blue, mostly like Arabian ones, but long trousers were also worn, and kepis in addition to the fez and *chechia*. There was also an Italian influence, and the Zouave Firemen wore Garibaldi shirts for a while, and the Garibaldi Guard wore a *Bersaglieri* uniform. The only German influence manifested itself in the frequently worn drill dress.

On service, Confederate troops wore a gray broad-brimmed hat, or a gray-blue kepi with blue band, short gray-blue jacket without colored distinctions, with black-piped pointed cuffs and yellow metal buttons; and brown leather equipment. The everyday uniform consisted of a double-breasted gray coat with blue collar, piping, pointed cuffs, and trousers, and kepi as before. Equipment was of black leather. In the southern states, too, some volunteer corps wore Zouave and drill uniforms. With the end of the Civil War, the distinctive Confederate uniforms came to an end.

The infantry uniform was altered in 1872. A new tunic with shorter skirts was introduced, with white collar patches bearing the regimental number, white shoulder straps, and double-scalloped white cuff patches. From this time, the coat was piped down the front. NCOs' lace was now made white. A blue cloth-covered chaco was adopted. The fir-cone-shaped pompon and the piping were white (Fig. 156a). The officers' chacos had drooping plumes. Officers also wore dark blue double-breasted coats without colored distinctions, with epaulettes. The cuffs were without patches, but had lace loops, pointed at the top. A gold-laced waistbelt replaced the black one. The crimson sashes hitherto worn were abolished. On the gray trousers were broad dark blue stripes.

In 1881 a spiked helmet was introduced. All-white collars were added to the tunics, and the regimental numerals were removed. The pouch belt, worn over the shoulder, was abolished. Bandsmen wore white lace loops on the front of their tunics, and two white stripes on their trousers. The officers' uniform remained as before, but a single-breasted blue jacket with pockets in the breast and skirts, and passants, was introduced as well. A buttonless jacket with broad lace on the collar, down the front, around the hem, and on the hip vents, was adopted in 1896. From 1888 gaiters, laced up the sides, were worn on service. On their spiked helmets, officers wore a small chain which ran from high up on the right side to low down on the left side. Field officers wore a horsehair plume drooping to the rear, and a cord in *Waffenfarbe*. The peaked cap had a low, small crown (Fig. 156b). The men's jacket had altered little since 1861. With it was worn a soft gray hat, with a dent from front

Fig. 156. United States of America, 1872–1934.
a, b, c, d, f, g, h, k, l: infantry. e: cavalry.
d, k: officers. i: marine corps.

to rear. White cork helmets were worn on service in the tropics. A khaki uniform was adopted in 1898, at the time of the Spanish Civil War. The jacket had five buttons in front and patch pockets on the breast and skirts. A shirt, with passants for officers, was the usual wear in summer (Fig. 156d).

In 1903 the distinctive color of the infantry was changed back to light blue. Collar, shoulder straps, and cuffs were dark blue with light-blue piping. The cuff patches were abolished. In full dress, a plaited cord was worn across the breast. The stripes on the men's trousers were abolished. A flat-topped forage cap, with two light-blue bands around it, replaced the spiked helmet and the kepi (Fig. 156c). The officers retained their double-breasted frock coats. Officers' collar and cap bands were light blue with gold lace from that time. The epaulettes were replaced by plaited shoulder cords. The cuffs had a gold piping, with gold knots above according to rank, with the arm-of-service badge between them.

A few minor changes took place in 1912. The crown of the forage cap was broadened, and came nearer to resembling the British style. The felt hat was no longer pleated but had four dents (Fig. 156f). The service dress was olive drab, and underwent no basic changes during the Great War, except for the necessary adoption of the round, flat-brimmed steel helmet (Fig. 156g). The arm of service was denoted by the hat cord, which was light blue, and by a bronze button at each end of the collar, the right hand one having the initials "ULS" on it with the designation of the regiment below; that on the left with the arm-of-service badge—crossed rifles for infantry—and the company initial below. At both ends of the collar officers wore the initials "U.S." in bronze with the arm-of-service badge below. A fore-and-aft cap was adopted during the war (Fig. 156h), with the men's button, distinguishing the arm of service, on the left side of the turn-up. Officers had piping in *Waffenfarbe* around the edge of the turn-up—light blue for infantry—with the rank badges on the left side. The dress uniform was abolished after the Great War. The service dress was altered in 1926, the jacket thenceforth being made with an open neck, and the buttons and insignia becoming gilt instead of bronze. The arm of service buttons and the initials were placed on the lapels. Officers had brown leather equipment; that of the men was of gray-green webbing (Figs. 156k,l). The uniform was of the same style for all arms. All officers wore a medium-width dark brown cloth stripe around their cuffs. On the peaked forage cap, officers wore the national eagle, and other ranks wore their arm-of-service badge.

II. CAVALRY, ARTILLERY, AND ENGINEERS

During the Revolution, the cavalry units were dressed in varying uniforms. Only a few examples can be given. In 1775 the City of Philadelphia Cavalry wore brown coats with white distinctions, and black helmets (Fig. 155b); Lee's Cavalry was dressed in blue coats with white distinctions, white waistcoats, and black breeches. In 1776 part of the 1st Continental Regiment of Light Dragoons had blue coats and red distinctions; the rest had brown coats with green. In 1780 the 4th Regiment of Light Dragoons had red coats, and later, green coats with red lapels. Washington's Mounted Lifeguard had white uniforms with light-blue collars, lapels, and cuffs, skirts and waistcoats, and leather helmets with foxtails. Colonel Marion's Cavalry

(South Carolina) was noteworthy in that its leather helmets had a white metal scroll with the legend "Death or Liberty." In 1779 the light dragoons had blue coats with white distinctions; in 1800 green coats with black collars, lapels, and cuffs, with white linings, waistcoats and breeches, yellow metal shoulder scales and buttons, and yellow button loops. The leather helmets had black horsehair manes, with a yellow metal plate on the front; officers also had a green plume (Fig. 155e). In the period 1802–1810 the cavalry wore infantry uniforms. In 1812 they had white skirt turn-backs. In 1814 the dragoons adopted orange piping and lace loops, and the other cavalry regiments, yellow. The uniform underwent the same changes as that of the infantry, but the arm-of-service color was yellow, which the Confederate cavalry also wore during the Civil War, with the normal gray uniform. The cavalry adopted a white plume on the chaco in 1835. In 1846 a regiment of mounted riflemen was raised; its uniform was blue with green piping. In 1861 the entire mounted arm was reorganized as the 1st–6th Cavalry, and adopted a black felt campaign hat, turned up at one side, frequently with a black ostrich feather on it. The arm-of-service badge was two crossed sabers. In full dress, a short dark blue coat, piped yellow on all the seams, was worn. Two yellow embroidered button loops with a small button at the end ornamented the collar. The trousers were dark blue. The tunic worn from 1881 to 1903 was distinguished from the infantry's by the *Waffenfarbe* and by being piped around the hem as well; and the skirt pocket flaps were of a different pattern, with two buttons, the flaps themselves being of *Waffenfarbe*. The spiked helmet had a yellow plume falling to the rear, and yellow lines, for all ranks (Fig. 156e).

The Indian Scouts, raised around 1870, wore cavalry uniforms with white distinctions and red piping; the helmet plume was white and red. The arm-of-service badge consisted of crossed arrows with the initials "U.S.S." above, which they retained, along with the white and red hat cord on their uniforms up to the 1930s. The 1903-pattern cavalry uniform and the service uniform were distinguished from the infantry uniform only by the arm-of-service badge and by the yellow *Waffenfarbe* of the men.

Artillery (raised 1777): The artillery uniform as given in the regulations of 1779 consisted of a dark blue coat with red collar, lapels, cuffs, and skirt lining, and yellow metal buttons. The lapels and buttonholes, and the black tricorne hat, which had a red feather plume, were edged with narrow yellow lace. The breeches, and leather equipment, were white. In 1794 a black leather helmet with black crest reaching from front to back, and with a red plume on the left side, was introduced (Fig. 155d). In 1800 the plume was striped red and black; the officers' epaulettes were gold. In 1812 the artillery wore the infantry chaco, with crossed cannon barrels below the national eagle, and the infantry uniform, but with yellow piping and buttons. From 1835 the piping was red. The artillery retained this distinctive color on all their later changes of uniform, which were of infantry pattern. A red horsehair plume was worn on the chaco adopted in 1861 (Fig. 155l). In 1881 the horse artillery adopted cavalry-pattern tunics. The arm-of-service badge on the 1903 full-dress and service uniforms consisted of crossed cannon barrels.

Corps of Engineers: The uniform in general resembled that of the infantry and artillery. In 1780 they wore a blue coat with buff distinctions and undergarments. They retained these colors up to 1821, when engineer officers adopted black velvet collars and cuffs and, as a distinctive device, a star in a laurel wreath. The men wore yellow piping on their blue uniforms. In 1851 the badge was changed to a castle with three towers. In 1874 the distinctive color was changed to red, with white piping. The uniforms in general followed those of the infantry except for the insignia and *Waffenfarbe*. The Signal Corps was a separate arm of service dating from the Civil War. Its *Waffenfarbe* was orange, with white piping. The arm-of-service badge consisted of two crossed signal flags above a flaming torch.

III. GENERAL OFFICERS AND GENERAL STAFF; RANK DISTINCTIONS

From the beginning, general officers wore blue coats with buff distinctions and yellow metal buttons, buff undergarments, gold epaulettes with one to three five-pointed silver stars; black tricornes with a white feather plume for the commander in chief, black and white for a major general, and red and white for a brigadier general. From 1802 the hat was worn fore and aft. In 1808 a coatee was introduced with a row of ten buttons and vee-shaped loops down the front, with buff collar and round cuffs, with one button and loop on the cuff and three others on the sleeve above it. The feather plumes were abolished in 1812. In 1835 general officers wore a dark blue double-breasted coatee, with buttons arranged in twos or threes, according to rank. The collar, cuffs, skirt turnbacks, and lining were buff; the trousers, dark blue with broad buff stripes. In 1848 general officers, too, adopted chacos, with a gold pompon; from 1851 the chaco had a dark blue velvet band around the bottom. The buff distinctions on the coat and trousers were changed six years later for dark blue velvet collars and cuffs, which were embroidered with gold oak sprigs after 1903. From 1861, the full-dress headdress of a general officer was a black silk felt hat, with black ostrich feather plumage, and a gold loop on the right side. General officers had buff sashes: these were worn over the left shoulder in full dress up to the 1890s, and later over the right shoulder; and around the waist on service. The dark blue service jacket and kepi, worn from the Civil War, were only distinguished from the uniform of other officers by the rank insignia on the passants, and by the initials "U.S." in a laurel wreath on the kepi. General officers wore dark blue trousers, with broad gold lace down them for social occasions. With the 1903 uniform, general officers, too, adopted a peaked cap with dark blue top, and black velvet band. The band and the peak were embroidered with gold oakleaves. The service dress of general officers was only distinguished from that of other officers by the rank badges.

Up to about 1820 general staff officers wore the uniform of general officers, with the appropriate rank badges: and from then to 1851 they had dark blue collars and cuffs with buff collar patches. Up to 1861 they had single-breasted, and later double-breasted, tunics with buff piping on the collar. Their arm-of-service badge was a five-pointed star with an eagle on it. Black sleeve stripes were worn on the service dress.

As a distinction of rank, epaulettes of button color, with stiff bullions, were ordered for officers in 1780. A major general wore two gold epaulettes, bearing two gold stars; brigadier generals had only one star. Field officers wore two plain epaulettes; captains, one on the right shoulder; subalterns, one on the left. Sergeants had two worsted epaulettes; corporals, one, on the left shoulder; these were probably of button color. From 1832 all officers wore two epaulettes, of a different pattern for company officers. These were retained on the full-dress uniform up to 1861. About the same time, rank distinctions were prescribed for the everyday dress, and these remained unaltered on the dress uniform up to the Great War. They took the form of passant-type cloth stripes of distinctive color, edged with gold embroidery, worn across the outer ends of the shoulders. On the strap, general officers had one to three silver stars; colonels, a silver spread eagle; lieutenant colonels, an oakleaf at each end in silver; majors, the same in gold; captains, two silver bars at each end; 1st lieutenants, one; 2nd lieutenants had no badges of rank. On the 1881 uniform, a new type of epaulette was introduced on the social dress of officers. The strap and crescent pad were of gold plaited cord. The crescent was of cloth of *Waffenfarbe*, with the regimental number and rank badges in silver. General officers' epaulettes were unaltered, all gold, with one to three silver rank stars. The rank of general, revived in the event of war, wore a large silver star between two smaller silver stars, on both the epaulettes and passants. On the 1903 uniform the epaulettes worn by general officers remained unaltered; in place of them, all other officers adopted triple gold plaited shoulder cords, with the silver rank stars on a plain gold underlay. On the 1903-pattern full-dress tunic, officers' rank was denoted by one to five gold cords in trefoil form; while general officers wore one to three silver stars above their cuffs.

From 1847 the distinctions of the other ranks consisted of chevrons of *Waffenfarbe* worn on the upper arms, reaching from the forearm seam to the hindarm seam, point down (point up from 1861). They were greatly reduced in size in 1903. The senior ranks of NCOs wore additional arcs joining the lower ends of the chevrons.

On the field service dress, officers' rank badges remained unchanged and were worn on the pointed shoulder straps. The rank of general, restored during the Great War, was denoted by four five-pointed silver stars. From 1918 2nd lieutenants wore a single gold bar on their shoulder straps. The rank insignia of NCOs and men remained unchanged in number and arrangement, and consisted of khaki stripes on a dark blue backing. The rank of warrant officer, created at that time, wore an officers'-style uniform without rank badges on the shoulder straps, but with the eagle arms in dull gold in place of the arm-of-service badges at the ends of the collar. In service dress, general officers wore a medium and a narrow black silk stripe, 3 centimeters apart, around both cuffs. The silver rank stars were placed side by side between them.

On their gray uniforms, the NCOs and men of the Confederate army wore chevrons of *Waffenfarbe* on the upper arms, of the same type and number as in the Union army. Officers' ranks were indicated by gold cords forming a trefoil on the lower arms: lieutenants, one; captains, two; field officers, three; general officers, four. In addition, company officers wore at the ends of the collar one to three short horizontal gold stripes, one above the other; field officers had one to three gold five-pointed stars side by side; and generals, three gold stars in a gold oak wreath. The double-breasted coats had collar and pointed cuffs of *Waffenfarbe*: infantry, light blue; cavalry, yellow; artillery, red; general officers and general staff, buff.

THE
NAVIES

The study of the historical development of the uniforms of the navies presents difficulties much greater than in the case of the armies. The sources available are very sparse, and difficult to elicit; and as the principal components of the armed forces of the Great Powers have been the armies, the study of naval uniforms has been relegated to the background. For a long period, naval dress was not the subject of such exact regulations as in the case of the armies, from the mid-eighteenth century onward. On the other hand, the problem is simplified, insofar as from about 1860 the naval uniforms of the maritime powers tended to become very similar; and in the main, the same items of uniform, in almost the same style, were worn in all navies. The standard development of uniforms was based on British patterns. The British navy, which dominated the seas in the nineteenth century, had and retained a very strong influence on the development of naval dress. Especially after 1900, naval uniforms came more and more to resemble the British model, as regards both the style of the individual items of dress and the form of rank distinctions. It will be helpful, and at the same time serve as an introduction to the reader, to begin with a description of the main items of uniform generally worn in navies, taking 1860 as a conservative date for the introduction of naval uniforms, for the entire period to the late 1930s. Following this, the development of uniforms in the earlier period and the various differences will be dealt with under the respective countries.

In the first place, the basic color of all items of naval dress was dark blue, often verging on blue-black. In summer and in the tropics, white linen was worn instead. Buttons, rank distinctions, lace, etc., were basically gold in all navies, silver badges and buttons mainly being confined to administrative officers. The principal items of dress, almost identical in all navies, were as follows.

Hat: Black dressed felt turned up at two sides, with the points worn fore and aft. The British hat had two rounded fans; the French one was low, rectangular. The

443

former had a vertical gold loop in the center of the fan; on the latter, the loop ran from the right, forward to the center. Gold tassels were worn at the ends. Flag officers in most navies had broad gold lace around the edges of the fans; and often also had black or white ostrich feather plumage.

Full-Dress Coat: Double-breasted, fastened right up, with a stand collar, cut as a frock coat or coatee, with rich embroidery or lace edging on the collar; and rank stripes and/or embroidery on the cuffs.

Full-Dress Trousers: Long dark blue trousers with broad gold lace down the outer seams, according to rank.

Sword: Slightly curved, with gilt hilt and ivory grip; black leather scabbard with gilt mounts; worn on a black leather or silk waistbelt, which was often embroidered, worn over the full-dress coat.

Epaulettes: Naval epaulettes were always gold, with an embroidered crescent, and stiff, or fairly stiff, bullions. A foul anchor was often worn on the crescent (i.e., an anchor with the cable twisted around it).

Officers' Caps: Dark blue flat-topped caps with black patent leather peak and chinstrap; black silk or mohair band, on the front an anchor or the national cockade in an oak wreath with crown or national badge above. This cap was also worn by warrant officers, but without the oak wreath. The upper part was broad or close-fitting, according to fashion. Many countries copied the British pattern, on which flag officers and senior officers had a double or single row of gold oakleaf embroidery around the edge of the peak, according to rank. In the Latin countries, laurel leaves were often worn instead of oakleaves.

Frock Coat: Long-skirted, with two rows varying between three and six buttons, which usually bore an anchor device. In many navies it was worn buttoned right up, until the end of the nineteenth century. In the British navy and in countries following its fashions, it was worn open at the top, like a civilian coat. In the late 1920s and early 1930s the fashion was to have a few buttons and very long lapels. At the back were skirt pocket flaps, with two or three buttons. Gold lace stripes, according to rank, were worn on the cuffs (see table). In many navies gold passants were worn; but not in the British navy, nor in those navies that followed its lead.

Jacket: Double-breasted, cut like the frock coat, but with skirts varying in length between medium and short. No buttons at back; rank lace worn only on the sleeves. It was also frequently worn by warrant officers and chief petty officers.

Sailors' Cap: Dark blue; white for summer, with flat top and narrow band. This was surrounded by a black silk ribbon or tally, on which was printed, in gold or yellow lettering, the name and/or type of ship. The ends of this silk band hung down, or were tied in a small bow on the left or right side. The top was stiffened at the front on the German cap, and all around on the British one.

Jumper: Of dark blue worsted or serge; of white linen in summer; with a broad collar hanging down at the back, and forming a deep vee on the chest, usually worn tucked into the trousers like a shirt; but worn outside in some navies. With it was worn a light- or medium-blue collar, hanging down over the shoulders at the back, with three narrow white stripes around the edge. The shirt, which was visible at the neck, was white, usually with a blue edging; or striped blue and white horizontally. Under the collar was a black silk tie, worn in a knot on the chest. In the German navy, it had a medium-blue diagonal stripe, which was visible running above the

Fig. 157. Navies, 1750–1935.

Great Britain—a: admiral. c: officer. d, k: sailors. France—b,
e: sailors. i: officer. Austria-Hungary—f: officer. Japan—g: officer.
Russia—h: officer. U.S.A.—k: sailor.

center of the knot. The knot was often secured to the collar by a small white loop (Fig. 157l).

Pea Jacket: Short double-breasted overcoat reaching to the hips, with a flat turndown collar, open in front, with broad lapels. With this jacket, the jumper collar was worn underneath.

Trousers: Dark blue, closed with a flap in front. The legs were traditionally bell-bottomed, and almost covered the shoes.

Sailors' Jacket (German navy): Short double-breasted waist-length jacket, fastened in front only by a button link, so that the jumper was visible. The light-blue collar was worn on the outside (Fig. 158k).

Mess Jacket: Short jacket without skirts, with two rows of three buttons, worn open like a smoking jacket, with a very low-fronted waistcoat, stiff white shirt and collar, and black silk bow tie. Rank stripes on cuffs. In a few navies, shoulder cords or epaulettes were worn with it on formal occasions. Blue trousers, with or without gold lace stripes, were worn, according to the occasion.

Cloak: Long dark blue flared cloak with turndown collar; light-gray or black silk lining; fastened across the front by a chain with lion's head bosses. It was worn without rank distinctions in almost all navies. In the German service it was called a *Spanier*.

White Clothing: In summer, and in the tropics, almost all items of dress were duplicated by similar ones made of white linen. Instead of their normal frock coats or jackets, officers wore a single-breasted tunic or jacket, which, after the Great War, almost always had patch pockets with a small button and pleat, on the breast and skirts.

Rank Stripes Worn on the Sleeves by Naval Officers in 1913 and 1934

In the following table, "n" = narrow stripes, 0.7–1 cm wide; "m" = medium stripes, 1.3–2.2 cm wide; "b" = broad, those of more than 5.3 cm wide. They were invariably gold, and are here counted from the lowest up.

COUNTRY	SUBLIEUTENANT LIEUTENANT LIEUTENANT COMMANDER	COMMANDER COMMANDER CAPTAIN	REAR ADMIRAL VICE ADMIRAL ADMIRAL (ADMIRAL OF THE FLEET)	REMARKS APPROXIMATE RANKS ONLY
Argentina	1m 1n + 1m 3n	1m + 1n + 1m 3m 4m	1b + 1–3m	curl on top stripe; engineers, light blue underlay to stripes
Austria-Hungary (1913)	1–3n	1m + 1–3n	1b + 1–3n	executive officers had curl; flag officers, gold crown above curl
Brazil (1913)	1–3n	4–6n	2 and 3 five-pointed stars together	3 small buttons vertically on sleeve seam
Brazil (1934)	1m 1n + 1m 2m	1m + 1n + 1m · 3m 4m	1b + 1–2m	executive officers, engineers, airmen, curl; engineers with globe above; airmen, an eagle
Chile	1–3n	1m + 1n + 1m 3m 4m	1b + 1–2m	five-pointed star above top stripe; engineers, blue underlay
China	1m 1m + 1n 2m	2m + 1n 3m 4m	1b + 1–3m	executive officers, gold open wreath; airmen, eagle above; engineers, dark blue underlay
Denmark	1m 2m 1m + 1n + 1m	1m + 2n + 1m 2m + 1n + 1m 4m	2m + 1b + 1m 1m + 2b + 1m 3b + 1m	curl on top stripe; engineers, red underlay
Estonia	1m 2m 1m + 1n + 1m	1m + 2n + 1m 3m 4m	1b + 1m	curl on top stripe; engineers, purple underlay
Finland	1m 2m 1m + 1n + 1m	3m 2m + 1n + 1m 4m	1b + 1b–3m	lion rampant above stripes; engineers, purple underlay
France	1–3n	5n (2 and 4 silver) 5n	2) 3 } five-pointed silver 4) stars	no curl or badge; between third and fourth stripes, double
Germany (1913)	1n 1m 2m	3) 4 } m 4)	1b + 1–4m	imperial crown above top stripe; engineers, black velvet underlay
Germany (1934)	1m 2m 1m + 1n + 1m	3) 4 } m 4)	1b + 1–4m	branch badge above top stripe; executives, five-pointed star; engineers, cog wheel
Great Britain (1913)	1m 2m 1m + 1n + 1m	3m 4m	1b + 1–4m	executive and engineer officers only had curl; engineers, purple between stripes
Great Britain (1934)	1m 2m · 1m + 1n + 1m	3m 4m	1b + 1–4m	curl for all officers; engineers, between stripes

(continued)

COUNTRY	SUBLIEUTENANT LIEUTENANT LIEUTENANT COMMANDER	COMMANDER COMMANDER CAPTAIN	REAR ADMIRAL VICE ADMIRAL ADMIRAL (ADMIRAL OF THE FLEET)	REMARKS APPROXIMATE RANKS ONLY
Greece	1m 2m 1m + 1n + 1m	3m 2m + 1n + 1m 4m	1b + 1–3m	curl on top stripe for executive officers; engineers, violet underlay
Hungary	1–3n	1m + 1–3n	1b + 1n	curl for executive officers; engineers, carmine underlay; flag officers, gold crown in oak wreath above curl
Italy	1–3n	1m + 1–3n	*Greca* lace and 1–4n	curl on top stripe; engineers, carmine underlay
Japan	1m 1n + 1m 2m	1n + 2m 3m 4m	2b + 1–3m	curl on top stripe; engineers, violet underlay
Latvia	1m + 1–3 five-pointed stars	2m + 1 and 2 four-pointed stars	3m + 3 four-pointed stars	curl on top stripe; rank stars side by side above curl
Mexico	1m 1n + 1m 2m	1m + 1n + 1m 3m 4m	gold laurel leaf embroidery + 1–3m	executive officers, five-pointed star above top stripe; engineers, propeller
Netherlands	1m 2m 1m + 1n + 1m	3m 4m 4m	1b + 1m; above, 2, 3, or 4 silver stars	curl on top stripe
Norway	1m 2m	3m 4m 1b + 3m	1m + 1b + 1–3m	curl on top stripe
Poland	1–3n	1m + 1–3n	1b vandyked + 1–3n	curl on top stripe; engineers, violet underlay
Portugal	1–3n	1m + 1–3n	1b + 1n; 3 silver; 3, 4, gold, five-pointed stars below stripes	curl for executive officers; engineers, violet underlay
Rumania	3n	1m + 1–3n	1b + 1m + 1–3n	curl on top stripe; engineers, violet underlay
Russia (1913)	—	—	—	no cuff stripes (See text.)
U.S.S.R. (1934)	1m 1m + 1n 2m	2m + 1n 3m 4m	1b + 1–3m	red five-pointed enameled star above stripes
Sweden (1913)	1–3n	1–n + 1m above	1b + 1–3 silver stars	curl for executive officers; engineers, purple underlay
Sweden (1934)	1m 2m	3m 1m + 1n + 2m 4m	1b + 1–3 silver stars	curl for executive officers; engineers, triangle, point down, and purple underlay
Spain	1m 2m 1m + 1n + 1m	3m 4m 4m	1b + 1 and 2m	executive officers, star above; engineers, green underlay
Turkey	1m 2m 1m + 1n + 1m	3m 2m + 1n + 1m 4m	1b + 1–4m	curl on top stripe
United States	1m 1m + 1n 2m	1m + 1n + 1m 3m 4m	1b + 1–3m	executive officers, five-pointed star above
Yugoslavia	1–3n	1m + 1–3n	1b + 1n with 1–3 stars above	curl on top stripe; engineers, silver gray underlay

AUSTRIA-HUNGARY

After the uniform regulations of 1815, the naval officers' dress exactly resembled the army uniform of the period but was of dark blue cloth, with light-blue distinctions. A gold foul anchor badge was worn horizontally at the ends of the collar. Buttons were yellow metal. The greatcoat was dark blue with light-blue cuffs. Senior officers wore lace according to rank on the cuffs, as in the army. All officers wore the hat fore and aft, army style; but it was rather taller; all the other items, including the sash, were as for the army. The *Matrosenkorps* (Sailor Corps) wore a round leather hat, with a crowned anchor on the front, and at the top on the left, the black and yellow rosette. They also had a dark blue double-breasted jacket with yellow metal buttons; with short tails at the back for petty officers; a yellow foul anchor was worn horizontally on the stand collar; and dark blue trousers. The marine infantry had army uniforms in light blue with light-red distinctions, yellow metal buttons, and round hats. In 1820 these latter were replaced by chacos; the artillery wore a hat *à la corse*. In the same year, marine infantry and artillery officers were ordered to wear gold epaulettes. Naval officers adopted an all-dark-blue greatcoat in 1827. On board ship, a dirk in a black leather scabbard with gilt mounts was worn instead of the sword. Warrant officers had dark blue double-breasted coats with a stand collar, and no further distinctions. In 1836 buttons bearing an anchor on them were introduced; the naval artillery adopted chacos; naval officers took into wear gold passants, and senior officers, two epaulettes with stiff bullions; junior officers, a bullion epaulette on the right shoulder, and a crescent on the left. In 1849 marine uniforms underwent the same change as in the army. The dark blue tunic had two rows of yellow metal buttons, a light-blue stand collar, round cuffs, and piping around them, army-pattern rank distinctions, and two epaulettes for officers, with thick bullions for senior officers, and thin ones for others. On board ship, the coat was often worn open with a blue or white waistcoat fastened right up; and dark blue trousers, which were only gold-laced for full dress. In addition to the hat, which no longer had a feather plume, a dark blue flat-topped cap with gold band, black leather peak, and black and gold rosette on the front of the upper part was introduced. In 1852 the sailors' uniform was assimilated to that generally worn: a dark blue jumper, white in summer, with light-blue collar falling over the shoulders, with one to three stripes, and stars in the corners, according to rank; double-breasted dark blue jacket, dark blue trousers, and sailors' cap with black silk band lettered in gold at the front, and ends hanging down at the back. The uniform of the marine infantry was of army pattern, all dark blue with red piping. In 1859 a long dark blue civilian-style double-breasted frock coat was introduced for officers. A white shirt and black bow tie were worn with it. It had gold passants, and on formal occasions, gold epaulettes as before; rank was denoted by gold stripes on the cuffs: junior officers, one to two narrow ones; senior officers, one medium and one to two narrow; flag officers, one broad and one to two narrow stripes. On the epaulettes were one to three silver stars, with a gold crown above, in addition, for flag officers. In 1866 the tunic was made with a turndown collar, and the light-blue distinctive color was changed to dark blue. From that time it was worn only in full dress. The rank stars were removed from the officers' epaulettes; and at the same time, a cap was introduced for wear on board ship, which remained a distinctive feature of the Austrian navy up to the beginning of the present century. It is shown in Fig. 157f. In addition to the frock coat, a dark blue double-breasted jacket was worn, with rank distinctions on the cuffs, and gold passants. In 1890 the cuff bands on the frock coat and jacket were: for junior officers, one to three narrow horizontal stripes; with, for senior officers, one medium, and for flag officers, one broad, stripe below. One to three narrow gold stripes, according to the grade of the officer, were worn around the black cap band. The British-style tall hat was retained. Warrant officers wore officers' caps without the lace; and on the sleeves of the frock coat, one to three yellow silk cords, placed horizontally. Petty officers and ratings took into wear the gold Imperial crown and ribbons on the upper edge of their sailors' caps. Dark blue shoulder straps, with lace on them as on the cuffs, were introduced for wear on the officers' white uniform. Around 1900 flag officers adopted one to three large six-pointed gold stars above the broad cuff stripe, instead of the narrow stripes; and the same in silver on their epaulettes, on the straps of which all officers wore a gold crowned anchor. In 1908 the officers' cap was changed to one like the British type; with the cipher "F.J.I." in gold on a gold anchor in a crowned laurel wreath on a black field, on the front. Warrant officers wore the cipher in a circle with the Imperial crown above, on a black ground. The top row of the officers' cuff lace now formed a curl; flag officers' stars were abolished, and replaced by one to three narrow stripes, with a large gold crown above the curl on the top stripe. Warrant officers adopted two or three medium-width gold lace loops 11 centimeters long, worn horizontally on the cuffs, with a small button at the front ends. Petty officers wore one to three cloth stars in the corners of their collars. They and the ratings wore qualification badges on the left upper arm in yellow, with a crown above for petty officers, e.g., a foul anchor, propeller, anchor and crossed cannon barrels, and so on.

DENMARK

The uniforms of the Danish navy followed the usual lines. The band on the ratings' cap was tied in a small bow on the right side, on the center of which was the red-white-red national cockade. Rank and qualifications badges were worn on the right upper arm: in red for the ratings and gold for petty officers, with the crown above. The various ranks of petty officer were indicated by one to three short chevrons below. Warrant officers had officers'-type frock coats and jackets, with their crowned qualifications badges in gold at the ends of the collar; and on their forearms, a triple lace chevron on red with one or two gold buttons above the point. Executive officers wore double-breasted full-dress coatees with red collar and pointed cuffs; with gold embroidery on them, as in the army, for flag officers. The hat was like the French pattern, with black ostrich feather plumage. The officers' cap badge was a gold foul anchor in a rope circle on a red background, surrounded by an oak wreath, with crown above. A silver anchor was worn on the strap of the gold epaulettes.

ESTONIA

The greatcoat was double-breasted; and the rank stripes were worn on the pointed shoulder straps. The officers' cap badge consisted of an anchor in an oak wreath with the national arms above. Senior officers and flag officers wore embroidery on the cap peak, as in the British navy. The ratings' cap had no pendant tails.

FINLAND

The officers' hat had a white and blue silk cockade and gold loop on the right side. Flag officers had broad patterned gold lace around the edges. Senior officers and flag officers had a single and double row of oakleaf embroidery around their cap peaks; and on the front the red cockade and gold lion rampant, within a gold oakleaf wreath, surmounted by a gold embroidered foul anchor. The gold epaulettes bore the Finnish heraldic lion in silver on the crescents, and had stiff bullions for flag officers, semistiff for senior officers, and thin ones for junior officers. The frock coat had gold passants. Officers wore a sash like the army's. On board ship and off duty, a dirk in a black leather brass-mounted scabbard was worn, on a black silk belt. Warrant officers wore officers'-pattern frock coats and jackets, with one to three narrow chevrons, point up, with the branch badge above, on the lower arms. Their cap badge was the blue and white cockade with two gold laurel leaves below, and foul anchor above. The sailors' cap was like the German one, with the white-blue-white national cockade on the upper part; and the ends of the gold-lettered silk band hanging down at the back. The branch badge was in red embroidery: a foul anchor for the seamen's branch; propeller for engineers. These were worn on the left upper arm of the jumper and short greatcoat; leading seamen wore one and two narrow red chevrons below. Petty officers wore officers' jackets and white shirts, and on the left upper arm, the branch badge and two to four narrow, and one broad, chevron, below, according to rank, all in gold. The badge on their peaked cap was the national cockade with the anchor above in a rope circle.

FRANCE

Dark blue was adopted as the basic color for French naval uniforms in the last third of the eighteenth century; but for long the waistcoats and undergarments were red. Around 1786 the officers were dressed as follows: black tricorne with gold edging and white cockade; dark blue single-breasted long-skirted coat without lapels or turnbacks, round red cuffs with three buttons, gold epaulettes varying by rank as in the army, turndown (later standing) collar, in the squadron color; red waistcoat and breeches, and white stockings, black shoes; and a sword. The squadron colors were: 1st, carmine; 2nd, white; 3rd, green; 4th, lemon yellow; 5th, light blue; 6th, orange; 7th, violet; 8th, fawn; and black for the marines. Seamen wore dark blue double-breasted open jackets, red waistcoats, dark blue trousers, white shirts, black round leather hats, or hats turned up at the sides; black leather belts; and on board ship, red and white, or blue and white, striped shirts and overalls were often worn. This uniform remained essentially the same throughout the Napoleonic era. The leather hat had a brim varying in width, with a brass anchor badge on the front (Fig. 157b). Around 1812 the sailors' jacket was made entirely dark blue and was double-breasted, fastened right up, with a stand collar. A yellow loop and cockade were added on the left side of the hat; they were changed to white again in 1815. In 1848 the sailors wore a white shirt with black tie, and a blue sailor's collar, the front corners of which were all white, a distinction retained into the present century. The dark blue double-breasted jacket, which had broad lapels and round cuffs with three gilt buttons, was worn with dark blue trousers, and a black leather hat turned up all around, or a dark blue sailors' cap with soft top, and red pompon on the top, and black silk band with long dependent ends. This uniform altered very little thereafter. Fig. 157e shows the uniform of 1870.

A distinctive feature of the sailors' cap, in addition to the red pompon, was the white strap running over the top of the cap, which was retained up to the present century. In 1890 the French navy wore the following uniform: flag officers—same hat as for general officers, but with no gold lace edging or ostrich feather plumage; full-dress coat—coatee worn fastened up, with one to three sprigs of oakleaf embroidery on the collar and round cuffs for flag officers; and for other officers, ornamented with lace around the outside edges, and embroidered anchors in the corners. There were no rank distinctions on the sleeves. The gold epaulettes followed the army patterns, but had a gold foul anchor on the crescent. The double-breasted frock coat was still worn closed up after the Great War, and had two rows of gold buttons, gold passants, and gold cuff stripes as given in the table (Fig. 157i). Flag officers wore silver stars instead. The cap had rank stripes on the band, with a gold anchor above. Flag officers wore the same oakleaf embroidery as on the bands of general officers' kepis, around their caps, with their silver rank stars on the front. Warrant officers wore officers'-pattern frock coats, with narrow gold stripes, with a red interweave, on the cuffs; and their epaulettes had a red longitudinal stripe. Petty officers had the short jacket with the branch badge in the corners of the collar, and one to three gold diagonal stripes on the lower arms. Ratings wore red embroidered branch and-qualifications badges on the upper arm of the jumper and greatcoat, and one to two red diagonal stripes on the lower arms. Equipment was of black leather. From 1934 British-style officers' frock coats and jackets were worn, and a British type cap, with a stiff top. The cap badge at that time was a gold anchor in a laurel wreath. Flag officers wore their rank stars above. The embroidery on the peak was similar to that worn by the British navy. The sailors' cap was piped red around the top and bottom of the band. Petty officers' jackets were single-breasted with a stand-and-fall collar.

Warrant officers, in full dress, wore double-breasted frock coats fastened up to the neck; with, on the lower arms, a narrow gold stripe with a silver and a gold, or just a gold, cord below. Their peaked cap had a medium-width gold stripe around the center of the band, and above, a cap badge of officers' pattern in reduced size. Petty officers wore no rank stripes on the cap band. Midshipmen wore a narrow cuff stripe with diagonal light-blue stripes at regular intervals through it.

GERMANY

Only Prussia among the German states had a navy worthy of note, from the beginning of the nineteenth century. In 1849–1852, an attempt was made to found a *Reichsmarine*, or German national navy. In 1867 the Prussian navy become part of that of the North German Confederation, which, after the proclaiming of the German Empire in 1871, became the *Kaiserlich Deutsche Kriegsmarine* (Imperial German Navy). The cockade was black and white up to 1874, and black, white, and red from that date. The navy of 1849–1852 wore black, red, and gold cockades.

Up to about 1840 the uniforms of the navy were strongly influenced by those of the army. The officers wore single-breasted, later double-breasted, coatees with red Brandenburg cuffs and blue three-button patches, dark blue collar piped red, with a gold-embroidered foul anchor placed horizontally at the ends; and dark blue trousers with red triple stripes. The hat and sash were of army pattern. Buttons were yellow metal. Ratings wore short dark blue jackets with three rows of brass buttons, and in the first third of the nineteenth century, red collars and cuffs; and round black leather hats with a broad flat brim, and later a round upturned brim. The ship-borne infantry and artillery wore blue coatees with three rows of buttons, red collar and Brandenburg cuffs, and red skirt turnbacks; chacos; and black leather equipment. A small corps of *Gardemariniers* was maintained for duty on the royal vessels on the Potsdam Havelsee. In full dress they wore a dark blue double-breasted jacket, with dark blue collar with two yellow loops of guard lace, red Brandenburg cuffs with blue patches, red shoulder straps and skirt turnbacks; black leather equipment, and guard chacos with cords. In everyday dress a single-breasted waist-length jacket, ornamented like the coatee, was worn; and dark blue flat-topped caps with a dark blue band and red piping. About 1844 the collar, cuffs (by then of Swedish type), and officers' skirt linings were changed to white. Senior officers wore gold embroidery around the outer edges of the collar and cuffs, and gold epaulettes. From the same time, officers off duty wore a dark blue peaked cap with broad gold lace band and black leather chinstrap; and a short cutlass on a black waistbelt. The ratings' uniform was all dark blue (Fig. 158a). The uniform of the *Reichsmarine* of 1849–1852 resembled that of the Prussian navy, but had a black, red, and gold cockade. In 1860 the uniform of the Prussian navy was as follows.

The officers' full-dress headdress was a black dressed felt hat turned up at both sides, with a cockade and gold loop on the right. The body was rather low-crowned. Flag officers had broad gold lace around the outer edges. A dark blue double-breasted coatee was worn in full dress. Flag officers' collars, and round cuffs with three gilt buttons, were ornamented with gold oakleaf embroidery, like that worn by Prussian general officers. The lapels were worn buttoned back at the top. They were faced white and had gold lace, of varying widths according to rank, around the outer edges. Flag officers had gold aiguillettes; other officers wore gold epaulettes with a

452

Fig. 158. German Navy and Colonial Troops, 1848–1936.
a: sailor, German navy. b: marine (Prussia). c: officer (North German
Confederation). d: rear admiral. e: German Southwest Africa. f: *Askari,* East
Africa. g: marine infantry. h: officer, naval regiment. i: warrant officer. k: sailor.

silver foul anchor, and bullions for all ranks. The collar for all officers below flag
rank was edged with broad gold lace; and around the cuffs, below the three buttons,
were one to four medium-width stripes. There were broad gold stripes on the dark
blue trousers. The naval sword, worn up to 1939, was similar to the usual pattern,
with a gilt hilt, in a black leather gilt-mounted scabbard. The lion's head pommel had
one green and one red eye. The sword knot was as in the army. In formal dress and
evening dress, the coatee was worn open, with epaulettes, and rank stripes on the
cuffs. It was also worn by flag officers. Service dress consisted of a dark blue double-
breasted frock coat worn open; or a similar shorter jacket; with dark blue or white
waistcoat, white shirt, and black bow tie; dark blue trousers; and a dark blue peaked
cap with a gold band. No cuff stripes were worn on the everyday coat, but it had
shoulder straps like those of the Prussian hussars (Fig. 158c). From the same time,
sea cadets and midshipmen wore a small dirk with a white grip, in a brass scabbard.
The latter wore a short silver and black lace loop with a button at the rear, at the ends
of the collar of the jacket and coatee. Warrant officers wore officers'-style uniforms
without rank stripes or shoulder cords; but had a gold crowned foul anchor at the
ends of the collar. The cap had a rather narrow gold band. Petty officers and ratings
wore blue or white shirts with a black tie, and a medium-blue shirt collar with three
white stripes around the edge; dark blue double-breasted jackets worn open; dark
blue trousers; and a short greatcoat which had two rows of horn buttons. Their dark
blue sailors' caps had a small soft top, and black silk band, with the ends hanging
loose, with the words *"Königliche Marine"* (Royal Navy) on the front. A round
black lacquered leather hat with the edge turned up all around was worn in full dress.
The rank badges consisted of a gold anchor and the branch badge, with a crown
above for *Obermaate* (chief petty officers), on the left upper arm.

During the period 1874–1888 the uniform was not very different from that

453

previously worn. The black, white, and red cockade of the Confederation, and now of the German Empire, was adopted in place of the Prussian one. The full-dress coatee was abolished for officers below flag rank. The officers' dark blue double-breasted frock coat, which corresponded with the tunic of the army, was at that time worn fastened right up, and had a dark blue turndown collar, and two rows with six gilt buttons in each, with the crowned anchor on them; and silver, black, and red passants on the shoulders; and for full dress, epaulettes according to rank. Around the cuffs (above the three buttons, which were later abolished) were the rank stripes; *Unterleutnants zur See* wore one narrow gold stripe; *Leutnants zur See*, one medium stripe; *Kapitänleutnant*, two; *Korvettenkapitän*, three; *Kapitän zur See*, four; *Konteradmiral*, a broad one; with one medium stripe for *Vizeadmiral*, and two medium stripes for *Admiral*, above (Fig. 158c). Later the branch badge was worn above the stripes. The *Seeoffizierkorps* (executive officers) had a six-pointed star; *Marinestab*, a six-leaved rose; *Admiralstab*, an Imperial crown. Engineers wore no branch badge, but their rank stripes were backed with black velvet, and the collar of the frock coat was also velvet. A silver, black, and red hussar-type sash was worn with the frock coat. It was tied on the left front in a bow, with the two tassels on long cords, pushed through. In full dress, dark blue trousers with broad gold lace were worn. The hat and cap remained unchanged, except for the adoption of the black, white, and red cockade. In undress and off duty, a dark blue double-breasted civilian-style topcoat was worn, along with a dark blue single-breasted waistcoat. Cuff stripes were not worn on it, only the branch badge. Rank was shown on the silver, black, and red shoulder cords. The cap was always worn with this. On board ship, officers had a double-breasted dark blue jacket, which also had shoulder cords, and had no cuff stripes. The epaulettes were all gold; with thick bullions for flag officers and senior officers, thin ones for *Kapitänleutnant* and *Leutnant zur See*, and none for *Unterleutnant zur See*. A silver foul anchor was worn on the crescent, with rank stars as in the army; with a silver eagle with crown above for flag officers. The crescent was edged with silver, embroidered with black and red. The engineers' epaulettes had a black velvet crescent and strap, with the branch badge in gold; a plain anchor with a cog wheel on it; which badge was also worn on the shoulder cords. Warrant officers did not have a coatee, but wore the frock coat without cuff lace or shoulder cords. The rank badges were worn at the front ends of the collar, and took the form of the branch badge, with crown above for senior warrant officers: *Bootsmann*, a foul anchor; *Feuerwerker*, a plain anchor and crossed cannon barrels; *Maschinist*, a plain anchor and cog wheel; *Meister*, a plain anchor. Cadets and sea cadets, which corresponded to the later ranks of *Seekadett* and *Fähnrich zur See* (midshipman), had short jackets, worn open, with two rows of seven buttons, and round cuffs with three large buttons bearing an anchor device. In addition, *Fähnrich zur See* wore a narrow silver, black, and red lace loop, with a small button at the rear, at the ends of the collar. *Seekadetten* wore officers' caps, and *Kadetten* wore a dark blue peaked cap with the cockade on the front, and a narrow gold cord around the top of the dark blue band. The ratings' uniform was practically the same as that worn up to 1939. The short double-breasted greatcoat worn by petty officers and ratings had a fairly broad turndown collar, with medium-blue rectangular patches at the ends. These had one small silver, black, and red embroidered stripe for *Unterof-*

fiziere, and two for *Feldwebel* and *Obermaate*, at the upper edge. Engineering personnel wore silver buttons and rank distinctions on the sleeves. The bandsmen's badge took the form of two yellow chevrons—gold for buglers—on the lower arm of the jacket and shirt. The top one formed a loop. Leading seamen wore a cloth chevron, point down, in yellow (in blue on the white uniform), on the left upper arm.

The next major series of changes in uniform took place in 1889–1890, at the beginning of Kaiser William II's reign. The full-dress coatees of flag officers, and the coatees of other officers, were abolished, and a long dark blue double-breasted frock coat was introduced, with a self-colored stand collar, which was ornamented with gold oakleaf embroidery for flag officers, while other officers had broad gold lace around the outer edges. The lapels, worn turned back, were faced with white, and edged with gold lace, varying according to rank. The sleeves had a long white three-button scalloped slash, with gold lace edging. The rank stripes ran underneath it. Flag officers had round cuffs with rich oakleaf embroidery up to 1911. All executive branch officers adopted the Imperial crown in gold embroidery, worn above the rank stripes, as their distinctive badge. The hussar sash was superseded by a silver, black, and red laced waistbelt with gilt buckle, bearing the crowned Imperial cipher on a plain anchor, later with an oakleaf surround. The sword was worn on this belt. Hat, trousers, and epaulettes remained unaltered. The frock coat was now cut on civilian lines and was no longer worn fastened right up (Fig. 158d). Shoulder cords took the place of epaulettes for everyday wear. The rank of *Fregattenkapitän* (corresponding to a lieutenant colonel in the army), created in the meantime, wore four medium-width cuff stripes, and a star on the epaulettes and shoulder straps. On the jacket, rank was thenceforth only denoted by the cuff stripes, and the shoulder straps were abolished. A black mohair cap band was introduced. The Imperial cockade in a gold crowned oakleaf wreath was worn on the front of the cap, which was the same for all ranks from *Fähnrich zur See* upward. The dark blue double-breasted greatcoat had dark blue roll cuffs, six-button scalloped skirt pocket flaps, and a half belt. No shoulder cords or rank distinctions were worn with it; but flag officers had their lapels faced cornflower blue. Warrant officers adopted officers' caps, but only wore the black, white, and red cockade, with the Imperial crown and ribbons above. The distinctions of rank on the collar of the frock coat were abolished; and dark blue pointed shoulder straps were introduced, bearing the branch badge in gold, with a crown above for *Overdeckoffiziere*. The cuffs were round, with three buttons. The jacket was similar to the officers', with the appropriate shoulder straps, which were also worn on the greatcoat. In 1901, following the Russian example, executive branch officers adopted a short dirk, with ivory grip, and an Imperial crown pommel, in a brass scabbard, worn on a black silk belt with two slings. From 1874 the sword knot was silver, with black and red silk threads running through it. The only change in the ratings' dress was that the torpedo boat divisions adopted red piping on the collar patches of the greatcoat and around the tops of their caps. The crew of the Imperial yatch *Hohenzollern* had white collar patches. The officers' evening dress was a short British-type mess jacket, with rank lace on the cuffs. Midshipmen, now called *Seekadetten*, wore only the black, white, and red cockade on their caps. The lace worn by *Fähnriche* on their collars was also worn on the shoulders and on the short pea jacket as well.

Feldwebel and *Wachtmeister*, the highest petty officer grades in the *Land-marine*, had a special uniform. They wore warrant officers' caps, and in full dress, the jacket of an *Obermaat*; with their rank badges on the left upper arm, and the additional lace of a *Feldwebel* around the cuffs. They also had white shirts and black bow ties; blue trousers; and a sword and sword knot. On service, a double-breasted jacket with the rank badges on the left upper arm was worn instead.

During the Great War, uniforms altered very little, except that double-breasted jackets, with the dirk buckled underneath, and white shirt and black tie, became the usual dress for officers; it was worn off duty as well. Officers and ratings in U-boats and airships adopted black double-breasted leather jackets worn buttoned right up, with a navy blue cloth turndown collar. Officers' and warrant officers' ranks were denoted by shoulder cords and straps. Petty officers wore a gold anchor and the branch badge on the left upper arm. Black leather trousers and caps with black leather tops were also worn. The navy always had black leather equipment. In 1916 naval officers were ordered to wear shoulder cords on the greatcoat. The *Matrosenregimenter* (naval regiments) raised during the war, and which fought with gallantry in Flanders, wore, to begin with, field gray sailors' uniforms; officers had plain jackets and field gray forage caps with a black band (Fig. 158h). Later they wore the 1915-pattern jacket as worn by the army, with sailors' caps, which always had a field gray top. Steel helmets were not worn. Officers' rank was denoted partly by shoulder straps or cuff stripes, and partly by both in conjunction. As a rule, petty officers retained their rank badges, but on the 1915 jacket adopted short chevrons at the ends of the collar as well.

Immediately after the war, all Imperial insignia were abolished, but the shoulder straps, passants, sash, and sword knot were retained as before, and did not become all silver until 1933. The belt buckle had an anchor in a laurel wreath on it. The full-dress frock coat and, for domestic reasons, the epaulettes of executive officers were abolished. A five-pointed gold star was introduced for the executive branch in place of the Imperial crown, above the cuff stripes. Officers of other branches had a badge appropriate to their department: engineers wore a cog wheel. Flag officers' epaulettes were made with a plain silver strap and crescent, on which was a gold foul anchor and the rank stars. Officers' cuff stripes were altered, so that a *Leutnant* now had one medium stripe; *Oberleutnant*, two; and *Kapitänleutnant*, two, with a narrow one between. The badges on the shoulder straps remained as before. The crown on the cap was abolished. Up to 1933 an oval yellow cockade and black eagle were worn instead of the black, white, and red one. The oak wreath was made higher, and curved inward at the top. The ranks of warrant officer gradually died out. The newly created ranks of *Feldwebel—Feldwebel* and *Oberfeldwebel*—wore officers' jackets and greatcoats with pointed self-colored shoulder straps, with gold lace edging around them, with a silver anchor and the branch badge in the center, and one or two silver stars in addition. All officers, and petty officers having the *portepee*, adopted a dirk for wear ashore. This had, at first, a black grip, and a round pommel instead of the Imperial crown, and a knot. On the ratings' uniform, only the cockade was changed, and the red piping for torpedo boat personnel was abolished. The engineering branch took into wear yellow metal buttons and insignia. *Obermaaten* adopted a short gold chevron, point down, in place of the Imperial crown, below the branch badge on the left upper arm. The ratings' grades were denoted by one to four gold chevrons, point down; with the branch badge above, which was worn by all sailors: seamen's branch, a five-pointed star; engineering branch, a yellow cog wheel.

The Coast Defense Detachments, later Marine Artillery Detachments, wore field gray uniforms similar to those of the army, with yellow metal buttons and rank distinctions, and gray collar lace on a yellow patch. The peaked cap had a dark green band and piping around the top. Officers were distinguished only by their shoulder cords. The ratings' shoulder cords bore two plain anchors crossed, in yellow embroidery.

In 1933 the black, white, and red cockade was reintroduced, and in the following year the eagle and swastika badge was adopted, worn on the cap above the cockade, and on the right breast (Figs. 158i,k). The red center stripe on the belt was abolished. In 1936 gold embroidery was taken into wear on the cap peaks: narrow lace, waved on the inside, for junior officers; and of single and double oakleaf embroidery for senior officers and flag officers respectively. The newly created rank of *Generaladmiral* was indicated by four medium stripes above the broad stripe on the cuffs, and by three stars, arranged in a triangle, on the shoulder straps and epaulettes.

In 1850 a *Marinirkorps*, two companies strong, was raised in the Prussian navy. It was called the *Seebataillon* from 1854. It was composed of infantry and artillery carried on board ship. Later, a 2nd was raised; and in 1898 a 3rd, which was based at Tsingtau. The *Seebataillon*, collectively referred to as marine infantry, were Confederation troops from 1867 and Imperial troops from 1871, and accordingly wore cockades, shoulder cords, sashes, and sword knots in the Imperial colors. From 1850 the uniform consisted of a dark blue tunic with self-colored collar and Brandenburg cuffs. The collar, the front of the coat, and the three-button scalloped skirt pocket flaps were piped white. Officers wore a loop of old guard lace on the collar and had white-piped cuff patches. There was a foul anchor badge on the white shoulder straps and officers' epaulettes, which had white straps and crescents. The leather equipment was black. The trousers were dark blue with white piping (Fig. 158b). The headdress up to 1862 was a helmet like that worn by the line artillery, with a yellow metal plate; and from then up to 1883, a blue-covered felt chaco with black leather peak. The badge was a bronze anchor with the motto *"Mit Gott für König und Vaterland"* (With God for King and Country). In 1875 the plate was altered, and the flying eagle was placed on the anchor; and brass chinscales were fitted. Leather front and back peaks were added in 1883. The chaco was of black cloth for officers and of lacquered leather for the men. A black plume—red for bandsmen—was worn in full dress. At first, dark blue flat-topped caps with white piping around the top of the band were worn, with the initials "K.M." on the front. The national cockade was worn from 1854. Officers' caps had a black leather peak and chinstrap. White bands, and piping around the top, were introduced on the dark blue flat-topped caps in 1875. The following alterations took place to the tunic.

From 1875 white collars and cuffs were worn. In 1888 officers and men adopted two loops of guard lace on the collar and three on the cuff patches, in gold and yellow respectively. Two crossed anchors, with the Imperial crown above, were worn on the shoulder straps and epaulette crescents. Later, to indicate the battalion,

Roman numerals were added below. Officers only had a gold Imperial crown on their shoulder straps (Fig. 158g).

The same greatcoat was worn as in the army. From 1906 the lapels for officers of the *Seebataillon* were faced with white. The III *Seebataillon* in Kiauchow wore, on service in China, khaki uniforms with a stand-and-fall collar, with the same shoulder straps as on the tunic; brown leather equipment; and khaki tropical helmets with the eagle in yellow metal on the front. In 1856–1867, there existed a special *Seeartillerieabteilung*. It wore the uniform of the *Seebataillon*, but with black collar and cuffs. Anchors with two crossed cannon barrels above them were worn on the shoulder straps. On the 1910 service dress, the *Seebataillon* wore white piping on the collar, cuffs, shoulder straps, and front of the coat, yellow guard lace on the stand-and-fall collar and cuff patches; and yellow letters on the shoulder straps. On their 1915-pattern jackets, the men had yellow lace on a white collar patch. At the reorganization of the armed forces in 1919, marine infantry ceased to exist.

GERMAN COLONIAL TROOPS (SCHUTZTRUPPEN)

GERMAN EAST AFRICA

Troops were raised, under the authority of the *Reichskommissar*, in 1889–1891. The European officers and NCOs wore white tropical helmets with the black, white, and red cockade on the front; and in full dress, a dark blue tunic (white for service wear) with turndown collar; black, white, and red twisted shoulder cords, and one to three gold rank stripes on the cuffs, the top row of which formed a loop; brass buttons; and silver, black, and red embroidered sashes and sword knots for officers. A khaki-colored service dress of the same pattern was also worn. NCOs' ranks were denoted by one to three chevrons on the left upper arm. The native troops wore single-breasted khaki jackets, turban, or red fez with a blue tassel, blue puttees, and brown leather equipment. After being taken into the Imperial service, the *Schutztruppen* of 1891–1896 wore the following uniform.

Officers, full dress: black leather helmet with yellow metal Imperial eagle plate, spike, and chinscales; dark blue single-breasted tunic with yellow metal buttons, with white piping on the turndown collar, tunic front, Brandenburg cuffs, and skirt pocket flaps, and a gilt Imperial crown at the ends of the collar. The shoulder straps and sash were like those of the *Seebataillonan*. The trousers were dark blue with white piping. The everyday uniform was white, of the same pattern, with breast and skirt pockets, and dark blue piping instead of white. A white tropical helmet with brass plate and spike was worn with it, or a white cap with a dark blue band, and the cockade on the front. The service dress was khaki, of the same style as the white uniform, and had yellow piping, and the Imperial crown at the ends of the collar. The NCOs' rank badges were of British type. The uniform of the native Askaris remained unchanged. In 1896 a general-pattern uniform was introduced for *Schutztruppen*. The home service uniform was made of light-gray cord with stand-and-fall collar, Swedish cuffs, and piping in the color of the colony, which was white for German East Africa; light-gray trousers with white piping; and a broad-brimmed gray hat with band and binding in the color of the colony. The hat was turned up at the right side, with a large black, white, and red cockade on the flap. There was white guard lace (silver for officers) with a red patch, on the collar and cuffs of the jacket. The shoulder straps, sash, and sword knot were like those of the army, in the Imperial colors. In full dress officers wore a double silver aiguillette on the left shoulder. The leather equipment was brown. General officers had red distinctions with gold embroidery, Prussian style, and gilt buttons, and gold hat binding. The service dress of European colonial troops consisted of a khaki jacket with a row of white metal buttons, turndown collar, round cuffs, all piped blue, with no lace; khaki trousers; and a khaki tropical helmet, with the cockade on the front. The Askaris also wore khaki jackets with turndown collar and white metal buttons; a khaki fez with neckshade, with the silver Imperial eagle on the front; brown leather equipment; dark blue puttees; and brown footwear (Fig. 158f).

GERMAN SOUTHWEST AFRICA

In 1889–1893 the troops under the *Reichskommissar* wore jackets of gray cord and trousers and hat of the later colonial pattern without colored distinctions; and brown leather equipment. In 1893–1896, after they came into Imperial service, the same was worn, but with a light-blue collar, and pointed cuffs, with a white loop of guard lace (silver for officers) on a red patch. Up to 1895 a small kepi was worn with a blue band and piping around the top, and a black rectangular leather peak, with the black, white, and red cockade above; and from 1896 the general *Schutztruppen* uniform with light blue as the distinctive color. On service, brown drill uniforms were worn, as in German East Africa. The tunic was cut like the home service uniform, but in gray cord (Fig. 158e).

CAMEROONS

The distinctive color of the *Schutztruppen* uniform was red, as were the rank chevrons and bandsmen's wings worn by the native troops. The police troops in Togo wore the same uniform.

GREAT BRITAIN

In 1748 George II ordered the uniforms of naval officers to be blue and white, with gold lace; and these have remained unchanged since then. The cut of the uniform generally followed the fashion of the period (Fig. 157a). At first, long double-breasted or single-breasted coats were worn, with white or blue lapels and round or slash cuffs, according to rank. The undergarments were blue or white. In 1783 one to three broad rank stripes were introduced on flag officers' cuffs. Generally speaking there were no distinctions of rank, the shape and color of the cuffs and lapels denoting this. Epaulettes with thick bullions were introduced in 1795; with one to three silver stars for flag officers; post captains, two epaulettes with plain straps; captains under three years, one epaulette on the right shoulder; commanders, one on the left shoulder; junior officers wore none. The white facings were not worn between 1795 and 1812. In that year, all senior officers adopted two epaulettes: post captains, with a silver crown and anchor; junior captains, with a silver anchor only; commanders, two plain epaulettes. Lieutenants adopted one on the right shoulder. The collar, whose development in size followed that of the army, was white from 1812. From then to 1827 the cuffs were white, and were changed in the latter year to dark blue with white scalloped slashes with three buttons. In the period 1830–1843 officers wore red collars and cuffs. Double-breasted coatees were adopted by officers of the executive branch in 1827; and single-breasted ones by civil officers (Fig. 157c). In 1847 two gold epaulettes were introduced for lieutenants, and at the same time a frock coat, which could be worn either open or closed, with a white shirt, and a blue peaked cap with a gold band. The ratings' uniform of the period consisted of a short dark blue jacket worn open, with two rows of brass buttons; white or dark blue trousers; white shirt, black silk tie; black leather round hat, which later became lower with the brim turned up all around; and in summer a yellow straw hat of similar shape. The officers' overcoat was worn without epaulettes, but had cuff stripes: captains, three; commanders, two; lieutenants, one. From 1856 a curl was formed on the top stripe. In 1861 sublieutenants adopted one stripe; lieutenants, two; commanders, three; captains, four. About this time, officers' caps had a black mohair band with a silver anchor in a gold crowned oak wreath, on the front. In 1891 double and single oakleaf embroidery around the outer edge of the cap peak was introduced for flag officers and senior officers. A crowned anchor badge was worn on the left arm, as a rank distinction for petty officers, and later, the branch badge, with gold service chevrons below. Up to 1939 a full-dress double-breasted coatee was worn, fastened up to the neck, with a white stand collar with broad or narrow gold lace edging, white, scalloped three-button cuff slashes edged with gold lace, and gold lace around the skirt pocket flaps and around the hip buttons. Flag officers had rich oakleaf embroidery on the collar and cuff slashes. The rank stripes ran under the slashes on the cuffs. Midshipmen and cadets wore officers' caps, with a white collar patch having a small gilt button at the end. These distinctions were also worn on the short single-breasted dress jacket. They also had a small dirk with gilt mounts, in a black leather scabbard. Fig. 157l shows the ratings' uniform. The officers' epaulettes had straps of gold check and vellum lace, with thick bullions down to the rank of lieutenant. On the strap was a silver foul anchor; with silver star in addition, for a lieutenant commander; and a crown for commanders. Captains had a crown and star; and post captains and commodores, a crown and two stars. On their straps, flag officers had a crossed sword and baton with one to three stars and crown above. The epaulette badge for an admiral of the fleet was the same as that worn by a field marshal. On the double-breasted greatcoat, the rank distinctions took the form of stripes on the shoulder straps. Flag officers' shoulder straps were entirely covered with gold lace, with the epaulette badges on them. These straps were also worn with the white uniform.

Under the admiralty, from the mid-eighteenth century, were the Royal Marines, which later consisted of the Royal Marine Artillery and the Royal Marine Light Infantry, up to 1922. The light infantry uniform generally followed that of the army: the tunic was red with dark blue facings. The R.M.A. had dark blue coats with red facings. The Royal Marines' badge was a globe and laurel wreath. From 1922 they wore dark blue single-breasted jackets with the badge at the end of the collar, and dark blue trousers. In full dress, white equipment and white tropical helmets with a brass plate were worn. The rank badges were, generally speaking, the same as in the army.

HUNGARY

The Danube flotilla maintained by Hungary was dressed like the earlier Austrian navy in its basic style and rank distinctions. The officers' cap badge consisted of a silver anchor in a gold oak wreath, with a gold St. Stephen's crown above.

ITALY

The uniform of the Italian navy, from its formation up to the late 1930s, changed little in essentials. The officers' hat was like the British pattern; flag officers had broad gold embroidery around the edges, with black ostrich feather plumage. The full-dress garment was a coatee with two rows of five buttons, four of which buttoned, with rank stripes on the sleeves; and the silver regular service star at the ends of the collar, in gold for flag officers. On the shoulders, flag officers wore gold twisted cords, with hanging cords on the right shoulder; the other officers had passants: of plain gold lace for junior officers; of dark blue cloth for senior officers, with a gold edging, and a gold anchor cable in the middle; and gold shoulder scales with a plain or vandyked edging and thin or thick bullions respectively. The dress trousers had gold stripes. The frock coat had the star at the ends of the collar, and rank stripes on the cuffs; it was double-breasted, with two rows of five buttons, and passants, like the double-breasted jacket, which had only three buttons in each row in the 1930s. In the late 1930s the double-breasted greatcoat also had lace on the cuffs. Officers' caps had a gold crowned anchor in a laurel wreath above the peak, and the fairly wide band had the same stripes as on the cuffs, around it. They also wore a light-blue sash, as in the army. Warrant officers wore officers' caps without the rank lace. Their jackets had dark blue passants with one to three gold lace stripes on them; and on the frock coat, they wore a single medium-width cuff stripe with the branch badge above. Petty officers wore one to three gold chevrons, point down, on the upper arms. Ratings had the star in the corners of their blue collars, which had only two white stripes around the edges. The cap band was tied in a small bow on the left side. Branch badges, and the chevrons denoting rank, were worn on both upper arms, in red embroidery.

In the Italian navy, the Battalion San Marco took the place of marines. The men wore a gray-green sailors' uniform with a red patch on the cuffs bearing the winged lion of San Marco in white embroidery. Up to 1934 officers wore army uniforms, with a red stand collar, and to the rear of the star, the lion in gold embroidery. From that year, they wore jackets as in the army, with rank denoted by cuff stripes; and red patches with the silver star, on the collar; and above, the gold embroidered lion of San Marco. The officers' badge was worn on the peaked cap, and on the left side of the service beret.

JAPAN

The uniforms of the Japanese navy were similar to the British ones. On the flag officers' coats and on the cap badges, gold cherry leaves were, however, worn instead of oakleaves. The jacket worn prior to 1939 was like the American style (Fig. 157g). The cuff stripes on it were of black lace, with the top row forming a curl. The number of stripes on the cuffs remained unchanged from the 1890s to the late 1930s.

LATVIA

A distinctive feature of Latvian naval uniform was its black basic color. Further, the sailors' collar was edged with two narrow dark red stripes with a white one between. On the officers' everyday dress, pointed black shoulder straps bearing a gold anchor were worn; in full dress, officers had gold twisted cords with a silver anchor on them. The silk bands of the sailors' caps hung down at the back. Warrant officers had one broad gold chevron on the upper arm; petty officers had one to three narrow gold ones. The branch badges worn above them were in dark red.

MEXICO

The uniforms worn by the navy between the wars showed a strong United States influence. Gold epaulettes with fairly thick bullions were worn by all ranks and had two crossed silver anchors on the crescent for flag officers; a foul anchor for senior officers; and plain crescents for junior officers. Warrant officers wore one to three narrow stripes around the cuffs; petty officers had narrow gold chevrons, point up, on the upper arm, with the branch badge below.

NETHERLANDS

The first regulations for the Dutch navy date from 1792 and were augmented in 1798. The flag officers' full dress consisted of a dark blue coat with dark blue collar, lapels, and round cuffs; both the latter were edged with broad single and double gold lace respectively. White waistcoats and knee breeches were worn; and black gold-laced

462

tricornes, with red, white, and blue ostrich feathers. In undress, a dark blue double-breasted coatee with stand-and-fall collar, and round dark blue cuffs, was worn. The gold epaulettes had thick bullions and one or two silver stars on the crescents. Trousers were white or dark blue. The hat had no feathers. The lapels and skirt lining were red for captains and 1st lieutenants, and dark blue for commanders and lieutenants. Junior officers wore one or two longitudinal stripes on the crescents of their gold epaulettes. The hat and undress coatee were the same as for flag officers, with the appropriate epaulettes. Warrant officers wore officers'-pattern hats, and blue single-breasted long-skirted frock coats with stand collar and round cuffs with three anchor buttons and no further ornamentation; and blue undergarments. In 1808, under French control, the red distinctions disappeared, and the collar, cuffs, and lapels were changed to dark blue. The uniforms of flag officers remained as before. French-pattern epaulettes were worn by all officers. At that time, the sailors wore dark blue open jackets, with two rows of brass buttons, red waistcoats, white or blue trousers, and round caps. In 1824 officers' full dress consisted of a dark blue double-breasted coatee with red stand collar, edged with broad gold lace for flag officers, and narrower lace for senior officers. The round cuffs were red, and similarly laced. Junior officers had dark blue cuffs without lace on them or on the collar. Epaulettes were gold with thick bullions: flag officers had two and three silver stars; captains, plain crescents; commanders had a silver longitudinal stripe on the crescents; 1st and 2nd lieutenants had a single epaulette with bullions, on the right shoulder. The sword was worn in a black scabbard with gilt mounts. Broad gold lace stripes were added to the dark blue trousers for full-dress wear in 1835. With full dress a black hat was worn, with on the right side a large orange silk cockade and gold loop. Flag officers had white ostrich feather plumage in their hats.

In undress, all officers wore a double-breasted frock coat with gold passants, worn open or buttoned across, with a dark blue single-breasted waistcoat. In 1831 1st and 2nd class lieutenants adopted two gold epaulettes with bullions, with a silver longitudinal stripe for the latter. In 1835 a dark blue peaked cap with small top and a wide, red-edged gold stripe on the band was introduced for wear on board ship. After the introduction of the tunic into the army, officers took into wear a double-breasted coat fastened right up, with medium-length skirts, stand collar, and round cuffs, which was worn in full dress. Epaulettes were worn with it; flag officers had rich gold embroidery on the collar and cuffs; other officers had only a horizontal anchor and gold leaves at the ends of the collar. Rank lace, as given on page 446, was worn on the cuffs, with the top stripe forming a curl. Gold passants were worn; and officers' epaulettes were now made with a plain strap and crescent, with thick bullions for senior officers and thin ones for junior officers. The hat remained unaltered. Gold passants and epaulettes were worn in addition to the cuff stripes, on the long civilian-style frock coat. The characteristic device on this and on the jacket was a gold crowned foul anchor worn at the ends of the collar; engineers wore a crowned flambeau on two crossed arrows. Up to the Great War, officers wore a cap similar to the contemporary Austrian naval pattern (Fig. 157f). It had a straight leather peak, with the branch badge (as worn on the collar) in a gold oak wreath on the front. Immediately after the war, British-style officers' caps were taken into wear instead, with peak embroidery for senior officers and flag officers. Officers in the

Naval Air Service had a rotary engine with a propeller and a crown above, as their branch badge. Otherwise the uniform was the same as for naval officers. The development of the ratings' uniform followed the usual lines. Branch badges were worn on the left arm: a plain anchor for the seamen's branch; two crossed torches for engine room staff, in red; for petty officers, in gold with crown above.

A corps of marines was established in 1814, similar to the later German *Seebataillon*. At first it wore a dark blue army-pattern coat with yellow collar, cuffs, and piping, yellow metal anchor buttons, and chaco; from 1817 dark blue double-breasted coats with yellow metal buttons, red stand collar, and dark blue slash cuffs piped red were worn; and dark blue trousers with red piping, and a leather hat turned up at the left side with orange cockade, yellow loop, and red feather plume. Officers wore gold epaulettes, according to rank. In 1830 a single-breasted coat was introduced, which had two yellow lace loops (gold for officers) on each side of the red collar. The cuffs were pointed, with red piping. The army-pattern chaco had a red pompon and small tuft, and on the front, crossed anchors with the crown above. Epaulettes were worn, according to rank. After the introduction of the tunic in the 1860s, the collar was altered to dark blue, piped red all around, and the edges of the men's cuffs were piped red. The chaco, which followed the variations of the army pattern, had a badge consisting of crowned crossed anchors. On their tunic the men wore dark blue shoulder straps piped red; officers had gold shoulder cords, and rank lace like that of naval officers, on the cuffs; and orange silk sashes. At the end of the nineteenth century, the chaco was superseded by a British-type dark blue cloth-covered cork helmet with brass fittings and chin chain, and on the front, the Dutch lion in a laurel wreath on crossed anchors on a crowned eight-pointed star. This uniform was retained for full dress up to the late 1930s. On board ship, the tunic gave way to a dark blue single-breasted service jacket with stand-and-fall collar. NCOs' rank distinctions were as in the army; and they wore officers'-style caps, with a plain vertical anchor crowned, on the front.

NORWAY

During the period of the union with Sweden down to 1905, Norwegian naval uniform differed little from the Swedish pattern. From that date, it remained much the same as before, except for the national cockade on the officers' hats.

POLAND

In the 1930s Polish naval officers wore a tall hat, like the British one; with a large white and red silk cockade, and gold lace loop vertically over it, on the right side. It was the same for all ranks, including flag officers. Officers had no full-dress coat. The civilian-style long double-breasted frock coat had gold passants; and in formal dress, plain gold epaulettes were worn, with thick bullions for flag officers and senior officers, and thin ones for junior officers, in addition to the cuff stripes, for which see page 446. The sword, of the usual pattern, in a black leather scabbard with gilt mounts, was worn on a black silk waistbelt with a gilt buckle. A white shirt and a bow tie were worn with the jacket. On service and in everyday dress, a dark blue flat-topped cap with black mohair band, and black lacquered leather peak and chinstrap, was worn. Junior officers wore a single row of plain gold lace around the cap peak; senior officers, two; and flag officers had broad vandyked gold lace around the edge. The cap badge, on a black cloth backing, consisted of two crossed laurel sprigs, with the silver Polish eagle crowned, on a gold anchor, in the center. In summer a white cap cover was worn. The double-breasted civilian-style jacket with rank distinctions on the sleeves, and no passants, was worn in undress and for walking out, with a white turndown collar and black tie; and a small dirk with ivory grip, in a gilt-mounted black leather scabbard. The greatcoat was double-breasted and had rank stripes on the dark blue blunt-ended shoulder straps, as on the jacket cuffs. Warrant officers wore officers'-pattern jackets. Their distinctions took the form of one or two small gold chevrons, point down, on the lower arms. The senior grade of warrant officer wore a narrow gold stripe on a red underlay around the arm below these. The same rank distinctions were worn on the black shoulder straps of the greatcoat. With it, they wore an officers'-pattern cap, with the Polish eagle in silver on a gold anchor. The same badge was worn on the top front of the ratings' dark blue cap, the gold-lettered silk band of which had no pendent ends. Their rank distinctions, on the blue or white jumper, and the short double-breasted overcoat, consisted of one to three short gold diagonal stripes piped red, on the left upper arm, with, above, the branch or qualifications badges: e.g., a ship's propeller on a cog wheel, crossed cannon barrels, etc., in red embroidery. On duty under arms, brown leather equipment and short white galters were worn.

PORTUGAL

In 1890 the admiral wore a black felt hat with black ostrich feather plumage. In full dress, a double-breasted tunic buttoned to the neck, with gold embroidery on the collar and round cuffs, was worn. The rest of the officers' uniform items were similar to those of the British navy. The cuff stripes were of the same number and width as then worn in the army; flag officers, however, had three broad stripes with one medium one above, the top stripe forming a curl. Warrant officers wore a short dark blue double-breasted jacket, with the gold branch badge crowned, in the corners of the collar. Later, the uniforms, and the officers' cuff stripes, were copied from the British patterns.

RUMANIA

In 1852 the Wallachia river flotilla wore green tunics with green collars and slash cuffs, all piped white, brass buttons, gold epaulettes for officers, gold guard lace on the cuff patches, and a horizontal gold anchor at the ends of the collar; brown leather equipment; dark green trousers piped white; and black leather chacos with a white metal eagle plate, and brass chinscales. About 1870 officers adopted a single-breasted coatee in dark blue, worn open at the top, for full dress; with gold epaulettes and cuff stripes, and at the ends of the stand collar, a horizontal gold anchor. They also wore dark blue trousers with gold stripes; and a black French-style hat with a red, yellow, and blue cockade, and gold loop. Their sword, which resembled the usual naval pattern, was worn on a gold full-dress waistbelt. For everyday use, a long double-breasted frock coat with gold passants and cuff stripes was worn, with a white shirt and black bow tie; and crowned anchors in the corners of the collar, which was also the badge on the dark blue peaked cap. In full dress, ratings wore a black leather or straw hat, with a broad brim turned up all around, with a black silk band which had long hanging tails. For everyday dress, they had a dark blue sailors' cap with red pompon on the top, like the French one. The rest of the uniform was similar to the usual pattern. French styles continued to influence the uniform. After the Great War, the uniform, even to the cuff stripes, was modeled exactly on that of the British navy. The branch and rank badges of ratings and petty officers were worn on the left upper arm, in red and gold embroidery respectively. Warrant officers wore a single-breasted jacket fastened right up, with their branch badges in gold embroidery on the pointed shoulder straps; and the rank badges—one to three plain gold chevrons—on the upper arm. The warrant officers' cap badge was similar to the officers', but without the oakleaf embroidery. In addition to the sword, officers had a small dirk with ivory grip, in a brass scabbard.

RUSSIA

From the early nineteenth century, down to its demise in 1917, the Russian navy was organized on the pre-Napoleonic French lines, in flotillas, each of which consisted of a ship of the line and several small vessels. The Guard Flotilla, stationed at St. Petersburg, wore a special uniform.

Up to the end of the 1850s the navy was dressed exactly like the army. Officers and men wore a chaco with a brass anchor on the front, and dark green coats and trousers, piped white, like the army uniform. The rank distinctions, too, were as in the army. The leather equipment was black. From then on, it began to more closely resemble the general naval dress; but many peculiarities were retained, most notably the dark green basic color. The black dressed felt hat was quite tall, with a diagonal gold loop and a white, orange, and black silk cockade on the right. The dark green full-dress tunic was double-breasted, and had medium-length skirts; and for flag officers, a stand collar and slash cuffs with thick gold oakleaf embroidery. The other officers had a horizontal foul anchor on the stand collar, and two loops of gold guard lace on the Swedish cuffs; gold epaulettes with embroidered crescents, and thick bullions. Flag officers had one to three black enamel eagles on the crescent. Senior officers had thin bullions; captains, none; commanders, three five-pointed silver stars; lieutenants and sublieutenants, no bullions, and three and one silver stars respectively, on the crescent. There were no further distinctions of rank. The dark green trousers had broad gold stripes. The sword, in a black scabbard with gilt mounts, was worn on a black leather belt with a gilt buckle. On service, an all-dark-green peaked cap with chinstrap, and white piping around the top and around the band, was worn. On the front of the band was worn an oval cockade of silver, orange, and black. In summer the cap had a white cover. The long double-breasted frock coat, cut on civilian lines, was of dark green cloth and was worn with a white shirt and black tie. It had two small buttons on the sleeve seam, no rank stripes, but black shoulder straps with gold lace as in the army, and rank distinctions as on the epaulettes. The trousers had no gold stripes. The dirk, with ivory grip, was worn on a belt outside the coat. In formal day dress, the hat and epaulettes were worn. On board ship, a double-breasted jacket with shoulder straps was worn, which was fastened up to the neck to the end of the nineteenth century (Fig. 157h). The great-coat was dark green, with two rows of yellow metal buttons, and a turned-down collar. The ratings wore a dark green sailors' cap of the usual type, with white piping around the top, and an oval cockade on the top front, with a black silk gold-lettered band, with the ends hanging loose. They also had a blue, and white, jumper, with the usual light-blue collar, and a blue and white horizontally striped vest; dark green trousers; black leather equipment; and a short greatcoat worn fastened right up, with pointed shoulder straps, on which the initials of the flotilla were painted in yellow. The Guard Flotilla had red shoulder straps, white collar piping, yellow guard lace on the collar and round cuffs; and orange and black horizontal stripes on the cap band. The petty officers and leading seamen wore one to four narrow yellow stripes across the shoulders or shoulder straps. Warrant officers wore a double breasted jacket, fastened to the top until about 1900, and a white shirt; and a broad gold lace stripe running across the shoulder straps; and the branch badges at the ends of the collar: an anchor; crossed cannon barrels; for engineers, a cog wheel and ship's propeller; and an officers' cap with the men's cockade on the band. The engineers had silver buttons, epaulettes, and shoulder straps on a red backing; otherwise they were dressed like executive officers.

U.S.S.R.

After the Revolution, Russian naval uniforms displayed a profusion of red distinctions: cockade, cap band, and collar among others. In the late 1920s and early 1930s, however, their uniform came much closer to the Western European patterns; and dark blue was introduced as the basic color. Officers' rank distinctions are given in the table. The officers' cap badge consisted of a gold anchor on a red enameled button, surrounded by two gold laurel sprays, with a red five-pointed enamel star above. Warrant officers wore a similar badge, but without the laurel sprays. On the lower arms they had one to four very small gold cords, with a red enameled star above.

SPAIN

One distinguishing feature of the uniform, which differed little from the general type, was the officers' full-dress coatee. It had a red collar, broad buttoned-back lapels, and round cuffs, which were edged with gold lace of varying breadth, according to rank.

SWEDEN

Around 1800 the Stockholm Boatmen's Company wore black round hats with a yellow band, dark blue double-breasted jackets lined with yellow, and yellow collar and round cuffs, yellow waistcoat, and dark blue trousers. In 1830 the sailors wore dark blue peakless caps with a soft flat top. From the mid-nineteenth century, the general pattern of uniform was worn. The sailors' cap had a fairly small soft top, and a silk band with yellow lettering, tied in a small bow at the left side, with dependent ends. The branch badges were worn in yellow embroidery on the left upper arm of the jumper and short greatcoat. These took the form of crossed cannon barrels, crossed signal flags, ship's propeller, etc. Short yellow stripes denoting the men's rank were worn below. Petty officers and warrant officers wore double-breasted officers'-pattern jackets, with two to three short chevrons, point up, on the lower arms, with the branch badge in gold below. Coxswains had a foul anchor or ship's wheel. They wore officers' caps with a gold foul anchor badge between three crowns in a crowned rope circle. Officers had the same cap badge, but with an oakleaf wreath in place of the rope circle. Flag officers wore a broad gold cap band instead of the black mohair one. Officers' rank stripes were worn on both lower arms and on the double-breasted greatcoat as well.

In Sweden the coast artillery formed part of the navy, and, generally speaking, was dressed like the navy. All the yellow distinctions of the latter were, however, in red for the former. The cap badge for officers and warrant officers was two crossed cannon barrels. The top stripe of the officers' cuff lace formed an elongated loop. Officers also had a dark blue single-breasted full-dress tunic, with gold epaulettes, as in the army. The collar was piped gold around the edge. Gold rank stripes were worn on the sleeves.

Naval and coast artillery officers wore a hat of the usual type, with a yellow silk cockade and gold loop; flag officers had gold lace around the edge, and black ostrich feather plumage. They also wore a double-breasted full-dress coatee, with stand collar and slash cuffs richly embroidered in gold. The lapels were worn buttoned back to show the white facings; and the skirts, too, were lined with white.

A regiment of marines existed up to about 1890. They wore dark blue tunics with white lace on the collar and cuffs, and white piping around the latter; and head-dress as for the army. On the spiked helmet, they wore a ball instead of a spike, and they had white leather equipment and dark blue trousers with white piping.

TURKEY

Up to the Great War, the Turkish navy wore a red fez. The double-breasted officers' frock coat had gold passants and epaulettes, and British-style rank lace, with a curl on the top stripe. The ratings wore a dark blue collar with a red stripe around the edge, on their dark blue, and white, jumpers. Petty officers' chevrons, and branch badges, were worn in red, on the left upper arm. During the Great War, officers wore dark blue stiff peakless kepis, with a badge on the front, and rank stripes around the bottom edge. After the war, the uniforms were copied exactly from those of the

British navy. The cap badge was a silver anchor, latterly in a gold rope circle, surrounded by two gold oakleaf sprigs, with the star and crescent above, in gold. Double and single oakleaf embroidery was worn on the cap peak by flag officers and senior officers respectively. Gold epaulettes, with a silver anchor on the crescent and one to three rank stars on the crescent, were worn in full dress up to the 1930s, with thick, medium-thick, and thin bullions according to grade. Cocked hats were not worn in the Turkish navy. Latterly, the epaulettes were superseded by gold plaited shoulder cords, with one to three gold bars across the outer ends according to grade, and one to three gold stars above, to denote the actual rank: e.g., a captain wore two bars, with three stars above. These were also worn on the shoulder straps of the white uniform.

Small collar patches, pointed at the rear, with a small button, were worn at the ends of the collar of the frock coat and jacket—dark blue for executive branch officers, and medium blue with a black diamond for engineers. The rank distinctions on the cuffs of junior officers were changed to one medium; one narrow and one medium; and two medium stripes. In addition to the sword, which was of the usual pattern, a dirk with an ivory grip, in a brass scabbard, was worn on a black silk belt.

UNITED STATES OF AMERICA

By 1766 officers were wearing dark blue uniforms. The collar and cuffs, and the lapels, which were worn closed up to the 1830s, were red at first, later white; buff was also often worn, and from 1830, dark blue. Rank was denoted by epaulettes, as in the army. In 1840 the ratings had a dark blue cloth jacket, dark blue trousers, and a white shirt with large blue collar, and a black leather hat. Up to about 1850, officers wore a dark blue double-breasted frock coat, fastened right up, on duty, with a turndown collar; and a white shirt; and in full dress, a black hat and gold epaulettes; otherwise, a peaked cap, and dark blue passants edged with gold, with a silver foul anchor and rank distinctions as in the army on them, were worn. At the time of the Civil War, the rank stripes on the cuffs were arranged as follows: junior officers, one to three narrow stripes; lieutenant commanders, four narrow, with a space between the third and fourth; commanders, five, with spaces between the first and second, and fourth and fifth; captains, six, with a space between the third and fourth; commodores, seven, with spaces between the third and fourth, and fourth and fifth; rear admirals, eight, with spaces between the first and second, fourth and fifth, and seventh and eighth. Executive officers had a five-pointed gold star above. The ratings wore uniforms like those of the British navy. Petty officers had a white eagle and anchor, according to rank, on the right or left upper arm. The Confederate States navy wore gray uniforms, with medium-width gold cuff stripes, the top one forming a curl: flag officers, four stripes; captains, three; commanders, two; lieutenants, one; and the same number of stars as stripes were worn on the light-blue gold-edged passants. The rank stars were also worn on the cap, above a foul anchor in an oak wreath. Flag officers had gold cap bands. The seamen wore a white shirt, black silk tie, gray jacket and trousers, and a black hat; petty officers wore a foul anchor in black silk on the right upper arm. About 1870 officers adopted a double-breasted coatee for full dress, with gold epaulettes, bearing silver rank stars as in the army; and as their everyday dress, a black high-buttoned jacket with a stand collar, edged all around with broad black lace, something like Fig. 157g, but with gold rank stripes on the cuffs and silver rank distinctions on the collar, of the same number and form as in the army. Flag officers' rank stripes were at that time of varying width: one broad; one broad with one medium above; and two broad with one medium between, respectively. The officers' cap was like the contemporary Austrian naval one (Fig. 157f). The cap badge consisted of a flying eagle above a shield, in silver, on two crossed foul anchors, in gold. After 1900 a British-type cap was introduced. The buttoned-up jacket was worn until after the Great War and only then superseded by a British-type double-breasted jacket with cuff stripes. Warrant officers and senior warrant officers wore officers'-pattern uniforms, but with narrow and medium-width rank lace respectively, broken by three broad vertical blue bands. The cap badge for both was crossed foul anchors in gold. Distinctive features of the more recent U.S. ratings' uniforms were: the white cap, always worn with the blue uniform, with turned-up edge all around; the black silk tie with long ends; and the white stars in the corners of the collar (Fig. 157k). Petty officers' rank distinctions were worn on the upper arm, in the form of chevrons with the eagle in white above. Petty officers wore a vertical gold foul anchor badge on their caps.

The U.S. Marine Corps existed from the formation of the navy. By 1797 it had a dark blue uniform with red distinctions, which colors it retained. The development of its uniform in general followed that of the army. Officers were distinguished by rich gold lace on the collars and cuffs of their uniforms. Their rank badges resembled those of the army. The trousers were light blue with red piping for the men, and stripes for officers. The leather equipment was white. The Marine Corps badge consisted of the globe on a diagonal anchor, with the eagle above. This badge was also worn on the service dress, which was like that of the army, but the cloth was of a darker olive green color. On board ship and off duty, the dark blue single-breasted uniform with stand-and-fall collar with the Marines' badge was worn; with brass buttons; light-blue trousers with red stripes; white belts; and dark blue caps with the badge on the top front (Fig. 156i, page 438).

THE
AIR FORCES

Up to the Great War, military aviation had not advanced very far. From the 1880s, however, many countries, especially the more important ones, had formed captive balloon detachments, which were not separate units but were attached to the engineers, and wore their uniforms. This connection between the engineers and military aviation remained, in all armies, up to about the same time. The unforeseen development during and especially after the war caused the flying corps to be re-formed as separate services and, later, to become equal members of the armed forces, along with the armies and navies. In only a few countries were the air forces ordered to retain the engineer uniform, with only their special insignia to distinguish them. These will not be specially mentioned here. The majority of countries created a dress differing considerably from the army uniforms then worn. Up to the last war, there was a considerable international similarity in the uniforms of the youngest service; and air force uniforms, untrammeled by tradition, became an up-to-date, practical, and at the same time handsome military dress. The prevailing style of uniform, recognizably of British origin, was a four-button civilian-type jacket, with as large as possible patch pockets on the breast and skirts; colored shirt or, off duty, a white one; long trousers, usually with turnups; and a forage cap with peak and chinstrap.

ALBANIA

The 1929-pattern air force uniform was the same as the infantry uniform, with the addition of rectangular yellow patches at the front lower ends of the collar. On the 1936-pattern uniform, the *Waffenfarbe* was yellow. Officers wore a flying eagle badge in gold at the ends of the collar. The rest of the dress was like that worn in the army.

ARGENTINA

The uniform was the same as that worn by the army. The *Waffenfarbe* was royal blue velvet. The flying badge was the national arms between two eagle's wings, in gold, and was worn on the right breast.

AUSTRIA

The *Luftwaffe* was re-formed in 1935 and embraced flying troops and air defense troops.

The uniform differed completely from the traditional Austrian army dress and took after the international fashion. The service uniform consisted of a field gray jacket with four field gray buttons, and patch pockets with scalloped flaps and buttons. The badge was worn embroidered above the right breast pocket: between two stylized eagle's wings (which were in gold for officers, silver for NCOs, and dark blue silk for rank and file), for flying personnel, a red button with a gold edge, with a white triangle on it; for air defense troops, a red, white, and red button with a bow and arrow on it. The shirt was field gray or white; the tie, black. Stone gray breeches and trousers, without piping, were worn. The field gray greatcoat was double-breasted, Ulster style, with black collar patches, and red-lined lapels for general officers. Rank distinctions were worn on both lower arms of the jacket and greatcoat, in the form of horizontal stripes, 8 centimeters long. Officers had a curl in the top stripe. Junior officers had one to three stripes, each 1 centimeter broad; field officers wore a 4-centimeter-wide stripe below these; and general officers had one 5.3 centimeters wide. All the stripes were gold. NCOs wore silver lace with no curl; a *Wachtmeister* had a narrow chevron, and higher grades wore one to three very small ones above it. The rank and file had one to three blue silk chevrons, worn point up. The field cap was the same as for the army; and a field gray forage cap with black peak was also worn. On the front was a flying eagle, or a bow and arrow, in an oak wreath, of the color of the rank stripes, and the cap cord was of the same color. On the field gray cap band, general officers wore three narrow gold stripes; field officers had the two lower ones, junior officers the lowest, and NCOs a single one, in silver; those of the rank and file were in dark blue silk. On the upper part of the cap was the red, white, and red cockade. All officers and flying personnel wore a dirk with an ivory grip, hung from a belt below the jacket.

In lieu of the full-dress army tunic, an all-dark-blue uniform was worn, with a white shirt. There were two rows of three buttons on the jacket, and slit pockets; and the twisted shoulder cords were the same color as the rank badges on the sleeves.

BRAZIL

In 1921 an olive green jacket with yellow buttons and dark brown shoulder straps was worn, with a light-khaki shirt and tie, olive green trousers without colored stripes, black footwear, and light-brown leather equipment. The forage cap was like the United States pattern, and had an olive top, dark brown band, and light-brown peak and chinstrap. The rank badges were the same as those in the army. The summer service uniform was a light-khaki color. The 1931-pattern uniform was the same as the army uniform in style. The flying badge was an upright winged sword. The *Waffenfarbe* on the gray and dark blue uniforms was light blue.

CHILE

The uniform was the same as for the army. The *Waffenfarbe* was yellow, and the buttons were white. In 1929 officers adopted a four-button jacket without collar patches, and a gray shirt and tie. The full-dress colored uniform was light blue, as for the cavalry, but with yellow distinctions and silver buttons. The arm of service badge on the collar was a flying eagle, possibly with a numeral above.

CZECHOSLOVAKIA

The uniform was the same as the general army pattern. The *Waffenfarbe* was light blue. Officers wore a four-button jacket, and a double-breasted Ulster-style great-coat, neither having colored collar patches. The shirt and tie were gray-green; off duty, a white shirt and black tie were worn. Airmen wore a dirk with an ivory grip, in a gilt mounted brown leather scabbard, buckled below the jacket. The trousers had a light-blue piping. The flying badge was a winged sword in a linden leaf circle, in silver, worn on the right breast. From 1936 the basic color was gray-blue.

DENMARK

Officers seconded to the air force wore the uniform of their former arm—mainly the 1923-pattern uniform—with the flying badge above the right breast pocket. This consisted of a cannon barrel on crossed rifles, with crown above, between two stylized eagle's wings, in gold embroidery.

EIRE

An army-style uniform was worn. The gold collar badge depicted an eagle flying off from a cliff, within a pierced circle. The officers' full-dress uniform was a medium-blue cloth tunic, with scarlet collar and cuffs, and yellow metal insignia.

FINLAND

The 1922-pattern uniform was in general similar to that worn by the army; for officers, wholly of dark blue cloth. The trousers had broad light-gray stripes. The naval-type cap for officers had a flying eagle above the red cockade in a gold oak wreath. The men's uniform consisted of a light-gray jacket with dark blue collar, field cap, and trousers; the cuffs were round; the shoulder straps, black, piped light blue. The air force badge was a winged propeller. The 1927-pattern uniform was in the same style as that for the army, but all in dark blue cloth. With it was worn a gray-blue shirt and collar.

FRANCE

Before 1914, and for the first part of the Great War, the engineer uniform was worn, with the specialist badges in red or gold embroidery on the right upper arm: a winged propeller for airmen, and a winged anchor for balloon troops. Toward the end of the war, airmen adopted the horizon blue uniform, with orange collar patches, with black chevrons and numerals on them; balloon troops had black patches with orange letters—gold for NCOs and officers. The chevrons were variously colored: balloon troops, orange; fighter squadrons, green; bomber squadrons, red; observation squadrons, light blue; ground troops, violet; meteorological service, white.

From 1934 officers and NCOs, and from 1935 the men, wore a new uniform, of dark blue cloth, but the officers usually wore black cloth. Buttons and rank distinctions were in yellow and gold. Officers and senior NCOs (adjutants) wore a jacket like that in Fig. 159d, but without the cloth belt and collar patches, and with only four buttons down the front. The rank distinctions were the same as in the army. In full dress, gold twisted shoulder cords, widening toward the outer end, were worn by all ranks of officers. The waistbelt, shoulder brace, and pistol holder were of dark blue leather; the air force dirk had a white grip, yellow metal mounts, and a dark blue leather scabbard. It was worn on a belt under the jacket. The cap was of the same type and color as that worn by the navy. The gold embroidered badge was worn on the upper part of the front of the cap, and on the right breast; two stylized eagle's wings with the unit number above; colonial troops wore a foul anchor; and the general staff, a five-pointed star. The men's uniform was as in Fig. 159d, without the belt and passants; the rank badges were in orange; the collar patches had the same color and ornamentation as before. Leather equipment, only worn on duty under arms, was brown. The shirt was gray-blue. The cap band was black mohair with orange piping top and bottom. The air force badge was in gold embroidery. In summer a white cap cover was worn. NCOs wore gold rank stripes on the cuffs; and the officers' cap without rank stripes, but with a narrow gold cord around the top edge of the band. In the tropics a uniform of similar style was worn, but in light-khaki-colored material. Off duty, officers had a white uniform; and an evening dress, which consisted of a dark blue naval-type coatee with gold embroidery around the cuffs, gold lace shoulder straps with the flying eagle, and dark blue rank stripes running diagonally; and dark blue full-dress trousers with broad gold lace stripes.

GERMANY

The *Luftschifferabteilung* (airship detachment), formed in 1887, and later expanded into two battalions, adopted the uniform of the *Gardepioniere* with a yellow "L" on the red shoulder straps; and from 1895 wore a *Jäger* chaco, with white metal plate and black plume. After the reorganization of the transport troops in 1911, the shoulder straps were changed to light gray with a red letter, and, in addition to the "L," the battalion number, from 1 to 5. *Luftschifferbataillone* 3 to 5 had neither guard lace nor hair plumes. The four Prussian *Fliegerbataillone* (flying battalions) raised for the Great War adopted the same uniform, but with only one loop of lace on the collar, and a winged propeller and the batallion number on the shoulder strap. The Bavarian formations had two loops of guard lace. The 1910 service dress had black piping on the collar and cuffs, white metal buttons, dun-colored piping on the shoulder straps, red letters, and white lace on a black patch on the collar and cuffs. Officers had one collar patch of black velvet with red piping and a silver lace loop. The 1915 service dress had white lace on the collar, on a white patch, with a black light; *Fliegerbataillone* 1 to 4 wore one lace loop and shoulder straps entirely of light gray, with red letters.

The formation of the *Luftwaffe* was announced in 1935. It was given a uniform entirely different from all previous patterns. The basic color for all garments was a dark blue-gray. The jacket was cut like the prevailing style with a row of four buttons, rectangular collar patches, piped in *Waffenfarbe* around the outside of the collar and the round cuffs. With it was worn a dove gray shirt, white for off-duty wear, with a black tie and turndown collar. Officers had dark brown leather equipment, which included a shoulder brace; the men wore brown, later black, leather equipment and footwear. The breeches were not piped, but the long trousers had piping in *Waffenfarbe*; general officers had triple stripes. The cap was like that of the *Reichswehr*, with a black leather peak and chinstrap, and black mohair band piped in *Waffenfarbe* around the top and bottom. On the band was the black, white, and red cockade within a small oak wreath between two stylized eagle's wings. Above, on the upper part, was the flying eagle and swastika, which device was also embroidered above the right breast pocket. The top part of the cap was piped in *Waffenfarbe*. Officers and flying personnel wore a dirk with inverted quillons in a blue leather sheath. The steel helmet was of the army pattern (Fig. 159a). On service, a flying jacket was worn, with piping on the collar and shoulder straps, and collar patches as on the jacket (Fig. 159b). A field cap was worn with it, which was piped around the flap in *Waffenfarbe*, with the cockade, and the eagle and swastika above on the upper part. The greatcoat was double-breasted, with collar patches in *Waffenfarbe* and shoulder straps as on the jacket, but without colored piping. General officers' lapels were lined with white. There was a belt with two buttons at the back.

Fig. 159. Air Forces, 1936.

Germany—a: officer. b: airman, service dress. Great Britain—c: officer, full dress. France—d: NCO. Italy—e: officer. Poland—f: officer. Sweden—g: NCO.

The rank distinctions on the shoulder straps and cords were the same as those worn by the army. NCOs wore their lace around the outer edges of the collar of the jacket, and on the flying jacket and greatcoat, around the lower and outer edges of the patches. In addition, one to four double wings were worn on the collar patches, which for officers were edged with metal cord; below the wings, junior officers wore two oak sprigs, while senior and general officers had a complete circle of oak leaves. The buttons, embroidery, and all metal devices were gold for general officers, and white (silver) for the others. The *Waffenfarbe* were: general officers and Göring Regiment, white; flying personnel, golden yellow; antiaircraft artillery, red; air signals troops, gold brown; Air Ministry, black. All officers had aluminum cord instead of piping in *Waffenfarbe*, except for general officers, who wore gold. In full dress, all officers wore a silver waistbelt, with black and red lines. The silver double cord aiguillette, when worn, was on the right shoulder. The long-bladed *Luftwaffe* sword was worn in a blue leather scabbard. In summer a white cap cover and white trousers were worn, and officers had a white jacket.

Officers also had an evening dress of basic color, with shoulder cords and silver or gold collar piping, cut like a mess jacket; with broad silver or gold lace stripes on the trousers.

GREAT BRITAIN

The Royal Air Force was formed on 1 April 1918 by an amalgamation of the Royal Flying Corps (raised 1912) and the Royal Naval Air Service (formed in 1914). The RFC wore a khaki double-breasted jacket, fastened right across the front, with the buttons concealed in a fly; a fore-and-aft cap; and breeches. Officers seconded from the army wore their usual service dress uniform with breeches, with the flying badge on the left breast: the initials "RFC" crowned, between two eagle's wings, all in white. RNAS officers wore normal naval uniforms, with an eagle above the sleeve rings and on the cap for officers, and at the tops of the sleeves, and on the cap, for ratings. Ratings wore blue peaked caps, blue jackets, breeches and puttees, and white collar and black tie.

The RAF adopted a khaki service dress of army pattern for the duration of the war. It was worn with or without a cloth belt, and had four patch pockets but no shoulder straps. Naval-type cuff rings were used to denote rank. These were khaki with a light-blue center stripe; and a crowned eagle was worn above in lieu of the curl. The buttons were yellow metal. The initials "RAF" were introduced in the flying badge.

The first distinctive RAF service dress was of the same pattern as the khaki one, but in French blue, with gold cuff rings. This was superseded late in 1919 by a darker blue-gray uniform, which had black cuff rings with a light-blue center stripe, the rings being of varying widths according to rank, as in the navy. Stripes were not worn on the trousers, except in mess dress. Officers wore white or light-blue shirts and black ties. The blue forage cap had a cloth peak, but group captains and air officers wore leather peaks with single or double oakleaf embroidery respectively, according to rank, and a black mohair band with a gold crowned eagle above two laurel sprigs, or on a laurel wreath, for air officers. In full dress a light-blue tunic (Fig. 159c) was worn. It had gold lace around the collar, with gold oakleaf embroidery varying according to rank at the ends, gold cuff rings, and a light-blue waistbelt and slings with two gold stripes. The flying badge was embroidered in gold and silver. The sword had an eagle's head pommel, and was carried in a black leather scabbard. The headdress was a formalized flying helmet of black leather trimmed with black fur, with a light-blue plume, and gold twisted cords flecked with light blue, in front. The men wore a blue-gray jacket buttoned right up, and blue forage caps with a black leather peak, and brass badge on the black mohair band. Embroidered light-blue eagles on black rectangular patches were worn on both sleeves just below the shoulder. NCOs wore light-blue army-style chevrons. Breeches and puttees were worn at first, and trousers later. In 1936/37 jackets with open necks, and collars and ties, were introduced, and all ranks adopted a blue fore-and-aft field service cap, with the badge on the left in reduced size, and later with light-blue piping around the edges for air officers.

ITALY

At first the engineers' uniform, with special badges, was worn; but from the beginning of the twentieth century, they had a gray-blue uniform (Fig. 159e). In the late 1930s the buttons and rank badges were the same as on the 1934-pattern army uniform. The top rank stripe formed a diamond. The collar was of basic color, with the regular star in the corners. The collar was of basic color, with the regular star in the corners. The cap badge was a flying eagle in a crowned oak wreath. Officers also wore their rank stripes on the cap band; and had light-blue silk sashes, and naval-pattern swords.

LATVIA

The style of uniform and the rank distinctions were the same as in the army, but the basic color was black. All piping was blue, and the collar patches and cap band were a dark cherry color.

LITHUANIA

The same uniform was worn as in the army, but the basic color was blue-black. The distinctive color was black.

MEXICO

The army uniform was worn. The arm-of-service badge was a winged propeller.

NETHERLANDS

The men wore infantry service dress uniforms with the arm-of-service badge—a rotary engine and propeller—in yellow on the collar. The officers wore the uniform of their former arm, with the arm-of-service badge in gold embroidery. On the blue-black uniform, the badge was worn on the collar. There was no colored piping on the tunic and trousers.

POLAND

The air force adopted the 1919 army uniform, with dark yellow collar patches and cap band. The evening dress trousers were light blue with dark yellow triple stripes. The flying badge was a silver flying eagle, worn by officers and NCOs on the left breast, and on the left upper arm by the men.

In 1936 a new uniform, of gray basic color, was introduced. The four-button jacket had patch pockets on the breast and skirts; and officers had a black silk stripe around their round cuffs. The shirt was gray or white, with a black tie. The rank distinctions on the shoulder straps were the same as in the army. The forage cap had a gray top and black mohair band, on which were placed the rank stars. The black lacquered leather peak had a single or double lace binding for officers, according to rank, and vandyked lace for general officers. On the upper part was the Polish eagle, between two formalized upright eagle's wings. Buttons, metal insignia, and rank badges were silver. The gray trousers had black stripes. A brown waistbelt was worn (Fig. 159f).

RUMANIA

In 1923–1925 the air force adopted the khaki army uniform with light blue as its distinctive color; yellow metal buttons; and a forage cap with, as a badge, a crowned flying eagle over the royal cipher in an oak wreath.

In 1931 the basic color was changed to gray-blue. The men wore army-pattern service jackets, greatcoats, and trousers, with spearhead-shaped patches on the greatcoat and jacket collar: fighter squadrons, dark green; bomber squadrons, red; observation squadrons, light blue; balloon troops, brown; schools of instruction, orange; staffs, dark blue; engineers, royal blue; naval airmen wore yellow anchors instead of patches. A dark blue beret was worn, with the cap badge in yellow silk, in reduced size. Officers and NCOs had four-button jackets with patch pockets on the breast and skirts, and at the ends of the collar, patches like the men's; likewise on the double-breasted Ulster-style greatcoat. A gray-blue or white shirt was worn, with a black tie. In addition to the beret, a British-type forage cap in gray-blue was worn, with the badge in gold on the front, and a black leather peak and chinstrap. Officers had a dark blue mohair band. Senior officers and general officers respectively wore one and two rows of gold oakleaf embroidery around the outside of the peak. The officers' rank distinctions were worn on both forearms of the jacket and greatcoat, and took the form of gold stripes, as in the navy. The top stripe formed a diamond. NCOs had one to three short gold stripes on the right upper arm. In summer officers wore a white uniform with the rank stripes on the gray-blue shoulder straps and a cap with a white cover.

SWEDEN

The air force was first administered by the engineers. Officers on flying duty wore the uniform of their former arm, with the flying badge—a gold winged propeller and crown—on the breast. From 1930 they had their own pattern of uniform, of dark blue cloth (Fig. 139g). Officers wore a single-breasted jacket with four yellow metal buttons and patch pockets; NCOs and men wore buttoned-up ones with a stand collar, and brown leather equipment. Flying personnel wore a dirk with an ivory grip, in a brown leather sheath. The double-breasted greatcoat was similar to the navy pattern. Rank distinctions were worn on both lower arms of the jacket, tunic, and great coat, in the same number and arrangement as in the navy. The top stripe did not have a curl; but the badge of the service was worn above: a winged propeller surmounted by a crown; this badge was also worn on the cap peak. The ranks of the NCOs and men were denoted by horizontal stripes.

SWITZERLAND

Before and during the Great War, the balloon troops wore the dress uniform of the engineers; the chaco badge was a winged yellow anchor. Flying officers wore the uniform of their former arm, with, on the left upper arm, an eagle's wing; observers wore a four-pointed star below, of the color of the buttons. On the field gray uniform, which was similar in style to that of the army, the air force wore yellow metal buttons, and black collars and cuff patches. On the latter the flying companies wore a winged propeller in light brown or gold embroidery.

UNION OF SOVIET SOCIALIST REPUBLICS

At first, a khaki-colored army-pattern uniform was worn. The arm-of-service color was light blue; the collar patches were piped black around the outside and had a winged propeller in white at the rear end. From 1935 the basic color was light blue and the coat was made like a jacket; the collar patches were retained. A dove blue or white shirt was worn with a black tie. On the sleeves, junior officers had one to three narrow red chevrons, point down; these were of medium width for senior officers, and in gold for general officers.

UNITED STATES OF AMERICA

During the Great War, the flying corps was attached to the signal corps and had the same uniform. The officers wore a silver winged shield on the left breast; the men had a four-bladed propeller in white on a dark blue backing, on the right upper arm below the shoulder. Later, the flying corps was formed into an independent arm, and wore the universal army-pattern uniform with, as its arm-of-service colors (worn on the hat cord), dark blue and orange; and as its badge, a winged propeller. Officers had the propeller in silver, with gold embroidered eagle's wings, at the ends of the collar. For the men, the arm-of-service badge was stamped on a round yellow metal button worn at the left end of the collar; while at the right end was the universal army button with the initials "U.S."

GLOSSARY

This is mainly a list of foreign retentions and explanations of translations, together with a few technical expressions. It is not intended to be a complete glossary of all the technical usages for organizations, uniforms, and weapons.

NOTE: (n) following a German term indicates plural ending.

air rank (air forces). Corresponds to the grade of general officer in armies.

Attila. Short-skirted tunic or jacket with cord or braid loops across the front; worn by hussars from about the mid-nineteenth century. Also called *husarka.*

basic color. Main color of a garment or uniform.

busby. Low-crowned fur cap worn by hussars, artillery, etc., only in Great Britain.

button color. Color of button metal and sometimes other insignia; usually yellow (brass, gilt, copper) or white (silver, nickel).

carabinieri (Italy). Police force, part of regular army.

chasseurs à cheval (France). Light cavalry; no exact British equivalent.

chasseurs à pied (France). Light infantry; no exact British equivalent.

chenille. Close-fitting caterpillarlike crest on comb of helmet.

chevau-légers. Light cavalry.

coatee. Close-fitting body coat cut across at the waist in front, with long tails at rear.

cockade. Bow of ribbon (later circular or oval insignia) bearing national colors or emblem; worn on headdress as an identifying feature.

colored uniform. Ceremonial uniform (as opposed to service dress uniform) worn after 1918.

crinière. Long, flowing crest attached to comb of helmet; often made of horsehair.

cuffs. *Brandenburg.* Round cuff with vertical rectangular patch and buttons.

French. Brandenburg cuff with the patch scalloped at the rear; also a deep, round cuff sewn on to the sleeve as on a greatcoat.

gauntlet. Round cuff deeper at the rear than the front, with vertical lace loops.

Polish. Pointed cuff.

Saxon. Round cuff with one button on it and one above on the sleeve, both on or near hind-arm seam.

slash. Round cuff with vertical plain rectangular or scalloped patch or slash on the outside.

Swedish. Round cuff edged or piped along the top and down hind-arm seam, often with vertical lace loops.

distinctive color. See *Waffenfarbe(n).*

dolman. Short, single-breasted body garment with loopings across the front, worn by hussars; can refer to waist-length jacket or one with short skirts. Superseded by *Attila* about mid-nineteenth century.

evening dress. Formal dress worn on evening social occasions; called mess dress in British forces.

facings, facing colors (British army). Regimental or corps distinctions usually denoted by collar, cuffs, or lapels of different color; more strictly, tailor's expression for inside front edge of a garment, seen when lapels are turned or buttoned back.

Fähnrich (Germany). Lowest rank of commissioned officer or prospective officer on probation prior to commissioning.

field mark. Ad hoc distinction for purposes of identification either where uniforms did not exist or where they were so similar as to cause confusion.

field service cap. Usually fore-and-aft-shaped undress cap; garrison cap.

flag officer (navies). Rank of admiral equivalent to general officer in armies.

flank companies. Companies that took up positions on the right and left flanks of a battalion drawn up in line; a place of honor, as such occupied by superior troops, usually grenadiers and light infantry or *voltigeurs*; often wore some distinctions, in embellishment or color.

Flügelmütze(n). Tall, tapering cap with cloth bandage or "wing" wound spirally around cap's body; worn by light cavalry in late eighteenth and early nineteenth centuries; "wing" could be worn hanging loose. Called *mirliton* in France.

forage cap. Low cloth cap with a broad crown all around and a peak.

fusilier. In France, center companies of a battalion. Also, in seventeenth century, troops armed with flintlock muskets as opposed to matchlocks; later a term of distinction, often with special differences in uniform.

gendarmerie (France). Police force part of regular army.

"German" regiment (Austria-Hungary). German-speaking regiments from Austria, as opposed to "Hungarian" regiments from Hungary.

grade. Groupings of officers:

General officers: ranks of field marshal or equivalent down to major (or brigadier) general or equivalent.

Field officers: colonels down to majors.

Company officers: captains and all commissioned ranks below.

Great War. World War I (1914–1918).

guides (Europe). Light cavalry.

hangar. Short sword, frequently curved, carried by infantry in addition to bayonet.

honved (Austria-Hungary). Reserve force in Hungary.

houpette (French army). Short, brushlike tuft on the front of comb of helmet worn by cuirassiers and dragoons.

husarka. See *Attila*.

Jäger zu Fuss. Light troops, usually clad in green; originally denoted those armed with rifles when that was a novelty.

Jäger zu Pferd. Light cavalry, usually dressed in green.

jumper (navy). Upper garment—frock, jumper, or shirt worn at different times by sailors.

junior officers. *See* senior officers.

Kaskett. Stiff leather cap or hat not as big or elaborate as a helmet.

kepi. Close-fitting small-crowned peaked cap usually of cloth; softer than a chaco and often worn instead of chaco in undress or on service.

kiver (Russia). Broad-crowned chaco.

konföderatka. Square-topped cap, at first with fur band, later a cap copied by lancers in most countries; originated in southern Poland in the late eighteenth century.

kurtka. Waist-length double-breasted jacket with short skirts at rear and often with lapels.

kutsma (Russia). Fur cap with cloth bag worn by hussars.

Landesschützen (Austria). Reserve force with low liability for service.

Landwehr (Germany). Territorially raised force of later Napoleonic Wars consisting of men up to age thirty-nine liable for service and not in regular army; later a reserve force ranked after the *Reserve. Landsturm* in both cases was in service below *Landwehr*.

Leib. Alone, untranslatable in military titles; carries the connotation of a lifeguard or bodyguard formation.

light (lace). Center of lace loop, often open enough to show a narrow rectangle of color.

light horse. Rough equivalent of term *chevau-léger*.

Litewka (Germany). Undress coat cut like a tunic with medium-length skirts, double- or single-breasted.

mirliton. See *Flügelmütze(n)*.

mounted rifles. Rough equivalent of *chasseur à cheval* or *Jäger zu Pferd*.

musketeer. Man of center or musketeer company of German infantry battalion; applied on occasion to larger formations. Equivalent to French fusilier company or British center or battalion company.

Opanken. Open leather sandals worn particularly in the Balkans.

passant. German *Passant* or French *bride*. Rectangle of cloth, lace, or cloth edged with lace, usually bearing officers' rank insignia; worn at the point of the shoulder and parallel to sleeve seam.

pelisse. Overgarment covered with loopings or braid usually edged with fur or imitation fur, carried by hussars; normally slung by a cord over left shoulder; essentially a practical garment worn over the dolman instead of a greatcoat.

plumage. Edging of feathers all around the brim or fans of hat, as opposed to plumage, or plumes fastened to a single point.

portepee (German navy). Sword knot usually of lace or cord carried by officers, warrant officers, some senior NCOs, and petty officers.

pulk. Tactical formation of eastern European countries or of troops from this area.

regular star. Five-pointed star worn on the collar by all ranks of Italian regular armed forces.

Reiter (Germany). Cavalry or cavalryman, usually heavy cavalry.

rifle cords. Cords attached on the shoulder and looped across the chest, with tags; worn in some armies to denote marksmen or merely riflemen or *Jäger*.

ros (Spain). Low chaco with broad crown higher at the front than back.

Sam Browne. System of leather equipment devised in the British army—a waistbelt with shoulder braces for supporting the sword and/or pistol; adopted in many countries during the early twentieth century.

Scharawaden. Leggings worn over breeches and reaching the thighs.

senior officers (naval and air force sections). Ranks of officers approximating field officers in the armies, i.e., captains and commanders; lieutenants and below are junior officers.

Superwest, Suprawest (French, *soubreveste*). "Cuirass" generally of cloth worn over the coat by guard formations.

tirailleur (France). Sharpshooter.

triple stripes. On trousers and breeches, piping down side seam with a broader stripe of same color at each side.

ulster. A long, ample, double-breasted greatcoat.

undergarments. Collective expression for waistcoat and breeches.

velites (Italy). Light infantry.

voltigeur (France, etc.). Light infantry.

Waffenfarbe(n). Distinctive color of an arm of service, or sometimes a regiment.